# SIEDLUNGEN DER BERLINER MODERNE

NOMINIERUNG FÜR DIE WELTERBELISTE DER UNESCO

# HOUSING ESTATES IN THE BERLIN MODERN STYLE

NOMINATION FOR THE UNESCO WORLD HERITAGE LIST

BRAUN

# INHALT

| | |
|---|---|
| Grußwort | 9 |
| Einführung | 13 |
| **1. Denkmalanlagen/Angaben zum Standort** | **33** |
| 1. A Land | 34 |
| 1. B Bundesstaat, Provinz oder Region | 34 |
| 1. C Bezeichnung der Anlagen | 35 |
| 1. D Geographische Koordinaten | 36 |
| 1. E Karten und Pläne mit Darstellung der Grenzen der nominierten Anlagen und der Pufferzonen | 36 |
| 1. F Flächen der nominierten Anlagen (ha) und der vorgesehenen Pufferzonen (ha) | 37 |
| **2. Beschreibung** | **67** |
| 2. A Beschreibung der Anlagen | 68 |
| 2. B Geschichte und Entwicklung | 98 |
| **3. Begründung für die Eintragung** | **119** |
| 3. A Kriterien, denen zufolge die Eintragung beantragt wird | 120 |
| 3. B Erklärung bezüglich des außerordentlichen universellen Wertes | 123 |
| 3. C Vergleichende Analyse | 139 |
| 3. D Integrität und/oder Authentizität | 154 |
| **4. Erhaltungszustand und Faktoren, die die Anlagen beeinflussen** | **165** |
| 4. A Gegenwärtiger Erhaltungszustand | 166 |
| 4. B Faktoren, die die Anlagen beeinflussen | |
|     (I) Entwicklungsdruck | |
|     (II) Umweltfaktoren | |
|     (III) Naturkatastrophen und Schutzvorkehrungen | |
|     (IV) Druck durch Besucher/Tourismus | |
|     (V) Anzahl der Einwohner innerhalb der Anlagen und der Pufferzonen | 180 |
| **5. Schutz und Verwaltung der Anlagen** | **185** |
| 5. A Eigentumsverhältnisse | 186 |
| 5. B Schutzstatus | 187 |

# CONTENTS

| | |
|---|---|
| **Message** | 9 |
| **Introduction** | 13 |
| **1. Identification of monument properties** | 33 |
| 1. A Country | 34 |
| 1. B State, province or region | 34 |
| 1. C Name of the property | 35 |
| 1. D Geographical coordinates | 36 |
| 1. E Maps and plans, showing the boundaries of nominated properties and buffer zones | 36 |
| 1. F Area of nominated properties (ha) and proposed buffer zones (ha) | 37 |
| **2. Description** | 67 |
| 2. A Description of property | 68 |
| 2. B History and development | 98 |
| **3. Justification for inscription** | 119 |
| 3. A Criteria under which inscription is proposed | 120 |
| 3. B Proposed statement of outstanding universal value | 122 |
| 3. C Comparative analysis (including state of conservation of similar properties) | 139 |
| 3. D Integrity and/or authenticity | 154 |
| **4. State of conservation and factors affecting the properties** | 165 |
| 4. A Present state of conservation | 166 |
| 4. B Factors affecting the properties | |
|     (I) Development pressures | |
|     (II) Environmental pressures | |
|     (III) Natural disasters and risk preparedness | |
|     (IV) Visitor/tourism pressures | |
|     (V) Number of inhabitants within the properties and the buffer zones | 180 |
| **5. Protection and Management of the properties** | 185 |
| 5. A Ownership | 186 |
| 5. B Protective designation | 187 |

# INHALT

| | |
|---|---:|
| 5. C Mittel zur Umsetzung von Schutzmaßnahmen | 188 |
| 5. D Bestehende Planungen der Gemeinde und der Region, in der sich die nominierten Anlagen befinden | 190 |
| 5. E Managementplan oder sonstiges System zur Verwaltung der Anlagen | 198 |
| 5. F Quellen und Umfang der Finanzierung | 208 |
| 5. G Fachwissen und Schulung bezüglich Denkmalpflege und Verwaltung | 209 |
| 5. H Besuchereinrichtungen und -statistik | 209 |
| 5. I Grundlagen und Programme für die Öffentlichkeitsarbeit | 210 |
| 5. J Vorhandenes Personal | 210 |

## 6. Überwachung     213

| | |
|---|---:|
| 6. A Schlüsselindikatoren zur Bestimmung des Erhaltungszustandes | 214 |
| 6. B Administrative Regelungen für die Überwachung der Anlagen | 215 |
| 6. C Ergebnisse früherer Berichterstattungen | 215 |

## 7. Dokumentation     217

| | |
|---|---:|
| 7. A Photographien, Dias, Bildnachweis und Bildrechte sowie sonstiges audiovisuelles Material | 218 |
| 7. B Texte, die sich auf den Schutzstatus beziehen, Kopien bestehender Planungen oder Managementsysteme und Auszüge aus sonstigen für die Anlagen relevanten Plänen | 219 |
| 7. C Form und Datum jüngerer Publikationen und Bestandsaufnahmen | 223 |
| 7. D Anschriften der Einrichtungen, bei denen Bestandsunterlagen, Berichte und Archivalien verwahrt werden | 229 |
| 7. E Bibliographie | 230 |

## 8. Angaben zu den zuständigen Behörden     243

| | |
|---|---:|
| 8. A Vorbereitung | 245 |
| 8. B Örtlich zuständige Einrichtung/Behörde | 245 |
| 8. C Sonstige örtliche Einrichtungen | 245 |
| 8. D Offizielle Internetadresse | 245 |

## Anhang     247

| | |
|---|---:|
| Architektenbiographien | 248 |
| Gutachten | 261 |
| Impressum | 270 |

# CONTENTS

| | |
|---|---|
| 5. C Means of implementing protective measures | 189 |
| 5. D Existing plans related to municipality and region in which the proposed properties are located | 190 |
| 5. E Property management plan or other management system | 198 |
| 5. F Sources and scope of financing | 208 |
| 5. G Sources of expertise and training in conservation and management techniques | 209 |
| 5. H Visitor facilities and statistics | 210 |
| 5. I Policies and programmes related to the presentation and promotion of the property | 210 |
| 5. J Staffing levels | 211 |

## 6. Monitoring 213

| | |
|---|---|
| 6. A Key indicators for measuring state of conservation | 214 |
| 6. B Administrative arrangements for monitoring property | 215 |
| 6. C Results of previous reporting | 215 |

## 7. Documentation 217

| | |
|---|---|
| 7. A Photographs, slides, image inventory and authorization table and other audiovisual materials | 218 |
| 7. B Texts relating to protective designation, copies of property management plans or documented management systems and extracts of other plans relevant to the property | 219 |
| 7. C Form and date of most recent records and inventory of property | 223 |
| 7. D Addresses where inventory, records and archives are held | 229 |
| 7. E Bibliography | 230 |

## 8. Contact Information of responsible authorities 243

| | |
|---|---|
| 8. A Preparer | 245 |
| 8. B Official local institution/agency | 245 |
| 8. C Other local institutions | 245 |
| 8. D Official Web address | 245 |

## Attachment 247

| | |
|---|---|
| Architect's biographies | 248 |
| Expert's review | 261 |
| Imprint | 270 |

# GRUSSWORT
## MESSAGE

**des Regierenden Bürgermeisters von Berlin, Klaus Wowereit**

Berlin zählt zu den wenigen Städten, die auf der Liste der UNESCO-Welterbestätten gleich mehrfach vertreten sind. Die bereits 1972 von der UNESCO verabschiedete Konvention zum Weltkultur- und Weltnaturerbe fand nach der deutschen Vereinigung rasch auch auf die wiedervereinigte deutsche Hauptstadt Anwendung.

Bereits 1990, in den Monaten des Mauerfalls, erfolgte die Eintragung der Schlösser und Gärten von Potsdam und Berlin in die Welterbeliste der UNESCO. Die Weltgemeinschaft würdigte mit diesem vielbeachteten Schritt die herausragende historische und künstlerische Bedeutung der Berlin-Potsdamer Residenzlandschaft. Die Aufnahme der im Kalten Krieg durch den „Eisernen Vorhang" gespaltenen historischen Kulturlandschaft von Potsdam und des Westteils von Berlin in die Welterbeliste symbolisierte aber auch eindrucksvoll die internationale Anteilnahme und Unterstützung, die der Prozess der Wiedervereinigung in den Wendemonaten erfuhr. Mittlerweile haben die Gremien der UNESCO einer zweifachen Erweiterung der Welterbestätte der Schlösser und Gärten auf dem Territorium Brandenburgs zugestimmt (1992, 1999), sodass heute mehr als 500 Hektar mit über 150 Bau- und Kunstwerken sowie Park- und Gartenanlagen in weitläufigen Natur- und Landschaftsräumen dem Schutz der UNESCO unterliegen.

*from the Governing Mayor of Berlin, Klaus Wowereit*

Berlin is one of the few cities represented by several sites on the UNESCO World Heritage List. The UNESCO convention, adopted back in 1972 for the protection of the world's cultural and natural heritage, was applied to Germany's now reunified capital city soon after the country's unification.

Already in 1990, just a few months after the fall of the Berlin Wall, the palaces and parks of Potsdam and Berlin were inscribed on the UNESCO World Heritage List. With this widely acclaimed decision, the international community paid tribute to the outstanding historical and artistic significance of the former royal residences in Potsdam and Berlin. Adding the historic cultural landscapes of Potsdam and West Berlin, once divided by the Cold War's "iron curtain", to the World Heritage List was also a striking demonstration of the international interest and support enjoyed by the reunification process after the fall of the Wall. UNESCO's committees have since approved two applications to extend the area covered by the World Heritage "palaces and parks" site in the federal state of Brandenburg (1992, 1999), which means that over 500 hectares with more than 150 buildings and monuments, along with park grounds and public gardens in spacious natural and landscaped settings, are now under the protection of UNESCO.

Im Jahr 1999 stimmte die UNESCO der Aufnahme der Berliner Museumsinsel in die Welterbeliste zu. Die internationalen Experten würdigten das Berliner Museumsquartier als einzigartiges Ensemble von Bau- und Kunstdenkmalen, das die Entwicklung der Museumsarchitektur und des Bildungsgedankens seit der Aufklärung bis ins frühe 20. Jahrhundert höchst eindrucksvoll dokumentiert. Die Welterbegremien hoben die zentrale städtebauliche Lage in der historischen Mitte einer Metropole und die unvergleichliche Dichte der in unmittelbarer Nachbarschaft überlieferten Bauwerke als besonderen Vorzug des Berliner Denkmalensembles hervor.

Aber nicht nur wegen des weltweit bekannten und anerkannten Denkmalbestands möchte man Berlin als eine Art UNESCO-Stadt bezeichnen. In das 1992 von der UNESCO initiierte Programm des Weltdokumentarerbes (Memory of the World) fand 1999 als erster deutscher Beitrag die Sammlung des Berliner Phonogramm-Archivs, des sogenannten Edison-Zylinders mit 140 000 Musikaufnahmen aus den Jahren 1893 bis 1952, Aufnahme. Auch der zwei Jahre später als Weltdokumentarerbe ausgezeichnete Stummfilmklassiker „Metropolis" – 1925/27 von Fritz Lang in Babelsberg und Berlin gedreht und uraufgeführt – unterstreicht die internationale Ausstrahlung, die historisch von Berlin ausging. Dass der Weltruf, den Berlin für seine künstlerische Kreativität und kulturelle Bildung bis heute genießt, keineswegs der Vergangenheit angehört, sondern höchst gegenwärtig ist, beweist die 2005 erfolgte Ernennung Berlins zur ersten europäischen UNESCO-Stadt des Designs und die Aufnahme von „Spree-Athen" in das moderne Netzwerk kreativer Metropolen. Die Berliner Erklärung zum UNESCO-Welterbe von 2005, mehr als eine Hand voll Berliner UNESCO-Projektschulen oder auch das Berliner Komitee für UNESCO-Arbeit e.V. seien stellvertretend für die hohe Präsenz angeführt, die der UNESCO in Berlin und die Berlin in den Aktivitäten der UNESCO zukommen.

Im Jahr 1997 beschloss die Ständige Kultusministerkonferenz der deutschen Länder, sechs Berliner Siedlungen der Zwischenkriegszeit für die Tentativliste der Bundesrepublik Deutschland bei der UNESCO anzumelden. Die Kultusministerkonferenz würdigte damit die herausragende Rolle, die Berlin als eine Metropole der Moderne in den 1920er Jahren auf dem Gebiet der Architektur und des Städtebaus spielte. Zu den bleibenden sozialen, urbanen und künstlerischen Leistungen, die weltweit Aufmerksamkeit und auch Nachahmung fanden, zählen die Siedlungen des Sozialen Wohnungsbaus, wie sie damals nach Plänen von Berühmtheiten wie Bruno Taut und Martin Wagner, Walter Gropius und Otto Rudolf Salvisberg, Otto Bartning und Fred Forbat sowie Hugo Häring und Hans Scharoun oder Leberecht Migge und Ludwig Lesser in Berlin entstanden. Viele Berliner Namen und Bauwerke aus den Jahren vor der NS-Diktatur haben international bis heute einen guten Klang bewahrt und Eingang in die Weltarchitekturgeschichte des 20. Jahrhunderts gefunden. Mit dem Welterbeantrag für sechs Siedlungen der Berliner Moderne bekennt sich die deutsche Hauptstadt nicht nur zu ihrer führenden historischen Rolle in der Architektur- und Städtebaudiskussion des letzten Jahrhunderts, sondern auch zu der politischen Vorbildwirkung, die von der Sozial- und Wohnungsreform der Weimarer Republik noch für Jahrzehnte ausgehen sollte.

In 1999, UNESCO approved the inscription of Berlin's Museum Island on the World Heritage List. The international experts evaluating it praised this complex of museums as a unique ensemble of structural and artistic monuments, documenting in an extraordinary way the evolution of museum architecture and of the educational idea from the Enlightenment to the early 20th century. The World Heritage committees emphasized the ensemble's central location in the historic heart of one of the world's metropolises and the exceptional concentration of historic buildings in the immediate vicinity as key assets of this Berlin monument.

Berlin can be regarded as a "UNESCO city" of sorts not only because of its world-famous collection of landmarks, however. In 1999, Germany's first contribution to the Memory of the World programme launched by UNESCO in 1992 was the collection of the Berlin Phonogram Archive (Berliner Phonogramm-Archiv), "Edison cylinders" with 140,000 musical recordings from 1893 to 1952. Fritz Lang's silent movie classic "Metropolis", shot at Babelsberg starting in 1925 and first shown in Berlin in 1927, was added to this documentary heritage list two years later. It, too, underscores Berlin's historical appeal worldwide. That Berlin's international reputation for artistic creativity and cultural education is not just a thing of the past, however, was demonstrated in 2005 when Berlin, sometimes referred to as "Athens on the Spree," was appointed the first continental European UNESCO City of Design and taken into the new global network of creative cities. The 2005 Berlin Declaration on UNESCO World Heritage sites, a number of UNESCO project schools in Berlin, and the Berliner Komitee für UNESCO-Arbeit e.V. (Berlin committee for UNESCO work) are representative of the high visibility of UNESCO in Berlin and of Berlin in UNESCO's activities.

In 1997, the German federal states' Standing Conference of Ministers of Education and Cultural Affairs decided to add six Berlin housing estates built in the interwar years to the UNESCO Tentative List submitted by the Federal Republic of Germany. This decision paid tribute to Berlin's pre-eminence in the area of architecture and urban planning in the 1920s, as a metropolis of the modern age. The social housing estates built in Berlin back then by celebrated architects like Bruno Taut and Martin Wagner, Walter Gropius and Otto Rudolf Salvisberg, Otto Bartning and Fred Forbat, Hugo Häring and Hans Scharoun, and Leberecht Migge and Ludwig Lesser are lasting social, urban planning, and artistic achievements that were admired and imitated around the world. Many of the names and buildings associated with Berlin in the years before the Nazi dictatorship are known worldwide even today and figure prominently in the history of international architecture of the 20th century. With its application to have six housing estates in the Berlin modern style inscribed on the World Heritage List, Germany's capital city is underscoring not only the leading role it played in architectural and urban planning discourse in the last century, but also the political impact of social and housing reform in the Weimar Republic. These reforms served as a model for others for decades.

I would like to express my thanks to all those who have worked over the last few years to make Berlin's World Heritage application a reality. That includes the Senator for Urban Development and the Berlin State Office for the Pro-

Ich danke allen, die über die letzten Jahre am Zustandekommen des vorliegenden Berliner Welterbeantrags beteiligt waren. Dazu zählen die für Stadtentwicklung zuständige Senatorin und das Landesdenkmalamt Berlin ebenso wie die bezirklichen Gremien vor Ort, des weiteren sachverständige Architekten, Kunsthistoriker, Restauratoren und Gutachter wie das Berliner Büro Winfried Brenne Architekten oder Prof. Dr. Vladimir Slapeta und kompetente Kultureinrichtungen auf dem Gebiet der Baugeschichte und Denkmalforschung wie das Bauhausarchiv Museum für Gestaltung oder die Akademie der Künste Berlin-Brandenburg. Besonders herzlich danken möchte ich freilich den Eigentümern der Siedlungen, namentlich den Wohnungsgesellschaften BauBeCon, Berliner Bau- und Wohnungsgenossenschaft von 1892 e.G., GEHAG und GSW. Sie haben unsere Welterbeinitiative von Beginn an mit großem Verständnis unterstützt und mit eigenen Mitteln zum erfolgreichen Gelingen des vorliegenden Welterbeantrags beigetragen. Ihrer Traditionsverbundenheit und ihrem Denkmalverständnis verdanken wir in den meisten Fällen aber auch, dass diese Monumente des Sozialen Wohnungsbaus über Generationen und selbst in schwierigen Zeiten unterhalten, nach Kriegsschäden wiederaufgebaut, immer wieder mit viel Sorgfalt gepflegt, wo nötig behutsam modernisiert oder auch restauriert worden sind und sich heute Bewohnern und Besuchern überwiegend in einem ausgezeichneten Überlieferungszustand präsentieren.

Die vorliegende Dokumentation der für das Welterbe angemeldeten Siedlungen der Berliner Moderne mag Bewohnerinnen und Bewohnern dieser Denkmaladressen und auch interessierten Bürgerinnen und Bürgern von Berlin erstmals eine umfassende Information über dieses Kapitel der modernen Architektur- und Sozialgeschichte der deutschen Hauptstadt bieten. Der angestrebte Status einer Welterbestätte schließt freilich ein, dass die sechs Berliner Siedlungen auch im globalen Maßstab als Erbe der ganzen Menschheit begriffen und angeeignet werden können. Die deutsch-englische Veröffentlichung dieser Dokumentation versteht sich zugleich als Einladung und Orientierungsangebot an Besucherinnen und Besucher aus aller Welt, diesen lokalen Beitrag der Berliner Moderne aus eigener Anschauung kennen und als gemeinsames Erbe der Menschheit schätzen zu lernen.

Klaus Wowereit
Der Regierende Bürgermeister von Berlin
Governing Mayor of Berlin

tection of Historical Monuments, as well as the local borough authorities, architects, art historians, restorers, consultants like the Berlin firm Winfried Brenne Architekten and Prof. Dr. Vladimir Slapeta, and cultural institutions working in the field of architectural history and monument research like the Bauhaus Archive/Museum of Design and the Berlin-Brandenburg Academy of the Arts. I would especially like to thank the owners of the housing estates, the housing companies BauBeCon, Berliner Bau- und Wohnungsgenossenschaft von 1892 e.G., GEHAG, and GSW. They were extremely supportive of our World Heritage initiative from the very beginning and made their own contributions to helping this application succeed. In addition, we owe it in large part to their sense of history and their understanding of the importance of historical monuments that these landmarks of social housing were preserved over generations, even in difficult times, rebuilt after suffering war damage, maintained with great care, painstakingly modernized or restored where necessary, and passed on to today's residents in what is generally excellent condition.

This documentation of the housing estates in the Berlin modern style being recommended for inclusion in the World Heritage List is meant to be the first comprehensive look at this chapter of modern architectural and social history in Germany's capital city that residents and other interested Berliners have ever had. Because we are aiming at inscription on the World Heritage List, however, we must also ensure that these Berlin housing estates can be understood and experienced also on a global scale as the legacy of all humankind. The book based on this documentation that is being published in German and English should thus be regarded as an invitation to people from all over the world to visit these sites and as a guide to getting to know Berlin's modernist architecture personally and to appreciating these estates as the shared legacy of humanity.

# EINFÜHRUNG
## INTRODUCTION

Abb. 1: „Konservierung der Moderne?". Dokumentation der ICOMOS-Tagung von 1996. Titelblatt

Fig. 1: „Konservierung der Moderne?" (Conservation of Modern Architecture?) Documentation of the ICOMOS conference, 1996. Front page

„Berlin war, nach Paris, die zweite Kunstmetropole Europas, in der nicht nur interessante Werke entstanden, sondern darüber hinaus eine bemerkenswerte Gruppe talentierter Architekten tätig war. Kein anderes Zentrum in den 20er Jahren konnte sich rühmen, mehr als ein Dutzend progressiver Architekten zu haben mit mehr als durchschnittlichem Talent und Fähigkeiten, genügend beweglich in geistiger Hinsicht, um eine ästhetische Revolution vom Expressionismus zum Elementarismus hervorzubringen, und mit gleicher Energie und Sicherheit in beiden Richtungen zu arbeiten."

Reyner Banham, Theory and Design in the First Machine Age, London 1960

"As the second artistic capital of Europe, after Paris, Berlin was clearly likely to produce works of interest, but it contained, in addition, a remarkable group of architectural talents. No other centre in the early Twenties could have boasted, as Berlin could, more than a dozen progressive architects of more than average competence, sufficiently resilient in mental constitution to take in their stride a major aesthetic revolution, from Expressionism to Elementarism, and to design in either style with equal vigour and assurance."

Reyner Banham, Theory and Design in the First Machine Age, London 1960

## Das Erbe der Berliner Moderne – Großsiedlungsbau als Kulturleistung

Zwischen den beiden Weltkriegen, genauer: zwischen der deutschen Novemberrevolution 1918 und der nationalsozialistischen „Machtergreifung" im Januar 1933, entwickelte sich Berlin zu einer Metropole der modernen Kunst. „Gross-Berlin" war nach den Eingemeindungen von 1920 eine der flächenmäßig größten Städte der Welt mit 876 Quadratkilometern und mit 3,86 Millionen Einwohnern hinter New York und London die bevölkerungsreichste Stadt. Berlin galt als größte Industriestadt des Kontinents, als Verkehrsknotenpunkt und europäisches Luftkreuz, als internationaler Messe- und moderner Medienstandort.

Die legendären „Goldenen 20er Jahre" verbinden sich mit der Stellung Berlins als kulturelles und künstlerisches Zentrum von Weltgeltung. Hier lebten und arbeiteten Künstler von internationalem Rang. Die „Weltstadt" (Martin Wagner) der Weimarer Republik zählte zu den internationalen Hauptschauplätzen der künstlerischen Avantgarde und des kulturellen Diskurses zwischen Tradition und Moderne. Zahlreiche Künstler, Autoren und Publizisten, Maler und Bildhauer, Theater- und Filmemacher, Musiker und Schauspieler von internationaler Bedeutung, die damals von hier Anregungen empfangen beziehungsweise in der weltoffenen Stadt auf Resonanz hoffen konnten, besuchten die Stadt oder standen mit ihr in Kontakt, andere lebten und arbeiteten hier wenigstens auf Zeit oder auf Dauer.

Das Ende des Ersten Weltkriegs, der Zusammenbruch des Deutschen Kaiserreichs, der Sturz der Monarchie und die Proklamation der Republik weckten neue politische und künstlerische Hoffnungen, teilweise verbunden mit der Utopie vom Sozialismus. Rasch entstanden nach der Novemberrevolution kritische, meist antibürgerliche, oftmals auch international zusammengesetzte Künstlergruppen wie der „Club Dada" (1918, mit Richard Huelsenbeck, Raoul Hausmann, George Grosz, John Heartfield, Hannah Höch etc.), der „Kreis Berliner Konstruktivisten" (1922, mit Naum Gabo, El Lissitzky, Laszlo Moholy-Nagy, Oskar Nerlinger) oder die „Gruppe der Blauen Vier" (1924, mit Wassily Kandinsky, Lyonel Feininger, Paul Klee, Alexej Jawlensky), die teilweise auch am Bauhaus in Dessau (1925–1932) und Berlin (1932/33) tätig waren. Neben der Avantgarde der visuellen Künste war die Avantgarde der darstellenden und literarischen Künste in Berlin durch namhafte und innovative Persönlichkeiten vertreten, wie die Regisseure und Autoren Bertolt Brecht und Erwin Piscator, Alfred Döblin und Erich Kästner oder die Publizisten Carl von Ossietzky, Kurt Tucholsky und Egon Erwin Kisch. Komponisten und Musiker wie Max Bruch, Arnold Schönberg, Kurt Weill, Hanns Eisler bestätigten Berlins Ruf als ein Experimentierfeld innovativer ästhetischer und politischer Konzepte.

Neue Medien, außer dem jungen Rundfunk vor allem die sich rasant entwickelnde Film- und Kinobranche, fanden in der weltoffenen Großstadtkultur Berlins rasch ihre Produzenten und ihr Publikum. Aus der 1917 in Berlin gegründeten Universum Film AG (UFA) entwickelte sich das größte Unternehmen dieser Art außerhalb der USA, und Berlin galt nach Hollywood als bedeutendster Film- und Kinostandort der Welt. Regisseure und Schauspieler wie Friedrich Wilhelm Murnau, Fritz Lang und Marlene Dietrich

## The Legacy of the Berlin Modern Style – Large housing estates as a cultural achievement

The years between the two world wars – or more precisely between the November Revolution of 1918 and Hitler's seizure of power in January 1933 – were the years of Berlin's transformation into a metropolis of modern art. In 1920, after incorporating a number of surrounding towns and villages, "Greater Berlin" had become one of the world's largest cities (876 square kilometres), and in terms of population the world's third largest after New York and London, with 3.86 million inhabitants. It was considered to be the most important industrial city on the European continent, a traffic hub, a European air hub and an attractive location for international fairs and modern media institutions.

The legendary "Golden 20s" are indelibly associated with the image of Berlin as one of the world's leading centres for culture and the arts. Internationally renowned artists lived and worked here. The "Weltstadt" of the Weimar Republic, as town planner Martin Wagner called it, was a magnet for the international avant-garde and a focal point of the cultural debate between tradition and modern age. Many artists, authors and journalists, painters and sculptors, theatre directors and film makers, musicians and actors of international standing visited the city or had links to it, hoping to draw inspiration from it or to be well received in the city's cosmopolitan atmosphere. Others lived and worked here at least for a while or permanently.

The end of the First World War, the collapse of the German Empire, the fall of the monarchy and the proclamation of the Republic sparked new hopes in Germany's political and artistic circles, some of them related to a utopian dream of socialism. The years following the November Revolution

Abb. III: Eröffnung der 1. Internationalen Dada-Messe am 5. Juli 1920 in Berlin

Fig. III: Opening of the 1st International Dada Fair on 5 July 1920 in Berlin

Abb. II: „Berlin. Die Sinfonie der Grosstadt". Uraufführungsplakat 1927

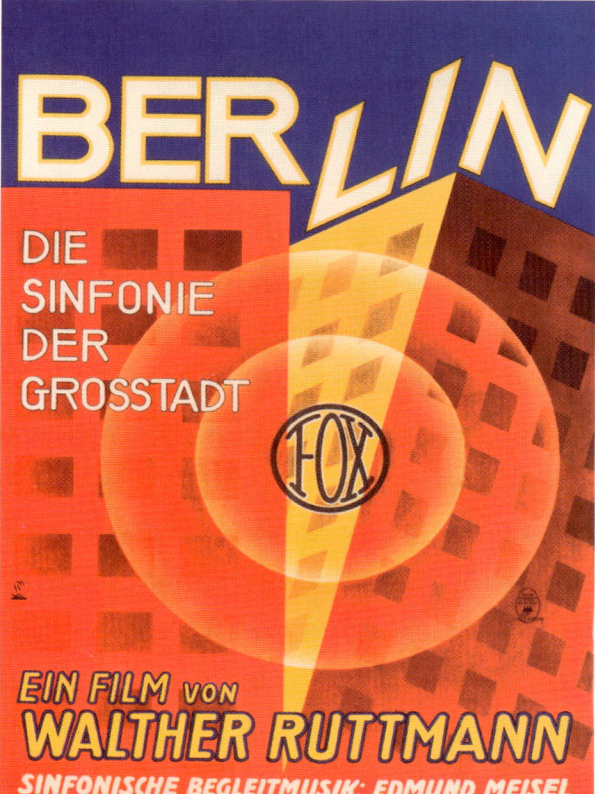

Fig. II: "Berlin. Die Sinfonie der Grosstadt". Premiere poster 1927

gaben ihr Debüt oder erlebten ihren künstlerischen Durchbruch in Berlin, ehe sie in die USA auswanderten. Ein Film- und Kinodenkmal der cineastischen Avantgarde setzte Walter Ruttmann der Stadt 1927 mit seinem Montagefilm „Berlin – die Sinfonie einer Großstadt". Der 1925/26 in Berlin von der UFA produzierte und 1927 hier uraufgeführte Film „Metropolis" von Fritz Lang ist 2001 von der UNESCO zum Weltdokumentarerbe (Memory of the World) erklärt worden. Legendäre Lichtspielhäuser der Berliner Moderne wie das Kino Babylon von Hans Poelzig oder das Universum-Kino von Erich Mendelsohn erinnern als Baudenkmale an den Aufstieg des neuen Mediums.

### Europäische Metropole der modernen Architektur

Eine Schlüsselrolle in der künstlerischen und sozialen Reformbewegung, die die Revolutionszeit 1918/19 und die kurze kulturelle Blütezeit der Weimarer Republik bis zur Weltwirtschaftskrise 1929/30 entscheidend prägen sollte, kam der Bau- und Stadtbaukunst zu. Wichtige Impulse für die Anfangsjahre und eine Art Katalysatorfunktion für die folgende Konsolidierungsphase gingen von der „Novembergruppe" aus, der neben bildenden Künstlern (Max Pechstein, Käthe Kollwitz, Cesar Klein, Rudolf Belling etc.) auch die Baukünstler Erich Mendelsohn, Ludwig Hilberseimer, Ludwig Mies van der Rohe, Hans Poelzig und weitere angehörten, oder von dem zeitgleich ins Leben gerufenen Berliner „Arbeitsrat für Kunst" (Karl Schmidt-Rottluff, Gerhard Marcks, Lyonel Feininger etc.) mit den jungen Architekten Bruno und Max Taut, Walter Gropius, Otto Bartning, Adolf Meyer und vielen anderen. Den revolutionären Impetus, mit dem die frühen Kunst- und Architekturmanifeste dieser Initiativen eine radikal neue Verbindung von Kunst und Leben forderten und der Baukunst eine führende Funktion

were characterised by the quick development of critical, usually anti-bourgeois and often international groups of artists such as Club Dada (1918 with Richard Huelsenbeck, Raoul Hausmann, George Grosz, John Heartfield, Hannah Höch etc.), the circle of the Berlin Constructivists (1922 with Naum Gabo, El Lissitzky, Laszlo Moholy-Nagy, Oskar Nerlinger), or the Blue Four (1924 with Wassily Kandinsky, Lyonel Feininger, Paul Klee, Alexej Jawlensky). Some of these artists were also involved with the Bauhaus movement, both in Dessau (1924–1932) and in Berlin (1932/33). But Berlin was not only a magnet for the avant-garde in the visual arts: It also attracted renowned and innovative personalities in the world of theatre, music and literature: directors and authors Bertolt Brecht and Erwin Piscator, Alfred Döblin and Erich Kästner, journalists Carl von Ossietzky, Kurt Tucholsky and Egon Erwin Kisch. Composers and musicians such as Max Bruch, Arnold Schönberg, Kurt Weill and Hanns Eisler confirmed Berlin's reputation as an incubator for innovative aesthetic and political concepts. The new media – not only the young world of radio broadcasting but also the rapidly growing cinema industry – quickly found producers and audiences in Berlin's open-minded and cosmopolitan culture. Universum Film AG (UFA), founded in Berlin in 1917, became the largest company of its kind outside the USA, and Berlin became known as the world's most important film and cinema location after Hollywood. Directors and actors such as Wilhelm Murnau, Fritz Lang and Marlene Dietrich made their debuts or experienced their breakthrough as artists in Berlin before emigrating to the USA. With his 1927 film montage "Berlin – die Sinfonie einer Großstadt", Walter Ruttmann created a memorial to the city and its cinematographic avant-garde. Fritz Lang's "Metropolis", produced by UFA in Berlin in 1925/26 and premiered there in 1927, was added to UNESCO's Memory of the World Register in 2001. Legendary cinemas in the Berlin Modern style – the Babylon, by Hans Poelzig, or the Universum, by Erich Mendelsohn, for instance – are architectural memorials to the early years of the new medium.

### A European metropolis of modern architecture

Architecture and urban development played a key role in the artistic and social reform movement that characterised the revolutionary period of 1918/19 and the short cultural upswing experienced by the Weimar Republic until the world economic crisis of 1929/30. The "November Group", which included artists (Max Pechstein, Käthe Kollwitz, Cesar Klein, Rudolf Belling etc.) as well as architects (Erich Mendelsohn, Ludwig Hilberseimer, Ludwig Mies van der Rohe, Hans Poelzig and others), and the Berlin "Arbeitsrat für Kunst" (Working Council for Art: Karl Schmidt-Rottluff, Gerhard Marcks, Lyonel Feininger and others), dating from the same period and including the young architects Bruno Taut, Walter Gropius, Otto Bartning, Adolf Meyer and many others, provided inspiration in the early years and fulfilled a catalyst function for the phase of consolidation which followed. Filled with a revolutionary spirit, these groups published manifestos calling for a radically new relationship between art and life and attributing a leading role to architecture in the construction of a new society and a new environment. This revolutionary impetus is reflected in an early appeal of the Working Council, formulated in 1918 by

im Aufbau einer kommenden Gesellschaft und Umwelt beimaßen, gibt ein – von dem Architekten Bruno Taut formulierter – früher Aufruf des „Arbeitsrats" aus dem Jahr 1918 wider: „Kunst und Volk müssen eine Einheit bilden. Die Kunst soll nicht mehr Genuss weniger, sondern Glück und Leben der Masse sein. Zusammenschluss der Künste unter den Flügeln einer großen Baukunst ist das Ziel. Fortan ist der Künstler allein als Gestalter des Volksempfindens verantwortlich für das sichtbare Gewand des neuen Staates. Er muss die Formgebung bestimmen, vom Stadtbild bis hinunter zur Münze und zur Briefmarke."

Die 1923/24 in Berlin durch Mies van der Rohe, Max Taut, Erich Mendelsohn, Hugo Häring, Hans Scharoun und anderen als „Zehnerring" – später „Zwölferring" – initiierte Architektenvereinigung „Der Ring" sollte sich ab 1926 reichsweit auf 27 Mitglieder erweitern und zu einer Art Sezession deutscher Architekten entwickeln. Sie bot ganz unterschiedlichen Strömungen der architektonischen Zwischenkriegsmoderne eine gemeinsame Plattform und vereinte Exponenten der Neuen Sachlichkeit und des Bauhauses ebenso wie Vertreter einer Organischen Architektur. Die Siedlung Siemensstadt, an der namhafte Ring-Architekten mitwirkten, erhielt im Volksmund die Bezeichnung „Ringsiedlung". Vor allem aber entfaltete der Architektenzirkel eine eminente Außenwirkung als Multiplikator moderner Architekturprogramme – und provozierte 1928 als stramm konservative Gegeninitiative den von Paul Bonatz, Paul Schmitthenner, Paul Schultze-Naumburg und anderen ins Leben gerufenen Zusammenschluss national gesonnener Kollegen im Architektenbund „Der Block".

Berlin entwickelte sich in den 20er Jahren zunehmend auch zu einer begehrten Bühne für namhafte auswärtige Baukünstler, die in der aktuellen Architekturdebatte durch Vorträge, Ausstellungen oder gebaute Beiträge Position beziehen wollten. Die von Hannes Meyer entworfene Bundesschule Bernau des Allgemeinen Deutschen Gewerkschaftsbundes (1928) vor den Toren Berlins oder das Shell-Haus (1930) von Emil Fahrenkamp erinnern bis heute daran. Seine Rolle als eine internationale Begegnungsstätte der Zwischenkriegsmoderne und als ein europäisches Zentrum des internationalen Architekturdiskurses verdankte Berlin einer kosmopolitischen Öffnung, die sich bereits vor dem ersten Weltkrieg angebahnt hatte und in den Revolutions- und Inflationsjahren rasch verbreitete. Gastvorträge und Gastausstellungen oder Studienaufenthalte in Berlin sowie Vortrags- und Studienreisen oder Arbeitsaufenthalte deutscher Planer und Architekten im Ausland intensivierten den internationalen Meinungs- und Erfahrungsaustausch. Kolonien ausländischer Künstler aus den europäischen Nachbarstaaten, namentlich aus Russland (Charlottengrad), Italien und Frankreich, aber auch aus Amerika waren sichtbare Zeichen eines neuartigen, weil grenzen- und gattungsübergreifenden Dialogs.

Hatte sich das Interesse der deutschen Reformbewegung in Architektur, Wohnungsbau und Kunstgewerbe während der Kaiserzeit auf „Das englische Vorbild" (Stephan Muthesius) konzentriert, also insbesondere die englische Gartenstadtbewegung, die „Arts and Crafts-Bewegung" und den bürgerlichen Hausbau auf der Insel im Auge, jedoch Entwicklungen in Frankreich, Belgien, Holland oder gar in den Vereinigten Staaten nur am Rande wahrgenommen, so

*architect Bruno Taut: "Art and the people must be united to form one entity. Art shall no longer be the preserve of a selected few but a source of happiness and life for the masses. The aim is to unite the arts under the umbrella of great architecture. From now on the artist, shaper of popular sensibilities, bears the sole responsibility for the visible appearance of the new state. He must define all design from urban architecture to coins and postal stamps".*

*The association of architects founded in 1923/24 by Mies van der Rohe, Max Taut, Erich Mendelsohn, Hugo Häring, Hans Scharoun and others under the name "Der Ring" (initially a ring of ten, then twelve, and finally 27 members nationwide as of 1926) developed into a kind of secession of German architects. It provided a common platform for many different movements of modern architecture between the two world wars and brought together representatives of Neue Sachlichkeit and Bauhaus as well as advocates of Organic Architecture. The Siemensstadt housing estate, designed by a number of leading members of the Ring, was soon nicknamed "Ring Estate". The greatest significance of this circle of architects, however, was its enormous external impact as a multiplier for modern architectural programmes. In 1928 its activities provoked a strictly conservative counter-initiative called "Der Block" – an association of nationalistic colleagues created by Paul Bonatz, Paul Schmitthenner, Paul Schultze-Naumburg and others.*

*In the 1920s, Berlin also increasingly attracted renowned architects from outside the city who wanted to take a stance in the ongoing architectural debate by giving lectures, holding exhibitions or designing buildings. Hannes Meyer's Bundesschule des Allgemeinen Deutschen Gewerkschaftsbundes (Federal School of the General German Trade Union Federation) in Bernau on the outskirts of Berlin (1928) and Emil Fahrenkamp's Shell-Haus (1930) are reminders of this trend to the present day. Berlin's role as an international meeting place for modern artists of the inter-war period and its position at the centre of the international architectural debate were the result of its open, cosmopolitan atmosphere, which had started before the Great War and developed rapidly during the years of revolution and inflation. Guest lectures and exhibitions in Ber-*

Abb. V: „Metropolis" von Fritz Lang, 1925/26

Fig. V: "Metropolis" by Fritz Lang, 1925/1926

Abb. IV: Shell-Haus, 1930/31 von Emil Fahrenkamp, Foto 1931

Fig. IV: Shell-house, 1930/31 by Emil Fahrenkamp, 1931

stand die Fachwelt der Berliner Architekten und Architekturpublizisten in der Weimarer Republik vor allem unter dem Eindruck russischer und holländischer Entwicklungen. In Holland hatte das Wohnungsbaugesetz von 1901 eine effektive Arbeit von Wohnungsbaugesellschaften ermöglicht und gefördert. Bruno Taut zum Beispiel bereiste 1923 die Niederlande, um staatlich geförderte Siedlungen zu studieren. Und Erich Mendelsohn wurde bereits 1920 zu einer Vortragsreise nach Holland eingeladen und hielt 1923 seinen programmatischen Vortrag „Dynamik und Funktion" in Amsterdam. J. J. P. Oud, Theo van Doesburg und El Lissitzky seien stellvertretend für zahlreiche ausländische Künstlerarchitekten genannt, die in Berlin während jener Jahre als besonders anregend wahrgenommen wurden.

„Das Neue Berlin" – so auch der Titel der 1929 von Stadtbaurat Martin Wagner (nach dem Frankfurter Vorbild von Ernst May) ins Leben gerufenen „Monatshefte für die Probleme der Großstadt" – verstand sich vor allem als Hauptstadt einer neuen Baukultur. In keiner anderen kulturellen Sparte profilierte sich Berlin so sehr als „avantgardistischer Nabel der Welt" wie auf dem Gebiet der Architektur und des Städtebaus. Ein Gutteil seiner kulturellen und urbanen Identität beruhte auf großangelegten städtebaulichen Projekten und Bauvorhaben der Zwischenkriegsjahre. Seinen Ruf als internationales Zentrum der Städtebaureform und der modernen Architekturbewegung verdankte Berlin kühnen und visionären Zukunftsentwürfen ebenso wie neuen, Aufsehen erregenden Bauwerken, die als programmatische Beiträge zu einer neuen Baukultur über Veröffentlichungen und Vorträge weite Verbreitung fanden.

lin and study visits to the city as well as lecture tours, study trips and working visits of German planners and architects abroad intensified this international exchange of opinion and experience. Colonies of foreign artists from neighbouring European states, in particular from Russia ("Charlottengrad" was the nickname given to the Berlin district of Charlottenburg), Italy and France and even from America, represented the visible signs of this new dialogue across national borders and art genres.

Under the Kaisers, the interest of the German reform movement in architecture, housing construction and crafts had focussed on the "English example" (Stephan Muthesius), in particular on the English Garden City Movement, the Arts and Crafts Movement and middle-class housing construction in Great Britain, while acknowledging only marginally developments in France, Belgium, Holland or especially in the United States. In the Weimar Republic, Berlin architects and architectural journalists, on the other hand, were mainly influenced by developments taking place in Russia and Holland. In Holland, the housing law of 1901 had laid the legal and financial foundations for efficient residential construction by housing associations. Bruno Taut travelled through the Netherlands in 1923 to study housing estates built with state subsidies. As early as 1920, Erich Mendelsohn had been invited on a lecture tour of Holland, and in 1923 he held his hallmark lecture on dynamics and function in Amsterdam. J.J.P. Oud, Theo van Doesburg and El Lissitzky are among the many foreign architects whose work was perceived as particularly inspiring in the Berlin of the 1920s.

Utopische, vorwiegend expressionistische Projekte wie Bruno Tauts Architekturphantasien (Auflösung der Städte, Die Stadtkrone, Alpine Architektur etc.) oder Hans Scharouns organischer „Volkshaus-Entwurf" trugen zu diesem Ruf bei, ebenso unrealisiert gebliebene Wettbewerbsbeiträge oder Entwurfsideen wie Mies van der Rohes Glashochhausprojekt für Berlin oder radikale urbanistische Neuordnungsvorschläge wie Ludwig Hilberseimers Großstadtarchitektur. Selbst später verloren gegangene Bild- und Bauwerke jener Jahre wie der expressionistische Zuschauerraum von Hans Poelzigs Großes Schauspielhaus oder Mies van der Rohes Denkmal für Rosa Luxemburg und Karl Liebknecht haben in das kollektive Bau- und Bildgedächtnis Eingang gefunden.

Vor allem aber sind es die ausgeführten und überlieferten Bauwerke oder städtebaulichen Ensembles selbst, die Berlins Geltung als Hauptschauplatz moderner Architektur und Stadtplanung begründeten. Zu den Inkunabeln der Weltarchitekturgeschichte des frühen 20. Jahrhunderts zählt Peter Behrens AEG-Turbinenhalle (1909) als Wegbereiter einer neuen Ästhetik im Industriebau. Nach dem Ersten Weltkrieg entstanden betont moderne Gewerkschaftshäuser von Bruno und Max Taut sowie von Erich Mendelsohn (ADGB-Haus Wallstraße, Verbandshaus der Buchdrucker Dudenstraße, DMV-Haus Alte Jakobstraße), Beiträge zu einer neuen Bürohausarchitektur von Peter Behrens und Bruno Paul (Alexander- und Berolina-Haus am Alexanderplatz, Kathreinerhaus am Kleistpark) oder das Haus des Rundfunks (Hans Poelzig) und der Funkturm (Heinrich Straumer) am Messegelände. Sie stehen gestalterisch für die radikale Abkehr von der Architekturauffassung des Kaiserreichs und funktional für ganz neuartige Bauaufgaben. Gemeinsam mit programmatisch gestalteten Schulbauten und öffentlichen Sozialeinrichtungen wie dem Strandbad Wannsee (Martin Wagner, Richard Ermisch) akzentuierten sie das Stadtbild im Sinne einer modernen, weltoffenen und egalitären Großstadtarchitektur.

Ihren städtebaulichen und sozialen Hauptbeitrag für ein modernes Stadt- und Gesellschaftsbild leistete die neue Architektur aber auf dem Gebiet des Wohn- und Siedlungsbaus. Vor allem sind hier die weitläufigen Mietwohnanlagen am Rand der inneren Stadterweiterungsgebiete und in den Außenbezirken zu nennen, wie sie der moderne Großstadtverkehr erschlossen und die Bildung von Groß-Berlin in das Weichbild der Metropole eingeschlossen hatte. Ungeachtet der exponierten Villen oder Wohnhausgruppen für aufgeschlossene bürgerliche Kreise oder auch bedeutender Künstler- und Architektenhäuser verkörpern die Großsiedlungen für breite Bevölkerungskreise den herausragenden bau- und sozialpolitischen Reformbeitrag der Zwischenkriegsjahre auf dem Gebiet des Städtebaus und des Wohnungsbaus. Nirgendwo hat die soziale Intention und Dimension der Architektur- und Städtebaudebatte der Zwischenkriegsmoderne sinnfälliger Gestalt angenommen als in den gemeinnützigen bzw. genossenschaftlichen Siedlungsbauprojekten jener Jahre.

Einen rasanten Aufschwung nahm die Wohnungsbauproduktion in Berlin seit Mitte der 20er Jahre, namentlich unter dem sozialdemokratischen Stadtbaurat Martin Wagner (1926–33), einem exzellenten Organisator und Multiplikator der Reformpolitik. Hauptvoraussetzung für die großartige Leistung war die gezielte Bündelung staatlicher Interven-

"Das Neue Berlin" (The New Berlin) – title of the "monthly journal for the problems of the city" founded in 1929 by the Berlin urban development councillor Martin Wagner following the example of Ernst May in Frankfurt – shows that Berlin understood itself above all as the capital of a new culture of architecture and building. In no other field of culture did Berlin make such a mark as the "avant-garde centre of the universe" as in the field of architecture and urban development. Much of its cultural and urban identity was based on the large-scale urban development projects and building activities of the inter-war years. Berlin owed its reputation as an international centre of urban development reform and the modern architecture movement to bold and visionary designs as well as to sensational new buildings popularised in publications and lectures as programmatic contributions to a new culture of building. Utopian and mainly Expressionist projects such as the architectural fantasies of Bruno Taut – Auflösung der Städte (dissolving the cities), Die Stadtkrone (the city crown), Alpine Architecture, etc. – or Hans Scharoun's organic design of the Volkshaus contributed to this reputation, as did unbuilt competition entries or design ideas such as Mies van der Rohe's glass high-rise building project for Berlin or the radical proposals for urban restructuring reflected in Ludwig Hilberseimer's city architecture. Even no longer existing sculptures and buildings from those years, for instance the Expressionist auditorium of Hans Poelzig's Grosses Schauspielhaus or Mies von der Rohe's monument to Rosa Luxemburg and Karl Liebknecht, have found their way into our collective memory of buildings and images.

Yet Berlin's reputation as a city of great modern architecture and urban planning is mainly founded on buildings and urban development projects that were actually implemented. One of the earliest examples of early twentieth-century world-class architecture is the AEG turbine hall by Peter Behrens (1909), which paved the way for a new type of aesthetics in industrial buildings. The structures erected after World War I were, for instance, emphatically modern trade union buildings by Bruno and Max Taut and by Erich Mendelsohn (the ADGB building on Wallstrasse, the printers' union building on Dudenstrasse, the DMV building on Alte Jakobstrasse), avant-garde office buildings by Peter

tions- und Förderinstrumente der Bau- und Wohnungsgesetzgebung sowie der Finanzierung und Bewirtschaftung umfangreicher Wohnungsbestände. Eine konsequente Typisierung und Normierung des Planungs- und Bauprozesses sowie die politisch forcierte Bildung hochrationeller Bauunternehmen und großer gemeinnütziger Wohnungsgesellschaften sorgten für die Umsetzung eines bis dahin für unvorstellbar gehaltenen Wohnungsbauprogramms: Waren in der Nachkriegsnot 1919 bis 1923 in Berlin etwa 9.000 öffentlich geförderte Mietwohnungen entstanden, wurden zwischen 1924 und 1930 noch einmal 135.000 Wohneinheiten fertiggestellt.

### Berlins Beitrag zum kulturellen Welterbe des 20. Jahrhunderts

Berlin sorgte in den 20er Jahren vor allem als Stadt der modernen Architektur für Furore und schrieb sich in das Buch der Weltarchitekturgeschichte des 20. Jahrhunderts ein. Reclams Kunstführer Deutschland, dessen Band „Berlin. Kunstdenkmäler und Museen", erstmals 1977 erschien, räumt der Neugestaltung Berlins im ersten Drittel des 20. Jahrhunderts Weltrang ein – „vielleicht ist es die einzige architektonische Leistung Berlins, die diesen Rang wirklich verdient." Im Unterschied zur Berliner Schinkel-Schule im 19. Jahrhundert oder auch zur fortschrittlichen „Amsterdamer Architekturschule" oder zur konservativen „Stuttgarter Architekturschule" im 20. Jahrhundert wirkte die Berliner Moderne der Zwischenkriegszeit freilich weniger geschlossen und schulbildend. Ihre transnationale, ja interkontinentale Ausstrahlung verdankt sie den vielfältigen biographischen Verflechtungen ihrer Hauptakteure, mehr noch ihrer äußerst aktiven Vortrags- und Publikations- sowie Reisetätigkeit und ihrer Lehrtätigkeit im In- und Ausland. Hinzu kommen zahlreiche Bauwerke, die ihre Protagonisten und Schüler in vielen Teilen der Welt hinterließen. Auslandsaufenthalte oder Auswanderung infolge der Weltwirtschaftskrise, vor allem aber dann die Verfolgung jüdischer, sozialistischer oder oppositioneller Künstler und Architekten unter dem Nationalsozialismus trugen zur weltweiten Verbreitung Berliner Beispiele der Zwischenkriegsmoderne bei. Bruno Taut (1880–1938), der 1931 mit einigen Mitarbeitern nach Russland ging, 1933 nach Japan emigrieren musste und 1936 einen Ruf nach Istanbul erhielt, oder Martin Wagner (1885–1957), der 1936 in die Türkei und 1938 in die USA emigrierte, um Stadtplanungsprofessor an der Harvard Universität zu werden, seien nur als exemplarische Lebensläufe angeführt.

Als um 1995 die Vorbereitungen zur Aktualisierung der deutschen Tentativliste für das UNESCO-Weltkulturerbe einsetzten, standen zwei Berliner Vorschläge zum Erbe des 20. Jahrhunderts auf der Agenda: zum einen das industrielle Erbe der „Elektropolis Berlin", also insbesondere die Industrie- und Technikdenkmale der einst weltweit führenden elektrotechnischen Industrie und Stromversorgungsunternehmen von Berlin aus dem ersten Drittel des 20. Jahrhunderts, zum anderen das Erbe der modernen Architektur und des sozialen Wohnungsbaus aus der Weimarer Republik. Die 1997 in der Kultusministerkonferenz der deutschen Länder erfolgte Prioritätensetzung für die Nominierung von sechs Großsiedlungen der Berliner Moderne aus den 20 Jahren erfolgte vor dem Hintergrund einer rund

Abb. VII: Großes Schauspielhaus, 1918/19 von Hans Poelzig. Foto 1920

Fig. VII: Großes Schauspielhaus, 1918/19 by Hans Poelzig, 1920

Abb. VI: Strandbad Wannsee, 1929/30 von Martin Wagner und Richard Ermisch. Foto 1931

Fig. VI: Strandbad Wannsee (beach resort Wannsee), 1929/30 by Martin Wagner and Richard Ermisch, 1931

Behrens and Bruno Paul (the Alexander and Berolina buildings at Alexanderplatz, the Kathreiner building at Kleistpark) or Haus des Rundfunks (the radio broadcasting house) by Hans Poelzig and the Funkturm, the radio telecommunication tower on the trade fair grounds, by Heinrich Straumer. In terms of design, they symbolise a radical break with the architectural views of the Empire, and functionally they reflect completely new tasks to be fulfilled by buildings and architecture. Together with school buildings and public social facilities such as the Wannsee Beach public bath (Martin Wagner, Richard Ermisch) with its programmatic design, they are the highlights of the new city and examples of a modern, cosmopolitan and egalitarian city architecture.

The new architecture's main urbanistic and social contribution to a modern image of cities and society, however, was made in the field of housing and estate construction. Particularly worthy of mention in this respect are the spacious rental housing estates at the edges of the inner city expansion areas and in the suburbs, which had been made accessible thanks to modern city transport and which had gradually become part of the fringe areas of the city as a result of the formation of Greater Berlin. Leaving aside the prominent residential villas and ensembles of the liberal bourgeoisie and notable houses of artists or architects, the large housing estates for the general population are the true embodiment of the reforms in building and social policies that took place between the two world wars in the field of urban development and housing. Nowhere else are the social intentions and dimensions of the debate on modern architecture and urban development between the two world wars more clearly reflected than in the non-profit and cooperative housing development projects of those years.

40-jährigen konservatorischen Erfahrung mit Wohnanlagen der Berliner Zwischenkriegsmoderne und im Wunsch nach einer Fortschreibung der Welterbeliste unter Einbeziehung des bis dahin unterrepräsentierten architektonischen Erbes des 20. Jahrhunderts und des großstädtischen Massenwohnungsbaus als Resultat von Industrialisierung und Urbanisierung.

Der auf internationalen ICOMOS Tagungen in Helsinki (1995) und Mexiko (1996) vorbereitete „Montreal Action Plan" von ICOMOS aus dem Jahr 2001 bestärkte die Berliner Initiative. Die im Februar 2004 von ICOMOS im Auftrag der UNESCO vorgelegte Studie zur Ausgewogenheit der Welterbeliste „The World Heritage List: Filling the Gaps – an Action Plan for the Future" konstatierte ebenfalls einen Mangel an Welterbeeintragungen aus dem letzten Jahrhundert und forderte die Unterzeichnerstaaten der UNESCO-Welterbekonvention auf, ihre Prioritätensetzungen im Dialog mit Experten von ICOMOS, DOCOMOMO, TICCIH etc. zu überprüfen und zu verbessern.

Die sechs als Welterbstätten nominierten Siedlungen der Berliner Zwischenkriegsmoderne zählen – auch im internationalen Vergleich – zu den Schlüsselzeugnissen des sozialen Wohnungsbaus im 20. Jahrhundert überhaupt. In den exemplarisch ausgewählten Siedlungen verdichten sich auf einzigartige Weise baukünstlerische und stadtbaukünstlerische Entwicklungslinien des modernen Massenwohnungsbaus, aber auch sozialpolitische und wohnungspolitische Reformansätze, die über Berlin und Deutschland hinaus auf die europäische Architekturdebatte ausstrahlten. Dabei handelt es sich weder um singuläre Modellbauvorhaben oder prototypische Einzellösungen, wie sie bereits die Weltausstellungen des 19. Jahrhunderts zur Lösung der Wohnungsfrage oder später die Bauausstellungen der Werkbundbewegung im 20. Jahrhundert als Musterkollektion präsentiert hatten, noch um Sonder- oder Insellösungen, wie sie philanthropische oder gemeinnützige Bestrebungen bereits vor dem Ersten Weltkrieg in industriellen

Housing construction in Berlin grew enormously after the mid-1920s, in particular under the Social Democratic urban development councillor Martin Wagner (1926–33), an excellent organiser and multiplier of the reform policies. The main precondition for this great achievement was the focussed bundling of instruments of state intervention and promotion with regard to building and housing legislation as well as to the financing and management of large numbers of flats. A housing programme of hitherto unimaginable scope could be implemented thanks to consistently standardised design, planning and construction and to political support for highly efficient construction companies and large non-profit housing associations. While Berlin had built approximately 9,000 subsidised rental flats during the hard post-war years between 1919 and 1923, another 135,000 units were built between 1924 and 1930.

## Berlin's Contribution to the Cultural World Heritage of the Twentieth Century

In the 1920s, Berlin was sensationally renowned as the city of modern architecture, thus securing its position in the annals of twentieth-century world architectural history. The first edition of the volume Berlin. *Kunstdenkmäler und Museen* (Berlin, Monuments and Museums), published in 1977 by Reclam as part of the "Kunstführer Deutschland" (Art Guide for Germany) series, claims that the re-design of Berlin during the first third of the twentieth century was of world standing – "Perhaps this is Berlin's only architectural achievement which really deserves this rank." Yet, in contrast to the Berlin Schinkel school of the nineteenth century or to the progressive "Amsterdam school of architecture" or especially the conservative "Stuttgart school of architecture" of the twentieth century, the Berlin Modern style of the years between the two world wars appears to be less closed and schoolish. Its transnational, indeed intercontinental influence was based on the manifold biographical intertwinings of its main actors and even more on their

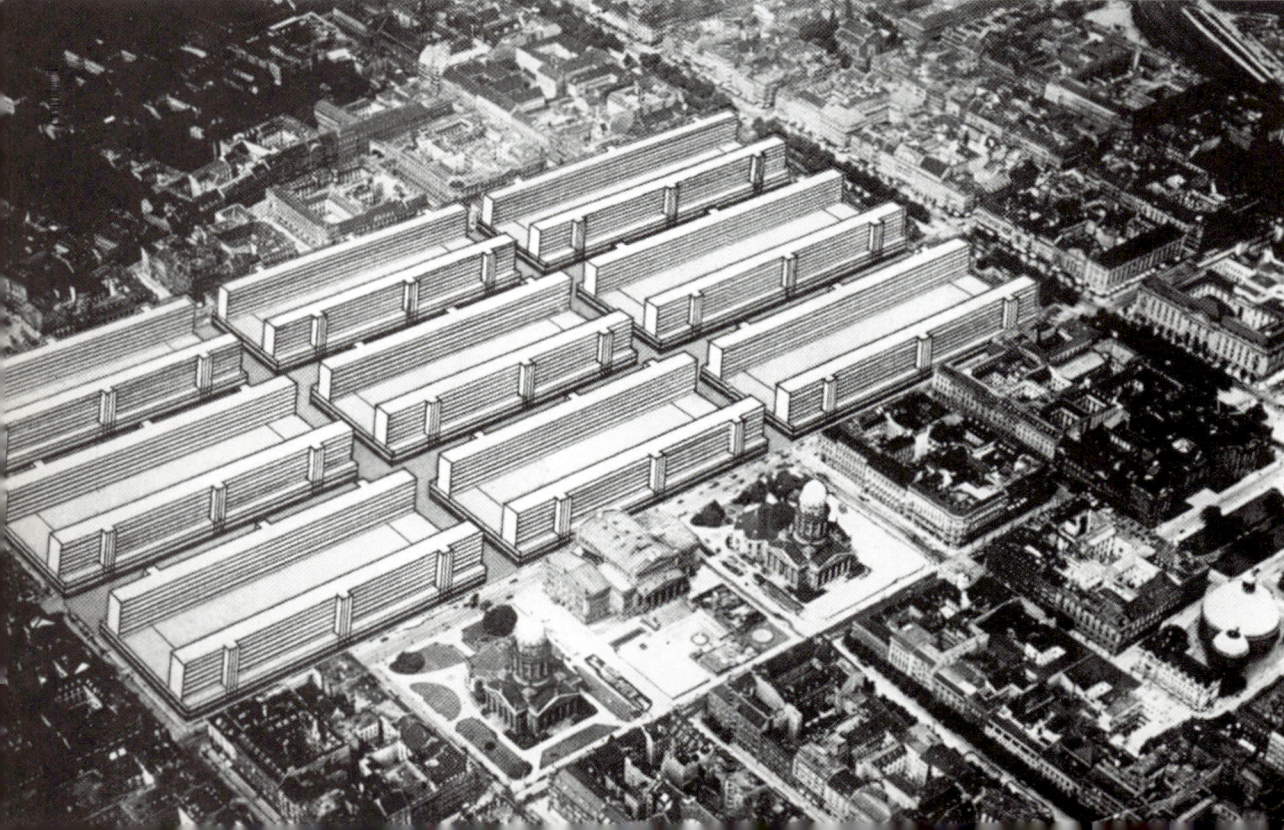

Abb. VIII: Ludwig Hilberseimer: Projektstudie zur Umgestaltung des Berliner Zentrums, 1928

Fig. VIII: Ludwig Hilberseimer: Design study for restructuring the Berlin city centre, 1928

Abb. IX: Siemensstadt

Fig. IX: Siemensstadt

oder großstädtischen Ballungsräumen realisiert und als Vorbilder propagiert hatten. Vielmehr stehen die sechs ausgewählten Siedlungen pars pro toto für eine Vielzahl von durchgrünten Siedlungsgebieten in Berlin, wie sie zwischen den beiden Weltkriegen raumgreifend und im städtebaulichen Maßstab als alternative Bau- und Wohnform zur hochverdichteten Mietskasernenstadt des 19. Jahrhunderts entstanden und bis heute erhalten sind.

Die zur Eintragung in die Welterbeliste vorgeschlagenen Berliner Siedlungen decken typologisch und funktional einen bislang unter den UNESCO-Welterbestätten des 20. Jahrhunderts nicht oder nur sehr unvollkommen repräsentierten Ausschnitt der Kulturgeschichte ab, nämlich die Bauaufgabe des Massenwohnungsbaus in zusammenhängend geplanten, ausgeführten und belegten städtebaulichen Einheiten. Lässt man die eminent bedeutenden historischen Stätten von Krieg und Frieden, von politischer Verfolgung und Widerstand im 20. Jahrhundert (Konzentrationslager Auschwitz-Birkenau, wiederaufgebaute Altstadt Warschau, Hiroshima Peace Memorial – Genbaku Dome) als Sonder-

enormous lecturing, publishing, travelling and teaching activity at home and abroad, not to forget the many structures built by its protagonists and students in many parts of the world. Visits to other countries or emigration due to the world economic crisis and in particular as a result of the persecution of Jewish, socialist or oppositional artists and architects during the Nazi years contributed to the spread of Berlin examples of modern inter-war architecture all over the world. Bruno Taut (1880–1938), for instance, who had gone to Russia together with some coworkers in 1931, had to emigrate to Japan in 1933 and got an appointment in Istanbul in 1936. Martin Wagner (1885–1957) emigrated to Turkey in 1936 and to the USA in 1938, where he was appointed professor for urban development at Harvard University.

When preparations for updating the German tentative list for the UNESCO world heritage began in 1995, two Berlin proposals for the heritage of the twentieth century were on the agenda. One of them was the industrial heritage of "Electropolis Berlin", in particular the monuments of in-

Abb. X: „Siedlungen der 20er Jahre". Dokumentation der Berliner Tagung 1985. Titelblatt

Fig. X: „Siedlungen der 20er Jahre" (Housing estates of the 1920s). Documentation of the Berlin conference, 1985. Front page

dustry and technology built in the first third of the twentieth century by Berlin electrical engineering and power-supply companies, the top global players in their market at the time. The other was the heritage of modern architecture and publicly assisted housing development in the Weimar Republic. In 1997, the German federal conference of state ministers of education and cultural affairs gave priority to six large housing estates built in the 1920s in the Berlin Modern style. This selection was based on the forty or so years of experience gathered in conserving the housing estates built in the Berlin Modern style between the two world wars and on the wish to complement the World Heritage List with examples of twentieth-century architectural heritage, which is still under-represented in the list, and of mass urban housing resulting from industrialisation and urbanisation.

The Berlin initiative was confirmed by the Montreal Action Plan of ICOMOS (2001), which had been prepared during the international ICOMOS conferences in Helsinki (1995) and Mexico (1996). The ICOMOS study on the representativity of the World Heritage List – "The World Heritage List: Filling the Gaps – an Action Plan for the Future" – presented in February 2004 at the request of UNESCO stated that there was a lack of items from the past century and requested the signatory states of the UNESCO World Heritage Convention to review and improve their priorities in a dialogue with experts of organisations such as ICOMOS, DOCOMOMO, TICCIH, etc.

Nationally and internationally, the six nominations – housing estates built in the Berlin Modern style between the two world wars – represent key products of twentieth-century publicly assisted housing development. The selected estates are outstanding combinations of architectural and urbanistic trends in modern mass housing construction and examples of the variety of approaches to social and housing policy reforms that influenced the European architectural debate even beyond Berlin and Germany. They are not unique model projects or individual prototypes like those presented as potential solutions to housing problems at nineteenth-century world exhibitions or as part of model collections at Werkbund exhibitions in the twentieth century. Nor are they special or isolated solutions for industrial centres or conurbations as had already been implemented and encouraged by philanthropic or non-profit measures before the First World War. Rather, these six chosen estates are typical of many Berlin housing areas mixed with green spaces as they were erected between the two world wars and still exist today. From an urbanistic point of view, these spacious estates represent an alternative form of development and housing to the extremely dense tenement buildings of the nineteenth century.

In terms of typology and functionality, the Berlin housing estates which have been proposed for entry in the World Heritage List cover a segment of twentieth-century cultural history which is not or only very insufficiently covered by the UNESCO World Heritage List: the task of developing mass housing facilities in coherently planned, erected and occupied urban units. Leaving aside the eminently significant historic locations of war and peace, of political persecution and resistance in the twentieth century (the concentration camp at Auschwitz-Birkenau

kategorie außer Acht, dann repräsentieren einige kulturelle Welterbestätten des 20. Jahrhunderts künstlerische Œuvrezusammenhänge und Vorformen oder Frühformen der Moderne, die ihre historische Wurzeln in den Jahren vor und nach 1900 (Stadthäuser von Viktor Horta, Brüssel, Belgien; das Werk von Antoni Gaudi, Barcelona, Spanien) haben. Andere Stätten sind im engeren Sinn dem industriellen und technischen Erbe des 20. Jahrhunderts (Zeche Zollverein, Essen, Deutschland; Radiostation Varberg, Grimeton, Schweden; Dampfpumpwerk Wouda, Niederlande) zuzurechnen. Auch das auf der bundesdeutschen Tentativliste für das Welterbe verzeichnete Fagus-Werk (Alfeld) von Walter Gropius lässt sich diesem speziellen Segment zuordnen.

Im Unterschied zu prominenten Denkmalen der modernen Architektur und Wohnkultur, die in der Welterbeliste durch herausragende künstlerische Einzelschöpfungen vertreten sind, wie das Rietveld-Schröder-Haus von Gerrit Thomas Rietveld (Utrecht, Niederlande), das Haus Tugendhat von Ludwig Mies van der Rohe, (Brünn, Tschechien) oder das Architektenhaus und Studio Luis Barragán (Mexiko Stadt, Mexiko), repräsentieren die vorgeschlagenen Berliner Siedlungen einen sozial orientierten Beitrag zur Lösung der großstädtischen Wohnungsfrage und Miethausreform für Arbeiter und das Kleinbürgertum. In urbanistischer Hinsicht nimmt die Auswahlgruppe Berliner Siedlungen einzelne Aspekte funktionalistischer Stadtplanungskonzepte und des „International Style" vorweg, wie sie die als Welterbestätten des 20. Jahrhunderts eingetragenen städtebaulichen Komplexe in Europa (Weiße Stadt Tel Aviv, Israel; Wiederaufbaustadt Le Havre, Frankreich) und Südamerika (Brasilia, Brasilien; Universitätsstadt von Caracas, Venezuela) auszeichnen. Unter völlig anderen typologischen und zeitlichen Vorzeichen könnte man vielleicht die auf der Tentativliste von Frankreich bzw. der Schweiz angemeldete Wohnhochhausscheibe der „Unités

Abb. XI: „Das Neue Berlin". Titelseite des ersten Heftes, Januar 1929

Fig. XI: "Das Neue Berlin". Front page of the first issue, January 1929

d'habitation" in Marseille (1950) aus dem Œuvre von Le Corbusier als interessantes Vergleichsobjekt der Nachkriegsmoderne und als in die Vertikale gehendes Gegenbeispiel diskutieren.

Die nominierten Berliner Wohnanlagen stehen in einer Traditionslinie mit frühindustriellen und frühsozialistischen Mustersiedlungen des 18./19. Jahrhunderts und der Gartenstadtbewegung, wie sie die utopische Siedlungsgründung New Lanark (Schottland) von Robert Owen oder auch das philanthropische Textilarbeiterdorf Saltaire (England) auf der Welterbeliste repräsentieren. Im Unterschied zu diesen Welterbestätten der Industriekultur, zu denen auch die Werkssiedlung Crespi d'Adda in Oberitalien gerechnet werden kann, handelt es sich allerdings nicht um idealstädtische Modellanlagen im ländlichen Raum, sondern um großmaßstäbliche und großserielle Lösungen im urbanen Verdichtungsraum einer Industriemetropole, wie sie für das 20. Jahrhundert charakteristisch werden sollten.

### Denkmalerhaltung als Wertschätzung des kulturellen Erbes

Hohe Wertschätzung als Zeugnisse der modernen Architektur und des modernen Städtebaus, aber auch als Denkmale des Sozialen Wohnungsbaus erfuhren die Siedlungen der 20er Jahre schon bald nach dem Zweiten Weltkrieg und der Befreiung vom Nationalsozialismus. Die für eine Eintragung in die Welterbeliste vorgeschlagenen Großsiedlungen sind bereits in den ersten Nachkriegsinventaren der seit 1948 geteilten Stadt als bedeutende Bau- und Kunstzeugnisse gewürdigt. Die Ringsiedlung Siemensstadt beispielsweise wurde schon in den Inventaren der „Bauwerke und Kunstdenkmäler von Berlin" für Stadt und Bezirk Charlottenburg (1961) sowie Stadt und Bezirk Spandau

(Oświęcim), the rebuilt centre of Warsaw, the Hiroshima Peace Memorial – Genbaku Dome), which form a category of their own, some cultural world heritage sites of the twentieth century represent ensembles of a particular architect's oeuvre or are precursors or early forms of modern architecture with historic roots in the years before and after 1900 (the Victor Horta townhouses in Brussels, Belgium, the work of Antoni Gaudí in Barcelona, Spain). Others represent in a narrower sense the industrial and technical heritage of the twentieth century (Zeche Zollverein in Essen, Germany, the Varberg radio station in Grimeton, Sweden, the D. F. Wouda steam pumping station in the Netherlands). The Fagus-Werk (Alfeld) by Walter Gropius on the German tentative list for world cultural heritage also belongs to this special segment.

In contrast to the outstanding monuments of modern architecture and residential culture represented on the World Heritage List by famous artistic creations such as the Rietveld Schröderhuis by Gerrit Thomas Rietveld (Utrecht, Netherlands), the Tugendhat Villa by Ludwig Mies van der Rohe, (Brno, Czech Republic) or the Luis Barragán house and studio (Mexico City, Mexico), the proposed Berlin housing estates represent a socially oriented contribution for solving urban housing problems and providing flats for workers and the emerging middle classes. With respect to urban planning, the Berlin estates anticipate individual aspects of functional urban planning and International Style as they are represented by World Heritage sites in Europe (the White City of Tel Aviv in Israel, Le Havre, the City Rebuilt in France) and South America (Brasília in Brazil, Ciudad Universitaria in Caracas in Venezuela). In a completely different typology and time context, Le Corbusier's high-rise residential Unités d'habitation in Marseille (1950), which appear on the tentative list of France and Switzerland, might

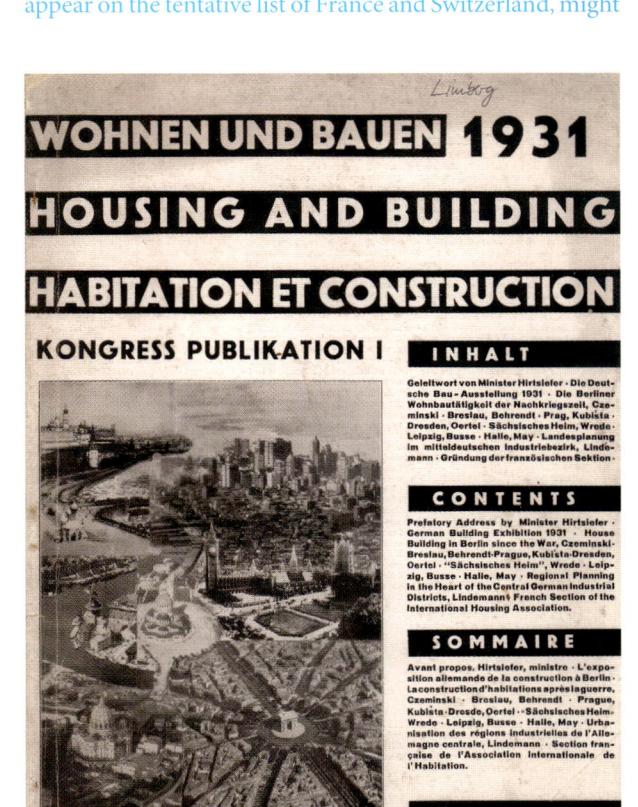

Abb. XII: „Wohnen und Bauen 1931". Tagungsband des Berliner Kongresses für Städtebau und Wohnungswesen. Titelblatt

Fig. XII: "Wohnen und Bauen 1931". Conference documentation of the Berlin Conference for urban development and housing. Front page

be seen as an interesting illustration of post-war modern style and a more vertically-oriented counter-example.

The nominated Berlin housing estates continue in the tradition of the model settlements of the early industrial and early socialist age of the eighteenth and nineteenth centuries and the Garden City Movement as represented in the World Heritage List by utopian settlements such as New Lanark (Scotland) by Robert Owen or the philanthropic textile workers' village of Saltaire (England). However, in contrast to these world heritage sites of industrial culture – which also include the company town of Crespi d'Adda in northern Italy – they are not model settlements in rural areas but city-scale solutions built in large series in the dense urban space of an industrial metropolis, and as such they have become characteristic for the twentieth century.

## Monument Conservation as Appreciation of Cultural Heritage

Soon after the end of the Second World War and liberation from Nazi rule, the housing estates of the 1920s met with high appreciation as monuments of modern architecture and urban development and also of publicly assisted housing. The large housing estates now being proposed for entry in the World Heritage List were already acknowledged as important monuments of building and art history in the first post-war inventories of the soon divided city. The Siemensstadt Ring Estate, for instance, is included in the list of *Bauwerke und Kunstdenkmäler von Berlin* (Berlin Buildings and Art Monuments) for the city and district of Charlottenburg (1961) and for the city and district of Spandau (1971). Parts of the estates were already legally protected and officially entered in the list of monuments prior to 1975, the European Monument Protection Year. Among them is the Siemensstadt section designed by Hans Scharoun and the central area of the Britz Horseshoe Estate (both entered in 1958) and the Weiße Stadt Estate in Reinickendorf (entered in 1971). The highly developed awareness of owners and residents and also of architects and politicians who identified with the achievements of the inter-war Modern style contributed decisively to ensuring that most of the estates were treated carefully even in the decades before they were legally protected, so that they have come down to us in a state of conservation which is truly rare.

In the 1970s series *"Berlin und seine Bauten"* (Berlin and its Buildings), the Berlin Association of Architects and Engineers published an initial scientific inventory of the entire city covering 171 Berlin housing estates built between 1919 and 1945. This inventory provided the basis for protecting further estates in the western part of the city. The legal opportunities were expanded with the GDR Monument Conservation Act of 1975 (Denkmalpflegegesetz) and the West Berlin Monument Protection Act of 1977 (Denkmalschutzgesetz), and these laws were used by curators on both sides of the Iron Curtain to protect the most important examples of publicly assisted housing built in the inter-war Berlin Modern style. As early as 1977, Gartenstadt Falkenberg (also known as the "paint-box estate", or "Tuschkastensiedlung") and Wohnstadt Carl Legien in the eastern part of the city were entered as monuments of supraregional signifi-

(1971) vorgestellt. Auch rechtskräftige Unterschutzstellungsverfahren und förmliche Eintragungen in die Denkmalliste erfolgten für einzelne Teilbereiche von Siedlungen bereits vor dem Europäischen Denkmalschutzjahr 1975, so etwa 1958 für den Bauabschnitt von Hans Scharoun in der Ringsiedlung Siemensstadt und für den Zentralbereich der Hufeisensiedlung Britz und 1971 für die Weiße Stadt in Reinickendorf. Das hochentwickelte Denkmalverständnis von Eigentümern und Bewohnern, aber auch von Architekten und Politikern, die sich mit den Errungenschaften der Zwischenkriegsmoderne identifizierten, hat entscheidend dazu beigetragen, dass die meisten Siedlungen auch in den Jahrzehnten vor einer gesetzlichen Unterschutzstellung pfleglich behandelt wurden und in einem selten guten Erhaltungszustand überliefert sind.

Eine erste gesamtstädtische wissenschaftliche Bestandsaufnahme von 171 Berliner Wohnanlagen und Siedlungen aus den Jahren 1919 bis 1945 veröffentlichte der Architekten- und Ingenieurverein zu Berlin 1970 in der Reihe „Berlin und seine Bauten". Aus dieser Bestandserhebung resultierten auch weitere Unterschutzstellungsverfahren im Westteil der Stadt. Die mit dem Denkmalpflegegesetz der DDR (1975) und dem Denkmalschutzgesetz von Westberlin (1977) erweiterten gesetzlichen Möglichkeiten nutzten die zuständigen Konservatoren auf beiden Seiten des Eisernen Vorhangs, um die wichtigsten Zeugnisse des Sozialen Wohnungsbaus der Zwischenkriegsmoderne als Flächendenkmale zu schützen. So erfolgte beispielsweise im ehemaligen Ostteil von Berlin schon 1977 die Eintragung der Gartenstadt Falkenberg (Tuschkastensiedlung) und der Wohnstadt Carl Legien als „Denkmal der Kultur und Lebensweise der werktätigen Klassen und Schichten" von überregionaler Bedeutung. Im ehemaligen Westteil wurden weitere Bereiche der Hufeisensiedlung Britz in Neukölln 1986 großflä-

Abb. XIII: „Tag des offenen Denkmals". Veranstaltungsbroschüre des Landesdenkmalamtes 2003. Titelblatt

Fig. XIII: "European Heritage Day". Brochure issued by the Landesdenkmalamt. 2003

Abb. XIV: Haus Lemke von Ludwig Mies van der Rohe, 1932/33

Fig. XIV: Haus Lemke (Lemke House) by Ludwig Mies van der Rohe, 1932/33

chig unter Denkmalschutz gestellt. Mit dem Fall der Berliner Mauer bzw. dem Gesetz zur Vereinheitlichung des Berliner Landesrechts (1990) und dem Inkrafttreten des Gesamtberliner Denkmalschutzgesetzes 1995 unterliegen alle sechs nominierten Siedlungen einem einheitlichen Schutz als Denkmalbereiche (Gesamtanlage, Ensemble), und zwar immer auch unter Einbeziehung aller konstituierenden Grün- und Freiflächen oder als Gartendenkmale geschützten Anlagenteile.

Kaum eine andere Stadt in Deutschland und wohl nur wenige in Europa haben so früh konservatorisches Neuland betreten und sich gezielt dem jungen Erbe des 20. Jahrhunderts zugewandt. Und kaum eine andere Stadt verfügt über vergleichbare Erfahrungen auf dem Gebiet der rechtlichen und praktischen Denkmalpflege von 20er Jahre-Siedlungen. Im Gefolge des Europäischen Denkmalschutzjahres (1975) und in Vorbereitung zum 750-jährigen Stadtjubiläum (1987) startete die Westberliner Denkmalpflege bereits 1978 vier Pilotprojekte zur vertiefenden Erfassung und Schadensanalyse sowie zur Entwicklung von denkmalgerechten Sanierungs- und Restaurierungstechnologien für das Erbe der 20 Jahre-Siedlungen. Daraus entstanden in Zusammenarbeit mit den zuständigen Wohnungsbaugesellschaften umfangreiche und detaillierte Dokumentationen aller wichtigen Bauteile und historischen Baustoffe und Baukonstruktionen als unentbehrliche Grundlage für die Sanierungsplanung und für die Entwicklung von langfristigen Denkmalpflegekonzepten.

Zu den Westberliner Modellprojekten, die in den 1970/80er Jahren in der Stadt ausgeführt und durch Publikationen, Ausstellungen und Vorträge im In- und Ausland weit über Berlin hinaus bekannt gemacht wurden, gehören auch drei für das Welterbe angemeldete Wohnkomplexe, nämlich die Hufeisensiedlung, die Ringsiedlung Siemensstadt und die Weiße Stadt Reinickendorf. Bereits im Jahr 1985 nahmen das Deutsche Nationalkomitee für Denkmalschutz

cance "to the culture and way of life of the working classes and strata". In West Berlin, further parts of the Britz Horseshoe Estate (Neukölln) were added to the list of protected monuments in 1986. Since the fall of the Berlin Wall and the adoption of the 1990 act standardising laws in the State of Berlin, and since the Gesamtberliner Denkmalschutzgesetz (Monument Protection Act for the Entire Berlin Territory) came into force in 1995, all six of the nominated settlements have enjoyed equal protection as monument sites (entire estate, overall design), in all cases also including all green spaces and outdoor facilities or the parts of the estates that are protected as historic gardens.

Hardly any other city in Germany and probably only few in Europe have embarked upon new roads in monument conservation as early as Berlin or started to deal with the legacy of the twentieth century in such a focussed manner. And hardly any other city has comparable experience in the field of legal and practical monument conservation of 1920s estates. In 1978, as a consequence of the European Monument Protection Year (1975) and in connection with preparations for the city's 750th anniversary (1987), the West Berlin monument conservation authority launched four pilot projects to encourage a more comprehensive stocktaking and analysis of damage as well as to develop restoration and repair technologies suitable for preserving the 1920s estates. In cooperation with the housing associations that own or manage the estates, it produced comprehensive and detailed documentations for all important building elements and historic building materials and designs, which now form an indispensable basis for planning refurbishment measures and developing long-term monument conservation concepts.

Among the West Berlin model projects of the 1970/80s that became known far beyond Berlin as a result of publications, exhibitions and lectures at home and abroad are also three of the estates now being proposed for entry in the

und der Gesamtverband gemeinnütziger Wohnungsunternehmen e.V. die fortgeschrittenen Berliner Erfahrungen zum Anlass, um eine interkommunale Tagung und bundesweite Dokumentation zur Denkmalpflege an Siedlungen der 20er Jahre durchzuführen. Nach dem Mauerfall 1990 konnten Denkmalpfleger und die rechtmäßigen Eigentümer der im Ostteil von Berlin gelegenen Siedlungen Gartenstadt Falkenberg und Wohnstadt Carl Legien methodisch und praktisch auf diesen Vorarbeiten aufbauen: Mit erheblicher öffentlicher Förderung versetzten die zuständigen Genossenschaften bzw. Gesellschaften ihre denkmalgeschützten Wohn- und Grünanlagen schrittweise ebenfalls wieder in einen historisch und künstlerisch angemessenen Zustand.

Die Berliner Bau- und Gartendenkmalpflege setzte in den letzten 25 Jahren deutschlandweit und im Dialog mit Konservatorenkollegen aus dem europäischen Ausland auch international Maßstäbe für die denkmalgerechte Pflege und Restaurierung von Siedlungen und Wohnanlagen der modernen Architektur. Am Internationalen Denkmaltag von ICOMOS im Jahr 2002 (International Day for Monuments and Sites) zum Thema „Conserving Monuments of the 20 Century Heritage" beteiligte sich das Landesdenkmalamt Berlin mit Führungen und Veranstaltungen zu den für die Welterbeliste nominierten Siedlungen der Zwischenkriegsmoderne. Berlin zählt zu den Initiatoren zur Einrichtung des Internationalen Wissenschaftlichen ICOMOS-Komitees „Erbe des 20. Jahrhunderts" (20th Century Heritage) und ist in diesem durch den Berliner Landeskonservator als Gründungsmitglied vertreten. Berlin bietet eine Plattform im Netzwerk der internationalen Denkmalkontakte und europaweiten Denkmal-Kooperationen. Zuletzt lenkte die sogenannte Berliner Erklärung der UNESCO (Berlin Appeal), die 75 Delegierte aus 40 europäischen Ländern im November 2005 zum „Periodic Reporting" der Welterbstätten (Periodic Reporting on the implementation of the World Heritage Convention) verabschiedeten, die internationale Aufmerksamkeit auf die deutsche Hauptstadt.

Die ausgewählten sechs Siedlungen sind nicht nur städtebauliche und architektonische Schlüsselzeugnisse des modernen Großsiedlungsbaus, sondern sie bestechen auch

World Heritage List: the Britz Horseshoe Estate, the Siemensstadt Ring Estate and the Weiße Stadt Estate in Reinickendorf. As early as 1985, the German National Committee for Monument Conservation (Deutsches Nationalkomitee für Denkmalschutz) and Gesamtverband gemeinnütziger Wohnungsunternehmen e. V. (a federation of non-profit housing companies) used the extensive Berlin experience as the basis for holding an inter-municipal conference and publishing a national report on monument conservation with regard to housing estates built in the 1920s. In 1990, after the border was opened, experts in monument conservation and the legal owners of the estates in the eastern part of the city (Gartenstadt Falkenberg and Wohnstadt Carl Legien) were able to fall back on this basis both with respect to methodology and in practice. Gradually and with the help of considerable public funding, the responsible housing cooperatives and housing companies restored East Berlin's protected residential buildings and outdoor facilities to their appropriate historic and artistic state.

During the past twenty-five years, the Berlin authority for the conservation of historic buildings and gardens has established new standards for the appropriate conservation and restoration of modern-style housing estates and residential ensembles both in Germany and, in a dialogue with colleagues from other European countries, internationally. Landesdenkmalamt Berlin participated in the 2002 ICOMOS International Day for Monuments and Sites, which was dedicated to the topic of "Conserving Monuments of the 20th Century Heritage", by offering guided tours and events presenting the inter-war estates built in the Berlin Modern style now nominated for entry in the World Heritage List. Berlin is one of the initiators of efforts to establish the ICOMOS International Scientific Committee on "20th Century Heritage", where it is represented as a founding member by the Berlin state curator. Berlin offers a platform in the network of international monument contacts and European monument conservation cooperation efforts. Most recently, UNESCO's so-called "Berlin Appeal" on periodic reporting on the implementation of the World Heritage Convention adopted in November 2005 by 75 representatives from 40 European countries attracted international attention for the German capital.

Abb. XV: Haus des Deutschen Metallarbeiter-Verbandes von Erich Mendelsohn, 1929/30

Fig. XV: "Haus des Deutschen Metallarbeiter-Verbandes" by Erich Mendelsohn, 1929/30

Abb. XVI: Haus des Deutschen Metallarbeiter-Verbandes von Erich Mendelsohn, 1929/30

Fig. XVI: "Haus des Deutschen Metallarbeiter-Verbandes" by Erich Mendelsohn, 1929/30

durch ihre weitgehend unverfälschte Authentizität. Sie sind bis heute im kulturellen Bewusstsein der Stadt verankert und als attraktive Wohnanlagen begehrt. Ihre Eintragung als Welterbestätte bedeutet für die politisch und konservatorisch zuständigen Stellen eine hohe Anerkennung und einen hohen Anspruch. Die Verantwortlichen in Berlin sind sich der mit einer Welterbeeintragung verbundenen Ehre und der daraus erwachsenden Verpflichtungen bewusst.

Prof. Dr. Jörg Haspel
Landeskonservator Berlin

The selected six settlements are not only key representatives of modern urban development and architecture; they also fascinate with their almost unadulterated authenticity. Even today they are firmly anchored in the city's cultural awareness and in great demand as attractive residential areas. Listing them as World Heritage sites would mean enormous recognition and further impetus for the politicians, conservation authorities and other parties involved in their preservation. The relevant parties in Berlin are fully aware of the honour connected with entry in the World Heritage List and of the obligations arising from it.

Prof. Dr. Jörg Haspel
State Curator of Heritage Conservation

| Nr. | Welterbestätten 20. Jahrhundert (Stand 2005) | Jahr der Eintragung |
|---|---|---|
| 1. | Konzentrationslager Auschwitz/Polen | 1979 |
| 2. | Altstadt von Warschau (Wiederaufbau)/Polen | 1980 |
| 3. | Das Werk von Antoni Gaudí in und bei Barcelona/Spanien | 1984/2005 |
| 4. | Stadt Brasilia/Brasilien | 1987 |
| 5. | Waldfriedhof Skogskyrkogården, Stockholm/Schweden | 1994 |
| 6. | Das Bauhaus und seine Stätten in Weimar und Dessau/Deutschland | 1996 |
| 7. | Hiroshima Peace Memorial (Genbaku Dome)/Japan | 1996 |
| 8. | Dampfpumpwerk Wouda, Lemmer/Niederlande | 1998 |
| 9. | Stadthäuser des Architekten Victor Horta, Brüssel/Belgien | 2000 |
| 10. | Rietveld-Schröder-Haus, Utrecht/Niederlande | 2000 |
| 11. | Universitätsstadt von Caracas, Venezuela | 2000 |
| 12. | Villa Tugendhat, Brünn/Tschechien | 2001 |
| 13. | Zeche Zollverein, Essen/Deutschland | 2001 |
| 14. | „Weiße Stadt", Tel Aviv/Israel | 2003 |
| 15. | Studio-Haus von Luis Barragán, Mexiko-Stadt/Mexiko | 2004 |
| 16. | Radiostation Varberg, Halland/Schweden | 2004 |
| 17. | Le Havre, die wiederaufgebaute Stadt von Auguste Perret/Frankreich | 2005 |

| No. | 20th Century World Heritage (state 2005) | Year of Inscription |
|---|---|---|
| 1. | Auschwitz Concentration Camp/Poland | 1979 |
| 2. | Historic Centre of Warsaw (Reconstruction)/Poland | 1980 |
| 3. | Works of Antoni Gaudí in and near Barcelona/Spain | 1984/2005 |
| 4. | City of Brasilia/Brazil | 1987 |
| 5. | Skogskyrkogården, Stockholm/Sweden | 1994 |
| 6. | Bauhaus and its Sites in Weimar und Dessau/Germany | 1996 |
| 7. | Hiroshima Peace Memorial (Genbaku Dome)/Japan | 1996 |
| 8. | Wouda Steam Pumping Station, Lemmer/Netherlands | 1998 |
| 9. | Major Town Houses of the Architect Victor Horta, Brussels/Belgium | 2000 |
| 10. | Rietveld Schröderhuis, Utrecht/Netherlands | 2000 |
| 11. | Ciudad Universitaria de Caracas/Venezuela | 2000 |
| 12. | Tugendhat-Villa, Brno/Czech Republic | 2001 |
| 13. | Zollverein Coal Mine Industrial Complex, Essen/Germany | 2001 |
| 14. | White City of Tel Aviv – the Modern Movement/Israel | 2003 |
| 15. | Luis Barragán House and Studio, Mexico City/Mexico | 2004 |
| 16. | Varberg Radio Station, Halland/Sweden | 2004 |
| 17. | Le Havre, the City Rebuilt by Auguste Perret/France | 2005 |

Abb. XVII: Welterbestätten des 20. Jahrhunderts (ohne Europa), Stand 2005

Fig. XVII: 20th Century World Heritage (without Europe), 2005

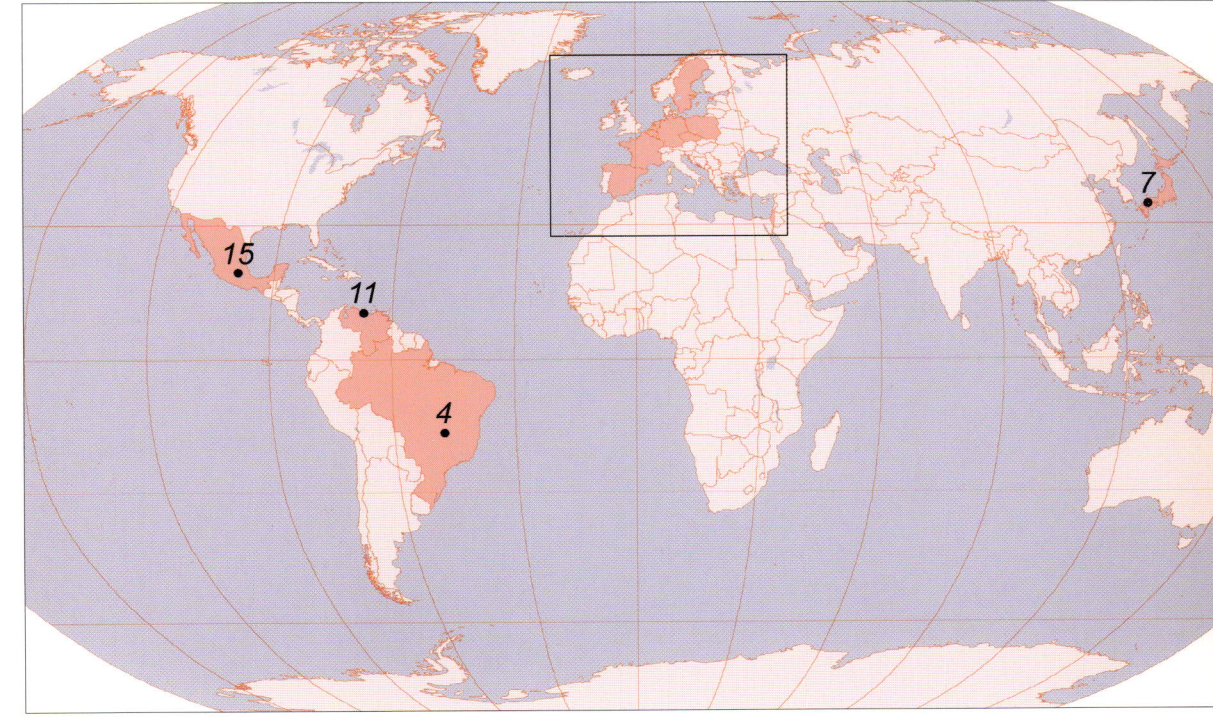

Abb. XVIII: Welterbestätten des 20. Jahrhunderts in Europa, Stand 2005

Fig. XVIII: 20th Century World Heritage in Europe, 2005

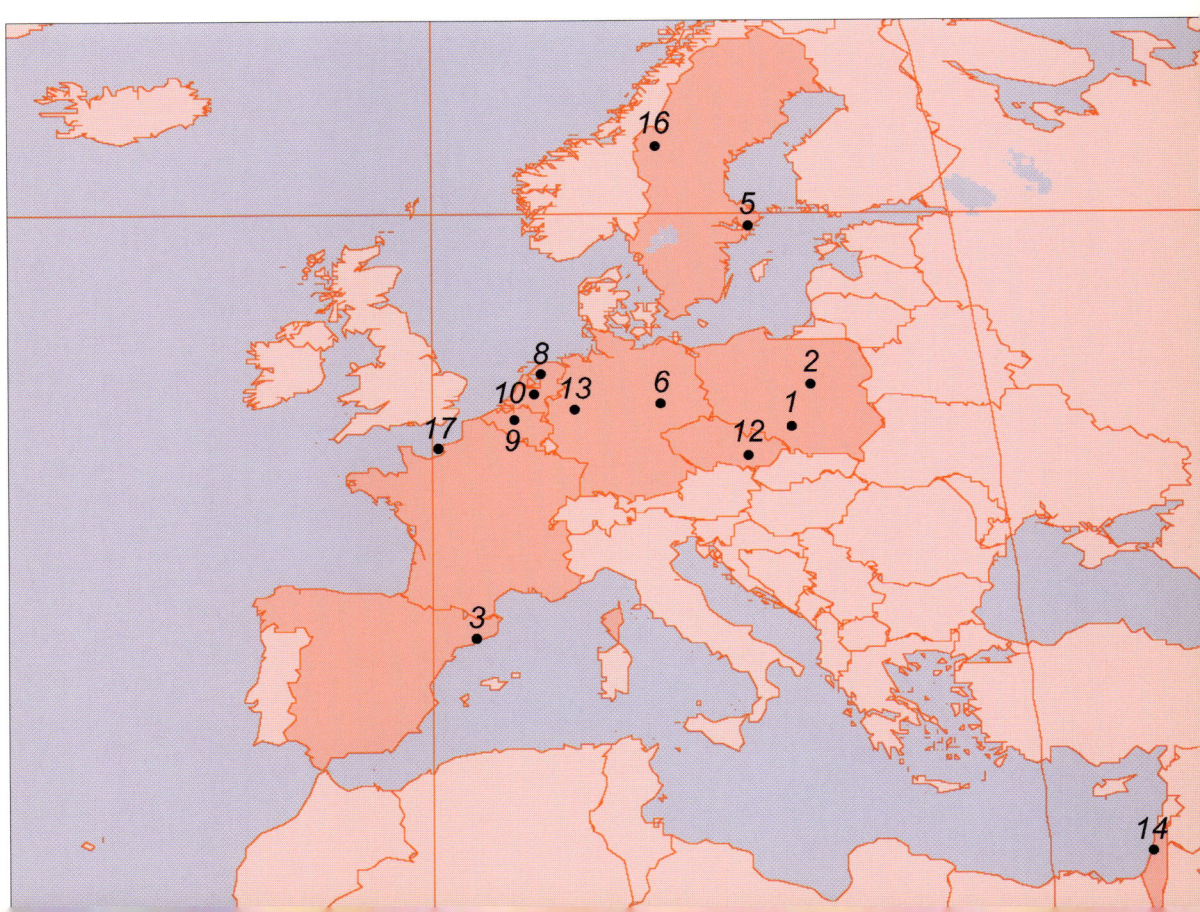

# 1
**DENKMALANLAGEN/ANGABEN ZUM STANDORT**
IDENTIFICATION OF THE MONUMENT PROPERTIES

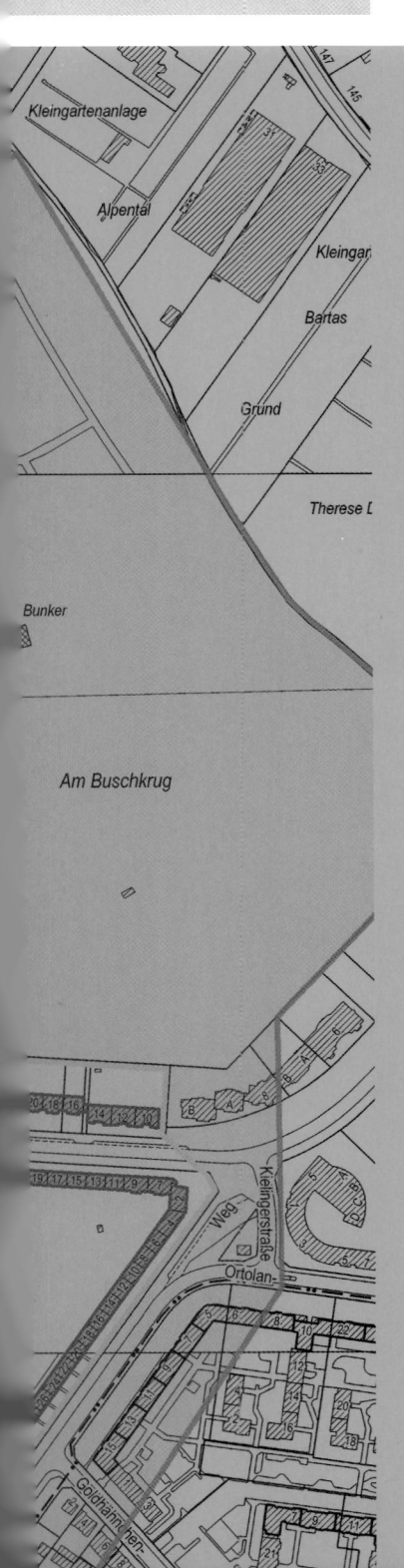

1.A **Land**

**Bundesrepublik Deutschland**

1.A Country

The Federal Republic of Germany

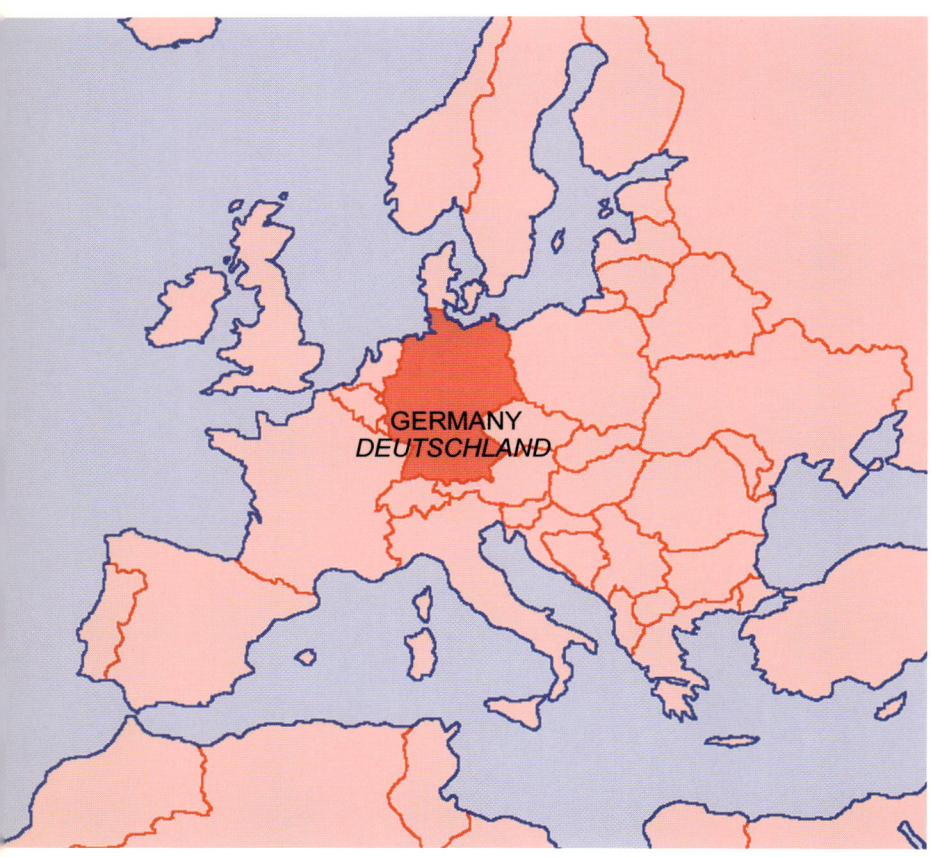

Abb. 1: Mitteleuropa mit Deutschland

Fig. 1: Central Europe with Germany

1.B **Bundesstaat, Provinz oder Region**

**Land Berlin**

1.B State, province or region

The Federal State of Berlin

Abb. 2: Deutschland mit Berlin

Fig. 2: Germany with Berlin

1.c **Bezeichnung der Anlagen**　　　　　　　1.c **Name of the property**

**Siedlungen der Berliner Moderne**　　　　　**Housing Estates in the Berlin Modern Style**

1 Gartenstadt Falkenberg　　　　　　　　　1 Gartenstadt Falkenberg
2 Siedlung Schillerpark　　　　　　　　　　2 Siedlung Schillerpark
3 Großsiedlung Britz (Hufeisensiedlung)　　　3 Großsiedlung Britz (Hufeisensiedlung)
4 Wohnstadt Carl Legien　　　　　　　　　4 Wohnstadt Carl Legien
5 Weiße Stadt　　　　　　　　　　　　　　5 Weiße Stadt
6 Großsiedlung Siemensstadt (Ringsiedlung)　6 Großsiedlung Siemensstadt (Ringsiedlung)

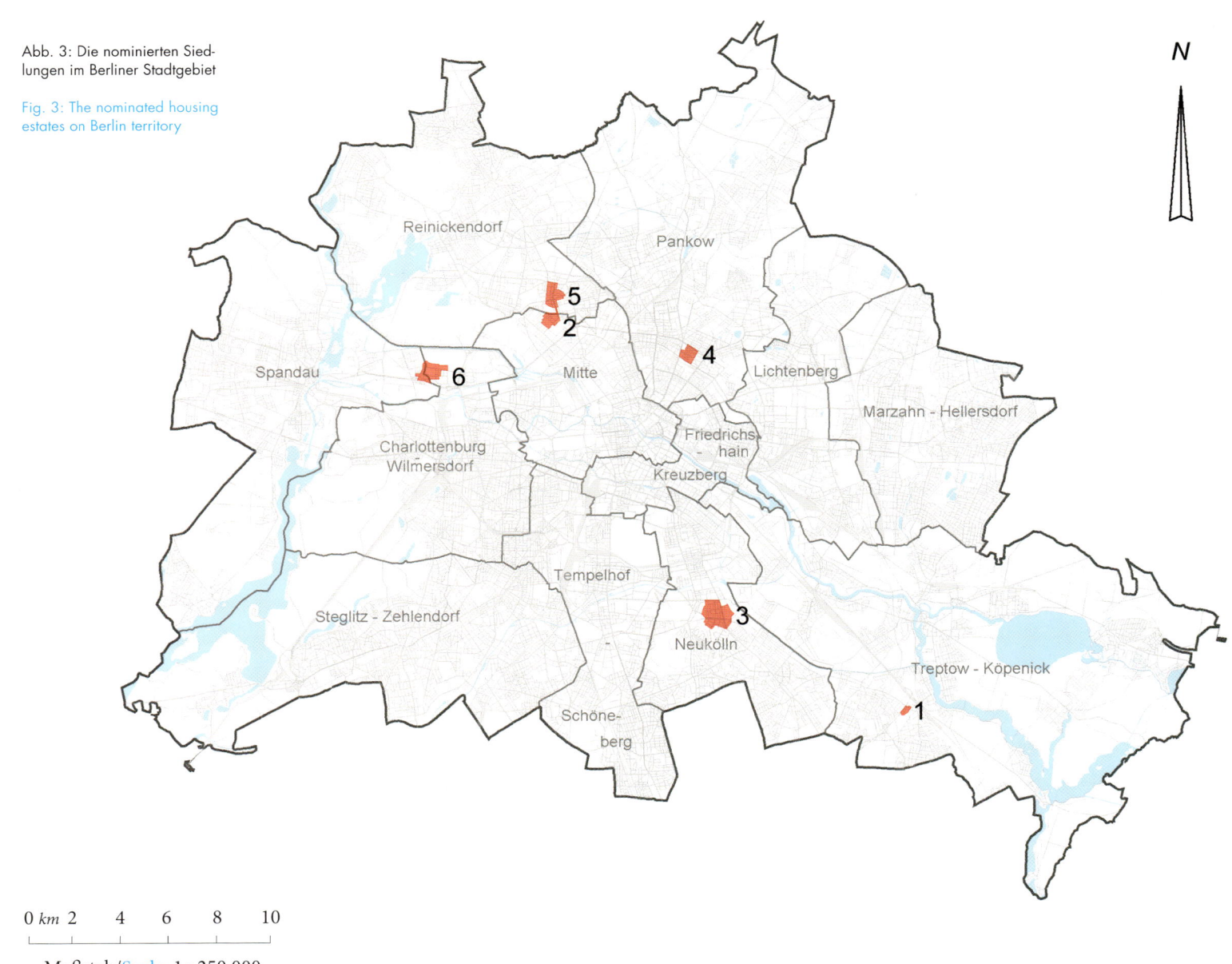

Abb. 3: Die nominierten Siedlungen im Berliner Stadtgebiet

Fig. 3: The nominated housing estates on Berlin territory

0 km 2　4　6　8　10

Maßstab/Scale 1 : 250.000

## 1.D Geographische Koordinaten / 1.D Geographical coordinates

**Fortlaufende Tabelle zu den nominierten Anlagen (Kennnummer 1239)** / **Serial nomination table ID–No. 1239**

| Kenn-Nr. / ID-No. | Gebietsbezeichnung / Name of the area | Bezirk / District | Zentrum (ha) / Core Zone (ha) | Pufferzone (ha) / Buffer Zone (ha) | Koordinaten / Coordinates geographische östl. Länge/ terrestrial longitude East geographische nördl. Breite/ terrestrial latitude North |
|---|---|---|---|---|---|
| 1239-001 | Gartenstadt Falkenberg | Treptow-Köpenick von/of Berlin | 4,4 ha | 6,7 ha | 13° 34' 00" 52° 24' 39" |
| 1239-002 | Siedlung Schillerpark | Mitte von/of Berlin | 4,6 ha | 31,9 ha | 13° 20' 56" 52° 33' 34" |
| 1239-003 | Großsiedlung Britz (Hufeisensiedlung) | Neukölln von/of Berlin | 37,1 ha | 73,1 ha | 13° 27' 00" 52° 26' 54" |
| 1239-004 | Wohnstadt Carl Legien | Pankow von/of Berlin | 8,4 ha | 25,5 ha | 13° 26' 01" 52° 32' 47" |
| 1239-005 | Weiße Stadt | Reinickendorf von/of Berlin | 14,3 ha | 41,1 ha | 13° 21' 03" 52° 34' 10" |
| 1239-006 | Großsiedlung Siemensstadt (Ringsiedlung) | Charlottenburg-Wilmersdorf von/of Berlin Spandau von/of Berlin | 19,3 ha | 46,7 ha | 13° 16' 39" 52° 32' 22" |
| | TOTAL | | **88,1 ha** | **225,0 ha** | |

## 1.E Karten und Pläne mit Darstellung der Grenzen der nominierten Anlagen und der Pufferzonen / 1.E Maps and plans, showing the boundaries of the nominated properties and buffer zones

**Liste der Pläne** / **List of the maps**

| Kenn-Nr. / ID-No. | Gebietsbezeichnung / Name of the area | Inhalt / Contents | Maßstab / Scale |
|---|---|---|---|
| 1239-001 | Gartenstadt Falkenberg | Lageplan/site plan | 1 : 5.000 |
| 1239-001 | Gartenstadt Falkenberg | Luftbild/aerial view | 1 : 5.000 |
| 1239-002 | Siedlung Schillerpark | Lageplan/site plan | 1 : 5.000 |
| 1239-002 | Siedlung Schillerpark | Luftbild/aerial view | 1 : 5.000 |
| 1239-003 | Großsiedlung Britz (Hufeisensiedlung) | Lageplan/site plan | 1 : 5.000 |
| 1239-003 | Großsiedlung Britz (Hufeisensiedlung) | Luftbild/aerial view | 1 : 5.000 |
| 1239-004 | Wohnstadt Carl Legien | Lageplan/site plan | 1 : 5.000 |
| 1239-004 | Wohnstadt Carl Legien | Luftbild/aerial view | 1 : 5.000 |
| 1239-005 | Weiße Stadt | Lageplan/site plan | 1 : 5.000 |
| 1239-005 | Weiße Stadt | Luftbild/aerial view | 1 : 5.000 |
| 1239-006 | Großsiedlung Siemensstadt (Ringsiedlung) | Lageplan/site plan | 1 : 5.000 |
| 1239-006 | Großsiedlung Siemensstadt (Ringsiedlung) | Luftbild/aerial view | 1 : 5.000 |

**1.F Flächen der nominierten Anlagen (ha) und der vorgesehenen Pufferzonen (ha)**
**Area of nominated properties (ha) and proposed buffer zones (ha)**

### Gartenstadt Falkenberg

| | |
|---|---:|
| Nominierungsgebiet/Area of nominated property: | 4,4 ha |
| Pufferzone/Buffer zone: | 6,7 ha |
| Gesamt/Total: | 11,1 ha |

### Siedlung Schillerpark

| | |
|---|---:|
| Nominierungsgebiet/Area of nominated property: | 4,6 ha |
| Pufferzone/Buffer zone: | 31,9 ha |
| Gesamt/Total: | 36,5 ha |

### Großsiedlung Britz (Hufeisensiedlung)

| | |
|---|---:|
| Nominierungsgebiet/Area of nominated property: | 37,1 ha |
| Pufferzone/Buffer zone: | 73,1 ha |
| Gesamt/Total: | 110,2 ha |

### Wohnstadt Carl Legien

| | |
|---|---:|
| Nominierungsgebiet/Area of nominated property: | 8,4 ha |
| Pufferzone/Buffer zone: | 25,5 ha |
| Gesamt/Total: | 33,9 ha |

### Weiße Stadt

| | |
|---|---:|
| Nominierungsgebiet/Area of nominated property: | 14,3 ha |
| Pufferzone/Buffer zone: | 41,1 ha |
| Gesamt/Total: | 55,4 ha |

### Großsiedlung Siemensstadt (Ringsiedlung)

| | |
|---|---:|
| Nominierungsgebiet/Area of nominated property: | 19,3 ha |
| Pufferzone/Buffer zone: | 46,7 ha |
| Gesamt/Total: | 66,0 ha |

## Gartenstadt Falkenberg

Die Gartenstadt Falkenberg liegt im Bezirk Treptow-Köpenick von Berlin, Ortsteil Bohnsdorf.

Akazienhof 1–26
Am Falkenberg 118–120
Gartenstadtweg 15–66, 68/72, 74–99

Die geographischen Koordinaten WGS 84 (GRS 80) sind:
1. Geographische östl. Länge 13° 34′ 00′′
2. Geographische nördl. Breite 52° 24′ 39′′

## Gartenstadt Falkenberg

Gartenstadt Falkenberg is situated in the district of Treptow-Köpenick of Berlin, borough of Bohnsdorf.

Akazienhof 1–26
Am Falkenberg 118–120
Gartenstadtweg 15–66, 68/72, 74–99

The geographical coordinates according to WGS 84 (GRS 80) are:
1. terrestrial longitude East 13° 34′ 00″
2. terrestrial latitude North 52° 24′ 39″

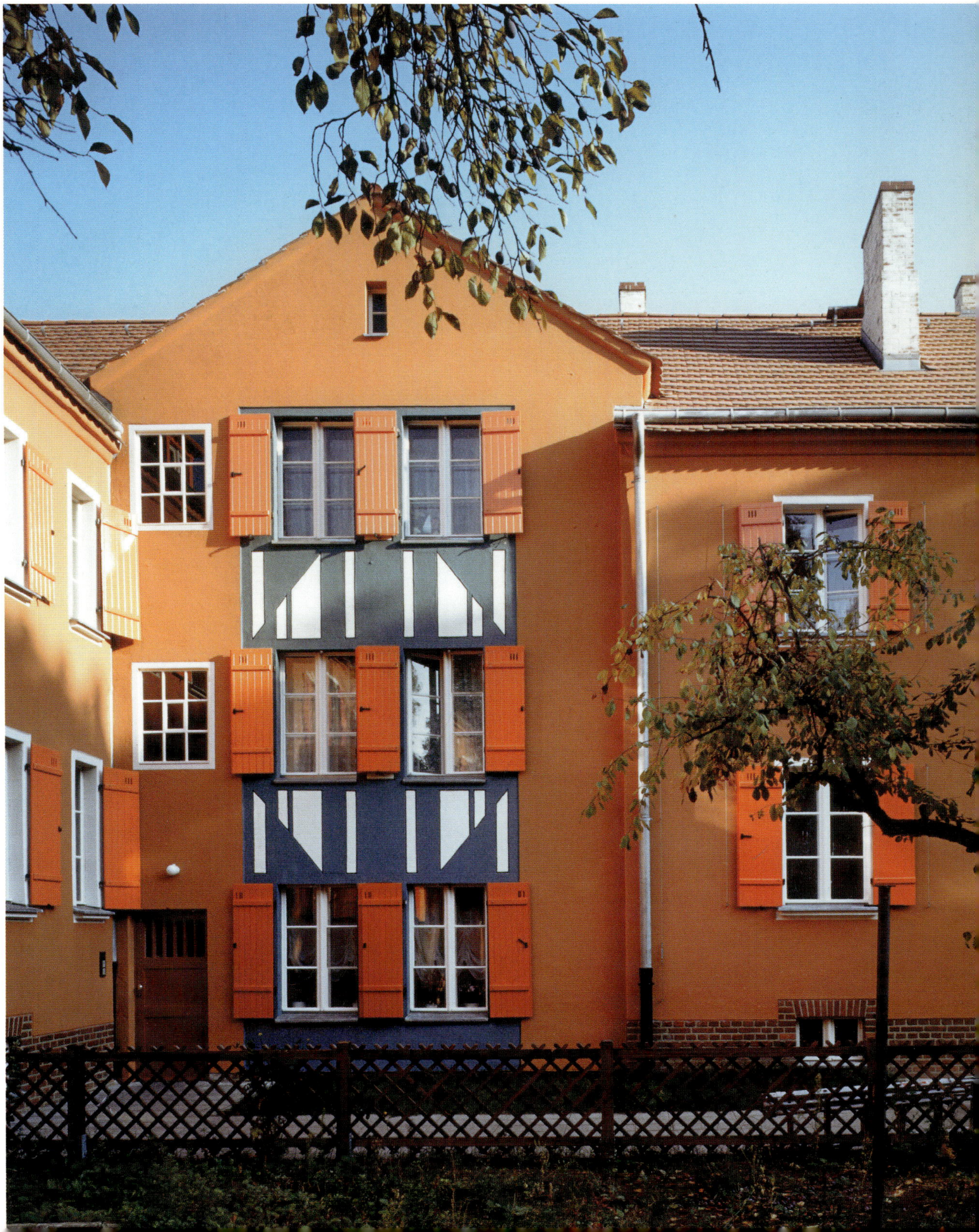

**Gartenstadt Falkenberg**

Luftbild/Aerial view
Landkarte/Land map

0 m   100   200   300   400   500

Maßstab/Scale 1 : 5.000
Kartengrundlage/Source plan: Bildflug Berlin, August 2004

Baudenkmal/Monument

Gartendenkmal/Listed garden

Nominierungsgebiet/
Aera of nominated property
Fläche/Surface         4,4 ha

Pufferzone/Buffer zone
Fläche/Surface         6,7 ha

Fläche Gesamt/
Surface total          11,1 ha

## Siedlung Schillerpark

Die Siedlung Schillerpark liegt im Bezirk Mitte von Berlin, Ortsteil Wedding.

Barfusstraße 23/31
Bristolstraße 1/17, 18/23, 25/27
Corker Straße 3/7, 19/29, 33/35
Dubliner Straße 62/66
Oxforder Straße 3–12, 14
Windsorer Straße 3–11

Die geographischen Koordinaten nach WGS 84 (GRS 80) sind:
1. Geographische östl. Länge 13° 20′ 56′′
2. Geographische nördl. Breite 52° 33′ 34′′

## Siedlung Schillerpark

The Siedlung Schillerpark is situated in the district of Mitte of Berlin, borough of Wedding.

Barfusstraße 23/31
Bristolstraße 1/17, 19/23, 25/27
Corker Straße 3/7, 19/29, 33/35
Dubliner Straße 62/66
Oxforder Straße 3–12, 14
Windsorer Straße 3–11

The geographical coordinates according to WGS 84 (GRS 80) are:
1. terrestrial longitude East 13° 20′ 56″
2. terrestrial latitude North 52° 33′ 34″

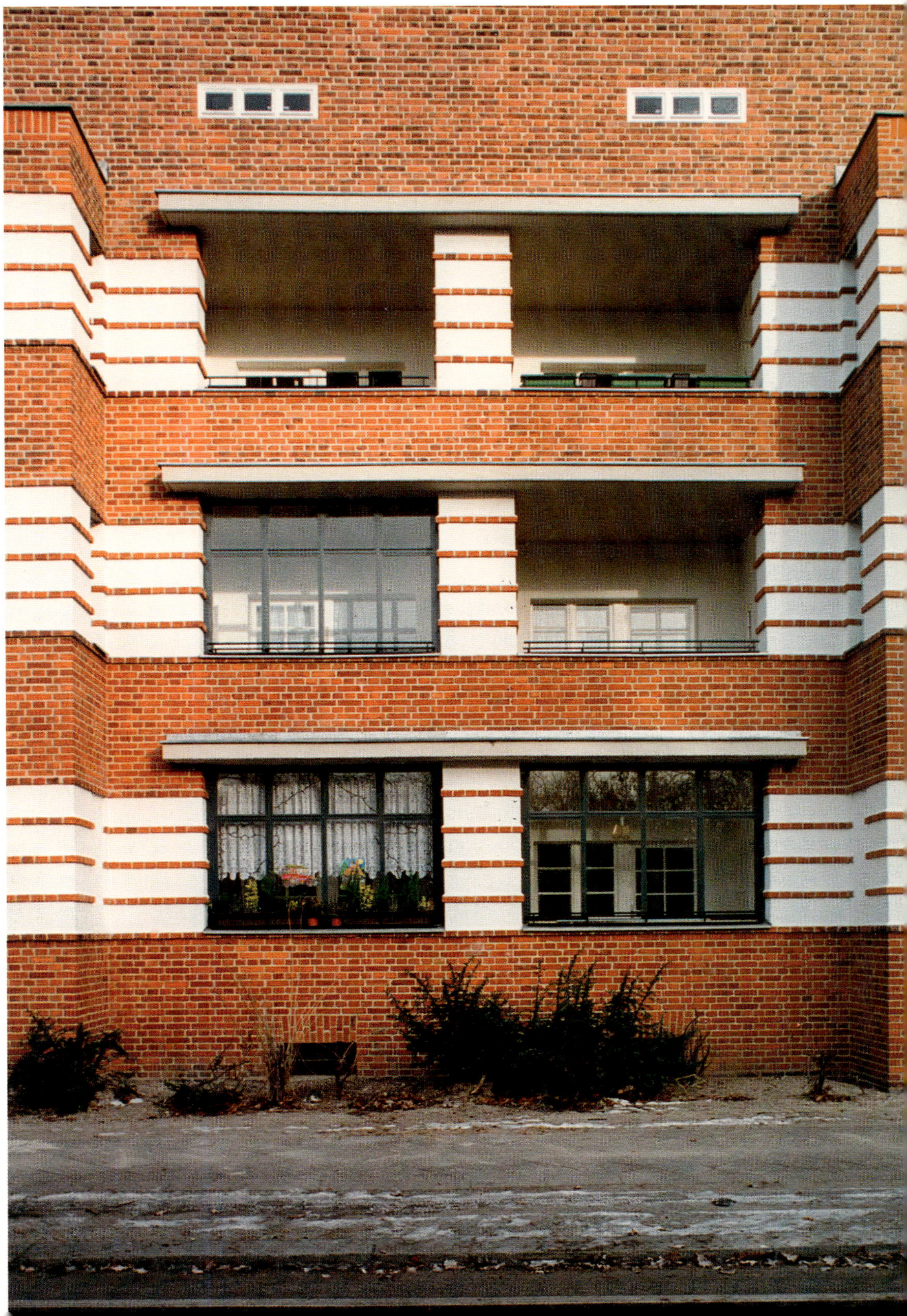

**Siedlung Schillerpark**

Luftbild/Aerial view
Landkarte/Land map

0 m   100   200   300   400   500

Maßstab/Scale 1 : 5.000
Kartengrundlage/Source plan: Bildflug Berlin, August 2004

Baudenkmal/Monument

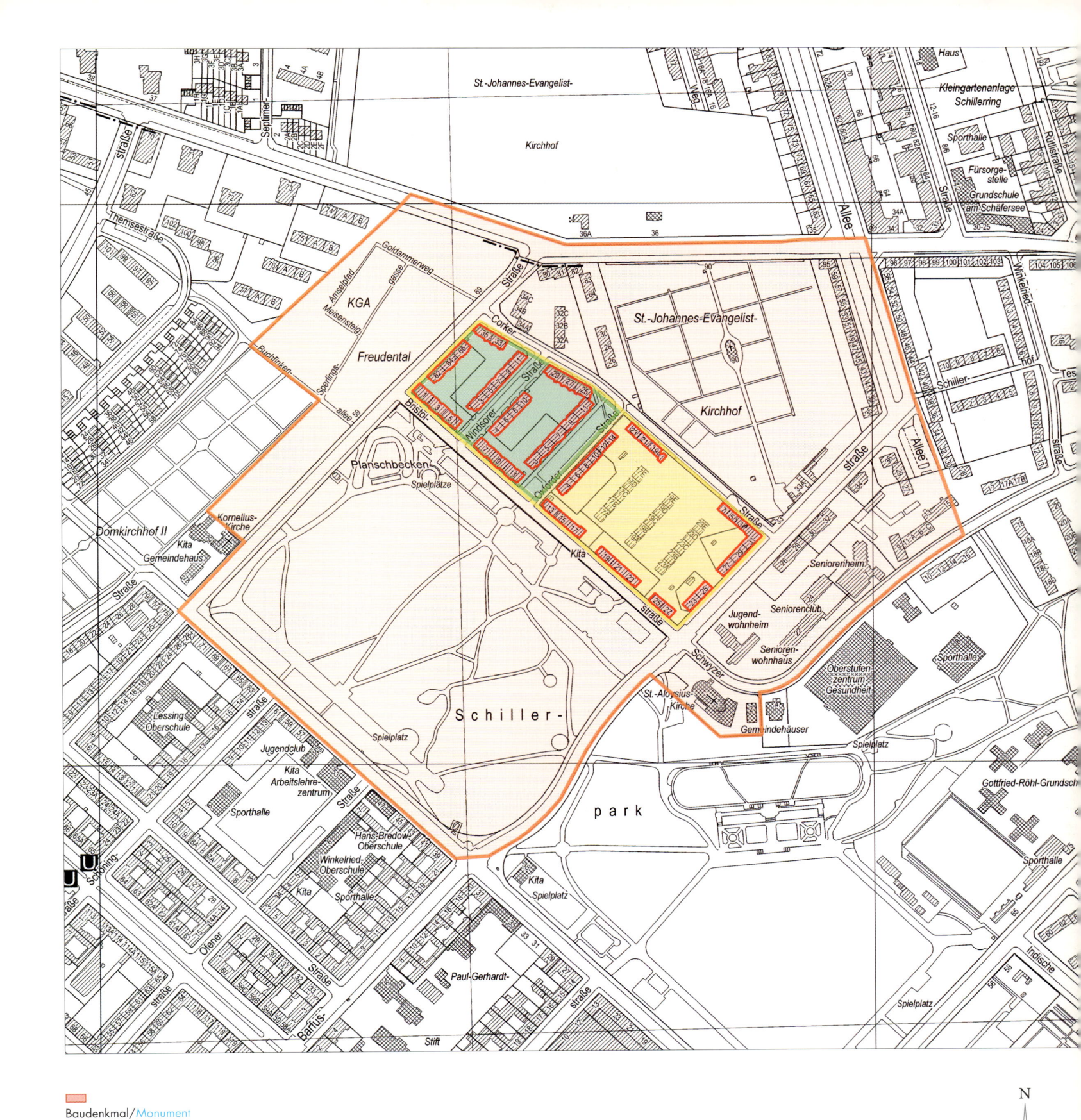

Gartendenkmal/Listed garden

Nominierungsgebiet/
Aera of nominatec property
Fläche/Surface          4,6 ha

Pufferzone/Buffer zone
Fläche/Surface          31,9 ha

Fläche Gesamt/
Surface total           36,5 ha

## Großsiedlung Britz (Hufeisensiedlung)

Die Großsiedlung Britz (Hufeisensiedlung) liegt im Bezirk Neukölln von Berlin, Ortsteil Britz.

Buschkrugallee 177/247
Dörchläuchtingstraße 1–10, 12/16, 18–50
Fritz-Reuter-Allee 2/72, 78/120
Gielower Straße 41–50
Grüner Weg 2/34
Hüsung 1–38
Jochen-Nüßler-Straße 1–45
Liningstraße 1–83, 85/87
Lowise-Reuter-Ring 1/47
Miningstraße 1–36, 38–86, 87–102
Onkel-Bräsig-Straße 1/11, 12–74, 79–143
Parchimer Allee 7, 9–30, 32, 66–70, 72–91, 92/104
Paster-Behrens-Straße 1–46, 48, 53/77
Stavenhagener Straße 4/32
Talberger Straße 2/12R

Die geographischen Koordinaten nach WGS 84 (GRS 80) sind:
1. Geographische östl. Länge 13° 27′ 00′′
2. Geographische nördl. Breite 52° 26′ 54′′

## Großsiedlung Britz (Hufeisensiedlung)

The Großsiedlung Britz (Hufeisensiedlung) is situated in the district of Neukölln of Berlin, borough of Britz.

Buschkrugallee 177/247
Dörchläuchtingstraße 1–10, 12/16, 18–50
Fritz-Reuter-Allee 2/72, 78/120
Gielower Straße 41–50
Grüner Weg 2/34
Hüsung 1–38
Jochen-Nüßler-Straße 1–45
Liningstraße 1–83, 85/87
Lowise-Reuter-Ring 1/47
Miningstraße 1–36, 38–86, 87–102
Onkel-Bräsig-Straße 1/11, 12–74, 79–143
Parchimer Allee 7, 9–30, 32, 66–70, 72–91, 92/104
Paster-Behrens-Straße 1–46, 48, 53/77
Stavenhagener Straße 4/32
Talberger Straße 2/12R

The geographical coordinates according to WGS 84 (GRS 80) are:
1. terrestrial longitude East 13° 27′ 00″
2. terrestrial latitude North 52° 26′ 54″

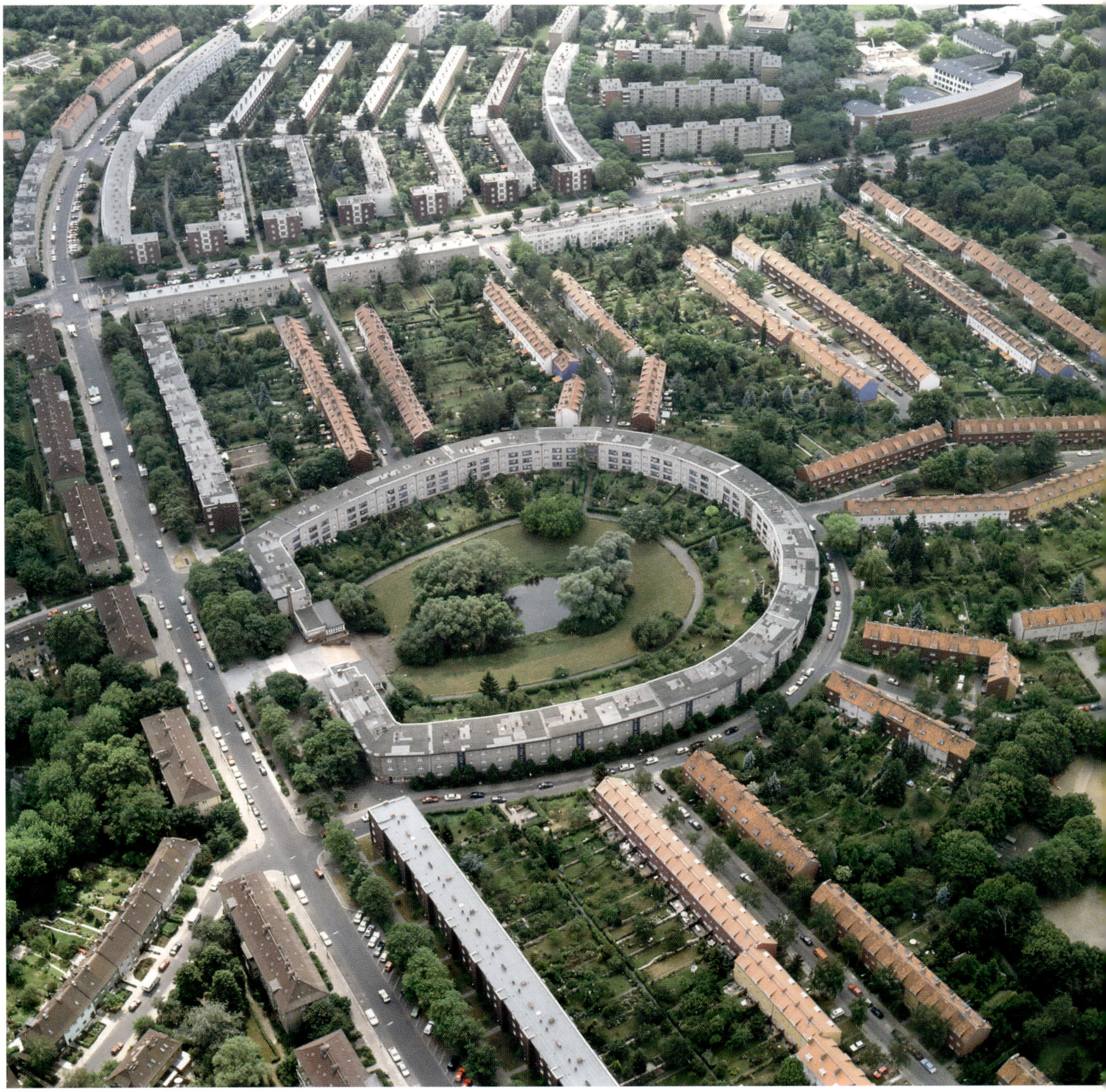

**Großsiedlung Britz
(Hufeisenseidlung)**

Luftbild/Aerial view
Landkarte/Land map

Maßstab/Scale 1 : 5.000
Kartengrundlage/Source plan: Bildflug Berlin, August 2004

| | |
|---|---|
| ▭ Baudenkmal/Monument | ▭ Nominierungsgebiet/Aera of nominated property |
| ▭ Gartendenkmal/Listed garden | Fläche/Surface 37,1 ha |
| | ▭ Pufferzone/Buffer zone |
| | Fläche/Surface 73,1 ha |
| | Fläche Gesamt/Surface total 110,2 ha |

N

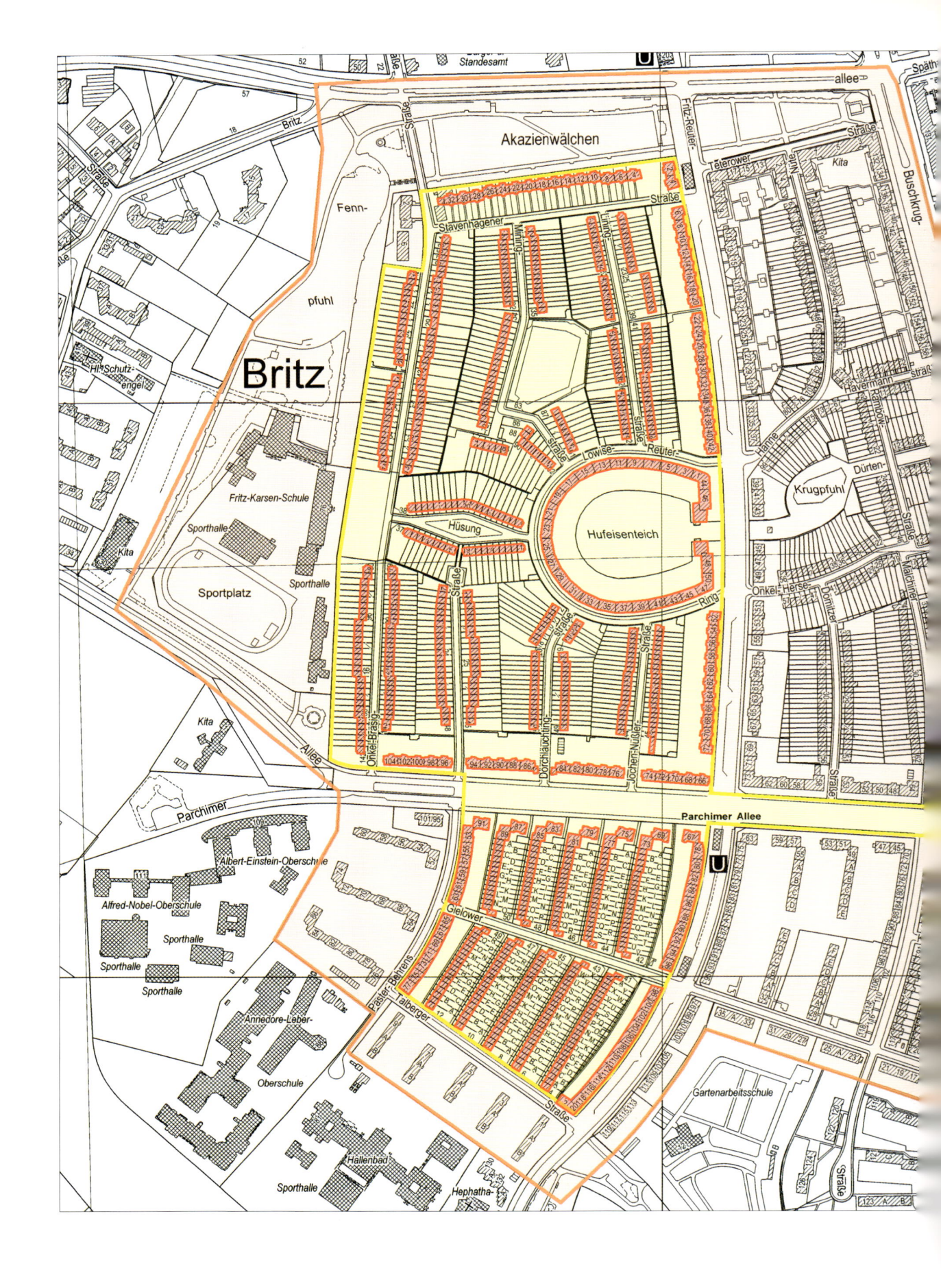

**Großsiedlung Britz
(Hufeisenseidlung)**

Luftbild/Aerial view
Landkarte/Land map

0 m  100  200  300  400  500

Maßstab/Scale 1 : 5.000
Kartengrundlage/Source plan: Bildflug Berlin, August 2004

Baudenkmal/Monument

Gartendenkmal/Listed garden

Nominierungsgebiet/
Aera of nominated property
Fläche/Surface     37,1 ha

Pufferzone/Buffer zone
Fläche/Surface     73,1 ha

Fläche Gesamt/
Surface total     110,2 ha

N

## Wohnstadt Carl Legien

Die Wohnstadt Carl Legien liegt im Bezirk Pankow von Berlin, Ortsteil Prenzlauer Berg.

Erich-Weinert-Straße 98/100, 101
Georg-Blank-Straße 1/5
Gubitzstraße 32–46
Küselstraße 4/6, 16/18, 28/30, 34
Lindenhoekweg 2/6, 12/16
Sodtkestraße 1–34, 36/46
Sültstraße 11–26, 30/44
Trachtenbrodtstraße 2–34

Die geographischen Koordinaten nach WGS 84 (GRS 80) sind:
1. Geographische östl. Länge 13º 26´ 01´´
2. Geographische nördl. Breite 52º 32´ 47´´

## Wohnstadt Carl Legien

Wohnstadt Carl Legien is situated in the district of Pankow of Berlin, borough of Prenzlauer Berg.

Erich-Weinert-Straße 98/100, 101
Georg-Blank-Straße 1/5
Gubitzstraße 32–46
Küselstraße 4/6, 16/18, 28/30, 34
Lindenhoekweg 2/6, 12/16
Sodtkestraße 1–34, 36/46
Sültstraße 11–26, 30/44
Trachtenbrodtstraße 2–34

The geographical coordinates according to WGS 84 (GRS 80) are:
1. terrestrial longitude East 13° 26' 01"
2. terrestrial latitude North 52° 32' 47"

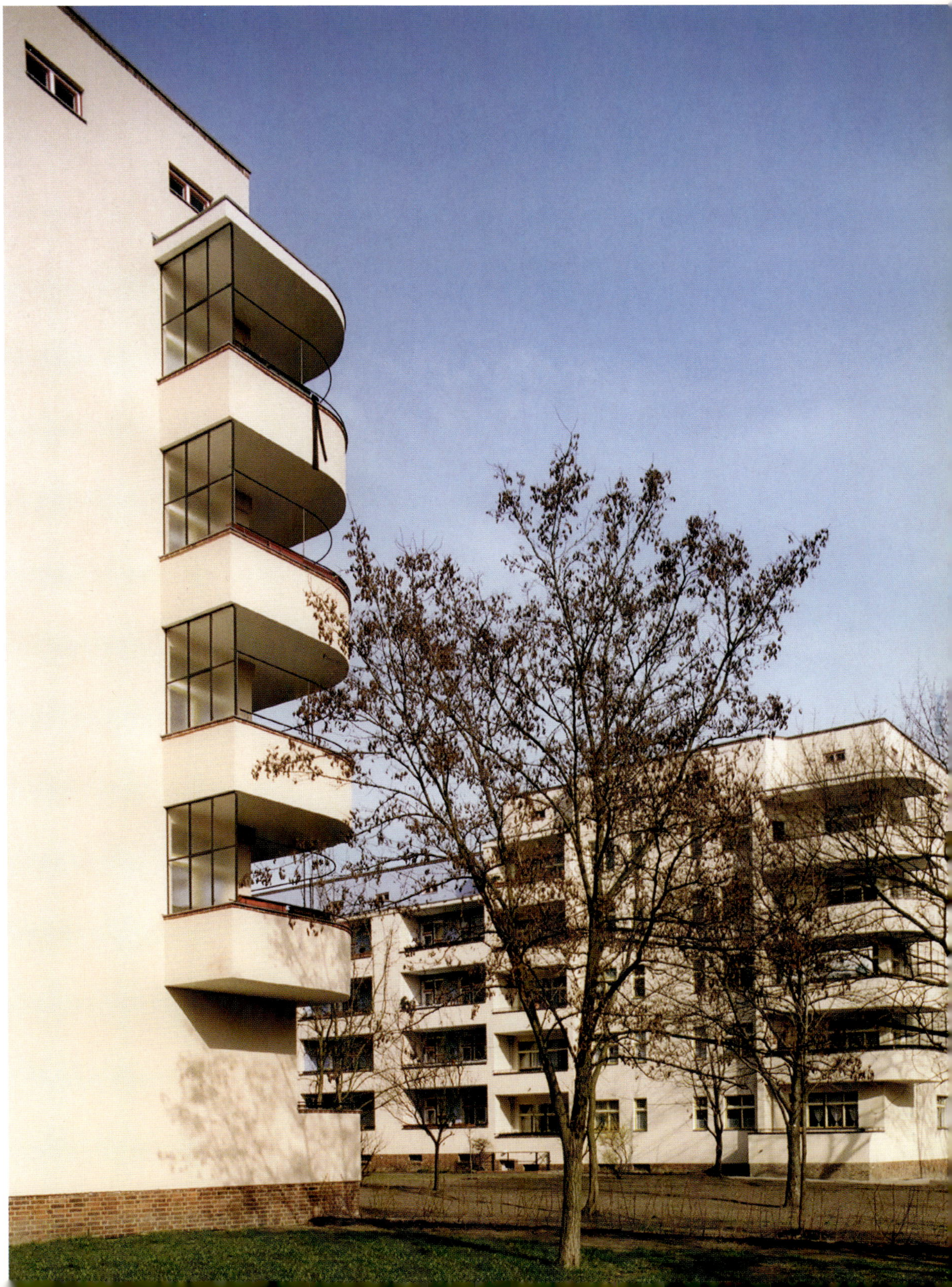

**Wohnstadt Carl Legien**

Luftbild/Aerial view
Landkarte/Land map

0 m   100   200   300   400   500

Maßstab/Scale  1 : 5.000
Kartengrundlage/Source plan: Bildflug Berlin, August 2004

Baudenkmal/Monument

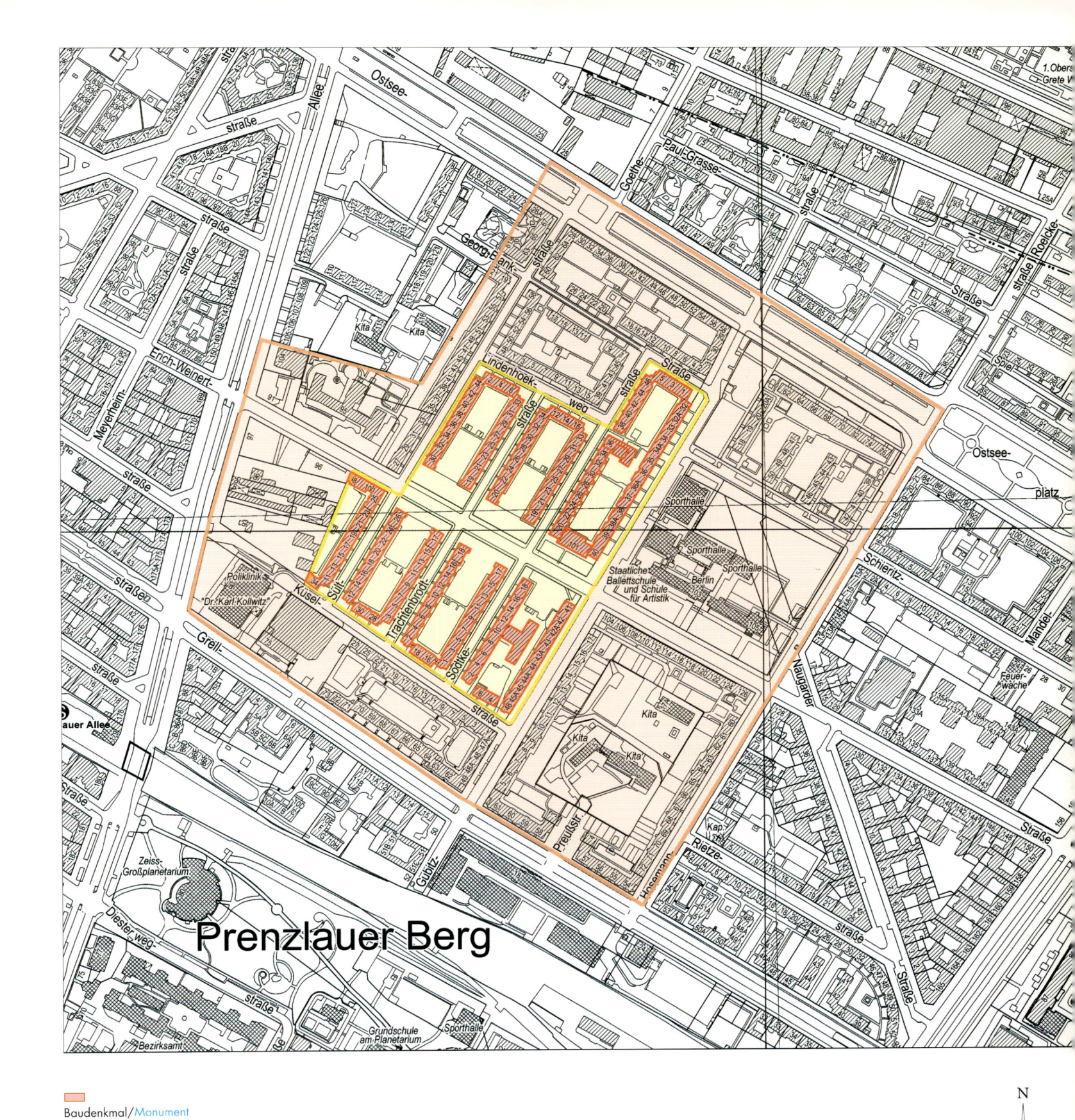

Gartendenkmal/Listed garden

Nominierungsgebiet/
Aera of nominated property
Fläche/Surface    8,4 ha

Pufferzone/Buffer zone
Fläche/Surface    25,5 ha

Fläche Gesamt/
Surface total    33,9 ha

## Weiße Stadt

Die Weiße Stadt liegt im Bezirk Reinickendorf von Berlin, Ortsteil Reinickendorf.

Aroser Allee 116/118, 121–153B, 154, 155/193
Baseler Straße 55/57
Bieler Straße 1/9
Emmentaler Straße 2–11, 13/37, 40–57
Genfer Straße 45/119
Gotthardstraße 4/8
Romanshorner Weg 54/82, 61/79, 96/212
Schillerring 3/31
Sankt-Galler-Straße 5

Die geographischen Koordinaten nach WGS 84 (GRS 80) sind:
1. Geographische östl. Länge 13° 21′ 03′′
2. Geographische nördl. Breite 52° 34′ 10′′

## Weiße Stadt

The Weiße Stadt is situated in the district of Reinickendorf of Berlin, borough of Reinickendorf.

Aroser Allee 116/118, 121–153B, 154, 155/193
Baseler Straße 55/57
Bieler Straße 1/9
Emmentaler Straße 2–11, 13/37, 40–57
Genfer Straße 45/119
Gotthardstraße 4/8
Romanshorner Weg 54/82, 61/79, 96/212
Schillerring 3/31
Sankt-Galler-Straße 5

The geographical coordinates according to WGS 84 (GRS 80) are:
1. terrestrial longitude East 13° 21′ 03″
2. terrestrial latitude North 52° 34′ 10″

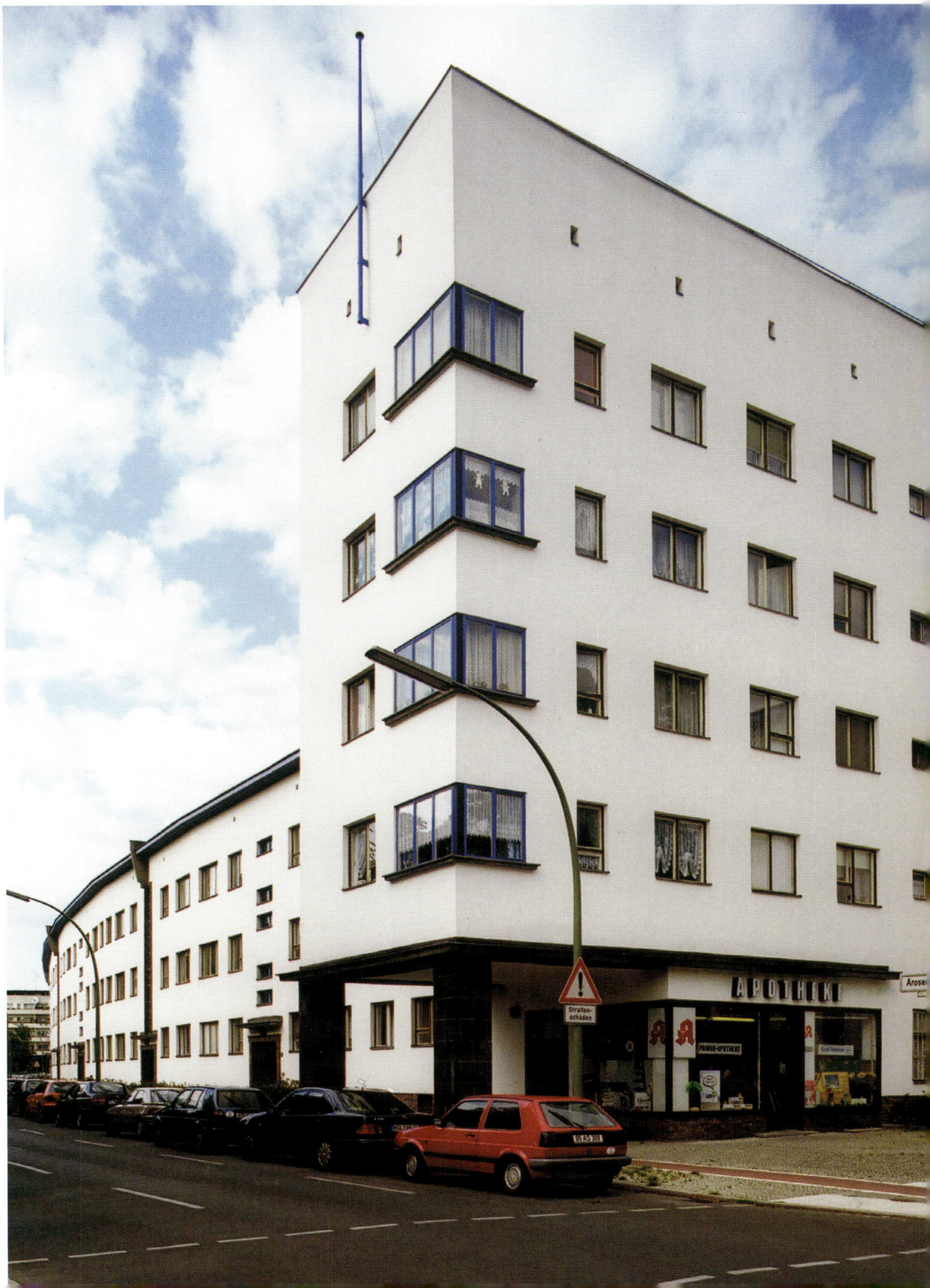
Straßen-
schäden

**Weiße Stadt**   Luftbild/Aerial view
Landkarte/Land map

0 m   100   200   300   400   500

Maßstab/Scale 1 : 5.000
Kartengrundlage/Source plan: Bildflug Berlin, August 2004

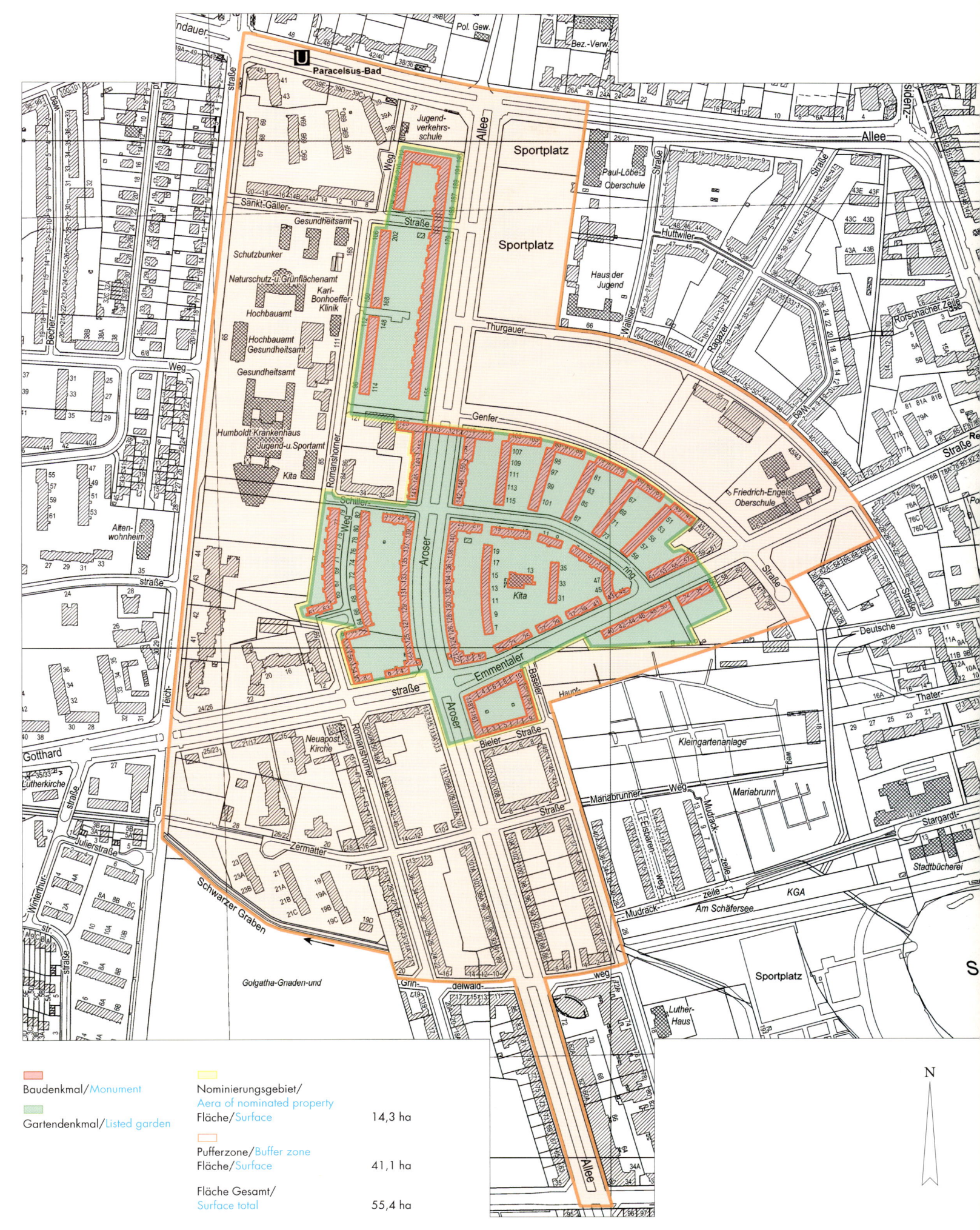

| | Baudenkmal/Monument | | Nominierungsgebiet/Aera of nominated property | |
|---|---|---|---|---|
| | | | Fläche/Surface | 14,3 ha |
| | Gartendenkmal/Listed garden | | Pufferzone/Buffer zone | |
| | | | Fläche/Surface | 41,1 ha |
| | | | Fläche Gesamt/Surface total | 55,4 ha |

N

## Großsiedlung Siemensstadt (Ringsiedlung)

Die Großsiedlung Siemensstadt liegt im Bezirk Charlottenburg-Wilmersdorf von Berlin, Ortsteil Charlottenburg, und im Bezirk Spandau von Berlin, Ortsteil Siemensstadt.

Geißlerpfad 1, 3–11, 13–29
Goebelstraße 1/9, 2/122, 11, 15, 19/25, 29, 35, 39, 45, 49, 51, 55, 61, 63, 69, 71, 75, 79, 83, 87, 91, 95, 99, 103, 107/113
Heckerdamm 283/299
Jungfernheideweg 1, 3–15, 16/20, 21–31, 33/45
Mäckeritzstraße 6/22

Die geographischen Koordinaten nach WGS 84 (GRS 80) sind:
1. Geographische östl. Länge 13° 16′ 39′′
2. Geographische nördl. Breite 52° 32′ 22′′

## Großsiedlung Siemensstadt (Ringsiedlung)

The Großsiedlung Siemensstadt is situated in the district of Charlottenburg-Wilmersdorf of Berlin, borough of Charlottenburg and in the district of Spandau of Berlin, borough of Siemensstadt.

Geißlerpfad 1, 3–11, 13–29
Goebelstraße 1/9, 2/122, 11, 15, 19/25, 29, 35, 39, 45, 49, 51, 55, 61, 63, 69, 71, 75, 79, 83, 87, 91, 95, 99, 103, 107/113
Heckerdamm 283/299
Jungfernheideweg 1, 3–15, 16/20, 21–31, 33/45
Mäckeritzstraße 6/22

The geographical coordinates according to WGS 84 (GRS 80) are:
1. terrestrial longitude East 13° 16′ 39″
2. terrestrial latitude North 52° 32′ 22″

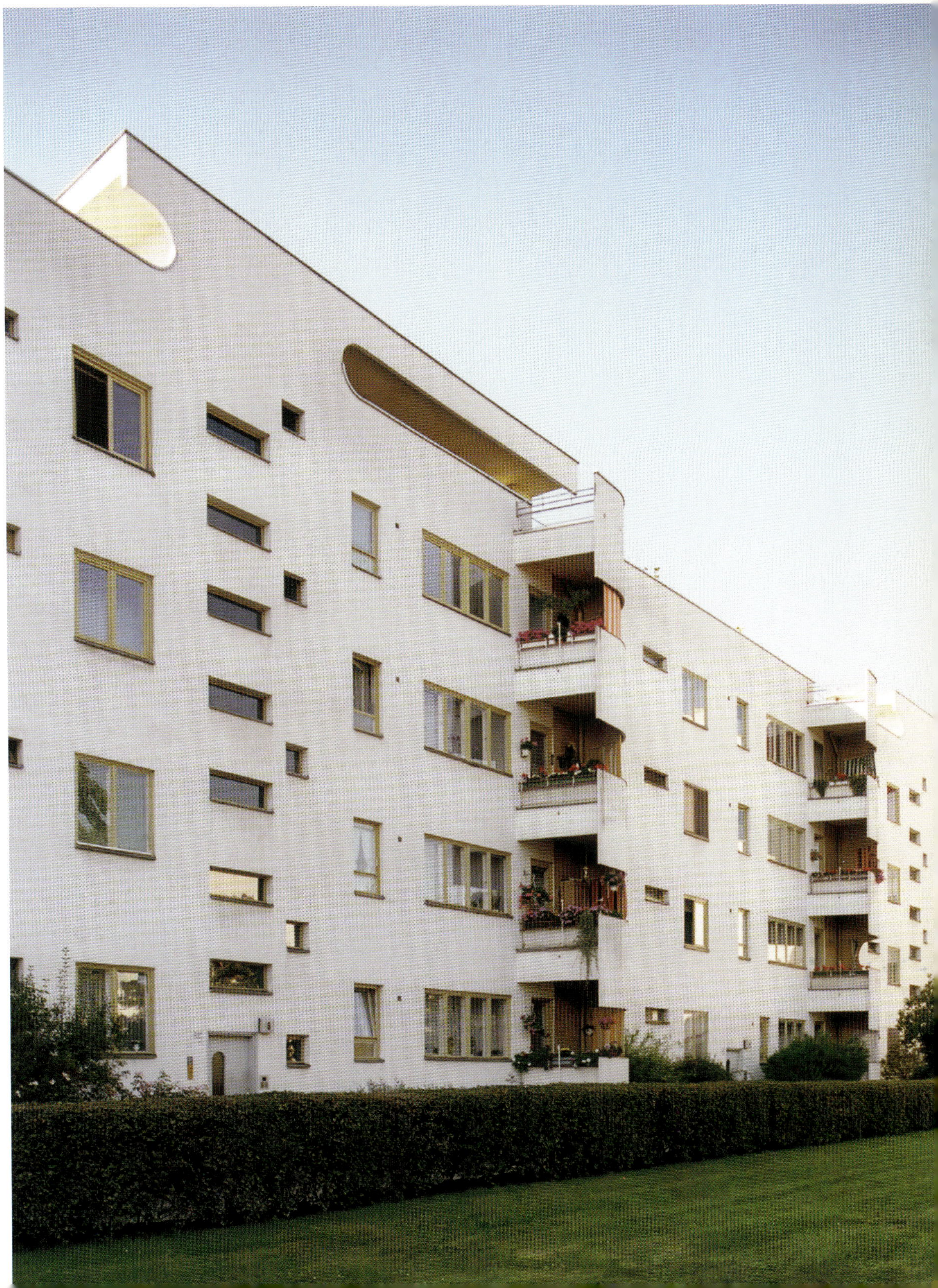

**Großsiedlung Siemensstadt
(Ringsiedlung)**

Luftbild/Aerial view
Landkarte/Land map

0 m    100    200    300    400    500

Maßstab/Scale 1 : 5.000
Kartengrundlage/Source plan: Bildflug Berlin, August 2004

Baudenkmal/Monument

Gartendenkmal/Listed garden

Nominierungsgebiet/
Aera of nominated property
Fläche/Surface           19,3 ha

Pufferzone/Buffer zone
Fläche/Surface           46,7 ha

Fläche Gesamt/
Surface total            66,0 ha

N

**Großsiedlung Siemensstadt
(Ringsiedlung)**

Luftbild/Aerial view
Landkarte/Land map

Maßstab/Scale 1 : 5.000
Kartengrundlage/Source plan: Bildflug Berlin, August 2004

Baudenkmal/Monument

Gartendenkmal/Listed garden

Nominierungsgebiet/
Aera of nominatec property
Fläche/Surface           19,3 ha

Pufferzone/Buffer zone
Fläche/Surface           46,7 ha

Fläche Gesamt/
Surface total            66,0 ha

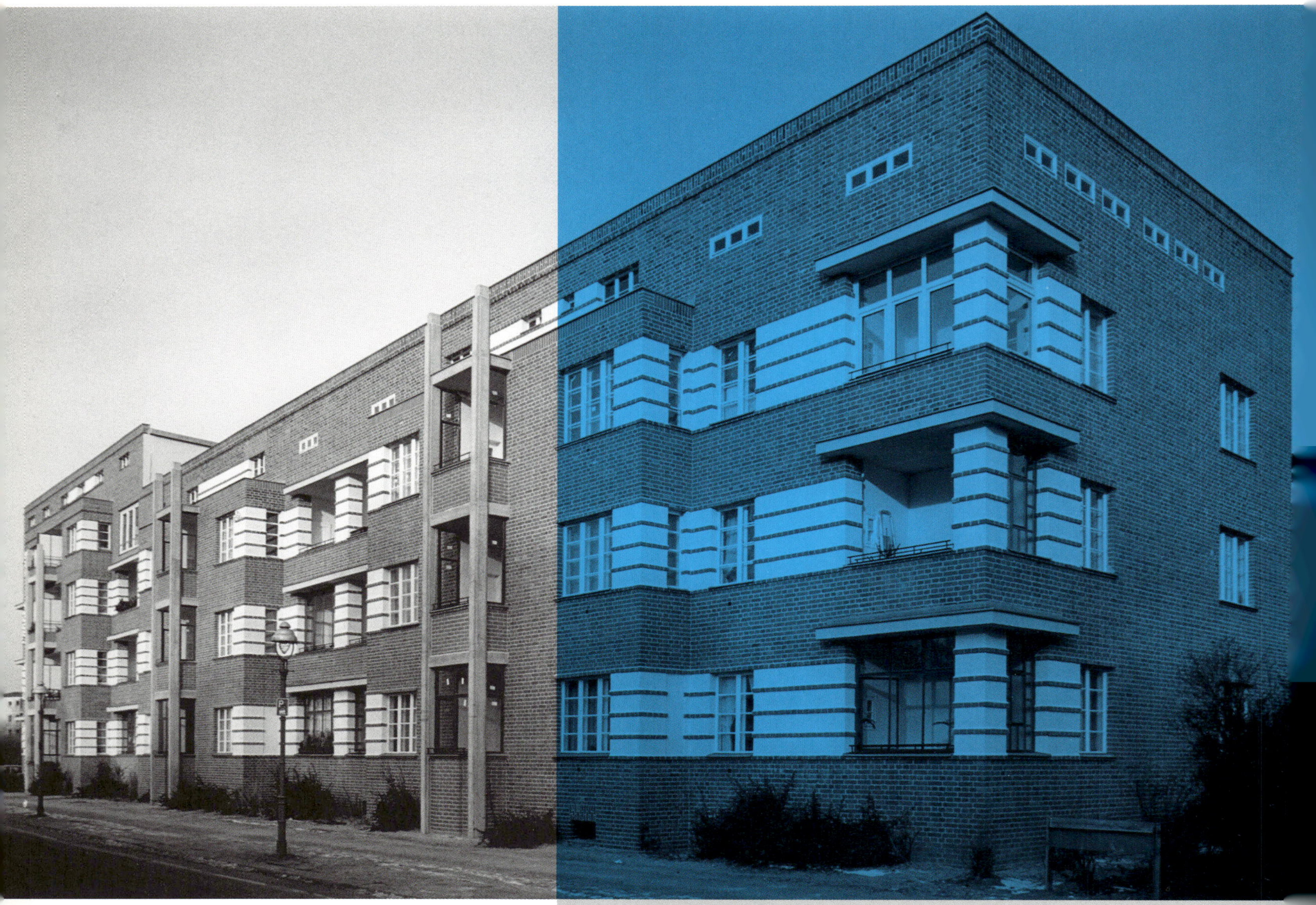

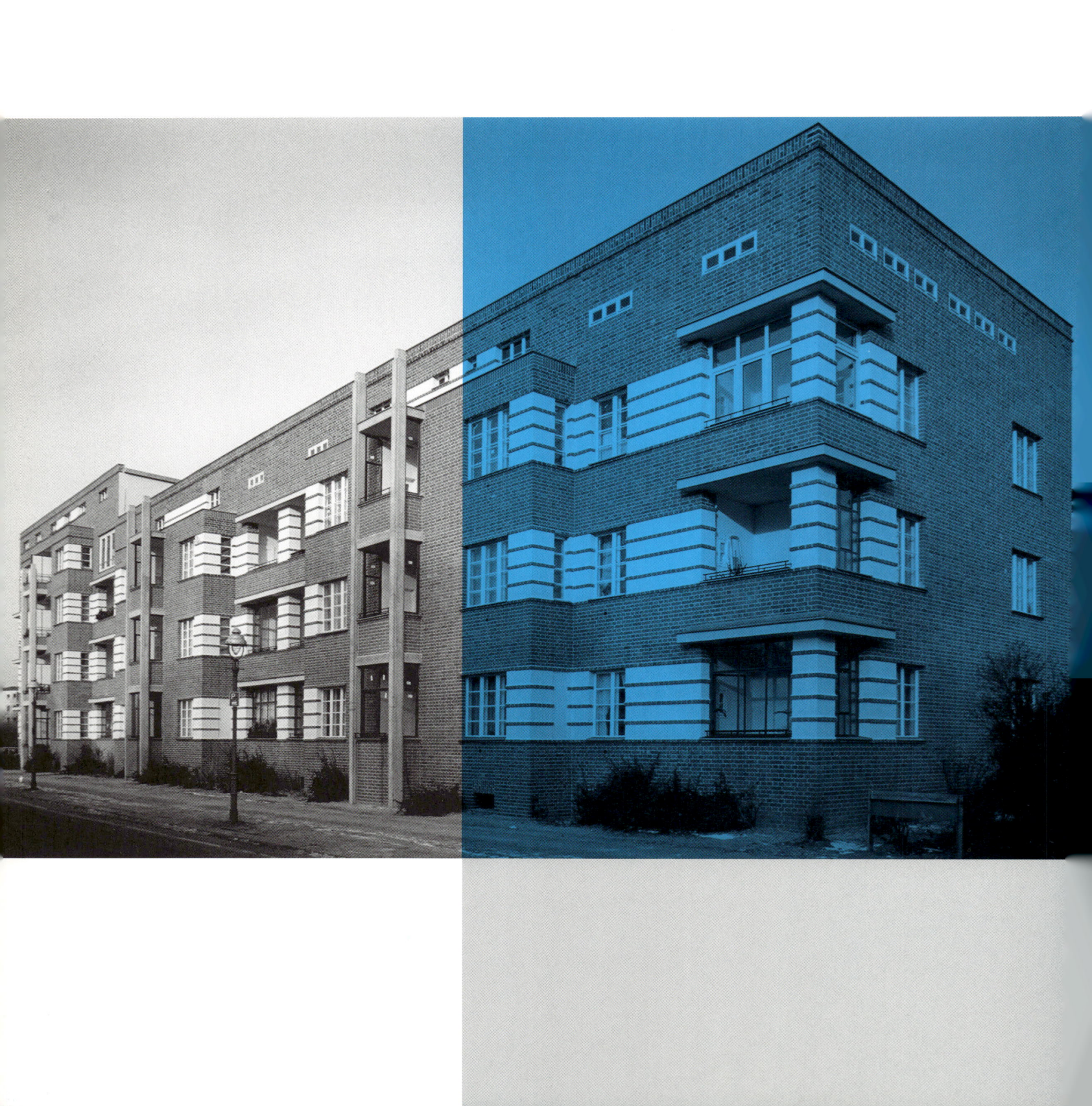

# 2

**BESCHREIBUNG**
**DESCRIPTION**

## 2.A Description of property

The reformed housing development of Berlin stands out from among that of other metropolises of the early 20th century by its high quality of architecture, an abundance of experimental forms of social housing and a large amount of buildings. These projects provided on a large scale healthy, hygienic and humane living conditions for the low income groups and demonstrated democratic housing development on a scale not seen again until Germany's social housing programmes after 1945.

The builders of the Berlin garden towns and large housing estates found the land they needed for implementing the housing policy in the intended quality in the rural outer districts of Berlin. It is quite obvious that the intense development on the margins of the city required the existence of the city itself with its economy and its strong infrastructure – the new housing estates were situated near the stations of the tightly knit and further expanding Berlin commuter transport network. Gartenstadt Falkenberg in the district of Alt-Glienicke, which was built shortly before the First World War, as well as the estates which were built later, i.e. Britz (in Neukölln), Weiße Stadt (in Reinickendorf) and Siemensstadt (in Charlottenburg and Spandau) were erected on the territory of former suburbs of Berlin which were merged with the core of the city thus forming Greater Berlin only in 1920. Solely the estate at Schillerpark (district of Wedding) and Wohnstadt Carl Legien (district of Prenzlauer Berg) are located at the margin of the city centre on building ground that had already been subdivided into parcels in 1918. The growing city has meanwhile reached or even overtaken all of these settlements and they are now islands of well-designed living within a city environment.

All nominated estates were built by cooperatives and non-profit organisations, which wanted to provide humane living conditions. All of these estates are based on a holistic settlement ground plan which reflects the respective model of housing reform of each of their developers. The closed tenements with densely packed structures were substituted by concepts of open housing aimed at creating garden towns and cities. These new concepts represent a radical

Fig. 4: Großsiedlung Britz at the outskirts of the city, aerial photograph montage, in approximately 1930

*Fig. 5: Gartenstadt Falkenberg, Akazienhof 5–8, row houses and multiple dwellings, 2005*

delt, eingebettet in gemeinschaftliche funktionale Grünräume. In diesen Siedlungen herrscht das zu geöffneten Blöcken und in Zeilen zusammengefasste mehrgeschossige Miethaus vor, das in erster Linie 2- bis 2½-Zimmerwohnungen hatte.

Neu war auch die hohe Bedeutung der Siedlungsfreiräume, die zu einem konstitutiven Bestandteil des Siedlungsplanes wurden. Die Grünanlagen haben wesentlichen Anteil an der freundlichen Gesamtwirkung, die heute noch spüren lässt, dass es den Erbauern nicht allein um eine neue soziale und räumliche Ordnung, sondern auch um die Schönheit der Anlagen und das Glück der Bewohner ging. Bereits in Falkenberg hatte Taut den angesehenen und ebenfalls sozial engagierten Gartenkünstler Ludwig Lesser für die Gestaltung der Freiflächen und Siedlergärten herangezogen. Nach Tauts Verständnis sollten den Bewohnern Gemeinschaftsflächen, „Außenwohnräume", wie er es nannte, eröffnet werden, die zum Aufenthalt im Freien, im Sonnenlicht und in frischer Luft einladen, um so den Wohnwert der Wohnungen zu erhöhen.

Lessers spätere weitläufige Gartenanlagen in den Höfen der Weißen Stadt sind vor allem den Bewohnern und ihren privaten Bedürfnissen nach Spiel und Aufenthalt im Freien zugedacht. Leberecht Migges Entwurfsidee um den vielzitierten eiszeitlichen Pfuhl im Zentrum des Hufeisens verbindet die Motive eines blühenden formalen Gartens mit der Idee einer Urlandschaft und hat wesentlichen Anteil an der bildhaft emblematischen Wirkung des Britzer Siedlungskernes für die gesamte Siedlungsbewegung. In Siemensstadt gelang dem Masterplaner Hans Scharoun und dem Gartenkünstler Leberecht Migge die Gestaltung einer Stadtlandschaft, deren weite Wiesenflächen und deren alter Baumbestand die Atmosphäre einer offenen „Parkstadt" erzeugen.

break with urban development of the 19th century, with its corridor-like streets and reserved spaces for squares.

The most important urban development designer in Berlin was Bruno Taut. His design of Gartenstadt Falkenberg focuses on the modest single-family house built as row or semi-detached house with a garden for supplying food for the inhabitants. Whereas Taut, after the First World War, again uses and re-defines elements of garden town design in a mixed structure of single-family and multi-storey buildings, the other estates of the Weimar Republic – Schillerpark, Carl Legien, Weiße Stadt and Siemensstadt – represent experiments with social housing in modern city mass residential development.

The ideal was to create housing for all income levels with equal standard and varying sizes, with dedicated bathrooms and kitchens and generous loggias and balconies that faced the sun. This intention was complemented by the desire to find a modern architecture which reflects the ground plan structure and treats both front and rear facades without hierarchy and to embed all this in communal functional green spaces. These housing estates are dominated by multi-storeyed blocks of flats arranged in open blocks or ribbons with flat sizes of usually 2 or 2 ½ rooms.

Another new aspect was that of the outdoor facilities which became an inherent part of the design of the estates. The green spaces are very important in creating the friendly impression which makes us feel even today that the developers of these estates were not aiming only at creating a new social and spatial order, but that they wanted to create beautiful facilities and make the inhabitants of these areas happy. As early as the planning of Falkenberg, Taut had invited Ludwig Lesser for designing the outdoor facilities and private gardens. Lesser had a very good reputation and was committed to social improvement. According to Taut's understanding, the inhabitants of the area should be offered common areas – he called them "Außenwohnräume" (outdoor living spaces) – which would invite them to come outside to enjoy sunlight and fresh air. With these spaces he wanted to enhance the use value of the flats.

## Die einzelnen Siedlungen

### Gartenstadt Falkenberg

Nahe der Stadtgrenze liegt im Südosten von Berlin die 1913 bis 1916 nach einem Entwurf von Bruno Taut erbaute „Gartenstadt Falkenberg". Sie wird im Norden von der Straße Am Falkenberg, im Osten von der Bruno-Taut-Straße und im Westen von der Schnellstraße B 96 a begrenzt. Unweit verläuft im Norden die Trasse der früheren Berlin-Görlitzer Bahn (1867 eröffnet) mit dem S-Bahnhof Grünau. Infolge ihrer Aufsehen erregenden Farbigkeit wurde die Gartenstadt im Volksmund bald nach ihrer Fertigstellung als „Tuschkastensiedlung" bezeichnet.

Landschaftlich reizvoll in unmittelbarer Nähe zum Forst Grünau und zur Dahme gelegen, wird das Gartenstadtgelände noch heute von bewegten eiszeitlichen Landschaftsformationen geprägt. An dem Übergang von der Niederung der Dahme und der Spree zur Hochfläche des Teltows liegt als höchste Erhebung der 25 m hohe Falkenberg, an dessen nördlicher Hangseite die „Gemeinnützige Baugenossenschaft Gartenvorstadt Groß-Berlin eGmbH" zwei Bauabschnitte einer größeren Siedlungsplanung verwirklichen konnte, bevor es kriegsbedingt zu einer Einstellung der Bautätigkeit kam. Im Norden und Osten schließen amorphe offene vorstädtische Siedlungsgebiete an, die geprägt sind von Gewerbe- und Industriebauten sowie villenähnlicher Bebauung aus dem späten 19. Jahrhundert. In den 1970er Jahren schob sich die vorstädtische Wohnbebauung bis an die Gärten der Gartenstadt heran.

Die in zwei Bauetappen entstandenen Siedlungsteile gruppieren sich in offener Bauweise um die beiden Wohnstraßen „Am Akazienhof" und „Gartenstadtweg", die von der nördlich verlaufenden Straße „Am Falkenberg" abzweigen. Der erste Bauabschnitt von 1913, ein intimer, mit zwei Reihen von Akazien bepflanzter Wohnhof, eben der „Akazienhof", umfasst insgesamt 34 Wohneinheiten, davon 23 in

The spacious garden grounds which Lesser designed later for the courtyards of Weiße Stadt were mainly supposed to satisfy the private needs of the inhabitants for playing and staying outdoors. Leberecht Migge's design idea for integrating the often-quoted glacial pond in the centre of the horseshoe combines the motives of a flowering formal garden with that of a primordial landscape. This design makes a major contribution to the symbol-like impact of the core of the Britz housing estate on the entire housing estate movement. At Siemensstadt master planner Hans Scharoun and the garden artist Leberecht Migge created an urban landscape whose wide lawns and old trees give it the atmosphere of an open "park town".

## The individual housing estates

### Gartenstadt Falkenberg

Gartenstadt Falkenberg, built between 1913 and 1916 according to a design by Bruno Taut, is located in the southeast of Berlin near the city boundary. Its limits are the street Am Falkenberg in the north, Bruno-Taut-Straße in the east and the thoroughfare B 96 a in the west. Not far from it in the north passes the line of the former Berlin-Görlitz railway (opened in 1867) with the commuter station of Grünau. Because of its sensational use of colours, people began calling the garden town "Tuschkastensiedlung" (paint-box housing estate) soon after its completion.

The garden town is located in an attractive landscape near the Grünau forest and the river Dahme. Still today, this landscape is characterised by lively glacial shapes. The hill Falkenberg (25 m high) is located at the transition from the lowland of the rivers Dahme and Spree to the highland of Teltow. At the northern slope of this hill, the "Gemeinnützige Baugenossenschaft Gartenvorstadt Groß-Berlin eGmbH" (Non-Profit Building Cooperative Garden Suburb Greater Berlin registered limited liability company) was able to

Abb. 6: Gartenstadt Falkenberg, Mehrfamilienhaus Gartenstadtweg 29/33, 2005

Fig. 6: Gartenstadt Falkenberg, multiple dwelling at Gartenstadtweg 29/33, 2005

Einfamilienreihenhäusern in mehreren Hausgruppen, acht in Mehrfamilienhäusern, zwei in einem Doppelwohnhaus und eine in einem Einfamilienhaus. Zwei freistehende villenartige Häuser fassen die schmale Zufahrt zum Wohnhof: das von Heinrich Tessenow entworfene „Haus Otto", Am Falkenberg 119, als sein einziger Beitrag zur Siedlung und ein Doppelwohnhaus, Am Falkenberg 120, von Bruno Taut. Hier steht auch ein weiteres Doppelwohnhaus von Taut, Am Falkenberg 118, das 1916 fertiggestellt, als einziges Gebäude des dritten Bauschnittes verwirklicht werden konnte.

*Der Akazienhof*
Im Akazienhof stehen sich an den beiden Längsseiten unterschiedliche, gruppierte Reihenhäuser gegenüber: an der Westseite zwei Gruppen mit je fünf eingeschossigen Kleinsthäusern in parataktischer Reihung unter einem Dach, der seinerzeit wirtschaftlichste Typ. Das sehr stark ausgeprägte geschweifte Traufgesims und die ins Dach hochgeführten breiten Drempelfenster – eines pro Hauseinheit – sind die einzigen plastischen Motive. An der Ostseite liegen zwei zweigeschossige Hausgruppen mit insgesamt zehn paarig angeordneten Hauseinheiten, die nebeneinander gerückten Hauseingänge werden von weiß gestrichenen Pergolen eingerahmt.

Bestimmend für die Raumwirkung des Akazienhofs ist die subtile Asymmetrie der Komposition. So ist am Kopfende des Hofes das raumschließende, in sich achsensymmetrische dreiteilige Haus aus der Raumachse verschoben, die östliche Häuserreihe endet in einem etwas vorgezogenen Mietshaus, die westliche Reihe ist durch ein weit zurückgesetztes Vierfamilienhaus aufgebrochen.

Die expressive Farbigkeit der Häuser überrascht immer wieder aufs Neue. Die Farbtöne, nach der jüngsten Restaurierung wiederum von großer Tiefe und Leuchtkraft, waren und sind noch immer als Gebäudefarben ungewohnt und reizvoll, besonders das tiefe, bräunliche Rot und das strahlende Ultramarinblau, das als „Taut-Blau" berühmt wurde und in seinen späteren Siedlungen immer wieder vorkommt. Es ist gewiss kein Zufall, dass Taut, der als junger Mann gezaudert hatte, ob er nun lieber Maler oder Architekt sein wollte, in Falkenberg auf Farbtöne zurückgriff, die er in seinen frühen Pastellzeichnungen verwendet hatte. Das Blau des Himmels in seinen Landschaftsbildern wird zur blauen Fläche auf den Falkenberger Reihenhäusern. Denn hier in Falkenberg ist die Farbe vollkommen flächig verwendet. Sie überzieht die gesamte Wand wie ein Tafelbild, dessen Rahmen das weiß gefasste geschweifte Traufgesims abgeben könnte.

Die Zuordnung der Farbtöne zu den Hauseinheiten artikuliert die kompositorischen Prinzipien der Reihung und Spiegelung und verstärkt die harmonische Asymmetrie der Anlage: weiß für das dreiteilige Haus am Kopfende, gelb und braun für die Etagenwohnhäuser und grün, gelb, blau, rot alternierend für die Reihen und Paare. Es entsteht eine farbige Komposition von individuellen Hauseinheiten, die gleichwohl solidarisch – ganz im Sinne, der auf Solidarität beruhenden Falkenberger Baugenossenschaft – den Hofraum umstehen.

complete two phases of a larger plan for housing estate development before they had to terminate the work due to the war. The housing estates north and east of it are amorphous suburbs characterised by commercial and industrial buildings as well as villa-like residential buildings from the late 19th century. During the 1970s, suburban residential development advanced up to the gardens of the garden town.

The housing estate was erected in two phases, and the houses of each phase form open groups around the two residential streets "Am Akazienhof" (acacia yard) and "Gartenstadtweg" which branch off in northern direction of the street Am Falkenberg. The first development phase began in 1913 and produced the intimate courtyard "Akazienhof", named after the double row of acacias planted in it. It has a total of 34 residential units. Twenty-three of them were erected as single-family terraced houses in several groups. Eight were built in multiple dwellings, two in a semi-detached house and one in a single-family house. Two separate villa-like houses frame the narrow access road to the courtyard: one is the house "Haus Otto" (Am Falkenberg 119) designed by Heinrich Tessenow, which is his only contribution to the housing estate, and the other is the semi-detached house Am Falkenberg 120 by Bruno Taut. Another twin house by Taut – Am Falkenberg 118 – is also located here. It was completed in 1916 and is the only building of the third phase to be completed.

*Akazienhof*
At Akazienhof groups of row houses in varying design face each other: along the western side stand two groups of five single-storey small houses each in paratactical sequence under one roof. At the time when they were built this was the most economical design. The very curved eaves cornice and the broad jamb wall window – one per unit – are the only plastic motives. Two double-storeyed groups of houses with a total of ten units arranged in pairs are located at the eastern side. Their paired entrances are framed by white painted pergolas.

The spatial impression of Akazienhof is determined by the subtle asymmetry of the composition. The house at the head of the yard, which is tripartite and axi-symmetric is shifted out of the spatial axis. The eastern row of houses ends with a somewhat projecting tenement house and the western row is interrupted by a far retreating quadrimonium.

The expressive colourfulness of the houses never ceases to surprise. The colours, which have regained their great depth and brightness with the most recent restoration, are still unusual and interesting as colours for buildings. This applies in particular to the deep brownish red and the bright ultramarine blue, which has become famous as "Taut blue" and appears again and again in his later designs. It is certainly not by chance that Taut, who as a young man found it hard to decide whether he wanted to become a painter or an architect, used colours at Falkenberg which he had used in his early pastel drawings. The blue of the sky in his landscape paintings returns in the blue faces of the Falkenberg row houses. Here at Falkenberg, he used the colours for entire faces. It covers entire walls as if they were panel paintings and the white painted eaves cornices might well be the paintings' frames.

*Der Gartenstadtweg*

Der zweite Bauabschnitt 1914 – 15 umfasst zwölf typisierte Hausgruppen, die beiderseits des zum Plateau des Falkenberges ansteigenden Gartenstadtwegs angeordnet sind. Hier nutzte Taut das hügelige Terrain, um den Straßenraum zu einem landschaftlich reizvollen Siedlungsbild zu modellieren. Die Straße ist als Hohlweg angelegt, beiderseits ergeben sich mehrfach terrassierte gestaltete Hänge, die mit Stützmauern, Treppen, und niedrigen Pflanzungen als Vorgärten für die von der Straße zurückgesetzten Häuserreihen dienen.

Wie im Akazienhof sind auch hier zweigeschossige Mehrfamilienhäuser mit ein- und zweigeschossigen Einfamilienhausreihen gemischt. Von den insgesamt 94 Wohnungen unterschiedlicher Größe – von der Einzimmerwohnung mit Kammer bis zur Fünfzimmerwohnung – liegen 54 in Kleinhäusern. 40 Etagenwohnungen verteilen sich auf vier Mietshausanlagen. Zwei Mehrfamilienhäuser auf der Ostseite der Straße leiten am Anfang des Gartenstadtwegs den Siedlungsabschnitt ein. Zu U- und L-förmigen Anlagen zusammengefügt bilden sie den Gegenpol zu den gegenüberliegenden Kleinhausreihen auf der Westseite. Kurz bevor der Gartenstadtweg die Hangkuppe erreicht, treten die Reihen an der Westseite von der Straßenflucht zur Hangkante zurück, um den Raum zu erweitern. Hier am Knick der Straße stehen, einander schräg gegenüber, die beiden anderen Mehrfamilienhäuser. Danach, wo flaches Gelände beginnt, folgen zu beiden Seiten die letzten beiden Reihen mit Kleinhäusern, die wieder dicht an die Straße gesetzt sind und die Siedlung etwas unvermittelt abschließen – hier sollte ja weitergebaut werden.

Am Gartenstadtweg wird Tauts Farbgestaltung noch kühner und unkonventioneller; hier kombinierte er insgesamt vierzehn verschiedene Farbtöne. Dabei zeichnen sich analog zu den städtebaulichen Raumbildungen abgestimmte Farbräume ab. Am Anfang des Weges bestimmen hellere Töne – gelb, ocker, rotbraun, leuchtend orange und weiß – das Siedlungsbild. Die Reihenhäuser mit von Haus zu Haus wechselnder Fassung, die Mehrfamilienhäuser mit einer Grundfarbe und teils sehr lebhaft kontrastierendem Ornament. Das Gelenk zum zweiten Raumabschnitt bildet der strahlend blaue Kopfbau am Ende der ersten Häuserreihe der Westseite.

Im räumlich erweiterten mittleren Abschnitt stehen zwei eher unspektakulären hellgrauen Häusern zwei außerordentlich markante, jeweils achtteilige Reihenhausgruppen gegenüber, deren Einheiten abwechselnd schwarz und rot gefasst sind. Der letzte Straßenabschnitt mit den beiden Einfamilienhausreihen und der winkelförmigen Mietshausgruppe ist in weiß-schwarz-dunkelgrau gehalten. Hier auf der Hanghöhe kulminiert die Farbgebung in dem Mehrfamilienhaus Gartenstadtweg 84/86, dessen völlig schwarze Fassaden einen aufreizenden Kontrast zu den weißen Fenstern und Fensterläden, roten Fensterrahmungen, rot-weiß gehaltenen Brüstungsfeldern und der roten Dachhaut mit den weißen Schornsteinen bilden.

Grundsätzlich erhalten die farbigen Wände in Falkenberg ihre volle Leuchtkraft erst durch die kontrastierenden Anstriche der Fenster und Fensterläden, der Gesimse, der Veranden und der hölzernen Balkonbrüstungen. Ein Rückgriff

The allocation of colours in the house units expresses the compositional principles of sequencing and mirroring and stresses the harmonic asymmetry of the place: white for the tripartite house at the head, yellow and brown for the double-storeyed houses and green, yellow, blue and red alternating for the rows and pairs. This creates a colour composition of individual housing units which nevertheless stand around the yard in solidarity – expressing the sense of solidarity that was the basis of the Falkenberg housing cooperative.

*Gartenstadtweg*

The second phase built in 1914 and 1915 includes twelve unitised groups of houses that are placed along both sides of Gartenstadtweg rising towards the plateau of Falkenberg. Here, Taut used the hilly landscape for modelling the roadside environment to turn it into an attractively designed housing estate. The street is designed as a defile. Along both of its sides it has landscaped slopes with multiple terraces which are formed by walls, stairs and low plants, and constitute the front gardens of the rows of houses which are retreated from the road.

As at Akazienhof, these houses are a mix of double-storeyed multiple dwellings and single-storeyed as well as rows of double-storeyed single-family houses. Fifty-four of the total 94 apartments of varying sizes (ranging from single-room apartments with one bedroom to five-room apartments) are located in small houses. Four tenement house units contain a total of 40 flats. Two multiple dwellings on the eastern side of the street start the housing estate section at the beginning of Gartenstadtweg. They are arranged in U- and L-shaped groups and form the complementary pole to the rows of small houses on the opposing western side. The rows at the western side retreat from the road building line shortly before they reach the summit of the hill where they form a wider space. Here, at the bend of the street and diagonally opposed, are the other two multiple dwellings. Where flat ground begins they are followed on both sides by the last two rows of small houses that are placed near the road again. These houses form a somewhat sudden end of the housing estate – originally more houses were planned to follow them.

auf das eigentlich bereits in der farbigen Fläche aufgegangene Ornament sind die bunten Wandmuster an den Mehrfamilienhäusern. Die schachbrettartig über die ganze Front gesetzten Farbfelder und die konzentrierteren geometrischen Motive sind vom gewohnten Architekturornament ebenso fern wie die Farbe von den gewohnten Architekturfassungen. Als quasi autonomer Dekor verstärken sie die bildhafte Wirkung der Hausfassaden.

Allen Haustypen gemeinsam ist neben einem individuellen Farbanstrich die Verwendung gleicher Baudetails: lebendiger, kreuzweise gestrichener Putz, rote Satteldächer in Biberschwanzkronendeckung mit stets gleicher Dachneigung, hochrechteckige Sprossenfenster, weiß gestrichene Schornsteine sowie hölzerne Elemente – Klappläden, Pergolen an den Hauseingängen, Spaliere, Nutz- und Zierspaliere, die den Gartenstadtcharakter betonen. Sie sind mit der Grund dafür, dass die Gartenstadt Falkenberg wegen ihrer Harmonie zwischen Architektur und Städtebau gerühmt wird.

*Siedlungsfreiraum*
Einen wesentlichen Beitrag zu dem einheitlichen, gleichwohl auch lebendigen Erscheinungsbild der Siedlung leistete der Gartenbaudirektor Ludwig Lesser, der als planender und beratender Gartenarchitekt von der Genossenschaft beauftragt wurde. Jede Wohnung verfügt über einen 135 bis 600 qm großen Garten, der ehemals unter dem Gesichtspunkt zur teilweisen Selbstversorgung angelegt war. Für die regelmäßigen Reihenhausgärten hatte Ludwig Lesser mit dem Ziel einer möglichst einheitlichen Gestaltung „Pflanzenauswahllisten" aufgestellt.

Die für das Siedlungsbild charakteristischen begrünten Dungwege dienen der Bewirtschaftung der Gärten mit den kleinen typisierten Ställen für die Kleintierzucht.

Abb. 7: Gartenstadt Falkenberg, Reihenhäuser Gartenstadtweg 68–74, 2005

Fig. 7: Gartenstadt Falkenberg, row houses at Gartenstadtweg 68–74, 2005

Abb. 8: Gartenstadt Falkenberg, „Blaues Haus" Gartenstadtweg 50, 2005

Fig. 8: Gartenstadt Falkenberg, "blue house" Gartenstadtweg 50, 2005

At Gartenstadtweg, Taut's colouring becomes even bolder and more unconventional. Here he combined a total of fourteen different shades of colours. In doing so he arranged colour spaces which coincide with the housing estate spaces. At the beginning of the street the housing estate's image is determined by light shades – yellow, ochre, red brown, bright orange and white. The colours of the row houses alternate from house to house. The multiple dwellings have one principal colour and sometimes very lively contrasting ornaments. The bright blue head building at the end of the first row of houses constitutes the joint with the second development phase.

In the spatially widened central section, two rather unspectacular light grey houses are opposed by two very striking groups of row houses, each with eight units, having alternatively black and red units. The last section at the street with the two single-family houses and the angular group of tenement houses is painted white, black and dark grey. Here at the summit of the hill, colouring culminates in the multiple dwelling (Gartenstadtweg 84/86) whose completely black facade is in strong contrast to the white windows and shutters, red window frames, red-white parapet areas and the red roofing with the white chimneys.

Actually all of the coloured walls at Falkenberg are given their full brightness by the contrasting colours of the windows and shutters, cornices, verandas and wooden balcony parapets. The colourful patterns on the walls of the multiple dwellings are recourses to the ornaments which actually have been absorbed in the coloured faces. The fields of colour which cover the front facades in chess board patterns and the clearly delimited geometric motives are as far away from the usual architectural ornament as the colour is from those conventionally used for buildings. As a quasi-autonomous decoration, they stress the visual impact of the facades.

What all types of houses have in common is an individual colouring and the use of the same architectural details: lively plaster in cross-wise application, red gable roofs made of single-lap crown tiles, all having the same pitch, high rectangular transom windows, white painted chimneys and wooden elements – shutters, pergolas at the entrances, trellises, trellises for use and others only for decoration, all of which stress the garden town character. They are part of the reason why the garden town of Falkenberg is praised for its harmony of architecture and urban development.

*Outdoor facilities*
The chief garden architect Ludwig Lesser made an important contribution to the both uniform and lively appearance of the housing estate. The cooperative had awarded him the contract as designing and consulting garden architect. Each apartment has a garden. The gardens' sizes vary between 135 and 600 sqm and were originally meant to be used for growing part of the inhabitants' food. For the regular row house gardens, Ludwig Lesser had established "lists of pre-selected plants" in order to lend them a uniform appearance.

The green alleyways that are typical for the housing estate serve the gardens with the small standardised stables for breeding small animals.

Eine Bepflanzung des Akazienhofs und des Gartenstadtwegs sah Lesser zur Verdeutlichung der städtebaulichen Intention Bruno Tauts in ausgewählten Abschnitten vor. Der Hof wurde mit Rasen und mit einer Doppelreihe niedriger, kugelförmig geschnittener Akazien begrünt. (Eigentlich „Robinia pseudoacacia", jedoch in den historischen Beschreibungen „Akazien" genannt.) Er erinnert, mehr durch die gärtnerische Gestaltung als durch die rechteckige Hofform, an brandenburgische Dorfanger.

Die gartenstädtische Konzeption Tauts für den zweiten Bauabschnitt, den ansteigend am Hang des Falkenberges verlaufenden Gartenstadtweg, bezieht die Vorgärten der Einfamilienhausreihen geschickt in den Straßenraum ein. Die Staffelung, die Vor- und Rücksprünge auch der Mehrfamilienhäuser ergeben unterschiedlich tiefe Vorgärten, die den Straßenraum erweitern. So blieb der mittlere Abschnitt mit den tiefen Vorgärten und der Abschnitt vor den Terrassengärten einseitig frei von Straßenbäumen, um das Gartenstadtbild nicht zu verunklaren. Die Höhendifferenz, besonders im stärker ansteigenden mittleren Abschnitt der Straße, wurde für die Anlage von Terrassenbeeten genutzt. Ihre differenzierte Bepflanzung nach Art von Steingärten, auch die Haustürpergolen und die zahlreichen Spaliere mit Obstgehölzen und Kletterpflanzen an den farbig voneinander abgesetzten Häuserfassaden tragen zum malerischen Straßenbild bei. Die Vorgärten und rückwärtigen Hausgärten wurden einheitlich mit Holz-, Drahtzäunen und Hecken eingefriedet.

## Siedlung Schillerpark

Im Norden der Innenstadt liegt im Ortsteil Wedding des Bezirks Mitte die 1924 bis 1930 nach Plänen von Bruno Taut für den „Berliner Spar- und Bauverein" errichtete „Siedlung Schillerpark". Sie bekam ihren Namen vom unmittelbar südwestlich der Bristolstraße angrenzenden großen Schillerpark, der 1909–1913 von der Stadtgemeinde als erster sogenannter Volkspark mit Spiel- und Liegeflächen angelegt wurde. Mit einer Laubenkolonie im Norden und dem St.-Johannes-Evangelist-Kirchhof im Osten liegt die Siedlung wie ein eigenständiger Block im Stadtgefüge, von den umgebenden Wohnquartieren abgerückt. Das von der Windsorer und der Oxforder Straße dreigeteilte Siedlungsgelände wird von der Bristolstraße, der Dubliner Straße, der Corker Straße und der Barfusstraße umfasst.

Am anschaulichsten zeigt sich das neuartige Städtebau- und Wohnkonzept in den zwei Baublöcken zwischen Dubliner und Oxforder Straße, die den beiden ersten Bauabschnitten von 1924 bis 1928 angehören. Ohne der Blockkante präzise zu folgen, stellt Taut dreigeschossige, ost-west und nord-süd orientierte Zeilenbauten um ruhige Gartenhöfe und lässt sie so als offene Blockrandbebauung erscheinen. Die Treppenhäuser liegen jeweils an der Nord- bzw. an der Ostseite, so dass ein Teil der Eingänge von der Straße, der andere vom Gartenhof aus zugänglich ist. Die großen Gartenhöfe müssen also auch öffentlich zugänglich sein. Hierfür sind jeweils an den äußeren Enden der Zeilen Durchgänge geschaffen, die durch Klinkermauern eingefasst werden und mit Gittertoren verschließbar sind. Selbst wenn die Tore offenstehen, ist so der Eindruck von räumlicher und sozi-

Lesser planned to carry out the planting at Akazienhof and Gartenstadtweg in selected sections as a way to stress Taut's intentions of urban development. Low acacias with crowns cut into ball shapes were planted in the Akazienhof yard. (Actually they are Robinia pseudoacaia, but in historic descriptions they are called acacias.) It is reminiscent of village greens as they can be found in villages of the region of Brandenburg – much more because of its garden-like design than its rectangular shape.

Taut's garden town concept of the second development phase, i.e. Gartenstadtweg at the slope of the hill Falkenberg, cleverly integrates the front gardens of the single-family houses into the road space. The staggering, projecting and retreating fronts also of the multiple dwellings produce front gardens with varying depths which widen the road space. At the central section with the deep front gardens and the section in front of the terraced gardens, no trees were planted in the street to avoid impeding the image of the garden town. The difference in elevation, especially in the central, more inclined part of the road was used for creating terraced gardens. Their varied planting in rock garden style, the pergolas at the front doors and the many trellises with fruit trees and climbers on the facades in different colours contribute to the picturesque image of the street. The front and the back gardens have uniform fencing of wood, wire and hedges.

## Siedlung Schillerpark

In the north of the city in the sub-district of Wedding, which is part of the district of Mitte (centre), sits the housing estate Schillerpark. It was built between 1924 and 1930 according to designs by Bruno Taut for "Berliner Spar- und Bauverein" (Berlin Savings and Building Association). It was named after the large Schillerpark, which is located at its southwestern border formed by Bristolstraße. This park was the first so-called public park with playgrounds and recreational areas built by the community in 1909–1913. With allotment gardens in the north and the St. John Evangelist churchyard in the east, the housing estate is separated from the surrounding residential quarters as if it were an autonomous block in the city's network. The housing estate area, which is cut into three parts by Windsorer and Oxforder Straße, is surrounded by Bristolstraße, Dubliner Straße, Corker Straße and Barfusstraße.

The two blocks between Dubliner and Oxforder Straße, which belong to the first two development phases erected between 1924 and 1928, show the novel urban development and residential concept most clearly. Without following the block line precisely, Taut places three-storey ribbon-buildings with east-west and north-south orientation around quiet garden courts to make them appear as open block boundary buildings. The staircases are located at the north or respectively at the eastern side so that some of them are accessible from the street and the others from the garden courts. This means that the large garden courts must also be publicly accessible. For this purpose passages have been provided at the extreme ends of the ribbons. They are bordered by clinker walls and can be closed with iron-barred gates. Even when the gates are open the ensembles give an impression of spatial and social self-con-

Abb. 9: Siedlung Schillerpark, Bristolstraße 1–5. Bauabschnitt I mit Dreispännerhäusern, 2005

Fig. 9: Siedlung Schillerpark, Bristolstraße 1–5, cevelopment phase I with houses with three back-to-back flats, 2005

aler Geschlossenheit im Sinne einer genossenschaftlichen Siedlergemeinschaft zur Anschauung gebracht.

Die halboffene Bauweise unterstützt nicht nur die von Taut angestrebte Verbindung der Wohn- und Freiräume, hier wird auch erstmalig im Stockwerksbau Tauts Prinzip des „Außenwohnraums" erprobt. Auch der angrenzende Schillerpark wird mit einbezogen: Taut legte auf der Höhe eines zentralen Parkzuganges, neben der Oxforder Straße, eine breite Grünschneise mit doppelter Baumreihe durch den Siedlungsbinnenraum und verband so den Park mit den halböffentlichen Grünflächen und dem nordöstlich angrenzenden Kirchhof.

Tauts städtebaulicher Entwurf nimmt Bezug auf die moderne Architektur Hollands, die er auf einer Studienreise Anfang der 20er Jahre kennengelernt hatte. Sein räumliches Konzept ist von den Siedlungsbauten von Jakobus Johannes Pieter Oud beeinflusst. In der Architektur mit ihrem roten Ziegelmauerwerk, den Flachdächern und der plastischen Durchbildung der Fassaden mit Loggien und Balkonen finden sich vor allem Anklänge an die Amsterdamer Schule mit ihren traditionsreichen, soliden Backsteinbauten.

Wie dort „an neuen Betonhäusern in Amsterdam und in Rotterdam gesehen, kombinierte er am Schillerpark den dunkelroten Backstein mit waagerecht unterteilten hellen Putzflächen zwischen einzelnen Fenstergruppen." (Kurt Junghanns, Bruno Taut 1880–1933. Berlin 1970, S. 64). Taut wählte hier erstmals das flache Pultdach mit Drempel

tainedness in the sense of a cooperative housing estate community.

The semi-open development does not only support the integration of residential and open space as desired by Taut. It is also the first test for Taut's principle of "outdoor living space" in a multi-storeyed environment. Even the adjacent Schillerpark is involved: At one of the main entrances to the park and along Oxforder Straße, Taut created a wide green corridor with a double row of trees which crosses the housing estate and thus connects the park with the semi-public green spaces and the churchyard in the northeast.

Taut's urban development concept is a reference to the contemporary Dutch architecture, which he got to know during a study trip in the early 1920s. His spatial concept was influenced by the housing estate buildings designed by Johannes Pieter Oud. The architecture with its red brick walls, flat roofs and plastic shapes of the facades with loggias and balconies, reflects in particular the Amsterdam school with its traditional, solid brick buildings.

As he had "seen there in the new concrete houses in Amsterdam and Rotterdam, at Schillerpark he combined dark red brick with horizontal subdivided light plaster areas between individual groups of windows." (Kurt Junghanns, Bruno Taut 1880–1933, Berlin 1970, p. 64). This was the first time that Taut used flat mono-pitch roofs with jambs for creating low attics with washkitchens and rooms for drying laundry, and parts of the facades of these attics were plastered and got a colour which differed from that of the

für ein niedriges Bodengeschoss mit Waschküchen und Trockenräumen, das teilweise verputzt und farbig abgesetzt wurde. Die Drempelfenster, zunächst in liegenden Formaten, setzte Taut im ersten Bauabschnitt über die gliedernden Achsen der Gebäude. Im zweiten und dritten Bauabschnitt sind sie quadratisch und erscheinen auf der gesamten Zeile in einer durchlaufenden Reihe. Sie bilden ein gestalterisch höchst wirksames gliederndes Element, das die spiegelsymmetrisch angeordneten Hauseinheiten zusammenfasst. Taut griff in späteren Entwürfen auf diese Idee zurück.

Vor allem die zuerst erbauten Zeilen von 1924–26, die mit zahlreichen Vor- und Rücksprüngen und dem bewegten Wechsel von Loggien und Hauslauben einen ausgefallen plastischen und kontrastreichen entwickelten Materialstil zeigen, erinnern an das holländische Vorbild. Ungewöhnliche expressionistische Details, wie die Eisenbetonstützen an den Hauslauben, die mit spitzen Aufsätzen fast bis zur Traufe durchlaufen, verstand Taut in Einklang mit der kubischen Strenge des Neuen Bauens zu bringen. Konsequent ist die Fassadengliederung aus dem funktionellen Aufbau der Wohnungen entwickelt, die mit ihren Loggien, Hauslauben und Balkonen dem Sonnenlauf zugewandt nach Südosten oder Südwesten orientiert sind. Die besondere Tiefe des Fassadenreliefs ergibt sich aus der Grundrissidee. Taut konzipierte eine Dreispänner-Anlage, wobei die dritte, kleinere Wohnung mit Fenstern nur zur besonnten Himmelsrichtung mitsamt der vorgestellten Hauslaube ein Stück aus der Mauerflucht hinausgeschoben wurde. Schmale Fenster an den Außenflanken der Vorsprünge sollten eine Art Querlüftung ermöglichen.

Ab 1925 ließen die Richtlinien der Wohnungsfürsorgegesellschaft keine Dreispännertypen im Stockwerksbau mehr zu. Bereits im 1928 bezugsfertigen zweiten Bauabschnitt finden sich ausschließlich Zweispännerhäuser mit paarweise zusammengefassten Loggien. Eine Ausnahme bildet der winkelförmige Block an der Oxforder Straße 3–11 Ecke Corker Straße, der an den zweiten Bauabschnitt nahtlos mit dem alten Aufbau anschließt.

Die Entwicklung der modernen Architektur mündete in ganz Europa gegen Ende der 20er Jahre in einen versachlichten und gelegentlich, wie bei Otto Haeslers Bauten in Celle, geradezu minimalistischen Stil. In der Abfolge der Bauabschnitte der Schillerparksiedlung tritt eine dieser Entwicklung entsprechende Vereinfachung der Formen ein, die auch wirtschaftlich begründet ist. Um die Kohärenz der Gesamterscheinung zu wahren, verwandte Taut auch im dritten Bauabschnitt (1929–30) weiterhin tiefroten Ziegel als Fassadenmaterial, verzichtete aber auf Putzgliederungen und abgesetzte Drempelzonen. Hervorgehoben werden lediglich die breiten Fenster mit einer Ziegelrahmung aus großen dunkelvioletten Steinen und die leicht vorspringenden Loggien mit ungestrichenen Sichtbetonbrüstungen. Die Häuser im unvollendet gebliebenen Block zwischen Barfusstraße und Oxforder Straße erscheinen so zum einen sachlicher, zum anderen aber auch massiver und kubischer und gewinnen so eine ganz eigene plastische Schwere.

Die Zusatzbebauung von Hans Hoffmann, Hausarchitekt der Genossenschaft, hat 1954 den südöstlichen Block –

rest of the facade. In the buildings of the first development phase, Taut placed the jamb windows – initially in horizontal shapes – above the structural axes of the buildings. In the second and third development phase they are square and appear along the entire front in an uninterrupted line. They are a very effective design elements providing structure and serving to group the housing units which are arranged in specular symmetry. In other designs made later in his life, Taut came back to this idea.

Especially the rows are reminders of the Dutch model. They were built in 1924–26 and show an unusual plastic and contrasting style with their many projections and retreats and the lively alternation between loggias and balconies. Taut managed to harmonise unusual expressionist details like the reinforced concrete pillars on the loggias, whose tipped attachments almost reach the eaves with the cubic strictness of Neues Bauen. The facade structure was developed consistently from the functional design of the apartments, whose loggias and balconies are orientated towards the sun, i.e. southeast or southwest. The particular depth of the facade relief results from the ground plan idea. Taut designed a tripartite arrangement. All the windows of the smaller flat in the middle face towards the sun and together with its loggia it projects a bit from the building line. Narrow windows in the flanks of the projecting part were supposed to provide for a kind of cross-ventilation.

As of 1925, the guidelines of the housing welfare society no longer allowed tripartite houses with more than one storey. Already in the second development phase, which was completed in 1928, we find only double-houses with paired loggias. The angular block at Oxforder Straße 3–11/Corker Straße is an exception. With its design, it creates a seamless connection with the buildings of the second phase.

At the end of the 20s, the development of modern architecture had reached a functional and occasionally almost minimalist style everywhere in Europe. The latter is represented in particular by the buildings designed by Otto Haesler in Celle. The subsequent development phases at the Schillerpark housing estate reflect this development by a simplification of the designs, which is also the result of growing economic restrictions. In order to preserve a coherent overall appearance, Taut continued using dark red bricks for the facades in the third phase (1929–30) as well, but stopped using plaster structures and distinguished jamb zones. Only the wide windows are highlighted by frames of large dark violet bricks and the slightly projecting loggias with unpainted parapets of architectural concrete. The houses in the uncompleted block between Barfusstraße and Oxforder Straße thus appear more functional but also more solid and cubic and acquire a plastic heaviness of their own.

The additional houses were designed by Hans Hoffman, company architect of the cooperative. They completed the south-eastern block – development phase III – in 1954, in harmony with Taut's concept, utilising the three rows of houses to densify the use of the very wide space between the blocks. The four additional buildings at the margin of the block complete its regular quadrangular shape. Hoffmann adapted the contours – three stories with jamb – and materials – plaster and partially brick – to the respective

Abb. 10: Siedlung Schillerpark, Oxforder Straße 10/12, rechts Erweiterungsbau 1954 von Hans Hoffmann, 2005

Fig. 10: Siedlung Schillerpark, Oxforder Straße 10/12, on the right additional building by Hans Hoffmann erected in 1954, 2005

Bauschnitt III – im Sinn des Tautschen Konzeptes vollendet und den sehr großen Blockinnenbereich mit drei Zeilen für eine Verdichtung genutzt. Die vier zusätzlichen Randbauten formten den Block zu einem regelmäßigen Viereck. Die Häuser von Hoffmann sind in Kontur – dreigeschossig mit Drempel – und Materialien – Putz und zum Teil Ziegel – dem Bild der jeweils benachbarten Tautschen Häuser soweit angepasst, dass nirgendwo ein gestalterischer Bruch entsteht. Hoffmann führte Tauts Konzept auf demselben hohen gestalterischen Niveau mit den stilistischen Mitteln der Architektur der 50er Jahre fort. So sind die Sonnenseiten als geschosshohe Fensterwände mit durchgehenden Balkonen transparent gestaltet und die Erdgeschosswohnungen verfügen über private Gärten mit Terrassen. Damit erreichte er auch für diesen Bauteil den für Taut wichtigen Bezug zum Außenwohnraum.

Die drei Zeilen im Blockinnern sind ähnlich konzipiert, jedoch viergeschossig und ohne Drempel. Leider wurden sie durch Wärmedämmmaßnahmen Anfang der 1980er Jahre in ihrem Erscheinungsbild stark verändert. Sie liegen mitten im Grün des Blocks, das der Gartenarchitekt Walter Rossow gestaltete.

### Siedlungsfreiraum
Das Neue Bauen mit einer halböffentlichen Bauweise am Blockrand verlangte ebenso eine klar gegliederte funktionelle Gestaltung der Freiflächen, die hier vermutlich auf entwurfliche Vorgaben Bruno Tauts zurückgehen. Eine besondere gärtnerische Fassung bekamen die beiden abgeschirmten Innenhöfe zwischen Dubliner und Oxforder Straße, wo augenfällig die Siedlung als Ganzes auch mit Vorgärten weit in die umgebenden Straßen- und Grünräume hineinwirkt und mit ihnen verflochten ist. Die Ausrichtung der Wohnungen nach dem Sonnenlauf ließ die Treppenhäuser oder die Loggien und Hauslauben mal zur Straße und mal zum Hof liegen, so dass bei den Block-

adjacent houses by Taut to such a degree that nowhere is there a break in the design. Hoffmann continued Taut's concept on the same high level of design using the architectural style of the 50s. The building facades facing the sun are executed transparently as storey-high window walls with uninterrupted lines of balconies and the flats on ground floor level have private gardens with terraces. Thus he created the link with outdoor living space which had also been so important for Taut.

The three rows inside the block are based on a similar concept but they have four storeys and no jambs. Unfortunately heat insulation that was added in the early 1980s has very much changed their appearance. They are located in the middle of the green space of the block designed by the garden architect Walter Rossow.

### Outdoor facilities
Neues Bauen, with its semi-public structures at the margins of the blocks, also required a clearly structured functional design of the outdoor spaces. Here the design is probably based on design requirements posed by Bruno Taut. The two enclosed courtyards between Dubliner and Oxforder Straße enjoy a particular garden design. The entire housing estate, including its front gardens, obviously influences the surrounding street and green spaces and is integrated in them. Since the flats are orientated towards the sun, the staircases or respectively the loggias and balconies alternatingly face the street or the yard. Therefore access had to be provided to the spaces inside the blocks. Here, edge courses of red brown clinker frame paths along the building fronts. These paths divide the yards into two areas of different sizes. The larger space with more or less rectangular shape is a lowered lawn with seams of trees along the longitudinal sides. The remaining eastern space provides children's playgrounds with sand-pits. This creates the architectural spatial structure and also the green "outdoor living spaces" which the tenants enjoy in their loggias and on balconies. This is supported by the trees along the roads, i.e. the whitebeams at Windsorer Straße and the original rows of pink hawthorns (now birches) at the wide green band at Oxforder Straße. They also connect Schillerpark with the clearly structured green spaces among and around the residential buildings.

Walter Rossow designed the green spaces around the postwar buildings by Hans Hoffmann which complete Taut's previously unfinished third phase. They are a combination of tenants' gardens and lawns with irregularly placed trees (mainly birches). The tenants' gardens make an exclusively private impression and they have been designed as recreational gardens, not as kitchen gardens. They were handed over with initial greenery in place. Hoffmann's building concept and Rossow's outdoor design are mutually related. Architecture and in particular the design of the flats and the positioning of the buildings interact with the outdoor spaces and alignment of the paths.

innenräumen eine Erschließung der Zeilen notwendig war. Hier gliedern mit Rollschichten aus rotbraunen Klinker eingefasste Randwege entlang der Fronten das Innere der Höfe in jeweils zwei unterschiedlich bemessene Flächen. Die größere Partie von annähernd rechteckigem Grundriss ist jeweils als abgesenkte Rasenfläche mit säumenden Baumreihen an den Längsseiten gestaltet, während der übrige östliche Teil für Kinderspielplätze mit Sandgruben vorbehalten ist. So entstehen die architektonische Raumfassung, aber auch die Wohnung erweiternde grüne „Außenwohnräume", die dem Mieter über Loggien, Balkone und Hauslauben erlebbar sind. Auch die Alleebäume der Straßen, die Mehlbeerbäume in der Windsorer Straße und die ursprünglichen Rotdornreihen – jetzt Birkenreihen – auf dem breiten Grünzug der Oxforder Straße wirken hierbei mit. Zudem verbinden sie den Schillerpark mit den klar gegliederten Wohngrünanlagen.

Die Freianlagen an den Nachkriegsbauten von Hans Hoffmann, die den unfertig gebliebenen Tautschen dritten Bauabschnitt komplettieren, entwarf Walter Rossow. Sie sind eine Kombination aus Mietergärten und durch unregelmäßige Baumpflanzungen, insbesondere Birken, geprägte Rasenflächen. Die Mietergärten vermitteln einen ausschließlich privaten Charakter und sind als Wohngärten, nicht als Nutzgärten konzipiert. Sie wurden mit einer Grundbepflanzung übergeben. Hoffmans Baukonzept und Rossows Freiraumplanung sind aufeinander bezogen. Architektur, insbesondere die der Gestaltung der Wohnung und die Stellung der Bauten sowie die Freiflächen und die Wegeführung bedingen einander.

## Großsiedlung Britz (Hufeisensiedlung)

Weit entfernt vom eigentlichen Kern der Mietskasernenstadt entstanden im Umfeld Berlins auf unbebauten Arealen der ehemaligen Vororte die großen Siedlungsanlagen der Weimarer Republik. Zu ihnen zählt, im Südosten der Stadt, die „Groß-Siedlung Britz", die auf den Flächen des früheren Rittergutes Britz in sechs Etappen von 1925 bis 1930 vollendet wurde.

Die schon während ihrer Fertigstellung wegen der markanten Hufeisenform ihres städtebaulichen Zentrums genannte „Hufeisensiedlung" umfasst 1.963 Wohneinheiten, die nach Entwürfen der Architekten Bruno Taut und Martin Wagner errichtet wurden. Unter der Bauherrschaft der „Gemeinnützigen Heimstätten-Spar- und Bau-AG", der GEHAG, entstand eine Großsiedlung für rund 5.000 Bewohner, die im Norden an das Akazienwäldchen längs der Blaschkoallee angrenzt, im Westen mit den Reihenhäusern längs der Onkel-Bräsig-Straße abschließt, im Osten von den Nord-Süd Straßenzügen Fritz-Reuter-Allee und Buschkrugallee tangiert wird und im Süden mit dem sechsten und letzten Bauabschnitt bis zur Talberger Straße reicht. Gegenüber, auf der anderen Seite der Fritz-Reuter-Allee, liegt die zur gleichen Zeit nach Plänen der Architekten Engelmann & Fangmeyer erbaute, siedlungstypologisch verwandte, mit ihrem expressionistischen Dekor stilistisch konservativere Wohnsiedlung der DeGeWo – die sogenannte „Eierteichsiedlung". Die Ein- und Mehrfamilienhäuser der „Hufeisensiedlung" beanspruchen mit ihren

## Großsiedlung Britz (Hufeisensiedlung)

On the outskirts of Berlin, far away from the actual core of the tenement house city, on unused land of the former suburbs, the large housing estates of the Weimar Republic were built. Among them is the Großsiedlung Britz in the southeast of the city. It was erected on the land of the former manor of Britz in six phases lasting in total from 1925 until 1930.

During its construction, the housing estate was named after the striking horseshoe shape of its centre. It comprises 1,963 housing units, which were built on the basis of designs by Bruno Taut and Martin Wagner. The "Gemeinnützige Heimstätten-Spar- und Bau-AG" (Non-Profit Housing Savings and Building Shareholding Company) was the client for the erection of the large housing estate for approximately 5,000 people which is delimited in the north by the acacia grove along Blaschkoallee. Its western border is formed by the row houses along Onkel-Bräsig-Straße. In the east, the north-south-lines of Fritz-Reuter-Allee and Buschkrugallee touch it, and in the south the buildings of the sixth and last phase reach Talberger Straße. Opposite, on the other side of Fritz-Reuter-Allee is the so-called "Eierteichsiedlung". It was erected at the same time according to designs by the architects Engelmann & Fangmeyer for DeGeWo (Deutsche Gesellschaft zur Förderung des Wohnungsbaus, The German Society for the Promotion of Housing Construction). This estate belongs to the same type, but its expressionist decoration is of a more conservative style. The single-family houses and multiple dwellings of the six phases of the "Hufeisensiedlung" occupy more than 29 hectares in the district of Neukölln at the northern margin of the sub-district of Britz.

Taut had been ordered to combine multiple dwellings with single-family row houses which resulted in him creating a particular quality of urban development. He reacted to the topography and the natural space and he integrated garden town elements like small houses and tenants' gardens as well as common functional and event spaces into social housing of the 20s, thus creating a completely novel housing estate landscape. The garden architect Leberecht Migge designed the private and public green spaces and areas. The works were executed according to plans by Ottokar Wagler, chief garden officer of Neukölln in partially altered form. From Migge's design, Wagler took over the shape of the pond and the alignment of the surrounding paths. The utilisation concept for the interior space of the horseshoe was altered.

### The Horseshoe

The integration of architecture and topography appears most clearly in the symbol of the housing estate: the horseshoe. Taut created a 350 m long, three-storey horseshoe-shaped row of buildings around a depression with a pond in the centre of the area. The row consists of 25 houses of the same type and forms a large common green space. According to the typology of urban development, the horseshoe is nothing but an original crossover between block margin and ribbon since the structure is just a 360 metre long ribbon that has been bent into the shape of a horseshoe. The residential rooms with loggias, which all have the same ground plan, are thus orientated towards the south, west or north respectively. All the entrances are at the ex-

Abb. 11: Großsiedlung Britz, raumschließende Wohnhäuser an der Stavenhagener Straße von Martin Wagner, 2005

Fig. 11: Großsiedlung Britz, residential buildings by Martin Wagner at Stavenhagener Straße, 2005, they enclose the space

sechs Bauabschnitten ein über 29 Hektar großes Neuköllner Stadtgebiet am nördlichen Rande des Ortsteils Britz.

Aus der Vorgabe, Stockwerks- und Einfamilienreihenhausbau miteinander verbinden zu müssen, entwickelte Taut die besondere Qualität seines städtebaulichen Entwurfs. Indem er auf Topographie und Naturraum reagierte und Gartenstadtelemente, wie Kleinhaus und Mietergarten, sowie gemeinschaftliche Funktions- und Erlebnisräume auf den sozialen Siedlungsbau der 20er Jahre übertrug, schuf er eine völlig neuartige Siedlungslandschaft. Der Gartenarchitekt Leberecht Migge entwarf die privaten und öffentlichen Grünräume und Plätze. Die Ausführung erfolgte nach Plänen des Gartenamtsleiters von Neukölln, Ottokar Wagler, zum Teil in veränderter Form. Von Migges Planung übernahm er die Formgebung des Pfuhls und die umlaufende Wegeführung. Das Nutzungskonzept im Inneren des Hufeisens wurde jedoch verändert.

### Das Hufeisen

Am augenfälligsten zeigt sich die Integration von Architektur und Topographie beim Wahrzeichen der Siedlung: beim Hufeisen. Taut legte um eine Teichsenke in der Mitte des Geländes eine 350 Meter lange dreigeschossige, hufeisenförmige Bebauung – gebildet aus der 25maligen Reihung nur eines Haustyps –, die einen großen gemeinschaftsbildenden Grünraum formt. Städtebautypologisch ist das Hufeisen eine origineller Zwitter zwischen Blockrand und Zeile, denn schließlich ist der Bau nichts anderes als eine 360 Meter lange Zeile, die so gebogen wurde, daß sie die Hufeisenform erhielt. Die Wohnräume mit Loggien, alle mit demselben Grundriss, sind also, dem Rund folgend, nach Süden, Westen oder Norden orientiert, die Eingänge liegen alle an der Außenseite des Runds. Nach Westen folgt eine weitere raumbildende Symbolfigur, ein angerförmiger rhombischer Wohnhof, Hüsung genannt, umstanden von Einfamilienhausreihen („De Hüsung" war ternal side of the horseshoe. In the west, another symbolic spatial arrangement follows – a diamond shaped courtyard, called Hüsung, surrounded by rows of single-family houses. "De Hüsung" was the right of domicile that farm hands and day-labourers had to obtain from landlords. Both shapes share an axis and together they form the central motifs of the first two development phases of the estate.

In seemingly free non-geometric composition, Taut placed streets and squares around the horseshoe and the Hüsung. These were supposed to function as external residential spaces, i.e. "outdoor living spaces". Narrow residential streets with rows of low single-family houses start at the horseshoe and point north and south. To these houses belong band-shaped tenants' gardens. Taut placed each row of houses into a finely structured system of shifted building lines, asymmetric positions and gaps which can hardly be perceived at first glance. Here he proved quite proficiently that the restriction to two types of houses for 472 single-family houses need not necessarily lead to monotonous repetition. Each street has a character of its own created by projecting and retreating groups of houses or head buildings which widen or narrow the space.

Colour is used as an element of design and for providing structure at the Britz estate even more than at Falkenberg. The uniform use of white and blue in the housing units along the horseshoe stresses its closed nature. On the inside only the internal walls of the loggias are blue, whereas on the outside blue colour has been used for jambs and staircases. For the surrounding single-family row houses, Taut abstained from using a uniform colour for each block. By means of differentiated colouring using bright red, yellow, white or blue integrally coloured stippling (sand-float finish), he makes urban and spatial correlations optically perceivable. Thus, each row or group of houses received its own colour, each street its own spatial colour identity.

das gutsherrliche Niederlassungsrecht, das Landarbeiter und Tagelöhner benötigten). Beide Figuren sind axial aufeinander bezogen und bilden die zentralen Motive der ersten beiden Bauabschnitte der Siedlung.

In scheinbar freier, ungeometrischer Komposition ordnete Taut im Bereich um das Hufeisen und den Hüsung Straßenräume und Plätze an, die nach seinem Verständnis außenliegende Siedlungswohnräume, also „Außenwohnräume" bilden sollten. Vom Hufeisen gehen strahlenförmig nach Norden und Süden schmale Wohnstraßen mit niedrigen Einfamilienhausreihen ab, zu denen Mietergärten in Streifenform gehören. Auf den ersten Blick fast unmerklich, stellte Taut jede Hausreihe in ein feingliedriges Bezugssystem aus Baufluchtversetzungen, asymmetrischen Anordnungen und Lückenbildungen. Meisterhaft führt er hier vor, dass die Beschränkung auf zwei Haustypen bei 472 Einfamilienhäusern nicht zwangsläufig zu monotoner Wiederholung führt. Jede Straße erhält einen eigenen Charakter durch vor- und zurückspringende Hausgruppen oder Kopfbauten, die den Raum aufweiten oder verengen.

Noch ausgeprägter als in Falkenberg wirkt in der Britzer Siedlung die Farbe raumgestaltend und städtebaulich disponierend. So verdeutlichen einheitlich weiß-blau gehaltene Hauseinheiten die geschlossene Form des Hufeisen-Runds, wobei im Inneren nur die Loggieninnenwände und zur Straße hin Drempel und Treppenhäuser blau gefasst sind. Bei den umgebenden Einfamilienreihenhäusern löste Taut sich von einer blockweisen einheitlichen Farbgebung. Mit Hilfe einer differenzierten Farbigkeit mit kräftig roten, gelben, weißen oder blauen durchgefärbten Strukturputzen (Madenputz) machte er städtebauliche und räumliche Zusammenhänge optisch erfahrbar. Jede Hausreihe oder –gruppe bekam so ihre eigene Farbe, jeder Straßenzug erhielt so seine eigene räumliche Farbidentität.

Die Reihenhäuser mit Steildächern und Gärten werden auf drei Seiten, zu den Hauptverkehrsstraßen hin, von dreigeschossigen, flachgedeckten Wohnblöcken stadtmauergleich abgeschirmt – ein städtebauliches Grundkonzept, das woh-

On three sides, three-storey flat-roofed blocks of flats were erected like screens or a town wall around the row houses with their steep-pitched roofs and gardens. This is a fundamental concept of urban development that applies reformist housing ideas from before the First World War, a result of the urban development contest of Greater Berlin of 1910.

### The "Red Front"

With a provocative gesture of delimitation, Taut opposed the traditionalist DeGeWo estate that was built at the same time according to designs by Engelmann & Fangmeyer. This gesture consists of two long rows of thirty equal three-storeyed housing units whose tower-like projecting staircases literally remind of military architecture. The two blocks with their blood-red plaster, called "Red Front" or "Chinese Wall", remind us of the fact that the dispute between modern and traditional architecture in the 1920s was not only carried out on paper. Yet, with a clever dialectical turn, Taut formulated precisely here an invitation to the residents and passers-by to enter the large housing landscape: the inside of the horseshoe. The head buildings of the horseshoe with brilliant white facades interrupt the "Red Front" at Fritz-Reuter-Allee. Here – flanked by community buildings – is the main entrance with the flight of outside steps down to the horseshoe pond.

The northern margin of the housing estate is formed by the transverse ribbon of residential buildings along Stavenhagener Straße. They were designed by Martin Wagner. At the outer side towards the green space, the "Akazienwäldchen" (acacia grove), blue double alcoves stand out from the white facades. Behind deep front gardens, the bastion-like projecting staircases face the street. Corner houses in deep yellow frame the long white building front.

### The development phases three through five

Along Buschkrugallee and Parchimer Allee and beyond the DeGeWo estate by Engelmann & Fangmeyer, the buildings of phases three through five are situated, which are exclusively multiple-storeyed dwellings built 1927–29. North of

nungsreformerischen Vorstellungen vor dem Ersten Weltkrieg folgt.

### Die „Rote Front"

Der traditionalistischen zeitgleichen DeGeWo-Siedlung von Engelmann & Fangmeyer entlang der Fritz-Reuter-Allee setzte Taut mit einer provozierenden Geste der Abgrenzung zwei langgestreckte Randzeilen mit dreißig gleichen dreigeschossigen Hauseinheiten entgegen, die mit ihren turmartig vorgezogenen Treppenhäusern geradezu buchstäblich an Wehrarchitektur erinnern. Blut-rot geputzt, als „Rote Front" oder „Chinesische Mauer" betitelt, erinnern die zwei Blöcke daran, dass der Streit um Modernität oder Traditionalismus im Siedlungsbau in den 1920er Jahren nicht nur auf dem Papier ausgetragen wurde. In einer klugen dialektischen Wendung formulierte Taut indes gerade hier die Einladung an Bewohner und Passanten, in das Innerste seiner großen Wohnlandschaft einzutreten: in die Landschaft innerhalb des Hufeisens. In ihrem leuchtendem Weiß unterbrechen die Kopfenden des Hufeisens die „Rote Front" an der Fritz-Reuter-Allee; hier liegt, von Gemeinschaftbauten flankiert, der Haupteingang mit Freitreppe hinab zum Hufeisenteich.

Den Nordrand der Siedlung bildet die von Wagner entworfene Wohnzeile an der Stavenhagener Straße. An der Außenseite zur Grünanlage, dem „Akazienwäldchen", setzen sich blaue Doppellauben vor der weißen Hauswand ab. Zur Straße liegen, hinter tiefen Vorgärten, die bastionsartig vortretenden halbrunden Treppenhäuser. Tiefgelbe Eckhäuser fassen die langen weißen Gebäudefronten ein.

### Der dritte bis fünfte Bauabschnitt

Jenseits der DeGeWo-Siedlung von Engelmann & Fangmeyer liegen längs der Buschkrugallee und der Parchimer Allee die ausschließlich aus Etagenwohnhäusern bestehenden Bauten der Etappen drei bis fünf, errichtet 1927–29. Nördlich der Parchimer Allee bilden sie eine hakenförmige Großform mit weitausgreifenden Flügeln und offener Innenfläche, die von abgezäunten Mietergärten eingenommen wird. Südlich der Allee sind die Hauseinheiten um einen geschlossenen Dreiecksblock mit gärtnerisch angelegtem Hof gestellt. Auch hier nutzt Taut die farblich abgesetzten Balkone, zu Paaren oder zu Bändern zusammengefasst, zur Strukturierung der Fassaden. Im Dreicksblock liegen sie bis auf wenige Ausnahmen zur ruhigen Hofseite, während Treppenhäuser die planen straßenseitigen Eingangsfronten rhythmisieren. In der hakenförmigen Anlage sind die Balkone im Südblock der Straße, im Westblock dem Hof zugewandt. Um das Blockhafte der Umbauung zu untermauern, sind die Fassaden aller Hausseiten gelb gefasst. Die davorgesetzten Balkonpaare sind leuchtend Blau. Statt der Sprossenfenster verwandte man nun eine Pfosten-Kämpfer-Fensterform, wobei die einzelnen konstruktiven Elemente des Fensters mit kontrastierenden Farbkombinationen gefasst wurden.

### Der sechste Bauabschnitt

Beim letzten 1929/30 erstellten Bauabschnitt südlich der Parchimer Allee stand Taut weniger Bodenfläche zur Verfügung. Daraufhin ordnete er Reihenhäuser und Stockwerkswohnungen beiderseits der Gielower Straße in zwei mal sieben parallel gestellten Zeilen an. Auch hier umgeben, wie bei den ersten beiden Bauabschnitten, höhere

Abb. 12: Großsiedlung Britz, Raumbildung im Hüsung, 2005

Fig. 12: Großsiedlung Britz, space inside the Hüsung, 2005

Abb. 13: Großsiedlung Britz, „Rote Front" an der Fritz-Reuter-Allee, 2005

Fig. 13: Großsiedlung Britz, "Red Front" at Fritz-Reuter-Allee, 2005

Parchimer Allee they have been arranged in a large hook-shape with far outreaching wings and an open courtyard used for tenants' gardens. South of Parchimer Allee the house units are built around a closed triangular block with a garden courtyard. Here, too, Taut uses balconies in colours which differ from those of the facades – either paired or arranged in bands – to structure the facades. In the triangular block they face the quiet yard with few exceptions, whereas the staircases give rhythm to the entrance fronts at the street side. In the hook-shaped arrangement, the balconies of the southern block face the street, while those of the western block face the yard. To highlight the block-type character of the buildings, the facades on all sides of the houses are yellow. The paired balconies in front of them are bright blue. Instead of the lattice windows, a post-impost window shape was used. The individual structural elements of the windows have been painted in combinations of contrasting colours.

### Construction phase six

Taut had less space for building the last development phase south of Parchimer Allee in 1929/30. This is why he arranged row houses and multi-storeyed blocks of flats in two by seven parallel ribbons along Gielower Straße. As in the first two development phases, higher multiple dwellings with three storeys surround an internal area with lower double-storeyed rows of single-family houses. At Parchimer Allee and Gielower Straße, Taut made one head building each project from the beginning of the row into the street and green space, thus avoiding the penetrability of the housing estate flanks which is so typical for ribbon housing estates. At Gielower Straße, this produces a very

dreigeschossige Mehrfamilienhäuser einen Innenbereich mit niedrigeren zweigeschossigen Einfamilienhauszeilen. An der Parchimer Allee und an der Gielower Straße schob Taut jeweils einen gegen den Zeilenanfang versetzten Kopfbau in den Straßen- und Grünraum vor, so dass die im Zeilenbau übliche Durchlässigkeit der Siedlungsflanken vermieden wurde. An der Gielower Straße ergibt sich damit eine sehr reizvolle Sequenz kleiner, kubischer Baukörper, die in ihrer klaren Kantigkeit und weißen Farbfassung dem „International Style", der weißen Moderne der Zeit um 1930 nahestehen. Die Kopfbauten zur breiteren, stärker befahrenen Parchimer Allee sind dreigeschossig und bilden mit ihrer tiefroten Fassung eine massive Abgrenzung zwischen dem öffentlichen Straßenraum und dem Inneren des Siedlungsabschnittes. Wohnwege verlaufen dicht vor den Westseiten der Häuserreihen. Die Hauseingänge liegen jedoch an den Ostseiten, der einzige Zugang zum Haus führt durch den parzellenbreiten – oder besser gesagt, den parzellenschmalen – Mietergarten.

Für die kompakte, nach Innen gekehrte Form dieses letzten Siedlungsabschnittes entwickelte Taut ein Farbkonzept mit vier Fassadenfarben – weiß, gelb, rot und türkisgrün. Zu jeder Fassadenfarbe gehört eine bestimmte Farbkombination für Fenster und Türen, so dass sich ein vielfältiger Farbwechsel ergibt. Durch eine gleichmäßige und einheitliche Tönung der Reihenhauszeilen wird im Inneren des Gebietes ein farblich geschlossenes Bild erzeugt. Eingangs- und Rückseite haben in allen Reihen einen abwechselnden roten oder gelben Putz erhalten. Die farblich abgesetzten Kopfbauten – weiß an der Gielower Straße, rot an der Parchimer Allee – wirken hierbei als Klammer, ähnlich wie die weiß gefassten Loggienbänder der Stockwerksbauten der beiden außen liegenden gebogenen Zeilen den Siedlungsteil abschirmen.

Durch den rationellen Einsatz weniger Bauelemente, die konsequente Verwendung des Flachdaches und den weitgehenden Verzicht auf Vor- und Rücksprünge der Baukörper zeigt sich dieser Siedlungsteil weitaus sachlicher. Dies kann auch, aber nicht nur, aus der Kürzung der Fördergelder aus dem Hauszinssteueraufkommen erklärt werden. Es war auch die allgemeine Entwicklung um 1930, die den „International Style" als Etappe in der Stilgeschichte der Moderne hervorbrachte.

*Siedlungsfreiraum*
Der städtebauliche Entwurf Bruno Tauts berücksichtigte in vorbildlicher Weise ein Zusammenwirken von Siedlungsstruktur, Architektur und privaten und öffentlichen Grünanlagen. Neben der Integration eines eiszeitlichen Pfuhls als formgebendes Element für den zentralen Teil der Siedlung wurde versucht, für alle Bewohner der Siedlung gleiche Wohnbedingungen zu schaffen. Jede Wohnung verfügt über eine Loggia oder einen Balkon, die stets den Gartenanlagen zugewandt liegen und zwischen Außen und Innen vermitteln. An die Einfamilienhäuser grenzen jeweils Gärten in der entsprechenden Hausbreite, zwischen den Häuserzeilen liegt jeweils ein 40–60 Meter breiter Gartenraum. Auch die Straßenräume sind als Wohnstraßen konzipiert.

Die Grünfläche im Inneren des hufeisenförmigen Zeilenbaus gliedert sich in einen öffentlichen Bereich im Zentrum und in private Mietergärten, die dem Gebäude vor-

Abb. 14: Großsiedlung Britz, Geschoßbauten des letzten Bauabschnitts an der Fritz-Reuter-Allee, 2005

Fig. 14: Großsiedlung Britz, multi-storey buildings of the last development phase at Fritz-Reuter-Allee, 2005

attractive sequence of small, cubic structural bodies whose clear cut edges and white facades resemble the "International Style" of the white modern architecture of the period around 1930. The head buildings towards the wider and busier Parchimer Allee have three storeys, and with their deep red facades, they create a massive delimitation between the public road space and the interior of this section of the estate. Residential paths run along the western fronts of the rows of houses at a short distance from the buildings. Yet, the house entrance doors are located on the eastern sides, and to reach them, people have to cross the tenants' garden, which is as wide – or rather as narrow – as a single property.

For the compact, introverted form of this last phase of the estate, Taut developed a colour concept with four facade hues – white, yellow, red and turquoise green. Each facade colour has a certain corresponding colour combination for windows and doors. This creates a lively change of colour sequences. The lines of row houses have an even and uniform colouring, such that the inside of this area has a uniform look as far as colour is concerned. In all rows, the front and rear sides have alternating red or yellow plaster surfaces. The head buildings in contrasting colour – white at Gielower Straße, red at Parchimer Allee – create the impression of framing the others, similar to the effect created by the white bands of the loggias at the multi-storeyed buildings of the two bent ribbons which screen the housing estate from the outside.

This part of the estate appears much more functional due to the rational use of less structural elements, the consistent use of flat roofs and the fact that almost all of the structural bodies were built along the building lines nearly without projecting or retreating houses. This can be explained to an extent, but not exclusively, by cutbacks of the grants from the mortgage servicing tax. It was also the result of the development around 1930 which produced the "International Style" as a stage in modern style history.

gelagert sind. Eine Hainbuchenhecke und ein umlaufender öffentlicher Weg trennen diese Bereiche. Im Zentrum der öffentlichen, parkähnlichen Anlage sahen Taut und Migge eine streng gefasste Teichanlage mit einer breiten Freitreppe vor – gleichsam inszeniert mit barocker Geste. Ursprünglich baumlos gedacht und mit einer Staudenpflanzung gerahmt, wird der Teich heute von Großbäumen bestimmt.

Die Gestaltung der Mietergärten geht auf eine von Leberecht Migge entworfene Grundausstattung zurück. Um eine möglichst einheitliche Gestaltung der meist von den Bewohnern selbst anzulegenden Mietergärten zu erreichen, wurden beispielhaft Mustergärten eingerichtet. So sind die Gärten durch markante Böschungen in drei Terrassenstufen eingeteilt. In den Gärten wurden vor allem Gemüsebeete und an den Terrassen Blumenbeete angelegt. Auf der unteren Ebene sah Migges Konzept Schattenmorellen und auf der mittleren Ebene Apfelbäume vor.

Wichtige Elemente wie die Vorgärten, die privaten Mietergärten und auch die Bepflanzung der Straßenräume mit Alleebäumen erfolgte weitgehend in einheitlicher Gestaltung. In Verbindung mit der städtebaulich-architektonischen Komposition der Baukörper gelang es, sowohl eine homogene zugleich aber auch lebendige Wirkung der Straßen- und Freiräume zu verwirklichen.

In das Gesamtgefüge der Siedlung harmonisch eingebettete gemeinschaftliche Funktions- und Erlebnisräume wie dem sogenannten „Paradies" mit einem Spielplatz an der Miningstraße oder dem „Hüsung", einer angerartigen Erweiterung mit einer Linde, prägen wesentlich den einzigartigen Charakter der Hufeisensiedlung. Wäschetrockenplätze, einheitlich gestaltete Müllhäuschen und Teppichklopfplätze und ein Netz aus Wirtschaftswegen berücksichtigen vorbildlich die funktionalen Bedürfnisse der Bewohner.

## Wohnstadt Carl Legien

Noch im Umkreis der Mietskasernenviertel liegt im Nordosten der Innenstadt die „Wohnstadt Carl Legien". Nahe der Wohnstadt, die zum dicht bevölkerten Ortsteil Prenzlauer Berg gehört, verläuft südlich der S-Bahnring. Die vier- bis fünfgeschossige Großstadtsiedlung entstand 1928 bis 1930 im Auftrag der „Gemeinnützigen Heimstätten-, Spar- und Bau-Aktiengesellschaft" (GEHAG) nach Plänen ihres Chefarchitekten Bruno Taut, der hier mit dem Leiter des Entwurfsbüros der GEHAG, Franz Hillinger, zusammenarbeitete. Mitten durch das Siedlungsgelände verläuft die breite Erich-Weinert-Straße in Ost-Westrichtung. Nach Norden reichen die Wohnblöcke bis zur Georg-Blank-Straße und zum Lindenhoekweg, nach Westen bis zur Sültstraße, nach Süden bis zur Küselstraße und nach Osten bis zur Gubitzstraße. Sie werden dort von Wohnanlagen der 1920er und 1930er Jahre begrenzt. Zur Fertigstellung bekam die GEHAG-Siedlung ihren Namen „Wohnstadt Carl Legien", zu Ehren des 1920 verstorbenen Gewerkschaftsführers.

Taut und Hillinger standen vor der Aufgabe, den hohen Grundstückspreis durch eine großstädtische Verdichtung zu kompensieren und dennoch sozial und stadthygienisch den Anforderungen an einen modernen Massenwohnungs-

### *Outdoor facilities*

In an exemplary way, Taut's design took into consideration an interaction of housing estate structure, architecture and private as well as public green spaces. Besides integrating a glacial pond as an element defining the shape of the central part of the estate, he also tried to create equal living conditions for all inhabitants of the housing estate. Each flat has a loggia or a balcony and all of these face the gardens and provide a connection between the outdoor and the indoor spaces. The single-family houses have adjacent gardens over their entire width and the rows of houses are separated by garden bands 40 to 60 metres wide. Even the road spaces are designed as residential streets.

The green space in the centre of the horseshoe-shaped row of houses is subdivided into a public area in the middle and private tenants' gardens in front of the building. A hornbeam hedge and a public path around the circumference separate these two areas from each other. For the centre of the public park-like area, Taut and Migge planned a strictly designed pond with a wide flight of stairs – almost like a baroque scene. According to the original design, the pond was to be surrounded by herbaceous plants without any trees. However, it is now dominated by large trees.

The design of the tenants' gardens is based on a primary layout by Leberecht Migge. Sample gardens were created for the purpose of achieving a uniform layout of the tenants' gardens, which were usually to be set up by the inhabitants themselves. Characteristic slopes divide the gardens into three terrace levels. The gardens were dominated by vegetable beds, and mainly flowers were grown on the terraces. According to Migge's concept, morello cherries were to be planted on the bottom level and apple trees on the middle level.

Important elements like the front gardens, the private tenants' gardens and the planting of trees along the streets usually had a uniform design concept. In combination with the urban development and architectural composition of the buildings, the designers created both a homogeneous and lively appearance of the streets and outdoor facilities.

Functional and event spaces like the so-called "Paradies" (paradise) with a playground at Miningstraße or the Hüsung – a village green-like extension with a lime tree – are harmonically embedded in the overall structure of the estate and give the Hufeisensiedlung its unique character. Areas for drying laundry, uniformly designed waste bin sheds and places for carpet beating as well as a network of service paths provide for the functional needs of the inhabitants in an exemplary fashion.

## Wohnstadt Carl Legien

In the vicinity of the tenement house quarters, the "Wohnstadt Carl Legien" is located to the northeast of the city centre. This estate belongs to the densely populated district of Prenzlauer Berg and near it in the south, the commuter railway ring line passes. The city estate with its four to five-storeyed houses was built in 1928 through 1930 by order of the "Gemeinnützige Heimstätten-, Spar- und Bau-Aktiengesellschaft" (GEHAG) (Non-Profit Housing, Savings

Abb. 15: Wohnstadt Carl Legien, offene Höfe an der Erich-Weinert-Straße, 2005

Fig. 15: Wohnstadt Carl Legien, open yards at Erich-Weinert-Straße, 2005

bau zu genügen. Dies war nur in einer konzentrierten Stockwerksbauweise zu realisieren. Auf dem Straßenraster des Hobrechtplans (Berliner Bebauungsplan des 19. Jahrhunderts) galt es, „den Mietskasernenstädtebau auf seinem eigenen Terrain zu schlagen und zu beweisen, dass man mit Hilfe der neuen Grundsätze auch besser städtisch bauen kann" (Kurt Junghanns, Bruno Taut 1880–1933. Berlin 1970, S. 70).

Taut kombinierte auch hier Zeile, Blockrand und Grünfläche zu einem neuartigen halböffentlichen Raumgefüge, womit es ihm gelang, inmitten der Stadt den Eindruck von aufgelockertem Wohnen im Grünen zu erzielen. Er bestimmte die Erich-Weinert-Straße zur durch Grünstreifen erweiterten kommunikativen Achse, zu der sich paarweise sechs U-förmige Wohnhöfe öffnen. Die Höfe, mit weiten Rasenflächen, Büschen und Bäumen gestaltet, bilden eine eindrucksvolle Sequenz von großzügigen, ineinander fließenden Siedlungsräumen. Sie übernehmen die Funktion von identitätstiftenden Sozialräumen, die das gemeinnützige Prinzip veranschaulichen – wie in Falkenberg der Akazienhof, am Schillerpark die halboffenen Innenhöfe und in Britz das Hufeisen und der Hüsung.

Die architektonische Gliederung und der durchdachte Einsatz von Farbe steigern die großartige Raumwirkung an der Erich-Weinert-Straße und stellen über die Straße hinweg visuelle Bezüge her. Markante, auf fünf Geschosse erhöhte Kopfbauten, die durch vertikale Loggienstreifen, Eckfenster und abgerundet über Eck gezogene Balkone kräftig gegliedert werden, lenken den Blick auf sich und leiten ihn in die Höfe. Hier liegen, abgewandt von den Verkehrsstraßen und konsequent den Grünhöfen zugewandt, die zentralen Wohnräume und geräumige, über die ganze Wohnungsbreite reichende Loggien oder vorgesetzte Hauslauben. Der Weite und lebhaften Gliederung der Höfe steht die Enge der schmalen Wohnstraßen gegenüber, denen die Häuser ihre völlig flachen Außenfronten zuwenden.

and Construction Shareholding Company). It was designed by the company's chief architect Bruno Taut, who cooperated in this case with Franz Hillinger, chief of the GEHAG design office. The wide street Erich-Weinert-Straße runs in an east-west-direction through the middle of the estate. The blocks of flats reach up to Georg-Blank-Straße and Lindenhoekweg in the north, Sültstraße in the west, Küselstraße in the south and Gubitzstraße in the east. There they are surrounded by estates from the 1920s and 1930s. When it was completed, the GEHAG estate was named in honour of Carl Legien, the trade union leader who had died in 1920.

The task of Taut and Hillinger was to compensate the high property price by setting the buildings densely to accommodate an urban setting and yet in line with modern mass residential development requirements in terms of social conditions and urban hygiene. This task could be fulfilled only by focussing on multi-storeyed buildings. The designers had to adhere to the street pattern designed by Hobrecht (designer of the Berlin urban development plan of the 19th century) and yet to "beat builders of tenement houses with their own weapons and to prove that the new principles allowed for better urban development" (Kurt Junghanns, Bruno Taut 1880–1933. Berlin 1970, p. 70).

Here, too, Taut combined rows of houses, block margins and green spaces to create a novel semi-public space structure. Thus he managed to create the impression of living in green spaces even in the middle of the city. He defined Erich-Weinert-Straße as an axis of communication that is extended by green bands and opens towards six paired U-shaped courtyards. The yards are covered with wide lawns, bushes and trees. They form an impressive sequence of generous, mutually linked housing estate spaces. They fulfil the function of social spaces which create identity and express the community principle as Akazienhof at Falkenberg, the semi-open courtyards at Schillerpark and the horseshoe and the Hüsung at Britz.

Abb. 16: Wohnstadt Carl Legien, roter Wohnhof mit breiten Balkonen, 2005

Fig. 16: Wohnstadt Carl Legien, red courtyard with broad balconies, 2005

Die Orientierung der Wohnungen zu den tiefen Höfen und die Anbringung von wohnungsbreiten, stark plastisch wirkenden Loggienreihen erinnern an die Rotterdamer „Tusschendijken-Siedlung" von 1919, von J. J. P. Oud. Taut entwickelte jedoch aus diesem Motiv eine über alle Geschosse reichende, umfassende Loggienfront, die farblich abgesetzt dem eigentlichen Baukörper vorgelagert ist. Seine originäre Erfindung war hierbei das Farbsystem der Fassaden, Fenster, Haustüren und Treppenhäuser, das heute überall nach den letzten Instandsetzungen wieder zu erfahren ist.

Ähnlich wie in Britz wird die Farbe zu einem konstitutiven Bestandteil der Architektur, hatte sie räumliche Zusammenhänge sinnfällig zu gliedern. So sind die engen Straßenräume in einem sonnigen Gelb gehalten, was sie optisch erweitert. Die hohen Kopfbauten an der Erich-Weinert-Straße sind in demselben hellen Ton gehalten, so dass über die Straße hinweg der räumliche Bezug der offenen Wohnhöfe zueinander betont wird. Die Gartenhöfe bilden eigene, intensive Farbräume. Um den Eindruck von Weiträumigkeit zu steigern, bekamen die einander gegenüberliegenden Höfe an Loggienrückwänden und Wandflächen jeweils den gleichen Anstrich – ein Hofpaar ist rotbraun, eines blau und eines dunkelgrün. Loggien und Hauslauben sind hier im gleichen Gelbton wie die Straßenfronten gestrichen, wodurch sie vor den dunkleren Rückwänden noch plastischer erscheinen.

Trotz innenstadtnaher Lage erhielt die Siedlung eine eigene Infrastruktur, mit einstmals zwei Wäschereien und einem Zentralheizwerk. Sie befinden sich im östlichen Siedlungsteil und stehen heute teilweise leer oder sind umgenutzt. Läden, ehemals auch ein Restaurant und Café, konzentrieren sich an der Erich-Weinert-Straße. Sie liegen bei den Kopfbauten oder in einer Ladenspange zwischen Sodtke- und Gubitzstraße.

### Siedlungsfreiraum
Gartenarchitektonisch dominant waren in der gesamten Siedlung die weiten, teppichartigen Rasenflächen, in die

The architectural structure and the clever application of colours enhance the spatial design at Erich-Weinert-Straße and create visual links across the street. Impressive head buildings with five storeys and a clear structure provided by vertical bands of loggias, corner windows and round corner balconies attract the eye and guide the view into the yards. The central residential rooms and large loggias as wide as the flats all face these yards and are thus shielded against the traffic on the roads. The width and lively structure of the yards is countered by the narrow residential streets and the totally flat facades.

The orientation of the flats towards the deep yards and the full-width loggias with their plastic appearance are reminiscent of the "Tusschendijken" housing estate of 1919 by J.J.P. Oud. Taut developed this motif into a front of loggias covering all storeys that lies in front of the actual building block and is painted in a contrasting colour. His original invention in this case is the colour system for facades, windows, entrance doors and staircases, which has been restored with the most recent refurbishment.

Similar as at Britz, colour became a constitutive part of architecture which was to provide a clear structure for spatial elements. Thus, the narrow residential streets are surrounded by yellow facades, making them appear wider. The high head buildings at Erich-Weinert-Straße are painted in the same light colour so that they underline the spatial link between the open courtyards across the street. The garden courtyards are intensely coloured spaces with a particular character. To make them appear wider, the rear walls of the loggias and walls in opposing courtyards were painted in the same colour – one pair of yards is reddish brown, one is blue and one is dark green. In these yards, the loggias are painted in the same shade of yellow as the street facades which makes them stand out with even more plasticity from the darker walls.

Despite its location near the city centre, the estate received its own infrastructure with two laundries originally and a

Abb. 17: Weiße Stadt, Siedlungsabschnitte und Architekten, M 1 : 5000

Fig. 17: Weiße Stadt, development sections and architects, scale 1:5000

■ Otto R. Salvisberg

■ Bruno Ahrends

■ Wilhelm Büning

nur einige wenige Solitärbäume eingefügt waren. Die Erschließung der Grünflächen innerhalb der Wohnhöfe verläuft parallel zu den Baukörpern, eine schmale und niedrige Strauchpflanzung setzt die Wege von den Fassaden ab. Die Erschließungswege verbinden die hofseitigen Kellerzugänge mit den zumeist zentral gelegenen Müllhäuschen, denen jeweils zwei Teppichklopfanlagen zugeordnet wurden und mit Sträuchern und Stauden eingefasst waren.

Die Rahmung der Rasenteppiche der Wohnhöfe mit einer niedrigen Feldahornhecke im Bereich der Erich-Weinert-Straße lässt diese wie in den Straßenraum hineingeschoben erscheinen, wodurch die verbindende Wirkung der zur Erich-Weinert-Straße geöffneten Wohnhöfe unterstützt wurde. Im Bereich der Kopfbauten an der Erich-Weinert-Straße wurden Robiniengruppen angepflanzt, die zum einen den als kommunikative Achse gedachten Straßenraum in der Ost-West-Perspektive als gartenarchitektonische Analogie zu den Kopfbauten fassten, gleichzeitig den Blick in die Wohnhöfe zuließen. Zusätzlich waren die Kopfbauten in der Erich-Weinert-Straße zum Teil mit Wein berankt, so dass die Wirkung einer grünen Fassung des Straßenraumes verstärkt wurde. In den engen Straßenräumen zwischen den U-förmigen Blöcken flankieren niedrige Ligusterhecken die schmalen Rasenspiegel der Vorgärten.

central heating plant. They are located in the eastern part of the housing estate, and are now either disused or used for other purposes. Shops and (in the past) a restaurant and café are concentrated at Erich-Weinert-Straße. They are located at the head buildings or in a row of shops between Sodtkestraße and Gubitzstraße.

*Outdoor facilities*

The garden architecture of the entire estate was dominated by the wide carpet-like lawns. Only a small number of solitary trees were planted in these areas. The paths through the green areas inside the courtyards run parallel to the buildings, and narrow bands of low bushes separate the paths from the facades. The paths connect the entrances to the basements located on the yard side with the primarily central waste bin sheds. The waste bin sheds are accompanied by two carpet beating places and they are surrounded by bushes and herbaceous plants.

At Erich-Weinert-Straße, the lawns of the courtyards are framed by field maple hedges such that they appear as if they were pushed towards the street space. This supports the connecting effect of the courtyards, which are opened towards Erich-Weinert-Straße. Groups of robinias were planted at the head buildings on Erich-Weinert-Straße. On the one hand, these groups of trees created a landscaping analogy to the head buildings in an east-west direction for the street space, which was designed as communicative axis,

Abb. 18: Weiße Stadt, Brückenhaus über die Aroser Allee von Otto R. Salvisberg, 2005

Fig. 18: Weiße Stadt, bridge house across Aroser Allee by Otto R. Salvisberg, 2005

## Weiße Stadt

Zwischen der Siedlung Schillerpark und Alt-Reinickendorf, ehemals ein Dorf weit außerhalb des Stadtkerns, zeichnet sich signifikant im Stadtgrundriss die geschlossene Figur der Großsiedlung „Weiße Stadt" ab. Wie zeitgleich in Siemensstadt bildete sich auch hier eigens für dieses städtische Wohnprojekt, das in den Jahren 1929 bis 1931 unter der Regie des Stadtbaurats Martin Wagner entstand, eine Arbeitsgemeinschaft aus den Architekten Otto Rudolf Salvisberg, Bruno Ahrends und Wilhelm Büning. Während der städtebauliche Entwurf bei Salvisberg lag, zog man für die Grünplanung den Gartendirektor Ludwig Lesser hinzu. Die Bauträgerschaft für die 1.268 Geschosswohnungen in größtenteils dreigeschossigen, durchweg flachgedeckten Stockwerksbauten übernahm die stadteigene „Gemeinnützige Heimstättengesellschaft Primus mbH".

Rationalität und Wirtschaftlichkeit bestimmten Bebauungsplanung, Haus- und Grundrissentwurf. Entsprechend dem Bedarf nach billigen Kleinstwohnungen war auch hier der Anteil der 1 bis 2 ½ Zimmerwohnungen mit mehr als 80 % sehr groß. Die städtische kommunale Finanzierung ließ aber in Reinickendorf, genauso wie bei der Großsiedlung Siemensstadt, ein Experimentieren bei der Grundrisstypisierung zu. So wurden vier Küchentypen mit weitgehend identischer Grundausstattung entwickelt. Daneben nahm man Rentabilitätsberechnungen über Gebäudeabmessungen und Erschließung vor, die zu einer einheitlichen Haustiefe und zur Vorfertigung von Bauteilen führten.

Mit Flachdächern, prägnanter kubischer Baukörpergliederung und vor allem mit ihrem membranhaft zarten Oberflächenweiß leuchten die Siedlungshäuser heute aus der gemischten älteren und neueren Bebauung der vorstädtischen Umgebung hervor. Salvisberg, Ahrends und Büning hatten die Architekturteile der Dachüberstände, Regenfallrohre, Eingangstüren und Fensterrahmen lebhaft farbig gefasst und so die Strahlkraft der weißen Wände noch verstärkt. Durch die in jüngerer Zeit erfolgten Res-

and on the other hand they permitted a view into the courtyards. Additionally, the facades of the head buildings at Erich-Weinert-Straße were partially covered with vines, which enhanced the impression of a green street space. Low privet hedges between the U-shaped blocks flank the narrow lawns of the front gardens.

## Weiße Stadt

Between the Siedlung Schillerpark and Alt-Reinickendorf, which used to be a village far away from the city centre, the self-contained shape of the large residential estate of "Weiße Stadt" stands out markedly in the city structure. This housing project was implemented between 1929 and 1931 under the leadership of urban development councillor Martin Wagner by a consortium consisting of the architects Otto Rudolf Salvisberg, Bruno Ahrends and Wilhelm Büning. This approach was the same as for the simultaneously built Siemensstadt. Salvisberg was responsible for designing the urban development while the green plan was designed by gardening director Ludwig Lesser. The client for the construction of the 1,268 flats was the "Gemeinnützige Heimstättengesellschaft Primus mbH" (Primus Non-Profit Housing Society with limited liability). Most of the buildings have three storeys and all of them have flat roofs.

The master plan and the design of the houses and flats were based on rationality and economy. Since people demanded very cheap, small flats, the estate has a rather high proportion of single-room apartments or apartments with a maximum of 2½ rooms (80 %). Yet, since the municipality provided financing for this project at Reinickendorf just as for that of Siemensstadt, the architects could experiment with various standardised ground plans. For instance, they designed four types of standard kitchens with largely identical basic facilities. Furthermore, they carried out calculations concerning the economic viability of building dimensions and servicing, which resulted in a uniform depth of the houses and prefabrication of structural elements.

Abb. 19: Weiße Stadt, verglaste Hauslauben im Siedlungsteil von Bruno Ahrends, Emmentaler Straße, 2005

Fig. 19: Weiße Stadt, glazed loggias in the development section by Bruno Ahrends, Emmentaler Straße, 2005

taurierungen konnte diese Farbigkeit wiedergewonnen werden.

Den nordsüdlich orientierten Siedlungsplan, der im wesentlichen auf dem bestehenden Straßennetz mit der auf den Dorfanger von Alt-Reinickendorf zulaufenden Promenade „Aroser Allee" aufbauen musste, gliedern klar die drei Bauteile der Architekten: im Süden, zwischen Emmentaler Straße, Gotthardstraße und Schillerring der Siedlungsabschnitt von Ahrends, in der Mitte die bis zur Genfer Straße reichenden radial gesetzten Zeilen von Büning und daran anschließend mit dem Brückenhaus über die Aroser Allee die Bauten von Salvisberg, die nach Norden bis an die Lindauer Allee heranreichen. Allen drei Abschnitten gemeinsam ist eine offene Binnenstruktur aus Rand- und Zeilenbauten mit ineinander fließenden Grünräumen.

Bruno Ahrends entwarf die auf den Bürgersteig vorgeschobenen Torbauten am südlichen Eingang zur Siedlung, die die Aroser Allee optisch einschnüren und den Blick in die Magistrale und zum Brückenhaus von Salvisberg lenken. Die um zwei Geschosse erhöhten Bauten gewinnen durch das hohe, nur mit einer Reihe winziger Fensterchen durchbrochene Drempelgeschoss eine beinahe wehrhaft anmutende Festigkeit. Die Fahnenstangen, eine Pathosform der Gewerkschaftsbewegung, die hier, ähnlich wie am Eckbau des Metallarbeiter-Gewerkschaftshauses in Berlin-Kreuzberg von Erich Mendelsohn, aus der Mitte der Schmalwände weit über die Dachkante aufragen, überhöhen das Siedlungstor zu einem Wahrzeichen der Siedlungsgemeinschaft.

Today the houses of this estate, with their flat roofs, marked cubic structures and in particular with their membrane-like delicate white surfaces, shine out from the mix of older and newer suburban buildings. Salvisberg, Ahrends and Büning had chosen lively colours for the roof overhangs, rain down pipes, entrance doors and window frames that enhanced the brightness of the white walls even more. The recent restoration re-established this colourfulness.

The housing estate exhibits a clear division into three parts corresponding to the three architects. It has a north-south orientation and its layout had to be based mainly on the existing road network with the avenue Aroser Allee heading towards the village green of Alt-Reinickendorf. The section in the south between Emmentaler Straße, Gotthardstraße and Schillerring was designed by Ahrends, the centre with its radially positioned ribbons up to Genfer Straße by Büning. The adjacent section starting with the bridge house crossing Aroser Allee up to Lindauer Allee was designed by Salvisberg. All three sections share an open internal structure of block margin buildings and rows of houses with interconnected green spaces.

Bruno Ahrends designed the gate-like buildings projecting into the pedestrian path at the southern entrance to the estate. They seem to narrow Aroser Allee and attract the view to the main road and the bridge house by Salvisberg. The buildings are two storeys higher than the others and the high jamb storeys which are interrupted only by a row of tiny windows give it a strong and almost military appearance. The flagpoles – a form of pathos of the trade union movement – reaching out from the middle of the narrow side far beyond the roof edge enhance this entrance and turn it into a symbol for the housing estate community. Similar flagpoles have been used at the corner block designed by Erich Mendelsohn as a seat of the metal workers union in Berlin-Kreuzberg.

The residential houses designed by Ahrends in long uninterrupted rows follow the bend of Aroser Allee and the parallel Romanshorner Weg. The fan-shaped area between Aroser Allee, Schillerring and Emmentaler Straße is framed by short ribbons on the margins. The children's home which was also designed by Ahrends is embedded in the open space between the two north-south rows of buildings. Ahrends gives his buildings individuality in particular by the design of the staircase windows and entrance doors which, with their expressionist brick frames, stand out impressively from the cool plain white facades. The loggias face the yards and their glass bodies give the facades a plastic structure.

Rows of houses dominate the section designed by Wilhelm Büning. However, his three-storeyed ribbons do not stand parallel with north-south orientation as the ribbon doctrine would have required, but rather are positioned radially starting from the bent Schillerring. They form the outer ring of the fan between Aroser Allee and Emmentaler Straße. The trapezoid areas between them are green spaces which are open towards the tree-filled Schillerring at their narrow ends and closed by short three-storeyed cross bars at the wider ends towards Genfer Straße. This creates a clear mark for the threshold between public road space and semi-public green space at the margin of the es-

Ahrends Siedlungshäuser folgen in langen geschlossenen Reihen dem gekrümmten Verlauf der Aroser Allee und dem parallel geführten Romanshorner Weg. Das fächerförmige Areal zwischen Aroser Allee, Schillerring und Emmentaler Straße ist mit kurzen Randzeilen eingefasst. Zwischen zwei eingestellten nord-südlichen Zeilen hat sich im Innenfeld, eingebettet in den Siedlungsfreiraum, das ebenfalls von Ahrends entworfene Kinderheim erhalten. Individualität zeigte Ahrends besonders bei der Gestaltung der Treppenhausfenster und Hauseingänge, die sich mit expressionistischen Ziegelrahmungen vom kühlen sachlichen Weiß der Eingangsfronten effektvoll abheben. Zur Hofseite richten sich die Hauslauben, die als gläserne Körper die Front plastisch gliedern.

Im Abschnitt Wilhelm Bünings dominiert die Zeilenbauweise. Seine dreigeschossigen Zeilen sind jedoch nicht parallel nord-südlich ausgerichtet, wie die Zeilenbaudoktrin es gefordert hätte, sondern radial, vom gebogenen Schillerring ausgehend. Sie bilden den äußeren Ring des Fächers zwischen Aroser Allee und Emmentaler Straße. Die trapezförmigen Zwischenflächen sind als Grünräume angelegt, an der engeren Seite zum baumbestandenen Schillerring offen, an der breiteren Seite zur Genfer Straße mit kurzen dreigeschossigen Riegeln abgeschlossen. So ist die Schwelle zwischen öffentlichem Straßenland und halböffentlichem Grün zum Rand der Siedlung hin klar markiert, nach innen jedoch aufgehoben. In ihrer unsentimentalen Architursprache vermitteln die Häuser mit Dachüberstand und breitem farbigen Dachgesims ruhige Bodenständigkeit. An der Emmentaler und Genfer Straße treffen die Zeilen auf zwei hohe fünfgeschossige Mietshäuser der Vorkriegszeit. Gekonnt schob Büning zwischen Alt- und Neubau einachsige Hochhausscheiben, die scharfkantig aus der Bauflucht vortretend hier den Beginn der Siedlung ankündigen.

Nach Norden riegelt das die Aroser Allee überspannende Brückenhaus von Otto Rudolf Salvisberg den südlichen Siedlungsteil ab und leitet zugleich den vom selben Architekten bearbeiteten nördlichen Abschnitt ein. Der 40m breite Stahlbetonbau ruht auf vier Stützenreihen mit schmalem Querschnitt und wirkt mit seinen vier Obergeschossen wie schwerelos eingespannt zwischen den fünfgeschossigen Anschlussbauten. Die Laubengänge auf der Nordseite und die durchlaufenden wohnungsbreiten Loggien auf der Südseite geben dem blendend weißen Bau Plastizität zu beiden Seiten – in seiner Funktion als Mitte der Siedlung durfte das Haus keine Rückseite haben. Die beiden Uhren in der Mitte des obersten Stockwerks auf der Nord- und Südseite übernehmen in der Siedlung die kommunale Funktion der Kirchturm- oder Rathausuhren. Dies war um 1930 von ganz praktischem Nutzen, denn nicht jeder verfügte über eine verlässlich funktionierende Armbanduhr. Weit entfernt von der Expressivität und Monumentalität konventioneller Siedlungsportale, die in Ahrends Torbauten am südlichen Ende der Magistrale immerhin anklingen, ist Salvisbergs Brückenhaus dem abstrakteren Ideal unbedingter Modernität verpflichtet. Der Typus des Brückenhauses lässt an den wohl berühmtesten Bau der klassischen Moderne in Deutschland denken: das 1925/26 von Walter Gropius und Adolf Mayer errichtete Bauhaus in Dessau, mit seinem aufgestellten zweigeschossigen Brückenhaus zwischen Werkstatt- und Klassentrakt.

tate and simultaneously abolishes this division for its interior. The functional architectural language of the houses, with their roof overhangs and broad, coloured eaves, expresses calm rootedness. At Emmentaler Straße and Genfer Straße, the rows of houses meet two five-storey high pre-war buildings. Büning artfully placed high-rise buildings with single axes between the old and the new houses, and these high-rises stand out with sharp edges from the building line, thus marking the beginning of the estate.

In the north, the bridge house by Otto Rudolf Salvisberg crosses Aroser Allee and closes the southern section of the housing estate while at the same time starting the northern section, designed by that same architect. The 40 m wide building of reinforced concrete rests on four rows of pillars with narrow cross-sections, and with its four upper storeys, it looks as if it is weightlessly floating between the five-storeyed adjacent buildings. The galleries at the northern side and the uninterrupted bands of loggias as wide as the apartments on the southern side give both sides of the shining white building a plastic structure: Due to its function as the middle of the housing estate, the house was not to have a rear side. The two clocks in the middle of the top storey on both the north and south sides fulfil the communal function of church or town hall clock for the housing estate. At about 1930, this was quite useful since not everyone had a reliable watch. Salvisberg's bridge house is dedicated to the rather abstract ideal of unconditional modernity, being thus far away from the expressiveness and monumental character of conventional housing estate portals which are at least hinted upon in Ahrends' gate houses at the southern end of the main road. This type of bridge house calls into mind that probably most famous building of classical modern architecture in Germany: the Bauhaus in Dessau – designed and built in 1925/26 by Walter Gropius

Abb. 20: Weiße Stadt, Wohnzeile von Wilhelm Büning, Balkone und Treppenhäuser auf einer Hausseite, 2005

Fig. 20: Weiße Stadt, residential ribbon building by Wilhelm Büning, balconies and staircases at one side of the house

Hinter dem Brückenhaus beginnt auf der Westseite der Aroser Allee eine 280 m lange Hauszeile, deren glatte, geschlossene Straßenfront gleichsam als festes Gegenüber für die mit Sport- und Schulanlagen besetzte weiträumige Freifläche auf der gegenüberliegenden Straßenseite wirkt. Hier sollten nach dem ursprünglichen Konzept neue Schulbauten entstehen. Im Gegensatz zur expressiven Prägnanz der Häuser von Ahrends, sind Salvisbergs Zeilen von fein gezeichneter Sachlichkeit, ein Bild zeitloser Modernität. Eine Besonderheit stellen die zwei Zeilen am Romanshorner Weg dar. Hier sind Reihenhaus- und Geschosswohnungs-Schema baukastenartig kombiniert: Unter je 2 Maisonetten, die das 1. und 2. OG einnehmen, liegt im EG jeweils eine Wohnung mit Zugang zum Garten.

Nicht nur für die damalige Zeit, sondern auch für den heutigen Städtebau einzigartig ist die Vielzahl der Versorgungseinrichtungen. Die Ausstattung mit 24 Läden, die nicht zentral, sondern an mehreren städtebaulich dominanten Punkten liegen, einem Kinderheim im Bauteil Ahrends und sogar mit einer Arztpraxis, dokumentiert den hohen sozialen Standard der Großsiedlung „Weiße Stadt". Das Fernheizwerk mit angegliederter Zentralwäscherei zwischen Genfer Straße und Schillerring, wurde bereits 1968/69 vor der Unterschutzstellung der Siedlung abgebrochen.

*Siedlungsfreiraum*
Die in enger Korrespondenz zur städtebaulichen Gliederung und zur Architektur der Siedlungsteile entwickelte Freiraum- und Gartengestaltung lag einem Konzept des Gartendirektors Ludwig Lesser zu Grunde. Wie bei anderen Großsiedlungen der Zeit zeigt sich auch in der Gestaltung der Freiräume das Bestreben zum rationellen und funktionellen Bauen. Die parkähnlichen Siedlungsfreiräume sollten von den Bewohnern vielfältig nutzbar sein. Die halböffentlichen und privaten Freiräume innerhalb der Baublöcke sollten auch einen Erlebniswert für die Öffentlichkeit aufweisen. Lessers sozial orientierte Gestaltungsprinzipien, sein ganzheitlicher Stil gaben dem Neuen Bauen der Siedlung einen passenden Rahmen.

Lessers grüne Siedlungsräume waren ganz auf die einzelnen räumlichen und baulichen Konstellationen abgestimmt. Beabsichtigt war, den Zusammenhalt von mehreren Gebäuden zu betonen und einzelne Hausreihen in ihrer Wirkung zu unterstützen. So wurden selbst blühende Blumensorten farblich derart ausgewählt, dass sie die Leuchtkraft der weißen Hausfronten und ihrer farbigen Architekturteile hervorhoben. Bei Salvisbergs Dreifamilienhäusern am Romanshorner Weg entstanden in strenger geometrischer Ordnung Mietergärten, getrennt durch einheitliche Wege und Pflanzungen. Ansonsten dominierten Rasenflächen, auf denen einzelne Bäume und Baumgruppen in freier Anordnung wuchsen. Sie schufen einen spannungsreichen Gegensatz zu den seriell gereihten Hoffronten. Darüber hinaus bekam jeder Grünraum einen Sitzplatz für Erwachsene und einen Kinderspielplatz sowie an günstiger Stelle Müllplätze. Teilweise waren sie hinter berankten Lattenwerk oder hohen Hecken verborgen. Zum Teil wurden sie abgesenkt und überschaubar in die Gesamtanlage integriert.

Früh begannen die Umänderungen. So sind heute die kleinen Mietergärten bei den Dreifamilienhäusern verschwunden, die Spiel- und Sitzplätze vielfach aufgelöst und das

and Adolf Meyer – with its double-storeyed bridge house supported on pillars and connecting the workshop and classroom sections.

Behind the bridge house on the western side of Aroser Allee starts a 280 m long row of houses, whose plain and closed front along the road looks like a solid counterpart to the large open space with its sports grounds and schools on the other side. According to the original concept, new school buildings were to be erected there. In contrast to the expressive clarity of the houses designed by Ahrends, the rows by Salvisberg possess a finely drawn functionalism. They are an image of timeless modernity. The two rows at Romanshorner Weg are very particular. They present a kit-like combination of row house and multi-storey patterns: On the ground floor level, a flat with access to a garden lies below each of two maisonettes occupying the 1st and 2nd floor.

The large number of service facilities is quite unique not only for the time when the estate was built, but also in comparison with today's standards. Twenty-four shops which are not concentrated at a central location but distributed over a number of dominating urban positions, a children's home in the section designed by Ahrends and even a medical practice document the high social standard of the Großsiedlung "Weiße Stadt". The district heating plant with its adjoining central laundry between Genfer Straße and Schillerring was demolished as early as 1968/69 before the housing estate was listed.

*Outdoor facilities*
The design of the open and green spaces was based on a concept by gardening director Ludwig Lesser and corresponds closely with the urban structure and the architecture of the estate's three sections. Similar to the landscaping of other large housing estates of the same period, the design of the outdoor facilities of Weiße Stadt also reflects the intention to produce rational and functional designs. The park-like outdoor facilities were to provide multiple uses for the inhabitants. The semi-public and private outdoor facilities within the blocks were also supposed to be attractive for the public. Lesser's socially orientated design principles and his holistic style created a suitable frame for the approach of Neues Bauen which is represented by this estate.

Lesser's green spaces were designed to fully harmonise with the individual spatial and architectural situations. His intention was to stress the coherence of several buildings and enhance the appearance of individual rows of houses. He went to the extent of choosing flowers according to the colour of their blossoms so that they would enhance the brightness of the white facades and the impression of their coloured elements. Salvisberg's three-family houses at Romanshorner Weg are accompanied by tenants' gardens in strict patterns. These gardens are separated by uniform lateral paths and planted bands. The remaining areas are dominated by lawns where solitary trees and groups of trees were liberally placed. They created an interesting contradiction to the serial rows of yard-side fronts. Moreover, each of the green spaces was equipped with a spot where adults could sit and a playground for children as well as waste bin areas at suitable locations. Some of the latter were hidden behind lattice work or high hedges. Others were placed in depressions and visibly integrated into the overall design.

Abb. 21: Weiße Stadt, Gartenhof im Siedlungsteil Ahrends östlich der Aroser Allee. 2001 Teilwiederherstellung nach dem Konzept von Ludwig Lesser, 2005

Fig. 21: Weiße Stadt, garden courtyard in section by Ahrends east of Aroser Allee. 2001 partial reconstruction according to concept by Ludwig Lesser, 2005

Pflanzkonzept durch andersartige Neuanpflanzungen und Wildwuchs verunklärt. Jedoch ist die enge Verzahnung zwischen öffentlichem und halböffentlichem Grün erkennbar geblieben und die gartenkünstlerische Absicht Lessers, soziale Siedlungsgärten zu schaffen, ist heute noch erlebbar.

### Großsiedlung Siemensstadt (Ringsiedlung)

Heute gehört die 1929–34 erbaute Großsiedlung Siemensstadt, am nordwestlichen Rande der Berliner Innenstadt gelegen, zu einem der größten Wohngebiete Berlins. Bezirksübergreifend erstreckt sich ein Ost-West-Wohnband zwischen der Spandauer Siemensstadt mit ihren Fabriken und Werkssiedlungen im Süden und Westen, dem Volkspark Jungfernheide im Norden, und reicht im Osten mit den Wohngehöften der Nachkriegszeit von Hans Scharoun bis zum Kurt-Schumacher-Damm heran. In der Mitte liegt das Gelände der Großsiedlung Siemensstadt, zwischen dem Heckerdamm am Volkspark und der Mäckeritzstraße im Süden.

Wie auch zeitgleich in Reinickendorf bildete sich unter der Regie von Stadtbaurat Martin Wagner eine Arbeitsgemeinschaft aus den Architekten Hans Scharoun, Walter Gropius, Fred Forbat, Otto Bartning, Paul Rudolf Henning, Hugo Häring und dem Gartenarchitekten Leberecht Migge. Die Bauträgerschaft der 1.370 Mietwohnungen in flachgedeckten Stockwerksbauten übernahm die stadteigene „Gemeinnützige Baugesellschaft Berlin-Heerstraße mbH".

Jeder Architekt erhielt einzelne Häuserzeilen zur Bearbeitung. So kommt ein überaus vielgestaltiges Siedlungsbild zustande. Exemplarisch zeigt sich die ganze Spannbreite des Neuen Bauens vom Funktionalismus Gropius', über die Raumkunst Scharouns bis zum organischen Formenreichtum Härings. Scharoun kam die Aufgabe zu, die verschie-

The first changes were introduced quite early. The small tenants' gardens at the three-family homes do not exist anymore, most of the playgrounds and seats have disappeared and the planting concept has been disturbed by newly planted greenery which deviates from the patterns or by wild growing plants. Yet, the close interaction of public and semi-public greenery remained visible and the intention of the garden architect Lesser to create social housing estate gardens can still be experienced.

### Großsiedlung Siemensstadt (Ringsiedlung)

Built in 1929–34, the Großsiedlung Siemensstadt at the northwestern margin of the city centre of Berlin belongs to one of the biggest housing areas of Berlin. Across the district limits, an east-west band of residential estates stretches across Siemensstadt, with its mix of factories and company housing estates in the district of Spandau in the south and west, the public park of Jungfernheide in the north and in the east its post-war courtyards by Hans Scharoun, reaching Kurt-Schumacher-Damm. The area of the Großsiedlung Siemensstadt is located in the centre of this entire area, between Heckerdamm at the public park and Mäckeritzstraße in the south.

Similar to the consortium formed simultaneously for the project at Reinickendorf, a working group was formed by the architects Hans Scharoun, Walter Gropius, Fred Forbat, Otto Bartning, Paul Rudolf Henning, Hugo Häring and the garden architect Leberecht Migge. The group was headed by urban development councillor Martin Wagner. The client for the project with 1,370 tenement flats in flat-roofed, multi-storeyed buildings was the "Gemeinnützige Baugesellschaft Berlin-Heerstraße mbH" (Non-Profit Limited Liability Building Society Berlin-Heerstraße) which was owned by the city.

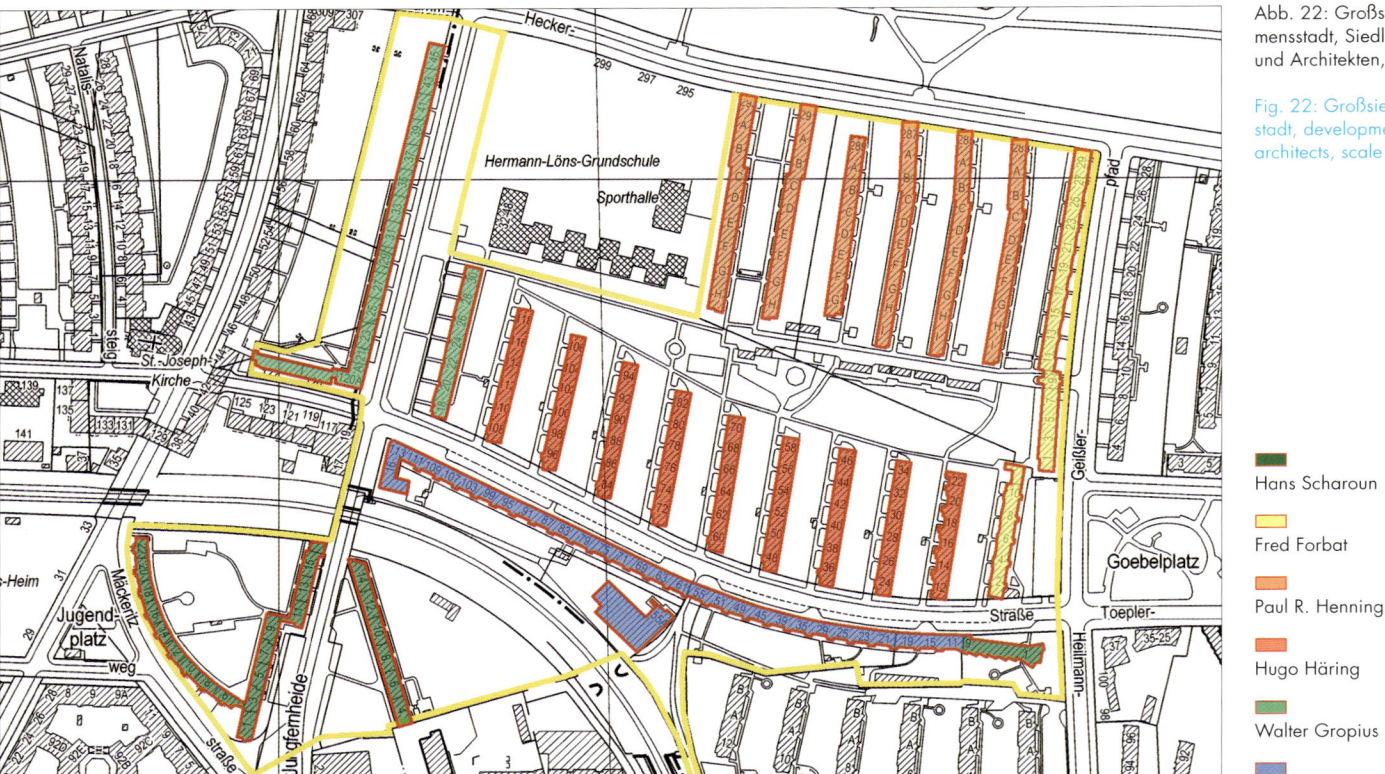

Abb. 22: Großsiedlung Siemensstadt, Siedlungsabschnitte und Architekten, M 1:5.000

Fig. 22: Großsiedlung Siemensstadt, development phases and architects, scale 1:5,000

■ Hans Scharoun
■ Fred Forbat
■ Paul R. Henning
■ Hugo Häring
■ Walter Gropius
■ Otto Bartning

denen Architekturen ganzheitlich städtebaulich zu fassen. Er entwickelte hier erstmalig sein auf den Lebensraum des Menschen bezogenes Leitmotiv der „Nachbarschaft". Nicht der starre funktionalistische Zeilenbau ist das Ideal, sondern eine auf die natürlichen Gegebenheiten des Geländes eingehende ungezwungene Raumgliederung mit Verengungen und Aufweitungen, Raumbegrenzung und Raumerweiterung, Abschirmung und Offenheit. Bei aller Freiheit der Komposition ist die in der Zeilenbaudoktrin geforderte Nord-Südorientierung beibehalten und sichert den Wohnungen viel Licht, Luft und Sonne. Der alte Baumbestand, den Scharoun zu schonen hatte, verstärkt seit Anbeginn den landschaftlichen Charakter der Gesamtanlage.

Den Eingang zur Siedlung von der Stadtseite her behielt Scharoun sich selbst vor. Hier, südlich der sogenannten Siemensbahn, galt es auf die geschlossene ältere Bebauung zu reagieren. Für die Gestaltung des Siedlungsauftaktes stand ein in die S-Bahnkurve geschmiegtes fächerförmiges Grundstück zur Verfügung, dessen Mitte der Jungfernheideweg durchschneidet. Scharoun bildete aus drei fünfgeschossigen Bauten beiderseits der Straße eine Art Trichter, der sich zur S-Bahnunterführung hin verengt. Die Binnenfläche nimmt ein von altem Baumbestand durchsetzter Gartenraum ein. Vor allem dem Kopfbau auf der Westseite des Jungfernheideweges, im Volksmund „Panzerkreuzer" genannt, gab Scharoun eine außerordentliche plastische Durchbildung, die mit Höhenstaffelung, tiefen Einschnitten für die Dachterrassen, Balkongondeln und kreisförmigen Fenstern Motive der Schiffsarchitektur aufgreift. Die ockerfarbige und gelbe Fassung der Balkon-Innenseiten lässt das dominierende Weiß der Wandflächen noch heller erstrahlen. Diesem lebhaft gegliederten Bau steht an der Ostseite eine ruhige Fassade gegenüber, die ihr subtiles räumliches Spiel mit Loggiasegmenten betreibt.

Each architect was allocated the design of individual rows of houses. The result is a very varied image of the housing estate. It contains examples of all styles of Neues Bauen, from the functionalism of Gropius through the spatial art of Scharoun up to Häring's organic wealth of shapes. Scharoun had the task of creating an architectural frame for all the different styles. Here, for the first time, he developed his leitmotif of "neighbourhood" which relates to the space in which people live. The ideal is not the strictly functional row of houses, but a casual spatial structure on the basis of the natural landscape and with narrowing, widening, delimitation and extension of space, screening and opening. Yet, despite all freedom of composition, the pattern preserved the north-south orientation required by the doctrine of building ribbon houses and thus assures that lots of light, air and sunshine reach the flats. Scharoun had to preserve the existing trees and, from the beginning, these trees strengthen the landscape character of the housing estate.

Scharoun reserved for himself the designing of the access to the estate from the city side. Here, south of the so-called Siemens railway line, he had to respond to the existing buildings with their closed pattern. The access of the estate was to be built on a fan-shaped property formed by the curve of the commuter railway line and cut through the middle by Jungfernheideweg. Scharoun designed a kind of funnel consisting of three five-storeyed buildings on both sides of the street and narrowing towards the railway line underpass. The interior space is occupied by a garden area with old trees. Especially for the head building on the western side of Jungfernheideweg, colloquially called the "armoured cruiser", Scharoun used a very plastic design with staggered heights, deep cuts for the roof terraces, balcony and circular windows, all of which give it the appearance of a ship. The ochre and yellow colour of the inner balcony walls makes the dominating white of the facades stand out

Hinter dem Damm der S-Bahn beginnt der eigentliche Siedlungsbereich, der am Heckerdamm in den Naturraum des Volksparks Jungfernheide übergeht. Der 338 m lange straßenbegleitende Bau von Otto Bartning entlang der leicht gebogenen Goebelstraße bildet die feste städtebauliche Kante im Süden, die als Lärm- und Sichtbarriere die Siedlung zur Trasse der „Siemensbahn" und zum Siedlungsheizwerk abschirmt. Zugleich wirkt er in seiner wenig gegliederten Wandhaftigkeit als Raumabschluss zu den gegenüberliegenden Häring-Zeilen. Die Rückseite der 26 identischen Hauseinheiten, von einem gemeinsamen Grünraum hinterfangen, zeigt mit gekoppelten Balkonen, die den einheitlichen Grundrissaufbau der Zweizimmerwohnungen widerspiegeln, ein lebhafteres Profil.

even brighter. This building, with its lively structure, is opposed in the east by a calm facade that plays a subtle spatial game with loggia segments.

The actual housing estate area starts behind the railway line and merges with the public park of Jungfernheide at Heckerdamm. The 338 m long building by Otto Bartning along the slightly bent Goebelstraße constitutes the firm architectural limit in the south and acts as a noise barrier and optical screen between the estate and the Siemens railway line as well as the estate's heating plant. Its relatively unstructured wall-type appearance also creates a delimitation from the opposite rows of houses by Häring. The rear facades of the 26 identical housing units with a common

Abb. 23: Großsiedlung Siemensstadt, östlicher Siedlungsteil von Walter Gropius am Jungfernheideweg, 2005

Fig. 23: Großsiedlung Siemensstadt, eastern section by Walter Gropius at Jungfernheideweg, 2005

Während der nach dem Krieg von Otto Bartning geleitete Wiederaufbau des östlichen Endes der Randzeile an der Goebelstraße und auch die gleichzeitige Ergänzung um drei Häuser (Goebelstraße 11–19) von Bartning sich streng am ursprünglichen Vorbild hielten, setzte sich Hans Scharoun mit seinem angrenzenden Kopfbau Goebelstraße 1–9 stilistisch effektvoll ab. Das 1955–56 über einem sägeblattartigem Grundriss erbaute Laubenganghaus leitet über zu den kühnen Form- und Grundrisserfindungen, die Scharoun in den 1960er Jahren im östlich anschließenden Siedlungsgebiet Charlottenburg-Nord umgesetzt hat. Bereits hier zeigt sich der stark differenzierende Entwurfsstil von Scharoun mit unregelmäßig geschnittenen Wohnungen. Die apartmentähnlichen Kleinwohnungen sind mit Küche, Essplatz und Toilette zum Laubengang an der Goebelstraße orientiert, während die verschachtelt angeordneten Schlaf- und Wohnzimmer mit breiten Fenstern sich zum Gartenhof öffnen.

green space behind them show a more lively profile with their coupled balconies which reflect the uniform ground plan of the two-room flats.

Post-war reconstruction of the eastern end of the marginal row on Goebelstraße, lead by Otto Bartning, and the simultaneous construction of three complementary houses (Goebelstraße 11–19) by Bartning strictly adhered to the original design. In contrast to this, Hans Scharoun chose a completely different style for the head building at Goebelstraße 1–9 (built 1955–56). The gallery block, with its sawblade shape, represents a transition to the boldly invented shapes and ground plans that Scharoun implemented in the adjacent residential estate of Charlottenburg-Nord on the eastern border of Siemensstadt after the war. This head building is an example of Scharoun's greatly differentiating style with irregular ground plans for the flats. The kitchens, dining areas and toilets of the apartment-like small flats are orientated towards the gallery at Goebelstraße, whereas the

Abb. 24: Großsiedlung Siemensstadt, Siedlungsteil Hans Scharoun. Eingang zur Siedlung am Jungfernheideweg, westlicher Bauteil, 2005

Fig. 24: Großsiedlung Siemensstadt, part designed by Hans Scharoun. Entrance to the Siedlung at Jungfernheideweg, western section, 2005

In den Konturen scharf und kantig, in der kühlen funktionellen Strenge der Reihung der identischen Hauseinheiten von schnittiger Eleganz, repräsentieren die beiden Gropius-Zeilen vor allen anderen Siedlungsbauten die programmatische Rationalität einer Großsiedlung des Neuen Bauens. Sie liegen am westlichen Rande des Siedlungsgeländes am Jungfernheideweg und leiten mit einem kurzen Laubenganghaus an der Goebelstraße zur benachbarten Siemenswerksiedlung „Heimat" von Hans Hertlein über, die zur gleichen Zeit erbaut wurde. Gropius' Technikästhetik entspricht die auf weiß-grau-schwarz reduzierte Farbigkeit der Baukörper. Die Stahlfenster der Treppenhäuser und Loggienverglasungen, alle Wohnungsfenster und die Schutzgitter vor den Dachgärten sind einheitlich schiefergrau gestrichen, so dass auf dem leuchtenden Weiß der Fassaden die bandartige Gliederung dieser Elemente klar zum Ausdruck kommt.

Zwischen Jungfernheideweg und Geißlerpfad stoßen, gegeneinander versetzt, die nord-südlich ausgerichteten Zeilen Hugo Härings von Süden und die sechs Zeilen Paul Rudolf Hennings von Norden auf einen breiten Grünstreifen – eine Promenade, die Kinderspielplätze, Kinderhort und Ruheplätze aufnehmen sollte. Die von Leberecht Migge gärtnerisch gestaltete „Grüne Mitte" der Siedlung, in die die Gartenanlagen der Zeilen einmünden, wirkt als gemeinschaftsbildender grüner Freiraum, ganz im Sinne von Scharouns Idee der Nachbarschaft. Im Osten schließen am Geißlerpfad die drei Wohnzeilen von Fred Forbat an. Nirgendwo kommt die der doktrinären Zeilenbauweise innewohnende Monotonie auf.

Naturhaft wirkende Baustoffe und Farben und vor allem die „weiche" Formgebung der weit vor den Baukörper tre-

interlaced bedrooms and sitting rooms with wide windows open towards the courtyard.

The two rows by Gropius, with their sharp and edgy contours, and the cool functional strictness of the sequence of identical, stylishly elegant housing units represent more than all the other residential buildings the programmatic rationality of the design of large housing estates in the Neues Bauen fashion. These rows are located on the western edge of the estate at Jungfernheideweg and, with a short gallery block, they provide a transition at Goebelstraße to the neighbouring company residential estate "Heimat", designed by Hans Hertlein and built at the same time. The colours of the buildings, which are limited to a pattern of white, grey and black, reflect Gropius' technical aesthetics. The steel frames of the windows of staircases and loggias, apartments and the protective railings of the roof gardens are all painted slate grey so that the band-like structure of these elements stands out clearly from the bright white of the facades.

Between Jungfernheideweg and Geißlerpfad, the rows of houses designed by Hugo Häring with their north-south orientation and the six rows of houses designed by Paul Rudolf Henning from the north meet at a wide green band in a staggered pattern. This green band is an avenue where playgrounds, a day care centre for children and resting places were to be installed. The "Green Centre" of the estate was designed by Leberecht Migge. Where the gardens of the rows of houses meet, it has the function of a community green and open space in the sense of Scharoun's idea of neighbourhood. In the east at Geißlerpfad lie the three rows of residential houses designed by Fred Forbat. Nowhere do we find the monotony that is inherent in doctrinaire ribbon architecture.

The architecture of functionalist Häring is characterised by natural looking materials and colours and especially the "soft" shapes of the kidney-shaped balconies standing out far from the building fronts. He is the only one to place balconies and staircases on the western side. The strong vertical element of the staircase windows harmonises with the dominating motif of the layered rounded balconies. This makes us see the facades in the rhythm of the plastic motifs that are mirrored at the staircase axis but not in that of the housing units. Häring explained the unusual shape of the balconies with a functional intention: On the one hand, he wanted the balconies as extensions of residential space to stand out as far as possible; on the other hand he wanted to reduce the shade they cause. The yellow-brown bricks, the beige smooth plaster, white window frames and dark brown entrance doors merge with their warm colours and the surrounding green into an overall image which demonstratively opposes the strictness and rationality of Gropius buildings.

Henning's six rows of houses have natural looking, reserved colours similar to those used by Häring. The same yellow plaster – here with a structured surface, the brick cladding in various shades of yellow and the window frames in light yellow give the group of buildings an air of a garden town and summer resort despite the ribbon pattern. This impression is enhanced by the fact that the ground floor apartments of the three eastern ribbons open to the green space

tenden nierenförmigen Balkone kennzeichnen die Architektur des organischen Funktionalisten Häring. Er ist der einzige, der Balkone und Treppenhäuser an die Westseite setzt. Das starke vertikale Element der Treppenhausfenster schließt sich mit dem dominierenden Motiv der geschichteten gerundeten Balkone zusammen. So sieht man die Fassade im Takt der um die Treppenhausachse gespiegelten plastischen Motive, aber nicht im Takt der Hauseinheiten. Häring begründete die ungewöhnliche Form der Balkone mit einer funktionellen Absicht. Er wollte einerseits die Balkone als Erweiterung des Wohnraums möglichst weit herausstrecken, andererseits den dadurch entstehenden Schatten verringern. Die gelb-braunen Ziegel, der beige Glattputz, der weiße Anstrich aller Fenster und die dunkelbraunen Haustüren, verbinden sich mit ihren warmen Farbtönen mit dem umgebenden Grün zu einem Gesamtbild, das sich demonstrativ von der Strenge und Rationalität der Gropiusbauten absetzt.

Ähnlich den Bauten Härings finden wir bei Hennings sechs Hausreihen naturhafte, verhaltene Farbtöne. Der gelbliche Putz, hier jedoch mit rauher Oberfläche, die gelb-bunte Ziegelverblendung und die hellgelb gestrichenen Fenster und Balkontüren verleihen der Baugruppe trotz des Zeilenschemas einen Zug von Gartenstadt und Sommerfrische. Dieser Eindruck wird dadurch verstärkt, dass sich die Erdgeschosswohnungen der drei östlichen Zeilen mit hausbreiten Terrassen zum Grünraum öffnen. Die breit hervortretenden Balkone mit ihren massiven Brüstungen und ihren starken Schattenwürfen bilden in der Reihung an der Westseite der langgestreckten Baukörper ein starkes expressives Element. Wesentlich karger, ganz ohne Balkone, Loggien und Terrassen, präsentieren sich die im letzten Bauabschnitt 1933–34 errichteten beiden Hausreihen im Osten. Die schlichten Fronten verdeutlichen den Wandel im öffentlichen Wohnungsbau nach der NS-Machtergreifung 1933, der zu wesentlichen Einschränkungen im Wohnungsstandard und zu Veränderungen in der Architektur führte.

Vielgestaltig zeigen sich die drei Hauszeilen von Fred Forbat, die am Geißlerpfad die Siedlung im Osten abschließen.

with terraces, which are as wide as the houses. The rows of widely projecting balconies with their solid parapets and heavy shadows on the western side of the buildings are a very expressive element. The two rows of houses in the east which were built during the last development phase in 1933–34 are much more austere and have no balconies, loggias or terraces. The plain facades reflect the change in public housing construction after the Nazis took power. They led to a deterioration of housing standards and changes in architecture.

The three ribbons of houses by Fred Forbat which complete the estate in the east at Geißlerpfad are quite varied. Similar to the buildings designed by Gropius, the clear geometric shapes of the buildings are dominated by a functional style with white facades and highlighting brick elements in various shades of yellow. Forbat's architecture is based on strict, carefully shaped simplicity and the stressing of closed contours which are enlivened by asymmetric highlights. The very long northern ribbon shows one of the most striking facade solutions in mass housing construction. Vertical walls and shallow curves form a projection-like frame for the entrances and vertical bands of the staircase windows. They give the entire front along the street an unusual, wave-like plastic structure.

### Outdoor facilities

Leberecht Migge was responsible for designing the outdoor facilities. Characteristic for his design is the creation of interconnected housing estate spaces, as well as the consistent integration of existing landscape elements like the trees of Jungfernheide. Especially in the section designed by Scharoun, the existing land was cleverly modelled for the purpose of preserving the trees and the landscape. As a result of these efforts, generous lawns with old trees create a park-like environment in the spaces between the ribbons and in particular in the area between the sections designed by Henning and Häring, which was to become a community facility. This effect was supported by the planting of herbaceous plants, low bushes and hedges in the small gardens in

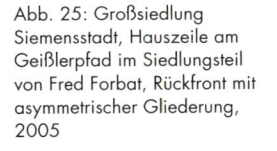

Abb. 25: Großsiedlung Siemensstadt, Hauszeile am Geißlerpfad im Siedlungsteil von Fred Forbat, Rückfront mit asymmetrischer Gliederung, 2005

Fig. 25: Großsiedlung Siemensstadt, ribbon at Geißlerpfad in the section by Fred Forbat, rear front with asymmetric structure, 2005

Abb. 26: Großsiedlung Siemensstadt, die „Grüne Mitte" zwischen den Zeilen von Henning und Häring, 2005

Fig. 26: Großsiedlung Siemensstadt, "Grüne Mitte" (green plain) between the ribbons by Henning and Häring, 2005

Ähnlich wie bei den Gropiusbauten bestimmt eine sachliche Formensprache mit weißen Fassaden und betont gesetzten gelbbunten Ziegelelementen die klaren geometrischen Baukörper. Forbats Architektur beruht auf strenger, sorgfältig geformter Einfachheit und auf der Betonung einer geschlossenen Konturwirkung, die durch asymmetrische Akzente belebt wird. Die besonders lange nördliche Zeile zeigt eine der markantesten Fassadenlösungen im Massenwohnungsbau. Die Eingänge und die vertikalen Bänder der Treppenhausfenster werden risalitartig von vorstoßenden Scheitwänden aus Ziegeln und flachen Rundungen gefasst. Sie verleihen der Straßenfront eine ganz ungewöhnliche wellenförmige plastische Gliederung.

### Siedlungsfreiraum

Charakteristisch für die Gestaltung der Freiräume, die in den Händen von Leberecht Migge lag, war die Schaffung zusammenhängender Siedlungsräume und die konsequente Einbeziehung vorgefundener landschaftlicher Elemente wie der Altbaumbestand der Jungfernheide. Für den Erhalt der Bäume und des Landschaftsbildes wurde vor allem im Bereich des Bauteils Scharoun das vorhandene Baugelände geschickt modelliert. So entstand zwischen den Zeilenbauten und vor allem in dem als Gemeinschaftsanlage geplanten Bereich zwischen dem Bauteil Henning und dem Bauteil Häring im Zusammenspiel großzügiger Rasenflächen mit dem alten Baumbestand ein parkähnlicher Charakter. Unterstützt wurde diese Wirkung durch die Bepflanzung der den Zeilenbauten vorgelagerten kleinen Gärten mit Stauden, niedrigen Sträuchern und Hecken, wie auch die Berankung zahlreicher Fassaden mit Wildem Wein.

Um die parkähnliche Wirkung durch die notwendigen Einbauten, insbesondere die Müllhäuschen nicht zu beeinträchtigen, wurden diese sorgfältig in die Gesamtanlage integriert. So entwarf Leberecht Migge für den Bauteil Häring front of the ribbon buildings and also by the fact that many facades are covered with Virginia creeper.

To prevent disturbing the park-like image by the necessary service facilities and in particular the waste bin sheds, these were carefully integrated into the overall design. For instance, for the section designed by Häring, Leberecht Migge designed waste bin sheds overgrown with green climbers and with green roofs where sunflowers and nasturtium grew. These sheds still exist today, although without the roof greenery. In Henning's section, these facilities were placed in depressions in the ground which preserved the transparency of the park-like, flowing green spaces and the view towards the public park Jungfernheide in the north.

Private and public housing estate areas were treated as equals and therefore the trees planted in the streets and in the front gardens, some of which reach out into the streets, were all integrated into the overall garden design concept. The Lombardy poplars which were planted in deliberate places were characteristic for the estate.

Between the sections designed by Henning and Häring, a generous park area was established with common playgrounds and meeting places creating a spatial connection between these two sections. In the "Green Centre", three differentiated meeting places and playgrounds were established which were linked with the surrounding buildings by various paths. These facilities were embedded into a spatial alternation of lawns and existing old trees. In the north and east, this area was surrounded by slopes.

Just as in the Großsiedlung "Weiße Stadt", the additionally established tenants' gardens in the section designed by Henning create a lively alternation of public, semi-public and private areas within the housing estate.

mit Kletterpflanzen begrünte und mit einer Dachbepflanzung aus Sonnenblumen und Kapuzinerkresse versehene Müllhäuschen, die bis heute, allerdings ohne Dachbegrünung erhalten geblieben sind. Im Bauteil Henning entschied man sich für eine abgesenkte Variante, welche die Durchsichtigkeit der parkartigen, fließenden Grünräume und die Sichtbeziehung zum nördlich gelegenen Volkspark Jungfernheide sicherstellte.

In einer gleichberechtigten Behandlung privater und öffentlicher Siedlungsräume wurden die Baumpflanzungen in den Straßenräumen und der zum Teil in den Straßenraum hineinragenden Vorgartenflächen mit in die gartengestalterische Konzeption integriert. Prägend für die Siedlung waren die pointiert gesetzten Pyramidenpappeln.

Zwischen den Bauteilen Henning und Häring wurde eine großzügige, mit gemeinschaftlichen Spiel- und Aufenthaltsbereichen ausgestattete Parkaue angelegt, die die beiden Bauteile räumlich miteinander verbindet. In der „Grünen Mitte" wurden drei differenziert gestaltete Aufenthalts- und Spielbereiche angelegt, die mit verschiedenen Wegeverbindungen an die einzelnen umliegenden Bauteile angeschlossen waren. Diese Anlagen waren in einen räumlichen Wechsel von Rasenflächen und ursprünglichen Altbaumbestand eingebettet. Nördlich und östlich war dieser Bereich durch Böschungen eingefasst.

Ebenso wie in der Großsiedlung „Weiße Stadt" wird durch die zusätzliche Anlage von Mietergärten im Bauteil Henning eine lebendige Abfolge von öffentlichen, halböffentlichen und privaten Bereichen in der Siedlung erreicht.

Abb. 27: Großsiedlung Siemensstadt, Siedlungsteil Hugo Häring, Treppenhaus mit Balkonen auf einer Zeilenseite, 2005

Fig. 27: Großsiedlung Siemensstadt, section by Hugo Häring, staircase with balconies at one side of the ribbon, 2005

Abb. 28: Großsiedlung Siemensstadt, Siedlungsteil Hugo Häring, Zeile mit Balkonen, 2005

Fig. 28: Großsiedlung Siemensstadt, section by Hugo Häring, ribbon with balconies, 2005

## 2.B Geschichte und Entwicklung

Der Aufstieg Berlins zur Metropole im 19. Jahrhundert war sowohl durch seine Hauptstadtfunktionen für Preußen und seit 1871 für das Deutsche Reich als auch durch seine Entwicklung zum Industrie- und Finanzzentrum Mitteleuropas bestimmt. Um 1900 hatte Berlin den Rang einer „Weltstadt" erreicht.

Allerdings waren die im Zuge dieser Entwicklung aufgetretenen sozialen Probleme nur unvollkommen gelöst worden. Es war nicht gelungen, die Masse der Bevölkerung in angemessenen Wohnungen unterzubringen. Der Wohnungsbau lag profitorientiert in den Händen von Einzelbauherren und Terraingesellschaften. In den Hinterhöfen, in Kellern und Kleinwohnungen der Mietskasernen musste die Arbeiterbevölkerung auf engstem Raum leben. Die Bevölkerungszahl Berlins hatte sich in einem Zeitraum von 25 Jahren verdoppelt. Zählte die Stadt 1849 412.000 Einwohner, waren es 1875 bereits über 960.000 und 1900 1,89 Millionen Einwohner.

Unter dem außerordentlichen Druck der Wohnungsnot und den elenden Verhältnissen in den hoffnungslos überbelegten Mietskasernen kam es schon ab den 1880er Jahren zu einer wahren Gründungswelle von Baugenossenschaften und gemeinnützigen Baugesellschaften – Berlin wurde zum Zentrum gemeinwirtschaftlicher Wohnungsfürsorge. Die Bismarck'sche Sozialgesetzgebung zwischen 1878 und 1889, die die Arbeits- und Lebensverhältnisse der Arbeiter erstmalig absicherte, begünstigte das Aufkommen des sozialreformerischen Wohnungsbaues. Zudem konnten nach der 1889 erfolgten Novellierung des Genossenschaftsrechtes und der Einführung der Gesellschaft mit beschränkter Haftung (GmbH) philantropisch gesonnene, wohlhabende Bürger Gesellschafter eines gemeinnützigen Wohnungsbauunternehmens werden, ohne mit ihrem gesamten Vermögen zu haften. Gleichzeitig wurde es möglich, aus den Rücklagen der neu eingerichteten Sozialversicherungskasse günstige Kredite für die Schaffung von Wohnraum für wenig Bemittelte zu erhalten. Außerdem begann der Staat die Initiative der Genossenschaften finanziell zu unterstützen, so dass den 38 Baugenossenschaften von 1890 in Deutschland im Jahre 1914 bereits 1.583 gegenüberstanden.

## 2.B History and development

Berlin's rise to a metropolis in the 19th century was based on both its function as capital of Prussia and later the German Reich (since 1871) and its development as a centre of industry and finance in central Europe. By approximately 1900, Berlin had finally become a cosmopolitan city.

However, the issues which had arisen in conjunction with this development had been solved only incompletely. No way had been found for providing decent housing for the masses of the population. Housing construction was profit-oriented and in the hands of individual builders and property companies. Working class people were forced to live in tiny flats in tenements and often these flats were located in backyards and basements of these blocks. Within a period of 25 years the population of Berlin had doubled. In 1849 the city had 412,000 inhabitants and in 1875 it had already grown to more than 960,000. By 1900 the city had 1.89 million inhabitants.

Due to the pressure of the lack of housing and the miserable conditions in the hopelessly overcrowded tenements, a genuine wave of housing construction cooperatives and non-profit housing construction societies were founded as

Abb. 29: Reformwohnungsbau des Berliner Spar- und Bauvereins. Wohnhof Sickingenstraße 7–8 von Alfred Messel, erbaut 1893–94

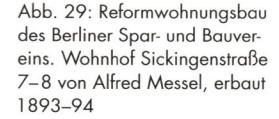

Fig. 29: Reform housing development of Berliner Spar- und Bauverein. Courtyard at Sickingenstraße 7–8 by Alfred Messel, erected 1893–94

Abb. 30: Berliner Kellerwohnung, Mietskaserne Sorauer Straße 27, um 1908

Fig. 30: Berlin basement flat, tenement block Sorauer Straße 27, approximately 1908

So waren die ersten Voraussetzungen für tiefgreifende und umfassende Innovationen im Wohnungsbau, namentlich für den Bau kleiner, in sich abgeschlossener und vollständig ausgestatteter Wohnungen gegeben. Der „Berliner Spar- und Bauverein", ein wesentlich von jüdischen Berliner Bürgern 1892 gegründeter Träger für den neuen Kleinwohnungsbau, beauftragte mit der Projektierung seiner ersten Wohnanlage, den Doppelhäusern in der Sickingenstraße in Berlin-Moabit, den Architekten Alfred Messel, der vor allem mit Warenhausbauten als Wegbereiter des modernen Bauens über Berlin hinaus bekannt wurde. Die Moabiter Wohnanlage und die wenig später folgende, ebenfalls von Messel entworfene Häusergruppe in der Proskauer Straße in Berlin-Friedrichshain, nach dem jüdischen Auftraggeber „Weisbach-Gruppe" genannt, waren sowohl für die Entwicklung rationeller Wohnungsgrundrisse als auch für die anspruchsvolle architektonische Gestaltung des Reformwohnungsbaus Maßstab setzend. Derselbe Spar- und Bauverein beauftragte später Bruno Taut mit der Errichtung der Gartenstadt Falkenberg und der Siedlung Schillerpark.

early as the 1880s. This development made Berlin the centre of communal housing welfare. Bismarck's social welfare laws, which came into force between 1878 and 1889 and were the first to provide some security for the working and living conditions of the working class, also had a favourable effect on the development of socially reformed housing construction. Furthermore, after the amendment of the cooperative law and the introduction of the limited liability company (GmbH) in 1889, it had become possible for well-to-do, philanthropically minded citizens to join non-profit housing construction societies without being liable with their entire property. At the same time, the possibility of acquiring low-interest loans was established from the reserves of the newly created social insurances for housing construction for low income groups. In addition, the state started to provide financial support for the cooperative's initiatives, such that the number of housing construction cooperatives in Germany grew from 38 in 1890 to 1,583 in 1914.

Abb. 31: Wohnhof in der Gartenstadt Falkenberg von Bruno Taut. Modell des ersten Bauabschnittes am Akazienhof, ausgeführt 1913

Fig. 31: Courtyard in Gartenstadt Falkenberg by Bruno Taut. Model of first development phase at Akazienhof, executed 1913

Im Sog der breiten Reformbewegung, getragen von Bodenreformern wie Adolf Damaschke und Wohnungsreformern wie Rudolf Eberstadt, gründeten sich um 1900 weitere gemeinnützige und genossenschaftliche Baugesellschaften, die erste Schritte zur Verwirklichung einer neuen sozialen Wohn- und Lebenskultur unternahmen. So die Baugenossenschaft „Freie Scholle", ebenfalls ein späterer Auftraggeber von Bruno Taut, der Vaterländische Bauverein und der Beamtenwohnungsverein, die mit ihren größeren und mittleren Wohnanlagen die Entwicklung von Grundrissen und städtebaulichen Großformen vorantrieben. Zum einen führten sie blockauflösende Innenstadtkonzepte vor, zum anderen suchten sie lebensreformerische Sied-

This had created the initial preconditions for thorough and comprehensive innovations in housing construction and especially for the construction of smaller, self-contained and completely equipped flats. The "Berliner Spar- und Bauverein" (Berlin Savings and Construction Association) was founded in 1892 for building small flats. Most of its members were Jewish citizens of the capital. Its contract for designing its first housing estate with semi-detached houses at Sickingenstraße in the district of Moabit went to the architect Alfred Messel, who also became famous outside Berlin as a pioneer of Neues Bauen, mainly for his department store designs. The Moabit estate created benchmarks both for the development of rational housing ground plans and also for attractive architecture in reformed housing

lungsprojekte an der Peripherie Berlins als Gegenentwurf zur Großstadt zu initiieren.

Ein solches lebensreformerisches Siedlungsprojekt war die 1913–1916 nach einem Entwurf von Bruno Taut von der „Gemeinnützigen Baugenossenschaft Gartenvorstadt Groß-Berlin eGmbH" geschaffene Gartenstadt Falkenberg in Alt-Glienicke. Die deutsche Gartenstadtgesellschaft wollte hier, nach dem Vorbild des englischen Gartenstadtkonzeptes von Ebenezer Howard und Raymond Unwin, neue Lebens-, Wirtschafts- und Wohnformen verwirklicht sehen. Es ging also um weit mehr als um das aufgelockerte, durchgrünte Siedlungsbild. Bodenspekulation und Mietwucher sollten ausgeschlossen sein und die Bewohner sollten aus allen Klassen der Gesellschaft stammen. Der umfängliche städtebauliche Entwurf Bruno Tauts wurde aufgrund des Krieges jedoch nur in wenigen Abschnitten ausgeführt.

Die gesellschaftspolitischen Folgen des Ersten Weltkrieges und die Gründung der Weimarer Republik prägten nachhaltig die Entwicklung der Stadt Berlin. Für die Stadtplanung Berlins bedeutete der Übergang zur Republik im Jahre 1918/19 eine wesentliche Veränderung der Rahmenbedingungen: Das demokratische Wahlrecht in den regionalen und lokalen Parlamenten öffnete den Weg einer stärker sozial bestimmten Bau- und Planungspolitik; auch lang hinausgeschobene Neuregelungen der Verwaltungsstruktur konnten jetzt durchgesetzt werden. So erfolgte 1920 der Zusammenschluss von 8 Städten, 59 Landgemeinden und 27 Gutsbezirken zur Einheitsgemeinde Groß-Berlin, wodurch das Gesamtgebiet nach einheitlichen Planungsgrundsätzen geordnet werden konnte.

Die wirtschaftliche Expansion Berlins, vor allem auf dem Gebiet der Elektroindustrie, sorgte ebenso wie die kommunalen Investitionen für den weiteren Aufstieg Berlins zu einer anerkannten Weltstadt. Trotzdem reichten die beschränkten finanziellen Möglichkeiten während der Weimarer Zeit nicht aus, größere städtebauliche Projekte in der

development. The same applies for the group of buildings on Proskauer Straße in the district of Berlin-Friedrichshain which was also designed by Messel and named the "Weisbach Group" after the Jewish client for whom it was built. The same Spar- und Bauverein later employed Bruno Taut to develop Gartenstadt Falkenberg and the estate Schillerpark.

In the wake of the broad reform movement, which was carried by land reformers like Adolf Damaschke and housing reformers like Rudolf Eberstadt, more non-profit and cooperative construction societies were founded around 1900. They made first steps towards implementing a new social culture of housing and living. One of them was the housing construction cooperative Freie Scholle (Free Land) which later awarded contracts to Bruno Taut. Others were Vaterländischer Bauverein (Patriotic Construction Association) and Beamtenwohnungsverein (Civil Servants Housing Association). Both supported the development of ground plans and large-scale urban development on their large and medium-sized estates. On the one hand they presented concepts for urban development which dissolved the closed blocks. On the other hand they tried to initiate housing estate projects which reformed living. They had these projects implemented in the periphery of Berlin. With them they opposed the metropolitan development conventional at the time.

One of these reformist projects was the design by Bruno Taut for Gartenstadt Falkenberg at Alt-Glienicke, which was built in 1913–1916 by the "Gemeinnützige Baugenossenschaft Gartenvorstadt Groß-Berlin eGmbH" (Non-Profit Building Cooperative Garden Suburb Greater Berlin registered limited liability company). Here, Deutsche Gartenstadtgesellschaft (German Garden Town Society) wanted to implement new forms of living, housing and commercial activities according to the model of the English garden town concept which had been developed by Ebenezer Howard and Raymond Unwin. So they wanted more than just spacious settlements with lots of greenery. They wanted to exclude property speculation and the charging of exorbitant rents, and inhabitants were to come from all social classes. However, due to the war, only parts of Bruno Taut's extensive urban development plan were implemented.

The socio-political consequences of the First World War and the founding of the Weimar Republic made a great impact on the development of the city of Berlin. For the urban development plan, the transition to the Republic in 1918/19 brought a major change of the framework conditions: The democratic electoral law for the regional and local parliaments opened the way towards a more social development and planning policy and the new order also made it possible to implement long overdue changes of the administrative structure. The year 1920 saw the merger of eight towns, 59 rural communities and 27 manor districts to form Greater Berlin. This created the precondition for applying uniform planning principles for the entire area.

The economic expansion of Berlin mainly in the field of electrical engineering, which was supported by the municipal investments, further facilitated Berlin's rise to the rank of an acknowledged international city. Yet, the limited financial resources that were available during the Weimar

Abb. 32: Martin Wagner, 1930

Fig. 32: Martin Wagner, 1930

Innenstadt zu verwirklichen. Im großen Umfang gelang es dagegen, den Reformwohnungsbau in den Randzonen der Stadt voranzutreiben.

Hierbei lag die Dominanz in Planungsfragen bei der zentralen Magistratsverwaltung. Im wesentlichen bestimmten die beiden Baustadträte Ludwig Hoffmann (1896–1924) und Martin Wagner (1926–1933) die wohnungspolitischen und stadtplanerischen Leitlinien. Vor allem Wagner war es, der als engagierter Sozialdemokrat und Architekt den notwendigen Bau von Reformwohnungen forcierte, hatte sich doch nach dem Krieg die Wohnungsnot in Berlin abermals verschärft. Die politischen und ökonomischen Folgen des Weltkrieges, verbunden mit einer neuen baurechtlichen Gesetzgebung der Weimarer Republik, hatten den rein privatwirtschaftlich organisierten Wohnungsbau zum Erliegen gebracht. Die neue Verwaltung von Groß-Berlin stand nun vor der Aufgabe, den dramatischen Mangel an Wohnraum so schnell wie möglich zu lindern. Der Bedarf an Kleinwohnungen belief sich auf 100.000 bis 130.000 Einheiten. Erst mit der nach Inflation und Währungsreform 1924 eingeführten Hauszinssteuer – eine Gebäudeentschuldungssteuer, mit der die von der Inflation begünstigten Hausbesitzer den sozialen Wohnungsbau finanzieren sollten – kam es zu einer raschen Belebung des Wohnungsbaues.

Grundlage für einen neuen sozialen Wohnungsbau bildete die 1925 in Kraft getretene Reformbauordnung für Berlin. Sie hatte die Auflockerung der Wohngebiete und eine klare Funktionstrennung der einzelnen Gebiete zum Ziel und teilte das gesamte Stadtgebiet in unterschiedliche Bauzonen: Von der Innenstadt mit einer 5-geschossigen Bauweise ausgehend nahm die Baudichte zu den Randgebieten, dort wo die Großsiedlungen entstanden, auf eine 2- bis 3-geschossige Bebauung ab. Hier setzte das Verbot der Errichtung von Quergebäuden und Seitenflügeln die Wohndichte drastisch herab.

Abb. 33: Titelseite der „Wohnungswirtschaft" mit der Hufeisensiedlung, 1927

Fig. 33: Front page of "Wohnungswirtschaft" with Hufeisensiedlung, 1927

Republic were not sufficient for implementing large-scale urban development projects in inner-city locations. In contrast to this, reformist housing construction could be done on a large scale in the marginal areas of the city.

The planning work was dominated by the Berlin central government. The guidelines of housing policy and urban development were mainly determined by the two urban development councillors Ludwig Hoffmann (1896–1924) and Martin Wagner (1926–1933). Wagner was a committed Social Democrat and architect, and he was the main force who pushed forward the necessary construction of reform housing estates. This was even more important because the lack of housing in Berlin had been further aggravated by the war. The political and economic consequences of the World War in conjunction with new building laws of the Weimar Republic had brought an end to purely private housing construction. The new administration of Greater Berlin was now facing the task of reducing the drastic lack of housing as quickly as possible. The demand for small flats amounted to 100,000 to 130,000 units. Housing construction was finally re-activated after inflation and currency reform by the introduction of the mortgage servicing tax in 1924. This mortgage servicing tax was a tax on the payments for redeeming mortgages, and it was introduced in order to make the house owners who had profited from inflation finance social housing construction.

The reform building regulations which came into force in 1925 provided the basis for a new social housing development. It was aimed at reducing the density of buildings in residential estates and at clearly separating the functions of individual zones, and it divided the entire area of the city into different development zones: Starting in the city centre where buildings were allowed to have 5 storeys, density decreased towards the margins where the large housing estates were built. Here buildings were allowed to have a maximum of 2 to 3 storeys. Building density was greatly reduced in these areas because it was forbidden to build cross buildings and wings.

Berlin now had the opportunity to implement housing development in accordance with the models of Neues Bauen – i.e. housing for the broad masses of the population. Within only seven years – from 1924 to 1931 – more than 146,000 flats were built. Such a volume of construction was never reached again, not even during the post-war period of the 1950s. The new social mass housing construction was financed by trade-union and cooperative, municipal or other non-profit construction societies. In 1924, trade unions and building cooperatives founded GEHAG ("Gemeinnützige Heimstätten-Spar- und Bau-AG", Non-Profit Housing Savings and Building Shareholding Company). It had been proposed by Martin Wagner and became the leading builders' society in Berlin and all of Germany. Thanks to its large business volume and the design achievements of its company architect Bruno Taut, GEHAG gained great influence on urban development and architecture in Berlin.

Taut's close friend Wagner had participated in designing the first phase of development of the Hufeisensiedlung before he was elected urban development councillor in 1926. He held this position until his removal from office by the

In Berlin bot sich nun die Chance, Siedlungsbau nach reformerischen Leitbildern des „Neuen Bauens" zu verwirklichen – ein Wohnungsbau für breite Schichten der Bevölkerung. In nur sieben Jahren, von 1924 bis 1931, wurden über 140.000 Wohnungen errichtet – ein auch während der Berliner Nachkriegszeit der 1950er Jahre nicht wieder erreichtes Bauvolumen. Träger des neuen sozialen Massenwohnungsbaues wurden gewerkschaftlich-genossenschaftliche, städtische oder andere gemeinnützige Baugesellschaften. Die auf Initiative von Martin Wagner von Gewerkschaften und Baugenossenschaften im Jahre 1924 gegründete „Gemeinnützige Heimstätten-, Spar- und Bau AG", die GEHAG, entwickelte sich zur führenden Bauträgergesellschaft in Berlin und dem übrigen Deutschland. Durch ihr großes Geschäftsvolumen und vor allem durch die gestalterische Leistung ihres Hausarchitekten Bruno Taut, gewann die GEHAG einen starken Einfluss auf den Städtebau und die Architektur des Berliner Siedlungsbaus.

Als enger Vertrauter Tauts hatte Wagner am ersten Bauabschnitt der Hufeisensiedlung mitgewirkt, bevor er 1926 zum Baustadtrat gewählt wurde. Er behielt diese Funktion bis zu seiner Absetzung durch die Nationalsozialisten im Jahre 1933. Wagner spielte eine zentrale Rolle für die gemeinwirtschaftliche Wohnungsfürsorge im Berlin der Weimarer Republik. Er schuf ein gemeinwirtschaftliches Verbundmodell, in dem die GEHAG für die Planungs- und Bauleitungsarbeiten zuständig war. Die Bauausführung lag bei sozialen Baubetrieben, wie der „Berliner Bauhütte". Wagner strebte einen wirtschaftlichen, rationalen Städtebau an; für die Entwicklung Berlins legte er ein polyzentrisches Stadtmodell zu Grunde, das zur Auflösung des Stadt-Land-Dualismus beitragen sollte. Im Einzugsgebiet der die Berliner Innenstadt einfassenden Ringbahn sollten dichte Wohnviertel in offener Geschossbauweise mit durchgrünten Siedlungsräumen die noch bestehenden Lücken im Stadtgefüge füllen. Zu ihnen zählen die Siedlung Schillerpark (1924–1930) im Wedding und die Wohnstadt Carl Legien (1928–1930) im Prenzlauer Berg, beide entworfen von Bruno Taut.

Erklärtes wohnungspolitisches Ziel war zur Zeit der Frühphase der Hauszinssteuerära die Errichtung kleiner Einfamilienhaus-Siedlungen in den Außenbezirken. Damit sollte der Proletarisierung im Massenwohnungsbau entgegengewirkt und die verlorengegangene Bindung des Menschen an Haus und Natur wiederhergestellt und den Siedlern die Möglichkeit zur teilweisen Selbstversorgung gegeben werden. Bei der Verteilung der Hauszinssteuermittel wurde daher anfangs der Flachbau, eine 1–2 geschossige Bauweise, bevorzugt und es sollten größtenteils Kleinwohnungen errichtet werden. So sollten außerhalb der Innenstadt, eingebettet in die märkische Landschaft, größere, stärker grün durchzogene Siedlungskomplexe in Flachbauweise entstehen. Hierzu gehört das erste Großprojekt der neuen Berliner Siedlungspolitik, die bald „Hufeisensiedlung" genannte Großsiedlung Britz. Sie wurde auf Initiative von Martin Wagner in den Jahren 1925 bis 1930 auf dem ehemaligen Britzer Gutsgelände nach Entwürfen von Wagner und Bruno Taut errichtet. Bauherrin war, ebenso wie für die Wohnstadt Carl Legien, die GEHAG.

Nazis in 1933. Wagner played a central role in non-profit housing welfare in Berlin during the Weimar Republic. He created a non-profit association model in which GEHAG was responsible for planning, design and control of the construction works. The works were executed by social construction companies like "Berliner Bauhütte". Wagner wanted to establish an economical and rational urban development. For the development of Berlin, he created a poly-centric model aimed at dissolving the division between town and countryside. Within the railway ring that surrounded the Berlin inner-city area, densely built residential quarters in open multi-storey design mixed with greenery were to fill the remaining gaps within the city's structure. Among them are the Siedlung Schillerpark (1924–1930) in the district of Wedding and Wohnstadt Carl Legien (1928–1930) in the district of Prenzlauer Berg. Both were designed by Bruno Taut.

During the early phase of the mortgage servicing tax era, the main purpose of housing policy consisted of developing estates with small single-family houses in the suburban areas. By this means, the responsible politicians wanted to counteract proletarisation in mass housing development and re-create the people's lost link with their houses and with nature. They also wanted to give the inhabitants of these housing estates the opportunity to become at least partially self-sufficient in food production. This is why initially a large proportion of the mortgage servicing tax income was preferably used for erecting low buildings (1 or 2 storeys) and mostly small flats. The general aim was to develop major housing estate complexes with low buildings mixed with lots of greenery outside the city's centre and embedded in the landscape of the Mark. One of them is the first large-scale project of the Berlin residential development policy: the Großsiedlung Britz, which soon was named Hufeisensiedlung. It was erected on the initiative of Martin Wagner in 1925 through 1930 on the premises of the former manor of Britz, and it was designed by Wagner and Taut. As for Wohnstadt Carl Legien, construction was financed by GEHAG.

Als die Einnahmen aus dem Aufkommen der Hauszinssteuer gegen Ende der 20er Jahre zurückgingen, mobilisierte die Stadt Berlin eigene Mittel, um die noch immer große Wohnungsnot mit weiteren Siedlungen zu lindern, die nun in mehrgeschossiger Zeilenbauweise errichtet wurden. Obwohl die Weltwirtschaftskrise von 1928/1929 Auswirkungen auf den Wohnungsbausektor zeitigte, konnte der Berliner Magistrat auf stadteigenem Gelände zeitgleich 1929–31 zwei Großsiedlungen erbauen: die Weiße Stadt in Reinickendorf und die Siedlung Siemensstadt in Charlottenburg und Spandau. Die Ausführung übernahmen stadteigene gemeinnützige Baugesellschaften, die Leitung lag bei Stadtbaurat Martin Wagner, der für den Entwurf zwei Teams aus renommierten Architekten des Neuen Bauens zusammenstellte, unter anderen Hans Scharoun, Walter Gropius, Hugo Häring, Otto Rudolf Salvisberg und Otto Bartning.

Mit der Großsiedlung Siemensstadt und der Weißen Stadt in Reinickendorf, jeweils in der Nähe von Industriestandorten, entstanden großzügige, moderne Wohnquartiere, durchzogen von gemeinschaftlichen Grünanlagen, die in geradezu idealtypischer Weise die Ziele der Congrès Internationaux d'Architecture Moderne (CIAM) verkörperten: Licht und Luft für ein gesundes Wohnen mit einem Raumkonzept für Wohnen und Freizeit, Arbeit und Verkehr nach menschlichem Maß. Die Weiße Stadt und die Großsiedlung Siemensstadt zählen zugleich zu den letzten Siedlungsvorhaben unter der Ägide des Berliner Stadtbaurats Martin Wagner, die dem Leitbild des Neuen Bauens und dem Ziel einer Erneuerung der städtischen Lebenskultur folgen, bevor es 1931 mit der Brüning'schen Notverordnung zur Streichung staatlicher Fördermittel kam.

Mit der Machtübernahme der Nationalsozialisten im Jahre 1933, die auch in der Stadtverwaltung zu völlig veränderten Organisations- und Personalstrukturen führte, endete in Berlin der demokratische, weitgehend von der Sozialdemokratie, von linken Gewerkschaften und Genossenschaften geprägte Wohnungsbau. Martin Wagner musste aus dem Stadtbauratsamt ausscheiden. Die Baupolitik der Nationalsozialisten folgte einer anderen Kunstauffassung, Modernität und Neues Bauen waren nicht mehr erwünscht, Bruno Taut, Martin Wagner, Walter Gropius und viele andere Protagonisten des modernen Siedlungsbaus mussten ins Exil gehen.

Alle Siedlungen blieben in den 1930er und 1940er Jahren von größeren Umbauten und Überformungen sowie von Kriegszerstörungen weitgehend verschont. Erste Instandsetzungsmaßnahmen nach dem Krieg, bei denen im Einzelfall auch nicht dem Original entsprechend verfahren wurde, führten zu Veränderungen im Erscheinungsbild. Ab den 1980er Jahren konnten im Rahmen denkmalgerechter Wiederherstellungen diese in großen Teilen rückgängig gemacht werden.

Die designierten Siedlungen haben ihre Bedeutung als vorbildliche soziale Wohnorte bewahrt. Bis heute zeichnet alle eine hohe Akzeptanz unter ihren Bewohnern aus. Die Wohnungen mit ihren noch immer als vorbildlich geltenden Grundrissen sind gefragt.

Abb. 34: Hufeisensiedlung im Bau, Anfang 1926

Fig. 34: Hufeisensiedlung under construction, early 1926

When the income from the mortgage servicing tax decreased in the late 20s, the city of Berlin mobilised its own finances for alleviating the still pressing shortage of housing with further housing estates, whose houses were now built as multi-storey ribbons. Although the world economic crisis of 1928/1929 had an impact on housing construction, the Berlin government was able to have two large estates erected simultaneously on city-owned land in 1929–31. One of them was Weiße Stadt in the district of Reinickendorf and the other was Siemensstadt in the districts of Charlottenburg and Spandau. The works were executed by city-owned non-profit construction companies. Urban development councillor Martin Wagner was in control and he had formed two teams of renowned Neues Bauen architects to complete the designs. The teams included for instance Hans Scharoun, Walter Gropius, Hugo Häring, Otto Rudolf Salvisberg and Otto Bartning.

Both the Großsiedlung Siemensstadt and Weiße Stadt at Reinickendorf were spacious, modern residential quarters located near industrial centres. The estates had common green spaces which were virtually ideal reflections of the aims of the Congrès Internationaux d'Architecture Moderne (CIAM): light and air for healthy living with a humane spatial concept for living and leisure, work and transport. Weiße Stadt and Siemensstadt are both among the last housing projects built under the auspices of urban development councillor Martin Wagner in line with the model of Neues Bauen and with the purpose of renewing the culture of urban living. In 1931 the emergency laws by Brüning lead to severe cuts in state grants.

When the Nazis took power in 1933, this resulted in completely changed structures of organisation and personnel in the municipal administration of Berlin and ended the democratic housing development, which had largely been influenced by social democracy, left-wing trade unions and cooperatives. Martin Wagner had to resign from office. The building policy of the Nazis was based on a different idea of arts. Modernity and Neues Bauen were no longer desired, and Bruno Taut, Martin Wagner, Walter Gropius and many other protagonists of modern housing development were forced to emigrate.

In the 1930s and 1940s, no major changes or distortions were made in any of the housing estates and they hardly suffered any destruction during the war. Their appearance was occasionally altered by early repair work after the end of the war when, in individual cases, the work did not re-establish the original design. As of the 1980s, many of these changes could be undone by new efforts in re-establishing the monument status of the buildings.

The designated housing estates have preserved their significance as exemplary areas of social housing. Up to the present, all of them are very well accepted by their inhabitants. There is a considerable demand for their flats with their ground plans, which are still considered to be exemplary.

## Die einzelnen Siedlungen

### Gartenstadt Falkenberg

Die Gartenstadt Falkenberg entstand von 1913 bis 1916 auf Initiative der „Deutschen Gartenstadtgesellschaft", die eigens zur Errichtung der Siedlung einen genossenschaftlich organisierten Bauträger, die „Gemeinnützige Baugenossenschaft Gartenvorstadt Groß-Berlin eGmbH" gründete. Die deutsche Gartenstadtbewegung propagierte in Anlehnung an das englische Vorbild ein umfassendes lebens-, sozial-, kultur- und wohnungsreformerisches Stadtmodell. In Dresden-Hellerau und in Karlsruhe-Rüppurr wurden seit 1907/08 die ersten deutschen Projekte dieser Reformbewegung geplant und bald darauf verwirklicht. In Berlin gründeten 30 Baugenossen, darunter vor allem freie Gewerkschafter, Sozialdemokraten und reformerisch eingestellte Idealisten, am 12. April 1910 die „Baugenossenschaft Gartenvorstadt Groß-Berlin". Ihr Ziel war, wie das der gleichzeitig in Berlin gegründeten anderen Genossenschaften „Freie Scholle" in Tegel, „Ideal" in Neukölln und „Paradies" in Bohnsdorf, die Bekämpfung des Mietskasernen-Elends der Großstadt Berlin.

Nach langwierigen Verhandlungen erwarb die Genossenschaft 1913 das circa 70 ha große, weitgehend unerschlossene Gut Falkenberg in Alt-Glienicke, auf dem unter Friedrich II. erfolglos eine Maulbeerbaum-Plantage betrieben worden war. Das Terrain zeichnete sich durch seine hügelige Beschaffenheit aus, mit dem Falkenberg als höchster Erhebung. Dieses bewegte Gelände galt es mit angepassten Straßenzügen zu erschließen ohne seinen landschaftlichen Charakter zu zerstören. Außerdem waren baupolizeiliche Vorschriften der Gemeinde zu berücksichtigen, die nur

## The individual housing estates

### Gartenstadt Falkenberg

Gartenstadt Falkenberg was built from 1913 to 1916. The project had been initiated by the "Deutsche Gartenstadtgesellschaft" (German Garden Town Society), which founded a special-purpose cooperative called "Gemeinnützige Baugenossenschaft Gartenvorstadt Groß-Berlin eGmbH" (Non-Profit Building Cooperative Garden Suburb Greater Berlin registered limited liability company) to construct this housing estate. The German garden town movement followed the English example in propagating a housing estate model for comprehensively reforming living and social conditions, culture and housing. Since 1907/1908 the first German projects of this reformist movement were planned and also soon implemented at Dresden-Hellerau and Karlsruhe-Rüppurr. Thirty partners – most of them free trade union members, Social Democrats and idealists with reformist ideas – founded the "Baugenossenschaft Gartenvorstadt Groß-Berlin" (Building Cooperative Garden Suburb Greater Berlin) in Berlin on 12th April 1910. With the other cooperatives that were founded at the same time in Berlin ("Freie Scholle" [Free Land]) at Tegel, "Ideal" at Neukölln and "Paradies" [Paradise] at Bohnsdorf), they intended to fight the tenement misery in the city of Berlin.

After tedious negotiations, in 1913 the cooperative purchased the largely unserviced estate Gut Falkenberg with a size of approximately 70 ha. Under the rule of king Friedrich II, it had been an unsuccessful mulberry plantation. The estate was characterised by a hilly landscape with the hill Falkenberg being the highest elevation. This rough landscape had to be made accessible by adapting streets to

Abb. 35: Gartenstadt Falkenberg, Akazienhof mit der Robinienallee, 1930er Jahre

Fig. 35: Gartenstadt Falkenberg, Akazienhof with rows of robinias, 1930s

Abb. 36: Gartenstadt Falkenberg, Gartenstadtweg 44/50. Terrassierung der Vorgärten mit Betonfuttermauern, um 1915

Fig. 36: Gartenstadt Falkenberg, Gartenstadtweg 44/50. Terraced front gardens with concrete retention walls, approximately 1915

eine offene Landhausbebauung mit Villen an der Straße „Am Falkenberg" gestattete. Mit möglichst verschiedenartigen Grundrisslösungen beabsichtigte man Variationsmöglichkeiten des Kleinhauses mit Garten vorzuführen, um so in Form einer Mustersiedlung den Gartenstadtgedanken zu veranschaulichen.

Bereits 1912 hatte Hans Bernoulli einen von der Landgemeinde abgelehnten Siedlungsplan vorgelegt, den er jedoch aufgrund seiner Übersiedlung nach Basel nicht weiter bearbeiten konnte. An seine Stelle trat Bruno Taut, damals beratender und leitender Architekt der Deutschen Gartenstadtgesellschaft. Sein visionärer Siedlungsentwurf sah eine den Landschaftsformationen angepasste weiträumige Gartenstadt für insgesamt 7.500 Bewohner aller Bevölkerungsschichten vor, für die etwa 1.500 Wohnungen – vom kleinen Etagenwohnhaus mit Küche, Stube und Kammer bis zum villenartigen Bürgerhaus – erbaut werden sollten. In Abweichung von den Idealen der englischen Gartenstadtbewegung sollte in Falkenberg nicht eine autarke Stadtgründung mit eigenen Produktionsstätten realisiert werden, sondern es sollte vielmehr eine weitläufige Vorstadtsiedlung mit eher vorstädtischer Infrastruktur und klarer Anbindung an die nahe Großstadt entstehen. Kultur- und Sozialbauten, wie Volksfesthaus und Ledigenheim, sollten als zentrale identitätsstiftende Bestandteile das Siedlungsgefüge ergänzen.

it without disturbing its character. Furthermore, the planners had to take into account regulations of the community's construction authority, which only permitted an open country-house development with villas along the street Am Falkenberg. The planners intended to show the possible variations of a combination of small houses and gardens by presenting various ground plan solutions. Their aim was to represent the idea of the garden town in a kind of model housing estate.

As early as 1912, Hans Bernoulli had presented a housing estate plan that was rejected by the community, and since he moved to Basel he was not able to process it further. He was substituted by Bruno Taut, who was at that time consulting and chief architect of Deutsche Gartenstadtgesellschaft. Taut's visionary housing estate design envisaged a spacious garden town, which was adapted to the landscape and would house a total of 7,500 inhabitants from all walks of life in approximately 1,500 flats – from small multi-storeyed houses with flats consisting of a kitchen, sitting room and bedroom up to villa-like town-houses. In deviation from the ideals of the English garden town movement, Falkenberg was not to be a self-sufficient town with its own production facilities. Rather, it was to be a spacious suburban housing estate with a suburban infrastructure and obvious connection to the nearby city. Cultural and social facilities like the public festival house and a home for single adults were meant to complement the housing estate structure as components lending the complex its own identity.

Abb. 37: Siedlung Schillerpark. Wohnhäuser des ersten Bauabschnittes an der Bristolstraße, 1929

Fig. 37: Siedlung Schillerpark. Residential houses of the first development phase at Bristolstraße, 1929.

Tatsächlich entstanden jedoch, infolge kriegsbedingter Einstellung der Bautätigkeiten, zunächst nur 128 Wohnungen in zwei Bauabschnitten – neben sechs Mehrfamilienwohnhäusern überwiegend in Gruppen gefasste kleine typisierte Einfamilienhäuser: 34 Wohneinheiten 1913 um den „Akazienhof" und 94 Wohnungen 1914–15 auf dem anschließenden Gelände am Gartenstadtweg. Für das Einzelwohnhaus (Am Falkenberg 119) des Generalsekretär Adolf Otto, konnte Heinrich Tessenow gewonnen werden, der durch seine Bauten für die Gartenstadt Hellerau bereits ein angesehener Architekt war. Alle anderen Siedlungshäuser entwarf Bruno Taut. So auch das als einziges realisierte Doppelwohnhaus des dritten Bauabschnitts, das trotz des Krieges neben dem „Haus Otto" 1916 fertiggestellt werden konnte.

Für die Gestaltung sämtlicher Kleingärten und vermutlich auch für die gemeinschaftlichen Freiflächen zog man den Berliner Gartendirektor Ludwig Lesser hinzu, der seit 1902 in Berlin wirkte und zur gleichen Zeit auch für die Gartenstadt Staaken tätig war. Lessers Konzept für Falkenberg sah eine einheitliche Anlage kleiner Siedlungsgärten vor, die der teilweisen Selbstversorgung der Mieter dienen sollten. Damit ist die Gartenstadt Falkenberg wohl die erste Siedlung, in welcher den Kleingärten eine so große Bedeutung zugestanden wurde, dass man diese bereits in die Planung mit einbezog.

Nach dem Ersten Weltkrieg musste die „Gemeinnützige Baugenossenschaft Falkenberg" mit dem „Berliner Bau- und Sparverein 1892", 1942 umgenannt in „Berliner Bau- und Wohnungs-Genossenschaft von 1892", aus wirtschaftlichen Gründen fusionieren. Da die „1892" den Schwerpunkt ihrer Bautätigkeit auf innerstädtische Projekte, wie die ab 1924 errichtete „Siedlung Schillerpark" legte, war zunächst

However, due to the First World War, work had to be discontinued and therefore initially only 128 flats were built in two phases – in addition to six multiple dwellings, small standardised single-family houses were built, most of which were arranged in groups: in 1913, 34 housing units were built at "Akazienhof" and in 1914–15 94 flats on the adjacent land at Gartenstadtweg. Heinrich Tessenow, who was already a renowned architect at that time since he had designed the buildings for Gartenstadt Hellerau, was employed to design the individual house (Am Falkenberg 119) for the general secretary Adolf Otto. All other houses of the housing estate were designed by Bruno Taut. Among them is the only double house of the third phase that was completed in addition to the "Haus Otto" in 1916 despite the war.

All private gardens and probably also the common outdoor facilities were designed by the Berlin gardening director Ludwig Lesser. He had been working in Berlin since 1902 and was involved in the development of Gartenstadt Staaken at the same time. Lesser's concept for Falkenberg required the creation of small, uniform private gardens where the inhabitants were to produce part of their food. This makes Gartenstadt Falkenberg probably the first housing estate where the private gardens were given so much significance that they became part of the design.

After the end of the First World War, the "Gemeinnützige Baugenossenschaft Falkenberg" was forced to merge for economic reasons with "Berliner Bau- und Sparverein 1892" (Berlin Construction and Savings Association). The society which resulted from this merger was renamed in 1942 and became "Berliner Bau- und Wohnungs-Genossenschaft of 1892" (Berlin Construction and Housing Cooperative of 1892). Since the "1892" cooperative focussed on inner-city projects like Siedlung Schillerpark, whose con-

Abb. 38: Siedlung Schillerpark, Hofseite Corker Straße 33/35, zweiter Bauabschnitt, um 1930

Fig. 38: Siedlung Schillerpark, yard-side of Corker Straße 33/35, second development phase, approximately 1930

an einen Weiterbau in Falkenberg nicht gedacht. Auch die ab 1926 von Taut wiederaufgenommene Erweiterungsplanung blieb aufgrund der geänderten Verteilungspolitik der Hauszinssteuermittel auf Projekte mit städtischen Mehrfamilienwohnhäusern und sodann aufgrund der Weltwirtschaftskrise unausgeführt. Auch während der NS-Herrschaft erfolgte keine ergänzende Bautätigkeit.

Ab 1951 kam die Siedlung, nun auf dem Territorium der DDR gelegen, in die Verantwortung der „Kommunalen Wohnraumverwaltung", die ihre gesellschaftlichen und geschichtlichen Bedeutung erkannte und sie gemäß den damaligen Möglichkeiten bewahrte und pflegte. Nach der Wiedervereinigung übernahm 1991 die „Berliner Bau- und Wohnungs-Genossenschaft von 1892" wieder die Verwaltung. Bald darauf leitete sie eine detaillierte denkmalpflegerische Untersuchung und Instandsetzung in die Wege, die 2002 abgeschlossen werden konnte.

### Siedlung Schillerpark

Erst nach dem Ersten Weltkrieg und den Jahren der Inflation konnte der „Berliner Spar- und Bauverein" die Realisierung seines Wohnbauprojektes am Schillerpark in Angriff nehmen. Schon 1913 hatte der 1892 gegründete traditionsreiche Bauverein, der bereits vor dem Krieg mit Projekten von Alfred Messel zu den Schrittmachern des reformierten Mietwohnungsbaues zählte, das im Norden Berlins gelegene Baugelände erworben. 1914 folgte für das städtebaulich attraktiv am gerade eröffneten ersten Volkspark Berlins, dem Schillerpark, befindliche Terrain auch ein erstes Bebauungskonzept, das im Sinne des Reformwohnungsbaues dieser Zeit eine geschlossene fünf-

struction began in 1924, it did not initially intend to continue the development at Falkenberg. Due to the amended distribution policy with respect to income from the mortgage servicing tax, the extension designed by Taut as of 1926 was not executed. The grants from the mortgage servicing tax were at that time focussed on urban multiple dwellings. Later the world economic crisis prevented Taut's plans from being implemented. During Nazi rule the housing estate was also not extended.

As of 1951, the "Municipal Housing Administration" became responsible for the settlement which was now situated on the territory of the German Democratic Republic (East Germany). This organisation understood its social and historic significance and conserved and maintained the housing estate as far as possible under the conditions of that time. After re-unification, the "Berliner Bau- und Wohnungs-Genossenschaft von 1892" (Berlin Construction and Housing Cooperative of 1892) once again took over management of the estate in 1991. Soon after that, it started a detailed investigation and refurbishment for preservation of the monument. These works were completed in 2002.

### Siedlung Schillerpark

"Berliner Spar- und Bauverein" had to wait until the end of the First World War and the period of inflation before they could start to implement the housing project at Schillerpark. The housing association, which had been founded in 1892 and had long-standing traditions, had purchased the property in the North of Berlin as early as 1913. Already before the war, the association had been one of the pacemakers of reformed housing development with projects designed by Alfred Messel. In 1914, the first master plan

geschossige Blockrandbebauung ohne Seitenflügel und Quergebäude mit großen begrünten Innenhöfen vorsah.

1924 bekam Bruno Taut, der durch sein Engagement für die Gartenstadt Falkenberg mit dem Berliner Spar- und Bauverein verbunden war, den Auftrag für eine Neuplanung des Geländes. In den veränderten gesellschaftlichen Verhältnissen und mit der vor der Verabschiedung stehenden neuen Reformbauordnung Berlins (am 1. Dezember 1925 in Kraft getreten) bot sich nunmehr erstmalig in Berlin die Chance, eine soziale Wohnsiedlung nach den Städtebauvorstellungen des Neuen Bauens und mit Mitteln des gerade eingeführten Förderprogramms der Berliner Wohnungsfürsorgegesellschaft zu verwirklichen.

Bis zum September des selben Jahres unterbreitete Taut zwei Siedlungsentwürfe, die sich jedoch aufgrund der von ihm gewünschten Zeilenbauweise baupolizeilich nicht durchsetzen ließen. Der folgende endgültige Vorschlag sah eine halboffene Randbebauung mit vier Blöcken zwischen Dubliner Straße und Barfusstraße vor, die ebenfalls nur mit behördlichen Dispensen umzusetzen war. Im Dezember 1924 erfolgte die Grundsteinlegung für den ersten Bauabschnitt, den man 1926 abschloss. Mit der 1928 vollendeten zweiten Etappe konnten die beiden Gevierte zwischen der Dubliner Straße und der Oxforder Straße umbaut und im Inneren mit begrünten Höfen versehen werden. Dagegen blieb der dritte Bauabschnitt 1929–30 auf dem entgegen Tauts Siedlungsplan nicht mehr geteilten großen Bauplatz östlich der Oxforder Straße mit vier Randzeilen nur ein Fragment, das erst 1953–57 mit Zeilenbauten von Hans Hoffmann ergänzt wurde.

Insgesamt konnten 303 Wohnungen mit 1½ bis 4½ Zimmern, alle mit Bädern und Loggien, errichtet werden, die zuletzt bezogenen Wohnungen auch mit Zentralheizung. 1930 entstand ein eigenes Waschhaus sowie ein Siedlungskindergarten in einem der Mietshäuser. Die Lebensmittelversorgung übernahm ein von der Genossenschaft geleiteter Konsumladen. Die Mieterschaft war ausgesprochen sozialdemokratisch und gewerkschaftlich organisiert – kein Wunder, da vor allem die Wohnungen des dritten Bauabschnittes für Mitglieder des Baugewerksbundes und des Metallarbeiterverbands reserviert waren.

Auch die Baubetreuung und Bauausführung erfolgte anfangs in einem gewerkschaftlich-genossenschaftlichen Verbundmodell. Während der genossenschaftliche „Berliner Spar- und Bauverein" als Bauherr auftrat, übernahm zunächst die gerade als eine Tochter der von Gewerkschaften geschaffenen DEWOG (Deutsche Wohnungsfürsorge A.G. für Beamte, Angestellte und Arbeiter) gegründete GEHAG (Gemeinnützige Heimstätten-, Spar- und Bau A.G.) die Baubetreuung. Ein Jahr später schied sie aus dem Verbund wieder aus. Die Bauabwicklung zog daraufhin der Spar- und Bauverein alleine an sich, jedoch blieb Bruno Taut, inzwischen Chefarchitekt der GEHAG geworden, weiterhin planender Architekt der folgenden Bauabschnitte.

Das moderne programmatische Leitbild der Siedlung, ihr Modellcharakter für eine gemeinschaftliche Wohnungsfürsorge und nicht zuletzt ihre Lage im sozialdemokratisch und kommunistisch geprägten Arbeiterbezirk Wedding zog eine bunt gemischte Mieterschaft aus Arbeitern, Intel-

for the property at Schillerpark followed. Its location at the recently opened first public park of Berlin was very attractive from the point of view of urban development. The design envisaged block margin buildings forming closed green courtyards without wings and cross buildings. This was in line with the ideas of reformed housing development at that time.

In 1924, Bruno Taut was ordered to design a new master plan for the estate. He was linked with Berliner Spar- und Bauverein since his commitment for Gartenstadt Falkenberg. Under the new social conditions and shortly before the new construction reform ordinance for Berlin came into force (on 1st December 1925), it was possible for the first time in Berlin to erect an estate for social housing on the basis of the urban development ideas of Neues Bauen and with the finances of the recently introduced support programme of the Berlin Housing Welfare Society.

By September of the same year, Taut presented two draft master plans. However, they were not approved by the construction authorities since he wanted to erect ribbon buildings. The final proposal which followed envisaged four semi-open blocks between Dubliner Straße and Barfusstraße that also required special approval by the authorities. The foundation stone for the first phase was laid in December 1924 and work on this phase was finished in 1926. With the completion of the second phase in 1928, two squares between Dubliner Straße and Oxforder Straße were framed and inside them green courtyards were created. In contrast to them, the third phase of 1929–30 remained incomplete with only four ribbons at block margins. This large building site east of Oxforder Straße was not divided as Taut had proposed. It was finally complemented by ribbon buildings designed by Hans Hoffmann in 1953–57.

The completed houses provided 303 flats with sizes ranging from 1½ to 4½ rooms. All of them had bathrooms and loggias and the last flats built also had central heating. In 1930 a laundry and a kindergarten were installed in one of the blocks of flats. Food was available in a cooperative shop. Most of the tenants were members of the Social Democratic Party and of trade unions. This is no surprise for those who know that especially the flats of the third phase were reserved for members of the building workers and metal workers unions.

Initially the construction services and execution of the construction were also carried out by a consortium consisting of trade union and cooperative representatives. The cooperative "Berliner Spar- und Bauverein" acted as a client and GEHAG "Gemeinnützige Heimstätten-, Spar- und Bau-Aktiengesellschaft" (a non-profit housing, savings and construction shareholding company), which only recently had been founded as a subsidiary of DEWOG (Deutsche Wohnungsfürsorge A.G., German Housing Welfare Shareholding Company) by the trade unions, took over the construction services. One year later it withdrew from the association. Consequentially, the Spar- und Bauverein took over full control of the execution of the project. Meanwhile, Bruno Taut had become chief architect of GEHAG, yet he also remained the designing architect for the following development phases.

lektuellen, Angestellten, Partei- und Gewerkschaftsfunktionären sowie Künstlern an, die der Siedlung am Schillerpark bald den Nimbus einer roten „Künstlerkolonie" verlieh. So wohnten hier nebeneinander der Arbeiterdichter Max Barthel, der Mediziner Willibald Pschyrembel und die Geigerin Irmgard Schnell.

Die Siedlung wurde im Zweiten Weltkrieg in kleinen Bereichen beschädigt und Anfang der 1950er Jahre wieder aufgebaut. Die Rekonstruktion des fast vollständig zerstörten Endhauses Bristolstraße 1/Ecke Dubliner Straße übernahm 1951 Max Taut, der Bruder von Bruno Taut. Er hielt sich überwiegend am originalem Vorbild, erhöhte aber das Haus durch des Ausbau des Drempelgeschosses.

Der Baublock III (Bauabschnitt III) konnte 1954 verdichtet werden, nachdem man auf die schräg einschneidende Straße endgültig verzichtet hatte. Hans Hoffmann, Architekt und Vorstandsmitglied der Berliner Bau- und Wohnungsgenossenschaft von 1892, ergänzte den Blockrand um die Wohngebäude Bristolstraße 25/27 sowie Corker Straße 3/7 und 19/23 und errichtete im Gartenhof die drei Hauszeilen Bristolstraße 17 A–E, 19 A–E und 23 A–E. Im Gegensatz zum Bauteil der 1920er Jahre, für den Bruno Taut der wesentliche Urheber der Freiraumgestaltung war, wurde die Erweiterung nun im Zusammenarbeit mit dem Gartenarchitekten Walter Rossow gemeinsam entworfen. So vollendet Hoffmanns Zusatzbebauung den dritten Tautschen Bauabschnitt südöstlich der Oxforder Straße. Eine denkmalgerechte Sanierung der Häuser von Taut und Hoffmann begann 1991 und hält bis heute an.

The estate attracted a lively mix of tenants – workers, intellectuals, clerks, party and trade union officials as well as artists, and it soon gave the estate the reputation of being a red "artists' colony". This was due to the modern programmatic model of the housing estate, its model character for communal housing welfare and last but not least its situation in the mainly social democratic and communist working class district of Wedding. The working class poet Max Barthel, the physician Willibald Pschyrembel and the violinist Irmgard Schnell lived close together here.

During the Second World War small parts of the estate were damaged and rebuilt in the early 1950s. The house at the corner of Bristolstraße (number 1) and Dubliner Straße had been almost completely destroyed and was rebuilt by Bruno Taut's brother Max Taut. He rebuilt it almost as it had been. The only change he made was to add a full fledged jamb storey.

In 1954 it became possible to densify Phase III after the street cutting diagonally into it had been cancelled. Hans Hoffmann, architect and executive member of Berliner Bau- und Wohnungsgenossenschaft von 1892, complemented the blocks around the residential buildings of Bristolstraße 25/27 and Corker Straße 3/7 as well as 19/23 and in the garden courtyard he erected the three ribbons of Bristolstraße 17 A–E, 19 A–E and 23 A–E. In contrast to the sections erected in the 1920s where Bruno Taut had been the main designer for the outdoor facilities, these were now designed in cooperation with the garden architect Walter Rossow. Hoffmann's complementary buildings completed Taut's third project phase southeast of Oxforder Straße. The rehabilitation works for conserving the monuments designed by Taut and Hoffmann began in 1991 and continue to date.

Abb. 39: Großsiedlung Britz, Eingang zum Hufeisen, um 1928

Fig. 39: Großsiedlung Britz, entrance to the horseshoe, approximately 1928

Abb. 40: Großsiedlung Britz, Hufeisenrund mit Mietergärten, 1930er Jahre

Fig. 40: Großsiedlung Britz, horseshoe with tenants' gardens, 1930s

## Großsiedlung Britz (Hufeisensiedlung)

Im Winter 1924 beschloss die Stadt Berlin, aus den Mitteln der neu eingeführten Hauszinssteuer eine erste Großsiedlung zu errichten. Für das erste Berliner Siedlungsprojekt dieser Zielsetzung wurde noch im gleichen Jahr ein Teil des Rittergutes Britz angekauft.

Initiator und Förderer des Britzer Projekts war Martin Wagner, der in der Nachkriegszeit eine zentrale Rolle in der gemeinwirtschaftlichen Wohnungsfürsorge einnahm. Er entwickelte ein gewerkschaftlich-genossenschaftliches Verbundmodell, zu dem 1924 die Gründung der „Gemeinnützigen Heimstätten-, Spar- und Bau AG", der GEHAG, zur Durchführung der Planungs- und Bauleitungsarbeiten und von sozialen Baubetrieben, den Bauhütten, gehörte. Die GEHAG unterhielt ein eigenes Architekturatelier, dessen künstlerische Leitung in den Händen von Bruno Taut lag, der, wie sein Freund Martin Wagner, seit der Vorkriegszeit bereits reiche Erfahrung im Bereich des Siedlungsbaus gesammelt hatte. Bis zum Weggang Wagners von der GEHAG 1926 – er wurde der neue Berliner Stadtbaurat – war Wagner zusammen mit Taut am architektonischen wie städtebaulichen Entwurfsprozess der Britzer GEHAG-Siedlung beteiligt. Das Britzer Bauvorhaben sollte das erste Großprojekt der von Wagner geschaffenen sozialen Bauorganisation werden: Die GEHAG übernahm die Bauträgerschaft, der Berliner Bauhütte übertrug man die Bauarbeiten und die Architekten waren Taut, Wagner und der im Siedlungsbau erfahrene Gartengestalter Leberecht Migge.

Migge, der sich mit der seriellen Gestaltung von Mietergärten und der Planung der Siedlungs-Freiflächen für Großsiedlungen konzeptionell auseinandersetzte, übernahm die Planung sowohl der öffentlichen wie privaten Freiflächen. Da allerdings für die Gestaltung der Grünflächen nach einer vertraglichen Vereinbarung im Rahmen des Geländeverkaufs von der Stadt Berlin an die GEHAG das Gartenamt Neukölln zuständig war, wurden vom damaligen Gartenamtsleiter Ottokar Wagler neue Pläne erstellt. Teilweise orientierten sie sich an den Planungen Leberecht Migges, teilweise stellten sie eigenständige Lösungen dar.

## Großsiedlung Britz (Hufeisensiedlung)

In winter 1924, the city of Berlin decided to erect the first large housing estate using finances acquired by the mortgage servicing tax. In the same year, GEHAG bought part of the manor of Britz to implement the first housing estate project.

This project was initiated and promoted by Martin Wagner, who played a central role in communal housing welfare after the war. He developed a model of joint work of trade unions and cooperatives which included the founding of GEHAG ("Gemeinnützige Heimstätten-Spar- und Bau-AG", Non-Profit Housing Savings and Building Shareholding Company) in 1924 and of social construction enterprises called "Bauhütte". The tasks of GEHAG consisted of carrying out the construction services (design, planning and control). GEHAG ran its own architects' office. Bruno Taut was its art director. Like his friend Martin Wagner, he had already gathered lots of experience in housing development before the war. Until Wagner left GEHAG in 1926 – he became the new Berlin urban development councillor – Wagner cooperated with Taut in the architectural and urban development design works for the GEHAG housing estate at Britz. The project at Britz was to be the first large project of the social construction organisation created by Wagner: GEHAG acted as a client, Berliner Bauhütte was employed for executing the works and the architects were Taut, Wagner and Leberecht Migge – a garden architect with a wealth of experience in residential development.

Migge designed both the public and the private outdoor facilities and dealt with the serial design of tenants' gardens as well as with designing outdoor facilities for large housing estates. However, since an agreement, which was signed in connection with the sale of the land by Berlin to GEHAG, stipulated that the public gardens department of Neukölln was responsible for designing the green spaces, Ottokar Wagler, at that time head of that department, produced new designs. To an extent he based them on Leberecht Migge's designs, but parts of them presented independent solutions.

Nach einem Generalbebauungsplan des Städtebauamtes teilte das in Aussicht genommene Gelände eine bogenförmige Erschließungsstraße, der Grüne Ring, die heutige Fritz-Reuter-Allee, in zwei Hälften: Die westliche war der GEHAG und die östliche auf Intervention der konservativen Magistratsparteien der DeGeWo (Deutsche Gesellschaft zur Förderung des Wohnungsbaus) zur Bebauung überlassen worden. Jede Gesellschaft sollte 1.000 Wohnungen in dreigeschossiger Bebauung am Rande und zweigeschossiger Einfamilienhausbebauung im Inneren der Anlage errichten. Die DeGeWo bebaute ihren Abschnitt 1925–27 nach Entwürfen der Architekten Engelmann & Fangmeyer. Wie später in der Berlin-Zehlendorfer GEHAG-Siedlung am Fischtal stehen sich auch hier seitdem als Abbild ideologischer Gegensätze der Weimarer Zeit ganz verschiedene Architektur- und Städtebauvorstellungen gegenüber.

Beide Bauträger stellten eigene Bebauungspläne auf, wobei beide Pläne von den vorhandenen eiszeitlichen Pfuhlen bestimmt wurden. Auf dem GEHAG-Gelände entstand von 1925–27 der signifikante Kern der Britzer Siedlung mit der namensgebenden hufeisenförmigen Umbauung eines der Teiche. Er umfasste in zwei Bauetappen zwischen Parchimer Allee und Stavenhagener Straße 1.027 Wohneinheiten, wovon fast die Hälfte in Einfamilienhäusern lagen. Der lange Baublock an der Stavenhagener Straße stammt von Martin Wagner, der wohl auch bis zu seinem Ausscheiden 1926 entwurflich bei der Randbebauung an der Fritz-Reuter-Allee und einigen Einfamilienhäusern beteiligt war.

Weit entfernt vom Hufeisen folgten 1927–29 die Bauabschnitte III bis V längs der Buschkrugallee und Parchimer Allee mit ausschließlich Stockwerkswohnungen, während die letzte, sechste Etappe von 1929–30 – wiederum in gemischter Bauweise mit Einfamilienhäusern und mehrgeschossigen Miethäusern – die Bebauung der ersten beiden Siedlungsteile südlich der Parchimer Allee fortsetzte. Die neuen Bauetappen spiegeln die wirtschaftlichen Probleme Ende der 20er Jahre wider. War die zugeteilte Bodenfläche anfangs noch großzügig, wird sie ab 1926 immer geringer. Als Folge entstehen im letzten Abschnitt 1930 relativ eng stehende Zeilen ohne größere Platz- und Straßenräume. So konnte auch nicht mehr Tauts visionäre Erweiterungsplanung im Anschluss an den sechsten Abschnitt umgesetzt werden, die nach dem Satellitenstadt-Schema Ebenezer Howards als eine selbstständige Gartenstadt mit 2.000 Wohnungen geplant war. Damit bildete sich in Britz kein homogenes Siedlungsbild, sondern es entstanden drei größere räumlich abgeschlossene Siedlungsteile.

Insgesamt waren innerhalb von knapp fünf Jahren eine Wohnstadt mit 1963 Wohneinheiten für über 5.000 Menschen entstanden. Weder neue Baumaterialien noch moderne Bautechniken, wie die Plattenbauweise, kamen in Britz zur Anwendung. Es galt in Britz vielmehr bei konventioneller Bauweise eine Senkung der Baukosten durch Beschränkung auf wenige Grundrisstypen unter Verwendung genormter Einzelteile zu erreichen und zugleich mit einer straffen Organisation und dem Einsatz moderner Maschinen die Bauabläufe reibungslos zu koordinieren. Auch der soziale Anspruch, Wohnraum für das Proletariat zu schaffen, konnte aufgrund der Baukosten und gestiegenen Hypothekenzinsen nicht eingehalten werden. Vorwiegend An-

According to a master plan produced by the urban development department, the project area was divided in two parts by a curved access road – the Green Ring, now Fritz-Reuter-Allee: The western part had been given to GEHAG for development and, upon intervention by the conservative parties of the Berlin government, the eastern part was given to DeGeWo (Deutsche Gesellschaft zur Förderung des Wohnungsbaus, German Society for Promoting Housing Construction). Each of the two societies was to erect 1,000 flats in buildings with three storeys at the margin and single-family houses with two storeys in the interior of the estate. DeGeWo built its part in 1925–27 on the basis of designs by the architects Engelmann & Fangmeyer. Entirely different ideas of architecture and urban development oppose each other in these two parts and reflect the ideological contradictions of the Weimar Republic. Another example for these contradictory ideas is the GEHAG housing estate Am Fischtal in the district of Zehlendorf.

Both clients established their own master plans that were both determined by the existing glacial ponds. On the GEHAG area, the significant core of the Britz housing estate was built in 1925–27 with the horseshoe-shaped ribbon around one of the ponds that gave it its name. The core comprised two construction phases between Parchimer Allee and Stavenhagener Straße with a total of 1,027 flats. Nearly half of them were built as single-family houses. The long block on Stavenhagener Straße was designed by Martin Wagner who was probably also involved in designing the ribbon along Fritz-Reuter-Allee and some of the single-family houses until he left in 1926.

Phases III to V, with only blocks of flats, were built in 1927–29 far away from the horseshoe along Buschkrugallee and Parchimer Allee. The sixth phase with again a mix of single-family houses and multi-storey blocks of flats was built in 1929–30, continuing the development of the two sections south of Parchimer Allee. The new phases of development reflect the economic problems of the late 20s. During the early phases the allocated parcels were still quite generous but from 1926 they became ever smaller. In consequence, the last phase – built in 1930 – shows relatively closely packed ribbons without much space for squares and roads. Another result is that Taut's visionary extension, which was to follow Phase VI, could not be erected. He had designed it as an independent garden town with 2,000 flats following the model of the satellite town by Ebenezer Howard. Thus, Britz did not acquire a homogeneous housing estate image. We now find three large separate housing estate spaces.

Within less than five years, a residential estate with 1963 flats for more than 5,000 people had been built. At Britz, no new building material or modern technologies like prefabricated elements had been used. The point had rather been to reduce costs for conventional construction by restricting the design to a small number of ground plan types with standardised elements and to achieve optimal coordination of the construction works by strict organisation and the use of modern machines. Due to the construction costs and the increased mortgage rates it was not possible to fulfil the original social intention of creating housing for the proletariat. Mostly clerks, public servants and craftsmen moved into the flats. Nevertheless, it was the first time that under

gestellte, Beamte und Handwerker bezogen die Wohnungen. Dennoch war unter schwierigen gesellschaftlichen und wirtschaftlichen Bedingungen erstmals ein Großprojekt gewerkschaftlicher Wohnungsfürsorge nach dem Leitbild des Neuen Bauens umgesetzt worden, das man den privatwirtschaftlich-staatlichen Siedlungen gegenüberstellen konnte, und das modellhaft auf kommende gemeinwirtschaftliche Projekte wirkte.

Ohne die Mitwirkung von Taut begann 1932 die GEHAG mit dem VII. Bauabschnitt östlich der Fritz-Reuter-Allee und südlich der Parchimer Allee. Die Brüningschen Notverordnungen zwangen zu kleinsten Wohnungen mit 1 bis 2 Zimmern. Als Ausgleich boten die breiten Abstände zwischen den 1933 fertiggestellten Zeilen Mietergärten zur Selbstversorgung. Weit abgelegen von Industrie und dem Stadtkern erfuhren die Siedlungsteile nur geringe Kriegsschäden. Nur die Eckbebauung Buschkrugallee 245–247 und Grüner Weg 32–34 mußte vollständig wiederaufgebaut werden. Seit 1984 läuft ein denkmalpflegerisches Erneuerungsprogramm, das bis jetzt anhält und große Teile der Hufeisensiedlung erfaßt hat. Mit dem Jahr 2000 begann eine Privatisierung der Einfamilienhäuser in der Siedlung.

## Wohnstadt Carl Legien

Die „Wohnstadt Carl Legien" (1929 bis 1930) zählt zu den letzten gewerkschaftlich-genossenschaftlichen Großsiedlungen unter der Ägide des Berliner Stadtbaurats Martin Wagner, bevor es 1931 mit der Brüning'schen Notverordnung zur Streichung staatlicher Fördermittel kam. Bauherrin der bereits zur ihrer Entstehungszeit nach dem 1920 verstorbenen Vorsitzenden des Allgemeinen Deutschen Gewerkschaftsbundes (ADGB) benannten Wohnsiedlung für rund 4.000 Bewohner war die „Gemeinnützige Heimstätten-, Spar- und Bau-Aktiengesellschaft", die GEHAG. Architekten waren Bruno Taut und der Leiter des Entwurfsbüros der GEHAG Franz Hillinger. Beide gaben später als Beginn der Planung das Jahr 1925 an, obwohl die

difficult social and economic conditions a large-scale project of trade union housing welfare following the model of Neues Bauen had been implemented. It could now be presented as a counter-model to state and privately financed development projects and it fulfilled a model role for future communal projects.

In 1932, GEHAG started to build phase VII east of Fritz-Reuter-Allee and south of Parchimer Allee. This time Taut was not involved. The emergency decrees by Brüning forced them to build only tiny flats with 1 or 2 rooms. To compensate for this, the wide distances between the ribbons which were completed in 1933 offered room for tenants' gardens so that they could produce some food. Since the estate was far away from any industry and from the city centre, it suffered only minor damage during the war. Only the building on the corner of Buschkrugallee (numbers 245–247) and Grüner Weg (numbers 32–34) had to be rebuilt completely. A renewal programme for maintaining the monument was started in 1984. It continues to date and has covered a large part of the Hufeisensiedlung up to now. In 2000, privatisation of the single-family houses in the housing estate began.

## Wohnstadt Carl Legien

"Wohnstadt Carl Legien" (1929 to 1930) is one of the last large trade union and cooperative housing estates built under the leadership of Berlin urban development councillor Martin Wagner, before the emergency decrees by Brüning in 1931 lead to the abolishment of all state grants. The client for whom this estate for approximately 4,000 people was erected was the "Gemeinnützige Heimstätten Spar- und Bau-Aktiengesellschaft" GEHAG. Right from the start, the estate was named after the chairman of the Allgemeiner Deutscher Gewerkschaftsbund (General German Trade Union Confederation, ADGB). Its architects were Bruno Taut and Franz Hillinger, head of the design office of GEHAG. Later both stated that the design works began in

Abb. 41: Wohnstadt Carl Legien, um 1930

Fig. 41: Wohnstadt Carl Legien, approximately 1930

Abb. 42: Wohnstadt Carl Legien, raumverbindende Wohnhöfe an der heutigen Erich-Weinert-Straße, 1930er Jahre

Fig. 42: Wohnstadt Carl Legien, courtyards which create combined spaces at today's Erich-Weinert-Straße, 1930s

GEHAG das unbebaute und mit Kleingärten und Lauben besetzte 13,5 ha große Grundstück, das sogenannte Bötzowgelände an der Carmen-Sylva-Straße (heute Erich-Weinert-Straße), erst 1929 erwarb und die frühesten bekannten Bebauungspläne aus dem Jahr 1928 datieren.

Sicherlich war die Benennung „Wohnstadt" von der GEHAG bewusst ausgewählt, da im Unterschied zur Hufeisensiedlung in Britz und zur Waldsiedlung in Zehlendorf das übernommene Terrain innerstädtisch im Norden des dicht bevölkerten Mietskasernenbezirks Prenzlauer Berg nahe am S-Bahnring lag. GEHAG und Architekten sahen sich vor die Aufgabe gestellt, über eine verdichtete Stockwerksbauweise und eine größtmögliche Ausnutzung des Geländes den hohen Grundstückspreis auszugleichen, und zugleich den reformerischen Leitbildern des Neuen Bauens zu genügen. Begünstigt wurde das Vorhaben durch die neue Berliner Bauzonenordnung, die innerstädtisch bis zu fünf Geschosse zuließ. Der größte Teil der Straßen, war bereits angelegt.

Geplant waren drei Bauabschnitte, aber nur der erste und zweite Bauabschnitt konnte bis 1930 umgesetzt werden. Die nördlich anschließende dritte Etappe mit 400 Wohnungen blieb unausgeführt. Insgesamt entstanden 1.149 Wohnungen mit 1½ bis 4½ Zimmern, wobei die Kleinstwohnungen mit bis zu zwei Zimmern mit einem Anteil von mehr als 80 % überwogen. Alle Wohnungen in den vier- und fünfgeschossigen Zweispännerhäusern verfügten entsprechend den Richtlinien der Wohnungsfürsorgegesellschaft, die das Unternehmen mit Hypothekengeldern unterstützte, über einen kleinen zentralen Verteilerflur, ein Bad mit WC, eine Küche und eine großzügige Loggia, Laube oder einen Balkon.

Die nur zum Teil mit Zentralheizung und Warmwasser ausgestatteten Wohnungen, die das Siedlungsheizwerk im südlichen Hof zwischen Gubitz- und Sodtkestraße versorgte, waren sehr begehrt. Zur sorgfältig geplanten Infrastruktur gehörte für jeden Bauabschnitt eine Zentralwäscherei, wobei das größere Waschhaus mit dem Heizwerk zu einem T-förmigen Komplex zusammengefasst wurde. Die Läden für den alltäglichen Bedarf konzentrierten sich

1925 although GEHAG only bought the 13.5 ha of land in 1929, and the earliest known master plans are dated 1928. When GEHAG bought it there were no buildings on the land. It was covered by allotment gardens and huts. The area was called "Bötzow premises" and was located at Carmen-Sylva-Straße (today Erich-Weinert-Straße).

Certainly GEHAG had chosen the name "Wohnstadt" (residential town) for a particular purpose, since the property was located in the city's centre in the north of the densely populated tenement house district of Prenzlauer Berg near the commuter railway ring. Thus it was completely different from the Hufeisensiedlung at Britz and the forest housing estate at Zehlendorf. GEHAG and the architects were facing the task of balancing the high property price by densely packed flats and a maximum use of the available area while fulfilling the requirements of the reformist models of Neues Bauen. The situation was improved by the fact that the new Berlin zoning ordinance permitted buildings with up to five storeys to be erected within the city. Most of the roads existed already.

Three development phases were planned, but only the first and the second phases could be implemented by 1930. The third phase with 400 flats, which was planned for the adjacent area in the north, could not be built. The estate got a total of 1,149 flats with 1½ to 4½ rooms. More than 80 % were very small flats with up to two rooms. In accordance with the guidelines of the housing welfare society that supported the project with mortgage money, all flats in the four- and five-storeyed houses with duplex flats had a small corridor, a bathroom with WC, a kitchen, and a generous loggia or balcony.

The demand for these flats was enormous, although not all of them had central heating and hot water supply provided by the estate's own heating plant in the southern courtyard between Gubitzstraße and Sodtkestraße. The carefully planned infrastructure included a central laundry for each development phase. The larger laundry was combined with the heating plant and accommodated in a T-shaped complex. The shops for satisfying inhabitants' daily needs were

Abb. 43: Weiße Stadt, Blick auf das Brückenhaus vom ehemaligen Dorf Alt-Reinickendorf, um 1930

Fig. 43: Weiße Stadt, view to the bridge house from the former village of Alt-Reinickendorf, approximately 1930

entlang der Erich-Weinert-Straße, die als breite begrünte Magistrale die Siedlung ost-westlich durchzieht. Die Geschäfte waren in den Kopfenden der Blockflügel untergebracht oder zusammengefasst mit einem Restaurant und Café in einer eingeschossigen Ladenspange, die die zwei Wohnriegel zwischen Gubitz- und Sodtkestraße miteinander verbindet. Ähnliche verbindende Pavillons – gedeckte Gänge mit Läden vor den anderen zur Erich-Weinert-Straße sich öffnenden Blöcken – hatte Taut anfangs geplant, hatte sie jedoch aus ästhetischen und städtebaulichen Gründen verworfen; sie hätten die straßenübergreifenden Raumbezüge gestört.

Zu Anfang setzte sich die Mieterschaft zu rund zwei Dritteln aus Arbeitern und zu einem Drittel aus Angestellten und Beamten zusammen. In der Zeit des Nationalsozialismus wurde die Siedlung in „Wohnstadt Flandern" umbenannt, die Architektur galt nunmehr als ein Abbild linker vaterlandsloser Gesinnung. Bauliche Veränderungen fanden jedoch nicht statt. Auch der Zweite Weltkieg brachte keine größeren Schäden. Nur das kleinere Waschhaus und einige Häuser an der Trachtenbrodtstraße 22–34 waren teilzerstört.

Nach der Teilung der Stadt verlor die GEHAG ihren Hausbestand in den östlichen Berliner Bezirken. Die Wohnstadt ging in die kommunale Wohnungsverwaltung über. Nach der Wiedervereinigung fielen die Häuser in den Besitz der GEHAG zurück, die auch Mitte der 1990er Jahre die ersten denkmalgerechten Instandsetzungen vornahm. Heute gehört die Wohnstadt Carl Legien der BauBeCon Wohnen GmbH aus Hannover, die auch den übrigen Haus- und Freiflächenbestand bis 2004 auf der Grundlage denkmalpflegerischer Auflagen modernisieren und restaurieren ließ. Nur für ein aus der Erbauungszeit der Siedlung stammendes Waschhaus steht die Grundsanierung noch aus.

concentrated along Erich-Weinert-Straße, which is a wide main street with greenery crossing the estate in an east-west direction. The shops were accommodated in the ends of the block wings or respectively arranged as a bracket-like single-storey line, including a restaurant and café, which connects the two residential cross bar buildings between Gubitzstraße and Sodtkestraße. Initially Taut had planned similar connecting pavilions, roofed passages with shops in front of the other blocks that are open towards Erich-Weinert-Straße. For aesthetic and urban development reasons, he later withdrew this idea – these buildings would have disturbed the spatial connections across the street.

Initially two-thirds of the tenants were workers and one-third clerks and public servants. During Nazi rule, the estate was renamed "Wohnstadt Flandern". Its architecture was now considered to be a symbol of left-wing, stateless convictions. Yet, the buildings were not altered. The Second World War did not cause major damage, either. Only the small laundry and some houses at Trachtenbrodtstraße (numbers 22–34) were partially destroyed.

After the division of the city, GEHAG lost its properties in the eastern Berlin districts. The estate became the property of the municipal housing administration. After re-unification, GEHAG got the houses back and in the mid 1990s it started the refurbishment of the monuments. Today Wohnstadt Carl Legien is the property of BauBeCon Wohnen GmbH. This company is located in Hanover. By 2004 it had modernised and restored the remaining houses and outdoor facilities in line with the requirements for maintaining monuments. Only a laundry building from the period when the estate was built still has to undergo fundamental refurbishment.

## Weiße Stadt

Als Ende der 1920er Jahre die Hauszinssteuermittel geringer wurden, legte die Stadt Berlin auf Initiative von Stadtbaurat Martin Wagner ein Sonderbauprogramm mit 15 Millionen Reichsmark auf, das den Bau von 2.080 Wohnungen in Reinickendorf an der Schillerpromenade, heute Aroser Allee, und in Siemensstadt vorsah. Beide Großsiedlungsprojekte finanzierte die Stadt zum ersten Mal aus laufenden Haushaltmitteln und ermöglichte so ein von den baulichen Bedingungen der Hauszinssteuer-Hypotheken befreites experimentelles Planen und Bauen. Die Fördermittel und damit auch die Zahl der Wohnungen verteilte man zu gleichen Teilen auf die beiden Vorhaben, die möglichst in Zeilenbauweise mit ausschließlich Geschosswohnungen zu realisieren waren.

In Reinickendorf stand südlich des Dorfangers als Baugelände ein bereits vor dem Krieg von der Landgemeinde Reinickendorf erschlossenes städtisches Terrain beiderseits der Aroser Allee zur Verfügung, das noch wenig bebaute sogenannte „Schweizer Viertel". Wie für Siemensstadt bildete Wagner auch in Reinickendorf eine Arbeitsgemeinschaft aus mehreren Architekten, denen jeweils einzelne Bauabschnitte übertragen wurden. Die Durchführung lag bei der stadteigenen „Gemeinnützigen Heimstättengesellschaft Primus mbH". In Kooperation arbeiteten die Architekten Otto Rudolf Salvisberg, der bereits über Erfahrung im Siedlungsbau verfügte und auch die städtebauliche Planung übernahm, Bruno Ahrends und Wilhelm Büning sowie der Architekt und Architekturjournalist Friedrich Paulsen, den man wegen seines Fachwissen über wirtschaftliche und rationelle Baumethoden hinzuzog, und der Gartenarchitekt Ludwig Lesser. Salvisberg hatte bei seiner Bebauungsplanung das bestehende Straßennetz des „Schweizer Viertels" zu berücksichtigen, da sämtliche Veränderungen und Neuanlagen zu Lasten der „Primus" gingen. Nach dreijähriger Bauzeit der beiden Bauabschnitte konnten 1931 die letzten der 1.268 Wohnungen bezogen werden.

Umfangreich und vorbildlich war die Austattung mit gemeinschaftlichen Einrichtungen und Läden für den täglichen Bedarf. Ein Zentralheizwerk versorgte die Wohnungen mit Wärme und Warmwasser. Zwei zentrale mechanische Wäschereien, 24 Läden, ein Café, ein Kinderheim und eine Arztpraxis waren ein demonstrativer Ausdruck für das sozialreformerische Bestreben Martin Wagners und der Architekten.

Aufgrund ihres leuchtend weißen Anstriches bekam die neue Wohnsiedlung schon bald den Namen „Weiße Stadt". Die Nähe zu Industriestandorten in Alt-Reinickendorf war vermutlich für Kriegszerstörungen mitverantwortlich, die aber nur einzelne Häuser betrafen. Der Wiederaufbau, verbunden mit einer Grundrenovierung, die unter Beratung Wilhelm Bünings stand, fand in den Jahren von 1949 bis 1954 nach originalem Vorbild statt. Seit 1982 läuft ein denkmalpflegerisches Erneuerungsprogramm, das bereits große Teile der „Weißen Stadt" erfasst hat. Die Umwandlung von Mietwohnungen zu privaten Eigentumswohnungen erfolgt seit einigen Jahren.

## Weiße Stadt

When the income from the mortgage servicing tax decreased in the late 1920s, urban development councillor Martin Wagner initiated a special housing fund comprising 15 million Reichsmark for the construction of 2,080 flats in the district of Reinickendorf at Schillerpromenade (today Aroser Allee) and Siemensstadt. For the first time, the city financed the building of both large housing estates with current budget means and thus provided the basis for experimental design and construction free from the conditions connected with the mortgages based on the mortgage servicing tax. Both projects got an equal share in the grants and thus also equal numbers of flats were to be built – if possible exclusively in multi-storeyed ribbon buildings.

On both sides of Aroser Allee south of the Reinickendorf village green, the so-called "Schweizer Viertel" (Swiss Quarter) was available. It was a sparsely built-up property that the village of Reinickendorf had already developed before the war. For the Reinickendorf project, Wagner created a working group of several architects just as he had done for Siemensstadt and each of the architects was responsible for an individual phase of development. The city-owned "Gemeinnützige Heimstättengesellschaft Primus mbH" (Primus Non-Profit Housing Society with limited liability) was responsible for executing the project. The architects Otto Rudolf Salvisberg, Bruno Ahrends and Wilhelm Büning, the architect and architecture journalist Friedrich Paulsen and the garden architect Ludwig Lesser cooperated for the Reinickendorf project. Salvisberg had some experience in developing residential estates and was also responsible for designing the urban development plan. Paulsen was invited because of his special knowledge of economical and rational methods of construction. In developing his master plan, Salvisberg had to conserve the existing road network of the Swiss Quarter since Primus would otherwise have had to pay all costs for changes or new roads. In 1931, after three years of construction work to complete the two phases of development, the last of the 1,268 flats were ready for tenants to move in.

The equipment of the estate with communal facilities and shops for satisfying the daily needs of tenants was comprehensive and exemplary. A central heating plant supplied heat and hot water for all flats. Two central mechanised laundries, 24 shops, a café, a children's home and a medical practice demonstrate the desire of Martin Wagner and the architects to introduce social reforms.

Soon after it was completed, the new estate was named "Weiße Stadt" because of the bright white facades. Individual houses of it were destroyed during the war. This was probably due to the fact that it is close to industrial estates at Alt-Reinickendorf. In 1949 through 1954 the houses were rebuilt and the estate underwent thorough refurbishment, re-establishing the original state. Wilhelm Büning acted as adviser for these works. A renewal programme for maintaining the monument was initiated in 1982. It continues to date and has already covered a large part of the Weiße Stadt. Several years ago, the privatisation of the rented flats began.

## Großsiedlung Siemensstadt (Ringsiedlung)

Das ca. 14 ha große Siedlungsgelände entstand auf dem früherem Terrain der baumbestandenen Jungfernheide, das seit der Eingemeindung 1920 vom Verlauf der Bezirksgrenze der beiden ehemaligen Städte Spandau und Charlottenburg gekennzeichnet wird. Für den Standort einer Großsiedlung waren hier mit der expandierenden Industrie- und Wohnstadt Siemensstadt im Süden, dem Natur- und Erholungsraum des Volksparks Jungfernheide im Norden und der 1929 eröffneten „Siemensbahn", die mit einem Dammbogen das Baugelände durchzog, optimale infrastrukturelle Bedingungen gegeben.

Für die städtebauliche und architektonische Bearbeitung wählte Wagner wie bei der Reinickendorfer Großsiedlung die Form der Arbeitsgemeinschaft. Es gelang ihm mit Hans Scharoun, Walter Gropius, Hugo Häring, Fred Forbat, Otto Bartning und Paul Rudolf Henning Baukünstler zu verpflichten, die zur Avantgarde des Neuen Bauens zählten. Bis auf Henning und Forbat gehörten alle zur Architektenvereinigung „Der Ring", wovon sich später der Name „Ringsiedlung" ableitete. Außer Walter Gropius und Hugo Häring verfügte allerdings keiner der ausgewählten Architekten über ausreichende Erfahrungen im Siedlungsbau. Als beratender Haustechniker konnte für die rationale Anordnung von Küchen, Bädern und der wirtschaftlichsten Lage der Hausinstallationen der Ingenieur Max Mengeringhausen gewonnen werden. Mit der Wahl von Leberecht Migge, dem im modernen Siedlungsbau maßgeblichen Gartenarchitekten seiner Zeit, vervollkommnete Wagner auf das Trefflichste das Team.

Die Baubetreuung übernahm die stadteigene „Gemeinnützige Baugesellschaft Berlin-Heerstraße mbH". Nach dreijähriger Bauzeit der beiden Bauabschnitte Siemensstadt I und II konnten 1931 die letzten der 1.370 Wohnungen bezogen werden. Entsprechend dem Bedarf in Berlin an billigen Kleinstwohnungen war auch hier der Anteil der 1 bis 2½- Zimmerwohnungen mit mehr als 90 % sehr groß. Die städtische Finanzierung ließ aber in Siemensstadt, genauso wie bei der Großsiedlung „Weiße Stadt", ein Experimentieren bei der Grundrisslösung zu. So wurden Wohnküchen, appartmentähnliche Aufteilungen und variable Grundrisse erprobt. Zusammen mit dem letzten, unvollendet gebliebenen Abschnitt Siemensstadt III, der u. a. aus den beiden 1933–34 realisierten Henning-Zeilen am Heckerdamm 292–293 bestand, war eine moderne Wohnstadt für 5.000 Bewohner mit Fernheizwerk, Zentralwäscherei, Schule, Spielplätzen und Läden entstanden.

Den Bau der Schule am Jungfernheideweg 32/48, deren Standort westlich der Henningzeilen und nördlich des Bauteils von Häring bereits im ersten städtebaulichen Entwurf von Scharoun vorgesehen war, übernahm 1930–31 die Hochbauabteilung des Bezirks Charlottenburg. Walter Helmcke entwarf eine Volksdoppelschule mit zwei langen eingeschossigen Flügeln, an die abwechselnd nach beiden Seiten Pavillons angefügt und die mit einem höheren Querriegel verbunden sind. Von dem geplanten Schulbaukomplex konnte nur der südliche Flügel realisiert werden. Die damalige 13. Volksschule galt als erste Schule Berlins im modernen Pavillonsystem; bei gutem Wetter fand der Unter-

## Großsiedlung Siemensstadt (Ringsiedlung)

The estate was built on approximately 14 ha of the park Jungfernheide, where trees had previously stood. The area was incorporated into Berlin in 1920 and since that time it has been characterised by the border between the two former towns of Spandau and Charlottenburg which crosses it. In the south, the industrial and residential areas of Siemensstadt expanded. The nature and recreation resort of Jungfernheide borders it in the north and the "Siemens railway line" opened in 1929 crosses the site on an elevated track. All of this provided for an optimal infrastructure for a large residential estate.

As for the large residential estate Reinickendorf, Wagner established a working group to design the urban development plan and architecture. He managed to employ members of the vanguard of Neues Bauen: Hans Scharoun, Walter Gropius, Hugo Häring, Fred Forbat, Otto Bartning and Paul Rudolf Henning. Except for Henning and Forbat, they belonged to the architects' association "Der Ring" (the Ring) which later gave the estate its name. However, with the exception of Walter Gropius and Hugo Häring, none of the involved architects had sufficient experience in residential development. The engineer Max Mengeringhausen was employed as a consultant for technical house installations. He assured that the kitchens and bathrooms were positioned rationally and that the house installations were arranged economically. Wagner completed the team excellently by choosing Leberecht Migge, the leading garden architect in modern residential development of that time.

The general construction services were provided by "Gemeinnützige Baugesellschaft Berlin-Heerstraße mbH" (Non-Profit Limited Liability Building Society Berlin-Heerstraße) which was owned by the city. In 1931, after three years of construction work to complete Phases I and II of development, the last of the 1,370 flats were ready for tenants to move in. Since people in Berlin demanded cheap, very small flats, the estate has a rather high proportion of single-room apartments or apartments with a maximum of 2½ rooms (90 %). Yet, since the municipality provided financing for this project at Siemensstadt just as for that of Reinickendorf, the architects could experiment with various ground plans. They tried combined kitchen and living rooms, apartment-like structures and variable ground plans. Together with the last development phase (Siemensstadt III), which remained incomplete and consisted of the two ribbon buildings by Henning built in 1933–34 at Heckerdamm (numbers 292–293), a modern residential estate for 5,000 people had been erected. It had a central heating plant, a central laundry, a school, playgrounds and shops.

The school at Jungfernheideweg 32/48 was built in 1930–31 by the civil engineering department of the district of Charlottenburg. Its location west of the ribbon buildings by Henning and north of the buildings designed by Häring had already been defined in Scharoun's first urban development plan. Walter Helmcke designed a duplex primary school with two single-storey wings. Pavilions were attached on both sides of them. The wings are connected by a higher cross bar building. Only the southern wing of the proposed school complex was able to be completed. The

Abb. 44: Großsiedlung Siemensstadt, Eingang zur Siedlung am Jungfernheideweg, Siedlungsteil von Hans Scharoun, 1930

Fig. 44: Großsiedlung Siemensstadt, entrance to the housing estate at Jungfernheideweg, section by Hans Scharoun, 1930

richt im Freien statt. Der bereits 1933–34 erweiterte Schulbau erlitt im Zweiten Weltkrieg schwere Beschädigungen.

Die Beseitigung der Kriegsschäden in der Siedlung und der Wiederaufbau zerstörter Gebäudeteile war 1955 abgeschlossen. Das östliche Ende der Bartningzeile wurde, nachdem der Wiederaufbau der kriegsbeschädigten Häuser Goebelstraße 21–25 in den Jahren 1951–52 abgeschlossen war, 1955–56 nach Bartnings eigenem Entwurf um die Häuser Nr. 11–19 verlängert. Um dieselbe Zeit entstand der abschließende Kopfbau Goebelstraße 1–9 bis zum Heilmannring, den Hans Scharoun als Laubenganghaus entwarf. Die im sozialen Wohnungsbau der 50er Jahre finanzierten Wohnungen sind entsprechend kleinteilig mit 2 und 2½ Zimmern.

Seit 1982 läuft ein denkmalpflegerisches Erneuerungsprogramm, das bereits große Teile der Großsiedlung Siemensstadt erfasst hat.

13th primary school at the time was considered to be Berlin's first school built with the modern pavilion system. When the weather was fair, classes were held outdoors. The building was already extended in 1933–34. It was severely damaged during the Second World War.

Repair and reconstruction work in the housing estate was completed in 1955. After reconstruction had been completed of the houses at Goebelstraße 21–25, that had been damaged during the war (1951–52), the eastern end of the ribbon designed by Bartning was extended by the houses Bartningzeile numbers 11–19 in 1955–56. Approximately at the same time, the final head building was built on Goebelstraße 1–9 up to Heilmannring. Hans Scharoun had designed it as a gallery block. The flats built with social housing financing in the 50s are small (with 2 or 2½ rooms).

A renewal programme for maintaining the monument was initiated in 1982. It continues to date and has already covered a large part of Siemensstadt.

# Die Gehag-Wohnung 1931

**WOHNSTADT CARL LEGIEN**
ERRICHTET VON DER GEHAG

CONDITOREI
EINFAMILIENHAUS BRITZ

**AUSSTELLUNG DER GEHAG** GEMEINNÜTZIGE HEIMSTÄTTEN-, SPAR- UND BAU-A.-G.
IN DER **STÄNDIGEN BAUWELT-MUSTERSCHAU**
BERLIN W 8 • WILHELMSTRASSE 92/93
FEBRUAR 1931

# 3

**BEGRÜNDUNG FÜR DIE EINTRAGUNG**
**JUSTIFICATION FOR INSCRIPTION**

## 3.A Criteria under which inscription is proposed

The nominated property …
(II) exhibits an important interchange of human values, over a span of time or within a cultural area of the world, on developments in architecture or technology, monumental arts, town-planning or landscape design

The six Berlin estates are examples of the paradigm shift in European housing construction, since they are an expression of a broad housing reform movement and, as such, made a decisive contribution to improving housing and living conditions in Berlin. Thanks to their exemplary character, their influence was felt all over Europe. With modern flats equipped with bathrooms, kitchens and sunny balconies in houses with spacious recreation spaces and playgrounds and without multiple courtyards and wings, these housing estates set a hygienic and social standard far removed from Berlin's inhumane tenement system of densely packed blocks of flats. Shortly before the First World War, ninety per cent of Berlin's population lived in tenements with four or five storeys. Nearly half of the flats were located in rear buildings and nine out of ten flats did not have a bathroom.

During the Weimar Republic, the worsening shortage of housing and the collapse of privately financed housing development also made housing construction a social policy challenge in Berlin. With political support from Germany's Social Democrats and from the trade unions, trade union cooperatives and municipal and other non-profit societies began financing new social housing in Berlin.

The construction of housing estates is an urban planning and architectural response to social problems and housing policy issues arising in regions with high population density. Novel housing estate forms developed in particular during the first decades of the 20th century in big European cities and metropolises. Building authorities, architects and urban planners often cooperated on these new housing estates, which created better living conditions for

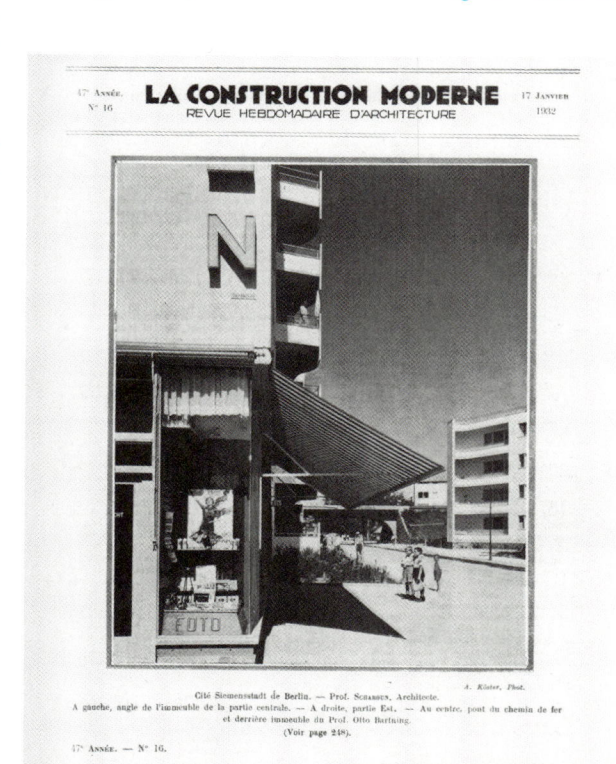

Abb. 45: International appreciation of the Großsiedlung Siemensstadt. Front page of "La Construction Moderne" of 1932 showing buildings designed by Hans Scharoun

Abb. 46 : Großsiedlung Britz, Luftaufnahme von Südosten, 1930

Abb. 46: Großsieclung Britz, aerial view from scutheast, 1930

In Berlin wurde der soziale Siedlungsbau in den 1920er Jahren von bedeutenden Planern, von städtischen Behörden und Wohnungsbaugesellschaften auf ein im internationalen Vergleich hervorragendes Niveau entwickelt. Es wurden die sozialpolitischen, ökonomischen, architektonischen und rechtlichen Instrumente geschaffen, um Hunderte von Siedlungsprojekten zu realisieren. Das Wohnungsbauproblem, das vorher fast ausschließlich Bauspekulanten überlassen worden war, wurde nun mit dem Anspruch der Gemeinnützigkeit systematisch, auf der Höhe der modernsten architektonischen, städtebaulichen, hygienischen und sozialwissenschaftlichen Erkenntnisse von ausgewiesenen Fachleuten angegangen.

Die nominierten Siedlungen waren Teil eines breit angelegten Wohnungsbauprogramms in Berlin, das innerhalb weniger Jahre zum Neubau von 140.000 Wohnungen führte. Dabei war der entstehende Massenwohnungsbau eng verknüpft mit neuen Konzepten zur räumlichen und sozialen Ordnung der Stadt. Der damalige Berliner Stadtbaurat Martin Wagner entwickelte ein modernes Städtebaukonzept, dem ein funktional entmischtes Stadtmodell zu Grunde lag und das zur Auflösung des in Berlin besonders ausgeprägten Stadt-Umland-Dualismus beitragen sollte. Während im unmittelbaren Einzugsgebiet der Großstadt dichte Wohnviertel in offener Geschossbauweise mit durchgrünten Siedlungsräumen noch bestehende Lücken im Stadtgefüge füllten (Siedlung Schillerpark, Wohnstadt Carl Legien), entstanden an der Peripherie, eingebettet in die märkische Landschaft, großzügig durchgrünte Großsiedlungen (Hufeisensiedlung Britz, Weiße Stadt, Großsiedlung Siemensstadt).

**(IV) ist ein herausragendes Beispiel eines Typus von Gebäuden oder architektonischen oder technischen Ensem-**

the poorer strata of the population in particular. Their quality of urban development, architecture and landscape design, as well as the housing standards that were developed during this period, served as a guideline for social housing constructed after the end of the Second World War, and they retained their exemplary function during the entire 20th century.

Berlin was a city whose population had multiplied in just a few decades as a result of industrialisation, and into the 1920s it was characterised by a shortage of housing and miserable living conditions in hopelessly overcrowded tenements. In this situation, the housing reform movement was able to generate initial momentum mainly in housing projects organised on a cooperative basis. Gartenstadt Falkenberg had already been built before the First World War. It was a housing estate project that aimed at creating a new way of living, and with its standardised house forms and ground plans for flats, it served as an important model for others.

In the 1920s, renowned designers, municipal authorities and housing societies in Berlin developed social housing construction to a level that was outstanding by international standards. The creation of social policy, economic, architectural and legislative instruments made it possible to implement hundreds of development projects. Housing construction had previously been left almost entirely to speculators. Proven experts now approached it systematically, in the interest of benefiting the public and on the basis of the most advanced knowledge of architecture, urban development, hygiene and social science.

The nominated housing estates were part of a broadly based housing construction programme in Berlin that led to the building of 140,000 flats within just a few years. This mass

bles oder einer Landschaft, das (einen) bedeutsame(n) Abschnitt(e) in der menschlichen Geschichte darstellt

Diese Berliner Siedlungen sind ein außergewöhnliches Beispiel des Siedlungsbaus in den ersten Jahrzehnten des 20. Jahrhunderts mit Vorbildwirkung für das großstädtische Wohnen und Leben in der modernen Industriegesellschaft.

International renommierte Architekten wie Bruno Taut, Walter Gropius, Otto Rudolf Salvisberg und Hans Scharoun entwickelten modellhaft neue Siedlungsstrukturen, die nicht nur gesunde und mit ansprechenden Standards ausgestattete Wohnungen ermöglichten, sondern darüberhinaus neuen Wohn- und Lebensformen Raum boten. Vom sozialen Experiment einer genossenschaftlich geprägten Gemeinschaft über das Prinzip des „Außenwohnraums" von Taut bis hin zum Scharounschen Konzept der „Nachbarschaft" erhielten diese Siedlungen neben einer vorbildlichen sozialen und versorgungstechnischen Infrastruktur mit Gemeinschaftseinrichtungen ein breites Spektrum gemeinschaftlicher Funktions- und Erlebnisräume. Von den beteiligten Architekten wurden neue Haus- und Wohngrundrisstypen entwickelt, die modernen Wohnbedürfnissen entsprachen.

Die besten in dieser Zeit entstandenen Siedlungen brachten hervorragende Lösungen für das Zusammenleben vieler Menschen auf engem Raum. Außergewöhnliche architektonische Gestaltung und Vielfalt in den Siedlungsstrukturen und Gebäudeformen wurden kombiniert mit einer geschickten städtebaulichen Einbindung, um brauchbare und variantenreiche Wohnungen in gesunder Umgebung zu schaffen. Licht, Luft und Sonne hießen die Schlagworte. Diesen folgte auch die Gestaltung der Siedlungsfreiräume mit Gemeinschaftsanlagen wie Spielplätze, großzügige Frei-

housing development was closely linked to new concepts for the spatial and social structure of the city. Martin Wagner, the city's urban development councillor at the time, developed a modern urban planning concept based on a model of functional separation. This model was to contribute to breaking up the contrast between city and countryside, a contrast that was especially marked in Berlin's case. In the city itself, dense residential quarters with open structures of multi-storeyed buildings dotted with green spaces filled gaps in the urban structure (Siedlung Schillerpark, Wohnstadt Carl Legien), while large housing estates with spacious green areas were embedded in the landscape of Mark Brandenburg on the outskirts of the city (Hufeisensiedlung Britz, Weiße Stadt, Großsiedlung Siemensstadt).

**(IV) is an outstanding example of a type of building, architectural or technological ensemble or landscape which illustrates (a) significant stage(s) in human history**

These Berlin housing estates are extraordinary examples of the housing developments built during the early decades of the 20th century and were models for housing and living in the big cities of modern industrial society.

Internationally renowned architects like Bruno Taut, Walter Gropius, Otto Rudolf Salvisberg and Hans Scharoun developed new and exemplary housing estate structures. These not only facilitated the provision of healthy flats with attractive amenities, but also offered a basis for new forms of housing and living. These housing estates were designed with community facilities offering an exemplary social and service infrastructure and a wide range of communal functional and event spaces, spanning models like the experiment of a cooperative-based community, Taut's "outdoor living space" and Scharoun's concept of "neighbourhood". The participating architects developed new types of ground plans for houses and flats that responded to modern demands on housing.

The best of the housing estates built during this period produced excellent solutions to the problem of designing housing for many people living together in limited space. They combined extraordinary architectural designs and a diversity of housing estate structures and building forms with intelligent integration into urban structures in order to develop useful and varied flats in healthy environments. Light, air and sunshine were key words. They also provided guidelines for the design of the housing estates' communal facilities, such as playgrounds, spacious outdoor facilities and tenants' gardens. Renowned garden architects like Ludwig Lesser and Leberecht Migge ensured that these reformist ideas were implemented in an outstanding way.

### 3.B Proposed statement of outstanding universal value

The social housing settlements built in Berlin during the 1920s are a heritage that unites all the positive achievements of early modernism. They represent a period in which Berlin was respected worldwide for its political, social, technical and cultural progressiveness. This creative environment facilitated the development of housing estates that can be regarded both as works of art and as health and

Abb. 47: Broschüre zur Ausstellung der GEHAG-Siedlungen auf der Bauwelt-Musterschau, 1931

Fig. 47: Brochure for the exhibition on the GEHAG-housing estates on the Bauwelt model exhibition, 1931

Abb. 48: Kleinster GEHAG-Wohnungstyp von 43 qm, 1½ Zimmer mit Bad, Küche, Flur und Balkon, etwas größer verwendet in der Großsiedlung Britz.

Fig. 48: Smallest GEHAG apartment type with 43 sqm, 1 ½ rooms with bathroom, kitchen, corridor and balcony, used in a slightly larger size in the Großsiedlung Britz

flächen und Mietergärten. Für eine qualitative Umsetzung der reformerischen Ideen standen renommierte Gartenarchitekten wie Ludwig Lesser und Leberecht Migge.

### 3.B Erklärung bezüglich des außerordentlichen universellen Wertes

Mit den Siedlungen des sozialen Wohnungsbaus der 1920er Jahre hat die Stadt Berlin ein Erbe zu bieten, das alle positiven Züge der frühen Moderne auf sich vereinigt. Sie künden von einer Zeit, in der sich Berlin weltweit durch politischen und sozialen, technischen und kulturellen Fortschritt auszeichnete. Dieses kreative Milieu ermöglichte die Entstehung von Siedlungen, die als Kunstwerke ebenso gut bestehen können wie als Werke der Gesundheits- und Sozialpolitik. Mit der Gewinnung der besten Architekten und Gartenarchitekten des Landes stieg der Siedlungsbau – mit jahrzehntelanger Nachwirkung – zum Leittypus und eigentlichen Medium der Architekturentwicklung auf.

Die politischen und wirtschaftlichen Umwälzungen in Deutschland nach dem verlorenen Ersten Weltkrieg machten den Siedlungsbau zum Gegenstand sozialpolitischer Zielvorstellungen. In Berlin gewann nach der Bildung der Einheitsgemeinde 1920 die Sozialdemokratie immer mehr Einfluss auf die kommunale Stadtplanung. Die ihr nahe stehenden neuen gewerkschaftlich-genossenschaftlichen Bauorganisationen, wie die GEHAG, propagierten einen modernen sozialen Wohnungsbau. Groß-Berlin mit seinen weitläufigen Flächenreserven wurde zum Experimentierfeld für die moderne Volkswohnung. Als der Architekt und Sozialdemokrat Martin Wagner im Jahre 1926 zum Stadtbaurat gewählt wurde, verkörperte er in Personalunion beide Bewegungen: die politische und die fachlich-reformerische.

Die Berliner Siedlungen, schon in ihrer Entstehungszeit in der Fachwelt und Fachpresse weithin beachtet und gewürdigt, gewannen auch im Diskurs über die Architekturgeschichte des 20. Jahrhunderts emblematischen Wert: Neben dem Bauhaus und den Bauten des Neuen Frankfurt erschienen sie in allen einschlägigen Publikationen als beispielhafte Leistungen der architektonischen und städtebaulichen Moderne. Indes gehören sie nicht nur der Geschichte an: Vom Zweiten Weltkrieg und von unsachgemäßen Erneuerungsmaßnahmen nur wenig betroffen, stehen sie noch heute, umgeben von großzügigem Grün ihrer Gärten und Freiflächen – attraktive Wohngebiete, deren Bewohner ihre Mietverträge oft von Generation zu Generation weitervererben.

Mit den Siedlungen, die zum großen Teil, aber nicht ausschließlich, außerhalb der in James Hobrechts Bebauungsplan von 1862 trassierten Stadt errichtet wurden, gewann in Berlin ein neues Konzept der räumlichen und sozialen Ordnung Gestalt. Die weniger bemittelten Bewohner der Stadt sollten nicht mehr in den schlechteren, kleineren und ungesünderen Wohnungen in den Souterrains, Seitenflügeln, Quergebäuden, Dachgeschossen, in überbelegten Mietshäusern der verdichteten Innenstadt verschwinden. Sie sollten nun sichtbar eigenen Raum erhalten, sowohl für die Privatheit ihrer Familien als auch für die öffentliche

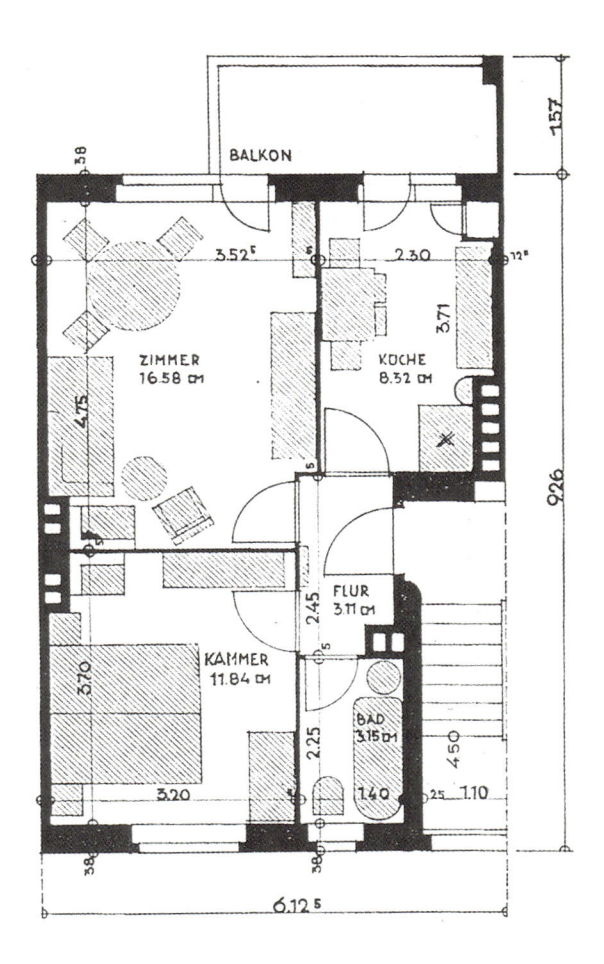

| | |
|---|---|
| Zimmer | 16,58 qm |
| Kammer | 11,84 qm |
| Küche | 8,32 qm |
| Bad | 3,15 qm |
| Flur | 3,11 qm |
| Wohnfläche | 43,00 qm |
| Balkon | 5,00 qm |

social policy achievements. When the best architects and garden architects of Germany became involved, housing estates became the model and actual instrument for the development of architecture. Their influence could be felt even decades later.

The political and economic transformations in Germany after it had lost the First World War made the development of housing estates the subject of social policy. After Berlin's incorporation of surrounding communities to form one large city in 1920, the Social Democrats acquired ever more influence on municipal urban development. The new trade union and cooperative building societies like GEHAG, which were their close allies, propagated the modern social housing development. Greater Berlin, with its spacious undeveloped properties, became the site of experiments in developing modern flats for the people. When the architect and Social Democrat Martin Wagner was elected urban development councillor in 1926, he embodied both movements at the same time: the political movement and that of the reformist experts.

The Berlin housing estates, which had attracted the attention of experts and of the specialised press even when they were first built, also acquired a symbolic value in the dis-

Repräsentation als gesellschaftliche Klasse und zur Veranschaulichung der Siedlungsgemeinschaften.

Die entwurfskünstlerische Phantasie der Architekten richtete sich sowohl auf die Entwicklung funktionaler, der Gesundheit und dem Familienleben förderlicher Wohnungsgrundrisse als auch auf die Anordnung der Baukörper in größeren städtebaulichen Figuren, stets in Bezug auf die Himmelsrichtungen und die Sonneneinstrahlung. Den Bewohnern sollten mit Gemeinschaftsflächen „Außenwohnräume" (Taut) eröffnet werden, die zum Aufenthalt im Freien, im Sonnenlicht und in frischer Luft einluden und nicht zuletzt der Bekämpfung der auch in Berlin noch immer grassierenden Tuberkulose dienten. Einer dieser Außenwohnräume, gefasst von einer besonders einprägsamen, kraftvollen städtebaulichen Figur, ist zum Wahrzeichen der Siedlungsbewegung geworden: das Hufeisen, Zentrum der von Bruno Taut und Martin Wagner 1925–30 errichteten Hufeisensiedlung in Britz.

Unter den zahlreichen größeren und kleineren Berliner Siedlungen und Wohnanlagen eine Auswahl zu treffen, ist nicht leicht. Viele sind erhalten, die meisten reizvoll, alle verschieden, manche urban verdichtet, andere offen und grün durchzogen, manche im künstlerischen Entwurf konservativ im Sinne der Heimatschutzbewegung, andere in expressionistischer Formensprache. Die getroffene Auswahl folgt im Wesentlichen vier Leitkriterien:

Der besonderen künstlerischen Bedeutung im Hinblick auf den architektonischen Entwurf und die Prägnanz der städtebaulichen Figur

Der guten Überlieferung der originalen Substanz

Der sozialpolitischen Intention ihrer Erbauer

Der internationalen Rezeption und Anerkennung

Es ergibt sich, gewiss nicht zufällig, eine bestimmte Konzentration auf die Werke Bruno Tauts. Sein Name ist, wie kein zweiter, mit der Glanzzeit des sozialen Wohnungsbaus der Weimarer Republik in Berlin verbunden. Seine Zusammenarbeit mit dem Berliner Stadtbaurat Martin Wagner führte zu beispielhaften Erfolgen. Aus seinem reichen Œuvre in Berlin wurden vier Siedlungen ausgesucht, die in ihrer Verschiedenheit die Etappen seiner künstlerischen Entwicklung als Architekt und Städtebauer verdeutlichen:

Die Gartenstadt Falkenberg (1913–1916), als ein baugenossenschaftliches Siedlungs- und Lebensreformmodell, entstanden aus der Kritik an der Großstadt und dem Berliner Mietskasernensystem

Die Siedlung Schillerpark (1924–1930), als erstes großstädtisches Wohnprojekt nach dem Ersten Weltkrieg in Berlin, das in idealtypischer Weise alle Merkmale des neuen sozialen Bauens aufweist wie auch das Leitbild einer modernen städtischen Lebenskultur verkörpert

Die Großsiedlung Britz (Hufeisensiedlung, 1925–1930), als erste deutsche Großsiedlung nach dem Krieg und der Inflation, die mit unterschiedlichen Wohnformen ein würdiges, gesundheitlich-hygienisches und menschen-

course on the history of 20th century architecture: Along with Bauhaus and the buildings of Neues Frankfurt, they appeared in all relevant publications as exemplary achievements of modernist architecture and urban development. However, they are not just part of history. They suffered little damage during the Second World War or from improper renovation, and thus are still standing today, surrounded by spacious gardens and green areas: attractive residential areas whose tenants often pass on leases from one generation to the next.

A new concept of spatial and social structure was implemented in Berlin with these housing estates. Most but not all of them were erected outside the city that was laid out in James Hobrecht's master plan of 1862. No longer were the city's less prosperous inhabitants to be hidden away in the smaller, less healthy, worse flats in the basements, wings, cross buildings, attics and overcrowded tenements of the densely built-up city centre. They were to get visible space for themselves both for the privacy of their families and for their public representation as a social class, as well as for presenting the housing estate communities.

In their design work, the imagination of the architects aimed both at developing functional floor plans for flats that would promote health and family life and at arranging the buildings in larger urban structures, while always keeping in mind the points of the compass and insulation. Common spaces were to offer tenants "Aussenwohnräume" (outdoor living spaces) (Taut), which would invite them to spend time outside enjoying the sunlight and fresh air and, last but not least, would help fight tuberculosis, still rampant in Berlin at the time. One of these outdoor living spaces formed by a particularly impressive and powerful urban structure has become the symbol of the housing estate movement: the horseshoe, centre of the Hufeisensiedlung built by Bruno Taut and Martin Wagner in Britz from 1925 to 1930.

Choosing between the many larger and smaller Berlin housing estates and residential estates is not easy. Many of them have been preserved, most of them are attractive, and all of them are different. Some of them have a dense urban structure, others are open and dotted with green spaces, some are based on a conservative artistic design in the spirit of the Heimatschutzbewegung (movement for the preservation of regional culture), others have a more expressionist style. The choice was made mainly on the basis of the following four criteria:

The particular significance of the architectural design and of the urban structure from the point of view of the arts

The good condition of the original structure

The social policy intentions of the developers

International awareness and recognition

It is certainly no coincidence that most of the housing estates chosen are works by Bruno Taut. Like no one else's, his name is linked with the heyday of social housing construction in Berlin during the years of the Weimar Republic. His cooperation with Berlin urban development councillor

Abb. 49: Außenwohnraum: raumbildene aufgelockerte Bauweise an der Onkel-Bräsig-Straße/Ecke Hüsung, veröffentlicht 1931 in Bruno Tauts Artikel „Der Außenwohnraum"

Fig. 49: Outdoor living space: creating space by dispersed buildings at Onkel-Bräsig-Straße and its corner with Hüsung, published in 1931 in Bruno Taut's article "Der Außenwohnraum".

freundliches Wohnen auch für untere Bevölkerungsschichten ermöglichen sollte

Die Wohnstadt Carl Legien (1928–1930), als städtischste und kompakteste Großsiedlung Berlins, die trotz ihrer hohen Wohndichte mustergültig mit einer Licht und Luft geöffneten Bauweise den Eindruck von aufgelockertem Wohnen im Grünen vermittelt

Andere Richtungen der Entwurfskunst und des Städtebaus vertreten die beiden gleichzeitig entstandenen Großsiedlungen:

Die Weiße Stadt (1929–1931), als eine Großsiedlung städtischen Typus in Zeilenbauweise mit durchgrünten Räumen, in der fern von jeglicher Monotonie freie abstrakte Raumfigurationen des Siedlungsbaus der Moderne erprobt wurden

Die Großsiedlung Siemensstadt (Ringsiedlung, 1929–1931), als eine funktionelle Wohnsiedlung, die den Weg zum internationalen modernen Städtebau weist und so das Modell einer aufgelockerten, gegliederten und durchgrünten Stadt bereits vorausnimmt

Die Weiße Stadt (1929–1931) entwarfen der Schweizer Otto Rudolf Salvisberg, der auch den städtebaulichen Gesamtentwurf verantwortet, und die beiden Berliner Architekten Bruno Ahrends und Wilhelm Büning. In Siemensstadt wirkte vor allem Hans Scharoun, der auch den städtebaulichen Plan schuf. Die Bauten stammen von Walter Gropius, Hugo Häring, Otto Bartning, Fred Forbat, Paul Rudolf Henning und Hans Scharoun selber. Beide Siedlungen sind über Berlin hinaus zum Symbol der Internationalen Moderne avanciert. Sie repräsentieren nicht nur einen Paradigmenwechsel in Architektur und Städtebau sondern auch einen gesellschaftlichen Strukturwandel, wie er sich mit monofunktionalen Trabantensiedlungen bei einer klaren Trennung von Wohn- und Arbeitsstätte offenbarte.

Martin Wagner yielded exemplary successes. Four housing estates were chosen from his rich oeuvre in Berlin. They are all different from each other, and their differences illustrate the stages of Taut's artistic development as an architect and urban developer:

Gartenstadt Falkenberg (1913–1916), developed by a building cooperative as a model for reforming housing estates and living, which emerged as the result of criticism of big city life and the Berlin tenement house system

Siedlung Schillerpark (1924–1930), one of the first urban residential projects built after the end of the First World War in Berlin; an ideal combination of all the features of the new social housing developments that also embodies the model of a modern culture of urban life

Großsiedlung Britz (Hufeisensiedlung) (1925–1930), the first large German housing estate built after the end of the First World War and the years of inflation; aimed at providing humane, healthy and hygienic living conditions, also for low-income groups, by offering various forms of housing

Wohnstadt Carl Legien (1928–1930), which, as the most urban and most compact large housing estate in Berlin, manages – despite its density – to create a housing environment that appears green and open, thanks to a building design opened up to light and air in an exemplary way

The following two large housing estates were erected at the same time and represent other approaches to design and urban development:

Weiße Stadt (1929–1931), which was built as a large housing estate with an urban character, consisting of ribbon buildings with green spaces in between; anything

Damit waren führende Architekten der klassischen Moderne im Berliner Siedlungsbau engagiert. Mit den vier Siedlungen Bruno Tauts, der Weißen Stadt und Siemensstadt wird die Entwicklung von der Gartenstadt zur großstädtischen Stadtlandschaft im Sinne Hans Scharouns abgeschritten. Jede Siedlung vertritt eine andere Etappe, eine andere, ganz spezifische Variante im breiten Spektrum der städtebaulichen und architektonischen Gestaltungsmöglichkeiten. Alle erlangten internationales Renommee, fanden in der internationalen Fachpresse Widerhall, wurden bereits zur damaligen Zeit von Fachinteressierten häufig besucht.

Die Nichtaufnahme anderer, qualitätvoller Wohnanlagen etwa der Architekten Mebes & Emmerich, Erwin Gutkind und Jean Krämer, begründet sich aus dem Gedanken, mit einer exemplarischen Auswahl das Ganze zu repräsentieren. Auch die Waldsiedlung Zehlendorf (auch Onkel-Tom-Siedlung genannt) von Bruno Taut, Otto Rudolf Salvisberg und Hugo Häring ist nicht zur Nominierung ausgewählt worden. Zum Zeitpunkt der Anmeldung der „Siedlungen der Berliner Moderne" 1999 zur Aufnahme in die Tentativliste der Bundesrepublik Deutschland war das Erscheinungsbild der Waldsiedlung noch stärker gestört als heute. Diese Beeinträchtigung der Authentizität traf vor allem für die Mehrzahl der in Privateigentum befindlichen 809 Reihenhäuser zu, die bereits kurz nach Errichtung als Eigenheime verkauft wurden. Zudem verkörpert die inmitten Zehlendorfer Villen liegende Waldsiedlung nicht im gleichen Maße die soziale Intention einer „Arbeitersiedlung" wie etwa die Hufeisensiedlung Britz oder die Wohnstadt Carl Legien. Überdies stellt sie auch städtebaulich und architektonisch keine Weiterentwicklung zur etwas älteren Britzer Hufeisensiedlung dar.

but monotonous, free and abstract spatial designs for modernist housing estates were tried out here

Großsiedlung Siemensstadt (Ringsiedlung, 1929–1931), a functional housing estate pointing the way to international modern urban development and thus anticipating the model of a spacious, structured city dotted by green spaces

Weiße Stadt (1929–1931) was designed by the Swiss architect Otto Rudolf Salvisberg, who was also responsible for the master plan, and the two Berlin architects Bruno Ahrends and Wilhelm Büning. Siemensstadt was mainly designed by Hans Scharoun, who also generated the master plan. Walter Gropius, Hugo Häring, Otto Bartning, Fred Forbat, Paul Rudolf Henning and Hans Scharoun himself designed the buildings. Both housing estates have become symbols of international modernist design in Berlin and beyond. Not only do they represent a paradigm shift in architecture and urban development, they also reflect a change in social structures, which was expressed by the development of mono-functional satellite housing estates with a clear division between spaces for living and working.

This meant that leading architects of classical modernism were involved in developing housing estates in Berlin. Bruno Taut's four housing estates, Weiße Stadt, and Siemensstadt reflect the development from garden town ideas to cityscapes in the spirit of Hans Scharoun. Each of the housing estates represents another stage, another and very specific variation within the broad range of urban and architectural design possibilities. All of them achieved international renown, were discussed by the international specialised press, and were frequently visited even at that early stage by interested experts.

The fact that other high quality estates – for instance by the architects Mebes & Emmerich, Erwin Gutkind and Jean Krämer – have not been included results from the idea that the chosen examples should stand for the entirety. Waldsiedlung (Forest housing estate), which is also called Onkel-Tom-Siedlung (Uncle Tom housing estate), by Bruno Taut, Otto Rudolf Salvisberg and Hugo Häring has not been nominated either. When the "housing estates of the Berlin Modern Age" were selected for entry in the provisional list of the Federal Republic of Germany, the appearance of Waldsiedlung was less true to the original than it is now. This impairment of authenticity referred mainly to the majority of the privately owned 809 row houses, which had already been sold to private owners shortly after they had been built. Moreover, Waldsiedlung, with its location right in the middle of Zehlendorf villas, does not reflect the social intention of a "working class housing estate" as much as is the case with the Hufeisensiedlung at Britz or Wohnstadt Carl Legien. In addition to this, it does not represent a higher stage in urban development and architecture in comparison with the slightly older Hufeisensiedlung at Britz.

Abb. 50: Gartenstadt Falkenberg, Haus Am Falkenberg 118 mit Spalieren, 2005

Fig. 50: Gartenstadt Falkenberg, trellises at semi-detached house Am Falkenberg 118, 2005

Abb. 51: Gartenstadt Falkenberg, Reihenhäuser Gartenstadtweg 16–30, 2005

Fig. 51: Gartenstadt Falkenberg, row houses at Gartenstadtweg 16–30, 2005

### Die einzelnen Siedlungen

### Gartenstadt Falkenberg

Die Gartenstadt Falkenberg in Berlin ist unter den Gartenstädten Europas die Farbige. Sie entstand 1913–1916 als Frühwerk des Architekten Bruno Taut, der hier erstmals kräftige, leuchtende Farben – Rot, Grün, Blau, Gelb – und auch Braun, Ocker, Schwarz und Weiß – in bis dahin nicht gewagten Kombinationen für den Außenanstrich von Siedlungshäusern anwandte. Damit gab Taut dem aus England übernommenen sozialen und städtebaulichen Modell der Gartenstadt, deren Verbreitung sich die Deutsche Gartenstadtgesellschaft, Initiatorin der Falkenberger Baugenossenschaft, verschrieben hatte, einen ganz eigenen künstlerischen Ausdruck. „Wir müssen die Farbe als absolut gleichberechtigt neben der Form anerkennen… Verachtet mir nicht dieses herrliche Gottesgeschenk, die reine, ungebrochene Farbe." (B. Taut, Architektonisches zum Siedlungswerk. In: Der Siedler (1)1918, S. 255)

Farbe, in der von Taut gewählten Intensität, soll die Sinne der Bewohner ansprechen, die in die knapp bemessenen, aber klug geschnittenen Reihenhäuser und Etagenwohnungen einziehen. Preiswerter als auch der einfachste skulpturale Schmuck, soll der Farbanstrich auf den Hauswänden, Gesimsen und Türen nicht nur Ausdruck, sondern auch Mittel einer grundlegenden Reform der Lebens- und Wahrnehmungsgewohnheiten sein. Die Berliner reagierten seinerzeit auf die provokative Farbenpracht der neuen Siedlung zunächst mit Unverständnis und versahen sie mit dem Spottnamen „Tuschkastensiedlung". Später gewöhnte man sich an die Farbigkeit und behielt die Bezeichnung bei.

In drei Bauabschnitten – 1913, 1914–15 und 1916 – entstanden zwei deutlich unterscheidbare Siedlungskomplexe, die einst Teile eines viel weiter ausgreifenden, nicht ver-

### The individual housing estates

### Gartenstadt Falkenberg

Among Europe's garden towns, Falkenberg is the most colourful. It was built in 1913–1916 as an early work by the architect Bruno Taut. For the first time, here he used full, bright colours: red, green, blue, yellow and also brown, ochre, black and white. He used them in combinations in which no one had dared using them to that date for painting the outside of residential buildings. In this way, Taut gave his very own artistic expression to the social and urban development model of the garden town which had been taken over from England. The purpose of the Deutsche Gartenstadtgesellschaft (German Garden Town Society), which had initiated the founding of the Falkenberg construction cooperative, was to further the dissemination of the garden town ideas. "We must accept colour as absolutely equal to form … Don't despise this marvellous gift of God: pure, unadulterated colour." (B. Taut, Architektonisches zum Siedlungswerk. In: Der Siedler (1) 1918, p. 255)

Colour in the intensity in which Taut used it is supposed to stimulate the senses of the inhabitants moving into the small but intelligently designed row houses and flats. Colour is cheaper than even the simplest plastic decoration, and the colourful painting of house walls, cornices and doors was to be not only an expression, but also a means of fundamentally reforming the habits of living and perceiving. Berliners at first did not understand this new provocative blaze of colour and called the estate "paint-box housing estate". Later they got used to its colourfulness and kept the name.

Two clearly different residential complexes were erected in three phases: 1913, 1914–15 and 1916. Originally they were to be parts of a much larger development that was not able to be built. Taut used patterns of urban development, which

wirklichten Gesamtentwurfes werden sollten. Die städtebaulichen Muster, die Taut zu Grunde legte, sind aus anderen Gartenstadtplanungen vertraut: der geschlossene Wohnhof (Akazienhof) und die der Geländesteigung folgende gebogene Wohnstraße (Gartenstadtweg). Jedoch finden sich auch hier schon das städtebaulich fein abgestimmte Bezugssystem aus kaum merklichen axialen Verschiebungen und die über raumbildende Fluchtlinien erreichte Einbeziehung des Straßenraumes, den Taut später als „Außenwohnraum" definierte. Der Akazienhof selber erscheint als Siedlungsbinnenraum, der, wie später das Hufeisen in der Großsiedlung in Britz, das genossenschaftliche Gemeinschaftsprinzip bildhaft vor Augen führen sollte.

Im Sinne eines kostensparenden, rationalisierten Bauens sind Hausformen und Grundrisse typisiert. Die Wohneinheiten sind klein, die Räume kleiner als in den durchschnittlichen Wohnungen in den Mietshäusern der Innenstadt Berlins, aber jede ist vollständig ausgestattet mit Küche, Bad und Garten. Die Hauseinheiten werden nur durch den Farbanstrich hervorgehoben. An den Mehrfamilienhäusern markierte Taut Eingänge und Wandfelder mit abstrakten geometrischen Mustern in lebhaft kontrastierender Farbgebung.

Bemerkenswert für die damalige Zeit ist die Beauftragung eines renommierten Gartenarchitekten wie Ludwig Lesser mit der Gestaltung der Gärten und der öffentlichen Freiräume. Lesser gelang es mit Straßenpflanzungen – gliedernden Alleen, Hecken und Baumreihen – die architektonisch markierten Raumwirkungen am Akazienhof und am Gartenstadtweg zu akzentuieren. Spaliere an den Fassaden mit Obstgehölzen und Kletterpflanzen führen zu unterschiedlichen Farbwirkungen in den Jahreszeiten.

Die Gärten sind ein wesentliches Element des besonderen Falkenberger Siedlungsbildes. In der planmäßigen Anlage von Kleingärten leistete Lesser Pionierarbeit. Durch die enge Zusammenarbeit mit Bruno Taut wurde erstmals dem Kleingarten eine große Bedeutung zugestanden und dieser in die Gesamtplanung mit einbezogen. Für die Bepflanzung der wohnungsbezogenen Nutzgärten, die im Sinn des Gartenstadtgedankens auch zur Selbstversorgung dienen sollten, stellte Lesser Vorschlagslisten zusammen und versuchte durch Vorträge auf die Gestaltung und die Nutzung der Gärten der Genossenschaftsmitglieder Einfluss zu nehmen. Auch wenn die Gärten unterschiedliche Größen aufwiesen und als reine Nutzgärten geplant und angelegt wurden, erfüllten sie doch den Anspruch, in Form von Gartenarbeit ein Gegengewicht zu der einseitigen Berufstätigkeit der Bewohner zu ermöglichen und zusätzlich einen bescheidenen Nutzen abzuwerfen. Die Wohnräume und die Küche liegen dementsprechend nach Möglichkeit zu ebener Erde, um einen bequemen Austritt ins Freie zu erreichen.

Die Gartenstadt Falkenberg ist in ihrer Mischung von Gartenstadtmustern und innovativer Farb- und Raumkomposition, ein einmaliges Zeugnis für den Variantenreichtum im Reformwohnungsbau und die Experimentierbereitschaft des Architekten und des Auftraggebers in der Zeit kurz vor 1914. Die vollkommen unkonventionelle Farbwahl und die ausdrücklich untektonische, malerische Farbkomposition rückt die Häuser der Gartenstadt als Kunstwerke in die Nähe der zeitgleichen expressionistischen

are familiar from other garden town developments: the closed courtyard (Akazienhof) and the curved residential street following the slope of a hill (Gartenstadtweg). However, we already find here the finely tuned urban structure of axes shifted so that it is hardly noticeable and the integration of the road space by means of building lines that create spaces. Taut defined this later as "Aussenwohnraum" (outdoor living space). Akazienhof itself seems to be a housing estate interior which was to reflect the cooperative community principle just like the horseshoe of the Großsiedlung Britz did later.

Houses and ground plans are standardised for saving money and rationalising construction. The residential units are small and the rooms are smaller than in the average flats in the tenement houses in the inner-city areas, but here at Falkenberg each of the flats has a kitchen, a bathroom and a garden. Only the difference in colour marks the limits of the residential units. For the multiple dwellings, Taut marked entrance doors and wall sections with abstract geometrical patterns in colours that stood out in lively contrast.

At that time it was quite remarkable that the renowned garden architect Ludwig Lesser was employed for designing the gardens and public outdoor facilities. By means of green spaces accompanying the streets – avenues, hedges and rows of trees – Lesser managed to highlight the spaces created by architecture at Akazienhof and Gartenstadtweg. Trellises on the facades bearing fruit trees and climbers make the colours change with the seasons.

The gardens are an essential element of the particular Falkenberg housing estate image. Lesser was a pioneer in designing small gardens (allotment gardens). His close cooperation with Bruno Taut ensured that for the first time the allotment gardens were treated as very important and therefore included in the master plan. Lesser produced lists proposing plants to be planted in the gardens for partial self-sufficiency in the sense of the garden town idea and he tried to influence garden design and use by the cooperative members by holding lectures. Although the sizes of the gardens varied and they were originally designed and created as pure kitchen gardens, they still fulfilled the claim of providing a counterweight to the one-sided employment of the inhabitants and making a modest contribution to their self-sufficiency in food supply. In order to facilitate stepping outside, the living rooms and kitchens are usually located on ground floor level.

With its mix of garden town patterns and innovative composition of colour and space, Gartenstadt Falkenberg is a unique example for the wealth of variation in reform housing development and the interest in experimenting of architects and clients shortly before 1914. With the completely unconventional choice of colours and the expressly non-tectonic picturesque combination of colours, the houses of Gartenstadt Falkenberg are close to the contemporary expressionist paintings in which artists like Marc, Kandinsky or Nolde used brilliant "false" colours – blue riders and horses, red and green cows, yellow figures of Christ. The closest analogy is a painting by Kandinsky – "Dame in Moskau" (Lady in Moscow) from 1912 – which shows a complex dream vision in which two rows of low

Abb. 52: Siedlung Schillerpark, rotbunte Ziegelfassade mit Betonelementen an der Bristolstraße, 2005

Fig. 52: Siedlung Schillerpark, facade of bricks in various shades of red with concrete elements at Bristolstraße, 2005

Bildkunst, in der Maler wie Marc, Kandinsky oder Nolde ihre Gegenstände mit leuchtend-"falschen" Farben – blaue Reiter und Pferde, rote und grüne Kühe, gelbe Christusfiguren – darstellten.

Die Falkenberger Baugenossenschaft verdankte ihre Entstehung einer Initiative der „Deutschen Gartenstadtgesellschaft", die Kern und ideologisches Zentrum der Gartenstadtbewegung war und deren Protagonisten Hans und Bernhard Kampffmeyer, Adolf Otto, Hermann Salomon und Albert Kohn der Baugenossenschaft vorstanden. Den bürgerlich-gemäßigten Reformideen der Gartenstadtbewegung folgend, dachten die Erbauer von Falkenberg keineswegs daran, nur Bewohner aus minderbemittelten Bevölkerungskreisen vorzusehen. Ihr Leitbild war ein Gemeinwesen, in dem ohne Klassenschranken auf einer genossenschaftlichen Basis zusammengelebt wird und die Bewohner im Idealfall auch gemeinsam im Handwerk, in Landwirtschaft und Industrie ihren Lebensunterhalt erarbeiten. Dies erfordert Wohnungsangebote mit unterschiedlichen Maßen und Grundrissen, damit jeder nach seinem Bedarf und seinen Mitteln leben kann. Die Gartenstadt Falkenberg sollte nach dem Willen ihrer Gründer möglichst verschiedenartige Grundrisslösungen und Variationsmöglichkeiten des Kleinhauses mit Garten vorführen, als eine Art Mustersiedlung, die den Gartenstadtgedanken veranschaulichen und für ihn werben sollte.

### Siedlung Schillerpark

Die 1924–30 von Bruno Taut in drei Abschnitten geschaffene Siedlung Schillerpark belegt mit ihren stark gegliederten Ziegelfassaden den Einfluss der Schule von Amsterdam auf die Baukunst Bruno Tauts: Die bevorzugt abgebildete Baufront an der Bristolstraße zeigt eine expressive und zugleich sachliche Architektur, detailreicher als seine späteren Entwürfe.

houses in "false" colours, each of them with a different colour, frame the middle ground.

The Falkenberg construction cooperative had been founded on the initiative of the "Deutsche Gartenstadtgesellschaft", which was the core and ideological centre of the garden town movement and whose protagonists Hans and Bernhard Kampffmeyer, Adolf Otto, Hermann Salomon and Albert Kohn were the executive members of the cooperative. In line with the bourgeois moderate reform ideas of the garden town movement, the builders of Falkenberg did not intend at all to erect it only for people from the low income groups. Their model was a community in which people lived together without class divisions on a cooperative basis and in which ideally the inhabitants of the housing estate would earn their living in a cooperation of trades, agriculture and industry. This required housing facilities with a variety of dimensions and ground plans so that everyone would have a space for living in line with his/her needs and means. At Gartenstadt Falkenberg, its founders wanted to present as much variation as possible of ground plans and small houses with gardens so that the estate could become a kind of sample housing estate representing the garden town idea while advertising for it.

### Siedlung Schillerpark

The Siedlung Schillerpark was created by Bruno Taut in three phases in 1924–30. Its very structured brick facades reflect the influence of the Amsterdam school on Bruno Taut's architecture: The building front at Bristolstraße, which is a favourite for photos of the estate, shows both expressive and functional architecture with more wealth of detail than his later designs.

Schillerpark is the first cooperative large urban housing estate in Berlin that unites in it nearly ideally all the typical features of Neues Bauen. The builder "Berliner Spar- und Bauverein" (Berlin Savings and Construction Association), together with their architect Bruno Taut, were pioneers of reform housing. Here, within this Wedding housing estate, they tested for the first time the model of a modern urban housing estate under the conditions of the new Berlin building regulations and the grant system of the mortgage servicing tax. The unconventional flat-roofed buildings were to represent the "New Berlin" as it had been proclaimed by urban development councillor Martin Wagner.

At Schillerpark, Taut transferred the achievements of reform housing development created since 1892 for the Berlin construction associations and cooperatives by Alfred Messel, Paul Kolb, Erich Köhn, Paul Mebes and others to a new stage of modernisation of urban development, types of ground plans and styles. He did preserve the block margin pattern of the traditional Berlin building regulation to the extent of arranging the buildings parallel to the street and creating large courtyards inside the blocks. However, these blocks are open at their joints and the ribbons of buildings at the block margin are arranged in parallel pairs: two in a north-south direction with entrances in the west and balconies in the west and two in a west-east direction with entrances in the north and balconies in the south. With this systematic integration of block margin and rib-

Schillerpark ist das erste baugenossenschaftliche großstädtische Wohnprojekt Berlins, das in geradezu idealtypischer Weise alle Merkmale des Neuen Bauens vereinigt. Der „Berliner Spar- und Bauverein", nahm als Bauherr zusammen mit seinem Architekten Bruno Taut eine wohnungsreformerische Vorreiterrolle ein. Hier auf dem Weddinger Siedlungsgelände wurde erstmals unter den Bedingungen der neuen Berliner Bauordnung und dem Fördersystem der Hauszinssteuer das Modell einer modernen städtischen Wohnanlage erprobt. In den unkonventionellen, flachgedeckten Siedlungshäusern sollte sich das „Neue Berlin" offenbaren, so wie es Stadtbaurat Martin Wagner verkündet hatte.

Am Schillerpark führte Taut die Errungenschaften des Reformwohnungsbaus, die Alfred Messel, Paul Kolb, Erich Köhn, Paul Mebes und andere seit 1892 für Berliner Bauvereine und Genossenschaften entwickelt hatten, in ein neues Stadium der städtebaulichen, grundrisstypologischen und stilistischen Modernisierung. Er behielt das Blockrandschema der traditionellen Berliner Bauordnung insofern bei, als er die Baukörper parallel zur Straße anordnete und im Inneren große Wohnhöfe anlegte. Allerdings sind die Baublöcke an den Gelenkstellen geöffnet, und die Häuserzeilen am Blockrand paarweise parallel geordnet: zwei nord-südlich, mit Eingängen im Westen und Balkonen im Osten und zwei west-östlich, mit Eingängen im Norden und Balkonen im Süden. Mit dieser systematischen Integration von Blockrand- und Zeilenbauschema ist Taut innovativ, bleibt aber der Tradition der Reformarchitektur verpflichtet.

Taut plante in der Schillerparksiedlung Wohnungen für verschiedene Einkommensschichten bei gleichem Standard und unterschiedlichen Größen, mit separaten Bädern und Küchen und großzügigen, zur Sonne orientierten Loggien und Balkonen. Die Hausfronten spiegeln den Grundrissaufbau wider, die aus der steinernen Stadt des 19. Jahrhunderts vertraute fassadenhafte Höherbewertung der Straßenseite ist überholt. Die Bauten erscheinen als umschreitbare Körper, sind von allen Seiten gleichermaßen schön. Bei der Grundsteinlegung im Jahr 1924 verkündete Taut mit der Losung „Für die neue Volkswohnung – für die neue Baukunst Berlins!" den Beginn einer neuen Ära des Mietwohnungsbaus. Die Schillerparksiedlung wurde zum Leitbild des sozialen Siedlungsbaus der 1920er Jahre in Berlin.

Die übersichtliche Gestaltung der Grünräume und ihre Gliederung in Funktionsbereiche harmonisiert ausgezeichnet mit der rationalen Siedlungsarchitektur. Wie in allen Siedlungen Tauts sind die öffentlichen und halböffentlichen Flächen integraler Teil eines ganzheitlichen sozialen Raumkonzepts. Höfe oder andere umbaute Grünräume dienen hier nicht nur zur solidarischen Identifikation der genossenschaftlichen Bewohner mit ihrer Siedlung. Sie sind auch elementarer Teil des von Taut definierten Außenwohnraumes. Es entstand eine eigene siedlungstypische Binnenstruktur mit einer engen Verzahnung von Innen- und Außenwohnräumen, verdeutlicht durch axiale Blickbeziehungen, und vor allem durch dem Grün zugewandte Loggien und Balkone vor den großen Wohnräumen. Exemplarisch wird ein neuartiges Siedlungsbild mit ineinander verflochtenen Grünräumen vorgeführt, wie wir es im Siedlungsbau der 1950er Jahre wiederfinden.

bon patterns, Taut is innovative and yet he continues the tradition of architectural reform.

For the Schillerpark estate, Taut planned flats for various income levels with uniform standards and various sizes, having dedicated bathrooms and kitchens and spacious loggias and balconies orientated towards the sun. The house facades reflect the ground plans. He does not treat the street front facades with preference as was done in the stone cities of the 19th century. The buildings appear as bodies for walking around. All of their sides are equally beautiful. When the foundation stone was laid in 1924, Taut proclaimed the beginning of a new era in rental housing development with the slogan "For a new popular flat – for a new architecture of Berlin". Schillerpark became the model for social residential development of the 1920s in Berlin.

The clear design of the green spaces and their subdivision into functional spaces harmonise very well with the rational architecture of the houses. As in all housing estates designed by Taut, the public and semi-public areas are an integral part of the holistic social concept of space. Yards and other green spaces surrounded by buildings not only support the identification and solidarity of the inhabitants with their housing estates. They are also an essential part of the outdoor living space as defined by Taut. The result is a characteristic type of internal structure of the housing estates with a close integration of indoor and outdoor living spaces. This is emphasised by axial views and especially by loggias and balconies in front of the main living rooms looking out at the green spaces. The estate is an exemplary presentation of a novel housing estate image with integrated green spaces as we find it again in the residential developments of the 1950s.

Hans Hoffmann, chief architect of the construction cooperative, introduced a new model – that of "transparent living" – with his buildings which were constructed after the

Abb. 53: Siedlung Schillerpark, Blocköffnung zur Oxforder Straße, 2005

Fig. 53: Siedlung Schillerpark, block opening towards Oxforder Straße, 2005

Ein neues Leitbild, das des „transparenten Wohnens", führte Hans Hoffmann, Chefarchitekt der Baugenossenschaft, mit seinen ergänzenden Siedlungsbauten für den unfertig gebliebenen dritten Bauabschnitt in der Nachkriegszeit ein. Hoffmann entwickelte eine originelle Komposition aus Taut'scher sowie eigener Architektursprache. Mit großflächiger, geschoßhoher Verglasung, durchgehenden Balkonen und begehbaren Blumenfenstern erzielte er eine hohe Transparenz der Fassaden – definierte so den für Taut wichtigen Bezug zum Außenwohnraum, zum Siedlungsfreiraum, auf eine zeitgemäße Weise. Mit entscheidend für das klare, in seiner scheinbaren Sparsamkeit ästhetisch höchst wirksame Bild sind die Treppenhausachsen. Sie liegen als gläserne Membran in der Mauerflucht, wobei geschossübergreifende Stahlsprossen die Leichtigkeit und Transparenz der Wirkung noch verstärken.

Die von dem Gartenarchitekten Walter Rossow gestalteten Freiräume unterstützen die Wirkung der feingliedrigen Architektur Hans Hoffmanns. Charakteristisch ist der durch die Blickbeziehungen erlebbare rhythmisierte Wechsel von offenen und geschlossenen bzw. öffentlichen, halböffentlichen und privaten Räumen wie den Mietergärten. Dies wurde durch die Verwendung unterschiedlicher Materialien und Gestaltungselemente wie Bossenmauern und Geländemodellierungen und vor allem durch die größere Vielfalt und Staffelung in den Pflanzungen unterstützt.

Bei der zusammenhängenden Betrachtung der Außenanlagen in der Siedlung Schillerpark sind die einzelnen Epochen in der Entwicklung der Freiflächengestaltung gut ablesbar. Die streng funktionalistischen Taut-Höfe kontrastieren mit der Gestaltung des Außenraumes an der Oxforder Straße von Hans Hoffmann und Walter Rossow mit den locker eingestellten Birken und dem in die Rasenfläche integriertem Spielbereich.

### Großsiedlung Britz (Hufeisensiedlung)

Das Hufeisen, städtebauliches Zentrum der „Großsiedlung Britz", gilt seit langem geradezu als Wahrzeichen des Berliner Siedlungsbaus der 1920er Jahre. Die Siedlung, 1925–30 von Bruno Taut und Martin Wagner geschaffen, ist die erste deutsche Großsiedlung mit mehr als 1.000 Wohnungen. Sie wurde unter dem einprägsamen Namen „Hufeisensiedlung" zum Inbegriff eines neuen sozialen Städtebaus, der auch für untere Bevölkerungsschichten ein würdiges, gesundes und menschenfreundliches Wohnen ermöglichen sollte.

Die Hufeisensiedlung ist die erste Mustersiedlung der GEHAG, einer Gründung von Sozialdemokraten und freien Gewerkschaften. Die „Gemeinnützige Heimstätten, Spar- und Bau-Aktiengesellschaft" (GEHAG), Teil eines von Wagner initiierten Netzwerkes gemeinwirtschaftlicher Wohnungsfürsorge, entwickelte sich in enger Teamarbeit mit ihrem Chefarchitekten Bruno Taut zum maßgeblichen Träger für das Modell der Großsiedlung in Berlin. Mit der Hufeisensiedlung sollte die Verbundorganisation genossenschaftlicher und gewerkschaftlicher Unternehmen als Gegenmodell zur Privatwirtschaft und als leistungsstärkere Variante zur staatlichen Wohnbaupolitik erprobt werden.

war to complement the incomplete third phase of the development. Hoffman created an original composition from Taut's and his own style of architecture. Large glass panels over the entire height of the storeys, gallery-like balconies and walk-in flower windows make the facades very transparent. This is how Hoffmann defined in a contemporary way the link with outdoor living space and open space in an estate that had been so important for Taut. One of the decisive factors for this image, which is very efficiently aesthetic for all its apparent economy, are the staircase axes. They are embedded in the walls' fronts like glass membranes and the steel lattices reaching over several storeys increase this impression of weightlessness and transparency.

The outdoor facilities were designed by the garden architect Walter Rossow and support the image created by Hans Hoffmann's finely structured architecture. The rhythmic change between open and closed or respectively public, semi-public and private spaces, like the tenants' gardens that can be experienced visually, is characteristic for this image. The impression is supported by the use of various kinds of material and design elements like bossed walls and landscaping and especially by a greater variety and staggering of plants.

When considering the outdoor facilities of the Siedlung Schillerpark in their entirety, it is easy to discern the individual phases of their development. The strictly functional yards by Taut contrast with the design of outdoor spaces at Oxforder Straße by Hans Hoffmann and Walter Rossow, with their scattered birches and the playground that is integrated into the lawn.

### Großsiedlung Britz (Hufeisensiedlung)

The horseshoe at the centre of "Großsiedlung Britz" has been virtually the symbol for Berlin residential development in the 1920s for quite a long time already. The housing estate was created in 1925–30 by Bruno Taut and Martin Wagner and is the first German large housing estate with more than 1,000 flats. Under the name of "Hufeisensiedlung" (Horseshoe Estate), which is very easy to remember, it has become the symbol for a new social form of urban development that was intended to also provide decent, healthy and humane housing for people with low incomes.

The Hufeisensiedlung is the first model estate of GEHAG founded by Social Democrats and free trade unions. GEHAG ("Gemeinnützige Heimstätten-Spar- und Bau-AG", Non-Profit Housing Savings and Building Shareholding Company), which had a close cooperation with its chief architect Bruno Taut and which was part of the network for non-profit housing welfare initiated by Wagner, had become the main developer of the model large housing estates in Berlin. With the Hufeisensiedlung, they wanted to test the association of cooperative and trade union companies as a model in opposition to private developers and they wanted to show that it was more efficient than state housing programmes.

Taut and Wagner developed an extraordinarily impressive urban development plan for this estate. The buildings designed by Taut in conjunction with the open green spaces

Der von Taut und Wagner entworfene Siedlungsplan ist von außerordentlicher städtebaulicher Prägnanz. Die Bauten Bruno Tauts und die von Leberecht Migge entworfenen und von Wagler ausgeführten offenen Grünräume und Mietergärten fügen sich heute, gut 70 Jahre nach der ersten Pflanzung, zu einer Wohnlandschaft zusammen, deren Entwurfsqualität in Europa ihresgleichen sucht.

Taut konnte hier seine in Falkenberg erprobte Entwurfsmethodik verfeinern: das Versatzspiel mit Symmetrie und Asymmetrie der Baugruppen und Straßenräume, die unmerklichen axialen Verschiebungen und behutsamen räumlichen Verfremdungen, den elementaren Einsatz von Farbe zur Raumgestaltung. Das politisch und organisatorisch Neue der genossenschaftlichen Großsiedlung fand indes vor allem in dem zentralen, raumbildenden Hufeisenrund einen kraftvollen architektonischen Ausdruck. In ihm manifestieren sich ebenso Fortschrittsglaube und Rationalisierung des Neuen Bauens wie Kollektivität und Solidarität der Genossenschaftsidee. An der offenen Ostseite des Hufeisens legte Taut einen repräsentativen Siedlungseingang an, der mit breiter Freitreppe hinab in die vom Baukörper eingefasste Grünanlage führt. Es ist die von Leberecht Migge aufgegriffene Topographie, die einen eiszeitlichen Teich zum Zentrum der gartenkünstlerischen Inszenierung macht.

Ebenso wie Bruno Taut und Martin Wagner durch Typisierung eine Rationalisierung im Siedlungsbau und somit die Senkung der Baukosten zu erreichen versuchten, tritt Migge für eine Übertragung dieser modernen Arbeitsmethoden auf die Anlage der Siedlungsgärten ein. Der Siedlergarten sollte möglichst in vielen Teilen normiert, in der Gestaltung rationalisiert aufgebaut und unter Zuhilfenahme verfeinerter Organisationsmethoden im Arbeitsprozess möglichst seriell erstellt werden.

and tenants' gardens designed by Leberecht Migge and built by Wagner have, within the 70 years since the first greenery was planted, become a residential landscape with a design quality that is unique in Europe.

Here, Taut was able to refine the design method which he had tested at Falkenberg: the playing with symmetry and asymmetry of groups of buildings and street spaces, the barely discernible shifts of axes, the subtle spatial alienations and the elementary use of colour for creating spaces. Yet, the novel political and organisational aspects of the cooperative large housing estate find its powerful architectural expression primarily in the central horseshoe that determines the spatial shape. This horseshoe expresses both the belief in progress and rationalisation of Neues Bauen as well as the collectivity and solidarity in the cooperative model. On the open eastern side of the horseshoe, Taut created a representative entrance to the housing estate with a wide sweep of stairs going down into the green space which is surrounded by the ribbon of buildings. Leberecht Migge used the existing topography and turned the glacial pond into the centre of an artistic scenery of garden architecture.

Bruno Taut and Martin Wagner tried to rationalise housing construction and thus reduce construction costs by means of standardisation. Migge applied these modern working methods to the creation of the gardens. He planned largely standardised gardens for inhabitants, gardens with rational design that were to be created as far as possible in serial production by means of refined methods of organising the working process.

In the Hufeisensiedlung, Taut was able to create a highly artistic fusion of the already existing urban development idea of the garden town and the more novel concept of the large housing estate. While the horseshoe, formed by a flat-roofed 360-metre long curved ribbon of buildings with a

Abb. 54: Großsiedlung Britz, Gartenstadtatmosphäre, Hausgärten im Bauabschnitt I/II, 2005

Fig. 54: Großsiedlung Britz, garden town atmosphere, house gardens in development phase I/II, 2005

Mit der Hufeisensiedlung gelang Taut die kunstvolle Verschmelzung der städtebaugeschichtlich älteren Gartenstadt-idee mit dem neueren Konzept der Großsiedlung. Während das Hufeisen, eine flach gedeckte, 360 Meter lange, gebogene Wohnzeile mit streng seriellem Grundriss, für das Bild der landschaftlich konzipierten Großsiedlung steht, ist der westlich anschließende, rhombenförmig umbaute kleine Platz, der nicht zufällig „Hüsung" benannt wurde, mit seinen Satteldachreihenhäusern und seinem Baumbestand in der Platzmitte ein Gartenstadtmotiv. Es ist mit Tauts Akazienhof in der Gartenstadt Falkenberg verwandt und darf mit den ostdeutschen Angerdörfern assoziiert werden.

Ganz im Sinne seiner Abneigung gegen dogmatische Festlegungen spielte Taut souverän mit den Vorzügen und Eigenarten der Gartenstadt und den abstrakteren Mustern der Großsiedlung, wobei er Blockrand-, Zeilen-, und Reihenfigurationen stets so einsetzte, dass eine klare Abgrenzung von privaten, halböffentlichen und öffentlichen Räumen entstand. Dort, wo er, wie im Umfeld des Hufeisens, zu größeren Einheiten zusammengefasste Reihenhäuser straßenbegleitend anordnete, rückt er sie gruppenweise zur Straße oder zum Garten, mal parallel, mal gespiegelt und schuf so abwechslungsreiche Wohnstraßen. Dort, wo er Reihenhäuser in Zeilen parallel stellte, wie im sechsten Bauabschnitt südlich der Parchimer Allee, schob er jeweils einen Kopfbau an den Anfang der Zeile so in den Straßen- und Grünraum vor, dass die sonst im Zeilenbau übliche Durchlässigkeit der Siedlungsflanken vermieden wird.

Hier in Britz, weit außerhalb der Mietskasernenviertel, konnte Taut seine Vision eines offenen, durchgrünten Städtebaus in einem größeren Maßstab umsetzen. Die künstlerische Forderung nach Modernität und Sachlichkeit der Form und die soziale Forderung nach Licht, Luft und Sonne werden hier gleichermaßen eingelöst. So begründeten Bruno Taut und Martin Wagner mit der Hufeisensiedlung ihren internationalen Ruf als sozialreformerische Architekten und Stadtplaner der 1920er Jahre.

Abb. 55: Großsiedlung Britz, Hufeisen mit eiszeitlichem Pfuhl, 2000

Fig. 55: Großsieclung Britz, horseshoe with the glacial pond, 2000

strictly serial ground plan, represents the image of the large, landscaped housing estate, the small adjacent diamond-shaped square to the west with its gable-roofed row houses and the trees in its middle is a garden town motif. It is not for nothing that it is called "Hüsung". This square is a relative of Taut's Akazienhof at Falkenberg and can be associated with the East German village greens.

Taut never liked dogmatic fixation and thus competently toyed with the advantages and features of the garden town and the more abstract patterns of the large housing estate. In doing so, he always used block margin, ribbon and row houses in such a way that they created clear separations between private, semi-public and public spaces. Where he arranged groups of row houses along the streets (for instance near the horseshoe), he placed these groups alternatingly closer to the street or to the gardens, parallel or mirrored – thus creating residential streets with varying patterns. Where he arranged row houses in parallel ribbons as in the sixth development phase south of Parchimer Allee, he always made one head building at the beginning of the row project into the street and green space so as to avoid the penetrability of the flanks, which is otherwise so typical for ribbon development.

Here at Britz, far away from the tenement quarters, Taut had the opportunity to implement on a large scale his vision of open urban development mixed with green spaces. Here he fulfils the artistic demand for modernity and functionality and, to an equal extent, the social demand for light, air and sunshine. With the Hufeisensiedlung, both Bruno Taut and Martin Wagner established their international reputation as architects and urban planners in the 1920s who supported social reforms.

## Wohnstadt Carl Legien

Of the Berlin housing estates of social housing development during the Weimar Republic, "Wohnstadt Carl Legien" is the most urbane and compact one. It occupies a special position among the works by Bruno Taut. Shortly before Brüning's emergency laws came into force in 1930, which deprived these trade union and non-profit residential developments of the necessary grants, Taut was able once more to present in a programmatic way the most important innovations of modern mass housing development. This project was also financed by GEHAG. On the edge of the inner-city district of Prenzlauer Berg and in the neighbourhood of densely packed tenements, Taut proved that the principles of Neues Bauen also made it possible to build "urban" estates.

Here it was not possible to use an open composition as at Britz or the Waldsiedlung at Zehlendorf. In this case, Taut was obliged to use the inner-city patterns of spatial structure consisting of blocks and streets which he expressly rejected. Moreover, he had to do so in an area whose main structure had been defined in the master plan by Hobrecht in 1862. The particular achievement of Taut's urban development plan is that he was able to invent a structure for the streets and blocks which provides the inhabitants with spaciousness, outdoor facilities and air with lots of green spaces despite the fact that the design is close to the spatial

## Wohnstadt Carl Legien

Die „Wohnstadt Carl Legien" ist die urbanste und kompakteste unter den Berliner Siedlungen des sozialen Wohnungsbaus der Weimarer Republik. Sie nimmt im Schaffen Bruno Tauts eine Sonderstellung ein. Kurz vor der Einführung der Brüning'schen Notverordnung 1930, die derartigen gewerkschaftlich-gemeinnützigen Wohnprojekten die Fördermittel entzog, gelang es Taut im Auftrag der GEHAG noch einmal, die wichtigsten Neuerungen des modernen Massenwohnungsbaus programmatisch vorzuführen. Am Rand des innerstädtischen Bezirks Prenzlauer Berg, in der Nachbarschaft dichter Mietshausviertel bewies Taut, dass man mit den Grundsätzen des Neuen Bauens auch „städtisch" bauen kann.

Eine freie, offene Siedlungskomposition wie in Britz oder in der Waldsiedlung Zehlendorf war hier nicht möglich. Taut musste also mit Block und Straße die innerstädtischen Raumordnungsschemata nutzen, die er ausdrücklich ablehnte. Und das in einem Gebiet, dessen Struktur durch die Hobrecht'sche Bebauungsplanung von 1862 großräumig festgelegt war. Die besondere städtebauliche Leistung Tauts besteht darin, dass es ihm gelang, eine Straßen- und Blockeinteilung zu erfinden, die den Bewohnern trotz der räumlichen und typologischen Nähe zur Stadt des späten 19. Jahrhunderts und trotz der aus wirtschaftlichen Gründen erforderlichen hohen Dichte die Großzügigkeit, Offenheit und Luftigkeit einer durchgrünten Siedlung bietet.

Er gliederte das große, rechteckige Baugebiet, dessen Querachse durch die Carmen-Sylva-Straße, die heutige Erich-Weinert-Straße, bereits festgelegt war, durch drei rechtwinklig über die Achse gelegte schmale Erschließungsstraßen in sechs sehr tiefe, rechteckige Baublöcke. Langgestreckte Zeilen bilden an den Erschließungsstraßen Blockränder, dazwischen liegen recht weite und blocktiefe Gartenflächen, die an den äußeren Enden mit Querriegeln geschlossen sind, sich jedoch zur Mitte hin öffnen. Es ergibt sich eine Figur aus je drei U-förmigen Wohnhöfen beiderseits der Erich-Weinert-Straße, die durch begleitende Grünanlagen zu einer Art Siedlungsboulevard aufgeweitet ist.

Taut griff mithin im städtebaulichen Entwurf auf das ältere Schema der Blockrandbebauung zurück, vertauschte dabei aber die Seiten und stellte gleichsam das alte hierarchische Mietskasernensystem auf den Kopf. Die gärtnerisch gestalteten Höfe wurden zum Mittelpunkt des Wohnens, während die schmalen Straßen nachrangige Bedeutung erhielten. Konsequent legte Taut alle Wohnräume mit ihren wohnungsbreiten Loggien oder vorgestellten Lauben an die Gartenhöfe und Nebenräume wie Bad oder Küche an die Straße. Im Sinne der Orientierung aller Wohnungen zum Garten sind die Zeilengrundrisse also gespiegelt und nicht gereiht.

Zum Erkennungsbild der Wohnstadt wurde die Ansicht der großzügig bemessenen und bepflanzten Erich-Weinert-Straße mit der Sequenz der fünfgeschossigen Kopfbauten an den Enden der Wohnzeilen. Die geschwungenen Eckbalkone leiten den Blick von den Straße in die Wohnhöfe. Die Fassaden der Schmalseiten sind zu Schildwänden erhöht, die die Schräge der Pultdächer und die Dachtraufen unsichtbar machen. Die Steigerung der Baumassen und die

structures and types of the late 19th century city and also despite the fact that the economic situation required considerable density.

The axis of the large square site had already been defined: Carmen-Sylva-Straße, today's Erich-Weinert-Straße. Taut divided the square into six very deep rectangular blocks by three narrow access roads, which he placed at right angles to the axis. Long ribbons form block margins along the access roads and between them are quite wide garden spaces, which are as deep as the blocks and closed at the extreme ends by cross bar buildings. Towards the middle, these blocks remain open. This creates a figure of three U-shaped courtyards on either side of Erich-Weinert-Straße, which is turned into a kind of boulevard by the accompanying green spaces.

This shows that Taut reverted to the older urban development pattern of block margin development, but he exchanged sides, thus turning the old hierarchical tenement system upside down. The garden-like courtyards became the centres for living, whereas the significance of the narrow streets was reduced. Taut consistently arranged all living rooms with the full-width balconies or loggias in front of the rooms on the courtyard side, and auxiliary rooms such as bathrooms or kitchens are orientated towards the streets. This means that in order to ensure that the living rooms are orientated towards the gardens, the ground plans of the ribbons are mirrored and not sequenced.

The view of the generously dimensioned Erich-Weinert-Straße with lots of greenery and the sequence of five-storeyed head buildings at the end of the ribbons became the symbol for this residential estate. The rounded balconies at the corners guide the view from the street into the courtyards. The facades on the narrow sides are designed as shield walls. They are higher than the single-pitch roofs and eaves, thus making them invisible. In this main view with the increased volumes and the concentration of architectural motifs on both sides of Erich-Weinert-Straße, the estate gains a monumental urban quality that emanates far into its environment.

Abb. 56: Weiße Stadt, Torbauten von Bruno Ahrends fassen die Aroser Allee am südlichen Eingang zur Siedlung ein, 2005

Fig. 56: Weiße Stadt, gate buildings designed by Bruno Ahrends frame Aroser Allee at the southern entrance to the housing estate, 2005

Konzentration architektonischer Motive beiderseits der Erich-Weinert-Straße verleihen der Wohnstadt in dieser Hauptansicht eine urbane Monumentalität, die weit in die umgebenden Stadträume ausstrahlt.

Nur der nord-östliche Hof ist durch eine vorgestellte eingeschossige Ladenzeile geschlossen. Im Übrigen ist die Grenze zwischen Siedlungsboulevard und den Gärten im Inneren der Blöcke nur durch die Bepflanzung markiert, der Blick der Bewohner soll aus ihrer Loggia bis zur Straße und in den gegenüberliegenden Gartenhof schweifen. So erzeugte Taut auf dem engen verfügbaren Raum einen Eindruck von Weite und Durchlässigkeit. Die im Grundriss optimal organisierten Kleinwohnungen mit ihren geräumigen Sonnenloggien wurden zu einem Sinnbild der neuen Wohnkultur, ein völlig neuer Typus von Großstadtwohnung, dessen Wohnqualitäten noch heute überzeugen.

Die Gestaltung der Freiräume der Wohnstadt Carl Legien fügte sich nicht nur in die städtebauliche Komposition der Anlage ein oder unterstützte die Wirkung der Architektur, sondern bildete mit ihr eine untrennbare Einheit. Die konsequente Anwendung städtebaulicher und architektonischer Vorstellungen des modernen Siedlungsbaus in Bezug auf die Gestaltung der Fassaden und der klaren räumlichen Gliederung der Baukörper wurden hier augenscheinlich von Bruno Taut auf die Freiräume übertragen. Ähnlich der Akzentuierung der einheitlichen Fassadenfronten durch das farbliche Absetzen der Fenster, Haustüren und Treppenhäuser oder der markanten Loggien und Balkone ließen die mit dezenten und minimalen gartenarchitektonischen Gestaltungselementen (in Höhen gestufte Hecken, einige wenige Solitärbäume und den Robiniengruppen an den Kopfbauten an der Erich- Weinert-Straße) gegliederten Rasenteppiche eine klare und einheitliche, aber ebenso lebendige Raumwirkung entstehen.

## Weiße Stadt

Die 1931 vollendete Großsiedlung Schillerpromenade ist unter der Bezeichnung „Weiße Stadt" schon bald nach ihrer Fertigstellung als Inbild des modernen Siedlungsbaus gefeiert worden. Ob nun unter den Begriff „Neues Bauen", „Funktionalismus" oder „International Style" subsummiert – die Siedlung passte in den Fortschrittsdiskurs der Architektur-

Abb. 57: Wohnstadt Carl Legien, Siedlungsboulevard Erich-Weinert-Straße. 2005

Fig. 57: Wohnstadt Carl Legien, housing estate-boulevard Erich-Weinert-Straße, 2005

Only the northeastern yard is closed by a single-storey ribbon of shops that were placed in front. Otherwise the limit between the boulevard and the gardens inside the blocks is marked only by the greenery, such that the inhabitants of the flats have an open view from their loggias to the street and into the opposite garden courtyard. In this way, Taut created the impression of spaciousness and penetrability within the rather limited space. The small flats with their optimally organised ground plans and spacious sunny loggias became symbols for a new culture of living – an entirely new type of city flat whose qualities are convincing even today.

The design of the outdoor facilities of Wohnstadt Carl Legien was not only integrated into the urban composition of the estate or supported the impact of its architecture, but it was an inseparable part of architecture. Obviously Bruno Taut transferred here to the outdoor facilities his consistent application of urban development and architectural ideas of modern residential development, which he had used in designing the facades and the clear structures of the buildings. Just like he used colour for windows, entrance doors and staircases or the shapes of loggias and balconies to vary the uniform facades, he created clearly structured, uniform and yet lively spaces by means of unobtrusive and minimal garden design elements (hedges with staggered heights, a small number of solitary trees and groups of robinias at the head buildings at Erich-Weinert-Straße) within lawn carpets.

## Weiße Stadt

Soon after its completion in 1931, the large estate was celebrated as a symbol of modern residential development. Its original name had been Schillerpromenade, but it became known as "Weiße Stadt". No matter what you called it – Neues Bauen or functionalism or international style – the housing estate fit into the dispute about progress in architecture as precisely as the artfully exalted sequences of images showing clear, cubic, white buildings which were published worldwide in books and journals around 1930 and later. Under the guidance of urban development councillor Martin Wagner, the Berlin architects Wilhelm Büning and Bruno Ahrends, as well as their Swiss colleague Otto Rudolf Salvisberg, worked here. The outdoor facilities were designed by Ludwig Lesser.

Otto Rudolf Salvisberg's urban development plan combines with great skill some quite traditional motifs of urban spatial structure and orientation with new and more abstract arrangements first introduced in residential development in the 1920s. The width and alignment of Aroser Allee were predefined, and he designed it as a main road with accompanying block margin buildings. At its beginning, he placed two buildings, which are higher than the ribbons, along the road and create the impression of a gate opening into the estate. He concluded the main road, which has a slight but noticeable bend towards the north, with a transverse building in the form of a bridge that lies across the entire width of Aroser Allee. The bridge house does not constitute the end of the estate, but rather defines its middle and is a viewpoint from both directions. A large clock in the middle of the top floor on either side shows the time.

Abb. 58: Weiße Stadt, Gartenhof im Siedlungsteil von Bruno Ahrends, 2001 instand gesetzt, 2005

Fig. 58: Weiße Stadt, garden courtyard in development section by Bruno Ahrends, restored in 2001, 2005

publizistik ebenso gut, wie in die kunstvoll überhöhten Bildsequenzen von klaren, kubischen, weißen Baukörpern, die in der Zeit um und nach 1930 in Büchern und Zeitschriften in der ganzen Welt erschienen. Unter der Regie von Stadtbaurat Martin Wagner wirkten hier die Berliner Architekten Wilhelm Büning und Bruno Ahrends und der Schweizer Otto Rudolf Salvisberg, die Gartenanlagen entwarf Ludwig Lesser.

Der städtebauliche Entwurf von Otto Rudolf Salvisberg kombiniert mit großem Geschick einige durchaus traditionelle Motive der stadträumlichen Ordnung und Orientierung mit neuen, im Siedlungsbau der 1920er Jahre erstmals geprägten Figurationen abstrakterer Art. Die in Breite und Verlauf festgelegte Aroser Allee inszenierte er als Magistrale mit begleitender Blockrandbebauung, die er am südlichen Eingang zur Siedlung effektvoll mit zwei erhöhten Torbauten beginnen ließ. Die Magistrale, in leichter aber merkbarer Biegung nach Norden verschwenkt, schloss er mit einem Querriegel, der als Brücke über die gesamte Breite der Aroser Allee gelegt ist. Das Brückenhaus markiert nicht etwa schon den Ausgang der Siedlung, es markiert ihre Mitte und dient als Point de Vue von beiden Richtungen. Je eine große, mittig auf der Wand des obersten Stockwerks angebrachte Uhr gibt zu beiden Seiten die Zeit an.

Torbauten, Achse und Brückenhaus sind raumbeherrschende und hierarchisierende Elemente von starker bildhafter Wirkung, sie fassen und repräsentieren die Siedlungsgemeinschaft. Beiderseits dieser bedeutungsvollen Mitte bildete Salvisberg aus Blockrändern, radial gestellten Zeilen und abschließenden Riegeln andere Raumfiguren, die auf nichts anderes als auf sich selbst verweisen. Die Weiße Stadt steht in ihrer Gesamtanlage für einen Städtebau, der aus den hygienischen und sozialen Zielen des Neuen Bauens Raumkonzepte entwickelte, die vom innerstädtisch verdichteten Blockrandschema ebenso weit entfernt sind wie von den auf Ländlichkeit oder kleinstädtischer Gewachsenheit zielenden Gartenstadtmustern.

The gate buildings, the axis and the bridge building are elements that dominate the space and create a hierarchy. They define the image and both create and represent the housing estate community. On either side of this meaningful centre, Salvisberg created other spatial structures consisting of block margin buildings, radially placed ribbons and concluding cross bar buildings. These other structures point at nothing but themselves. The entirety of Weiße Stadt stands for a form of urban development which, on the basis of the hygienic and social requirements of Neues Bauen, created spatial concepts that are as far away from the typical inner-city block margin pattern as the garden town patterns which try to express a rural character or the natural growth of small towns.

Reinickendorf was one of the suburban districts of Berlin that had been merged with Berlin in 1920 and was a suitable area for the experiments of the new and social urban development as it was propagated by urban development councillor Martin Wagner and progressive architects. The development at Reinickendorf differed from those of the GEHAG estates at Britz or Zehlendorf in as much as it was the test for a modern inner-city type of development that consisted exclusively of flats in multi-storey buildings. The small tenants' gardens were replaced by commonly used housing estate gardens that constituted a new type – functional green spaces with recreational areas and playgrounds.

Ludwig Lesser managed to create a structure of the outdoor facilities that harmonised with the urban development and architectural programme of the estate and fulfilled the requirements of Neues Bauen. By placing individual bushes or trees in the courtyards, which are dominated by lawns, he generated open spatial structures that offer room for various uses. He thus created a functional subdivision of the spaces as well as connections between the individual parts. The exemplary creation of outdoor facilities with many common areas set benchmarks for later residential development projects.

Hier in Reinickendorf, einer der Randgemeinden Berlins, die nach der Eingemeindung 1920 zu Verwaltungsbezirken zusammengelegt wurden, lag eines der geeigneten Experimentierfelder des neuen sozialen Städtebaues, wie er vom Stadtbaurat Martin Wagner und fortschrittlichen Architekten propagiert wurde. Anders als in den großen GEHAG-Siedlungen in Britz oder Zehlendorf wurde auf der ehemaligen Reinickendorfer Flur ein moderner großstädtischer Siedlungstyp erprobt, der nur Wohnungen in Geschossbauten vorsah. An die Stelle des kleinen Mietergartens trat hier mit gemeinschaftlich nutzbaren Siedlungsgärten ein neuer Typus – funktionelle Grünräume mit Sitz- und Kinderspielplätzen.

Ludwig Lesser gelang damit passend zum städtebaulichen und architektonischen Programm der Siedlung eine dem Anspruch des Neuen Bauens gerecht werdende Strukturierung der Freiflächen. Durch das Einfügen von einzelnen Strauch- und Baumpflanzungen in die einzelnen, von Rasenflächen dominierten Höfe, werden offene Raumstrukturen geschaffen, die verschiedene Nutzungen aufnehmen können. Es entsteht sowohl eine funktionale Gliederung der Räume als auch eine verbindende Wirkung. Die vorbildliche Ausstattung der Siedlungsfreiräume mit zahlreichen gemeinschaftlichen Plätzen setzte Maßstäbe für spätere Wohnsiedlungsprojekte.

### Großsiedlung Siemensstadt (Ringsiedlung)

Die 1929–31 erbaute Großsiedlung Siemensstadt hatte von Anbeginn auch die Funktion einer Architekturausstellung in großem Maßstab, die allerdings auf einen einzigen Bautyp festgelegt ist: die Großzeile, für die Varianten der Anordnung, Grundrissanlage, Erschließung und Gestaltung vorgeführt werden. Berühmte Architekten begründeten ihren frühen internationalen Ruhm. Beteiligt waren Walter Gropius, Hugo Häring, Otto Bartning, Hans Scharoun, Fred Forbat und Paul Rudolf Henning. Die Arbeitsgemeinschaft wurde von Stadtbaurat Martin Wagner geleitet, einem der vehementesten Verfechter des rationellen Großsiedlungsbaues. Er gab jedem der Architekten die Möglichkeit, seine individuelle Interpretation des neuen sozialen Bauens unter großstädtischen Bedingungen modellhaft umzusetzen. Rationalität und Wirtschaftlichkeit des Zeilenbaus konnten ebenso erprobt werden, wie ein organhaftes und stoffliches Bauen.

Radikal bricht der Bebauungsplan von Hans Scharoun mit den Städtebauvorstellungen des 19. Jahrhunderts. Im Brennpunkt steht jetzt die Gestaltung des Räumlichen und die Verknüpfung von Innen- und Außenraum. Hier lösen sich Straße, Wohnblock und Naturraum aus ihren bisherigen städtebaulichen Schemata und verschmelzen zu einer neuen, bisher nicht gekannten Komposition, deren Kern eine großzügige, vom Gartenarchitekten Leberecht Migge gestaltete Aue bildet.

Die Großsiedlung Siemensstadt weist den Weg zum internationalen modernen Städtebau, dessen Gliederungen als abstrakte Kompositionen keinerlei Rückbezug auf die städtebaulichen Motive der Vormoderne suchen. Das für die Zeit nach dem Zweiten Weltkrieg im europäischen Städtebau maßgebliche Modell der aufgelockerten, gegliederten

Abb. 59: Großsiedlung Siemensstadt, weiträumiger Gartenhof zwischen den Zeilen im Siedlungsteil von Paul R. Henning, 2005

Fig. 59: Großsiedlung Siemensstadt, spacious garden courtyard between the ribbons in the section by Paul R. Henning, 2005

### Großsiedlung Siemensstadt (Ringsiedlung)

From the beginning, the Großsiedlung Siemensstadt, built in 1929–31, also had the function of a large-scale exhibition of architecture which nevertheless concentrated on only one type of building: large ribbons presented in various arrangements and with varying ground plans, servicing and designs. Famous architects gained early international fame. Walter Gropius, Hugo Häring, Otto Bartning, Hans Scharoun, Fred Forbat and Paul Rudolf Henning participated in this project. The working group was headed by urban development councillor Martin Wagner, who was one of the most committed supporters of rational large housing estate development. He gave each of the architects the opportunity to create models presenting his individual idea of new social development in a big city. The architects had the opportunity to test the rationality and economy of erecting ribbon buildings and also organic and material design.

The master plan by Hans Scharoun constitutes a clear break with the ideas of urban development of the 19th century. His plan focuses on designing spaces and connecting indoor and outdoor spaces. He dissolves past patterns of street, block and natural space and merges these spaces to form a new unprecedented composition around the spacious central landscape designed by garden architect Leberecht Migge.

The Großsiedlung Siemensstadt paves the way towards an international modern urban development whose structures are abstract compositions and do not look at urban development motifs of pre-modern periods. This estate presents the model of a structured city with lots of green spaces, which came to dominate urban development in Europe during the period after the Second World War. Siemensstadt is a modern cityscape in the sense of Hans Scharoun's reconstruction concept of 1946.

The pioneering design of the outdoor facilities of Siemensstadt may also be understood as being exemplary for the design principles in modern European urban development.

The outdoor facilities, with their social and sanitary functions, were considered to function as a balance for the hard living and working conditions. The park-like design of the outdoor facilities, the creation of a central common space

und durchgrünten Stadt ist hier vorgeprägt: Siemensstadt ist eine moderne Stadtlandschaft im Sinne von Hans Scharouns Wiederaufbau-Konzept von 1946.

Auch in der wegweisenden Gestaltung der Freiräume der Siemensstadt können exemplarische Gestaltungsprinzipien für den modernen europäischen Städtebau abgelesen werden.

Die Freiräume mit ihren sozialen und sanitären Funktionen wurden als Ausgleich zu den schweren Lebens- und Arbeitsbedingungen verstanden. Die parkähnliche Gestaltung der weiträumigen Freiflächen, die Anlage eines zentral gelegenen Gemeinschaftsbereiches mit Spiel- und Sitzgelegenheiten als auch die sorgfältig integrierten Müllplätze folgten diesem Anspruch. Vorrangig waren die Schaffung zusammenhängender Grünflächen und die Sicherung des vorhandenen Baumbestandes. Die Anlage von Mietergärten beschränkte sich auf einen kleinen Teilbereich.

Durch die klare Differenzierung der einzelnen Funktionsbereiche und Gartenräume versuchte Leberecht Migge eine schlichte und rationale Freiraumgestaltung durchzusetzen, die sowohl die Baukosten als auch die späteren Pflegekosten minimieren sollten.

Ein weiteres, wichtiges gestalterisches Element der Siemensstadt wird in der Einbeziehung der öffentlichen Straßenräume deutlich. Mit Pappelpflanzungen an den wichtigsten Wegeverbindungen wurden die räumliche und funktionale Anbindung der neu zu schaffenden Freiräume an das übergeordnete Grünsystem erreicht.

with recreational facilities and playgrounds as well as the carefully integrated waste disposal facilities fulfil this demand. Creating a network of connected green spaces and maintaining the existing trees were primary concerns. Only a small part of the land was used to create tenants' gardens.

Leberecht Migge tried to implement a plain and rational design of the outdoor facilities by using a clear differentiation between the individual functional areas and the garden areas. In this way, he wanted to minimise both the cost of construction and future maintenance costs.

Another important design element of Siemensstadt is represented by the integration of the public street spaces. The newly created outdoor facilities were spatially and functionally linked with the overall green network by poplars planted along the most important streets.

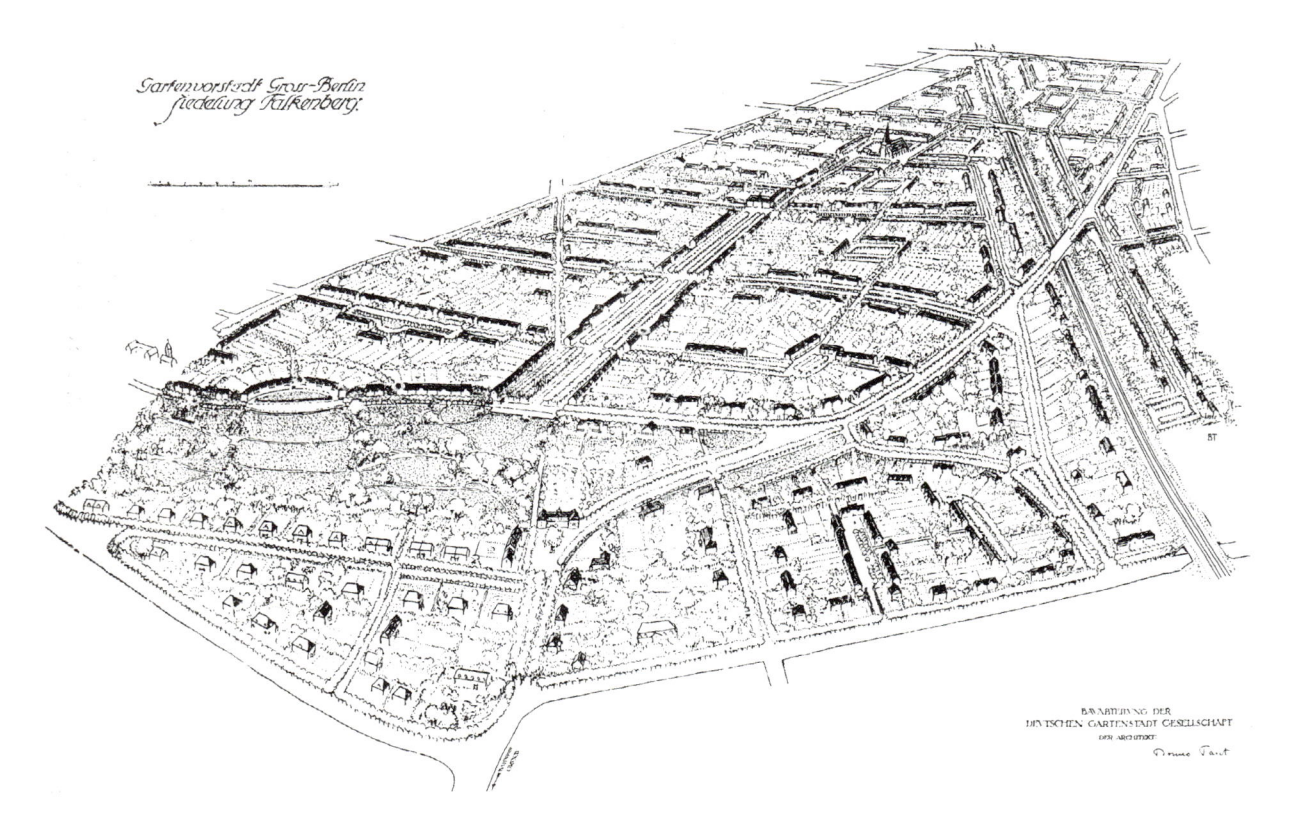

Abb. 60: Siedlungsplan von Bruno Taut für die Gartenstadt Falkenberg, 1913. Nur der Akazienhof, unten rechts, wurde nach diesem Plan realisiert.

Fig. 60: Design by Bruno Taut for Gartenstadt Falkenberg, 1913. Only Akazienhof (bottom right) was built according to this design.

## 3.c Comparative analysis (including state of conservation of similar properties)

**Concepts for mass residential development in Germany and Europe**

*From garden towns to housing estate development during the 1920s*

Since the first half of the 19th century, solving the housing question had been one of the greatest social challenges in most of the European countries. This referred in particular to the rapidly growing and densifying big cities. In those places where in the 19th century social impoverishment was greatest as a consequence of urbanisation and industrialisation, the first counter-movements and reforming activities began in urban and housing development. Especially in England, the first company settlements with healthier flats and social facilities soon appeared as results of initiatives of philanthropically-minded entrepreneurs. A milestone of social and industrial history was the industrial settlement of New Lanark in Scotland, which included several facilities for the working people – among them in particular educational facilities. This settlement was erected by Robert Owen – the social reformer and owner of a cotton spinning mill. A comparable model settlement of the early Industrial Age is Saltaire in Yorkshire, founded in the middle of the 19th century by the textile entrepreneur Titus Salt. Other examples for English industrial settlements of this kind are Cadbury's Bournville or Port Sunlight. In other European countries, too, industrial settlements were erected that represented noticeable progress in the living conditions of the working people. One example is the factory and workers' village of Crespi d'Adda near Capriate San Gervasio in the Italian province of Bergamo (Lombardy). It was named after the family Crespi who owned the cotton factory and who had the village with the factory, the settlement and social facilities erected from 1878. The settlements of New Lanark, Saltaire and Crespi d'Adda have been entered in the World Heritage List of UNESCO.

The industrial housing estates, which had been erected on the initiative of individual entrepreneurs, remained singular establishments created for improving the living conditions of the workers in the respective factories. The garden city model of Ebenezer Howard was the first to present an urban development idea in contrast to the big cities – a model which tried to overcome the disadvantages of city life. In his book "Garden Cities of Tomorrow", Howard presented the city embedded in green spaces which tried to merge city and nature into a holistic model of living by developing independent housing estates of reasonable size. All vitally important realms of life (housing, working, utilities, leisure and recreation) were to be closely combined and made visible in an urban form of housing estate that was to reflect the spirit of community and social reform.

Howard's ideas about the garden city were soon also disseminated beyond England with the founding (on his initiative) of the "Garden City Association" in 1899. In practice this resulted in the founding of garden cities like Letchworth (1903), Hampstead (1907–1910), both according to plans by Barry Parker and Raymond Unwin, as well as Welwyn (1920) by Louis de Soissons. However, in the

sie in den Sog Londons gerieten und eher den Charakter von Trabanten- oder Schlafstätten annahmen.

Der englische Gartenstadtgedanke hatte auch in Deutschland seine Anhänger. Schon 1902 wurde in Berlin die „Deutsche Gartenstadtgesellschaft" gegründet, der neben Sozialreformern und Gesundheitshygienikern auch Volkswirtschaftler und Architekten angehörten. Der Blick der Deutschen Gartenstadtgesellschaft richtete sich aber eher auf die Siedlung am Stadtrand, die Gartenvorstadt, als Erweiterung zur bestehenden Stadt. Mit der Gartenvorstadt als städtebauliches Leitbild vermied die Deutsche Gartenstadtgesellschaft von vornherein den utopistischen Anspruch der Howard'schen Idealstadt. Viele neugegründeten Siedlungen, z.B. Hellerau bei Dresden (1906–1908, Architekten: Tessenow, Riemerschmid, Muthesius) oder die Margarthenhöhe bei Essen (ab 1909 / Architekt: Georg Metzendorf), trugen zwar den Namen „Gartenstadt", waren aber eher vorstädtische Siedlungen nach dem Verständnis von Tony Garniers Cité Industrielle von 1904.

Andere wichtige Impulse für den Reformwohnungsbau in Deutschland kamen aus der Baugenossenschaftsbewegung, die mit dem Genossenschaftsgesetz von 1889 einen Aufschwung erlebte. Es entstanden zahlreiche gemeinnützige Baugenossenschaften auf der Grundlage gemeinschaftlichen Eigentums. Außer den rechtlichen und wirtschaftlichen Bedingungen des Wohnens gaben die Baugenossenschaften auch in architektonischer und hygienischer Hinsicht eine neue Richtung für die Form des Wohnens vor.

Im Werkswohnungsbau, in der Gartenstadtbewegung und im baugenossenschaftlichen Wohnungsbau lagen die Wurzeln für den europäischen Siedlungsbau des frühen 20. Jahrhunderts. Grundrisslösungen für Kleinwohnungen, den Gemeinschaftssinn fördernde Versorgungseinrichtungen sowie eine soziale Freiraumplanung waren die Neuerungen und Weiterentwicklungen der großen Siedlungen, die in den 1920er Jahren am Stadtrand der Großstädte entstanden. Unter den europäischen Großstädten entwickelte sich besonders Berlin zum Zentren eines ambitionierten, reformorientierten Wohnungsbauprogramms, das sich zudem in stadtplanerischer, architektonischer und bautechnischer

end these housing estates were not real garden cities according to Howard's definition since they got caught up in the maelstrom of big city life of London and rather turned into satellite or dormitory suburbs.

The English garden city idea also found followers in Germany. As early as in 1902, the first "Deutsche Gartenstadtgesellschaft" (German Garden City Society) was founded in Berlin, and its members included social reformers and experts in health hygiene as well as economists and architects. Yet, the view of Deutsche Gartenstadtgesellschaft was directed more towards the housing estate at the margin of the cities – the garden suburb – than towards extending the existing cities. In choosing the garden suburb as the urban development model, Deutsche Gartenstadtgesellschaft avoided from the outset the utopian claim raised by Howard's ideal city. Many of the newly founded housing estates – for instance Hellerau near Dresden (1906–1908, architects: Tessenow, Riemerschmid, Muthesius) or Margarthenhöhe near Essen (from 1909; architect: Georg Metzendorf) were indeed called garden cities, yet, they were rather suburban housing estates according to the model of Tony Garnier's Cité Industrielle of 1904.

Other important incentives for reform housing development in Germany came from the building cooperative movement which gained more impetus with the law on cooperatives of 1889. Many non-profit building cooperatives were founded, which were based on common ownership. In addition to the legal and economic conditions of housing, the building cooperatives also showed a new direction of development for housing with respect to its architecture and hygienic conditions.

Company housing development, the garden city movement and the building cooperatives are the roots of European housing estate development in the early 20th century. Ground plans for small flats and facilities that promote community spirit as well as social outdoor facility design were the innovations and further development of the large housing estates erected during the 1920s on the outskirts of the big cities. Among the large European cities, especially Berlin became one of the centres of an ambitious, reformist housing programme which represented the state of the art of urban development, architecture and construction of that time and involved many renowned planners, designers, architects and engineers of Neues Bauen.

*Housing estate development in European cities*
After the end of the First World War, the need for creating healthy and good quality housing for the broad masses was not restricted to Germany. Many countries had a similar shortage of housing, in particular those neighbouring countries that were undergoing the social transformations that followed the First World War. In many European big cities like Vienna, Amsterdam and Rotterdam, similar housing programmes were created with a claim for social reform supported by public funding. Yet, in many respects, the urban development and architectural concepts generated there were more conservative than those in Berlin. Furthermore, their flats were relatively small and had a comparatively low standard. In Berlin the architects were able to implement a comparatively high standard of housing and relatively comfortable flats on the basis of the new

Abb. 61: Gartenstadt Falkenberg, Akazienhof, 1913

Fig. 61: Gartenstadt Falkenberg, Akazienhof, 1913

Sicht unter Beteiligung namhafter Planer, Architekten und Ingenieure des Neuen Bauens auf der Höhe der Zeit befand.

*Siedlungsbau in europäischen Großstädten*
Die Notwendigkeit gesunden und qualitätsvollen Wohnraum für die breite Masse zu schaffen, war nach dem Ersten Weltkrieg nicht auf Deutschland beschränkt. In vielen Nachbarstaaten, besonders in den Ländern, die von den gesellschaftlichen Umwälzungen nach dem Ersten Weltkrieg betroffen waren, gab es eine vergleichbare Wohnungsnot. In den europäischen Großstädten wie Wien, Amsterdam und Rotterdam entstanden mit Hilfe staatlicher Fördermittel verwandte Wohnungsbauprogramme mit sozialreformerischem Anspruch. Die dort entwickelten städtebaulichen und architektonischen Konzepte waren allerdings in mancher Hinsicht konservativer als das in Berlin der Fall war. Auch hatten die relativ kleinen Wohnungen einen vergleichsweise niedrigeren Standard. In Berlin dagegen konnten die Architekten auf der Grundlage der neuen Bauordnung und den Richtlinien der Wohnungsfürsorgegesellschaft einen verhältnismäßig höheren Wohnungsstandard und Wohnkomfort verwirklichen mit zum Teil zentraler Warmwasser- und Wärmeversorgung sowie Waschhäusern in den Siedlungsgebieten.

In den Niederlanden wurden schon um 1900 die rechtlichen Grundlagen für einen sozial verpflichteten Wohnungsbau geschaffen. Nach 1918 verschärften sich die Wohnungsprobleme auch in Holland, so dass der Staat den Bau von sozial

building regulations and the guidelines of the housing welfare societies. Some of these flats had central heating and hot water supply as well as laundries in the residential quarters.

As early as around 1900, the Netherlands created the legal foundations for residential development on the basis of social concepts. After 1918, the housing shortage also worsened in Holland, so that the state paid even more subsidies for social housing development. In residential architecture, two opposing movements existed which have become manifest in the two cities of Amsterdam and of Rotterdam.

Abb. 62: Wohnhäuser an der Coöperatiesstraat in Amsterdam von P. L. Cramer, um 1925

Fig. 62: Residential buildings at Coöperatiesstraat at Amsterdam by P. L. Cramer, approximately 1925

In Amsterdam, where row houses embedded into the city structure represented the traditional standard, both urban and residential development concepts were determined by the aesthetics of the "Amsterdam school". Its conservative character is due to the fact that its designers adhered to regional traditions of housing development. On the basis of Hendrik Petrus Berlage's plan for Amsterdam South from 1915, dense multi-storey blocks of brickwork accompanying the streets dominated until the 1930s. The baroque city structure of Amsterdam was the benchmark. Everywhere, rows of houses with even fronts, some of which had expressive plastic decorations, were erected along wide avenues. The fact that many of these residential buildings were erected by private builders slowed down the development of functional ground plans and the optimisation of

verträglichen Wohnungen noch stärker subventionierte. In der Wohnbauarchitektur standen sich zwei Bewegungen gegenüber, die sich in der Wohnungsbaupolitik der Städte Amsterdam und Rotterdam manifestierten.

In Amsterdam, wo traditionell das ins Stadtgefüge eingebundene Reihenhaus der Standard war, waren Stadtplanung und Wohnbaukonzepte von der Ästhetik der „Amsterdamer Schule" geprägt. Ihr konservativer Zug gründet sich im Festhalten an regionalen Bautraditionen. Aufbauend auf Hendrik Petrus Berlages Plan für Amsterdam-Süd aus dem Jahre 1915 wurde bis in die 1930er Jahre hinein der straßenbegleitende, mehrgeschossige enge Block in Backstein vorherrschend. Maßstabbildend war die barocke Stadtstruktur von Amsterdam. Es entstanden überall gleichmäßige, zum Teil expressiv plastisch durchgestaltete Häuserfronten an breiten Alleen. Da die Wohngebäude häufig von Einzelbauherren errichtet wurden, hemmte dies eine funktionelle Grundrissentwicklung sowie die Optimierung der Wohnungsstandards. Auch gab es keinen in dieser Stringenz von der Kommune umgesetzten sozialen Wohnungsbau mit vergleichbaren Richtlinien für den staatlich geförderten Wohnungsbau wie in Berlin.

In Rotterdam, wo es kein vergleichbares Miethaussystem wie in Berlin gab, entstanden, losgelöst von der historischen Stadt, größere Siedlungskomplexe. Seit 1918 wirkte dort vor allem Jacobus Johannes Pieter Oud als Stadtplaner, der nach pragmatischen Lösungen im Flach- und Hochbau suchte. Er konnte nachweisen, dass man im Flachbau und in der Reihe kostengünstig Wohnungen auch für wenig verdienende Bevölkerungsschichten errichten kann. Beeinflusst durch die Architektur Le Corbusiers und „de Stijl" sind seine Entwürfe dem Neuen Bauen verpflichtet. Wie in den Berliner Siedlungen von Bruno Taut wollte sich Oud mit einer intensiven Farbigkeit seiner Häuser von der bestehenden Stadt absetzen. Die größeren Wohnblöcke folgen dem Blockrand und sind jedoch ähnlich wie bei Taut geöffnet. Während Taut jedoch Balkone oder Loggien je nach örtlicher Gegebenheit mal zur Straße, mal zum Hof legt, bleiben bei den Anlagen von Oud die straßenbegleitenden Fassaden flächig, während er die Hofseiten mit Balkonbändern plastisch durchbildet. Zudem gibt es – wie bereits erwähnt – ausschließlich streifenförmige Mietergärten und keine gärtnerisch gestalteten Freiräume.

Auch der kommunale Wohnungsbau der Stadt Wien hat nach dem Zusammenbruch der Donaumonarchie und der Gründung der Republik überragende Leistungen auf dem Gebiet des sozialen Wohnungsbaus hervorgebracht. Wie in Berlin war das Wiener Stadtparlament durch eine sozialdemokratische Mehrheit bestimmt und die Wohnungsnot besonders hoch. Die kommunale Verwaltung unter dem Bürgermeister Karl Seitz und dem Stadtbaurat Karl Ehn (1926–30) reagierte darauf bereits 1923 mit einem Wohnungsbauprogramm mit Mitteln aus dem Aufkommen der Wohnbausteuer.

Von 1923 bis 1934 entstanden etwa 63.000 kommunale Wohnungen, die größtenteils in riesigen innerstädtischen Wohnblocks, sogenannten „Superblocks", lagen. Man orientierte sich an der historischen Stadtstruktur Wiens. Monumentalität und Axialität im Sinne Otto Wagners, malerische Platzbildung nach Camillo Sitte, Randbauten

the housing standards. Further, the municipality did not have any strictly-implemented directives for social residential development as was the case in Berlin.

Rotterdam did not have a tenement system like Berlin, and larger housing estate complexes were erected there that were separate from the historical city. Since 1918, Jacobus Johannes Pieter Oud had been an urban development planner at Rotterdam, and he searched for pragmatic solutions for both single-storey and multi-storey buildings. He was able to prove that it was possible to keep building costs low and erect single-storey buildings and row houses with flats for the low income population. He was influenced by the architecture of Le Corbusier and "de Stijl", and his designs thus apply the principles of Neues Bauen. Oud wanted to mark the difference between the existing city and his houses by the intense colours of the facades just as Bruno Taut intended in Berlin. The major residential blocks follow the block margin but, similar to those by Taut, they are open. Depending upon the local situation, Taut had positioned the balconies and loggias either on the street side or the yard side, whereas Oud keeps the street side facades plain and develops a plastic design for the yard sides using galleries of balconies. Moreover – as we have mentioned before – the houses only have strip-shaped tenants' gardens and no outdoor facilities designed by garden architects.

The municipal housing development programme in Vienna, too, made enormous achievements in the field of social residential development after the collapse of the Danube monarchy and the founding of the Republic. As in Berlin, the Vienna city parliament had a Social Democratic majority, and housing shortage was extreme. The municipal administration under mayor Karl Seitz and the urban development councillor Karl Ehn (1926–30) reacted as early as 1923 with a housing programme financed by housing construction tax income.

Between 1923 and 1934, approximately 63,000 municipal flats were built. Most of them were located in huge inner-city residential blocks, the so-called "super blocks". Their structure reflected the historic city structure of Vienna. The designers preferred monumental and axial designs in the spirit of Otto Wagner, picturesque squares in the spirit of Camillo Sitte, block margin buildings with steep-pitched roofs and gates, battlements, bays, and towers to modern settlement areas which open and flow. The political aim was to create large estates that supported the forming of communities and fit into the existing city structure, offering comprehensive collective facilities for people who shared social and political views. However, except for the green courtyards, these projects did not have a greenery policy that might be compared with that of Berlin or Frankfurt, where functional outdoor facilities were integrated with an overall urban open space concept.

On the other hand, the municipality of Vienna wanted to keep rent very low, lower than in Berlin, so that it would be able to also offer appropriate flats to workers and clerks with low incomes. In order to achieve this, the flats had to be comparatively small – not more than 50 square metres always in houses with several back-to-back flats, such that cross ventilation was rather bad. Most of the flats had no bathrooms. This had been prevented in Berlin by the tech-

Abb. 63: Karl-Marx-Hof in Wien, 1926–30 von Karl Ehn, um 1975

Fig. 63: Karl-Marx-Hof at Vienna, 1926–30 by Karl Ehn, approximately 1975

mit Steildächern und mit Toren, Zinnen, Erker, Türme und nicht moderne, sich öffnende und fließende Siedlungsräume wie in Berlin wurden bevorzugt. Politisches Ziel waren gemeinschaftsbildende Großanlagen, die sich in das bestehende Stadtgefüge einfügten, mit umfassenden kollektiven Einrichtungen für sozial und politisch Gleichgesinnte. Es gab jedoch außer den begrünten Innenhöfen nicht eine mit Berlin oder Frankfurt vergleichbare Grünpolitik, die funktionelle Siedlungsfreiräume einband in ein gesamtstädtisches Freiflächenkonzept.

Allerdings war die Kommune Wien bedacht, die Mieten äußerst niedrig zu halten, niedriger als in Berlin, um auch für Arbeiter und Angestellte mit niedrigem Einkommen eine angemessene Wohnung anbieten zu können. Hierfür mussten die Wohnungen vergleichsweise klein sein – nicht größer als 50 qm – in durchweg mehrspännigen Häusern, was zu einer schlechten Querlüftung der Wohnungen führte. Auch hatten die Wohnungen meistens keine Bäder. Dies war in Berlin aufgrund der technischen Richtlinien der Wohnungsfürsorgegesellschaft ausgeschlossen worden. Zugelassen waren nur Zweispännerhäuser und alle Wohnungen mussten separate Bäder und Küchen sowie Balkone oder Loggien haben.

*Zentren des modernen Siedlungsbaus in Deutschland*
Unter den Städten Deutschlands zeichnen sich nach Quantität und Qualität neben Berlin besonders Frankfurt am Main, Hamburg und Magdeburg als Zentren des sozialen Reformwohnungsbaus nach dem Ersten Weltkrieg aus. Noch am ehesten vergleichbar mit den Berliner Siedlungen sind die großen Siedlungsprojekte, die in Frankfurt unter der Ägide von Ernst May (1925–1930) realisiert werden konnten. Wie in Berlin entstanden sie in einer sozialdemokratisch regierten Kommune und sind von einem Baudezernenten maßgeblich konzeptiert worden. Die Modernisierung der Großstadt, wozu die Siedlungen gehörten,

nical directives of the Wohnungsfürsorgegesellschaft (Housing Welfare Society). They permitted only houses with one pair of flats back-to-back and all flats had to have dedicated bathrooms and kitchens as well as balconies and loggias.

*Centres of modern housing development in Germany*
Among the German cities, Berlin can be considered one of the centres of social reform housing development after the First World War in terms of both quantity and quality. Others are Frankfurt/Main, Hamburg and Magdeburg. The Berlin housing estates can best be compared with the large housing projects which were realised in Frankfurt under the auspices of Ernst May (1925–1930). As in Berlin, they were built in a municipality with a Social Democratic government, and the urban development councillor played a major role in drafting their design. The modernisation of the big city, which included the settlements, was propagated by adding the buzzword "new" (the "new Frankfurt") as it happened in Berlin. Like Martin Wagner, May also wanted to separate the functions of the 19th century city with large housing estates that were separated from the historical city centre. From 1925, the city of Frankfurt erected approximately 15,000 flats in a number of housing estates. Most of them were embedded in the topography of the Nidda valley. The programme was planned to run for ten years. The flats had an exemplary standard with built-in kitchens, bathrooms and showers.

In contrast to the Berlin settlements, the flats were smaller since the benchmark consisted of flats on subsistence level to keep rents as low as possible. Moreover, development in Frankfurt focussed on rational construction with prefabricated and standardised parts. For the estates built at the end, around 1930, this meant that they were composed consistently of ribbon buildings. Under Wagner's influence, this was refuted in Berlin as being dogmatic. Today many

Fig. 64: Siedlung Römerstadt in Frankfurt a. M., 1927–28 von Ernst May, um 1929

Fig. 64: Römerstadt at Frankfurt am Main, 1927–28 by Ernst May, approximately 1929

wurde in derselben Weise mit dem Schlagwort „neu" – das „Neue Frankfurt" – propagiert. Auch strebte May wie Martin Wagner mittels Großsiedlungen – losgelöst vom alten Stadtkern – eine funktionelle Entmischung der Stadt des 19. Jahrhunderts an. Mit dem auf zehn Jahre angelegten Wohnungsbauprogramm ließ die Stadt Frankfurt ab 1925 eine Vielzahl von Wohnsiedlungen mit rund 15.000 Wohneinheiten errichten, meist unter Einbindung der Topographie des Nidda-Tals. Die Wohnungen zeichneten sich durch einen vorbildlichen Wohnungsstandard aus, mit Einbauküchen, Bädern oder Duschen.

Im Gegensatz zu den Berliner Siedlungen waren die Wohnungen jedoch kleiner, da man sich mehr an der Wohnung für das Existenzminimum orientierte, um die Mieten möglichst niedrig zu halten. Auch stand in Frankfurt das rationelle Bauen mit vorgefertigten und normierten Bauteilen im Vordergrund. Dies führte bei den zuletzt um 1930 erbauten Anlagen zu einer konsequenten Anwendung des Zeilenbausystems, was man in Berlin unter dem Einfluss von Wagner als Dogma ablehnte. Heute haben ein Großteil der Frankfurter Siedlungsbauten ihre Authentizität verloren. Viele der charakteristischen Gestaltungselemente wie Putz, Farbigkeit, Türen und Fenster sind verloren gegangen. Auch gibt es keine grundlegenden denkmalpflegerischen Erneuerungsprogramme zur Wiederherstellung der Siedlungen.

Im ebenfalls sozialdemokratisch regierten Magdeburg legte Bruno Taut während seiner kurzen Zeit als Stadtbaurat (1921–23) die Grundlage für einen von der kommunalen Verwaltung vorangetriebenen sozialen Siedlungsbau, der wie in Frankfurt die dezentralisierte Stadt zum Ziel hatte. In Zusammenarbeit mit Konrad Rühl entwickelte Taut einen Generalsiedlungsplan, der weit ins Umland von Magdeburg reichte. Hier waren in den Vororten gartenstadtähnliche Ansiedlungen zur Entlastung des zu erwartenden Stadtwachstums geplant, während in Zwischenzonen städtische Siedlungskomplexe bis zu drei Geschossen mit großzügigen Grünflächen für eine Verknüpfung sorgen sollten. Nach dem Weggang von Taut 1923 konnten Rühl und später Stadtbaurat Johannes Göderitz auf dem Plan aufbauen

of these buildings and estates in Frankfurt have lost their authenticity. Several of their characteristic design elements, such as plaster, colour, doors and windows, have been lost. Neither has the city programmes for a thorough restoration of these settlements.

In Magdeburg, which also had a Social Democratic government, Bruno Taut created the basis for a social housing development during his short term in office as urban development councillor (1921–23). This programme was aimed at decentralising the city, as was the concept in Frankfurt. In cooperation with Konrad Rühl, Taut developed a general development plan that also reached out far into the area around Magdeburg. To reduce the pressure of urban development on the city, this concept envisaged garden town-like housing estates in the suburbs, whereas in the zones between the centre and these suburbs, urban housing estate complexes consisting of buildings with a maximum of three storeys embedded in spacious green spaces were to create a kind of link. After Taut had left in 1923, Rühl and later urban development councillor Johannes Göderitz were able to use this plan and advance urban development with specific, large housing estates. These estates were erected between 1924 and 1930 mainly by Magdeburg non-profit construction societies and comprised approximately 12,000 newly built flats. Most of them were major housing estates which were usually designed by private Magdeburg architects and had spacious courtyard gardens. Their architecture was both functional and traditional, using plaster and brick contrasts. Although the hygienic conditions and the standard of the houses built by non-profit organisations in Magdeburg were on an equal level with those of Berlin, the housing estates did not reach the architectural quality of the Berlin housing estates.

In Hamburg, the urban development director Fritz Schumacher pursued other concepts for mitigating the housing shortage than those applied in Berlin, Magdeburg and Frankfurt. The target in Hamburg was to give the big city the same quality as the large housing estates, and the model was not to separate the functions by dissolving the city. Under the guidance of Schumacher, who designed some

Abb. 65: Siedlung Dammerstock in Karlsruhe, 1928/29 von Otto Haesler, Walter Gropius, 1929

Fig. 65: Dammerstock at Karlsruhe, 1928/29 by Otto Haesler, Walter Gropius, 1929

und die Stadtentwicklung mit konkreten großen Siedlungsprojekten vorantreiben. Die vor allem von Magdeburger gemeinnützigen Baugesellschaften errichteten Wohnsiedlungen zwischen 1924 und 1930 hatten ein Neubauvolumen von rund 12.000 Wohnungen. Es entstanden zum Teil größere Siedlungsanlagen, meist entworfen von Magdeburger Privatarchitekten, mit Wohnblöcken, die großzügige Gartenhöfe umfassten und einer sachlichen und zugleich traditionsgebundenen Formensprache mit Putz- und Ziegelkontrasten verpflichtet waren. Der gemeinnützige Siedlungsbau in Magdeburg, im wohnhygienischen Standard der Häuser und Wohnungen Berlin durchaus ebenbürtig, erreichte aber nicht die architektonische Qualität der Berliner Siedlungen.

In Hamburg verfolgte der Baudirektor Fritz Schumacher zur Linderung der Wohnungsnot andere Konzepte als sie in Berlin, Magdeburg und Frankfurt praktiziert wurden. In Hamburg war das Ziel, der Großstadt die Wohnqualität der Großsiedlungen zu geben, wobei die Auflösung der Stadt durch Funktionstrennung nicht das Leitbild war. Bis 1933 wurden unter der Leitung von Schumacher, der selbst einige der Anlagen entwarf, 65.000 Wohneinheiten, vorwiegend Kleinwohnungen, im Massenwohnungsbau errichtet. Gebaut wurde überwiegend am Blockrand in Klinkerbauweise in einer regional und lokal gebundenen Bautradition. Platzfassaden und Eckbetonung bestimmen die großen Blöcke mit gemeinsam benutzten Höfen.

Im Vergleich zu Martin Wagner in Berlin ging es Schumacher weniger um die Organisation der Großstadt durch die Demonstration funktionalistischer Städtebauprinzipien als vielmehr um die Schaffung homogener Stadtbilder. Ein städtebaulicher Paradigmenwechsel war in Hamburg weniger ausgeprägt als in Berlin. Auch wurden dort keine Siedlungskonzepte nach den Prinzipien des „International Style" verwirklicht, wie sie in der Weißen Stadt und der Großsiedlung Siemensstadt zu finden sind. Auch kam es aufgrund der stadträumlichen Situation nicht zur demonstrativen Einbeziehung von Natur und Topographie wie bei einigen Berliner Siedlungen.

estates himself, 65,000 flats were built, most of them small flats in mass housing projects until 1933. Most of the buildings were block margin buildings of clinker bricks on the basis of a regional and local tradition. The large blocks are characterised by facades towards squares, stressed corners and commonly used courtyards.

In contrast to Martin Wagner in Berlin, Schumacher was not so much aiming at organising the big city by demonstrating functionalist urban development principles. He rather wanted to create homogeneous urban cityscapes. The change of paradigm in urban development was less marked in Hamburg than in Berlin. Neither did Hamburg implement residential development concepts in line with the principles of International Style as they are reflected in Weiße Stadt and Siemensstadt. Due to the urban topography, the designs also did not include the demonstrative integration of nature and topography as it happened with some of the Berlin housing estates.

### "International Style" in Berlin

Weiße Stadt and the Großsiedlung Siemensstadt are products of the period "around 1930" and represent the "International Style", which for a long time has been considered by historians of architecture to be the actual representative of the Modern Age. The decisive factors for this assessment were the flawlessly white walls, which seemed to ideally represent a turning away from history, tradition, and ornament and were therefore stressed in an idealising manner in texts and photographs. The particular white of Weiße Stadt is also highlighted by the use of bright colours for windows, doors and cornices. In general, international research makes it ever clearer that the pure white of the International Style is a product of black and white photography.

In urban residential development, the phase around 1930 is considered to be a phase of an increasingly more scientific and functional approach. Large projects like the Reichsforschungssiedlung (Research Housing Estate of the Reich) in Berlin Haselhorst were supposed to support the development of an optimal concept for ribbon buildings and for

145

## „International Style" in Berlin

Als Produkte der Zeit „um 1930" repräsentieren die Weiße Stadt und die Großsiedlung Siemensstadt die Richtung des „International Style", die in der Architekturgeschichtsschreibung lange Zeit als die eigentliche Moderne gesehen wurde. Entscheidend für diese Bewertung waren die makellos weißen Wände, die auf idealtypische Weise die Abwendung von Geschichte, Tradition und Ornament zu verkörpern schienen und die deswegen in Texten und Fotos idealisierend hervorgehoben sind. Das besondere Weiß der Weißen Stadt tritt im Übrigen durch stark farbige Fenster, Tür und Gesimsprofile erst so richtig hervor. Überhaupt erweist sich das reine Weiß des „International Style" in der internationalen Forschung mehr und mehr als Produkt der Schwarzweiß-Fotografie.

Im Siedlungsbau wird die Phase um 1930 als Zeit der Verwissenschaftlichung und Versachlichung aufgefasst. Großprojekte wie die Reichsforschungssiedlung in Berlin-Haselhorst sollten der Ermittlung des optimalen Zeilenbaukonzeptes und der besten und zugleich wirtschaftlichsten Grundrisse dienen. Architekten wie Otto Haesler traten mit dem Konzept der Wohnung für das Existenzminimum hervor. In der Dammerstocksiedlung bei Karlsruhe (1928–29) entstand nach den städtebaulichen Entwürfen von Otto Haesler und Walter Gropius eine Zeilenbausiedlung, die ganz der Doktrin der Ausrichtung nach Morgen- und Nachmittagssonne folgen sollte.

Experimentell sind auch die beiden Anlagen „Weiße Stadt" und „Siemensstadt". Beide wurden direkt von der Stadt Berlin finanziert. Den mitwirkenden Architekten wurde bei der Grundrissentwicklung große Freiheit gelassen. Selbst die inzwischen grundsätzlich verpönte Wohnküche wurde gestattet, so in der geschwungenen Langzeile von Otto Bartning in Siemensstadt und in Teilen der Wohnzeilen von Wilhelm Büning in der Weißen Stadt. Hans Scharoun entwarf in seinen eigenen Bauten in Siemensstadt erstmalig eine Wohnung mit offenem Grundriss, deren Wohnraum sich zu beiden Seiten der Hauses öffnet. Gropius entwickelte seinen Kastengrundriss mit Mittelflur, den er später immer wieder verwendete, bis hin zu seinem Beitrag zur Interbau 1957 im Berliner Hansaviertel. Hugo Häring legte als einziger die Treppenhäuser und die „organisch" geformten Balkone nach Westen, wagte also eine höchst ungewöhnliche Konzentration aller plastischen Motive auf der besonnten Seite seiner Zeilen, die nicht umsonst das am häufigsten abgebildete Motiv in Siemensstadt geworden sind. Neu und ungewöhnlich war auch Salvisbergs Baukastensystem für seine Zeilen am Romanshorner Weg in der Weißen Stadt: über einer größeren Wohnung mit Garten im Erdgeschoss stehen je zwei Maisonettewohnungen mit Balkon und Außenzugang, ein Schema, das in den Siedlungen des London County Council im Großraum Londons nach dem Zweiten Weltkrieg wiederkehrt.

Die städtebaulichen Entwürfe von Otto Rudolf Salvisberg für die Weiße Stadt und von Hans Scharoun für Siemensstadt sind auf höchst signifikante Weise verschieden. Die Weiße Stadt bietet mit den erhöhten Rahmenbauten an der Aroser Allee, die den Blick in die leicht geschwungene, mit straßenbegleitenden Blöcken gefasste zentrale Achse lenken – die moderne Adaption eines traditionellen städtebaulichen Ordnungs- und Abgrenzungsmotivs – Turm

finding the best and simultaneously most economic ground plans. Architects like Otto Haesler presented concepts for a flat at subsistence level. The Dammerstocksiedlung (Dammerstock housing estate) near Karlsruhe (1928–29) was a ribbon building estate built on the basis of designs by Otto Haesler and Walter Gropius and was supposed to be built completely on the basis of the doctrine of orientation towards morning and afternoon sunshine.

Weiße Stadt and Siemensstadt, too, are experimental estates. Both were financed directly by the city of Berlin. The involved architects enjoyed enormous freedom when designing the ground plans. Even rooms that combined living rooms and kitchens were allowed (for instance in the long curved ribbon by Otto Bartning at Siemensstadt and in some of the residential ribbons by Wilhelm Büning at Weiße Stadt). For his buildings, Hans Scharoun designed for the first time for Siemensstadt a flat with an open ground plan whose living room opens towards both sides of the house. Gropius developed his box-type ground plan with a central corridor, which he kept on using even in his contribution for Interbau 1957 at Hansaviertel (Hansa Quarter) in Berlin. Hugo Häring was the only one who placed all the staircases and the "organically" shaped balconies on the western side. In doing so, he made the very unusual endeavour to concentrate all the plastic motifs on the sunny side of his ribbons, and it is not without reason that these buildings are the most frequently photographed houses of Siemensstadt. Also, Salvisberg's kit system was novel and unusual. He used it for his ribbons on Romanshorner Weg in Weiße Stadt. Above a larger flat on the ground floor level with a garden, there are two maisonettes with balconies and a separate entrance. This solution was used again in the estates built by the London County Council in the Greater London area after the Second World War.

There is a very significant difference between the designs by Otto Rudolf Salvisberg for Weiße Stadt and those by Hans Scharoun for Siemensstadt. With its higher, frame-like buildings along Aroser Allee that guide the view into the slightly bent central axis which is accompanied by blocks, Weiße Stadt is a modern adaptation of the traditional motif of order and delimitation using towers and gates. The bridge building that spans the central axis as a joint which can be viewed from both sides, with its artistic functionality, is a pure representation of International Style and fulfils the function of a centre that provides orientation. It is the point of view offering a target for the view

Abb. 66: Großsiedlung Siemensstadt, Blick vom Siemenswerk, um 1930

Fig. 66: Großsiedlung Siemensstadt, view from Siemens factory, approximately 1930

und Tor. Das Brückenhaus, das die zentrale Achse als nach beiden Seiten lesbarer Gelenkbau überspannt, in seiner kunstvollen Sachlichkeit die pure Verkörperung des „International Style", erfüllt die Funktion eines Orientierung gebenden Zentrums. Es ist der Point de Vue, der dem Blick auf der Mittelachse ein Ziel gibt – ganz im Sinne einer barocken Stadt- oder Gartenkomposition. So erhält die Weiße Stadt, bei aller Sachlichkeit und Funktionalität der Stockwerksbauten, eine klare räumliche Fassung. Die zwei Hauptansichten – Tor und Brückenhaus – sind außerordentlich einprägsam und werden gewöhnlich stellvertretend für das Ganze abgebildet.

Hans Scharoun ging mit seinem Entwurf für Siemensstadt einen ganz anderen Weg. Gleich weit entfernt von der steinernen Stadt des 19. Jahrhunderts und von allen Versuchen, das Kleinstädtische oder Dörfliche als Gegenbild zum Großstädtischen aufzubauen, schuf er hier eine Komposition aus parallelen und versetzten Zeilen, deren Beziehungen zueinander und zum großzügigen Grünraum keine Erinnerung an den vormodernen Städtebau wachrufen. Offene und bergende Räume, Verengungen und Aufweitungen folgen einem abstrakten Entwurf, in dem zwar Reihungen und Parallelen, nicht aber Achsen und Symmetrien vorkommen. In ihrer räumlichen Ausgewogenheit, der Einbeziehung existierender landschaftlicher Gegebenheiten und mit den von Leberecht Migge kongenial entworfenen offenen Grünräumen ist Siemensstadt eine moderne Stadtlandschaft, im Sinne des von Hans Scharoun erst in seiner Städtebaulehre nach 1945 explizit entwickelten Begriffes.

**„International Style" im Siedlungsbau in Frankreich, England und Holland**
Der Vergleich mit den großen Siedlungen der späteren 1920er Jahre in Europa stellt die Besonderheit der Weißen Stadt und der Großsiedlung Siemensstadt noch weiter heraus. Die großen Siedlungsprojekte der gleichen Zeit in Frankreich – etwa „La Butte Rouge" von Sivin, de Rutté und Bassompierre in Châtenay-Malabry, 1924–28 oder die Cité Jardin in Suresnes, 1921-29 von Alexandre Maistrasse, folgen zunächst dem Gartenstadtschema und dann einem Konzept stärkerer städtischer Verdichtung, in einer Stillage, die am ehesten mit Art Deco zu bezeichnen ist (Theater in Suresnes). Die damals sowohl stilistisch als auch städtebaulich avantgardistischen Projekte von Marcel Lods und Eugène Beaudouin – die „Cité du Champ des Oiseaux" in Bagneux (1930–32) und Drancy im Pariser Norden (1932–34) sind inzwischen entweder bis zur Unkenntlichkeit verändert (Bagneux) oder durch Abriss in ihrem Bestand stark reduziert (Drancy).

In England wird der „International Style" nur in wenigen Privat- und Sonderbauten greifbar. Die nach 1933 ins Exil getriebenen Architekten der Moderne aus Deutschland – u. a. Mendelsohn, Gropius, Gutkind, Fraenkel – hatten keine Gelegenheit, größere Wohnanlagen zu realisieren. Die große Zeit des modernen Siedlungsbaus in England beginnt erst in der Wiederaufbauzeit nach dem Zweiten Weltkrieg.

Stilistisch stehen den Berliner Projekten zweifellos die Großsiedlungen in Holland von J. J. P. Oud in Rotterdam und Hoek van Holland am nächsten, die für den Sied-

along the central axis and is thus fully in line with the spirit of a baroque urban or garden composition. Thus, Weiße Stadt has a clear spatial structure despite the non-emotional and functional character of its multi-storey buildings. The two main views – the gate and the bridge house – are extremely striking and are usually shown to represent the entire ensemble.

In his design for Siemensstadt, Hans Scharoun chose a completely different approach. Neither in the tradition of the stone city of the 19th century nor attempting to present small town or village developments as opposing the big city, here he created a composition of parallel and staggered ribbons whose relations to each other and the spacious green spaces do not recall any memories of pre-modern urban development. Open and containing spaces, narrowing and extending spaces follow an abstract design with rows and parallels, but not axes or symmetries. In their spatial balance, the integration of existing landscape situations and the green spaces that were ingeniously designed by Leberecht Migge, Siemensstadt is a modern urban landscape in the sense of a term that was explicitly developed by Hans Scharoun only in his urban development theory after 1945.

**"International Style" in housing estate development in France, England and Holland**
When comparing Weiße Stadt with the large European housing estates of the later 1920s, its peculiarities and those of Siemensstadt stand out even more clearly. The large housing estates, which were erected at the same time in France (for instance "La Butte Rouge" by Sivin, de Rutté and Bassompierre at Châtenay-Malabry, 1924–28 or Cité Jardin at Suresnes, 1921–29 by Alexandre Maistrasse), initially apply the garden town pattern and later a concept of greater urban density with a style which should most probably be called Art Deco (the theatre at Suresnes). The projects by Marcel Lods and Eugène Beaudouin – the Cité du Champs des Oiseaux at Bagneux (1930–32) and Drancy in the North of Paris (1932–34), which were vanguard projects both in terms of style and urban development have either been altered so much that they have become unrecognisable (Bagneux) or they were extremely reduced through the removal of buildings (Drancy).

In England the "International Style" was first used only in few private and special buildings. The German modern age architects driven into exile after 1933 – for instance Erich Mendelsohn, Walter Gropius, Erwin Gutkind, Rudolf Fraenkel – did not have an opportunity to realise major housing estates. The heyday of modern residential development started in England only with the period of reconstruction after the Second World War.

In terms of style, the large housing estates in Holland by J. J. P. Oud in Rotterdam and Hoek van Holland are probably closest to those in Berlin. These former housing estates have become symbols of the "white" modern age. Yet, the housing estates in Hoek von Holland (1924–27) and "De Kiefhoek" in Rotterdam (1925–29) present a completely different type and form of urban development concept than the two housing estates in Berlin. Oud stuck to the row house pattern for his long double-storey ribbons and placed his rows parallel without any sections with dominating

lungsbau der „weißen" Moderne emblematische Bedeutung gewonnen haben. Die Siedlungen in Hoek van Holland (1924–27) und „De Kiefhoek" in Rotterdam (1925–29) sind jedoch typologisch und städtebaulich ganz anders konzipiert als die beiden Berliner Anlagen. Oud blieb für seine langgestreckten zweigeschossigen Zeilen beim Reihenhausschema und stellte die Zeilen parallel, ohne Höhendominanten. Und, was in unserem Zusammenhang besonders wichtig wird: Die Freiflächen sind als Mietergärten streifenförmig abgeteilt. Für großräumige Gartenanlagen fehlten Raum und Mittel. Sein Projekt für die Großsiedlung Blijdorp (1931), das Geschosswohnungen in Zeilenbauten und große rechteckige Blocks mit Gärten im Inneren vorsah, wurde nicht verwirklicht.

**Der Siedlungsarchitekt Bruno Taut – Bauen mit Farbe in der Moderne**
Unter den Architekten, die sich im Siedlungsbau der 1920er Jahre engagierten, nimmt Bruno Taut eine herausragende Stellung ein. Er ist der Künstler unter den Siedlungsbauern, der mit alten und neuen Mustern und Typen souverän umgeht und aus Häusern in Blockrändern, Zeilen, Riegeln, Reihen und Gruppen immer neue Figuren bildet, die niemals schematisch irgendeinem alten oder neuen Dogma folgen. Wenn er, wie in der Schillerparksiedlung, die Gebäude in scheinbar traditioneller Weise am Blockrand stehen lässt, so öffnet er den Block an den Gelenkstellen und orientiert die Wohnräume und Balkone der Häuser zu den besonnten Seiten, nach Süden und Westen, macht sie also zu parallel stehenden Zeilen. Wenn er, wie in der Hufeisensiedlung, straßenbegleitende Reihenhausgruppen einander gegenüberstellt, versetzt er sie abschnittsweise nach vorn oder hinten, verschwenkt die Achsen, wenn auch nur um ein Geringes, schafft so Verengungen und Erweiterungen, die jede Straße als charakteristischen Raum formen. Das Hufeisen selber, grundrisstypologisch gesehen nichts anderes als eine langgestreckte, gebogene Zeile, bezieht wiederum seine besondere Kraft daraus, dass alle Wohnräume und Loggienbalkone nach innen, zur großen Grünanlage um den Hufeisenteich ausgerichtet sind, die damit zu einem auf das Wohnen bezogenen Freiraum wird, zugänglich für Besucher, aber zugehörig den Bewohnern.

Ganz anders wiederum in der Wohnstadt Carl Legien, die am Rand der Innenstadt an einer bereits bestehenden Achse zu entwickeln war. Hier ordnete Taut die Bauten U-förmig um je drei tiefe Gartenhöfe beiderseits der Straße an. Die Gartenseite ist die Hauptseite der drei Trakte, die breiten Loggien sind also auch hier nicht alle der besonnten Seite zugewandt, sondern dem gemeinsamen Gartenraum, der über die Straße hinweg mit dem Gartenraum des gegenüberliegenden Hofes zusammenfließt. So entsteht, mitten im verdichteten Innenstadtbezirk und ohne Verzicht auf die dem Ort angemessene Bebauungsdichte, eine großzügige, gartenstädtische Atmosphäre. Hier liegt auch der große Unterschied zwischen der Wohnstadt Carl Legien und der oft als Vorbild genannten Siedlung Tusschendijken von J. J. P. Oud (1920–24) in Rotterdam: Dort sind die Loggien in vergleichbarer Weise den Gartenhöfen zugewandt, aber die Höfe sind geschlossen, und überdies ist beiderseits ein Gutteil der Gartenfläche nach Art von Reihenhausgärten in schmalen Streifen abgezäunt. Die Atmosphäre ist freundlich, aber eng.

height. Another aspect is very important in this context: The outdoor facilities have been subdivided into strips of tenants' gardens. Unfortunately there was neither space nor means available for spacious gardens. Oud's design for the large housing estate of Blijdorp (1931) was not implemented. It envisaged flats in multi-storey ribbon buildings and large rectangular blocks around interior gardens.

**The housing estate architect Bruno Taut – Use of colour in Modern age building**
Bruno Taut stands out among the architects who were committed to housing estate development in the 1920s. He is the artist among the housing estate developers who competently uses old and new patterns and types and creates ever new patterns of houses along block margins, ribbons, cross bars, rows and groups, patterns that never schematically follow any old or new dogma. If he positions buildings in seemingly traditional patterns at the block margin as he did at the Schillerpark housing estate, he opens these blocks at their joints and orientates the living rooms and balconies of the houses towards the sunny sides, i.e. south and west, and thus turns the buildings into parallel ribbons. If he opposes groups of row houses along both sides of a street as he did in the horseshoe housing estate, he makes sections of them project or retreat, shifts their axes if only a little and thus creates narrower and wider parts which turn every street into a characteristic space. The horseshoe itself whose principle type is just a long, curved ribbon gains its special power from the fact that all living rooms and balconies are orientated towards the inside – the large green space around the horseshoe pond – turning this space into an open space which is related to living, accessible for visitors, but actually belonging to the inhabitants.

He found a completely different solution for Wohnstadt Carl Legien, which had to be developed at the margin of the city centre along an existing axis. Here, Taut placed the buildings in U-shapes around three deep courtyards on either side of the street. The garden side is the main side of the three blocks, which means that here, too, the loggias are not all orientated towards the sunny side but towards the common garden space, which merges with the garden space of the opposite courtyard across the street. This creates a spacious garden town atmosphere right in the middle

Abb. 67: Siedlung De Kiefhoek in Rotterdam, 1925–29 von J. J. P. Oud, um 1929

Fig. 67: De Kiefhoek at Rotterdam, 1925–29 by J. J. Oud, approximately 1929

Taut war auch Meister des farbigen Bauens. Er modellierte Baukörper und Siedlungsräume mit flächig aufgetragenen Farben, und das in Farbtönen und Farbdichten, die ungewöhnlich und stets aufs Neue überraschend intensiv wirken. Seine ersten farbigen Siedlungen sind die Gartenstadt Reform in Magdeburg und die Gartenstadt Falkenberg, seinerzeit – und auch heute noch – besonders aufsehenerregend, weil sie mit Abstand das farbigste Projekt war und blieb. Mit Lapislazuli-Blau, Schokoladenbraun, Orange, Türkis, Gelb, tief Braunrot, und gar Schwarz wählte Taut eine Palette, die nicht mit Hausanstrichen, sondern bestenfalls mit Tafelbildern assoziiert werden konnte. Am nächsten steht das farbige Falkenberg fraglos der expressionistischen Malerei, in der Tauts Zeitgenossen mit gleichfalls „fehlfarbenen" Gegenständen konfrontiert wurden – mit grünen Kühen, blauen Pferden, blauen Reitern, gelben Christusfiguren, die Maler wie Franz Marc, Wassili Kandinsky oder Emil Nolde in der Zeit um 1913 geschaffen haben. Es ist belegt, dass Taut vor allem die Gemälde Franz Marcs bewunderte. Als nächstgelegene Analogie sei Kandinskys Gemälde „Dame in Moskau" von 1912 genannt, das eine komplexe Traumerscheinung zeigt, in der zwei Reihen niedriger, „falsch"-farbener Häuser, jedes in einem anderen Farbton, den Mittelgrund einrahmen.

Bei einer europaweiten und nationalen Gegenüberstellung findet man keine vergleichbar farbigen Siedlungen vor dem Ersten Weltkrieg. Die Gartenstädte in England, Vorbilder für die städtebauliche Konzeption Falkenbergs, sind jedenfalls nicht vergleichbar farbig, ebenso wenig die Arbeitersiedlungen in den nordeuropäischen Industriegebieten, die Reformbauten in Berlin oder gar die ländliche Architektur Brandenburgs. Auch die zeitgleich entstandenen Gartenstädte in Deutschland wie die Siedlungen Hellerau bei Dresden (1908) und Staaken in Berlin (1913) zeigen nicht diese expressive Farbigkeit.

In der Taut-Forschung wird gelegentlich auf die Insel Burano bei Venedig hingewiesen, ohne dass klargestellt würde, ob Taut jemals, vielleicht in seiner Münchener Zeit, nach Venedig und Burano gereist ist oder wie er sonst von den bunten Fischerhäusern an der Lagune hätte Kenntnis erhalten können. Die Häuser, häufig in Reiseführern genannt und abgebildet, sind schmal, meist zweigeschossig, stehen mit der Traufseite zur Straße und sind farbig gestrichen, jedes in einem anderen Ton, mit starken, satt wirkenden Farben, so dass gelegentlich starke Kontraste entstehen. Es ist nicht bekannt, ob nun die Farben aus Resten von Schiffsanstrichen oder aus in Venedig erworbenen Pigmentresten gemischt wurden, und seit wann die Häuser derart farbig gestrichen werden. Sicher ist, dass die Leute von Burano für die Dekoration ihrer Häuser wenig Geld ausgeben konnten, ebenso wie Taut in Falkenberg. Ein flächenhafter Farbanstrich, auch ein stark farbiger – so Taut –, war billiger als der einfachste skulpturale Schmuck. Nachdem Taut in seinen publizierten Ausführungen zur Farbe nicht auf Burano verweist, muss die offensichtliche Analogie im Bild – in Erwartung weiterführender Forschungen – eine Randbemerkung zur Sache bleiben. Ähnliches gilt für die Buntheit skandinavischer Holzhäuser und die Farbigkeit osteuropäischer Volksarchitektur.

Auch in den 1920er Jahren bediente sich Taut der Farbe als architekturbildendes Element für seine zahlreichen Sied-

of a dense inner city district, even without losing any of the density of development that is appropriate for this location. This is the main difference between Wohnstadt Carl Legien and the housing estate Tusschendijken by J. J. P. Oud (1920–1924) in Rotterdam, which is often mentioned as a model. At this Rotterdam housing estate, the balconies are turned towards the courtyards, similar to the Carl Legien housing estate, but the yards of the former are closed and on either side quite a large part of the garden area is fenced in and subdivided into narrow bands like row house gardens. The atmosphere is friendly but close.

Taut was also a master of colour in building. He modelled buildings and housing estate spaces by means of coloured areas and used shades and densities of colour that are unusual and, again and again, surprisingly intense. His first colourful housing estates are the Gartenstadt Reform at Magdeburg and Gartenstadt Falkenberg. The latter was and is still today the most sensational because it was and has remained the most colourful of his projects. Lapis lazuli blue, chocolate brown, orange, turquoise, yellow, deep reddish brown and even black were the colours chosen by Taut, and they are normally not associated with facade colours but rather with panel paintings. The colourful housing estate at Falkenberg is probably closest to expressionist painting, in which Taut's contemporaries were confronted with things painted in "wrong colours": green cows, blue horses, blue riders, or yellow figures of Christ as they were created by painters like Franz Marc, Wassilly Kandinsky or Emil Nolde around 1913. It has been proven that Taut especially admired the paintings of Franz Marc. The closest analogy is a painting by Kandinsky – "Dame in Moskau" (Lady in Moscow) from 1912 – portraying a complex dream vision in which two rows of low houses in "wrong" colours, each in a different colour, frame the middle ground.

A European or national search does not yield any comparatively colourful housing estates built before the First World War. The English garden towns, which were the model for the urban development concept of Falkenberg, are not as colourful and neither are the workers' housing estates in the Northern European industrial areas, the reform buildings at Berlin nor the rural architecture of Brandenburg. The other German garden towns like Hellerau near Dresden (1908) and Staaken (1913) are not as expressively colourful, either.

Taut research occasionally mentions the island of Burano near Venice without clarifying, however, if Taut ever travelled to Venice and Burano – perhaps during his time in Munich – or how he might have come to know the colourful fishermen's huts on the lagoon. These houses are often mentioned and shown on photographs in tourist guides. They are narrow, usually have two storeys, their eaves are turned towards the street and they are each painted in a different colour. The colours are deep and saturated, such that some are in strong contrast with each other. It is not known whether the paint used was just left over from painting ships or whether residue pigments purchased at Venice were used or when the houses were painted so colourfully. What is known is that the people of Burano had little money to spend on decorating their houses and the same applied for Taut and the houses at Falkenberg. Taut found that a painted facade, even if very intense colours

Abb. 68: Wohnstadt Carl Legien, Wohnhof an der Erich-Weinert-Straße, historischer Farbdruck, um 1930

Fig. 68: Wohnstadt Carl Legien, courtyard with central heating plant at Erich-Weinert-Straße, historic colour print, approximately 1930

lungsprojekte. In der Hufeisensiedlung nutzte er die Farbe nicht nur flächig, für ganze Hauswände, sondern auch modellierend und gliedernd, wie etwa am Hufeisen selber, dessen Treppenhausachsen, Loggien und Drempel blau gefasst sind und optisch stark hinter die ursprünglich weiß gestrichenen Hauswände zurücktreten. Die Reihenhäuser färbte Taut in Gruppen, nicht alternierend, wie in Falkenberg. So entstehen größere Farbeinheiten, die ähnlich wie die Achsenabweichungen und Verschiebungen raumbildend wirken. In der Wohnstadt Carl Legien waren die einander gegenüberliegenden Gartenhöfe jeweils in einer Farbe gestrichen: ein Hofpaar tiefrot, eines grün, eines blau. Die Straßenseiten und die Kopfbauten zur Mittelachse waren leuchtend hellgelb, also ergab sich zu den Hofseiten auch hier ein starker Farbkontrast. Mit einer derart unkonventionellen Verwendung der Farbe stand Taut in Deutschland weiterhin allein. Das Bauhaus um Walter Gropius bevorzugte Primärfarben, wie die Gruppe „de Stijl". Taut galt als Außenseiter – wohl ein Grund dafür, dass er am internationalen publizistischen Ruhm der Bauhäusler keinen Anteil hatte.

### Farbe im europäischen Siedlungsbau

Nach 1918 ist Taut nicht mehr der einzige, der stark farbig baut: Die holländischen Künstler der Gruppe „de Stijl", namentlich Piet Mondrian, Gerrit Rietveld, Theo van Doesburg und auch J. J. P. Oud bekennen sich ausdrücklich zur Farbe in der Architektur. Sie verwenden sie aber in ganz anderer Weise als Taut: mit der Festlegung auf unvermischte Primärfarben – Rot, Blau, Gelb –, die gewöhnlich mit weißen Flächen kontrastierend vorkommen. So hat die Farblehre der Gruppe vielleicht mehr doktrinäre Klarheit geschaffen, dafür aber weniger Freiheiten gelassen als Taut sie mit seinen weiterhin außerordentlich kühnen künstlerischen Gestaltungen beanspruchte.

Auch Le Corbusier begann mit seinen Arbeiterhäusern des „Quartier Moderne Frugès", errichtet 1924 bis 1926 in Pessac bei Bordeaux, mit der Entwicklung einer stark farbigen

were used, was always cheaper than even the most simple sculptural decoration. Since Taut does not mention Burano in his published statements on colour, the obvious analogy in appearance must remain a marginal note in the matter until further research yields more results. Analogue conclusions apply for the colourfulness of Scandinavian wooden houses and the colourful eastern European national architecture.

Also during the 1920s, Taut used colour as an architectural element for his many housing estate projects. In the horseshoe housing estate, he used colour not only for full areas, i.e. walls of houses, but also for modelling and structuring, such as in the horseshoe itself, whose staircase axes, loggias and jambs are painted blue, making them retreat optically very much behind the house walls, which were originally painted white. Groups of row houses got the same colour. Their facades were not coloured alternatingly as at Falkenberg. Thus Taut created larger colour units that create spaces just as the shifted axes and building lines do. At Wohnstadt Carl Legien, the opposite courtyards were always painted in the same colour: One pair of yards was deep red, another one green and one was blue. The street-side facades and the head buildings at the central axis were painted in a brilliant light yellow that created a strong contrast to the yard sides. With this unconventional use of colour, Taut continued to stand alone in Germany. The Bauhaus Group surrounding Walter Gropius preferred primary colours like the group de Stijl. Taut was considered to be an outsider, which is probably one reason for the fact that he did not participate in the international fame of the Bauhaus-group.

### Colour in European urban development

After 1918, Taut was no longer the only one to use colour very much in architecture. The Dutch artists of the group "de Stijl", namely Piet Mondrian, Gerrit Rietveld, Theo van Doesburg and also J. J. P. Oud, expressly support the use of colour in architecture. Yet, they employ it in a completely

Architektur. Das Quartier Moderne ist als Gartenstadt angelegt, mit etwa 50 Häusern verschiedener Typen, einzeln stehend, in Gruppen und in Reihen. Nach Le Corbusiers eigener Darstellung entstand die Idee einer flächigen farbigen Fassung erst, als er die dichten Reihen betongrauer Häuser vor sich sah und nun die Dichte und vergleichsweise Enge der Bebauung mit den Mitteln einer farbigen Gestaltung mildern wollte. Manche Flächen sollten zurücktreten, quasi optische Rücksprünge bilden, andere sollten hervortreten und so die im Architekturentwurf angelegte skulpturale Tiefe der Bauten akzentuieren. Le Corbusier verwandte keine Primärfarben wie de Stijl, sondern starke Grundfarben, die er mit weißen Flächen kontrastierte.

Die Töne, die Le Corbusier seinerzeit wählte und die im Zusammenhang mit seinem Umgang mit Farbe in der unmittelbar vorangegangenen Phase des Purismus in seiner Malerei stehen – helles ultramarin-blau (bleu d'outremer clair), gebrannte Terra di Siena (terre de Sienne brulée), englischgrün (vert anglais), helles Terra die Siena (terre de Sienne claire) und weiß für die Wände, gebranntes Umbra (terre d'ombre brulée) für die Fensterrahmen, sind heute in ihrer ursprünglichen Farbwirkung schwer einzuschätzen, da Farbabbildungen aus der Bauzeit fehlen und der erste Farbenplan Le Corbusiers nicht aufgefunden werden konnte. Die Forschung hat sich bislang auf die erst 1931 von Le Corbusier selber entwickelten und von der Firma „Salubra" produzierten Farbklaviaturen gestützt und daraus auf die Zeit um 1925 rückgeschlossen. Für die Farbfassungen, die seit den 1980er Jahren an einzelnen Häusern in Pessac rekonstruiert wurden, konnte erst in jüngerer Zeit ein einheitliches Gesamtkonzept entwickelt werden, das auf ausführlichen bauhistorischen Studien, allerdings nicht auf restauratorischen Befundunsuchungen aufbaut. Man kann wohl sagen, dass die heute sichtbaren Töne – ein erdiges Rot, ein sehr blasses Grün, ein dichtes, aber stark mit Weiß aufgehelltes Blau – eine ganz andere Farbstimmung erzeugen als sie Taut in Falkenberg angestrebt hat.

Le Corbusier verwandte, ebenso wie Taut, starke und dichte Farben. Er färbte ganze Flächen in einem Ton und ließ genauso an den Hauskanten die Farbflächen ohne abgesetztes Profil hart aufeinander treffen. Auch Corbusier modellierte den Siedlungsraum mit den Mitteln der Farbgestaltung. Anders als Taut formte er auch die Baukörper durch farbige Rücksprünge, verwendete die Farbe also auch im Detail skulptural. In seinen theoretischen Äußerungen preist Le Corbusier die raumbildende und lichtmodellierende Kraft der Farbe – wie Bruno Taut.

Und natürlich wussten beide voneinander. Taut publizierte in seinem Buch „Bauen. Der neue Wohnbau" von 1927 fünf Abbildungen der „Arbeitersiedlung Pessac bei Bordeaux" und einen programmatischen Text Le Corbusiers. Die starke Farbigkeit der Siedlung ist auf den Schwarz-Weiß-Fotos unverkennbar. In Frankreich wiederum war Taut als Meister des sozialen und des farbigen Bauens kein Unbekannter. Im Archiv der „Fondation Le Corbusier" in Paris findet sich ein Artikel von Charles Petrasch aus „Le Monde" vom 28. September 1929, der unter der Überschrift „Bruno Taut" Leben und Werk des Architekten vorstellt. Dort heißt es u.a.:

Abb. 69: Besprechung der Siedlung Pessac von Le Corbusier in Bruno Tauts Buch „Bauen – Der Neue Wohnbau", 1927

Fig. 69: Review of the Pessac housing estate by Le Corbusier in Bruno Taut's book "Bauen – Der Neue Wohnbau", 1927

different way than Taut: They prefer unblended primary colours (red, blue, yellow), which they usually make contrast with white areas. So the chromatology of this group may have created more clarity, but it left less freedom that Taut continued to claim with his extremely bold artistic designs.

Le Corbusier also started developing a very colourful architecture when designing his workers' houses of the Quartier Moderne Frugès, which were built from 1924 through 1926 in Pessac near Bordeaux. The Quartier Moderne was designed as a garden town with approximately 50 houses of various types standing either alone or in groups or in rows. According to Le Corbusier's own statement, he got the idea of coloured walls only when he saw the dense rows of concrete grey houses and he wanted to mitigate the density and relative closeness of the buildings by using colour. Some areas were supposed to retreat, i.e. he wanted to create optical recesses, others were to project and thus highlight the sculptural depth of the buildings, which was part of the architectural design. Le Corbusier did not use primary colours like de Stijl, but rather deep primary colours, which he made to contrast with white areas.

The original impression created by the colours and shades, which Le Corbusier chose at that time and which are related to his use of colour in the immediately preceding phase of purism in his painting work, can hardly be assessed today, since there are no colour images from this time and his first colour scheme has not been found. He used light ultramarine blue (bleu d'outremer clair), burnt Terra di Siena (terre de Sienne brulée), lead chrome green (vert anglais), light Terra die Siena (terre de Sienne claire) and white for the walls, and burnt umber (terre d'ombre

„Bruno Taut est un des premiers a avoir su le mieux tirer parti de la peinture dans l'architecture allemande moderne. Il considère la couleur comme problème fondamental de toute construction. Jusqu'à lui, notre époque n'avait guère connu la couleur comme adjuvent de l'architecture. Cette idée possède des défenseurs dans chaque pays. Rappelons l'interview de Fernand Léger sur l'importance de la couleur, publié dans le n° 58 du Monde. Le Corbusier, Mallet-Stevens, Gevrekian, Lurçat, en France; Rietveld, Oud, en Hollande; Hoste, Bourgeois, Van de Swaelmen en Belgique, ont réalisés dans cet esprit de bâtisses et de jardins de grand intérêt."

Es muss offenbleiben, ob Le Corbusier seine Inspiration für eine farbige Siedlung ausdrücklich von Bruno Taut bezogen hat. Zu komplex ist bereits um die Mitte der 1920er Jahre das Bild in Europa. Nicht zu verkennen ist jedoch, dass Tauts Gartenstadt Falkenberg, unmittelbar nach Fertigstellung reichlich in der Fachpresse publiziert und diskutiert, gut ein Jahrzehnt vor Pessac entstand und dass auch Tauts theoretische Äußerungen zur Farbe bereits klare Konturen besaßen, bevor Le Corbusier begann, sich in Wort und Werk mit Farbe im Städtebau auseinander zu setzen. Die beiden Architekten erscheinen im Hinblick auf ihren Einsatz von Farbe im Städtebau durchaus ebenbürtig. Der wichtigste Unterschied wäre, dass für Taut die Schaffung sozialer Räume und überhaupt die funktionale und soziale Bindung der Architektur im Vordergrund stand, während Le Corbusier in Pessac, wie auch später mit der „Unité d'Habitation", mehr formalen und ästhetischen Leitlinien folgte.

Der soziale Wohnungsbau, in den 1920er Jahren europaweit einer der vordringlichsten Bauaufgaben, kennzeichnet das Œuvre Tauts, wie dies bei keinem anderen Architekten

brulée) for the window frames. To date, research relied on the colour ranges which were developed by Le Corbusier himself but not before 1931 and which were produced by the company Salubra. From these ranges, conclusions were reconstructed for the time around 1925. Only recently was a uniform general concept developed for the restoration of the colouring of the individual houses, which has been going on since the 1980s. This concept is based on comprehensive studies of the history of architecture, but not on investigations for restoration purposes of the existing houses themselves. We are certainly justified to say that the colours we can see today – an earthy red, a very pale green, a dense blue, which has been made lighter by adding a lot of white – create a totally different atmosphere than that intended by Taut for Falkenberg.

Just like Taut, Le Corbusier used deep and dense colours. He used one shade for an entire wall, and like Taut, he let coloured areas meet at house edges without any transitional profile. Le Corbusier also used colour for modelling urban spaces. But in contrast to Taut, he also modelled buildings with coloured recesses, so he also used colour in sculptural details. In his theoretical statements, Le Corbusier praises the power of colour for creating spaces and modelling light just as Bruno Taut does.

And of course the two knew about each other. In his book "Bauen. Der neue Wohnbau", 1927, Taut published five images of the "Workers' Housing Estate of Pessac near Bordeaux" and a programmatic text by Le Corbusier. The black and white photographs clearly reflect the intense colourfulness of the housing estate. Taut in turn was well known in France as the master of social and colourful architecture. The archives of the Fondation Le Corbusier in Paris include an article by Charles Petrasch from Le Monde of 28 September 1929 which introduces the life and work of the architect under the headline of "Bruno Taut". It reads for instance:

"Bruno Taut est un des premiers à avoir su le mieux tirer parti de la peinture dans l'architecture allemande moderne. Il considère la couleur comme problème fondamental de toute construction. Jusqu'à lui, notre époque n'avait guère connu la couleur comme adjuvent de l'architecture. Cette idée possède des défenseurs dans chaque pays. Rappelons l'interview de Fernand Léger sur l'importance de la couleur, publié dans le n° 58 du Monde. Le Corbusier, Mallet-Stevens, Gevrekian, Lurçat, en France; Rietveld, Oud, en Hollande; Hoste, Bourgeois, Van de Swaelmen en Belgique, ont réalisés dans cet esprit de bâtisses et de jardins de grand intérêt."

We cannot say whether Le Corbusier got his inspiration for a colourful housing estate expressly from Bruno Taut. The situation in Europe had become far too complex by the mid 1920s. However, it is quite obvious that Taut's Gartenstadt Falkenberg was very well covered and intensely discussed in the relevant press immediately after it had been completed and it had been built more than one decade before Pessac; also, Taut's theoretical statements on colour were already quite clear before Le Corbusier started to deal with colour in theory and practice in urban development. With respect to the use of colour in urban development, the two architects seem to be quite equal. The most important difference is

Abb. 70: Cover von Bruno Tauts Buch „Bauen – Der Neue Wohnbau", 1927

Fig. 70: Cover of Bruno Taut's book "Bauen – Der Neue Wohnbau", 1927

Abb. 71: Gartenstadt Falkenberg, hausweiser Farbwechsel, Akazienhof 1–4, 2005

Fig. 71: Gartenstadt Falkenberg, a different colour for each house at Akazienhof 1–4, 2005

jener Zeit der Fall war. Schon die geleistete Arbeit bei der Organisation, Planung und Ausführung von 10.000 Wohnungen in nur 10 Jahren verdeutlicht die ungeheure Schaffenskraft Tauts. Neben der Quantität ist in seinen Wohnanlagen und Siedlungen die soziale Verpflichtung des Architekten spürbar, dem es zudem trotz enger wirtschaftlicher Vorgaben im Massenwohnungsbau gelingt städtebaulich wie architektonisch einen hohen Gestaltungsanspruch umzusetzen. Im Werk von Bruno Taut sind auch die Entwicklungslinien im Reformwohnungsbau, von der Gartenstadt bis zur Großsiedlung, anschaulich dokumentiert. Sein ganz persönlicher Beitrag für die Geschichte des modernen Siedlungsbaus ist jedoch die Anwendung der Farbe als architekturbildendes Element. Seine farbigen Wohnanlagen und Siedlungen erregten schon zur Bauzeit großes Aufsehen, erfuhren international höchste Wertschätzung und avancierten bald zu vielbeachteten Anschauungsobjekten im Wohnungsbau.

Parallel zu seiner Tätigkeit als Siedlungsarchitekt gab es den Publizisten und Lehrer Bruno Taut, der sich als Mitglied in Architekten- und Künstlervereinigungen, als Hochschuldozent oder als Berater und Teilnehmer an Bauausschüssen und Bauausstellungen zu den diversen Fragestellungen des Städtebaus und der Architektur Gehör verschaffte. Zahlreiche Veröffentlichungen begleiteten sein umfassendes Wirken als anerkannter Architekt, dem sich auch nach seiner erzwungenen Emigration 1933 bald gute Arbeitsmöglichkeiten in Japan und der Türkei eröffneten. Bruno Taut – der Visionär, Stadtplaner, Architekt und Künstler – gilt zu Recht als einer der bedeutendsten Protagonisten des Neuen Bauens und Wegbereiter des modernen Siedlungsbaus.

Die zur Nominierung ausgewählten Berliner Siedlungen und Wohnanlagen repräsentieren nicht nur die unterschiedlichen Stufen und die Bandbreite der mitteleuropäischen Entwicklung im Siedlungsbau, in der Gartenkunst und Baukunst. Sie sind, als Gruppe, in ihrer Vielfalt und Originalität und ihrer außerordentlich hohen künstlerischen Qualität, im internationalen Vergleich tatsächlich einzigartig. Nicht zuletzt zeichnen sich die Berliner Siedlungen durch ihre bis heute erlebbare authentische Überlieferung aus, da sie von Kriegszerstörungen weitest gehend

that Taut focussed on creating social spaces and on the functional and social aspects of architecture, whereas Le Corbusier followed more formal and aesthetic guidelines both at Pessac and also later with the Unité d'Habitation.

Social housing development, which was one of the most important tasks in building in Europe during the 1920s, plays a greater role in Taut's oeuvre than in that of any other architect of that period. Taut's enormous creativity is already reflected by the work he did in organising, designing and executing 10,000 flats in only 10 years. In addition to their quality, the estates and housing estates he designed reflect the social responsibility of the architect who managed to create rewarding designs both of urban development and architecture despite the strict economic limits that applied for mass housing. Bruno Taut's work also documents the development of reform housing from the garden city to the large estate. However, his most personal contribution in the history of modern age settlement development is the use of colour as an architectural design element. His colourful housing estates and settlements attracted a lot of attention even while they were being built. They garnered the greatest international esteem and soon became very respected models for housing development.

Parallel to his work as a housing estate architect, Bruno Taut also worked as a publisher and teacher. He made his opinion heard concerning the various issues of urban development and architecture in his capacity as a member in architects' and artists' associations, of university teacher or respectively as a consultant and participant in building committees and exhibitions. He supplemented his comprehensive activity as a renowned architect with many publications and even after he had been forced to emigrate in 1933, he soon received favourable opportunities to work in Japan and Turkey. Bruno Taut the visionary, urban planner, architect and artist is very justly considered to be one of the most significant representatives of Neues Bauen and a pioneer of modern housing estate development.

The Berlin housing estates and housing estates which have been chosen for nomination not only represent the various phases and the scope of central European residential devel-

verschont blieben und konservierende bzw. restaurierende Instandsetzungsmaßnahmen den Erhalt der Originalsubstanz und des Erscheinungsbildes sicherstellten.

### 3.D Integrität und/oder Authentizität

Alle nominierten Berliner Siedlungen zeichnen sich durch ein hohes Maß an erhaltener historischer Substanz aus. Ideologisch begründete Eingriffe während der nationalsozialistischen Zeit beschränkten sich auf den neuen Fassadenanstrich der Siedlung Carl Legien. Da sich die Anlagen weitgehend außerhalb der Kernstadt Berlins befanden, blieben sie von größeren Zerstörungen im Zweiten Weltkrieg verschont. So haben die Gartenstadt Falkenberg, die Wohnstadt Carl Legien, die Weiße Stadt und die Hufeisensiedlung nur sehr geringe Kriegsschäden erlitten. Größer waren die Bombenschäden an den Siedlungen Schillerpark und Siemensstadt, die beide in der Nähe von Industrie- und Militärstandorten lagen. Aber auch hier blieben die Zerstörungen auf einzelne Häuser beschränkt. Die Wiederaufbauten sind eigenständige Leistungen, in Siemensstadt von Hans Scharoun und Otto Bartning selber, im Schillerpark von Max Taut. Sie haben das Gesamtbild der Siedlungen bereichert. Nirgendwo kam es nach 1945 zu baulichen Verdichtungen.

Durch den Auftrag von neuen Putzen nach 1945 gingen der für das Neue Bauen typische membranhafte Glattputz bzw. der für die ländlichen Kleinhäuser der Gartenstadt Falkenberg und der Hufeisensiedlung charakteristische durchgefärbte Strukturputz verloren. Damit verschwand zugleich in den Taut-Siedlungen Falkenberg, Britz, Schillerpark und Carl Legien die für die Architektur Tauts so überaus wichtige Farbgebung.

Die mit sorgfältig durchdachten, funktionellen Bereichen ausgestatteten Grünräume, die bei den meisten Siedlungen von eigens hierfür hinzugezogenen Gartenarchitekten gestaltet worden waren, haben sich in der Grundkonzeption trotz einiger Veränderungen bewahrt. Aufgrund veränderter Nutzungsansprüche wurden zusätzliche Spielplätze und Müllplatzanlagen, aber auch Parkplätze in die Anlagen eingefügt. Zusätzlich eingefügte Pflanzungen, zum Teil Wildwuchs oder die Umgestaltung der als Nutzgärten angelegten Mietergärten zu Wohn- und Ziergärten haben die räumlichen und sozialen Bezüge verunklärt.

## Die einzelnen Siedlungen

## Gartenstadt Falkenberg

In der Gartenstadt Falkenberg musste nur ein Reihenhaus am Gartenstadtweg (Nr. 50) wiederaufgebaut werden. Auch blieben die Siedlungshäuser in der Nachkriegszeit – die Gartenstadt lag nach der Teilung der Stadt in Ostberlin – vor gravierenden Anbauten und Veränderungen, wie Fensteraustausch oder Grundrissänderungen, bewahrt, so dass die Siedlung heute ein hoher Grad an authentischer Bausubstanz auszeichnet.

opment, garden architecture and building architecture. As a group, they are actually unique on an international level, considering their variation and originality and their excellent artistic quality. One of the most outstanding features of the Berlin housing estates is the fact that they are very authentic even today, since they suffered only very little damage during the war and conservation or respectively restoration works assure that their original fabric and appearance are preserved.

### 3.D Integrity and/or authenticity

The fact that the fabric of most of the historic buildings is preserved characterises all nominated Berlin housing estates. Any interference for ideological reasons during the Nazi period consisted only of the re-painting of the facades of Wohnstadt Carl Legien. Since most of the housing estates are not located within the central area of Berlin, they hardly suffered damage during the Second World War. Gartenstadt Falkenberg, Wohnstadt Carl Legien, Weiße Stadt and the Hufeisensiedlung experienced only little damage during the war. The Siedlung Schillerpark and Siemensstadt, which were both located near industrial and military locations, suffered more damage by bombing. Yet, even here only individual houses were damaged. The reconstruction works represent independent achievements. At Siemensstadt they were carried out by Hans Scharoun and Otto Bartning themselves, at Schillerpark by Max Taut. They have enriched the overall image of the housing estates. In none of the estates were additional houses built after 1945 to densify them.

After 1945, many of the houses were resurfaced and thus lost the smooth membrane-like finish typical for Neues Bauen and the pigmented stippling, which was characteristic for the rural small houses of Gartenstadt Falkenberg and the Hufeisensiedlung. The colouring, which was so very important for the Taut housing estates at Falkenberg, Britz, Schillerpark and Carl Legien, disappeared along with the plaster.

The fundamental concepts of the green spaces with their carefully designed, functional areas, designed by specially

Abb. 72: Gartenstadt Falkenberg, Akazienhof 5–7, nach der Wiederherstellung, 2003

Fig. 72: Gartenstadt Falkenberg, Akazienhof 5–7, after restoration, 2003

Mit der Neuverputzung um 1966 ging jedoch eine wesentliche Gestaltqualität verloren: der handwerklich aufgetragene Kellenputz mit seiner lebendigen Struktur. Auch die für das Gesamtbild der Siedlung entscheidenden Farbanstriche und Ornamente wurden fast vollständig entfernt. Ebenso wurden an vielen Häusern die Haustüren erneuert und die Dächer umgedeckt, wobei zum Teil die Schleppgauben verloren gingen. Auch war an einigen Häusern der Verlust der hölzernen Fassadenelemente wie Klappläden, Pergolen und Spaliere zu beklagen. Während der DDR-Zeit standen nur geringe Instandsetzungsmittel zur Verfügung. Daher bestand 1991 bei der Aufnahme der Erneuerungs- und Restaurierungsarbeiten ein hoher bautechnischer Modernisierungsbedarf.

Die seit Beginn der 1990er Jahre in Angriff genommene, in mehreren Etappen durchgeführte Grundinstandsetzung auf der Basis von denkmalpflegerischen Leitlinien konnte im Herbst 2002 abgeschlossen werden. Dabei sind nahezu alle Putzoberflächen erneuert, zahlreiche Türen, Fensterläden und z.T. auch Fenster gemäß Originalbestand nachgebaut worden. Die instand gesetzten Bauten zeigen die Taut'sche Farbenpracht, wie sie nach Befunduntersuchungen und Quellenstudium zu rekonstruieren war.

*Siedlungsfreiraum*
Das gartenstädtische Erscheinungsbild der Siedlung ist bis heute erhalten. Die Wegestruktur und die Struktur der Freiräume, einschließlich der Parzellierung ist bewahrt. Die Befestigung des Akazienhofes mit Asphalt und die Wegebeläge im Straßenraum sind bis auf Teilbereiche am Gartenstadtweg unverändert. Die ehemals mit einem Schotter-Sandgemisch befestigten inneren Erschließungswege, Dungwege und Terrassen wurden weitgehend von den Bewohnern mit unterschiedlichsten Materialien befestigt.

Am Gartenstadtweg ist die historische Terrassierung der Vorgärten erhalten, wenn auch die Betonmauern wohl bereits in den 1930er Jahren erneuert wurden.

Abb. 73: Siedlung Schillerpark, Treppenhaus und Hauseingang Dubliner Straße 62, Ziegeleinfassungen, Fenster und Türen original, 2005

Fig. 73: Siedlung Schillerpark, staircase and entrance at Dubliner Straße 62, brick frames, original windows and doors, 2005

employed garden architects for most of the estates, have been preserved with the exception of few changes. Since the demands for utilisation have changed, additional playgrounds and waste bin facilities and also parking lots were installed. Additional plants that partially grew wild or the conversion of the tenants' gardens, which had originally been designed as kitchen gardens, into recreational and ornamental gardens have reduced the clarity of the spatial and social relations.

## The individual housing estates

### Gartenstadt Falkenberg

At Gartenstadt Falkenberg, only one row house at Gartenstadtweg (no. 50) had to be rebuilt. After the division of Berlin, Gartenstadt Falkenberg belonged to the eastern part of the city and after the end of the war its houses did not become subject to major additions or changes like the replacement of windows or changes of the ground plans. For these reasons, most of the buildings now consist of the original fabric.

However, with the resurfacing in 1966, they lost an important design quality: the manually applied trowel plaster with its lively structure. The colourful painting and the ornaments, which were so decisive for the overall image of the housing estate, were also almost completely removed. The entrance doors of many houses were renewed and the roofs were re-covered, which led to the loss of many of the shed dormers. Some of the houses lost their wooden facade elements such as shutters, pergolas and trellises. During the existence of the GDR (German Democratic Republic), means for maintenance were scarce. For this reason, the houses were in enormous need of modernisation when renewal and restoration works began in 1991.

Thorough repair on the basis of restoration guidelines was started in the early 1990s. It was carried out in several phases and completed in autumn 2002. These works included the renewal of nearly all the plaster surfaces, and many doors, shutters and some windows were replaced by new ones that had been manufactured in the original design. The repaired buildings have Taut's colourfulness as it had been identified by studying the buildings and sources of information.

*Outdoor facilities*
The garden town character of the housing estate has been preserved. The structure of paths and outdoor facilities inclusive of the division into parcels has been maintained. The paving of Akazienhof with asphalt and the paving of the streets have not been changed with some exceptions at Gartenstadtweg. The interior paths, garden paths and terraces that had originally been paved with a mix of crushed stone and sand have largely been paved by the inhabitants, who used various materials.

At Gartenstadtweg, the historic terrace design of the front gardens has been preserved, although the concrete walls were probably already renewed during the 1930s.

Die Privatgärten wurden ursprünglich entsprechend dem Konzept des Gartenarchitekten Ludwig Lesser durch sogenannte Hausbäume (Obstbaum-Hochstämme), Spalierobst, Gemüsebeete und einheitliche Zäune oder Hecken geprägt. Hier hat sich in den letzten Jahrzehnten eine Wandlung vom Nutzgarten zum Wohn- und Ziergarten vollzogen mit starken Verlusten von Obstgehölzen. Mithilfe eines gartendenkmalpflegerischen Gutachtens und eines Merkblattes ist seit 2001 begonnen worden, diesen Prozess aufzuhalten. Die Ausstattung der Gärten mit typisierten Ställen für die Kleintierhaltung ist erhalten.

Die terrassierten Vorgärten am Gartenstadtweg und die Vorgärten im Akazienhof konnten durch die in jüngster Zeit erfolgten gartendenkmalpflegerischen Maßnahmen entsprechend dem historischen Erscheinungsbild wiederhergestellt werden.

## Siedlung Schillerpark

Die Siedlungsbauten aller drei Bauabschnitte zeichnet eine hohe Überlieferungsqualität aus. Das authentische Erscheinungsbild blieb über den Krieg und den Renovierungen der Nachkriegszeit hinweg bewahrt. Wo es Veränderungen gab – Betonteile, Loggien, Fenster u. a. –, sind die bestimmenden Gestaltelemente denkmalgerecht wiederhergestellt oder instandgesetzt worden.

Allerdings blieb die Siedlung aufgrund der Nähe zum Reinickendorfer Industriegebiet und zu Kasernenanlagen des Tegeler Schießplatzes nicht von Kriegsschäden verschont. Größere Zerstörungen durch Fliegerbomben beschränkten sich aber auf den Block 2 des ersten Bauabschnittes (Bristolstraße 1–5). Das Endhaus Bristolstraße 1/Ecke Dubliner Straße wurde fast vollständig vernichtet. Der Wiederaufbau 1951 stand unter der Leitung von Max Taut. Er hielt sich weitgehend an das originale Vorbild, erhöhte aber das Haus durch einen Ausbau des Drempelgeschosses, um mehr Wohnraum zu schaffen. Dabei wurden auch das Treppenhaus verändert und die Ziegelstreifen in den weißen Putzfeldern zwischen den Fenstern nicht wiederhergestellt.

Die übrigen Bauten überstanden den Krieg weitgehend unbeschädigt. Bei Instandsetzungsmaßnahmen der 1960er und 1970er Jahren sind nur geringe Eingriffe vorgenommen worden. So wurde in dieser Zeit der in der Siedlung ohnehin nur sparsam verwendete Putz erneuert. Gravierender waren der Verlust der farbigen Anstriche an den hofseitigen Treppenhausachsen und den Drempeln und die Vereinfachung der Eisenbetonpfeiler an den Balkonen einiger Blöcke des ersten Bauabschnittes. Hier entfernte man während der Betonsanierungen die Profilierung und die würfelförmigen Bekrönungen. Zwei Blöcke wurden damals durch eine die Baukörperkontur beeinträchtigende Wärmedämm-Maßnahme verändert. Die 1991 begonnenen denkmalpflegerischen Instandsetzungen haben die Gesamterscheinung der Siedlung im Sinne des originalen Zustandes korrigiert. So wurde auch bei der jüngst durchgeführten Restaurierung die Dämmung an einem der Blöcke wieder entfernt.

Auch bei der von Hans Hoffmann vorgenommenen Siedlungserweiterung von 1954 führten die Aufbringung von

According to the design by garden architect Ludwig Lesser, the private gardens had originally been dominated by so-called house trees (high-standing fruit trees), espalier fruit trees, vegetable patches and uniform fences or hedges. During the past decades, these kitchen gardens were converted into recreational and ornamental gardens and many fruit trees were removed. The process to stop this development was started in 2001 by means of an expert opinion on the restoration of the garden architecture and an information leaflet. The standardised sheds for small animals in the gardens were preserved.

In the recent past, it was possible to carry out conservation measures for reconstructing the terraced front gardens at Gartenstadtweg and the front gardens at Akazienhof in accordance with the historic design.

## Siedlung Schillerpark

The buildings of all three phases of development are well preserved. Despite the war and renovations, the authentic appearance was preserved. Wherever changes occurred – to concrete parts, loggias, windows, etc. – the characteristic design elements have been restored or repaired in line with the restoration requirements.

Unfortunately the housing estate suffered some damage during the war because it is located near the Reinickendorf industrial centre and the Tegel shooting range. However, damage by aerial bombs was restricted to the second block of the first development phase (Bristolstraße 1–5). The house on the corner of Bristolstraße 1 and Dubliner Straße was almost completely destroyed. Its reconstruction was headed by Max Taut. He rebuilt it almost as it had been. The only change he made was to extend the jamb storey to create more residential space. In connection with this, the staircase was changed and the brick bands in the white plaster squares between the windows were not reproduced.

Abb. 74: Siedlung Schillerpark, Fassade im dritten Bauabschnitt an der Barfusstraße, erhaltene Kastendoppelfenster und Ziegelrahmung, 2005

Fig. 74: Siedlung Schillerpark, facade in the third development phase at Barfusstraße, preserved box-type double windows and brick frames, 2005

Abb. 75: Großsiedlung Britz, Reihenhäuser des Bauabschnitts I/II, Fenster und Türen original, 2005

Fig. 75: Großsiedlung Britz, row houses of development phase I/II, original windows and doors, 2005

Wärmedämmung sowie weitere Modernisierungsmaßnahmen zu einem weitgehenden Verlust der architektonischen Qualität der drei Zeilen im Inneren des südlichen Blockes und bei zwei der Randzeilen. Die beiden anderen äußeren Randbauten von Hoffmann bewahrten dagegen ihre für die Architektursprache von Hoffmann charakteristische Transparenz der Fassaden mit flächig verglasten Treppenhausbereichen und breiten Verglasungen auf den Loggienseiten.

*Siedlungsfreiraum*
Die Grundrisse der den ersten und zweiten Bauabschnitt umfassenden beiden Gartenhöfe sind weitgehend original erhalten. Wesentliche Elemente wie die Unterteilung in schmale Vorgartenzonen, in umlaufende Erschließungswege, in von Baumreihen begleitete Rasenparterres sowie durch Hecken oder Baumreihen eingefasste grosse Sandspielflächen sind noch zu erkennen. Allerdings sind die originalen Pflanzungen nur noch teilweise vorhanden. Die Vorgärten bieten heute ein sehr heterogenes, unbefriedigendes Bild mit größtenteils die Fassaden und Eingänge der Gebäude störenden, verdeckenden hohen Pflanzungen. Beide Rasenparterres wurden ehemals von Baumreihen aus kugelig geschnittenen, eng gepflanzten Rotdornen begleitet, d. h., die strengen Fassaden erhielten als Korrespondenz architektonisch wirkende Pflanzbänder. Der Zustand der Haupterschließungswege mit Asphaltdecke und einer Einfassung aus gerundeten glasierten Klinkern entspricht der bauzeitlichen Situation.

Während die Windsorer Straße noch ihre Originalbepflanzung aus Mehlbeeren besitzt, ging die ehemals prägende Bepflanzung aus Rotdornen in der Oxforder Straße zu einem großen Teil verloren. Auch der wichtige Bezug zum Eingangsrondell des Schillerparks ist durch mangelnde Pflege des Parkrandes zur Siedlung verstellt. Hier wurde die ursprünglich als breite Promenade vorgelagerte Bristolstraße zum Teil mit Spiel- und Sporteinrichtungen überstellt.

The other buildings survived the war almost without damage. Repair works during the 1960s and 1970s caused only little changes. During this time the plaster was renewed. It had scarcely been used in this housing estate anyway. The loss of the coloured paint on the yard-side staircase axes and the jambs and the simplification of the reinforced concrete pillars on the balconies of some of the blocks of the first development phase were a greater loss. When the concrete was repaired, the workers removed the profile and the cubic crowning. At that time, two blocks were altered by the addition of heat insulation, which changed the contours of the buildings. The restoration works that began in 1991 have corrected the overall appearance of the housing estate and largely recreated the original designs. During recent restoration work, the insulation was removed from one of the blocks.

When the housing estate was extended by Hans Hoffman in 1954, the facades of the three ribbons in the interior of the southern block and of two of the ribbons at the margin were covered with heat insulation, and other modernisation measures were carried out. This led to an extensive loss of the architectural quality of these ribbons. In contrast to the above, the two outer buildings at block margins by Hoffmann were preserved with the transparency of the facades, which is characteristic for his architectural style using glass-fronted staircases and wide glass fronts on the loggia sides.

*Outdoor facilities*
The ground plans of the courtyards of the first and second development phases have largely been preserved in the original structure. Essential elements like the division into narrow front garden zones, access paths around the structures, flat lawns accompanied by rows of trees and large sand-covered playgrounds framed by hedges or rows of trees are still visible. However, a lot of the original plants and planting patterns do not exist anymore. The front gar-

## Großsiedlung Britz (Hufeisensiedlung)

Da die Britzer Siedlung nur geringfügige Kriegsschäden erlitt und die Einfamilienhäuser nach dem Krieg nicht an Einzeleigentümer veräußert wurden, weisen alle Siedlungsteile einen hohen Grad an originaler Substanz auf. Die chrakteristische gemischte Siedlungsform mit Geschossbauten und Einfamilienhäusern ist durch keinerlei An- und Neubauten verunklärt. Auch die Einfamilienreihenhäuser mit den schmalen und tiefen Gärten sind in ihrem authentischen Erscheinungsbild erhalten. Originale Fenster, Türen, Ziegelverkleidungen und Dachformen sind als elementare Gestaltmittel überall überliefert.

Der in allen Siedlungsteilen nahezu ausschließlich verwendete, mit Mineralfarben durchgefärbte und verriebene Strukturputz, der als Farbträger wesentliches zu den spektakulären Raumwirkungen beitrug, ist nicht mehr vorhanden. Bereits im Zuge der Instandsetzungen nach dem Zweiten Weltkrieg wurde er in vielen Siedlungsbereichen durch einen farblosen Rauhputz ersetzt. Ebenso gingen die Farbanstriche von vielen Fenstern und Türen verloren.

Auch im Rahmen der denkmalpflegerischen Erneuerungen, die in den 1970er Jahren zunächst ohne genauere Bestandsanalysen und restauratorische Befunduntersuchungen begannen, wurden erhaltene Putze aus wirtschaftlichen und bautechnischen Gründen abgeschlagen. Die neuen Putze entsprachen anfangs, wie bei den damals angestrichenen Stockwerksbauten Fritz-Reuter-Allee 6–42 und 52–72, nicht dem ursprünglichen durchgefärbten Vorbild. Mit der 1982 beginnenden Wiederherstellung wurden wieder mit Mineralfarben durchgefärbte Putze verwandt, deren Farbigkeit nach restauratorischen Untersuchungen festgelegt wurde.

### Siedlungsfreiraum

Die Flächenaufteilung und Wegestruktur der Freiflächen ist weitgehend erhalten, so dass der ursprüngliche Charakter der Siedlung, das funktionale und gestalterische Zusammenspiel der Gartenanlagen mit der städtebaulichen Anordnung der Baukörper bis heute erlebbar ist. Prägende Elemente wie die Gehwegbeläge, die wassergebundenen Wegeflächen und der historische Belag der Wirtschaftswege sind weitgehend erhalten.

Die ursprünglich weitgehend einheitliche Bepflanzung der Vorgärten und die einheitliche Ausstattung der Mietergärten mit Obstbäumen ist zu großen Teilen verloren gegangen. Die charakteristischen Alleepflanzungen in den Straßenräumen konnten zu großen Teilen bewahrt werden, jedoch wurden auch hier Nachpflanzungen vorgenommen, die nicht dem historischen Bild entsprechen.

Die historischen Müllhäuschen sind heute nicht mehr vorhanden, sie wurden auf den historischen Standorten durch Müllboxen aus Kieselwaschbeton ersetzt. Die ursprünglich vorhandenen Teppichklopfstangen wurden ebenfalls entfernt.

Die Vorgärten präsentieren sich heterogen und unbefriedigend, mit hohen Pflanzen, die zum großen Teil die Fassaden und Eingänge der Häuser verdecken und stören. Die beiden Rasenflächen wurden ursprünglich von dicht gepflanzten, kugelförmig geschnittenen Rotdornen begleitet. Das heißt, dass den strengen Fassaden entsprechende Pflanzenbänder mit architektonischer Wirkung entgegengesetzt wurden. Die Hauptwege mit Asphaltbelag und einer Einfassung aus gerundeten, glasierten Klinkersteinen sind wie ursprünglich gebaut.

Die Windsorer Straße hat noch die meisten ihrer ursprünglichen Mehlbeerbäume, aber viele der charakteristischen Rotdorne in der Oxforder Straße sind verloren. Die wichtige Beziehung zum Kreis, der den Eingang des Schillerparks markiert, wurde auch durch die mangelnde Pflege des Parkrandes gestört. Die Bristolstraße war ursprünglich eine breite Promenade vor dem Park, aber hier wurde sie teilweise durch Spielplätze und Sportanlagen überdeckt.

## Großsiedlung Britz (Hufeisensiedlung)

Since the housing estate at Britz suffered only little damage during the war and the single-family houses were not sold to individual owners after the war, all parts of this housing estate consist almost completely of the original fabric. The characteristic mixed housing estate form with multi-storey buildings and single-family houses has not been disturbed by any additions or new buildings. The appearance of the single-family row houses, with their narrow and deep gardens, is also still authentic. Original windows, doors, brick cladding and roof shapes as elementary design elements have been preserved everywhere.

The stippling, which had been coloured with mineral pigments and spread by rubbing and which was used nearly everywhere, contributing with its colours to the spectacular spatial impressions, no longer exists. Already during repairs after the end of the Second World War, it was replaced by uncoloured rough plaster on many facades. The coloured paint of many windows and doors is also lost.

During the restoration works, which were carried out in the 1970s, initially without analysing the original situation and studying it from the point of view of restoration, existing plaster was removed for economic and constructional reasons. Initially, the new plasters were not the same as the original pigmented plasters. Examples for them are the painted facades of the multi-storey buildings at Fritz-Reuter-Allee 6–42 and 52–72. With the restoration, which began in 1982, pigmented plasters were used again and their colours were determined on the basis of restorers' investigations.

### Outdoor facilities

The subdivision of areas and the structure of the paths through the outdoor facilities have largely been preserved, such that the original character of the housing estate and the functional and aesthetic interaction of the gardens with the arrangement of the buildings can still be experienced. Characteristic elements like the paving of the footpaths, the water-bound paths and the historic paving of the service roads have largely been preserved.

Abb. 76: Wohnstadt Carl Legien, Hoffront und Kopf eines U-förmigen Wohnblocks mit erhaltenen Fenstern, 2005

Fig. 76: Wohnstadt Carl Legien, yard-side facade and head building of one of the U-shaped blocks with preserved windows, 2005

## Wohnstadt Carl Legien

Bereits zur Olympiade 1936 nahm man aus ideologischen Gründen Veränderungen an den Fassadenfarben vor. Der Zweite Weltkrieg brachte nur geringfügige Zerstörungen unter den Wohnhäusern. Einige Häuser des Blocks E an der Trachtenbrodtstraße 22–34 weisen wohl stärkere Kriegsschäden auf, die man nach 1945 beseitigte, wobei man sich am ursprünglichen Vorbild orientierte. Fast vollständig vernichtet wurde jedoch das kleinere Waschhaus im Block an der nördlichen Gubitzstraße, das nach 1945 verändert wieder aufgebaut wurde.

Die Instandsetzungen nach 1945 führten dann zu einem großflächigen Verlust der originalen Edelputze und Mineralfarbenanstriche. Bei der Erneuerung waren verschiedene Putze verwendet worden (Glattputz, Strukturputz, Kratzputz). Auch die Fenster verloren ihren farbigen Aufbau und wurden – besonders die Einfachfenster der Bäder – teilweise ausgetauscht. Ebenso nahmen Mieter unterschiedliche Umbauten der Loggien zu Wintergärten vor. Allerdings fanden keine eingreifenden baulichen Veränderungen statt, so dass sowohl die städtebauliche Struktur als auch die Grundsubstanz und die architektonische Gliederung der Siedlungshäuser unversehrt blieben.

Anfang der 1990er Jahre begann die denkmalgerechte Instandsetzung der Fassaden nach restauratorischen Voruntersuchungen. Als Pilotprojekt wurde 1992–94 die Erneuerung der Fassaden Trachtenbrodtstraße 2–18 und Sodtkestraße 20–36 vorgenommen. Mit der Modernisierung der Wohnungen ab 2003 war auch die Weiterführung der denkmalgerechten Erneuerung der Siedlung verbunden. Dabei konnte ein Großteil der Fenster, vor allem die Fenster der Wohnungen nach den Höfen und in den Kopfbauten an der Erich-Weinert-Straße, erhalten bleiben. Jedoch mussten die straßenseitigen Kastendoppelfenster aufgrund bautechnischer Schäden gegen moderne Holz-Iso-Fenster ausge-

A lot of the originally, quite uniform planting schemes in the front gardens and the uniformly planted fruit trees in the tenants' gardens are lost. Most of the characteristic avenues of trees planted along the roads have been preserved, but some later additions of trees do not coincide with the original scheme.

The historic waste bin sheds do not exist anymore. They were replaced at the original locations by exposed-aggregate concrete boxes with a gravel surface. The originally existing carpet beating facilities were removed, too.

## Wohnstadt Carl Legien

For ideological reasons, colours of facades were already changed on the occasion of the Olympic Games in 1936. The Second World War caused only little damage to the residential buildings. Some houses of Block E on Trachtenbrodtstraße 22–34 seem to have suffered major damage, which was repaired after 1945. The repair works adhered to the original design. However, the smaller one of the two laundries that was located in the block at the northern section of Gubitzstraße had been almost completely destroyed and was rebuilt with a different design after 1945.

During the repairs that were carried out after 1945, a lot of the original patent plaster and mineral paint coating were lost. For the renewal, various types of plaster were used (smooth plaster, stippling, scraped rendering). The windows, too, lost their coloured design and some of them were exchanged. The latter happened in particular with the single windows of the bathrooms. Further, some tenants converted the loggias to conservatories. But no severely interfering constructional changes took place, such that both the urban structure and the buildings' fabric with their architectonic structure were preserved.

tauscht werden. Die neuen Fenster wurden in der Aufteilung und im Farbaufbau entsprechend dem originalem Vorbild nachgebaut.

Das große T-förmige Heiz- und Waschhaus im südöstlichen Hof zwischen Sodtke- und Gubitzstraße steht heute weitgehend leer. Es verlor aufgrund des Anschlusses aller Wohnungen an das Fernwärmenetz seine Bestimmung und wird nun z. T. als Fernwärmeübergabestation genutzt. Die ehemalige Zentralwäscherei ist innen und außen verändert, wobei die einstigen Großräume durch Vermauerungen der flächigen Verglasungen ihren lichten und transparenten Charakter verloren. Das kleinere Waschhaus ist 1992–94 dagegen im Rahmen der Fassadenrestaurierung der angrenzenden Blockseite an der Sodtkestraße in der Tradition des Neuen Bauens denkmalverträglich umgebaut worden.

Nach Abschluss der Bauarbeiten 2005 ist überall in der Wohnstadt das äußere Erscheinungsbild – auch das Farbkonzept nach Bruno Taut – zurückgekehrt.

### Siedlungsfreiraum

Die Analyse der Freiraumentwicklung zeigte seit der Zeit des Zweiten Weltkrieges einen schleichenden Niedergang der ehemaligen Freiraumqualität. Die ursprüngliche Intention Bruno Tauts, Licht, Luft und Sonne durch grosszügige, offene, von allen Mietern gemeinschaftlich zu nutzende Höfe mit gezielten betonenden malerischen Baumpflanzungen sowohl im Inneren der Höfe (Weiden), als auch an den Kopfbauten zur Erich-Weinert-Straße (Robinien) zu schaffen, wurde zunehmend bis in die 1990er Jahre durch mangelnde Pflege, Verwilderung, Vermüllung und Auflas-

In the early 1990s, restoration of the facades began after experts had carried out the necessary investigations. The pilot project was the renewal of the facades of Trachtenbrodtstraße 2–18 and Sodtkestraße 20–36 in 1992–94. When the flats were modernised starting in 2003, the restoration of the housing estate was continued, too. When these works were carried out, many windows were able to be preserved. This applies in particular to the windows of the flats, which are orientated towards the yards and those in the head buildings on Erich-Weinert-Straße. The box-type double windows on the street side had to be exchanged for modern wooden insulation windows due to constructional damage of the original ones. The new windows were manufactured with the same structure and colours as the original windows.

Most of the large T-shaped heating plant and laundry in the southern yard between Sodtke and Gubitzstraße is not in use today. When all of the flats were connected with the district heating system, it lost its function and part of it is now used as a long-distance heat intake. The former central laundry has been changed inside and outside and the previously spacious rooms lost their light and transparent character when the large glass panels were replaced by brickwork. In contrast to this, the smaller laundry was converted in observance of the restoration guidelines in 1992–94 when the facades of the block's side along Sodtkestraße were restored in line with the tradition of Neues Bauen.

When the works were completed in 2005, the settlement had regained the original appearance everywhere with the colour scheme that had been designed by Bruno Taut.

### Outdoor facilities

The analysis of the outdoor facilities shows that after the end of the Second World War, the quality of the outdoor facilities deteriorated gradually. The original intention of Bruno Taut to provide light, air and sunshine for the flats by means of spacious, open courtyards with purposefully and picturesquely planted trees both inside the yards (willows), which were to be used by all tenants in common, and also at the head buildings towards Erich-Weinert-Straße (robinias) was increasingly counteracted until the 1990s due to a lack of maintenance, overgrowing, littering and abandoning of the tenants' gardens which had been created to fight the misery of the war and post-war period.

Nevertheless, the structure of areas and paths has been mostly preserved in the entire housing estate, but the pavings and borders are only original in some places. Of most of the waste bin sheds, only parts have been preserved. Some of the original plants still exist and most of the borders and pavings for the house access paths have been preserved.

### Weiße Stadt

In all parts of the housing estate, the original fabric has been largely preserved. With the exception of the removal of the central heating plant in 1968–69, no major construction changes are visible despite the fact that individual houses had to be rebuilt after the war. The urban structure was also preserved and most of the design elements which

Abb. 77: Weiße Stadt, Treppenhaus im Bauteil O. R. Salvisberg an der Aroser Allee, Fenster und Kunststeinfassungen original, 2005

Fig. 77: Weiße Stadt, staircase in the section by O. R. Salvisberg at Aroser Allee, original windows and synthetic stone frames, 2005

sung der in den Notzeiten der Kriegs- und Nachkriegszeit entstandenen Mietergärten konterkariert.

In der gesamten Siedlung ist die Flächen- und Wegestruktur weitgehend erhalten, die Wegebeläge und Einfassungen entsprechen jedoch nur noch zum Teil der ursprünglichen Ausführung. Auch von den meisten Müllhäuschen sind nur noch Reste vorhanden. Teile der Originalbepflanzung als auch die Einfassungen und Wegebeläge für die Hauszugänge sind weitgehend erhalten.

## Weiße Stadt

Alle Siedlungsteile zeichnet ein hoher Grad an originaler Substanz aus. Gravierende bauliche Veränderungen, sieht man vom Abbruch des Zentralheizwerks 1968–69 ab, sind trotz einzelner Wiederaufbauten nach dem Krieg nicht zu erkennen. Auch die städtebauliche Figur blieb bewahrt und die das Gesamtbild prägenden Gestaltelemente – wie Fenster und Hauseingänge, Hauslauben, Dachüberstände, Betonteile und Ziegelrahmungen – haben sich überwiegend erhalten. Verloren ging jedoch der membranhafte dünne Glattputz mit seinem leuchtend weißen Anstrich und die Farbgebung einzelner Architekturteile. Sie waren infolge der Kriegsschäden und der Neuverputzung bei der Grundrenovierung bis 1955 und auch bei den weiteren Instandsetzungen in den 1970er Jahren zu einem großen Teil beseitigt worden.

Seit dem Beginn der denkmalpflegerischen Erneuerung der Siedlung 1982 konnte der entstellende Putz der Nachkriegszeit sukzessive durch neuen Glattputz mit weißem Mineralfarbenanstrich ersetzt werden. In einigen Fällen, so bei den Bauten von Ahrends an der Aroser Allee, wurde auf Wunsch der Siedlungsgesellschaft dünner Wärmedämmputz aufgebracht. Auch die verglasten Hauslauben im Siedlungsabschnitt von Ahrends wurden wärmegedämmt. Die bauzeitliche Eisen-Glaskonstruktionen mit dünnen, gemauerten Brüstungen mussten aufgrund bautechnischer Schäden neu aufgebaut werden. Man wählte eine dem ursprünglichen Zustand angenäherte Aluminiumkonstruktion mit Thermoverglasung und einer wärmegedämmten Brüstung. Dadurch ging aber die prägnante, präzise Kontur der Laubenreihen verloren.

### Siedlungsfreiraum

Die ursprünglich streng orthogonale Gestaltung Ludwig Lessers ist bezüglich Raumgliederung, Wegeführung, Materialien sowie Baumpflanzungen überwiegend noch nachvollziehbar, allerdings durch bauliche und pflanzliche Ergänzungen und Umgestaltungen der 1950er bis 1990er Jahre zum Teil überformt.

Im Abschnitt „Salvisberg" sind nur die zum Romanshorner Weg gelegenen Mietergärten erhalten und entsprechend der ursprünglichen Situation mit Hecken abgegrenzt, während die ehemals prägenden hofseitigen Mietergärten aufgelöst sind. Die Aroser Allee als grünes Rückgrat der Siedlung befindet sich nördlich der Straßenüberbauung weitgehend im Originalzustand; südlich davon ist leider die bis zum Schillerring ursprünglich baumlose, streng durch eine Hecke gefasste Mittelpromenade durch wahllose Birkenpflanzungen verstellt, welche die intendierte Wirkung des bau-

characterise the overall image – for instance windows and entrance doors, loggias, eaves, concrete parts and brick frames – have been preserved. The membrane-like thin smooth plaster with its brilliantly white paint coat and the colouring of individual architectural elements, however, have been lost. Most of them were removed when damage from the war was repaired and in connection with the new plaster-rendering during the thorough renovation until 1955 and also during later repair works in the 1970s.

Since restoration of the housing estate began in 1982, the disfiguring plaster of the post-war period was able to be replaced step by step by new, smooth plaster with white mineral paint coating. In some cases (e.g. the buildings at Ahrends along Aroser Allee), thin heat insulation plaster was used as requested by the estate community. The glazed loggias in the Ahrends houses also got heat insulation. The original iron and glass structures with thin parapets of brickwork had to be rebuilt because they exhibited constructional damage. They were substituted by aluminium structures with thermo-glazing and heat-insulated parapets whose appearance is similar to that of the original structures. Yet, the rows of loggias lost their characteristic, precise contours in the substitution.

*Outdoor facilities*
Ludwig Lesser had originally created a strictly orthogonal design. Most of its spatial structures, alignments of paths, materials and tree planting schemes do exist still. Yet, in some places the original situation has been disturbed by the addition and change of buildings and plants from the 1950s until the 1990s.

In the section, which had been designed by Salvisberg, only the tenants' gardens at Romanshorner Weg are preserved and they are still bordered by hedges as in the original design, but the formerly characteristic tenants' gardens on the yard side do not exist anymore. North of the bridge building, Aroser Allee largely still retains its original character of the estate's green backbone. South of the bridge house, the central promenade, which originally had no trees on the stretch down to Schillerring and which was bordered by an austere hedge, has been altered by irregularly planted birches that severely disturb the originally intended impression of the architectural ensemble. Regulations for the outdoor facilities were created in 2000, and on their basis, initial measures were carried out in 2001. They restored one yard in the section, which had been designed by Ahrends, and to an extent recreated the impression which Lesser had intended.

## Großsiedlung Siemensstadt (Ringsiedlung)

Since they are located near the large industrial estate of the Siemens company, the buildings of the Großsiedlung Siemensstadt suffered quite a lot of damage. Entire sections of the buildings designed by Scharoun and Gropius at Jungfernheideweg 1 and 21 as well as parts of the block margin by Bartning and of the ribbons by Häring at Goebelstraße 21–25 and 24 were destroyed. But the destruction had not been able to decisively change the authentic image of the large housing estate.

lichen Ensembles empfindlich beeinträchtigen. Auf der Grundlage des im Jahr 2000 aufgestellten Regelwerkes für die Freianlagen erfolgte 2001 eine erste Instandsetzung eines Hofes im Bauteil Ahrends, wobei die Lesser'schen Intentionen wieder stärker herausgearbeitet werden konnten.

## Großsiedlung Siemensstadt (Ringsiedlung)

Die Bauten der Großsiedlung Siemensstadt, da in unmittelbarer Nähe der weiträumigen Industrieanlagen der Fa. Siemens gelegen, trugen im Zweiten Weltkrieg zum Teil schwere Schäden davon. Von den Bauten Scharouns und Gropius' am Jungfernheideweg 1 und 21 sowie auch von Bartnings Randblock und Härings Zeilenbauten an der Goebelstraße 21–25 und 24 gingen ganze Gebäudeteile verloren. Die Zerstörungen konnten jedoch das authentische Bild der Großsiedlung nicht entscheidend verändern.

Beim Wiederaufbau Anfang der 50er Jahre wurde nicht immer der ursprüngliche Zustand vollständig wiederhergestellt. Für das Haus Jungfernheideweg 1 im Bauteil Scharoun entwarf Scharoun selbst einen 1949–50 entstandenen neuen Kopfbau. Auch die Eckbebauung mit der flachen Ladenspange Jungfernheideweg/Ecke Goebelstraße im Bauteil Gropius erfuhr 1955 einen vom Original abweichenden Wiederaufbau, der 1988/89 architektonisch nach einem Entwurf der Architekten Hilmer & Sattler im sachlich-funktionellen Stil der Gropiusbauten neu gestaltet werden konnte. Die Häuser Mäckeritzstraße 18–22 im Bauteil Scharoun errichtete man hingegen in Anlehnung an den Originalzustand.

Das östliche Ende des Bartningzeile wurde, nachdem der Wiederaufbau der kriegsbeschädigten Häuser Goebelstraße 21–25 in den Jahren 1951–52 abgeschlossen war, 1955–56 nach Bartnings eigenem Entwurf um die Häuser Nr. 11–19 verlängert. Um dieselbe Zeit entstand der abschließende Kopfbau Goebelstraße 1–9, den Hans Scharoun als

Abb. 79: Großsiedlung Siemensstadt, sanierte Balkone bei den Zeilen von Hugo Häring, 2005

Fig. 79: Großsiedlung Siemensstadt, restored balconies of ribbons by Hugo Häring, 2005

The reconstruction in the early 50s did not always completely re-establish the original state. Scharoun himself designed a new head building, which was erected in 1949–50, and replaced the house at Jungfernheideweg 1 in the section which he had designed. The building with the flat row of shops at the corner of Jungfernheideweg and Goebelstraße in the section designed by Gropius was also rebuilt in 1955 in a design that differed from the original. It was altered in 1988/89 and adapted to the functional style of Gropius on the basis of a design by the architects Hilmer & Sattler. The houses at Mäckeritzstraße 18–22 in the section by Scharoun were rebuilt in a design that resembled the original.

After reconstruction of the houses at Goebelstraße 21–25 that had been damaged during the war was completed (1951–52), the eastern end of the ribbon designed by Bartning was extended by the houses Bartningzeile numbers 11–19 in 1955–56. Approximately at the same time, the final head building at Goebelstraße 1–9 was built. Hans Scharoun had designed it as a gallery block. Its ground plan, which resembles a saw blade and the staggered facade structure, differ very much from the functional style of the Ringsiedlung.

The first refurbishment of the housing estate houses was completed in 1955. The estate was changed even more in the 60s and 70s when all houses were resurfaced with new plaster and a paint coating that did not coincide with the original situation. Many details were changed, too. In 1982, comprehensive restoration began with the rehabilitation of the ribbons by Häring. In 1984, many of the buildings by Scharoun followed, and subsequently the ribbons designed by Henning. The damaged elements were repaired and especially the plaster and the paint coating were renewed in concurrence with the original design. Changes were accepted only when they were necessary for constructional

Abb. 78: Großsiedlung Siemensstadt, 1949–50 unter der Leitung von Hans Scharoun verändert wiederaufgebauter Kopfbau Jungfernheideweg 1, 2000

Fig. 78: Großsiedlung Siemensstadt, head building at Jungfernheideweg 1, reconstructed with altered design under leadership of Hans Scharoun in 1949–50, 2000

Laubenganghaus entwarf. Mit seinem sägeblattförmigen Grundriss und der abgestuften Fassadengliederung ist er stark vom sachlichen Stil der Ringsiedlung abgesetzt.

Die erste Instandsetzungsphase der Siedlungshäuser war im Jahr 1955 abgeschlossen. Weitere Umwandlungen erfuhr die Siedlung in den 60er und 70er Jahren, als alle Häuser einen neuen Putz und neue Anstriche bekamen, die nicht mit dem Originalzustand übereinstimmten. Auch wurden zahlreiche Details verändert. Im Jahre 1982 begann mit der Sanierung der Zeilen von Häring eine umfassende denkmalpflegerische Erneuerung. 1984 folgte ein Großteil des Bauteiles von Scharoun, danach die Zeilen von Henning. Die schadhaften Elemente wurden instand gesetzt, vor allem der Putz und die Farbigkeit wurden originalgetreu erneuert. Nur wenn bautechnische Erfordernisse es unvermeidbar machten, wie bei der Reparatur der nierenförmigen Balkone an Hugo Härings Zeilen, nahm man Veränderungen in Kauf. Man entschloss sich, den Kopfbau von Hans Scharouns „Panzerkreuzer" am Eingang der Siedlung in der Nachkriegsvariante zu erhalten.

Die folgenden Instandsetzungen führten in den Bauabschnitten von Gropius und Bartning teilweise zu Veränderungen des bauzeitlichen Erscheinungsbildes. So nahm man bei der östlichen Randzeile von Gropius am Jungfernheideweg einen Austausch der eisernen Treppenhausfensterbänder vor. 1998 mußten die rückwärtigen Balkone der langen Bartningzeile an der Goebelstraße saniert werden, was zur Einfügung von Stahlrohren zur Stützung der schadhaften Balkondecken führte.

Insgesamt betrachtet ist die Ringsiedlung in ihrer städtebaulichen Komposition erhalten und zeichnet sich, vor allem seit den denkmalpflegerischen Instandsetzungen der 1980er/90er Jahre, auch in ihrer architektonischen Erscheinung durch eine hohe Authentizität aus.

### *Siedlungsfreiraum*

Wichtige gestalterische Elemente der Planungen von Leberecht Migge sind in der Großsiedlung Siemensstadt bis heute erhalten. Auch der ursprüngliche parkartige Charakter der Freiflächen ist in vielen Bereichen noch erlebbar, so dass eine denkmalgerechte Instandsetzung der Gartenanlagen in weiten Teilen der Siedlung grundsätzlich angestrebt wird.

Die Wegestruktur innerhalb der Siedlung und auch die Wegebeläge sind zum großen Teil erhalten. In der Wegestruktur im Straßenraum fanden Veränderungen vor allem durch die Anlage von Parkplätzen im Bereich der Goebelstraße und dem Vorplatz am Geißlerpfad statt. Die Struktur der Vegetationsflächen, zahlreiche Bäume des ursprünglichen alten Baumbestandes sowie die Fassadenbegrünung sind ebenfalls weitgehend noch vorhanden.

Abb. 80: Großsiedlung Siemensstadt, Siedlungsteil Scharoun, wiederhergestellte Balkone am „Panzerkreuzer", 1986

Fig. 80: Großsiedlung Siemensstadt, development section "Scharoun", restored balconies at the "Panzerkreuzer" (armored cruiser)

reasons as was the case for the kidney-shaped balconies by Hugo Häring. At that time, the decision was made to preserve the "Armoured Cruiser" by Hans Scharoun at the entrance of the housing estate in its post-war version.

The next repairs led to some deviations from the original design in the sections designed by Gropius and Bartning. In the eastern ribbon by Gropius at the block margin towards Jungfernheideweg, the iron strip windows of the staircases were replaced. In 1998 it became necessary to refurbish the rear balconies of the long Bartning ribbon on Goebelstraße. The ceilings of the balconies were damaged and steel pipes were installed to support them.

In general, the urban composition of Ringsiedlung has been preserved and especially since its restoration in the 1980s and 1990s, its architectonic appearance is also quite authentic.

### *Outdoor facilities*

In the Großsiedlung Siemensstadt, important elements of the design by Leberecht Migge have been preserved even until today. In many places the outdoor facilities still have their original park-like character, such that restoration is intended for many of the green spaces of the estate.

A lot of the path structure within the housing estate and also of the pavings have been preserved, too. The structure of the road spaces was altered mainly by the creation of parking lots at Goebelstraße and at the forecourt at Geißlerpfad. The structure of the vegetation areas, many of the original trees as well as greenery on the facades have also been preserved.

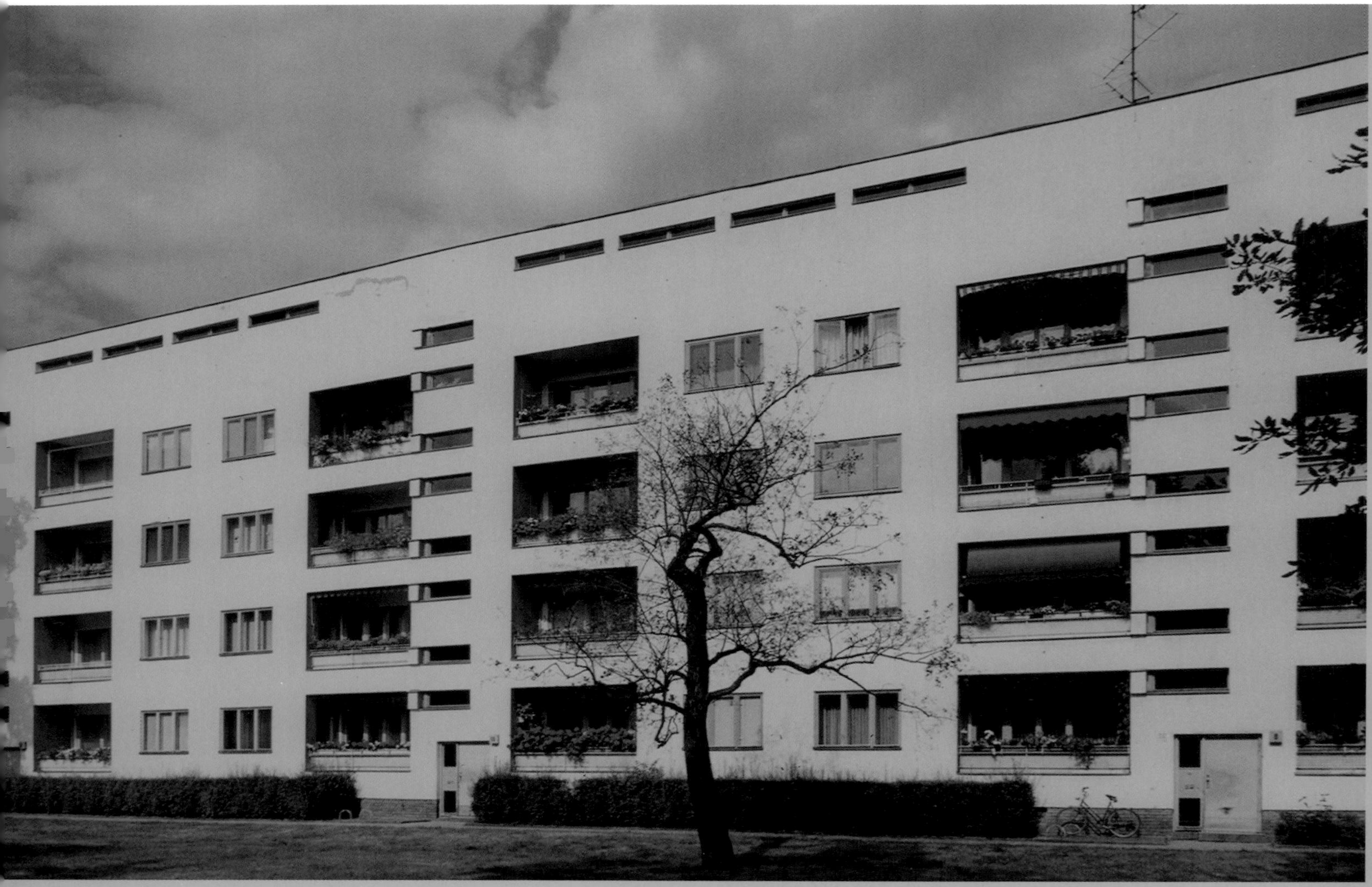

# 4

**ERHALTUNGSZUSTAND UND FAKTOREN, DIE DIE ANLAGEN BEEINFLUSSEN**
**STATE OF CONSERVATION AND FACTORS AFFECTING THE PROPERTIES**

Abb. 81: Gartenstadt Falkenberg, Akazienhof nach der denkmalgerechten Erneuerung, rechts die nachgepflanzte Robinienreihe, 2005

Fig. 81: Gartenstadt Falkenberg, Akazienhof after restoration, on the right hand-side the newly planted row of robinias

## 4.A Gegenwärtiger Erhaltungszustand

Zur Sicherung der Grundsubstanz wurden im Westteil Berlins ab den 1950er Jahren in der Großsiedlung Britz, der Siedlung Schillerpark, der Weißen Stadt und der Großsiedlung Siemensstadt Sanierungs- und Modernisierungsprogramme aufgelegt, die aber denkmalpflegerische Belange außer Acht ließen. In den Anlagen auf dem Gebiet von Ostberlin – also in der Gartenstadt Falkenberg und in der Wohnstadt Carl Legien – kam es nur zu vereinzelten Instandsetzungen. In den 1980er Jahren ist in enger Zusammenarbeit zwischen der Denkmalpflege, den Siedlungsgesellschaften und den beauftragten Architekten mit einer grundlegenden denkmalpflegerischen Erneuerung im Westteil der Stadt begonnen worden. In den östlichen Siedlungen begann dieser Prozess nach der Wiedervereinigung Deutschlands in den 1990er Jahren. Den denkmalgerechten Instandsetzungen gingen überall detaillierte Bestandsaufnahmen mit restauratorischen Befunduntersuchungen voraus.

Die denkmalpflegerischen Instandsetzungen sind in den nominierten Siedlungen unterschiedlich weit vorangeschritten. Bis jetzt konnten die Wiederherstellungsarbeiten in den Siedlungen Falkenberg und Carl Legien abgeschlossen werden. Die Arbeiten in der Gartenstadt Falkenberg wurden im Herbst 2002 beendet, in der Wohnstadt Carl Legien im Jahre 2005. Nach der streng nach Befund erfolgten Farbrekonstruktion zeigen die Siedlungshäuser wieder die reichen, starken Töne der Palette Bruno Tauts.

Auch die Erneuerungsarbeiten in der Siedlung Schillerpark fanden in allen vier Bauabschnitten bis heute zu einem großen Teil einen Abschluss. Lediglich die wenigen Fassadenteile, die ehemals farbig gestrichene Glattputze hatten, zeigen noch die Putze der Nachkriegszeit.

Die Großsiedlungen Britz (Hufeisensiedlung), Weiße Stadt und Siemensstadt haben etwa zu zwei Dritteln ihr ursprüng-

## 4.A Present state of conservation

Refurbishment and modernisation programmes were introduced in the 1950s to maintain the basic fabric of the housing estates of Britz, Schillerpark, Weiße Stadt and Siemensstadt in West Berlin, but those programmes did not take into account the requirements of monument restoration and conservation. In the estates on East Berlin territory, i.e. Gartenstadt Falkenberg and Wohnstadt Carl Legien, only occasional repair work was carried out. In the western part of the city, thorough restoration work began in the 1980s. These measures were conducted in close cooperation between the authorities and experts for the conservation of monuments, the estate communities and the architects contracted for these projects. This process started in the eastern parts of the city in the 1990s after the re-unification of Germany. Everywhere, restoration was preceded by detailed stock taking and investigations into the original state and development of the estates.

Restoration works have reached different stages of completion in the nominated housing estates. Up until now, restoration has been completed in the housing estates Falkenberg and Carl Legien. The measures at Gartenstadt Falkenberg were completed in autumn 2002. At Wohnstadt Carl Legien they were completed in 2005. After they were restored to their original colourfulness on the strict basis of research results, the houses of the housing estates once again display the rich, brilliant colours chosen by Bruno Taut.

Restoration work at the Siedlung Schillerpark has also largely been completed in all four of the development phases. Only the few parts of facades that originally had painted smooth plaster still have the post-war plaster rendering.

The large estates at Britz (Hufeisensiedlung), Weiße Stadt and Siemensstadt have regained about two thirds of their original appearance. Parts of these housing estates need more extensive restoration in particular, since the first res-

liches Erscheinungsbild wieder erlangt. Hier ist zum Teil ein höherer Wiederherstellungsbedarf zu erkennen, zumal die ersten denkmalpflegerischen Maßnahmen mehr als zwanzig Jahre zurückliegen und sich teilweise an diesen Bauteilen neue Schadensbilder zeigen (Bauteile Scharoun und Häring in der Ringsiedlung).

Den Standard der in den 1980er Jahren begonnenen denkmalpflegerischen Erneuerungen gilt es nun auf der Grundlage von Denkmalpflegeplänen zu halten und weiterzuführen. Es ist beabsichtigt, auch den noch nicht restaurierten Siedlungsteilen in dieser Form ihre Gestaltungsqualität zurückzugeben. Heute zeichnen sich aufgrund veränderter sozialer und wirtschaftlicher Rahmenbedingungen sowie durch Veränderungen auf der Eigentümerseite neue Herausforderungen für den Baubestand ab.

### Die einzelnen Siedlungen

### Gartenstadt Falkenberg

Die 1991 eingeleitete grundlegende denkmalpflegerische Erneuerung und Sanierung der Häuser erfolgte nach detaillierten Bestandsuntersuchungen anhand von denkmalpflegerischen Maßnahmekatalogen und wurde von restauratorischen Befunduntersuchungen begleitet. Das Ziel der denkmalpflegerischen Maßnahmen bestand in der weitestgehenden Wiedergewinnung der architektonischen Qualität der Siedlungsbauten einschließlich ihrer Farbigkeit und der zahlreichen für den Gesamteindruck wichtigen Details.

Aus restauratorischen Befunderhebungen und überliefertem Quellenmaterial konnte für nahezu jedes relevante Detail dessen ursprünglicher Farbton ermittelt werden.

toration works were carried out more than twenty years ago and some of the buildings, which were restored at that time, show new damage by now (buildings by Scharoun and Häring at the Ringsiedlung).

We now have to keep up the standard of the restoration measures as they were begun in the 1980s and continue these works on the basis of restoration plans. We also intend to use these schemes for re-establishing those parts of the housing estates that have not yet been restored to their proper quality. Today we are facing new challenges with respect to these housing estates because the social and economic situations have changed and changes have also occurred with respect to ownership.

### The individual housing estates

### Gartenstadt Falkenberg

The thorough restoration of the houses began in 1991 and was based on catalogues of restoration measures developed after detailed investigations into the original state and development from the restoration point of view. The purpose of the restoration measures consisted of re-creating as far as possible the architectonic quality of the buildings inclusive of the colourfulness and many of the details that are important for the general impression.

Based on the investigations and studies of source material, it was possible to determine the original colour for almost every relevant detail. In addition to the restoration or reproduction in line with the requirements for the conservation of monuments of windows, roofs, dormers, shutters, doors, chimney copings, trellises, pergolas, loggias and

Abb. 82: Gartenstadt Falkenberg, Stand der denkmalgerechten Wiederherstellung, Maßstab 1:5.000, 2005

Fig. 82: Gartenstadt Falkenberg, state of conservation, scale 1:5.000, 2005

Denkmalgerecht wiederhergestellt/Restored monument

Neben der Instandsetzung oder denkmalgerechten Nachbildung von Fenstern, Dächern, Gauben, Fensterläden, Türen, Schornsteinköpfen, Spalieren, Pergolen, Hauslauben und Gartenzäunen galt die besondere Aufmerksamkeit der Zurückgewinnung der ursprünglichen Putzart und der Mineralfarbenanstriche sowie der abstrakten Fassadenmalereien. Da die wenigen originalen Putze sowie die DDR-zeitlichen Putze bautechnisch in einem schlechten Zustand waren, mussten nahezu alle Putzoberflächen erneuert werden. Details, wie z.B. Dachanschlüsse, wurden nach heutigen technischen Standards denkmalverträglich ausgeführt.

2000 war die Restaurierung und Sanierung der Häuser des historisch zweiten Bauabschnitts am Gartenstadtweg zu Ende geführt. Ein Jahr später begann man mit dem ersten Bauabschnitt am Akazienhof, dessen Wiederherstellung 2002 abgeschlossen wurde. Damit hat die Gartenstadt Falkenberg ihr ursprüngliches farbenprächtiges Erscheinungsbild zurückerlangt.

*Siedlungsfreiraum*
Der von zwei Robinienreihen beherrschte, angerartige Akazienhof ist in den Jahren 2002/03 nach Ende der baulichen Restaurierung auch in seinen Außenanlagen vorbildlich instandgesetzt worden. Die fehlende Robinienreihe wurde ersetzt. Entsprechend dem historischem Bild wurden die Vorgärten mit Ligusterhecken und die Fassaden und Eingänge mit Spalierobst und Rankpflanzen versehen.

Seit Vorlage des gartendenkmalpflegerischen Gutachtens von 2001 wird versucht, durch das Entfernen störender Koniferen und unmaßstäblicher, immergrüner Gehölze aus den von den Mietern individuell umgenutzten Gärten und durch die Neupflanzung historischer Obstsorten als Hochstämme, den Nutzgartencharakter schrittweise wiederherzustellen. Ein in Abstimmung mit dem Landesdenkmalamt erarbeitetes Merkblatt für alle Genossenschaftler soll diesen Prozess unterstützen.

garden fences, special attention was paid to resurfacing the buildings with the original type of plaster and mineral paint as well as to re-creating the abstract paintings on the facades. Since the few plaster surfaces that were still original and also the plaster surfaces that had been produced during the GDR period were in a bad state of repair, nearly all of the plaster surfaces had to be renewed. Details like roof flashings were carried out in line with today's guidelines for the conservation of monuments.

Restoration and refurbishment of the houses in what was originally the second development phase at Gartenstadtweg was completed in 2000. One year later, work on Akazienhof, which had been the first development phase, began, and was completed in 2002. Thus Gartenstadt Falkenberg has been restored to its original colourful appearance.

*Outdoor facilities*
The outdoor facilities of Akazienhof with the dominating two rows of robinias were refurbished in 2002/03 in an exemplary manner after the restoration of the buildings had been completed. The missing row of robinias was replaced. In line with the original design, privet hedges were planted around the front gardens, and at the facades and entrances espalier fruit and climbers were planted.

Since the expert opinion on the restoration of the gardens was established in 2001, attempts have been made to abolish the coniferous trees and the oversized evergreen plants in the gardens, whose design was altered by the tenants on their own account, and to replace them with newly planted, high-standing trees of historical fruit varieties so as to re-establish the gardens in their original character as kitchen gardens. An information leaflet, which was produced in cooperation with the state conservation office and which is distributed to all members of the cooperative, is to support this process.

Abb. 83: Siedlung Schillerpark, Bauteil an der Bristolstraße nach der Sanierung der Fassade und der Betonteile, neue einheitliche Loggienverglasungen, 2005

Fig. 83: Siedlung Schillerpark, section at Bristolstraße after restoration of the facade and of the concrete elements, new uniform loggia glazing, 2005

Abb. 84: Siedlung Schillerpark, Stand der denkmalgerechten Wiederherstellung, M 1:5.000, 2005

Fig. 84: Siedlung Schillerpark, state of conservation, scale 1:5,000, 2005

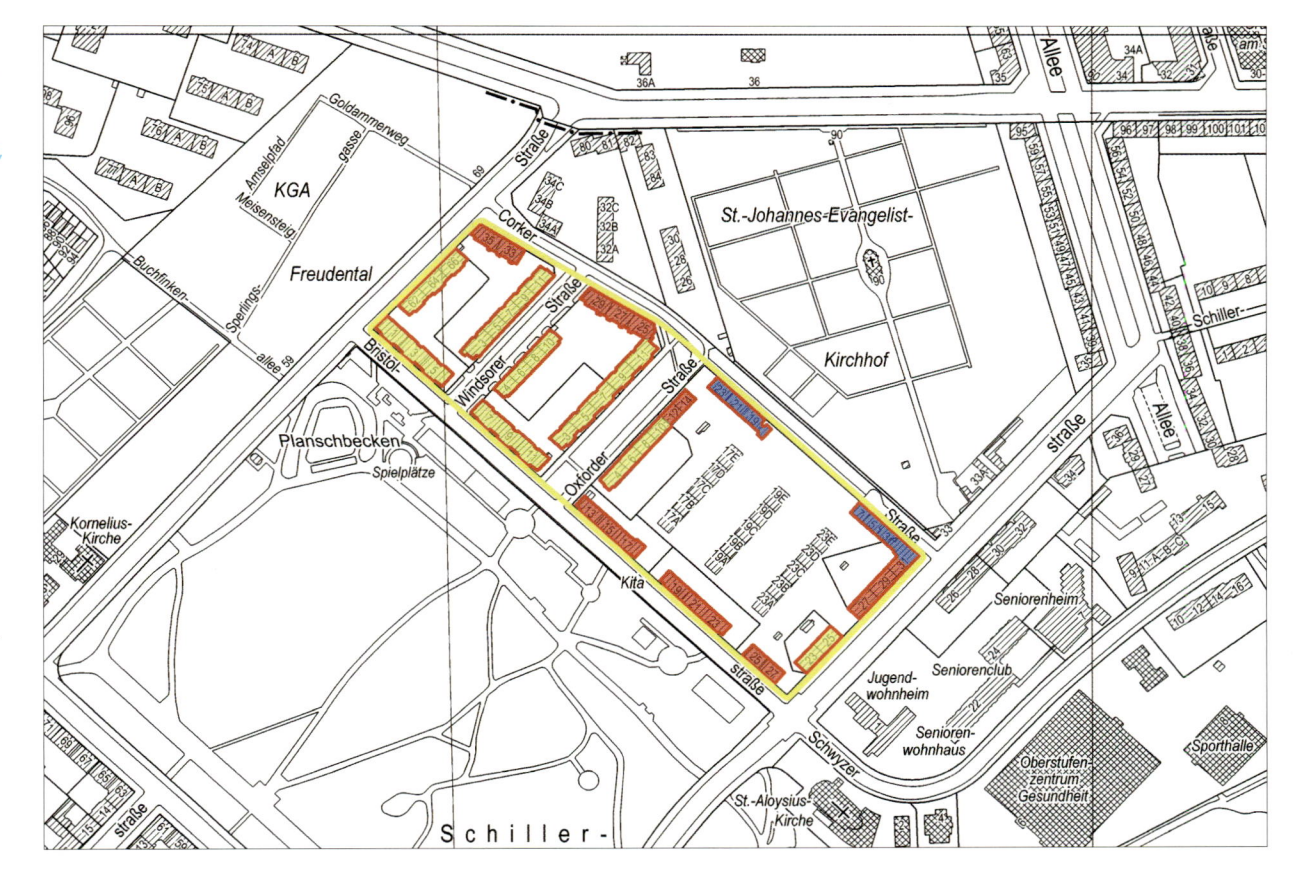

■ Denkmalgerecht wiederhergestellt/Restored monument

■ Geringer Handlungsbedarf/Minor need for conservation

■ Handlungsbedarf/Need for conservation

Die einheitlichen Zaunanlagen sind in den letzten Jahren bereits mit der Instandsetzung der Häuser wiederhergestellt worden. Ebenfalls wurden in jüngster Zeit Teile der Betonstützmauern der Vorgartenterrassen am Gartenstadtweg saniert und bepflanzt. Insgesamt präsentieren sich somit wichtige Teile der Außenanlagen wieder in einem denkmalgerechten Zustand.

The uniform garden fences were already rebuilt when the houses were restored during the past years. In the recent past, parts of the concrete retention walls of the front garden terraces at Gartenstadtweg were also repaired and the gardens were planted. As result of these efforts, important parts of the outdoor facilities have regained their original appearance.

## Siedlung Schillerpark

### Siedlungsabschnitt Bruno Taut

Die denkmalgerechte Instandsetzung wurde 1991 begonnen. Bis auf den Block Barfusstraße 23–25 sind alle Bauteile schrittweise nach originalem Vorbild weitgehend wiederhergestellt worden.

Grundlage der Wiederherstellung ist eine detaillierte Bestandsaufnahme mit einer anschließenden Ausarbeitung eines denkmalpflegerischen Instandsetzungskonzeptes, in das die Denkmalpflege, der Bauherr, die Mieter und das bauleitende Architekturbüro gleicherweise eingebunden sind.

Das Konzept sieht auch eine denkmalgerechte Lösung für die von den Mietern gewünschte Verglasung der Loggien vor, für die eine einheitliche filigrane Stahl-Glaskonstruktion entwickelt und dann sukzessive eingebaut wurde. Zur Unterscheidung von originalen und neuen Elementen strich man hier die alten seitlichen Windschutzelemente wieder in ihrer ursprünglichen Farbe Weiß, während die neuen Teile einen grauen Farbton bekamen.

Dem erforderlichen Lärmschutz – die Siedlung Schillerpark liegt in unmittelbarer Nähe zum Flughafen Tegel – wurde durch den Einbau von Schallschutzverglasungen

## Siedlung Schillerpark

### Section designed by Bruno Taut

Restoration began in 1991. Gradually all parts were restored in line with the original design, with the exception of the block at Barfusstraße 23–25.

The restoration was based on detailed stocktaking followed by the production of a concept for restoration in which the monument conservation authorities, the builder, the tenants and the responsible architectural office were equally involved.

The concept also envisages a solution in line with the requirements for monument conservation for the glazing of the loggias, which was requested by the tenants. For this purpose, a uniform filigree steel and glass structure was developed which was then installed step by step. The original lateral wind screens were painted in the original white colour, whereas the new parts were painted grey, such that the difference between the original and the new parts is obvious.

Since the Siedlung Schillerpark is located near Tegel Airport, it needed noise protection. This was provided by installing noise protection glazing in the inner wings of the

der inneren Flügel der Kastendoppelfenster Genüge getan. Dadurch konnten die für das äußere Erscheinungsbild der Siedlung wichtigen originalen Fenster erhalten werden. Noch nicht wiederhergestellt wurden dagegen die Glattputzflächen und ihre blau-weißen Mineralfarbenanstriche an den Treppenhausfeldern und den Drempelzonen. Hier erwies sich der in der Nachkriegszeit erneuerte Putz als so gut erhalten, dass eine Rekonstruktion nicht wirtschaftlich erschien. Es ist vorgesehen, bei zukünftigen Instandsetzungen einen Glattputz mit der ursprünglichen blauen Farbigkeit wiederherzustellen.

Eine gravierende Beeinträchtigung des Erscheinungsbildes bewirkte die in den 1970/80er Jahren vorgenommene Wärmedämmung zweier Baublöcke, wobei der Wärmedämmputz auf dem roten Verblendmauerwerk aufgebracht wurde. Während es gelang, beim Block Dubliner Straße 62–66 im Rahmen der denkmalpflegerischen Erneuerung die Wärmedämmung zu entfernen und das ursprüngliche Bild wiederherzustellen, musste beim Block Barfusstraße 23–25 bei der 2002–03 erfolgten Instandsetzung die alte Wärmedämmung aus bauphysikalischen Gründen erneuert werden. Allerdings nahm man nun eine Profilierung der Fassadenflächen mit Faschen und Schattenfugen vor, so dass sich typische Gliederungsmerkmale der Häuser dieses dritten Bauabschnittes ablesen lassen.

Die beeindruckende Farbigkeit mit schwarzen, roten und orangen Anstrichen im Innern der Treppenhäuser der ersten Bauetappe konnte jedoch restauriert werden. Auch die Betonpfeiler der vorgezogenen Loggien dieses Bauabschnittes bekamen nach einer grundlegenden Betonsanierung ihre ursprüngliche Ausbildung wieder. Ebenso wurden hier die fehlenden Ziegelstreifen der weißen Putzfelder bei den Bauten des ersten Bauabschnittes wieder ergänzt, so dass heute die expressive Gestaltqualität der Wohnsiedlung am Schillerpark eindrucksvoll vor Augen steht. Darüber hinaus ist von der Eigentümerin – der Berliner Bau- und Wohnungsgenossenschaft 1892 e.G. – geplant, in einer der Wohnungen die Farbigkeit nach Taut zu rekonstruieren.

**Siedlungsabschnitt Hans Hoffmann**
Die vier Randzeilen, die Hoffmann 1954 zur Vervollständigung des Blockes einfügte, befinden sich in einem unterschiedlichen Konservierungszustand. Während die beiden Bauteile Oxforder Straße 12/14 und Bristolstraße 25/27 im Rahmen der jüngsten Erneuerung der Taut-Häuser ebenfalls denkmalgerecht renoviert wurden, führte bei den zwei anderen Blöcken die Aufbringung von Wärmedämmung sowie der Austausch der flächig verglasten Treppenhausfensterbänder zu einem weitgehenden Verlust der architektonischen Qualität.

*Siedlungsfreiraum*
Die historische Wirkung der Baumreihen in den von Bruno Taut entworfenen Gartenhöfen ist durch die Vergrößerung der Pflanzabstände in den Rotdornreihen bzw. den nicht dem ursprünglichen Bild entsprechenden Ersatzpflanzungen eingeschränkt. Bisher ist lediglich im östlichen Hof zwischen Dubliner Straße und Windsorer Straße die ursprüngliche Rotdornpflanzung wiederhergestellt worden. Auch fassen die kleineren Spielplatzflächen am nördlichen Ende der Höfe wieder Hecken und Baumreihen aus Mehlbeerbäumen ein.

box-type double windows. This meant that the original windows, which are important for the appearance of the housing estate, were able to be preserved. The smooth plaster and the blue-white mineral paint coating of the staircase walls and jambs have not yet been restored. The post-war plaster is so well preserved that the restoration of these features appeared not to be economical. Yet, when any repair or maintenance works become necessary in future, the original blue smooth plaster will be restored.

When heat insulation was installed on two blocks in the 1970s/1980s, this created a severe disturbance of the appearance, since the heat insulation plaster was put on top of the red brick cladding. When the restoration works were carried out, it was possible to remove the heat insulation from the block at Dubliner Straße 62–66 and thus to re-establish the original appearance. For reasons of building physics, the heat insulation had to be renewed for the block at Barfusstraße 23–25 in 2002–03 when the building was restored. This time the facades received profiles consisting of white frames and dummy joints, such that typical structural elements of the houses of this third development phase are visible again.

The impressive colourfulness of black, red and orange paint coats inside the staircases of the houses of the first development phase has been restored. Also the concrete pillars of the projecting loggias of this development phase were restored with their original shapes when the concrete works were thoroughly rehabilitated. The missing brick bands of the white plaster squares on the buildings of the first development phase were also restored, such that the expressive design quality of the Siedlung Schillerpark has been re-established with its original impressiveness. Furthermore, the owner, i.e. Berliner Bau- und Wohnungsgenossenschaft von 1892 e.G., intends to paint one of the flats according to Taut's original colour scheme.

**Section designed by Hans Hoffmann**
The four ribbons at the margin, which Hans Hoffmann added in 1954 to complement the block, are in different states of repair and preservation. The two buildings of Oxforder Straße 12/14 and Bristolstraße 25/27 were renovated during the most recent restoration of the buildings by Taut, whereas the other two lost much of their architectural quality when their facades were covered with heat insulation and when the fully glazed staircase window bands were exchanged.

*Outdoor facilities*
The historic appearance of the courtyards designed by Bruno Taut with their rows of trees has been impaired by increasing the distance between the pink hawthorn trees and/or the replacement of plants by others that are not the same species as in the original design. Up to now the original pink hawthorn rows have been replanted only in the eastern courtyard between Dubliner Straße and Windsorer Straße. The smaller playgrounds at the northern ends of the courtyards are once more framed by hedges and rows of whitebeams.

In those parts which were designed by Hoffmann and Rossow, the increased density of trees impairs the spatial structure with its alternation of open and closed or respectively

In den von Hoffmann und Rossow geplanten Bereichen der Siedlung wird durch die höhere Baumdichte das Raumgefüge mit Wechsel von offenen und geschlossenen, bzw. öffentlichen und privaten Räumen und der durch eine eingeschränkte Artenverwendung erzielte ganzjährige Kontrast von Stammfarbe, Blattfarbe und Blühaspekt beeinträchtigt. Ebenso ist ein Verlust der Blickbeziehungen und eine Beeinträchtigung der Rasenflächen durch Verschattung zu verzeichnen.

Im Auftrag der Baugenossenschaft konnte 2003 ein Denkmalpflegeplan für die Freianlagen der 1920er und 1950er Jahre erarbeitet werden. Seit 2004 liegt darüber hinaus eine gartendenkmalpflegerische Entwicklungskonzeption für alle Siedlungsteile vor.

### Großsiedlung Britz (Hufeisensiedlung)

Die Anfang der 1980er eingeleitete und gegenwärtig noch andauernde grundlegende denkmalpflegerische Erneuerung und Sanierung der Häuser erfolgte anhand von detaillierten Bestandsanalysen und restauratorischen Befunduntersuchungen. Sie führte in allen Bauabschnitten zu einer Wiedergewinnung der architektonischen Qualität und der Farbräume, so dass der überwiegende Teil der Siedlung nach ursprünglichem Vorbild wiederhergestellt ist.

Die Britzer Hufeisensiedlung zeigt heute dennoch ein heterogenes Bild. Zum einen sind noch Siedlungsbereiche vorhanden – so etwa große Teile des Hufeisens und die mehrgeschossige Randbebauung an der Parchimer Allee 66–104 und Buschkrugallee 223–247 – die ohne denkmalpflegerische Zielsetzung in der Nachkriegszeit instand gesetzt worden sind und hierbei originalen Putz und ursprüngliche Farbe verloren. Zum anderen begann in den 1970er Jahren eine Erneuerung, die eine Wiederbelebung der Farbarchitektur Tauts zum Ziel hatte, die Restaurierung jedoch

public and private spaces and the year-round contrasts between the colours of the tree trunks, leaves and blossoms achieved through the selection of only a limited number of species. Furthermore, the higher density of trees disturbs views and impairs the lawns with too much shade.

In 2003, a plan for preserving the monument's outdoor facilities of the 1920s and 1950s was established by order of the building cooperative. Since 2004, a development concept for the restoration and preservation of the garden architecture has also been in existence.

### Großsiedlung Britz (Hufeisensiedlung)

The thorough restoration of the houses started in the 1980s and still continues. It is carried out on the basis of detailed analyses of the existing situation and investigations for restoration purposes. The result is that in all development phases, the architectural quality and colours were restored so that most of the housing estate has been re-established in its original design.

Yet, the Hufeisensiedlung at Britz still looks rather heterogeneous. On the one hand, there are still parts of the housing estate – for instance large parts of the horseshoe and the multi-storey buildings at the block margins at Parchimer Allee 66–104 and Buschkrugallee 223–247 – which had been repaired during the post-war period without consideration of their preservation as monuments and due to these repairs they lost their original plaster and colouring. On the other hand, a renewal was started in the 1970s with the intention of restoring Taut's coloured architecture, but this restoration was carried out on the basis of analyses of colours and materials that were not entirely correct. This particularly applies to the so-called "Red Front" at Fritz-Reuter-Allee 6–42 and 52–72, and as a result, the projecting staircases were not painted with the original pink colour.

Abb. 85: Großsiedlung Britz, Hufeisen Fritz-Reuter-Allee/ Ecke Lowise-Reuter-Ring, 2003 Erneuerung des Putzes und Farbanstrichs nach Befund, 2005

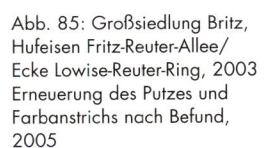

Fig. 85: Großsiedlung Britz, horseshoe at Fritz-Reuter-Allee/ corner with Lowise-Reuter-Ring, renewal of the plaster and paint coat according to investigation findings in 2003, 2005

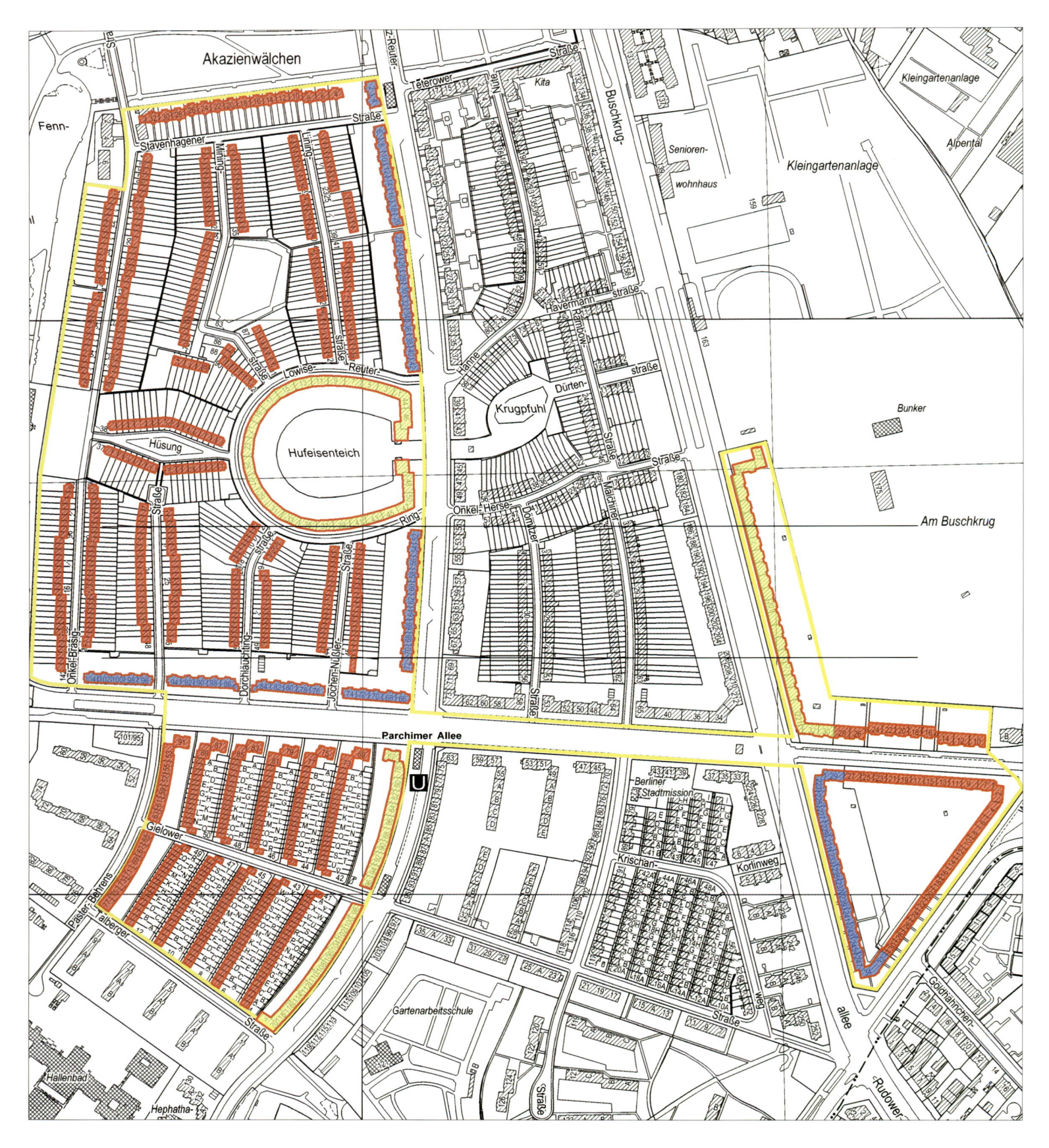

Abb. 86: Großsiedlung Britz,
Stand der denkmalgerechten
Wiederherstellung, Maßstab
1:5.000, 2005

Fig. 86: Großsiedlung Britz,
state of conservation, scale
1:5.000, 2005

■ Denkmalgerecht wiederhergestellt/Restored monument

■ Geringer Handlungsbedarf/Minor need for conservation

■ Handlungsbedarf/Need for conservation

teilweise auf der Grundlage von Fehlanalysen und falschen Materialien vollzog. Sie betrifft vor allem die sogenannte „Rote Front" an der Fritz-Reuter-Allee 6–42 und 52–72, bei der die vorgezogenen Treppenhäuser nicht wieder ihren rosafarbigen Ton bekamen.

Noch nicht vollständig restauriert ist das Hufeisen. Hier hatten zunächst Mitte der 1980er Jahre die Innenflächen der zum Teich gerichteten Loggien ihre blaue Farbe zurückbekommen. Mit der eigentlichen Erneuerung der Wandflächen und der Fensterfarbigkeit konnte 2000 begonnen werden. Bis 2001 wurde ein kleiner Abschnitt der weißblauen Außenfassade mit den Treppenhäusern – Fritz-Reuter-Allee 44–46 und Lowise-Reuter-Ring 1–9 – denkmalgerecht (Putz und Farbigkeit) erneuert. Ein hoher Sanierungsbedarf besteht beim Eingang zum Hufeisen an der Fritz-Reuter-Allee. Hier müssen die Treppenanlage mit den früheren Leuchtsäulen und der Vorplatz nach ursprünglichem Vorbild rekonstruiert werden.

Größere Fassadenschäden sind heute nur am Block Buschkrugallee 179–217 (Bauabschnitt III) festzustellen. Hier führten die in den 1970er Jahren vorgenommenen, nicht denkmalgerechten Renovierungen (falsche Farbigkeit und keine Mineralfarben) mit Dispersionsfarbanstrichen zu Folgeschäden. Bei der Instandsetzung nach originalem Vorbild wurden diese vor kurzem auf der Straßenseite beseitigt.

### Siedlungsfreiraum
Zur Zeit sind bedeutende Teile der Freianlagen in einem nicht denkmalgerechten Zustand. Eine denkmalpflegerische Wiederherstellung der Außenanlagen ist aufgrund der weitgehend vorhandenen Grundstruktur allerdings möglich. In dem Ende 2003 erarbeiteten gartendenkmalpflegerischen Gutachten wurden die wichtigsten Maßnahmen zur Wiederherstellung der Außenanlagen dargestellt.

Im zentralen Bereich der Siedlung, dem Hufeisen, ist das ursprüngliche gestalterische Konzept im Detail zu erkennen. Am ehemals baumlosen Teich sind hohe Bäume entstanden, der ehemalige, jahreszeitliche Höhepunkt eines blühenden Kranzes aus Sauerkirschen fehlt fast völlig und die Fassaden werden von hohen Koniferen verdeckt. Um eine denkmalgerechte Wiederherstellung dieser Anlage voranzutreiben, wurden zwischen der GEHAG und dem Bezirk Neukölln Verhandlungen geführt, um die gesamte Anlage des Hufeisens privat zu übernehmen.

Neben dem stark beeinträchtigten Erscheinungsbild der Grünflächen im Inneren des Hufeisens sind als wichtigste Defizite in der Siedlung die zum Teil fehlerhaft ergänzte Bepflanzung der Straßenräume und die individuelle Bepflanzung der Mietergärten zu nennen, so dass der Nutzgartencharakter dieser Bereiche weitgehend verloren ging. Die im Bereich der Fritz-Reuter-Allee eingefügten Hochbeete aus den 1960er/1970er Jahren und die in einigen Teilen der Siedlung vorgenommene Umwandlung von Vorgärten in Stellplätze stören ebenfalls das historische Bild.

Abb. 87: Großsiedlung Britz, Hofseite der Häuser Buschkrugallee 177–217, renoviert in den 1970er Jahren, 2005.

Fig. 87: Großsiedlung Britz, yard-side of the houses at Buschkrugallee 177–217, refurbished in the 1970s, 2005

The restoration of the horseshoe has not yet been completed. In the mid 1980s, the interior facades and the loggias that are orientated towards the lake were painted with the original blue colour. The actual renewal of the walls and of the window colours was started in 2000. By 2001, a small section of the white-blue facade with the staircases (at Fritz-Reuter-Allee 44–46 and Lowise-Reuter-Ring 1–9) was properly restored (both plaster and colour). The entrance to the horseshoe at Fritz-Reuter-Allee still requires major restoration works. The flight of stairs with the original pillar lights and the forecourt will have to be restored.

The block of Buschkrugallee 179–217 (Development Phase III) is the only one that still shows major damage of the facade. Repairs in the 1970s, which were not proper restorations (incorrect colours and no mineral paint) and in which dispersion paint was used, created subsequent damage. During recent restoration in line with the original state, this paint was removed on the street side facade.

### Outdoor facilities
Currently, large parts of the outdoor facilities are not in a proper state of restoration. However, proper restoration of the outdoor facilities is possible because their fundamental structure still exists. The expert opinion established in 2003 on the restoration of the garden architecture presents the most important measures for re-establishing the outdoor facilities in their original quality.

The core of the settlement – i.e. the horseshoe – still shows the design concept in detail. High trees have grown along the pond where originally no trees had been and the former seasonal climax created by a circle of blossoming morello cherry trees is almost non-existent. The facades are hidden

Fig. 88: Wohnstadt Carl Legien, 2004 wiederhergestellte Farbigkeit nach Befund, 2005

Fig. 88: Wohnstadt Carl Legien, colours restored according to investigation results in 2004, 2005

## Wohnstadt Carl Legien

Heute ist nach Beendigung der Sanierung 2005 das ursprüngliche Bild in allen Teilen der Wohnbauten wiederhergestellt. Entlang der Achse Erich-Weinert-Straße sind wieder die verschieden Farbräume der Höfe erfahrbar. In zwei Wohnungen konnte sogar die Originalfarbigkeit nach Taut rekonstruiert werden.

Als Pilotprojekt wurde 1992–94 nach restauratorischem Befund eine Putz- und Farbrekonstruktion der Häuser Trachtenbrodtstraße 2–18 und Sodtkestraße 20–36/Ecke Erich-Weinert-Straße durchgeführt, wobei beim Blockflügel an der Sodtkestraße der Kopfbau an der Erich-Weinert-Straße und die Straßenfront wiederhergestellt wurden. Auch der Putz konnte aus wirtschaftlichen Erwägungen dort nach originalem Vorbild erneuert werden, wo er stark beschädigt war. Die falschen Putze der 1960er Jahre wurden hingegen nur farblich angepasst. Die Fronten erhielten einen Mineralfarbenanstrich nach historischem Vorbild, wobei auch der Farbaufbau der Fenster und Haustüren und ein Treppenhaus rekonstruiert wurde. Die Erneuerung wurde mit Mitteln der Deutschen Stiftung Denkmalschutz gefördert. Zur gleichen Zeit erfolgte ein denkmalgerechter Umbau des ehemaligen kleineren, nach 1945 veränderten wieder aufgebauten Waschhauses im Block an der nördlichen Gubitzstraße zu Verwaltungsräumen.

Mit der Modernisierung der Wohnungen ab 2003 war auch die Weiterführung der denkmalgerechten Erneuerung der Siedlung verbunden, die heute abgeschlossen ist. Die denkmalgerechte Instandsetzung der Fassaden, Fenster, Türen und Treppenhäuser erfolgte nach restauratorischen Voruntersuchungen. Die in Teilen zum Baubeginn noch vorhandenen durchgefärbten originalen Glatt-, Schlepp- und feinkörnigen Kratzputze mussten aufgrund umfangreicher Hohllagen gänzlich nach Befund erneuert werden. Trotz

by high coniferous trees. To achieve proper restoration of this area, GEHAG and the district's municipal administration have entered into negotiations on taking the entire facility of the horseshoe into private care.

The green spaces inside the horseshoe are not the only ones that have been very much impaired. Other important deficits include the substitution of lost plants along the streets with some incorrect plants or species and the fact that inhabitants have changed the design and uses of their gardens such that a lot of these spaces are no longer the original kitchen gardens. The raised plant beds, which were built at Fritz-Reuter-Allee in the 1960s and 1970s, and the conversion of some front gardens into parking lots in some parts of the housing estate also disturb the historic appearance.

## Wohnstadt Carl Legien

Today, after the completion of the refurbishment in 2005, all parts of the residential buildings once again exhibit their original appearance. Along the axis of Erich-Weinert-Straße, the spaces with the various colours can again be experienced. It was even possible to restore two flats with Taut's original colour scheme.

In 1992–94, a pilot project was carried out in which the plaster and paint coats of the houses at Trachtenbrodtstraße 2–18 and Sodtkestraße 20–36 on the corner of Erich-Weinert-Straße were restored on the basis of restoration-based research. In the case of the block wing on Sodtkestraße, it was the head building and the street front at Erich-Weinert-Straße that were restored. For economic reasons, the plaster was able to be restored in the original quality and appearance only on those areas where it had been in a very bad state of repair, such that even the wrong plaster of the 1960s only got the correct paint coat. The facades were painted with mineral paint in line with the original coat and also the paint coats of the windows and entrance doors, as well as those of one staircase, were re-created. The restoration was supported by financing from the Deutsche Stiftung Denkmalschutz (German Foundation for Conservation of Monuments). Simultaneously, the former smaller laundry in the block at the northern part of Gubitzstraße, which had been rebuilt after 1945, although not in its original design, was converted into administration offices – this time in line with the requirements for preserving monuments.

When the flats were modernised from 2003 on, the restoration of the housing estate was continued, too, and it is completed now. The facades, windows, doors and staircases were restored on the basis of results of proper investigations. Since the original pigmented smooth, structured and fine-grain scraped renderings often were no longer properly attached to the facade surface, they had to be removed and the facades had to be completely resurfaced in line with the findings. The windows of the flats towards the yards and in the head buildings on Erich-Weinert-Straße had been somewhat protected against the weather by the full-width loggias, such that they could be preserved despite some constructional damage. However, the box-type double windows on the street side had to be exchanged for modern wooden insulation windows. The new windows

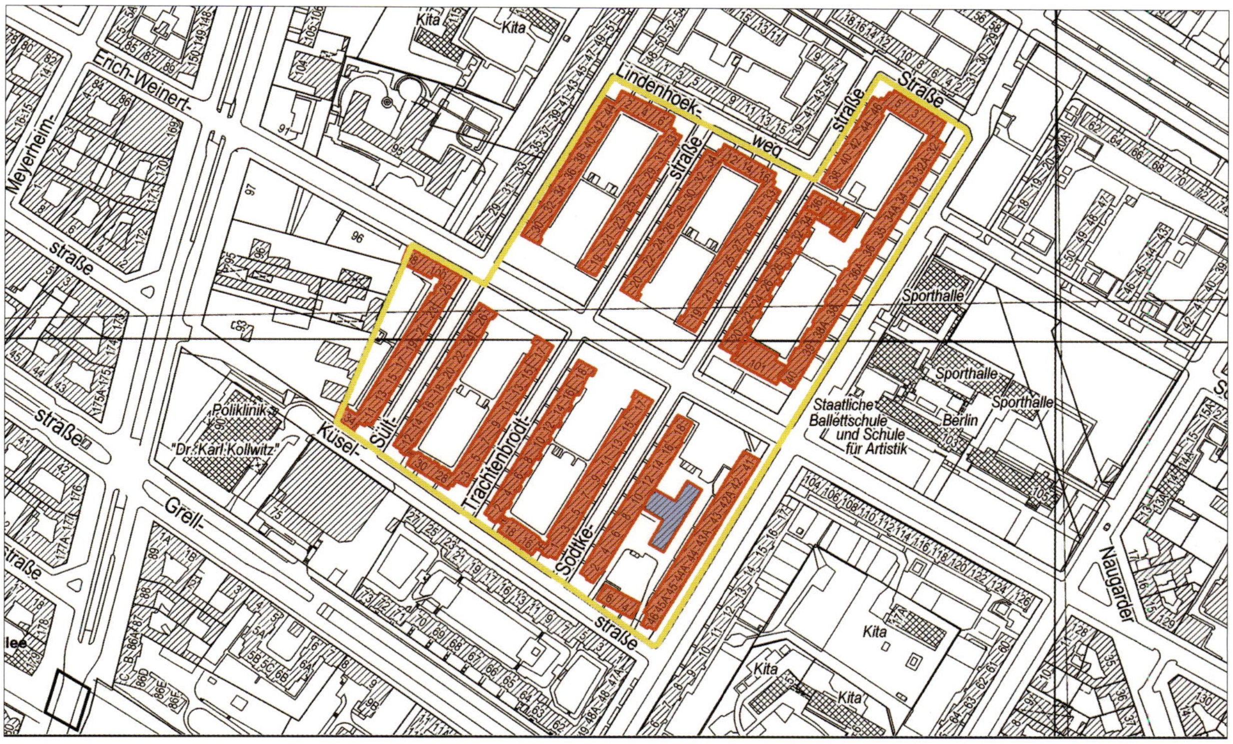

Abb. 89: Wohnstadt Carl Legien, Stand der denkmalgerechten Wiederherstellung, M 1:5.000, 2005

Fig. 89: Wohnstadt Carl Legien, state of conservation, scale 1:5.000, 2005

■ Denkmalgerecht wiederhergestellt/Restored monument

■ Geringer Handlungsbedarf/Minor need for conservation

■ Handlungsbedarf/Need for conservation

bautechnischer Schäden konnten die Fenster der Wohnungen nach den Höfen und in den Kopfbauten an der Erich-Weinert-Straße, die aufgrund der hausbreiten Loggien der Witterung weniger ausgesetzt waren, erhalten bleiben. Jedoch mussten die straßenseitigen bauzeitlichen Kastendoppelfenster gegen moderne Holz-Iso-Fenster ausgetauscht werden. Die neuen Fenster wurden in der Aufteilung und im Farbaufbau entsprechend dem originalem Vorbild nachgebaut.

Ein Instandsetzungs- und Wiederherstellungsbedarf besteht noch für das weitgehend leer stehende große T-förmige Heiz- und Waschhaus im südöstlichen Hof zwischen Sodtke- und Gubitzstraße. Während der DDR-Zeit verlor es aufgrund des Anschlusses aller Wohnungen an das Fernwärmenetz seine Bestimmung und wird nun im Untergeschoss als Fernwärmeübergabestation genutzt. Für das Haus ist die zukünftige Nutzung zu klären. Allerdings besteht bereits ein Konzept, das eine denkmalverträgliche Nutzung nachweist.

*Siedlungsfreiraum*
Korrespondierend zur Wiederherstellung der Fassaden sind nun auch die Freianlagen weitgehend denkmalgerecht wiederhergestellt und damit die ursprünglichen Gestaltungsideen wieder erlebbar. Für die Wiederherstellung wurden Bäume gefällt und nahezu sämtliche fehlenden historischen Bäume, Gehölze, Hecken und Stauden an den Originalstandorten in den Höfen und Vorgärten nachgepflanzt. Gleichzeitig wurden die früheren Sichtbeziehungen zwischen den Höfen behutsam geöffnet. Viele der verwilderten und zum Teil ungenutzten Mietergärten wurden unter Erhalt und Nachpflanzung von Obstbäumen aufgegeben und zugunsten gemeinschaftlich nutzbarer Rasen- und Spielflächen neu geordnet. Einhergehend wurde die ehemaligen Großzügigkeit der Flächen zurückgewonnen. Noch immer wirkt die Anlage durch den erhaltenen Altbaumbestand stark durchgrünt. Die Wege sind in ihrer

were manufactured with the same structure and colours as the original windows.

The T-shaped heating plant and laundry in the southeastern yard between Sodtke- and Gubitzstraße, which is mostly empty and disused, still requires major repair and restoration. When all of the flats were connected with the district heating system during the GDR era, it lost its function and its basement is now used as a long-distance heat intake. The future use of the house must still be defined. A concept exists for its use in line with the requirements for preserving it as part of the monument.

*Outdoor facilities*
Meanwhile the outdoor facilities have also been properly restored as had been done for the facades, and now the original design can once again be observed. Trees were felled and almost all missing trees, bushes, hedges and herbaceous plants which had been part of the original design were planted in the yards and front gardens to re-establish its historic appearance. These works also included the careful re-opening of the original views between the yards. Many of the overgrown and partially disused tenants' gardens were abandoned and integrated into lawns and playgrounds for communal use. In doing so, the fruit trees were preserved and missing ones were re-planted. This regenerated the original spaciousness of the areas. Thanks to the remaining old trees, the area is still very green. The paths have been repaved with the original materials (mastic asphalt or respectively Bernburg Mosaic grey stone paving) and waste bin areas as well as playgrounds were re-structured.

ursprünglichen Materialität mit Gussasphalt bzw. Bernburger Mosaik instand gesetzt, Müllplätze und Spielbereiche wurden neu geordnet.

## Weiße Stadt

Eine grundlegende denkmalpflegerische Instandsetzung der Siedlungsbauten begann 1982 auf der Grundlage einer 1980–81 durchgeführten detaillierten denkmalpflegerischen Bestandsaufnahme mit restauratorischen Analysen. Die bis heute anhaltende Erneuerung der Siedlung führte zu einer Wiedergewinnung der architektonischen Qualität in allen Siedlungsteilen. Vor allem der mit Mineralfarbe weiß gestrichene Glattputz und die farbigen Architekturelemente sind wieder nach Befund hergestellt worden.

Akute Bauschäden beschränkten sich auf die Konstruktion der verfensterten Hauslauben in den Bauteilen von Otto Rudolf Salvisberg und Bruno Ahrends. In den 1980er Jahren kam es vor allem bei den Häusern von Bruno Ahrends aufgrund bauphysikalischer Erfordernisse und auf Wunsch der Mieter und der Siedlungsgesellschaft zu einer Nutzungsänderung der ehemals als Wintergarten dienenden Lauben. Sie führte zu einer Beeinträchtigung der ursprünglichen Baugestalt. An die Stelle der Eisenkonstruktion trat eine Ausführung in Aluminium mit Wärmeschutzverglasung und eine Brüstung mit vorgesetzter Wärmedämmung, so dass die Lauben jetzt ganzjährig als zusätzlicher Wohnraum genutzt werden können.

Denkmalgerecht vollzog sich dagegen ab Ende der 1990er Jahre die noch fortwährende Sanierung der Hauslauben im Bauteil von Salvisberg. Schmalere Alu-Profile für die Iso-Verglasungen und der Verzicht auf eine Wärmedämmung sorgten für ein denkmalverträgliches Ergebnis. Auch die für das rationale Bauen wichtigen Betonfertigteile, die im

## Weiße Stadt

In 1982, a thorough restoration of the buildings began on the basis of a detailed stocktaking and analyses for restoration purposes which had been carried out in 1980–81. The restoration of the housing estate continues even today, and it has led to the recovery of the architectonic quality of all parts of the housing estate. Especially the smooth plaster with white mineral paint coating and the coloured architectural elements have been re-established in line with the findings.

Old damage existed in the structure of the glazed loggias in the buildings designed by Otto Rudolf Salvisberg and Bruno Ahrends. Especially in the houses designed by Bruno Ahrends, the loggias were originally used as conservatories, but in the 1980s their use was altered due to constructional needs and because the tenants and the estate society wanted it. This impaired the appearance. The iron structure was replaced by aluminium that was completed with thermo-glazing and a parapet with heat insulation attached in front, such that the loggias can now be used as additional living space throughout the entire year.

On the other hand, the loggias in the houses designed by Salvisberg have been restored in line with the requirements of monument conservation. This restoration started in the late 1990s and continues to date. The result of this restoration is more in line with the original appearance because the aluminium profiles for the thermo-glazing are narrower and because no heat insulation is attached to the fronts. The prefabricated concrete sections, which remained unpainted and frame the house entrances of the buildings designed by Büning, have recently been properly restored. These parts played an important role in rational building.

The gallery house by Salvisberg has also not yet been restored although a restoration concept exists for it. A small part of the garden side of the long ribbon by Salvisberg at

Abb. 90: Weiße Stadt, denkmalgerecht sanierte Hauslauben im Siedlungsteil von O. R. Salvisberg, 2005

Fig. 90: Weiße Stadt, restored loggias in section designed by O. R. Salvisberg, 2005

Abb. 91: Weiße Stadt, denkmalgerechte Sanierung der Kunststeineinfassung der Treppenhäuser und Hauseingänge im Siedlungsteil von Wilhelm Büning, 2005

Fig. 91: Weiße Stadt, restoration of the synthetic stone frames of the staircases and entrance doors in the section designed by Wilhelm Büning, 2005

Abb. 92: Weiße Stadt, Stand der denkmalgerechten Wiederherstellung, M 1:5.000, 2005

Fig. 92: Weiße Stadt, state of conservation, scale 1:5.000, 2005

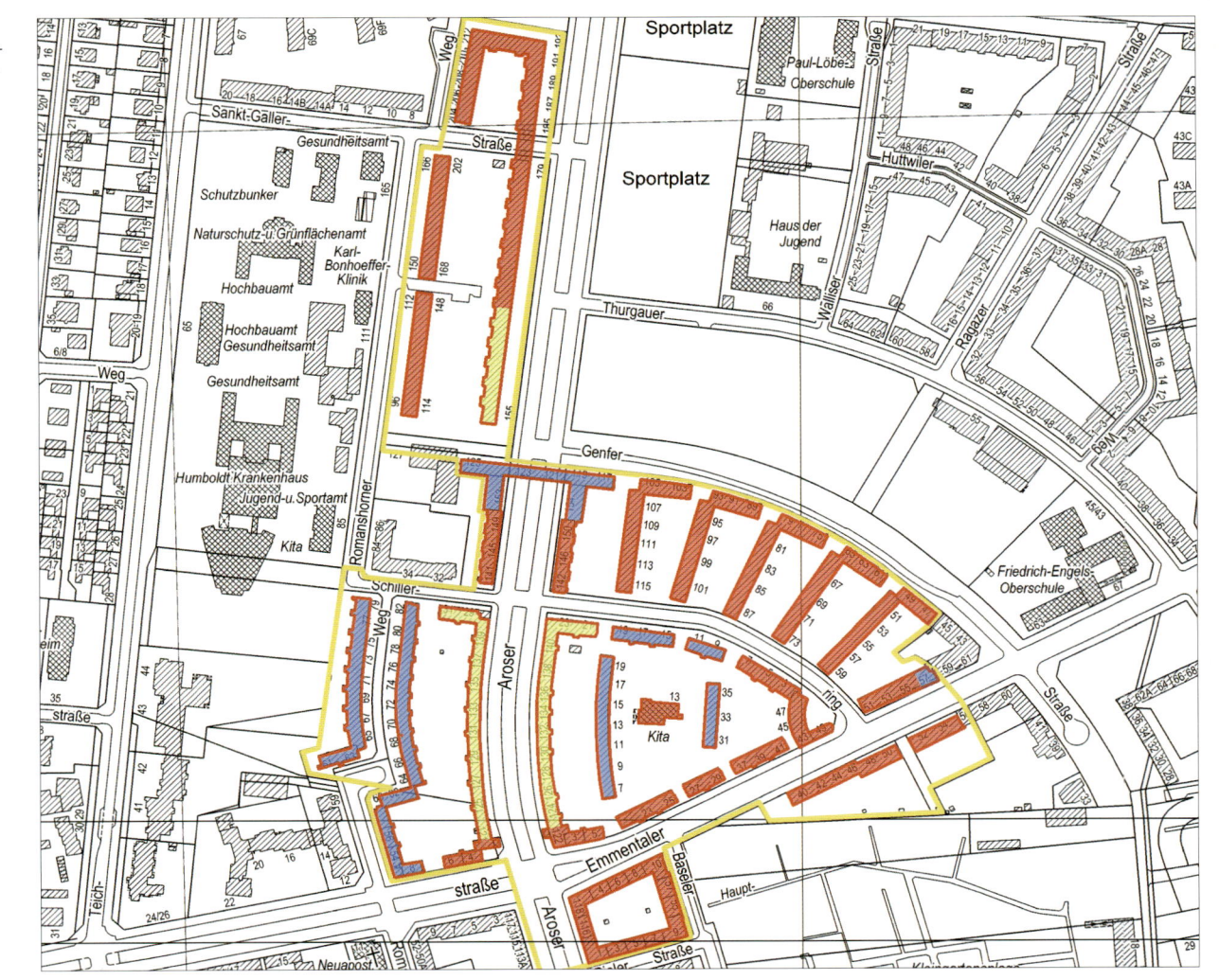

■ Denkmalgerecht wiederhergestellt/Restored monument

■ Geringer Handlungsbedarf/Minor need for conservation

■ Handlungsbedarf/Need for conservation

Bauteil von Büning ungestrichen die Hauseingänge rahmen, sind vor kurzem fachgerecht saniert worden.

Noch nicht restauriert worden sind das Laubenganghaus von Salvisberg, für das ein Instandsetzungskonzept vorliegt, ein geringer Teil der Gartenseite der langen Zeile von Salvisberg an der Aroser Allee sowie einzelne Blockteile des Abschnittes von Ahrends, wie die Randzeilen am Romanshorner Weg. Dies soll in den nächsten Jahren geschehen.

*Siedlungsfreiraum*
Auch die Gartendenkmalpflege begann parallel zu den baulichen Maßnahmen mit der Wiederherstellung der Grünflächen. Nur noch fragmentarisch ist heute das Konzept von Ludwig Lesser überliefert. Zwei der halböffentlichen Binnenhöfe bei den fächerförmig gegliederten Wohnzeilen im Abschnitt Büning konnten erneuert werden.

Auf der Grundlage des im Jahr 2000 erstellten Regelwerkes für die Freianlagen erfolgte 2001 eine denkmalpflegerische Rekonstruktion des Siedlungsfreiraums im großen östlichen Baublock des Abschnittes von Bruno Ahrends. Die ursprüngliche Konzeption Lessers konnte nicht vollständig wiederhergestellt werden, da die qualitätvollen Überformungen respektiert wurden. Es kam aus funktionellen Gründen zu Zugeständnissen bei den Wegebelägen. Das Ergebnis wird Vorbild für zukünftige gartendenkmalpflegerische Maßnahmen sein. Wiederhergestellt sind auch die Spiel- und Gartenanlagen bei der Kindertagesstätte.

Aroser Allee has also not yet been restored, as well as individual parts of blocks in the section designed by Ahrends and ribbons at block margins on Romanshorner Weg. These works will be carried out in the next few years.

*Outdoor facilities*
Restoration of the outdoor facilities began at the same time as renovation of the buildings with the re-creation of the green spaces. Only fragments of Ludwig Lesser's concept survived. Two of the semi-public courtyards at the ribbons with the fan-shaped structure in the section designed by Büning were able to be renewed.

The outdoor facilities in the large eastern block of the section by Bruno Ahrends were restored in 2001 on the basis of a set of rules for the outdoor facilities established in the year 2000. It was not possible to completely restore the original design by Lesser, since the high-quality changes were respected. For functional reasons, allowances were made with respect to the paving materials. The result will serve as a model for future restorations of outdoor facilities. Also, the playgrounds and outdoor facilities at the kindergarten were restored.

## Großsiedlung Siemensstadt (Ringsiedlung)

Die denkmalpflegerische Instandsetzung 1984–1986, die die Abschnitte von Scharoun, Häring und Henning betraf, strebte eine möglichst originalgetreue Wiederherstellung an. Grundlage war eine Bestandsaufnahme, verbunden mit restauratorischen Befunduntersuchungen. Jedoch erforderten bautechnische Schäden und wirtschaftliche Erwägungen in Teilen eine vom ursprünglichen Bild abweichende Erneuerung. Akute Bauschäden wurden vor allem bei der Konstruktion der nierenförmigen, Stahlrohr gestützten Balkone und beim Prüßwandmauerwerk der Dachgeschosse in den neun Häring-Zeilen festgestellt. Die Balkone mussten komplett saniert, die Stahlrohrstützen ausgetauscht und die Brüstungverblendungen in gelb-bunten Ziegeln erneuert werden. Der originale ungestrichene Kalkputz war nicht mehr zu erhalten. Alle Bauten bekamen einen neuen Glattputz mit einem beigen Mineralfarbenanstrich. So wurde ein annähernd der ursprünglichen Beschaffenheit entsprechendes Bild erzielt. Allerdings begann 2003–2004 eine erneute Sanierung der Balkone der Häring-Zeilen, wobei die charakteristische organische Baugestalt der Balkone bewahrt bleibt.

Ebenfalls stark geschädigt waren die leichten Brüstungsschalen der geschwungenen Balkone des Scharounbaus Jungfernheideweg 1/Ecke Mäckeritzstraße, die beim Wiederaufbau 1949–50 als dünne Rabitzwände ausgeführt worden waren. Die beiden Scharounblöcke am trichterförmigen Zugang der Siedlung konnten bisher nur in Teilbereichen 1985–86 denkmalpflegerisch erneuert werden. Die Straßenfronten am Jungfernheideweg und kleine Abschnitte der Hofseiten sind in Putz und Farbe wiederhergestellt. So besticht am Eingang zur Siedlung wieder Scharouns Konzept eines fein differenzierten Farbspiels von weißen, gelben und ockerfarbigen Fassadenelementen, wenn sich auch nach zwanzig Jahren wieder vereinzelte Putzschäden zeigen. Scharouns Kopfbau Jungfernheideweg 1 wurde damals in seiner von ihm autorisierten Wiederaufbaufassung bewahrt.

Zeitgleich nahm man auch ab 1984 die denkmalpflegerische Instandsetzung der Zeilen von Paul Rudolf Henning am Heckerdamm vor, die keine bautechnischen Probleme zeigten.

Noch vor der Unterschutzstellung aller Siedlungsteile 1995 kam es zu einer Renovierung der Treppenhausfensterbänder der östlichen Zeile von Walter Gropius am Jungfernheideweg. Anstelle der eisernen, schmalen Profile der bauzeitlichen Verglasung entstanden neue Treppenhausbereiche mit breiteren Alu-Profilen und anderer Fensterteilung. Bei der gegenüberliegenden Zeile hat sich dagegen die originale Treppenhausverglasung bewahrt. Bereits 1988/89 konnte hier die nach dem Krieg verändert wiederaufgebaute Eckbebauung Jungfernheideweg – Goebelstraße städtebaulich und architektonisch nach einem Entwurf der Architekten Hilmer & Sattler im sachlich-funktionellen Stil der Gropiusbauten neu geordnet werden.

1998 erfolgte die Balkonsanierung auf der Gartenseite der langen Zeile Goebelstraße 21–113 von Otto Bartning. Anstelle einer grundlegenden Erneuerung der schadhaften konstruktiven Betondecken erhielten die Doppelbalkone zusätzliche Stahlrohrstützen. Das bisherige leichte, schwebende Bild der Balkonreihen ging dadurch verloren.

## Großsiedlung Siemensstadt (Ringsiedlung)

The restoration of the sections designed by Scharoun, Häring and Henning in 1984–1986 was aimed at recreating the original appearance and quality as far as possible. It was based on stocktaking and investigations for restoration purposes. Unfortunately, the discovered constructional damage and economic considerations made it necessary to deviate occasionally from the original image. Severe constructional damage was discovered especially in the kidney-shaped balconies with steel-pipe structure and the pruesswand brickwork of the attics in the nine ribbons by Häring. The balconies had to be refurbished completely. Their steel-pipe structures had to be exchanged and the parapet cladding of brickwork in various shades of yellow had to be renewed. It was impossible to preserve the original unpainted lime plaster. All buildings got a new, smooth plaster with a beige mineral paint coat. Thus it was possible to create an appearance that is almost the same as the original one. In 2003–2004 another refurbishment of the balconies of the Häring ribbons began which preserves their characteristic organic shape.

In addition, the light parapet shell of the rounded balconies of Scharoun's building at Jungfernheideweg 1 on the corner of Mäckeritzstraße was severely damaged. They had been executed as plaster fabric wall during the reconstruction in 1949–50. Only parts of the two Scharoun blocks at the funnel-shaped entrance to the housing estate were able to be restored in 1985–86. Plaster and paint coats have been restored on the street fronts at Jungfernheideweg and in small sections on the yard sides. At the entrance of the housing estate, Scharoun's concept of carefully differentiated shades of white, yellow and ochre coloured facade elements makes a striking impact again even if now, twenty years after the restoration, some damage to the plaster is appearing again. The head building by Scharoun at Jungfernheideweg 1 has been preserved in the version in which it was rebuilt and which was authorised by Scharoun.

At the same time, in 1984, restoration of the ribbon buildings by Paul Rudolf Henning at Heckerdamm began. They did not have any constructional damage.

Before the entire housing estate became a protected monument in 1995, the staircase window band of the eastern ribbon by Walter Gropius at Jungfernheideweg was renovated. Instead of the narrow iron profiles of the original glazing, the staircases received new installations with broader aluminium profiles and a different subdivision of the window panes. The ribbon on the opposite side still has its original glazing. Already in 1988/89, it was possible to re-create the building at the corner of Jungfernheideweg – Goebelstraße, whose urban structure and architecture had been changed during reconstruction after the war. The restoration was based on a design by the architects Hilmer & Sattler that emulated the functional style of Gropius' design.

The balconies of the long ribbon by Otto Bartning (Goebelstraße 21–113) were refurbished in 1998. The concrete ceilings of the double balconies, which had developed constructional damage, were not thoroughly repaired but got additional steel pipe support structures. This destroyed the original image of light, floating rows of balconies.

Abb. 93: Großsiedlung Siemensstadt, Kopfbau 1955/56 von Hans Scharoun, Goebelstraße 1–9, farbliche Rekonstruktion nach Befund von 2000, 2005

Fig. 93: Großsiedlung Siemensstadt, head building 1955/56 by Hans Scharoun Goebelstraße 1–9, reconstruction of colour according to investigation results in 2000, 2005

Auch der 1955–56 von Hans Scharoun entworfene Kopfbau Goebelstraße 1–9 am östlichen Ende der Bartningzeile unterzog man 2000 einer Renovierung. Dabei entstand wieder die bauzeitliche Farbgebung mit einem rosafarbigen Anstrich und die kontrastierenden Farbfassungen der Brüstungen auf der Rückseite.

Die Erneuerung der 1980er und 1990er Jahre führte zu einer Wiedergewinnung des authentischen Erscheinungsbildes in diesen Siedlungsteilen. Noch keiner Erneuerung unterzogen sind neben den Bauteilen im Abschnitt von Hans Scharoun die Straßenseite des Bartning-Blockes, die Randbauten von Fred Forbat am Geißlerpfad und die beiden Zeilen von Walter Gropius. Es ist beabsichtigt, auch die restlichen Siedlungsabschnitte in den nächsten Jahren ebenfalls denkmalgerecht zu restaurieren.

*Siedlungsfreiraum*
Die Grundstruktur der Siedlungsräume ist auch in ihren pflanzlichen Elementen überliefert. Der ursprünglich parkartige Charakter der Freiflächen konnte durch regelmäßig vorgenommene Baumnachpflanzungen weitgehend erhalten werden.

Das Erscheinungsbild der „Grünen Mitte" wird jedoch durch nachträgliche Einbauten wie Garagen, Spielplätze und Müllstandorte gestört. Nachträgliche Baumpflanzungen gefährden zudem die bauzeitlichen Müllhäuschen. Durch das Entfernen der Pyramidenpappeln im Straßenraum ging ein wesentliches Gestaltungselement der Großsiedlung Siemensstadt verloren.

Ein 2003 erarbeitetes Parkpflegewerk hat alle Bestände der Pflanzungen, Wegematerialien und Ausstattungen erfasst, unter Würdigung der historischen Entwicklung bewertet und darauf aufbauend eine Entwicklungskonzeption erarbeitet, deren Umsetzung in den nächsten Jahren vorgesehen ist.

The head building of Goebelstraße 1–9 at the eastern end of the Bartning ribbon (designed in 1955–56 by Hans Scharoun) was renovated in 2000. This renovation restored the original pink colour and the contrasting colour of the parapets on the rear facade.

The renovations in the 1980s and 1990s recreated the authentic appearance of these parts of the housing estate. In addition to some parts of the section by Hans Scharoun, the street side of the Bartning block, the block margin buildings by Fred Forbat at Geißlerpfad and the two ribbons by Walter Gropius also still await restoration. The authorities intend to restore the remaining parts of the housing estate during the next few years.

*Outdoor facilities*
The principle structure of the spaces has been preserved, including with regard to the outdoor facilities. Thanks to the regular re-planting of trees to replace losses, it was possible to preserve the original park-like character of the outdoor facilities.

Yet, the appearance of the "Green Centre" has been disturbed by additions like garages, playgrounds and waste bin areas. Trees which were added later disturb the originally installed waste bin sheds. When the Lombardy poplars in the street area were removed, the estate of Siemensstadt lost an important design element.

In 2003, a park maintenance documentation was generated which took stock of all existing plants, paving materials and installations, assessed them with consideration of the historic development and, on this basis, elaborated a development concept which will be implemented during the next few years.

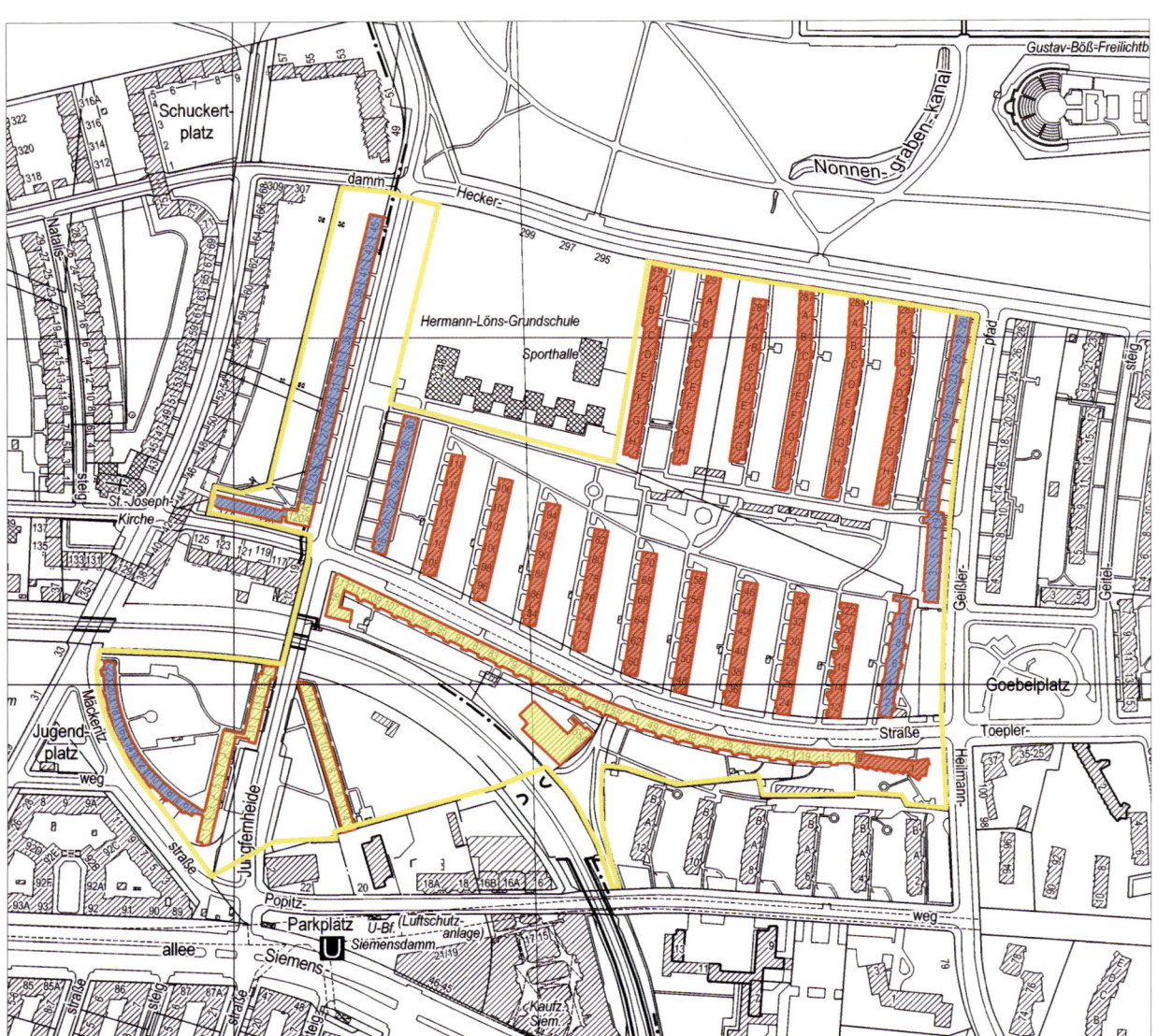

Abb. 94: Großsiedlung Siemensstadt, Stand der denkmalgerechten Wiederherstellung, M 1:5.000, 2005

Fig. 94: Großsiedlung Siemensstadt, state of conservation, scale 1:5.000, 2005

■ Denkmalgerecht wiederhergestellt/Restored monument

■ Geringer Handlungsbedarf/Minor need for conservation

■ Handlungsbedarf/Need for conservation

## 4.B Faktoren, die die Anlagen beeinflussen

Für alle nominierten Siedlungen besteht kein besonderer Veränderungsdruck, der sich aus regionalen Entwicklungsplanungen oder Verkehrskonzepten, aus Umwelteinflüssen, aus Naturkatastrophen oder aus einem verstärkten Tourismus ergeben könnte. Ein unbestimmtes Gefährdungspotenzial ist allenfalls für den authentischen Charakter der Siedlungen absehbar, wenn sich Nutzungen ändern, bautechnische Anpassungen erforderlich sind, auf Lärmschutzbestimmungen reagiert werden muss, es zu vermehrten Privatisierungen kommt, die zu einer individuellen Veränderung der Häuser und Gärten führen könnten oder ein geänderter Bedarf an Versorgungseinrichtungen (z. B. Müllplätze) besteht. Hieraus ergibt sich eine besondere Herausforderung für das Management des Welterbes, Instrumente zur Gefahrenabwehr vorzusehen (siehe dazu Ziffer 5.E).

## 4.B Factors affecting the properties

None of the nominated settlements is under major pressure to change, which might result from regional development plans or traffic concepts, environmental influence, natural catastrophes or increased tourism. The only risk potential for the authentic character of the settlements might arise from a change of use, need for constructional changes, need to react to noise protection requirements, increased privatisation, which might cause individual changes of houses and gardens, or a change in the need for service facilities (e.g. waste bin areas). This means that the management of the heritage must provide instruments for defence against risks (see also Item 5.E).

## (I) Entwicklungsdruck

### Gartenstadt Falkenberg

In den Randbereichen von Berlin, in denen es noch ausreichend Bauland gibt, besteht generell ein Entwicklungsdruck. Für die Gartenstadt Falkenberg ist allerdings mit der Arrondierung bzw. Erweiterung der angrenzenden Wohngebiete eine Bedrohung für den Denkmalbestand nicht zu erkennen. Die südlich angrenzende, in Entwicklung begriffende neue Gartenstadt Falkenberg der „Berliner Bau- und Wohnungsgenossenschaft von 1892" definiert im Sinn des Taut'schen Konzeptes den Gartenstadtgedanken zeitgemäß. Allerdings führt die Zufahrt zum neuen Siedlungsgebiet durch den Gartenstadtweg (2. Bauabschnitt der Taut-Siedlung). Hier kann es eventuell zu einer erhöhten Verkehrsbelastung kommen.

Da sich auch die Reihenhäuser der Gartenstadt in genossenschaftlichem Eigentum befinden, ist eine Gefährdung aufgrund von baulichen Eingriffen durch die Mieter nicht zu erwarten. Außerdem besteht eine verstärkte mietrechtliche Kontrolle seitens der Eigentümerin, der Baugenossenschaft von 1892.

Die Nähe zum im Ausbau befindlichen Flughafen Schönefeld, bzw. die Neuplanung eines internationalen Flughafens Schönefeld, wird vermutlich eine Lärmbelästigung für die Anwohner mit sich bringen. Auf die daraus abzuleitende Gefährdung des Baubestandes durch den Einbau von Lärmschutzfenstern ist im Rahmen des Managementplanes frühzeitig gestalterisch zu begegnen.

### Siedlung Schillerpark

Eine besonderer Veränderungsdruck, der den baulichen Bestand der Siedlung beeinträchtigen könnte, ist nicht erkennbar. Auch ist nicht vorgesehen, die genossenschaftlichen Häuser einer Privatisierung zuzuführen.

### Großsiedlung Britz (Hufeisensiedlung)

Für die Großsiedlung Britz ist ebenfalls absehbar, dass es keine städtebaulich störenden Einflüsse aus den umliegenden Wohn-, Sport-, Grün- und Kleingartenflächen geben wird. Allerdings entsteht durch die Privatisierung der Reihenhäuser ein Anpassungs- und Umnutzungsdruck, der zu baulichen Veränderungen führen kann.

### Wohnstadt Carl Legien

Da für das Gebiet der Wohnstadt und ihrer Umgebung eine über die Pufferzone hinausgreifende Erhaltungssatzung zur Sicherung des historisch bedeutenden Baubestandes besteht, sind keine negativen Veränderungen zu erwarten. Für ein kleines Gebiet am westlichen Zugang zur Wohnstadt an der Prenzlauer Allee, das durch einen amorphen, unterentwickelten Zustand auffällt, sieht ein bestehender Bebauungsplan hier als Puffer zur Wohnstadt einen schmalen Streifen mit einer Wohnnutzung vor, während an der Prenzlauer Allee ein Mischgebiet für Wohnen- und

## (I) Development Pressures

### Gartenstadt Falkenberg

There is a general development pressure on the outskirts of Berlin, where there is still an abundance of building land. For Gartenstadt Falkenberg, any rounding off or extension of the adjacent residential areas would not create risks for the existing monument. The new garden town Falkenberg, which is being developed on adjacent land in the south by "Berliner Bau- und Wohnungsgenossenschaft von 1892", redefines the garden town concept in the sense of Taut's ideas. However, access to the new residential area is through Gartenstadtweg (2nd development phase of the Taut settlement). This may cause an increased traffic load.

No constructional changes by the tenants need be feared, because the row houses of Gartenstadt are also owned by the cooperative. Additionally, the owner, i.e. the building cooperative Baugenossenschaft von 1892, exercises more control over the tenants.

Probably the inhabitants will be exposed to more noise, since the housing estate is located near the airport of Berlin-Schönefeld, for which plans for extension exist. The management plan will have to take timely precautions for the resulting need for noise-protection windows, which might become a risk for the appearance of the buildings.

### Siedlung Schillerpark

We cannot identify a particular pressure to change that might impair the existing housing estate. In addition, the cooperative does not intend to privatise the houses.

### Großsiedlung Britz (Hufeisensiedlung)

For the Großsiedlung Britz, we can also state that the surrounding residential, sports and green areas and allotment gardens will not create any urban development influence which might disturb the housing estate. On the other hand, the privatisation of the row houses creates pressure to adapt them and change their uses and this may lead to constructional changes.

### Wohnstadt Carl Legien

No negative impact need be expected for this housing estate, since the residential estate and a buffer zone reaching beyond its limits are protected by a regulation for preserving the historically important buildings. A small amorphous and underdeveloped area is located at the western access from Prenzlauer Allee to the residential estate. An existing development plan envisages a narrow band of residential buildings for this area to act as a buffer zone to Wohnstadt, whereas at Prenzlauer Allee the zoning plan shows a mixed area for housing and small commercial uses. In this respect, the urban development plans have to be revised.

Kleingewerbe ausgewiesen ist. Hier gilt es stadtplanerisch ordnend einzuwirken.

Die durchgeführte Grundsanierung der Siedlungshäuser hatte Mietpreiserhöhungen zur Folge, die zu einer Veränderung der sozialen Bewohnerstruktur hätte führen können. Um dem entgegen zu wirken, wurde mit der Erhaltungsverordnung 2003 auch eine Milieuschutzsatzung erlassen. (siehe Ziffer 5. c–d).

### Weiße Stadt

Akute oder längerfristige Gefährdungen der Anlage sind nicht zu erkennen. Aus der eingeleiteten Privatisierung ganzer Bauteile der Weißen Stadt könnte sich allerdings ein höherer Überwachungsbedarf ergeben, um die Einheitlichkeit der Großsiedlung zu gewährleisten und ihre Authentizität und Integrität zu sichern. Die umliegenden Flächen sind in ihrer denkmalverträglichen Nutzung durch den Baunutzungsplan bzw. Bebauungspläne abgesichert.

Auf der Südseite der Emmentaler Straße, gegenüber dem Bauteil von Bruno Ahrends, ist vor kurzem ein Supermarkt mit Parkplatz entstanden, der sich in seiner architektonischen Gestaltung dem sachlichen Stil der Siedlungsbauten anpasst. Nachfolgende ähnliche Einrichtungen an dieser Stelle sind nicht zu erwarten, da unmittelbar südlich ein aufgestellter Bebauungsplan das bestehende Kleingartengelände absichern soll.

### Großsiedlung Siemensstadt (Ringsiedlung)

Da der Baubestand der Ringsiedlung fast von allen Seiten von denkmalgeschützten weiteren Siedlungsanlagen umgeben ist, ist keine akute oder zukünfte Gefährdung festzustellen. Eine Beeinträchtigung für das Siedlungsbild ergibt sich heute nur durch die Gewerbebebauung (Supermarkt) beim südlichen Eingangsbereich, die die von Hans Scharoun geschaffene Torsituation am Jungfernheideweg/Ecke Popitzweg verunklart. Scharoun konnte hier sein städtebauliches Konzept, das auf eine damalige Verkehrsplanung einging, nicht verwirklichen. Die veränderte Verkehrserschliessung ließ an dieser Stelle eine Freifläche entstehen, die heute von Gewerbebauten genutzt wird, die zum Teil leerstehen. Für den gesamten Zugang zur Siedlung besteht daher ein städtebaulicher Gestaltungsbedarf.

### (II) Umweltfaktoren

Über das in einer Großstadt übliche Maß hinaus sind keine Beeinträchtigungen aller Siedlungen vorhanden. Besondere Schädigungen, die auf Umwelteinflüsse zurückgehen, sind nicht bekannt. Die umweltbedingten Verschmutzungen an Fassaden werden im Rahmen der Grundinstandsetzungen denkmalverträglich behoben. Besondere Lärmbelastungen sind in Teilen nur für die Gartenstadt Falkenberg und die Siedlungen Schillerpark und Weiße Stadt zu erkennen. Durch Lärmschutzwände entlang der Schnellstraße und Bahnstecke, die in der Gartenstadt Falkenberg an den Gärten der Häuser des Gartenstadtweges entlangführt, konnte die Lärmimmission reduziert wer-

After the thorough refurbishment and restoration of the houses, rents were increased. This might have led to a change in the social structure of the inhabitants. To counteract such a development, the authorities approved a regulation protecting the social environment together with the approval of the maintenance regulation in 2003 (see also Item 5. c–d).

### Weiße Stadt

We do not identify any current or long-term risks for the housing estate. However, since privatisation has started for entire sections of Weiße Stadt, the need for monitoring might increase in order for the uniform appearance of the large housing estate as well as its authenticity and integrity to be preserved. The land-use plan or respectively development plans assure that the surrounding areas will be used for purposes and in ways which do not endanger the monument.

A supermarket with car park was recently erected on the southern side of Emmentaler Straße opposite the section designed by Bruno Ahrends. Its design has been adapted to the functional style of the housing estate's buildings. There is no risk that more of these facilities will be erected at this place, since a development plan for the area to the immediate south of this land was established for preserving the existing allotment gardens.

### Großsiedlung Siemensstadt (Ringsiedlung)

Since the buildings of the Ringsiedlung are surrounded nearly on all sides by other housing estates which are protected as monuments, there is no current or future risk. The only existing impairment of the appearance of the housing estate results from the commercial buildings (supermarket) at the southern access area that disturb the gate-like impression designed by Hans Scharoun at the corner of Jungfernheideweg and Popitzweg. Scharoun was not able to implement his urban development concept here, which had been designed in line with a traffic plan of that time. The change of the traffic plan resulted in an open space at this location. This space was then used for erecting commercial buildings, some of which are not used now. This means that the access to the housing estate is in need of urban development measures.

### (II) Environmental pressures

None of the housing estates is exposed to any negative influence beyond the measure that is usual for big cities. Particular damage resulting from environmental impacts is not known. The soiling of the facades resulting from environmental pollution will be eliminated during thorough restoration measures. Particular exposure to noise can be identified only for parts of Gartenstadt Falkenberg and the Siedlung Schillerpark and Weiße Stadt. Noise emission has been reduced by noise barriers along the throughway and along the railway line that pass the gardens of the houses in Gartenstadtweg at Gartenstadt Falkenberg. Weiße Stadt and Schillerpark are exposed to noise caused by Tegel Air-

den. Lärmbelästigungen durch den Flughafen Tegel ergeben sich für die Siedlungen Weiße Stadt und Schillerpark. Bei der Siedlung Weiße Stadt führte der Fluglärm bisher nicht zum Einbau von Lärmschutzfenstern. Einige der Kastendoppelfenster der Wohnungen in der nicht weit entfernten Siedlung Schillerpark wurden denkmalverträglich durch innenliegende Schallschutzverglasungen ergänzt. Das äußere Erscheinungsbild blieb bewahrt. Im übrigen ist geplant, nach der Inbetriebnahme des neuen Flughafens Schönefeld den Flughafen Tegel zu schließen.

### (III) Naturkatastrophen und Schutzvorkehrungen

Berlin liegt in einer Region, in der keine Naturkatastrophen zu erwarten sind. Auch eine besondere Gefährdung durch Brände ist nicht zu erkennen.

### (IV) Druck durch Besucher/Tourismus

Bereits heute gibt es in allen Siedlungen regelmäßige Besuche von architekturinteressierten Gruppen, die keine Gefährdung des Denkmalbestandes darstellen. Berlin ist – insbesondere seit der Wiedervereinigung der beiden Stadthälften – eines der bedeutendsten Touristikzentren von internationaler Ausstrahlung. Aus der zu erwartenden wachsenden Besucherzahl ergeben sich ebenfalls keine besonderen Belastungen der Siedlungen. Ein Besuchermanagement soll in Zukunft eine Besucherbetreuung organisieren.

port. The noise exposure to date has not led to the installation of noise protection windows at the housing estate Weiße Stadt. Some of the box-type double windows of the flats at the nearby Siedlung Schillerpark have been complemented by noise-protection glazing which was attached inside. This is in line with the requirements for the preservation of monuments. This measure did not disrupt the appearance of the buildings. Moreover, the authorities intend to close down Tegel Airport after the new airport at Schönefeld has been opened.

### (III) Natural disasters and risk preparedness

Berlin is located in a region where there is no risk of natural catastrophes. There is no special fire risk either.

### (IV) Visitor/tourism pressures

Already, all housing estates are being visited by groups of people who are interested in architecture and do not represent a risk for the monuments. Berlin has become an important centre of international tourism (in particular after the re-unification of the two parts of the city). The expected increase of the number of visitors does not create any particular burden for the housing estates, either. In future, care for the visitors will be provided by a visitors' management organisation.

### (V) Anzahl der Einwohner innerhalb der Anlagen und der Pufferzonen/Number of inhabitants within the properties and the buffer zones

#### Gartenstadt Falkenberg
Einwohnerzahl/Number of inhabitants:

| | |
|---|---:|
| Nominierungsgebiet/Nominated area | 230 |
| Pufferzone/Buffer zone | 100 |
| Total/Total | 330 |
| Jahr/Year | 2005 |

#### Siedlung Schillerpark
Einwohnerzahl/Number of inhabitants:

| | |
|---|---:|
| Nominierungsgebiet/Nominated area | 740 |
| Pufferzone/Buffer zone | 890 |
| Total/Total | 1.630 |
| Jahr/Year | 2005 |

#### Großsiedlung Britz (Hufeisensiedlung)
Einwohnerzahl/Number of inhabitants:

| | |
|---|---:|
| Nominierungsgebiet/Nominated area | 3.100 |
| Pufferzone/Buffer zone | 3.500 |
| Total/Total | 6.600 |
| Jahr/Year | 2005 |

#### Wohnstadt Carl Legien
Einwohnerzahl/Number of inhabitants:

| | |
|---|---:|
| Nominierungsgebiet/Nominated area | 1.200 |
| Pufferzone/Buffer zone | 1.800 |
| Total/Total | 3.000 |
| Jahr/Year | 2005 |

#### Weiße Stadt
Einwohnerzahl/Number of inhabitants:

| | |
|---|---:|
| Nominierungsgebiet/Nominated area | 2.100 |
| Pufferzone/Buffer zone | 1.900 |
| Total/Total | 4.000 |
| Jahr/Year | 2005 |

#### Großsiedlung Siemensstadt (Ringsiedlung)
Einwohnerzahl/Number of inhabitants:

| | |
|---|---:|
| Nominierungsgebiet/Nominated area | 2.800 |
| Pufferzone/Buffer zone | 2.350 |
| Total/Total | 5.150 |
| Jahr/Year | 2005 |

(Angaben zu den geschätzten Einwohnerzahlen nach: Statistisches Landesamt Berlin, ZDC Regionales Bezugssystem)

(Source of estimated numbers of inhabitants: Statistisches Landesamt Berlin [office of statistics of Berlin], ZDC Regionales Bezugssystem [ZDC regional reference system])

Müllplatz

# 5

**SCHUTZ UND VERWALTUNG DER ANLAGEN**
**PROTECTION AND MANAGEMENT OF THE PROPERTIES**

## 5.A Eigentumsverhältnisse

### Gartenstadt Falkenberg
Alle Siedlungshäuser befinden sich im genossenschaftlichen Besitz der

Berliner Bau- und Wohnungsgenossenschaft von 1892 e. G.
Knobelsdorffstraße 96
14050 Berlin

### Siedlung Schillerpark
Alle Siedlungshäuser befinden sich im genossenschaftlichen Besitz der

Berliner Bau- und Wohnungsgenossenschaft von 1892 e. G.
Knobelsdorffstraße 96
14050 Berlin

### Großsiedlung Britz (Hufeisensiedlung)
GEHAG GmbH und
GEHAG Grundwert 1 GmbH & Co. KG
Mecklenburgische Straße 57
14197 Berlin

Seit einigen Jahren erfolgt eine schrittweise Überführung der Reihenhäuser in einzelnes Eigentum.

### Wohnstadt Carl Legien
BauBeCon Immobilien GmbH
Schützenallee 3
30519 Hannover

### Weiße Stadt
Fortimo GmbH
Mecklenburgische Straße 57
14197 Berlin

Seit einigen Jahren erfolgt eine schrittweise Überführung der Wohnungen in einzelnes Eigentum.

### Großsiedlung Siemensstadt (Ringsiedlung)
Gemeinnützige Siedlungs- und Wohnungsbaugesellschaft Berlin (GSW)
Kochstraße 22
10969 Berlin
und
Fortimo GmbH
Mecklenburgische Straße 57
14197 Berlin

aktualisiert Oktober 2006

## 5.A Ownership

### Gartenstadt Falkenberg
All buildings of the housing estate are owned by the cooperative

Berliner Bau- und Wohnungsgenossenschaft von 1892 e. G.
Knobelsdorffstraße 96
14050 Berlin
Germany

### Siedlung Schillerpark
All buildings of the housing estate are owned by the cooperative

Berliner Bau- und Wohnungsgenossenschaft von 1892 e. G.
Knobelsdorffstraße 96
14050 Berlin
Germany

### Großsiedlung Britz (Hufeisensiedlung)
GEHAG GmbH and
GEHAG Grundwert 1 GmbH & Co. KG
Mecklenburgische Straße 57
14197 Berlin
Germany

Several years ago, gradual privatisation of the individual houses began.

### Wohnstadt Carl Legien
BauBeCon Immobilien GmbH
Schützenallee 3
30519 Hannover
Germany

### Weiße Stadt
Fortimo GmbH
Mecklenburgische Straße 57
14197 Berlin
Germany

Several years ago, gradual privatisation of the individual flats began.

### Großsiedlung Siemensstadt (Ringsiedlung)
Gemeinnützige Siedlungs- und Wohnungsbaugesellschaft Berlin (GSW)
Kochstraße 22
10969 Berlin
Germany
and
Fortimo GmbH
Mecklenburgische Straße 57
14197 Berlin
Germany

last updated October 2006

## 5.B Schutzstatus

Alle sechs nominierten Siedlungen sind nach dem Denkmalschutzgesetz Berlin (DSchG Bln) vom 24. April 1995 als Denkmalbereiche (Gesamtanlage) gemäß §2 Abs. 3 DSchG Bln geschützt und in die Berliner Denkmalliste (§4 DSchG Bln) eingetragen (Amtsblatt für Berlin (51)2001, Nr. 29 vom 14. Juni 2001, S. 2261ff.). Zum Schutzgut zählen sämtliche baulichen Anlagen der Siedlung einschließlich der mit ihnen verbundenen Frei- und Wasserflächen.

Darüber hinaus sind die Freiflächen der Denkmalbereiche der Gartenstadt Falkenberg und der Weißen Stadt sowie eine Teilfläche des Denkmalbereichs der Siedlung Schillerpark als Gartendenkmal gemäß §2 Abs. 4 DSchG Bln geschützt und in die Berliner Denkmalliste eingetragen.

Im Folgenden ist für jede Siedlung dargelegt, seit wann sie als Ganzes oder Teile von ihr unter Denkmalschutz stehen.

### Gartenstadt Falkenberg

Die Gartenstadt Falkenberg wurde auf Beschluss des Ostberliner Magistrats (Magistratsbeschluss MG 432/77) vom 21. September 1977 in die Bezirksdenkmalliste Berlin-Ost aufgenommen und unterlag seitdem den Bestimmungen des Gesetzes zur Erhaltung der Denkmale in der DDR (Denkmalpflegegesetz) vom 19. 6. 1975. Nach der Wiedervereinigung der beiden deutschen Staaten 1990 wurde die Rechtswirksamkeit des Beschlusses bestätigt, die Siedlung als Baudenkmal gemäß den Bestimmungen des damals gültigen Denkmalschutzgesetzes Berlin (DSchG Bln) vom 22. Dezember 1977 anerkannt und in das Baudenkmalbuch übertragen. Die Gartenstadt Falkenberg ist seit der Novellierung des Berliner Denkmalschutzgesetzes 1995 als Denkmalbereich und als Gartendenkmal geschützt und in die Denkmalliste eingetragen.

### Siedlung Schillerpark

Die Siedlung Schillerpark ist als Baudenkmal am 2. Februar 1994 gemäß Denkmalschutzgesetz Berlin (DSchG Bln) vom 22. Dezember 1977 in das Baudenkmalbuch eingetragen worden. Sie ist seit der Novellierung des Berliner Denkmalschutzgesetzes 1995 als Denkmalbereich und als Gartendenkmal geschützt und in die Denkmalliste eingetragen.

### Großsiedlung Britz (Hufeisensiedlung)

Der Zentralbereich der Großsiedlung Britz (Hufeisensiedlung) ist gemäß Anlage zu §24 Abs. 2 der Bauordnung für Berlin in der Fassung vom 21. November 1958 erstmals als Baudenkmal geschützt und wurde mit Inkrafttreten des Denkmalschutzgesetzes Berlin (DSchG Bln) vom 22. Dezember 1977 in das Baudenkmalbuch eingetragen. Die Siedlung ist seit der Novellierung des Berliner Denkmalschutzgesetzes 1995 als Denkmalbereich geschützt und in die Denkmalliste eingetragen.

### Wohnstadt Carl Legien

Die Wohnstadt Carl Legien wurde auf Beschluss des Ostberliner Magistrats (Magistratsbeschluss MG 432/77) vom 21. September 1977 in die Bezirksdenkmalliste Berlin-Ost aufgenommen und unterlag seitdem den Bestimmungen des Gesetzes zur Erhaltung der Denkmale in der DDR (Denkmalpflegegesetz) vom 19. 6. 1975. Nach der Wiedervereinigung der beiden deutschen Staaten 1990 wurde die

## 5.B Protective designation

All six of the nominated housing estates are protected by the Denkmalschutzgesetz Berlin (Law on the Preservation of Historic Buildings and Monuments of Berlin) (DSchG Bln) of 24th April 1995 as monument areas (applying for the total premises) according to Section 2, Paragraph 3 DSchG Bln, and they have been entered in the Berlin Register of Historic Places (Section 4 DSchG Bln) (official gazette of Berlin (51) 2001, no. 29 of 14th June 2001, p. 2261 ff.) The protection covers all structures of the housing estate inclusive of the outdoor facilities and water bodies which are related to them.

Furthermore, the outdoor facilities of the monument areas of Gartenstadt Falkenberg and Weiße Stadt, as well as part of the monument area of Siedlung Schillerpark, are protected as historic gardens according to Section 2, Paragraph 4 DSchG Bln and entered in the Berlin Register of Historic Places.

Below, we indicate when protection for the entire area or parts of the area began for each of the housing estates.

### Gartenstadt Falkenberg

Gartenstadt Falkenberg was entered in the district Register of Historic Places of East Berlin on the basis of a resolution of the East Berlin government (government resolution MG 432/77) of 21st September 1977, and since then it has been subject to the stipulations of the law on the preservation of monuments in the GDR (Denkmalpflegegesetz – Law on the Preservation of Historic Places and Monuments) of 19/06/1975. After the re-unification of the two German states in 1990, the effectiveness of this resolution was confirmed and the housing estate was acknowledged as an architectural monument according to the stipulations of the Law on the Protection of Historic Places and Monuments of 22nd December 1977, applicable at the time, and entered in the Register of Architectural Monuments. Since the Berlin Law on the Preservation of Historic Places and Monuments was amended in 1995, Gartenstadt Falkenberg has been protected as an historic area and historic garden and entered as such in the Register of Historic Places.

### Siedlung Schillerpark

Schillerpark was entered as an architectural monument in the Register of Architectural Monuments on 2nd February 1994, according to the Law on the Preservation of Historic Places and Monuments (DSchG Bln) of 22nd December 1977. Since the Berlin Law on the Preservation of Historic Places and Monuments was amended in 1995, it has been protected as an historic area and historic garden and entered as such in the Register of Historic Places.

### Großsiedlung Britz (Hufeisensiedlung)

The central area of Großsiedlung Britz (Hufeisensiedlung) became protected as an architectural monument initially according to the annex to Section 24, Paragraph 2 of the Building Regulations of Berlin in the version of 21st November 1958, and when the Berlin Law on the Preservation of Historic Places and Monuments (DSchG Bln) of 22nd December 1977 came into force it was entered in the Register of Architectural Monuments. Since the Berlin Law on the Preservation of Historic Places and Monuments was

Rechtswirksamkeit des Magistratsbeschlusses bestätigt, die Siedlung als Baudenkmal gemäß den Bestimmungen des 1990 gültigen Denkmalschutzgesetzes Berlin (DSchG Bln) vom 22. Dezember 1977 anerkannt und in das Baudenkmalbuch übertragen. Sie ist seit der Novellierung des Berliner Denkmalschutzgesetzes 1995 als Denkmalbereich geschützt und in die Denkmalliste eingetragen.

Darüber hinaus ist die Wohnstadt Carl Legien seit 9. Oktober 2003 Teil des Erhaltungsgebietes „Ostseestraße / Grellstraße" mit Erhaltungssatzung nach §172, Abs.1 des Baugesetzbuches (BauGB) (siehe auch Ziffer 5.D).

### Weiße Stadt
Die Weiße Stadt ist gemäß Anlage zu §14 Abs. 6 der Bauordnung für Berlin in der Fassung vom 13. Februar 1971 erstmals als Baudenkmal geschützt und wurde mit Inkrafttreten des Denkmalschutzgesetzes Berlin (DSchG Bln) vom 22. Dezember 1977 in das Baudenkmalbuch eingetragen. Sie ist seit der Novellierung des Berliner Denkmalschutzgesetzes 1995 als Denkmalbereich und Gartendenkmal geschützt und in die Denkmalliste eingetragen.

### Großsiedlung Siemensstadt (Ringsiedlung)
Der im Bezirk Spandau liegende Teil der Großsiedlung Siemensstadt, drei Wohnblöcke von Hans Scharoun am Jungfernheideweg und an der Mäckeritzstraße, ist gemäß Anlage zu §24 Abs. 2 der Bauordnung für Berlin in der Fassung vom 21. November 1958 erstmals als Baudenkmal geschützt und wurde mit Inkrafttreten des Denkmalschutzgesetzes Berlin (DSchG Bln) vom 22. Dezember 1977 in das Baudenkmalbuch eingetragen. Mit der Novellierung des Berliner Denkmalschutzgesetzes 1995 wurden der in Spandau liegende Teil und der angrenzende Siedlungsbereich auf Charlottenburger Gebiet als zusammenhängender Denkmalbereich geschützt und in die Denkmalliste eingetragen.

### 5.C Mittel zur Umsetzung von Schutzmaßnahmen

Das Denkmalschutzgesetz Berlin (DSchG Bln) vom 24. April 1995 enthält Regelungen zu Aufgaben, Gegenstand und Organisation des Denkmalschutzes in Berlin (§§ 5–7 DSchG Bln), Allgemeine Schutzvorschriften (§§ 8–10 DSchG Bln) sowie Maßnahmen des Denkmalschutzes; öffentliche Förderung und Verfahrensvorschriften (§§ 11–15 DSchG Bln).

Die wesentlichen Bestimmungen zum Schutz und zur Erhaltung der Denkmale sind im folgenden zusammengefasst:

Mit der Erklärung zum Denkmal durch das Landesdenkmalamt Berlin und der Eintragung in die Denkmalliste ergeht die Verpflichtung des Denkmaleigentümers zum Erhalt des Denkmals (§8 DSchG Bln) und zum Schutz der unmittelbaren Umgebung des Denkmals (§10 DSchG Bln). Der Eigentümer eines Denkmals ist als Verfügungsberechtigter verpflichtet, das Denkmal im Rahmen des Zumutbaren instand zu halten und instand zu setzen, und dieses sachgemäß zu behandeln und vor Gefährdungen zu schützen. Er kann durch die zuständige Denkmalbehörde verpflichtet werden, bestimmte Maßnahmen zur Erhaltung durchzuführen. Ersatzweise und bei einer unmittelbar dro-

amended in 1995, the housing estate has been protected as an historic area and entered as such in the Register of Historic Places.

### Wohnstadt Carl Legien
Wohnstadt Carl Legien was entered in the district Register of Historic Places of East Berlin on the basis of a resolution of the East Berlin government (government resolution MG 432/77) of 21st September 1977, and since then has been subject to the stipulations of the law on the preservation of monuments in the GDR (Denkmalpflegegesetz – Law on the Preservation of Historic Places and Monuments) of 19/06/1975. After the re-unification of the two German states in 1990, the effectiveness of the Berlin government resolution was confirmed and the housing estate was acknowledged as an architectural monument according to the stipulations of the Law on the Protection of Historic Places and Monuments of 22nd December 1977, applicable at the time, and entered in the Register of Architectural Monuments. Since the Berlin Law on the Preservation of Historic Places and Monuments was amended in 1995, it has been protected as an historic area and entered as such in the Register of Historic Places.

In addition, Wohnstadt Carl Legien has been part of the preservation area "Ostseestraße/Grellstraße" since 9th October 2003 and subject to preservation statutes according to Section 172, Paragraph 1 of the Building Code (BauGB) (see also Item 5.D).

### Weiße Stadt
Weiße Stadt became protected as an architectural monument initially according to the annex to Section 14, Paragraph 6 of the Building Regulations of Berlin in the version of 13th February 1971, and when the Berlin Law on the Preservation of Historic Places and Monuments (DSchG Bln) of 22nd December 1977 came into force, it was entered in the Register of Architectural Monuments. Since the Berlin Law on the Preservation of Historic Places and Monuments was amended in 1995, it has been protected as an historic area and historic garden and entered as such in the Register of Historic Places.

### Großsiedlung Siemensstadt (Ringsiedlung)
The part of Großsiedlung Siemensstadt which is located in the district of Spandau, three blocks by Hans Scharoun at Jungfernheideweg and at Mäckeritzstraße became protected as an architectural monument initially according to the annex to Section 24, Paragraph 2 of the Building Regulations of Berlin in the version of 21st November 1958, and when the Berlin Law on the Preservation of Historic Places and Monuments (DSchG Bln) of 22nd December 1977 came into force it was entered in the Register of Architectural Monuments. Since the Berlin Law on the Preservation of Historic Places and Monuments was amended in 1995, the part of it which is located in Spandau and the adjacent area of the estate in the district of Charlottenburg have been protected as an overall historic area and entered as such in the Register of Historic Places.

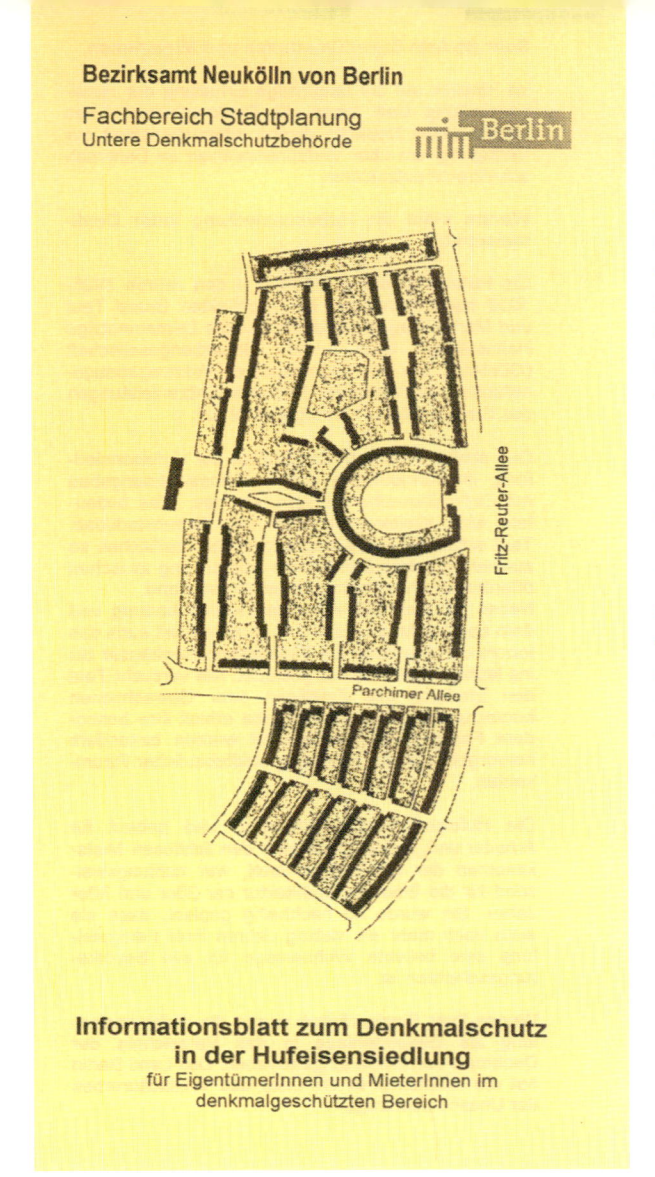

Abb. 95: Info-Faltblatt für die Bewohner der Großsiedlung Britz (Hufeisensiedlung)

Fig. 95: Information brochure for the inhabitants of the Großsiedlung Britz (Hufeisensiedlung)

## 5.c Means of implementing protective measures

### Protection and maintenance regulations

The Berlin Law on the Preservation of Historic Places and Monuments (DSchG Bln) of 24th April 1995 comprises regulations concerning the tasks, object and organisation of monument protection in Berlin (Sections 5–7 DSchG Bln), general regulations concerning protection (Sections 8–10 DSchG Bln) as well as measures for protecting and preserving monuments and historic places, public grants and procedures (Sections 11–15 DSchG Bln).

Below we summarise the most important regulations for the protection and preservation of monuments and historic places:

When the authority for the preservation of monuments and historic places of Berlin declares a place a monument or historic place and enters it in the Register of Monuments and Historic Places, its owner becomes obliged to preserve the monument (Section 8 DSchG Bln) and its immediate environment (Section 10 DSchG Bln). The owner of the monument in his position as the party authorised to dispose of it becomes obliged to take reasonable measures for preserving and repairing it, to treat it properly and protect it against risks. The relevant authority for the protection of monuments may require said owner to carry out certain measures for preserving the monument. Alternatively and in case of imminent danger to the existence of the monument, the relevant authority for the protection of monuments may have the necessary measures carried out on its own initiative.

Any alteration of the appearance, partial or complete removal, repair, reconstruction or change of use of the monuments requires the consent of the relevant authority for the protection of monuments. The same applies for accessories and equipment of the monument to the extent to which they form an entity together with the monument having monument value. If the immediate environment of a monument is of essential importance to its appearance, the law also prohibits said environment from being altered by erecting or changing structures, shaping the public or private areas which are not built up or by creating other changes in such a way that the characteristics and the appearance of the monument suffer essential impairment.

The immediate environment of a monument is that area within which any utilisation of properties or public areas for building or for other purposes has an essential impact on the monument. Any permits may be connected with conditions and requirements. Any changes and measures carried out at the monument must be documented. In case any measures are carried out without permission, the authority may stop the works and require that the previous state be re-established. The party which is authorised to dispose is obliged to grant the representatives of the monument protection authorities access to the properties, buildings and rooms and to provide the necessary information and documents to support these representatives in fulfilling their tasks. The authorities may impose large fines in case of violation of any of the above regulations.

henden Gefahr für den Bestand des Denkmals kann die zuständige Denkmalbehörde die notwendigen Maßnahmen selbst durchführen lassen.

Die Denkmale dürfen nur mit Genehmigung der zuständigen Denkmalschutzbehörde in ihrem Erscheinungsbild verändert, ganz oder teilweise beseitigt, instand gesetzt, wiederhergestellt oder in ihrer Nutzung verändert werden. Dies gilt auch für das Zubehör und die Ausstattung der Denkmale, soweit sie mit dem Denkmal eine Einheit von Denkmalwert bilden. Auch die unmittelbare Umgebung eines Denkmals, soweit sie für dessen Erscheinungsbild von prägender Bedeutung ist, darf durch Errichtung oder Änderung baulicher Anlagen, durch die Gestaltung der unbebauten öffentlichen und privaten Flächen oder in anderer Weise nicht so verändert werden, dass die Eigenart und das Erscheinungsbild des Denkmals wesentlich beeinträchtigt werden.

Als unmittelbare Umgebung eines Denkmals gilt der Bereich, innerhalb dessen sich die bauliche oder sonstige Nutzung von Grundstücken oder von öffentlichen Flächen auf das Denkmal prägend auswirkt. Die Genehmigungen können mit Bedingungen und Auflagen versehen werden. Alle Veränderungen und Maßnahmen am Denkmal sind zu dokumentieren. Im Falle der Durchführung ungenehmigter

Maßnahmen kann die Einstellung der Arbeiten oder Wiederherstellung des früheren Zustandes angeordnet werden. Der Verfügungsberechtigte ist verpflichtet, den Vertretern der Denkmalbehörden zur Erfüllung ihrer Aufgabe den Zugang zu Grundstücken, Gebäuden und Räumen zu gewähren sowie die erforderlichen Auskünfte zu erteilen und Unterlagen vorzulegen. Verstöße gegen die erwähnten Bestimmungen des Denkmalschutzgesetzes können mit hohen Geldbußen geahndet werden.

Die Genehmigungsbehörde ist das zuständige Bezirksamt von Berlin, vertreten durch die Untere Denkmalschutzbehörde. Sie entscheidet über das Bauvorhaben aus denkmalrechtlicher Sicht, sowohl im bauordnungsrechtlich genehmigungspflichtigen Verfahren, als auch bei bauordnungsrechtlich genehmigungsfreien Bauvorhaben nach dem Denkmalschutzgesetz Berlin. Die Entscheidungen der Unteren Denkmalschutzbehörde werden im Einvernehmen mit der Fachbehörde (Landesdenkmalamt Berlin) getroffen. Kann das Einvernehmen nicht hergestellt werden, entscheidet als oberste Denkmalschutzbehörde die Senatsverwaltung für Stadtentwicklung nach Anhörung der Unteren Denkmalschutzbehörde und des Landesdenkmalamtes.

Da die Wohnstadt Carl Legien im Geltungsbereich eines nach dem Baugesetzbuch (BauGB §172 Abs.1 Satz 1) förmlich festgelegten Erhaltungsgebietes liegt, unterliegt die Wohnstadt darüber hinaus einer 2003 erlassenen Erhaltungsverordnung (Gesetz- und Verordnungsblatt von Berlin (GVBl.) vom 2.4.2003, GVBl. 59.2003, Nr. 14, S. 150) und vom 8.10.2003 (GVBl. 59.2003, Nr. 35, S. 482). Danach „bedürfen in dem bezeichneten Gebiet der Rückbau, die Änderung oder die Nutzungsänderung baulicher Anlagen der Genehmigung." Genehmigungen erteilt hierfür das zuständige Bezirksamt Pankow von Berlin, Abteilung Stadtentwicklung, Stadtplanungsamt (siehe auch unter Ziffer 5.D).

## 5.D Bestehende Planungen der Gemeinde und der Region, in der sich die nominierten Anlagen befinden

**Bauleitplanung und Denkmalpläne**
In Deutschland ist die Bauleitplanung nach dem Baugesetzbuch (BauGB) das wichtigste Planungsinstrument zur Lenkung und Ordnung der städtebaulichen Entwicklung einer Gemeinde, wobei auch denkmalpflegerische Belange zu berücksichtigen sind (§ 1 Abs. 6 BauGB). Sie ist gegliedert in vorbereitende Bauleitplanung (Flächennutzungsplan / FNP, bezirklicher Bereichsentwicklungsplan / BEP) für das gesamte Gemeindegebiet und verbindliche Bauleitplanung (Bebauungspläne) für räumliche Teilbereiche des Gemeindegebietes, hier in Verbindung mit der Baunutzungsverordnung (BauNVO), in der Art und Maß der baulichen Nutzung, Bauweisen und die Überbaubarkeit von Grundstücken definiert sind. Das Baugesetzbuch regelt u.a. die Zulässigkeit von Bauvorhaben und sieht im besonderen Städtebaurecht die förmliche Festlegung von Sanierungsgebieten (§142 BauGB), Entwicklungsgebieten (§165 BauGB) und Erhaltungsgebieten (§172 BauGB) vor.

Die Teilung Berlins nach 1945 zog unterschiedliche bauplanungsrechtliche Entwicklungen in West- bzw. Ostberlin

The authority for approval is in each case the respective district office of Berlin, represented by the Lower Monument Preservation Authority. On the basis of the Law on the Preservation of Historic Places and Monuments, it will decide on the projects from the point of view of monument preservation both for projects which require a building permit and for projects which do not normally require a building permit under the building regulations. The Lower Monument Preservation Authority will make its decisions in agreement with the relevant special purpose authority (Landesdenkmalamt Berlin, State Monument Preservation Office of Berlin). In case the two authorities are unable to come to an agreement, the Berlin government Office for Urban Development in its capacity as supreme monument preservation authority will make a decision after having heard both the Lower Monument Preservation Authority and the State Monument Preservation Office.

Since Wohnstadt Carl Legien is part of a formally established preservation area (BauGB Section 172, Paragraph 1, Item 1) it is additionally subject to a preservation regulation of 2003 (Official Gazette of Berlin [GVBl.] of 02/04/2003, GVBl. 59.2003, no. 14, p. 150) and of 08/10/2003 (GVBl. 59.2003, no. 35, p. 482). According to this regulation, any "removal, alteration of structures or alteration of the utilisation of structures in the covered area require permission". The necessary permits will be granted by the district office of Pankow of Berlin, Department for Urban Development, Urban Planning Office (see also Item 5.D).

## 5.D Existing plans related to municipality and region in which the proposed properties are located

**Development plans and monument preservation plans**
According to the Baugesetzbuch (German Building Code, BauGB), development plans are the most important instruments for guiding and controlling the urban development of a community and they must also take into account the interests of monument preservation (Section 1, Paragraph 6 BauGB). The process of establishing development plans is divided into the preparatory phase of setting up non-binding development plans (consisting of a land-use plan and district area development plan for the entire territory of the community and a binding development plan for individual parts of the community's territory, here in connection with the Baunutzungsverordnung (Land-Use Act, BauNVO) which defines the kind and extent of structures, type of buildings and the degree to which the land may be built up. The Building Code regulates for instance the permissibility of projects and in the particular urban development legislation it stipulates the formal establishment of rehabilitation areas (Section 142 BauGB), development areas (Section 165 BauGB) and preservation areas (Section 172 BauGB).

Due to the division of Berlin after 1945, building legislation developed differently in East and West Berlin, and these differences still influence the currently valid building legislation even after the re-unification of the two German states. In the western districts, the Land-Use Plan of 1958/60 still applies, after it was transferred as a development plan to the Bundesbaugesetz (Federal Building Act,

nach sich, die auch nach der Wiedervereinigung der beiden deutschen Staaten von Bedeutung für das gültige Baurecht sind. So gilt für die westlichen Bezirke bis heute der Baunutzungsplan von 1958/60, nachdem dieser als Bebauungsplan nach Bundesbaugesetz (BBauG) von 1960, 1987 umbenannt in das Baugesetzbuch (BauGB), übergeleitet wurde. In der planungsrechtlichen Praxis fungiert der Baunutzungsplan heute als Ersatzbebauungsplan. Ein vergleichbares, fächendeckend wirksames Instrumentarium gibt es für die östlichen Bezirke nicht. Hier mussten nach 1990 erst rechtsverbindliche Bebauungspläne aufgestellt werden. In den nicht mit Bebauungsplänen beplanten Gebieten der östlichen Bezirke werden Baugenehmigungen nach § 34 Baugesetzbuch (BauGB) ausgesprochen.

Die Ausarbeitung und Aufstellung der Bebauungspläne erfolgt in der Stadtplanungsabteilung des jeweiligen Bezirksamtes, in Absprache mit anderen bezirklichen Stellen sowie mit den planenden Abteilungen der Senatsverwaltung für Stadtentwicklung Berlin und der Denkmalfachbehörde, dem Landesdenkmalamt Berlin.

Die Aufstellung von Denkmalpflegeplänen, von Maßnahmenkatalogen, Pflegewerken etc. (§ 8 Abs.3 DschG Bln) kann das Landesdenkmalamt bzw. die zuständige Denkmalbehörde anordnen.

Der Flächennutzungsplan von Berlin, letzte Fassung 2004, und die Bereichsentwicklungspläne der Bezirke stellen alle sechs Siedlungsgebiete als Wohnfläche dar. In den Siedlungsgebieten und Pufferzonen – außer in der Gartenstadt Falkenberg und der Wohnstadt Carl Legien – bestehen Bebauungspläne, die Art und Maß der vorhandenen Nutzungen, in erster Linie das Wohnen, sichern. Aber auch die umgebenen Grün- und Freizeitflächen innerhalb der Pufferzonen sind damit in ihrem Bestand abgesichert. Denkmalpläne sind vor allem für die zum Schutzgut gehörenden Gärten und Freiflächen vorhanden. Instandsetzungskonzepte und den Baubestand betreffende Maßnahmenkataloge sind ebenfalls für einige Siedlungen vorhanden. Grundsätzlich gibt es für alle sechs Siedlungen detaillierte Bestandsaufnahmen und restauratorische Befunduntersuchungen, auf deren Grundlage die Wiederherstellung des historischen Erscheinungsbildes der Siedlungen erfolgt. Im einzelnen existieren folgende Pläne:

BBauG) of 1960, renamed Baugesetzbuch (Building Code, BauGB) in 1987. In the practice of development law, the land-use plan now plays the role of alternative development plan. A comparable set of instruments that covers the entire area does not exist for the East Berlin districts. Legally binding development plans for these districts had to be established in 1990. In those areas of the East Berlin districts that are not covered by development plans, building permits are granted according to Section 34 of the Building Code (BauGB).

The urban development department of each district office establishes its own development plans in coordination with the other district authorities as well as with the development departments of the governmental urban development authorities and with the special purpose authority, i.e. the Landesdenkmalamt of Berlin.

The Landesdenkmalamt or the relevant monument preservation authority may require the establishment of monument preservation plans, catalogues of preservation measures, maintenance documentations, etc. (Section 8, Paragraph 3 DSchG Bln).

In the Land-Use Plan of Berlin in its latest version of 2004 and the district area development plans of the districts, all six housing estate areas are marked as residential areas. For the housing estate areas and their buffer zones (except Gartenstadt Falkenberg and Wohnstadt Carl Legien), development plans exist which guarantee the kind and extent of the existing uses, i.e. primarily residential use. These plans also guarantee the preservation of the green and leisure spaces within the buffer zones. Monument preservation plans exist mainly for the gardens and outdoor facilities that belong to the protected areas. For some of the housing estates, restoration concepts and catalogues of measures exist to be taken for the existing structures. In principle, there are detailed stocktaking documents and findings of investigations for restoration purposes for all six housing estates, which provide the basis for restoring the historic appearance of the estates. The following detailed plans exist:

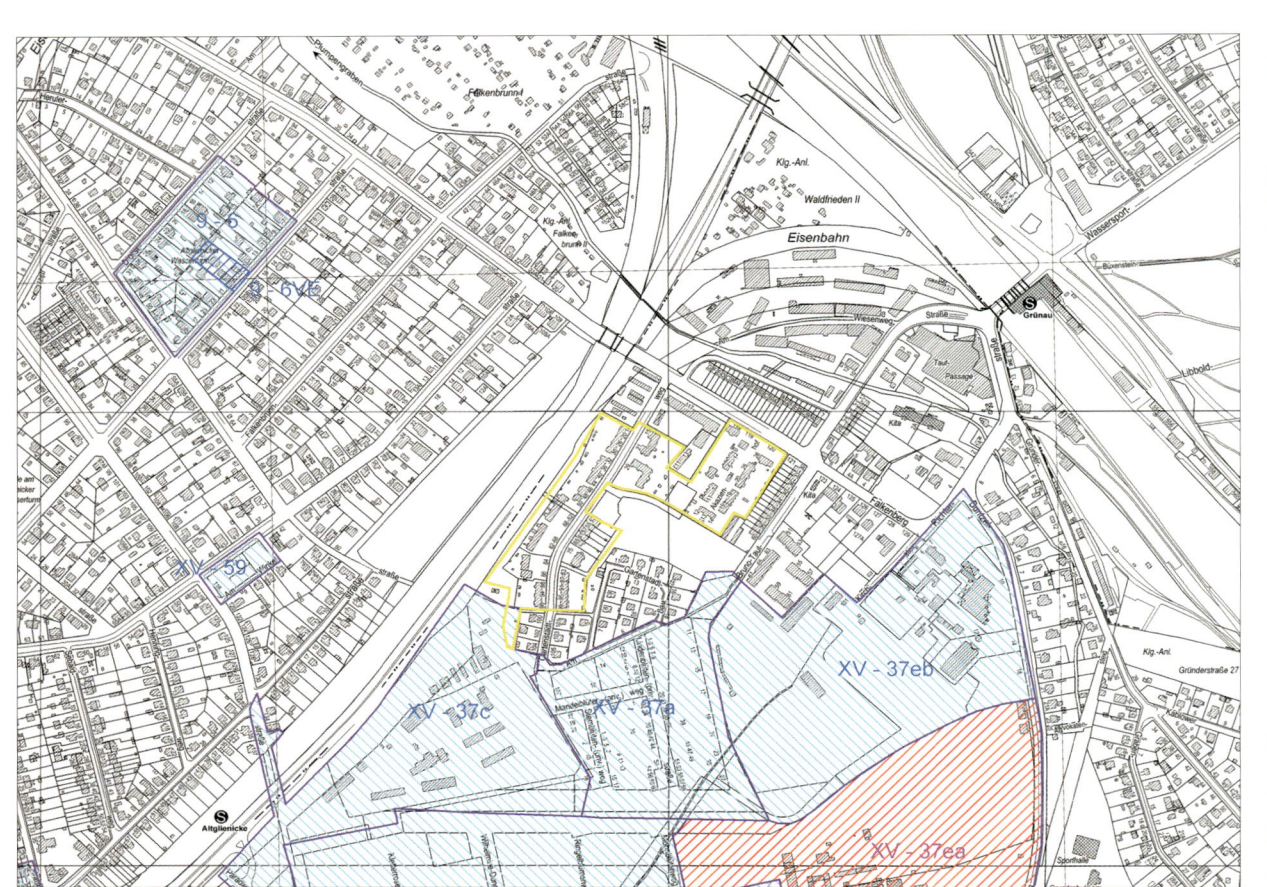

Abb. 96: Gartenstadt Falkenberg, Bebauungspläne im Nominierungsgebiet und in der Pufferzone, 2005

Fig. 96: Gartenstadt Falkenberg, development plans for the nominated area and the buffer zone, 2005

Festgesetzter Bebauungsplan/ Approved Development Plan

Bebauungsplan im Verfahren/ Development Plan in Progress

## Die einzelnen Siedlungen

### Gartenstadt Falkenberg

Für die südliche Gartenstadterweiterung, hier wird nur ein Teilgebeit der Pufferzone berührt, die zur Zeit auf der Grundlage eines städtebaulichen Realisierungswettbewerbs von 1992 durchgeführt wird, wurden ab 1994 für die einzelnen Bauabschnitte Bebauungspläne (XV-37a–XV-37e) aufgestellt. Sie sehen Wohngebiete mit offener, niedriger Bebauung und Grünbereiche vor, in Anlehnung an die Wohnstruktur der historischen Gartenstadt. Keiner der Pläne ist bisher förmlich festgesetzt.

Für die Freiflächen und Siedlergärten besteht seit 2001 ein denkmalpflegerischer Konzeptplan (s. Ziffer 7.c).

## The individual housing estates

### Gartenstadt Falkenberg

For the southern extension of the garden town that is currently being carried out on the basis of the results of an urban development competition of 1992, development plans for the individual development phases (XV-37a – XV-37e) were established as of 1994. This extension involves only part of the buffer zone. The development plans stipulate open, low structures and green spaces that emulate the residential structures in the historic garden town. To date, none of these plans has been formalised.

As of 2001, a monument preservation plan exists for the outdoor facilities and the gardens (see Item 7.c).

Abb. 97: Siedlung Schillerpark, Bebauungspläne im Nominierungsgebiet und in der Pufferzone, 2005

Fig. 97: Siedlung Schillerpark, development plans for the nominated area and the buffer zone, 2005

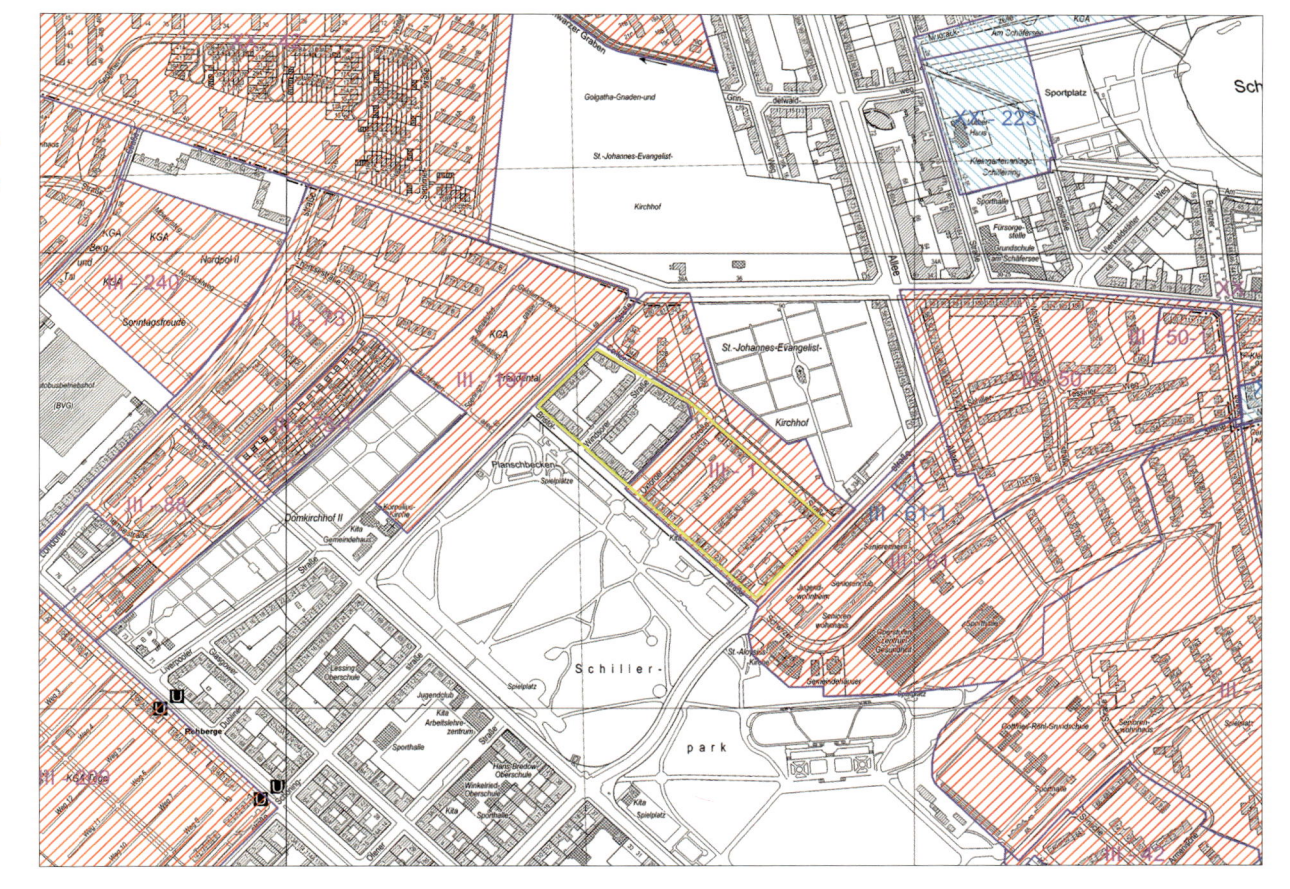

▨ Festgesetzter Bebauungsplan/ Approved Development Plan

▨ Bebauungsplan im Verfahren/ Development Plan in Progress

## Siedlung Schillerpark

Nur für den südöstlichen Teil, zwischen Oxforder Straße und Barfusstraße, des Nominierungsgebietes besteht seit 1954 ein festgesetzter Bebauungsplan (III-1), der Wohnbebauung als allein zulässige Bebauung festsetzt. Die beiden Baublöcke zwischen Dubliner und Oxforder Straße sind im Baunutzungsplan von 1958/60 als Wohngebiet ausgewiesen.

Die umgebenen Grün-, Friedhofs- und Kleingartenflächen sind ebenfalls in ihrer Nutzung gesichert. Der Schillerpark und der St. Johannes-Evangelist-Kirchhof sind im Baunutzungsplan von 1958/60 als Grünflächen festgesetzt, die Kleingartenkolonie „Freudental" ist 1992 im rechtsverbindlichen Bebauungsplan (III-197) festgesetzt worden.

Die Pufferzone schließt in südöstlicher Richtung ein von Barfusstraße und Schwyzer Straße begrenztes Areal ein, das eine Kirche, ein Jugendheim und Seniorenstätten aufnimmt. Es liegt im Geltungsbereich des 1975 beschlossenen Bebauungsplanes III-61, der ansonsten allgemeines Wohngebiet festsetzt.

Für die noch nicht vollständig denkmalgerecht erneuerten Wohnhäuser und Freiflächen bestehen Maßnahmenkonzepte (s. Ziffer 7.c). Für den Baubestand existiert seit 1991 ein Instandsetzungskonzept und für die Außenanlagen ein 2003 erstellter gartendenkmalpflegerischer Maßnahmenplan.

## Siedlung Schillerpark

A development plan (III–1) has been in existence since 1954 only for the southeastern part (between Oxforder Straße and Barfusstraße) of the nominated area, stating that residential buildings are the only permissible development. The two blocks between Dubliner Straße and Oxforder Straße are marked as residential areas in the Land-Use Plan of 1958/60.

Land-use is also defined for the green spaces, the churchyard and the allotment gardens. In the Land-Use Plan of 1958/60, Schillerpark and the churchyard St. Johannes-Evangelist are defined as green spaces. The allotment garden colony "Freudental" was defined in 1992 in the binding development plan (III–197).

The buffer zones include an area in the southeast surrounded by Barfusstraße and Schwyzer Straße which comprises a church, a youth home and homes for the elderly. This area is covered by Development Plan III-61, which was adopted in 1975 and otherwise defines the area as general residential area.

For the residential buildings and green spaces which have not yet been restored, concepts exist for restoration measures (see Item 7.c). Since 1991, a refurbishment concept has existed for the structures, and in 2003 a garden monument preservation plan was established for the outdoor facilities.

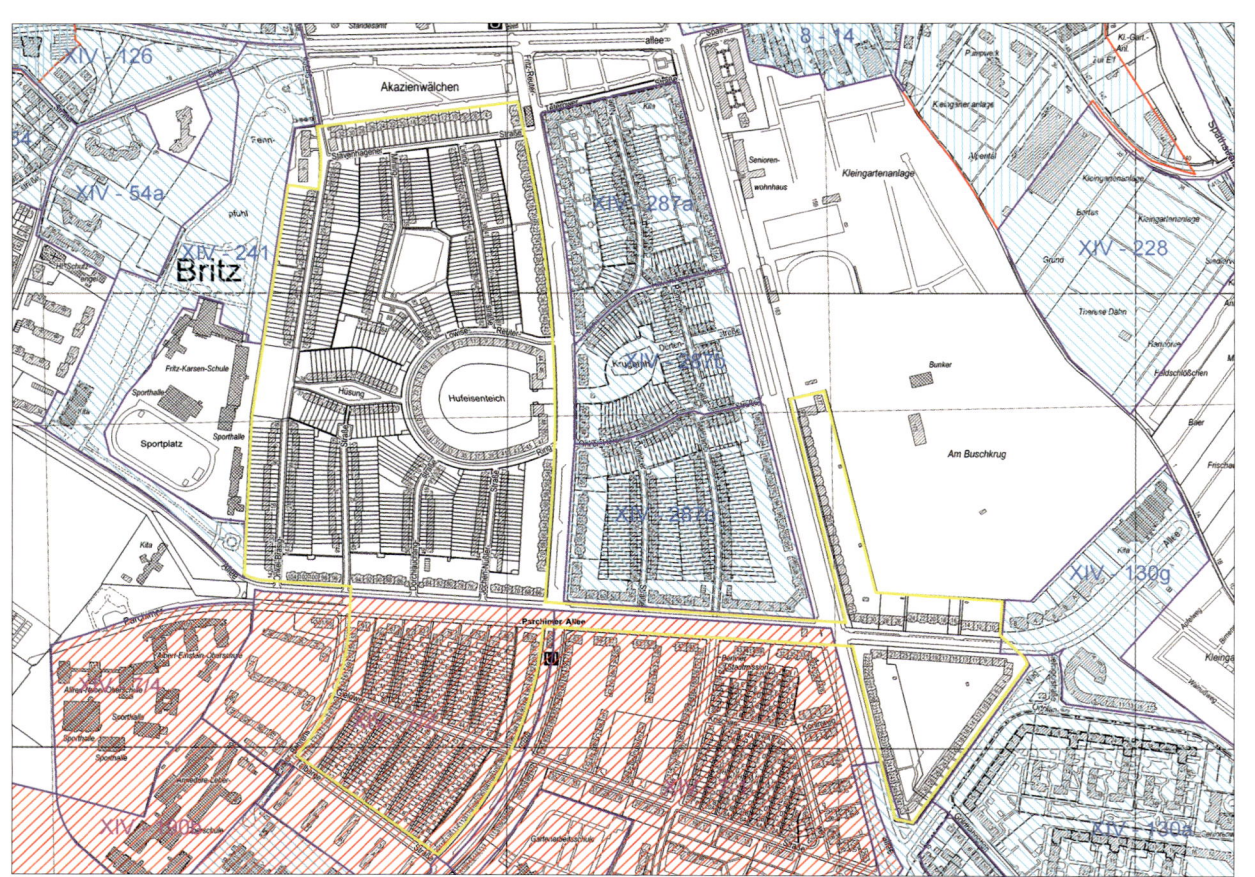

Abb. 98: Großsiedlung Britz, Bebauungspläne im Nominierungsgebiet und in der Pufferzone, 2005

Fig. 98: Großsiedlung Britz, development plans for the nominated area and the buffer zone, 2005

Festgesetzter Bebauungsplan/ Approved Development Plan

Bebauungsplan im Verfahren/ Development Plan in Progress

## Großsiedlung Britz (Hufeisensiedlung)

Das Hufeisen und die umliegenden Reihenhäuser bis zur Parchimer Allee (Bauabschnitt I und II) wie auch die Geschossbauten der Bauabschnitte III bis V östlich der Buschkrugallee sind im Baunutzungsplan flächendeckend als Wohngebiet festgesetzt. Der letzte Bauabschnitt VII, zwischen Parchimer Allee und Talberger Straße, liegt im Geltungsbereich des 1963 festgesetzten Bebauungsplans XIV-7/2, der diesen Siedlungsteil als Wohngebiet sichert.

Auch die Areale der Pufferzone sind in ihrer denkmalverträglichen Nutzung – Wohnen, Kleingarten-, Park- und Sportplatzflächen – durch Bebauungspläne oder durch den Baunutzungsplan gesichert.

Für den Umgang mit den Freiflächen der Hufeisensiedlung besteht seit 2003 ein Konzeptplan. Ein denkmalpflegerischer Maßnahmenkatalog zur Sicherung des historischen Erscheinungsbildes liegt für die Reihenhäuser des ersten und zweiten Bauabschnittes nördlich der Parchimer Allee seit 2001 vor. Die sukzessive Erneuerung der Siedlungshäuser erfolgte bisher auf der Grundlage eines 1984–1991 erstellten denkmalpflegerischen Bestandsgutachtens (s. Ziffer 7.c).

## Großsiedlung Britz (Hufeisensiedlung)

The land-use plan defines as a residential area the entire area of the horseshoe and the row houses around it up to Parchimer Allee (Development Phases I and II) as well as the multi-storey buildings of Development Phases III to V east of Buschkrugallee. The last development phase (VII) between Parchimer Allee and Talberger Straße is covered by Development Plan XIV-7/2 of 1963, which defines this area as a residential area.

The uses of the buffer zone areas (housing, allotment gardens, park, sport grounds) are also ensured by development plans or the land-use plan.

In 2003, a concept for the handling of the outdoor facilities of the Hufeisensiedlung was established. As of 2001, there is a catalogue of monument preservation measures for preserving the historic appearance of the row houses of the first and second development phases north of Parchimer Allee. To date, the gradual renewal of the houses has been carried out on the basis of the expert opinion on the existing monument of 1984–1991 (see Item 7.c).

Abb. 99: Wohnstadt Carl Legien, Bebauungspläne im Nominierungsgebiet und in der Pufferzone, 2005

Fig. 99: Wohnstadt Carl Legien, development plans for the nominated area and the buffer zone, 2005

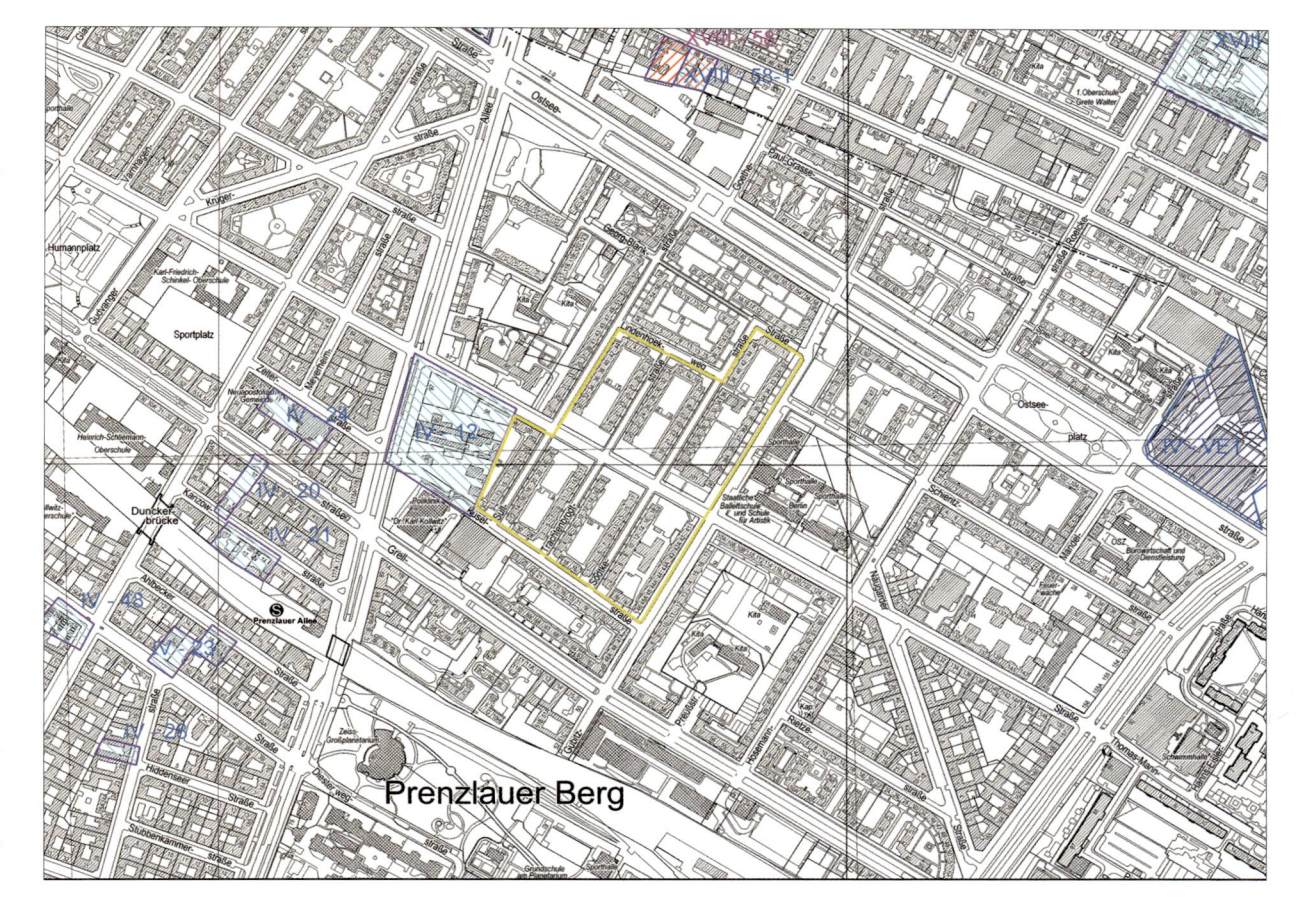

▨ Festgesetzter Bebauungsplan/
Approved Development Plan

▨ Bebauungsplan im Verfahren/
Development Plan in Progress

## Wohnstadt Carl Legien

Das Siedlungsgelände der Wohnstadt Carl Legien liegt im Geltungsbereich eines nach dem Baugesetzbuch (BauGB) 2003 förmlich festgelegten Erhaltungsgebietes, in dem die Vorschriften einer Erhaltungsverordnung gelten (s. Ziffer 5.c). Sie formulieren als Ziel den Erhalt der historischen Fassaden und Dächer mit ihren Elementen bzw. ihrer Materialität und Farbigkeit. Neubauten unterliegen bestimmten Gestaltungsgrundsätzen, die sich an der vorhandenen Bebauung orientieren.

Das Erhaltungsgebiet deckt sich bis auf ein kleines Gebiet zwischen Prenzlauer Allee, Erich-Weinert-Straße und Küselstraße mit dem Areal der Pufferzone. Für diesen Bereich ist 1993 ein Bebauungsplanverfahren (IV-12) eingeleitet worden, der ein Mischgebiet für Wohnen und nicht störendes Gewerbe sowie als Übergang zur Wohnstadt, einen ausschließlich für Wohnen bestimmten Geländestreifen vorsieht.

Für die noch nicht vollständig wiederhergestellten Freiflächen existiert seit 2001 ein gartendenkmalpflegerischer Maßnahmenplan (s. Ziffer 7.c). Die denkmalgerechte Sanierung der Etagenwohnhäuser konnte 2005 abgeschlossen werden.

## Wohnstadt Carl Legien

The housing estate area of Wohnstadt Carl Legien is located within a preservation area was formally defined in 2003 on the basis of the Building Code (BauGB), and within this area, the stipulations of a preservation regulation apply (see Item 5.c). They stipulate the preservation of the historic facades and roofs with their elements, materials and colours. For new structures, certain design principles apply which are based on the design of the existing buildings.

With the exception of a small area between Prenzlauer Allee, Erich-Weinert-Straße and Küselstraße, the preservation area coincides with the buffer zone. In 1993 a development planning procedure (IV-12) was initiated which stipulates a mixed area for residential purposes and non-interfering commercial use as well as a strip of land exclusively for residential purposes to function as a transition to the Wohnstadt.

As of 2001, a plan exists for the preservation and restoration of the historic garden which applies for the outdoor facilities that have not yet been completely restored (see Item 7.c). The restoration of the multi-storey residential buildings was completed in 2005.

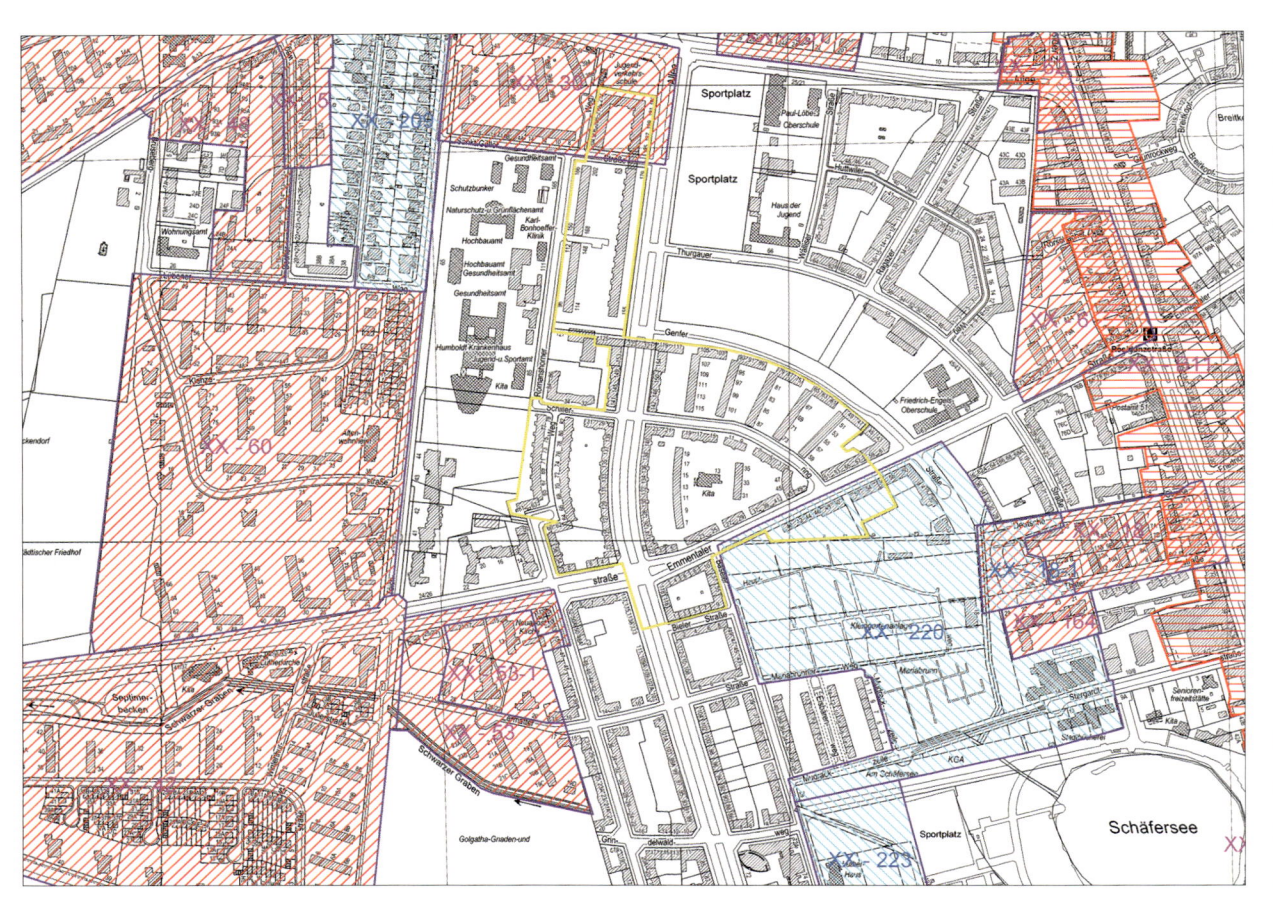

Abb. 100: Weiße Stadt, Bebauungspläne im Nominierungsgebiet und in der Pufferzone, 2005

Fig. 100: Weiße Stadt, development plans for the nominated area and the buffer zone, 2005

Festgesetzter Bebauungsplan/
Approved Development Plan

Bebauungsplan im Verfahren/
Development Plan in Progress

## Weiße Stadt

Zwei Bebauungspläne betreffen Bauteile der Weißen Stadt. Im Norden liegt ein Teil der Siedlungsbauten von Otto Rudolf Salvisberg im 1960 festgesetzten Bebauungsplan XX-30, der allgemeines Wohngebiet festsetzt. Im südöstlichen Bereich sind zwei Randzeilen von Wilhelm Büning auf der Südseite der Emmentaler Straße Teil des 1986 im Verfahren begonnenen Bebauungsplanes XX-220, der vor allem zur Erhaltung der hier liegenden Kleingartenkolonie „Mariabrunn" dient. Die übrige Fläche der Weißen Stadt wird durch den Baunutzungsplan als Wohngebiet gesichert.

Innerhalb der Pufferzone liegen zwei Bebauungspläne (XX-53 und XX-53-1), festgesetzt 1965 und 1971, die ebenfalls die Gebiete für eine Wohnnutzung sichern.

Für die gartendenkmalpflegerische Erneuerung der Freiflächen dienen 1984 und 2000 angefertigte Maßnahmenpläne. Die schrittweise Erneuerung der Siedlungshäuser erfolgte bisher auf der Grundlage eines 1981 erstellten denkmalpflegerischen Bestandsgutachtens (s. Ziffer 7.c).

## Weiße Stadt

Two development plans cover parts of Weiße Stadt. One part of the housing estate buildings by Otto Rudolf Salvisberg is located in the north. This part is covered by Development Plan XX-30 of 1960 in which it is defined as a general residential area. In the southeastern part, two ribbons at block margins by Wilhelm Büning on the southern side of Emmentaler Straße are covered by Development Plan XX-220, which mainly aims at preserving the allotment garden colony "Mariabrunn" and whose procedure started in 1986. The remaining area of Weiße Stadt is defined as a residential area by the land-use plan.

Within the buffer zone, two development plans (XX-53 and XX-53-1) of 1965 and 1971 apply which also define the areas as residential areas.

Action plans of 1984 and 2000 assure the restoration of the outdoor facilities. To date, the gradual renewal of the houses has been carried out on the basis of the expert opinion on the existing monument of 1981 (see Item 7.c).

Abb. 101: Großsiedlung Siemensstadt, Bebauungspläne im Nominierungsgebiet und in der Pufferzone, 2005

Fig. 101: Großsiedlung Siemensstadt, development plans for the nominated area and the buffer zone, 2005

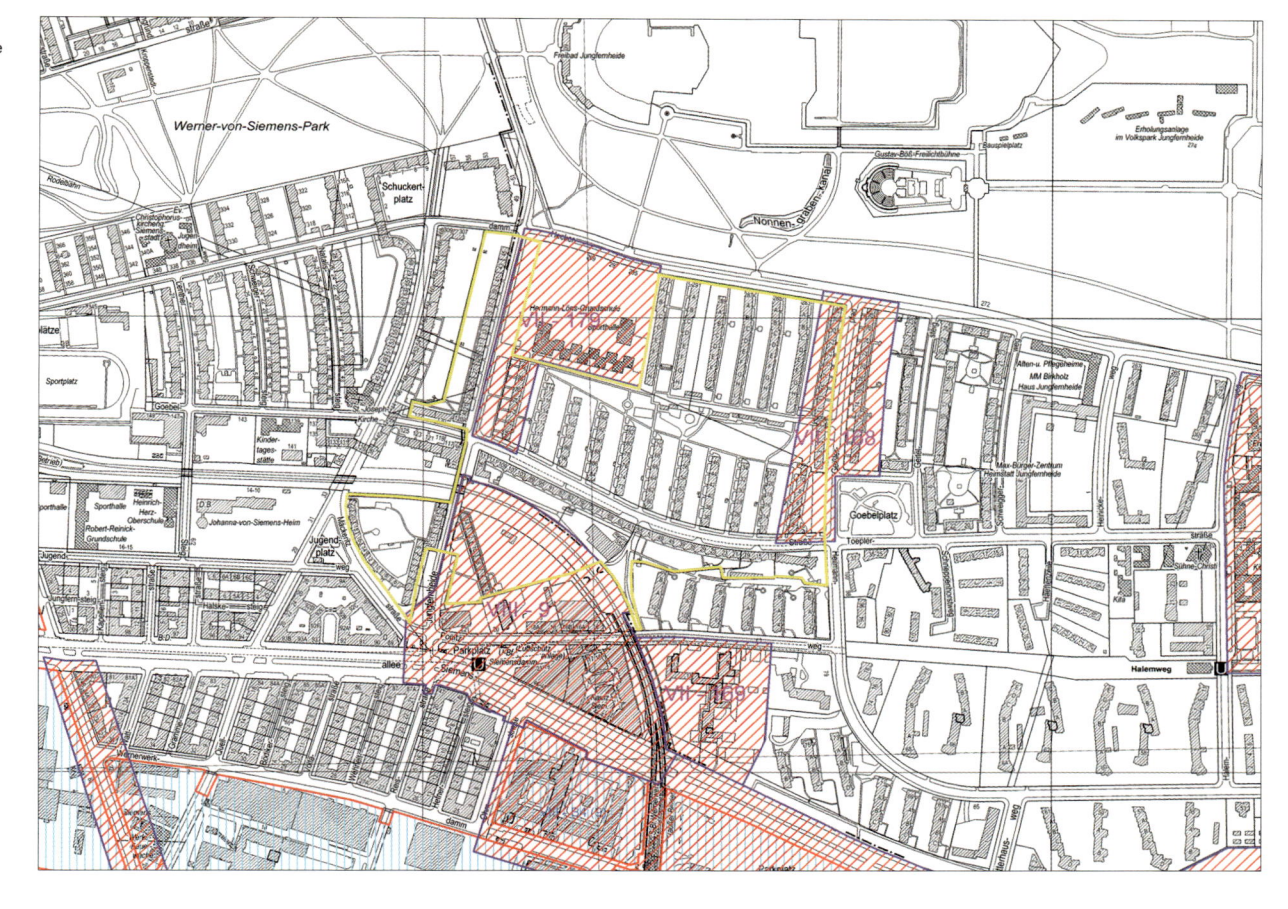

▨ Festgesetzter Bebauungsplan/
Approved Development Plan

▨ Bebauungsplan im Verfahren/
Development Plan in Progress

## Großsiedlung Siemensstadt (Ringsiedlung)

Bebauungspläne wurden nur für Teilbereiche der Siedlung aufgestellt. Der Großteil der Siedlung ist durch den Baunutzungsplan als allgemeines Wohngebiet gesichert. Die Bebauungspläne setzen die bestehende Nutzung fest: der Plan VII-168 von 1975 für den Bauteil von Fred Forbat am Geißlerpfad, der Plan VII-179 von 1973 am Jungfernheideweg für die östliche Randzeile von Walter Gropius. Beide Bebauungspläne sehen Wohnnutzung mit Gemeinbedarf (Schule) vor, beinhalten aber auch die Ausweisung von Stellplätzen, was sich im Vorgartenbereich der Forbatzeile am Geißlerpfad störend auf das Erscheinungsbild der Siedlung auswirkt.

Für den im Bezirk Spandau liegenden Siedlungsteil zwischen Siemensbahn, Jungfernheideweg und Siemensdamm weist der 1960 festgesetzte Bebauungsplan VIII-9 ein Mischgebiet für Wohnen und Gewerbe aus, unter ausdrücklicher Sicherung der zum Bauteil Scharoun gehörenden Wohnhauszeile am Jungfernheideweg 4–14. Allerdings wird durch diese Art der Festsetzung auch der im Eingangsbereich der Siedlung liegende Supermarkt in seinem Bestand gesichert.

Für die Siedlungsgärten der Ringsiedlung liegt ein 2003 erarbeitetes Pflegewerk mit Maßnahmenplänen vor. Die Erneuerung der Siedlungsbauten wird sich an einem 1984 erarbeiteten denkmalpflegerischen Bestandsgutachten orientieren (s. Ziffer 7.c).

## Großsiedlung Siemensstadt (Ringsiedlung)

Development plans have been established only for some parts of the housing estate. Most of the area of this housing estate is defined as a general residential area by the land-use plan. The development plans assure the current use: Plan VII-168 of 1975 for the buildings by Fred Forbat at Geißlerpfad, and Plan VII-179 of 1973 for the eastern ribbon by Walter Gropius at the block margin along Jungfernheideweg. Both development plans stipulate residential use with general services (school) but they also provide for parking lots. Where these have been established at the front gardens of the Forbat ribbon at Geißlerpfad, they disturb the appearance of the housing estate.

Development Plan VIII-9 of 1960 marks the area in the district of Spandau between the Siemens railway line, Jungfernheideweg and Siemensdamm as a mixed area for residential and commercial use and expressly protects the ribbon residential building by Hans Scharoun at Jungfernheideweg 4–14. However, the way in which the protection has been formulated also ensures the protection of the supermarket at the access to the housing estate.

In 2003, a maintenance documentation was adopted with action plans for the gardens belonging to the Ringsiedlung. The renewal of the buildings follows a 1984 expert opinion for restoration purposes on the existing monument (see Item 7.c).

## 5.E Property management plan or other management system

I. Fundamentals

II. Objectives
Conservation and development of the existing monuments
Assuring financial resources
Assuring residential use
Promotion of knowledge and acceptance of the housing estates

III. Actors
The controlling body
The owners
The inhabitants
The monument preservation authorities
External competence centres and experts
Politics and administrations in the districts
Cooperation partners

IV. Instruments and fields of action
Legal and planning bases
Financing
Monument preservation plans and other expert opinions
Public relations activities
Tourism concept

V. Control and reporting (monitoring)

### I. Fundamentals

Up to the present, the chosen housing estates of the Berlin Modern Style have preserved their significance as exemplary social residential areas with outstanding artistic quality. During the first decades of the 20th century, social mass housing development in Berlin produced new concepts for the spatial and social order of the city that have been preserved in the six nominated housing estates as they were handed down to us. Novel designs and a diversity of structure and building forms are combined with intelligent integration into urban structures to develop appropriate flats in healthy environments. The nominated housing estates are well accepted by their inhabitants and should preserve their character as has been described above.

The management plan aims at preserving these qualities. Its objective consists in sustainably preserving the nominated housing estates in the sense of the UNESCO convention on the protection of the heritage of humankind and in the sense of the international charters of Venice, Washington and Florence. This includes measures for protecting, preserving and restoring the housing estates as well as all necessary measures for preserving them as attractive residential areas. The objective is not to preserve them as museums, but to provide for their sustainable development as special monument sites and residential locations by adapting them to changing residential needs while adhering to the requirements of monument preservation.

Die Umsetzung des Managementplanes kann nur mit Hilfe eines abgestimmten Netzwerks gelingen, in das Eigentümer, Bewohner, Architekten, Landschaftsarchitekten, Planer, Fachleute und Behörden eingebunden sind. Aufgabe der Denkmalbehörden wird es sein, den schwierigen Prozess des Zusammenwirkens zu initiieren und zu moderieren. Der Kommunikation zwischen den Beteiligten kommt daher eine zentrale Bedeutung für die Erhaltung des Welterbes zu.

Der folgende Managementplan gibt eine aktuelle Fassung wieder und stellt grundsätzliche Ziele, die wichtigsten Akteure, Instrumente und Handlungsfelder sowie das Monitoring dar. Er bedarf einer Konkretisierung für jede einzelne Siedlung sowie hinsichtlich der Kooperationsprojekte. Er ist laufend zu überprüfen und ggf. durch Ergänzungen und Vertiefungen fortzuschreiben. Dies schließt die Information und Beteiligung der regional und lokal verantwortlichen politischen Gremien ein.

## II. Ziele
### Pflege und Entwicklung des Denkmalbestandes

Primäres Ziel des Managements ist der Schutz, die Pflege und Wiederherstellung des historischen Bau- und Freiflächenbestandes der Siedlungen einschließlich der Sozial- und Nutzungsstruktur:

Notwendige Veränderungsprozesse wegen bautechnischer Erfordernisse oder Sanierungen sind so zu steuern, dass die Authentizität und Integrität der Siedlungen einschließlich ihrer städtebaulichen Merkmale und Freiräume bewahrt bleibt

Überformte architektonische und freiräumliche Qualitäten sollen, soweit nötig, auf der Grundlage von Denkmalpflegeplänen wiedergewonnen werden

Zur Umsetzung der Denkmalpflegepläne sollen Maßnahmekataloge für den laufenden denkmalgerechten Bauunterhalt gemeinsam mit den Eigentümern entwickelt werden. Vorgesehene Neubebauungen in den Pufferzonen haben den Maßstab, die Gestaltung und die Nutzung des Denkmalbestandes der Siedlungen zu berücksichtigen

Privatisierungen wird es in einigen Siedlungen auch zukünftig geben. Die für diese Siedlungen zu konkretisierenden Managementpläne sollen auch auf Veränderungen der Eigentümerstruktur reagieren

Die öffentlichen Grün- und Verkehrsflächen sind als konstituierender Bestandteil der einzelnen Siedlungskonzepte zu erhalten. Das bedeutet auch, das Aussagen zu Straßenprofilen und zur Oberflächenbeschaffenheit sowie zu den Vegetationsstrukturen in die Managementpläne einzubeziehen sind

### Sicherung der finanziellen Ressourcen

Die Bereitstellung von finanziellen Mitteln für die Bauunterhaltung und die Erneuerung der Siedlungen, die in erster Linie den Eigentümergesellschaften obliegt, kann im Rahmen der laufenden Bewirtschaftung durch die Eigentümer als gesichert gelten. Dazu tragen auch die steuerlichen Abschreibungsmöglichkeiten bei erforderlichen Investitionen zur Erhaltung des Denkmalbestandes bei.

The management plan can only be implemented by means of a well adjusted network which includes owners, residents, architects, landscape architects, planners, experts and authorities. The monument preservation authorities are facing the difficult task of initiating and guiding the complex process of cooperation between all of these parties. So, communication between these parties plays a central role for preserving the world heritage.

Below we present the current version of the management plan and the fundamental objectives, the main actors, instruments and fields of action and monitoring as they are laid down in this plan. Specific stipulations are to be made for each of the housing estates and for the cooperation projects. The plan must be reviewed and if necessary supplemented and extended on an ongoing basis. This means that the responsible political bodies on a regional and local level must be kept informed and involved.

## II. Objectives
### Conservation and development of the existing monuments

The primary objective of the management is to protect, preserve and reconstruct the historic structures and outdoor facilities of the housing estates and their social and utilisation structure:

Changes that become necessary for constructional reasons or due to refurbishments must be controlled in such a way that they do not impair the authenticity and integrity of the housing estates and their urban features and outdoor facilities

Alterations to the architectural and outdoor features are to be reversed as far as necessary and on the basis of monument preservation plans

To ensure ongoing proper preservation of the buildings, we intend to develop action plans in cooperation with the owners. Any new development within the buffer zones must take into account the scale, design and utilisation of the existing monuments of the housing estates

In some of the housing estates, privatisation will continue in future. The management plans for those housing estates will have to also take into account the changing ownership relations

The public green and traffic areas will be preserved as essential parts of the individual housing estate concepts. This means that statements concerning the road profiles and surfaces as well as structures of vegetation will have to be taken into account by the management plans

### Assuring financial resources

We can assume that the financial means which are required for preserving and renewing the housing estates – tasks which largely have to be fulfilled by the owners – will be provided within the framework of regular management by the owners. The fact that investments that become necessary for preserving the monuments can be depreciated and thus reduce the tax burden contribute to assuring the finance.

Im Einzelfall wird aber auch der Einsatz öffentlicher Fördermittel sowie eine gezielte Einwerbung von Drittmitteln nötig sein, um die finanziellen Ressourcen zu stärken. Potentielle Welterbestätten erfüllen auch die Fördervoraussetzungen des Bundesprogramms „National wertvolle Kulturdenkmäler".

**Sicherung der Wohnnutzung**
Die Nominierungsgebiete werden ausschließlich vom Wohnen und seinen Folgenutzungen geprägt. Ziel ist es, keine Nutzung zuzulassen, die die vorhandene hohe Wohnqualität beeinträchtigen könnte, um auch Leerstand und soziale Instabilität sowie wirtschaftliche Probleme bei der Instandhaltung zu vermeiden. Dies gilt auch für die umgebenen Pufferzonen, die ebenfalls hauptsächlich durch Wohngebäude bestimmt sind oder denkmalverträgliche Nutzungen wie Parks, Friedhöfe und Sporteinrichtungen aufweisen. Auch werden weiterhin bauliche Verdichtungen in den Siedlungsgebieten ausgeschlossen.

**Förderung der Kenntnis und Akzeptanz der Siedlungen**
Zur Erhaltung und Pflege der nominierten Siedlungen ist es notwendig, das Bewusstsein für den Wert der Siedlungen zu vertiefen und ihre denkmalgerechte Erhaltung als allgemein anerkanntes Ziel zu etablieren. Die Identifikation der Bewohner sowie die vieler Berliner und Besucher der Stadt mit den Siedlungen soll durch eine vielfältige Öffentlichkeitsarbeit verstärkt werden.

Neben einer intensiveren Medienarbeit und Publikationstätigkeit werden Kooperationen mit anderen Welterbestätten sowie mit anderen Städten, die bedeutende Siedlungen der Moderne besitzen, angestrebt, um praktische Erfahrungen auszutauschen und die Bedeutung des Siedlungsbaus als kulturelles Erbe des 20. Jahrhunderts zu vermitteln.

In Zusammenarbeit mit wissenschaftlichen und kulturellen Einrichtungen der Berliner Region, die sich in ihrer Lehr- und Ausbildungstätigkeit auf dem Gebiet der Denkmalpflege und Welterbepflege oder in ihrer Forschungs-, Sammlungs- und Ausstellungstätigkeit besonders dem Neuen Bauen widmen, sollen Ausstellungen und andere Informationsvermittlungsangebote organisiert werden.

Der hohe Bekanntheitsgrad der Siedlungen in der Fachwelt ist eine gute Voraussetzung, sie durch ein noch zu entwickelndes Marketingkonzept auch für einen breiteren Besucherkreis interessant zu machen. Der Berlin-Tourismus bietet dabei vielversprechende Potenziale, da die Stadt eines der bedeutendsten Ziele des Städte- und Kulturtourismus in Europa ist und die Siedlungen durch den öffentlichen Nahverkehr gut erreichbar sind. Die touristische Übernutzung ist auch bei zunehmenden Besucherzahlen wegen der dezentralen Lage der Siedlungen und ihrer aufgelockerten Bebauungsstruktur nicht zu erwarten.

**III. Akteure**
Hauptakteure bei der Pflege und Entwicklung der Siedlungen sind die Eigentümer und die Denkmalbehörden sowie die Fachleute, die in ihrem Auftrag tätig sind. Unverzichtbare Partner sind darüber hinaus die Bewohner der Siedlungen sowie die politischen Verantwortlichen und Verwaltungen in den Bezirken, darüber hinaus aber auch

In individual cases, public grants and special purpose contributions from third parties may have to be acquired to enhance the financial resources. Potential world heritage locations fulfil the preconditions of the federal programme of "National wertvolle Kulturdenkmäler" (valuable national cultural monuments), thus entitling them to grants from this programme.

**Assuring residential use**
The nominated housing estates are used exclusively for residential and related purposes. The objectives include preventing any utilisation which might impair the excellent residential quality in order, for example, to avoid flats or houses becoming disused or the occurrence of social instability and economic difficulties related to maintenance. This also applies to the buffer zones which consist largely of residential buildings or of parks, graveyards or sports grounds – uses which do not impair the monuments. Any further densification of buildings in the housing estates is also excluded.

**Promotion of knowledge and acceptance of the housing estates**
In order to preserve and maintain the nominated housing estates, it is necessary to enhance the awareness of their value and to establish their preservation as monuments as a generally acknowledged objective. By means of comprehensive public relations activities, our goal is to ensure that many citizens and visitors of Berlin identify with the housing estates.

In addition to intensifying media and publication activities, we will try to establish cooperation with other world heritage locations and other cities with important Modern Style housing estates, so that we can exchange experience and disseminate knowledge about the significance of residential development as cultural heritage of the 20th century.

We will organize exhibitions and other offers for providing information in cooperation with scientific and cultural institutions of the Berlin region that focus on Neues Bauen in their training and education on the subject of monument or world heritage preservation or in their research, collections and exhibitions.

The fact that the housing estates are well known among experts is a good precondition for making them more widely known to visitors by means of a marketing concept which still has to be developed. Tourism in Berlin provides promising opportunities, since the city is one of the most important centres of urban and cultural tourism in Europe and the housing estates can be easily reached by public transport. Since the housing estates are not in central locations and have a low building density, there is no risk that they might suffer from excessive pressure by tourism.

**III. Actors**
The owners and the monument preservation authorities, as well as experts working by their order, are the main actors for preserving and developing the housing estates. Their indispensable partners are the inhabitants of the housing estates as well as the concerned political decision makers and district administrations and also the experts and insti-

Abb. 102: Erhaltungsverordnung Ostsee-/ Grellstraße für das Siedlungsgebiet der Wohnstadt Carl Legien, 2003

Fig. 102: Preservation regulation for the area Ostseestraße/ Grellstraße with Wohnstadt Carl Legien, 2003

**ERHALTUNGSVERORDNUNG OSTSEE-/ GRELLSTRASSE**

INFORMATIONEN ZUM ERHALTUNGSGEBIET

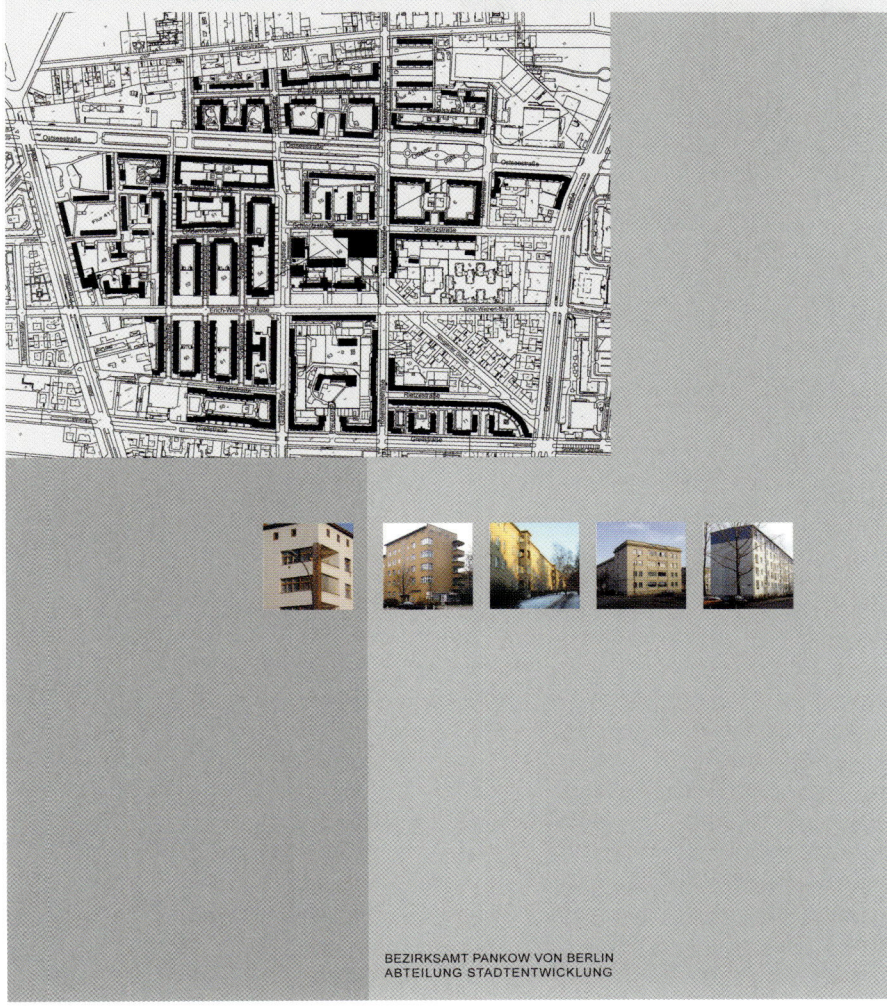

BEZIRKSAMT PANKOW VON BERLIN
ABTEILUNG STADTENTWICKLUNG

Spezialisten und Institutionen mit besonderer denkmalfachlicher Kompetenz und die interessierte Öffentlichkeit.

**Das Steuerungsgremium**
Die komplexen Managementaufgaben fordern die Bündelung von vielfältigem Sachverstand durch die Einbeziehung aller wichtigen Akteure in den Siedlungen sowie externer Fachleute und Kooperationspartner in einem arbeitsfähigen Gremium. Hilfreich kann darüber hinaus auch die Zusammenarbeit mit etablierten Gremien des Denkmalschutzes sein, wie dem Landesdenkmalrat und den Denkmalausschüssen der Kammern.

**Die Eigentümer**
Die Eigentümer tragen im Rahmen ihrer laufenden Bewirtschaftung den Hauptteil der Finanzierung zur Bauunterhaltung und zur denkmalgerechten Instandsetzung. Bei Bedarf übernehmen sie im Einvernehmen mit den Denkmalbehörden auch die Beauftragung von Fachleuten zur Erstellung von Fachgutachten und Denkmalpflegeplänen. Sie sind darüber hinaus in die Monitoringverfahren integriert, da sie über Schlüsselinformationen zur Höhe eingesetzter Mittel und zum Zustand der Siedlungen verfügen.

tutions with particular competence in the field of monument preservation and the interested public.

**The controlling body**
The complexity of the management tasks requires that the various forms of expertise be bundled and that all the important actors in the housing estates and external experts and cooperation partners be brought together in a well functioning body. Cooperation with established bodies of monument preservation like the Landesdenkmalrat (State Monument Council) and the commissions for monument protection of the chambers may also be helpful.

**The owners**
Within the framework of regular operation, the owners make the largest financial contributions for the ongoing maintenance and preservation of the monuments. When it becomes necessary they also employ experts for the generation of opinions and monument preservation plans. They agree on these kinds of decisions with the monument preservation authorities. The owners are also involved in the monitoring procedures, since they have the key information on the amount of financing used and on the state of conservation of the monuments.

For the housing companies, it is very important to communicate with their tenants and the purchasers of flats or houses in order to ensure that these inhabitants and individual owners take a positive attitude towards the efforts to preserve and restore the monuments. The housing companies are also important partners in public relations activities that aim at target groups outside the housing estates.

**The inhabitants**
With their behavior and their demands, the inhabitants exercise a decisive influence on the state of conservation as well as the development of the housing estates and their perception by the public. Thus, they are not only a target group for public relations activities, but one of our objectives is to motivate them to make their own contributions to preserving the monuments and act as multipliers, thus going beyond the satisfaction of their own demand for counselling and information. Involving them as partners in the management of the monuments is an important precondition for managing the monuments successfully.

**The monument preservation authorities**
According to the stipulations of the Berlin Law on the Preservation of Historic Places and Monuments, the monument preservation authorities must fulfil their legal obligations (see Items 5.B and 5.C), which range from protection under administrative law through expert counselling, providing financial resources in the form of tax privileges or grants up to urban research, publications and public relations activities.

They are to play the leading role in monitoring and other forms of reporting which may result from the inscription of the housing estates into the world heritage list. Furthermore, they must also initiate and accompany special tasks that may turn out to be necessary or desirable under this management plan.

Die Wohnungsunternehmen nehmen in der Kommunikation mit ihren Mietern sowie mit den Erwerbern von Einzeleigentum eine wichtige Rolle bei der Vermittlung einer positiven Einstellung gegenüber den Erhaltungs- und den Instandsetzungsbemühungen des Denkmalschutzes ein. Darüber hinaus sind sie auch wichtige Partner in der Öffentlichkeitsarbeit, die sich an Zielgruppen außerhalb der Siedlungen richtet.

### Die Bewohner

Die Bewohner der Siedlungen haben mit ihrem Nutzungsverhalten und ihren Nutzungsanforderungen prägenden Einfluss auf den Zustand und die Entwicklung der Siedlungen sowie auf deren öffentliche Wahrnehmung. Sie sind deshalb nicht nur Zielgruppe für Öffentlichkeitsarbeit, sondern sollen über die Befriedigung ihrer eigenen Beratungs- und Informationswünsche hinaus zu eigenen Erhaltungsbeiträgen motiviert und als Multiplikatoren gewonnen werden. Ihre partnerschaftliche Einbeziehung in ein denkmalbezogenes Management ist deshalb eine wichtige Voraussetzung für dessen nachhaltigen Erfolg.

### Die Denkmalbehörden

Nach den Bestimmungen des Berliner Denkmalschutzgesetzes haben die Denkmalbehörden ihre gesetzlichen Aufgaben wahrzunehmen (siehe Ziffern 5.B und 5.C) vom ordnungsrechtlichen Schutz über die fachliche Beratung, die Erschließung finanzieller Ressourcen in Form von Steuervergünstigungen oder Fördermittel bis hin zur siedlungsbezogenen Forschung, Publikationen und Öffentlichkeitsarbeit.

Sie haben federführend das Monitoring sowie die sonstigen Berichterstattungsaufgaben zu übernehmen, die aus einer Eintragung der Siedlungen in die Welterbeliste erwachsen werden. Darüber hinaus müssen sie auch initiierend und begleitend bei den speziellen Aufgaben mitwirken, die nach diesem Managementplan für die Siedlungen erforderlich oder wünschenswert sind.

### Externe Kompetenzzentren und Fachleute

Für die Erhaltung des Denkmalbestandes ist es unerlässlich, spezialisiertes Fachwissen heranzuziehen. Für die Untersuchung des Bestandes, die restauratorischen Analysen, die Aufstellung von Denkmalplänen und die Wiederherstellungsvorhaben sind die Fachkompetenz konservierungs- und restaurierungserfahrener Forschungs- und Entwicklungseinrichtungen sowie von denkmalerfahrenen Architekten, Landschaftsarchitekten und Fachleuten der Region hilfreich. Sie leisten mit ihrem Know-how und ihrer Kreativität wichtige Beiträge zur Problem- und ggf. auch Konfliktbewältigung bei den Managementaufgaben (siehe auch III. Kooperationspartner).

### Die Politik und die Verwaltungen in den Bezirken

Wegen ihrer vielfältigen kommunalen Zuständigkeiten und der sich daraus ergebenden besonderen Ort- und Problemnähe sind die politischen Akteure und die Verwaltungen in den Bezirken, in denen die Siedlungen liegen, wichtige Partner im Rahmen des Managements. Von ihnen wird erwartet, dass sie den Siedlungen eine über die geschäftsmäßig übliche hinausgehende Aufmerksamkeit und Fürsorge widmen. Dies schließt eine finanzielle Priorität-

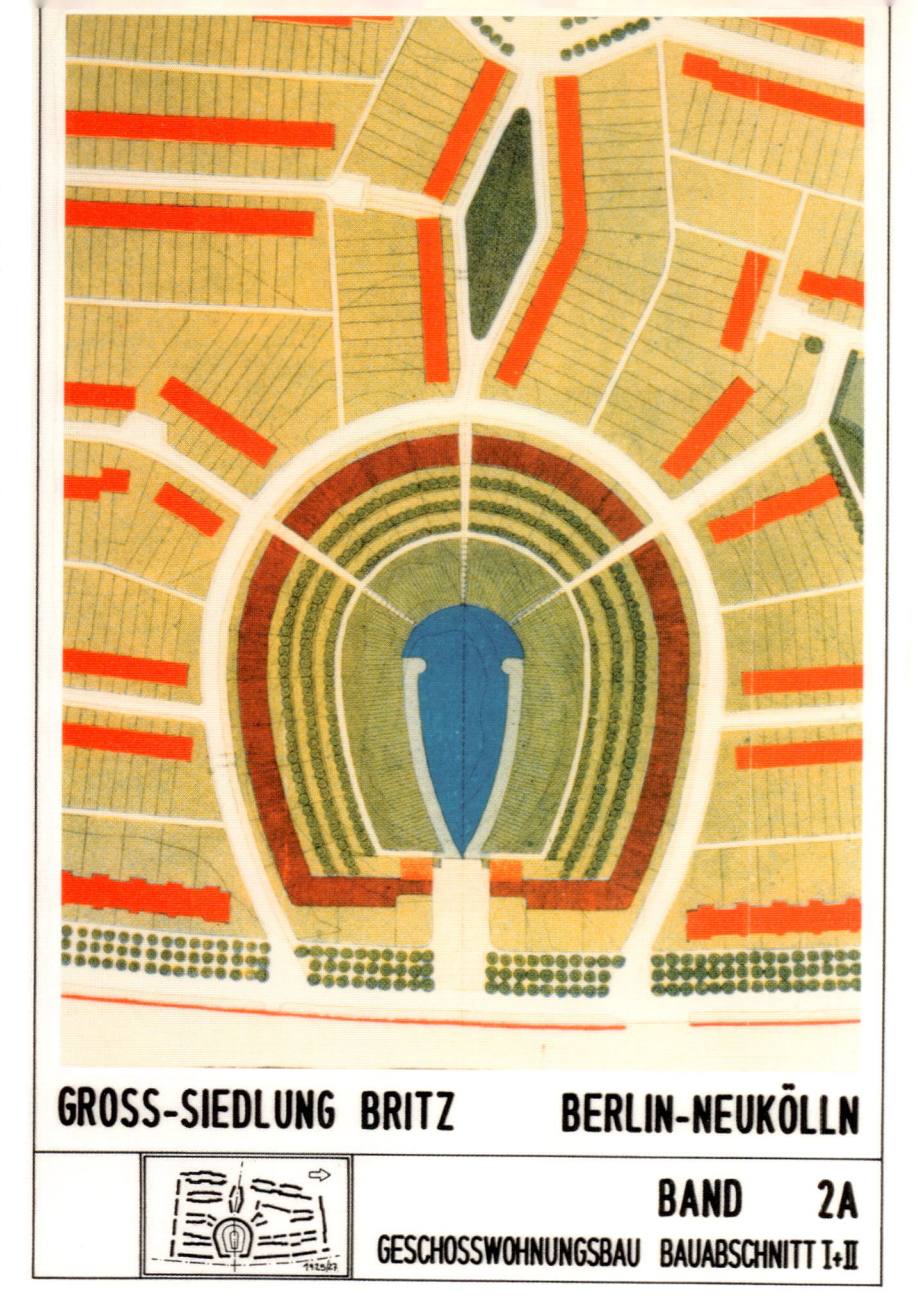

### External competence centres and experts

The preservation of the monuments makes it necessary to involve experts. For the investigation of the existing monuments, analyses for restoration purposes, generation of monument preservation plans, and restoration and reconstruction activities, we need the special competence of experts in conservation and restoration research and development facilities as well as that of architects, landscape architects and regional experts with experience in monument preservation and restoration. With their know-how and creativity, they make important contributions to solving problems or even conflicts that may occasionally arise from the management or in relation with it (see also III. Cooperation partners).

### Politics and administrations in the districts

The political actors and administrations in the districts where the housing estates are located are important partners for the management, since they are responsible for many municipal activities and also since they are close to the locations and thus to any issues that might arise. They are expected to treat the housing estates with more than the usual

tensetzung bei Pflegemaßnahmen und Instandsetzungsinvestitionen im Rahmen der knappen Haushaltslage ein.

Im Ausgleich für eine solch privilegierte Behandlung werden sich die Heimatbezirke der Siedlungen deren wachsender überregionalen Ausstrahlung und Anziehungskraft als einzigartige Kulturerbestätten erfreuen können.

**Kooperationspartner**
Die bewährte Kooperation mit renommierten Einrichtungen der Wissenschaft und Lehre auf dem Gebiet der Denkmalpflege und des Welterbemanagements garantieren ein hohes Problembewusstsein und ein hohes Niveau der Vorbereitung und Durchführung von Maßnahmen.

Berlin verfügt bereits über zwei Welterbestätten, die jeweils von einer leistungsfähigen Kulturstiftung getragen und gemanagt werden. Die Kooperation mit diesen sowie mit anderen nationalen und internationalen Welterbestätten wird eine selbstverständliche Aufgabe beim Management der Siedlungen sein. Dabei bieten sich sowohl regionale Schwerpunktsetzungen an als auch die thematische Konzentration auf Welterbestätten der Moderne.

Sinnvoll ist auch die Zusammenarbeit mit Städten, die bedeutende Siedlungsbestände der Moderne besitzen, wie beispielsweise Frankfurt am Main, Hamburg und Magdeburg in Deutschland oder Amsterdam, Rotterdam, Moskau und Wien in anderen Staaten.

Überregional und regional können Fördermittelgeber und Stiftungen zur finanziellen Unterstützung von Instandsetzungsmaßnahmen in den Siedlungen gewonnen werden.

Die Region Berlin-Brandenburg weist eine besondere Konzentration von Hochschulen auf, die über besondere Kompetenzzentren für die Erforschung des Kulturerbes der Moderne und den fachgerechten Umgang mit diesem verfügen. Hervorgehoben seien das Schinkelzentrum der TU Berlin, das Zentrum für europäische Kulturerbepflege an der Viadrina in Frankfurt/Oder sowie das Zentrum für Welterbemanagement an der BTU Cottbus. Hinzu kommen die Ausbildungsangebote des Aufbaustudienganges Denkmalpflege der TU Berlin sowie der Studiengänge Restaurierung an der FH Potsdam und der FHTW Berlin. Diese und weitere Hochschulen bieten sich als vielversprechende Kooperationspartner für das Management der Siedlungen an.

Berlin verfügt mit dem Bauhaus-Archiv, der Berlinischen Galerie sowie dem Stadtmuseum und den bezirklichen Museen über Kultureinrichtungen, die mit überregionaler, regionaler oder lokaler Wirkung die Geschichte und Bedeutung der Siedlungen der Berliner Moderne sowie ihres kulturellen und sozialpolitischen Umfeldes im Rahmen ihrer Ausstellungstätigkeit präsentieren können. Sie verfügen teilweise über eigene themenbezogene Sammlungsbestände sowie über bewährte Kontakte zu öffentlichen und privaten Sammlungen mit entsprechenden Beständen.

Als internationales Tourismuszentrum sind in Berlin leistungsfähige öffentliche und private Akteure der Tourismuswirtschaft aktiv, die in ihre Marketing- und Vertriebsangebote neben den beiden etablierten Welterbestätten in der

Abb. 103: Großsiedlung Britz, Bestandsgutachten 1989, Titelblatt

Fig. 103: Großsiedlung Britz, expert opinion, 1989, front page

care and attention. This includes the housing estates receiving priority in the allocation of financing for maintenance and refurbishment measures when resources are scarce.

In response to this kind of privileged treatment, the housing estates as a unique cultural heritage will attract attention to the districts where they are located which will reach far beyond the region.

**Cooperation partners**
Thanks to the long-standing cooperation with renowned scientific and educational institutions dealing with monument preservation and world heritage management, all involved parties are well aware of the special needs of the monuments, and any measures are prepared and carried out with excellent quality.

Berlin has already got two world heritage locations, each of which is operated and managed by a powerful cultural foundation. In managing the housing estates, we will of course cooperate with them and with other national and international world heritage locations. This cooperation will be carried out with a focus on both regional priorities and the topic of world heritage locations of the Modern Style.

It will furthermore be useful to cooperate with other cities that possess important housing estates in the Modern Style, such as Frankfurt am Main, Hamburg and Magdeburg in Germany or Amsterdam, Rotterdam, Moscow and Vienna in other countries.

Providers of grants and foundations may be involved as regional or supra-regional financial supporters of restoration measures in the housing estates.

The region of Berlin and Brandenburg has many institutions of higher education that have set up competence centres for research into the world heritage of the Modern Style and into methods and activities for their management. Among these institutions are in particular the Schinkelzentrum (Schinkel Centre) of Berlin Technical University (TU Berlin), the Zentrum für europäische Kulturerbepflege (Centre for the Preservation of Cultural Heritage) at Viadrina in Fankfurt/Oder and the Zentrum für Welterbemanagement (Centre for World Heritage Management) at BTU Cottbus. In addition to the above, the TU Berlin offers a post-graduate course in monument preservation and the FH (college) Potsdam and FHTW (Fachhochschule für Technik und Wirtschaft – College for Technology and Economics) Berlin offer restoration studies. These and other institutions of higher education offer themselves as promising partners for managing the housing estates.

Berlin has the Bauhaus-Archiv, the Berlinische Galerie and the Stadtmuseum as well as the various district museums. These are cultural able to present the history and significance of the housing estates of the Berlin Modern Style and their cultural and socio-political context in their exhibitions, and they enjoy local, regional and national attention. To an extent, they have their own collections related to the housing estates and they have long-standing contacts with public and private collectors with related inventories.

Stadtregion zukünftig auch die Siedlungen der Moderne sowie bedeutende Nachfolgeprojekte wie die Bauausstellungen von 1957 und 1987 einbeziehen können.

Die Siedlungen sind über den öffentlichen Nahverkehr gut erreichbar und liegen teilweise unmittelbar oder nahe an U- oder S-Bahnhöfen. Mit den Nahverkehrsbetrieben können deshalb vor Ort und in deren vielfältigen Informationsangeboten Hinweise auf die Siedlungen gegeben werden.

Neben dem Landesdenkmalrat gibt es auch in der Architekten- und der Ingenieurskammer Berlin engagierte Denkmalausschüsse, die als Fachgremien beratend und unterstützend in das Management der Siedlungen einbezogen werden können.

### IV. Instrumente und Handlungsfelder

Für einen nachhaltigen Schutz des Denkmalbestandes und für die Pflege der Siedlungsbauten stehen eine Fülle von Rechts-, Planungs- und Überwachungsinstrumenten zur Verfügung. Ergänzend sind Informationsangebote und Kooperationsprojekte mit vielfältigen Akteuren unverzichtbar für ein angemessenes Management der Siedlungen. Besonders dringlich ist ein Tourismuskonzept zu erarbeiten und umzusetzen.

### Rechts- und Planungsgrundlagen

Die Ziele des Managementplanes können auf der rechtlichen Basis des Baugesetzbuches, des Berliner Denkmalschutzgesetzes und der Berliner Bauordnung umgesetzt werden (siehe Ziffer 5.B bis 5.D). Für die unter Denkmalschutz stehenden Siedlungen gelten die Bestimmungen des Denkmalschutzgesetzes von Berlin (siehe unter Ziffer 5.C). Bauliche Veränderung bedürfen daher der denkmalrechtlichen Erlaubnis. Dieses betrifft auch die Gestaltung von Werbeanlagen. Größere bauliche Veränderungen und Nutzungsänderungen bedürfen darüber hinaus einer Baugenehmigung. Verstöße gegen die Bestimmungen des Denkmalschutzgesetzes können als Ordnungswidrigkeiten mit hohen Geldbußen geahndet werden. Um den Verfall von Teilen des Denkmalbestandes zu verhindern, bestehen darüber hinaus die denkmalrechtlichen Instrumente des Instandsetzungsgebotes, der Ersatzvornahme sowie des Wiederherstellungsgebotes.

Darüber hinaus bestehen für fast alle Siedlungen Bauleitpläne in Form des Baunutzungsplanes und von Bebauungsplänen oder zumindest des Flächennutzungsplanes, die das Wohnen als vorrangige Nutzung sichern. Für die Wohnstadt Carl Legien besteht kein Bebauungsplan. Sie liegt aber im Geltungsbereich eines nach § 172 Baugesetzbuch (BauGB) förmlich festgelegten Erhaltungsgebietes mit einer Erhaltungsverordnung (siehe unter Ziffer 5.D). Die Erhaltungssatzung schützt neben der Gestalt der Carl Legien Siedlung und ihres Umfeldes auch die soziale Struktur der Bewohnerschaft. Investitionen werden deshalb auch auf ihre mietsteigernde Wirkung geprüft und können ggf. reguliert werden, um Verdrängung von Mietern vorzubeugen.

### Finanzierung

Zur Realisierung der Ziele des Managementplanes sind hinreichende finanzielle Ressourcen notwendig. Für die Bauunterhaltung und Erneuerung aller sechs Siedlungen sind

Since Berlin is a centre of international tourism, its tourism industry has powerful public and private actors that can integrate the housing estates of the Modern Style and also significant follow-up projects like the Bauausstellung (Architecture Exhibition) of 1957 and 1987 into their future marketing and sales activities.

The housing estates can be easily reached by public means of transport, and some of them are located directly at or near underground or commuter train stations. Thus, the public transport companies can also refer to the housing estates at the respective locations and in their many different forms of information.

In addition to the Landesdenkmalrat, the Chamber of Architects and Engineers of Berlin also has very dedicated committees that may support the management of the housing estates and provide counselling.

### IV. Instruments and fields of action

A considerable number of legal, planning and monitoring instruments are available for providing sustainable protection of the monuments and preservation of housing estates. Supplementary offers of information and cooperation projects with many actors must complement the above to ensure the proper management of the housing estates. The most urgent task is to develop and implement a concept for tourism.

### Legal and planning bases

The legal basis for implementing the objectives of the management plan is the Baugesetzbuch (Building Code), the Berlin Law on the Preservation of Historic Places and Monuments and the Berlin Bauordnung (building regulations) (see 5.B through 5.D). For the housing estates that are protected as monuments, the stipulations of the Berlin Law on the Preservation of Historic Places and Monuments apply (see 5.C). This means that any constructional alterations require the consent of the monument preservation authorities. This also applies to the design of advertising facilities. Major constructional alterations and changes of use require a building permit. The authorities may impose large fines in case of violation of the regulations of the Law on the Preservation of Historic Places and Monuments. Other monument protection instruments prevent parts of the monuments from falling into a state of decay. They require monuments to be preserved, provide that the authorities may take actions for having them preserved in case this is not done by the owners and stipulate that unauthorized alterations must be reversed.

Furthermore, nearly all of the housing estates are covered by master plans established in the form of plans indicating the kind and degree of land use by buildings or development plans or at least as land-use plans which assure that they are primarily used for residential purposes. Wohnstadt Carl Legien is not covered by a master plan. However, it is part of a formally established preservation area according to Section 172 of the Building Code (BauGB) with a preservation regulation (see 5.D). The preservation regulation protects not only the appearance of the Carl Legien housing estate and of its environment but also the social structure of the inhabitants. This means that investments may be reviewed for their impact on the rents (increase)

nach dem Denkmalschutzgesetz Berlin die jeweiligen Eigentümer (vgl. Ziffer 5.A) im Rahmen ihrer wirtschaftlichen Leistungsfähigkeit zuständig. Sie bringen die erforderlichen Finanzmittel, wie bereits dargestellt, größtenteils aus Mieteinnahmen oder bei Selbstnutzung aus Eigenmitteln im Rahmen ihrer laufenden Bewirtschaftung auf. Außerdem haben Eigentümer die Möglichkeit, Aufwendungen für Maßnahmen zur Erhaltung oder zur sinnvollen Nutzung der Baudenkmale entsprechend der Einkommensteuergesetzgebung abzuschreiben.

Das Land Berlin beabsichtigt weiterhin im Rahmen dafür vorgesehener Haushaltsansätze, Fördermittel für denkmalpflegerische Mehraufwendungen oder für andere Vorhaben, die der Erhaltung und Bekanntmachung der Siedlungen dienen, bereit zu stellen. Fördermittel können auch aus dem Bundesprogramm „National wertvolles Kulturerbe" sowie bei der Deutschen Stiftung Denkmalschutz und weiteren Stiftungen beantragt werden.

**Denkmalpflegepläne und andere Fachgutachten**
Denkmalpflegepläne und Fachgutachten zur systematischen Erfassung der ursprünglichen Gestalt der Häuser und der Freiflächen dienen als fachliche Grundlage für Pflegemaßnahmen sowie für Instandsetzungs- und Restaurierungsvorhaben und sonstige Baumaßnahmen. Als Bestandteil des Managementplanes sind vor allem die Bestandserfassungen laufend fortzuschreiben (siehe Ziffer 7.C).

Mithilfe dieser Gutachten erfolgte bereits in vielen Siedlungsteilen eine denkmalgerechte Erneuerung der Fassaden, Dächer und Treppenhäuser. Im Einzelnen beziehen sich die Gutachten mit Material- und Farbangaben sowie Bestandszeichnungen auf folgende Elemente des Baubestandes:

- Oberflächenstruktur
- Fenster und Haustüren
- Treppenhäuser und Außentreppen
- Balkone und Loggien
- Dachausbildungen
- Terrassen
- Ställe und Müllhäuser
- Läden
- Wege und Plätze mit den Gartenanlagen
- Grundrisse

Zusätzlich bestehen Denkmalpflegepläne, die die Freiflächen und den Vegetationsbestand zum Inhalt haben. Zur Pflege und Wiederherstellung der Siedlungsgärten und Grünflächen sind für alle sechs Siedlungen Pflegekonzepte und Maßnahmenpläne aufgestellt worden, bezogen auf die Gestaltungselemente:

- Grundrissfigur der Anlagen
- Wege und Plätze
- Vorgärten, Mietergärten, Terrassen
- Raumeinheiten wie Spiel-, Sitz- und Müllplätze
- Materialien für Wege und Plätze
- Ausstattungen
- Vegetationsstrukturen und Baumbestände

Für den Reihenhausbestand des ersten und zweiten Bauabschnittes der Hufeisensiedlung existiert ein Leitfaden, der es dem Bezirksamt Neukölln erleichtert, auf den Ver-

and they may be regulated for preventing tenants from being driven out by rent increases.

**Financing**
The management plan can only be implemented if enough financing is available. According to the Berlin Law on the Preservation of Historic Places and Monuments, the owners of the six housing estates are responsible within the scope of their financial strength for preserving and renewing the monuments (see 5.A). They acquire most of the necessary financing within the framework of ongoing operation through the rents or from their own incomes if they use the monuments themselves. Furthermore, the owners may write off expenses for preserving or reasonably using the monuments of architecture in line with income tax regulations.

The State of Berlin intends to continue providing grants to cover expenses that go beyond the ordinary maintenance expenses because they are spent on monument preservation or for other projects that serve the preservation of the housing estates or make them better known. These provisions will be made within the state budget. More grants may also be requested via application from the federal programme of "National wertvolle Kulturdenkmäler" (Valuable National Cultural Monuments) and other foundations.

**Monument preservation plans and other expert opinions**
Monument preservation plans and expert opinions which provide systematic inventories of the appearance of the buildings and of the outdoor facilities provide the qualified basis for preservation measures and repair and restoration measures as well as other construction work. The inventories form a main part of the management plan and they must be updated regularly (see 7.C).

These expert opinions have already been the basis for the restoration of the facades, roofs and staircases in many parts of the housing estates. The expert opinions contain in particular information on the materials and colours as well as drawings of the following elements of the existing buildings:

- Surface structures
- Windows and entrance doors
- Stair cases and outdoor stairs
- Balconies and loggias
- Roof structures
- Terraces
- Stables and waste bin sheds
- Shops
- Paths and squares with greenery/gardens
- Floor plans

Other monument preservation plans cover the outdoor facilities and the vegetation. For all six housing estates, care concepts and actions plans have been established for assuring proper care and reconstruction of the gardens and green spaces. These concepts and plans refer to the following design elements:

- Ground plan of the outdoor facilities
- Paths and squares

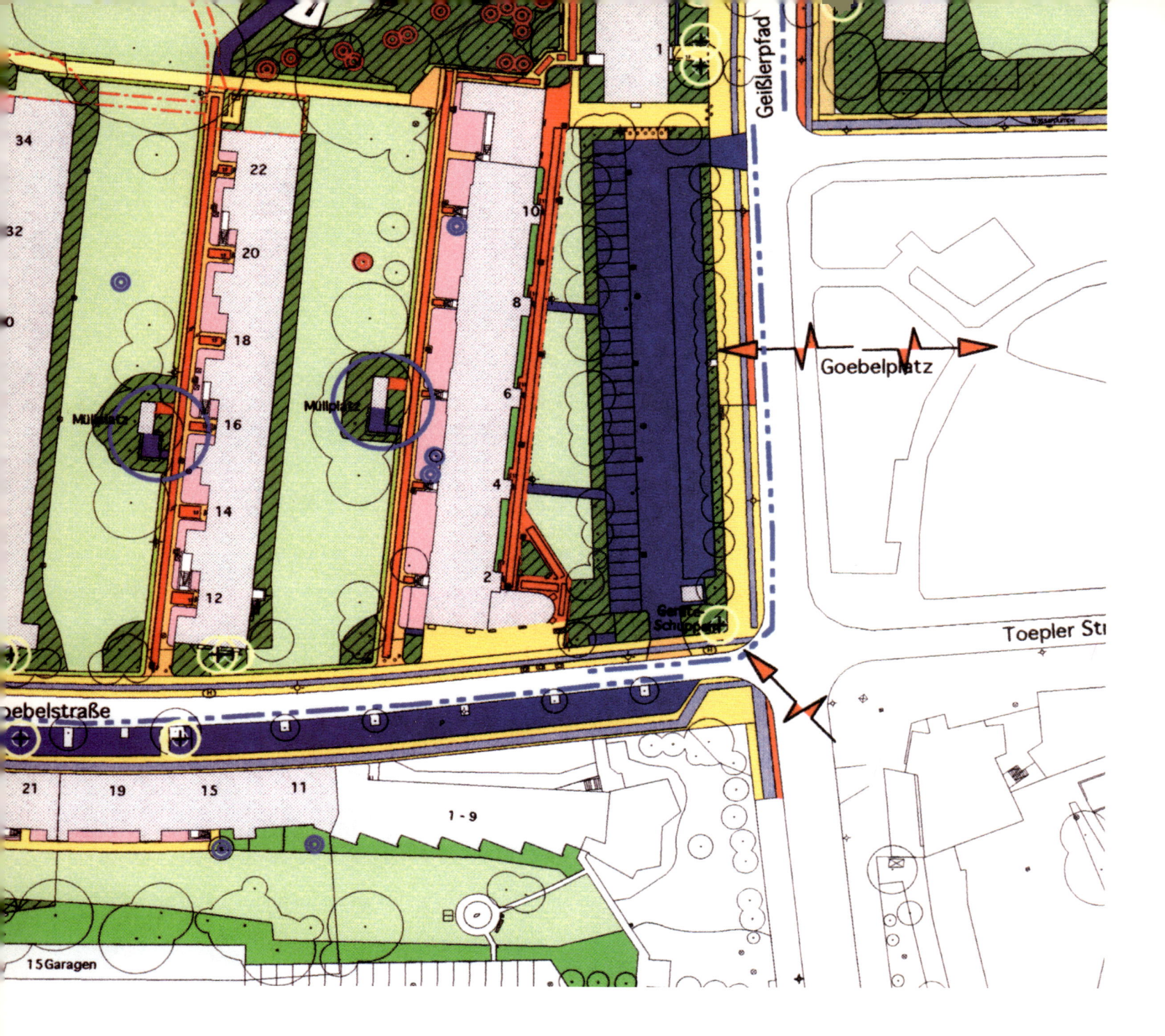

änderungsdruck zu reagieren, der sich aus der Reihenhausprivatisierung ergibt. Ein Denkmalpflegeplan, der auf bestehende Bestandsdokumentationen zur Siedlung basiert, ist in Arbeit.

**Öffentlichkeitsarbeit**
Vorgesehen sind bisher:

Eine umfangreiche Publikation, in der die Welterbe-Siedlungen mit dem dazugehörigen Antrag zur Aufnahme in die Welterbeliste vorgestellt werden

Broschüren zur Geschichte und Bedeutung der einzelnen Siedlung, zu ihrem Erhaltungszustand sowie zu Maßnahmen der Erneuerung

Faltblätter mit Hinweisen zum Umgang mit dem Denkmal, die den Einzeleigentümern ausgehändigt werden.

Front gardens, tenants' gardens, terraces
Special facilities like playgrounds, resting places and waste bin areas
Materials used for paving the paths and squares
Equipment
Vegetation structures and trees

The row houses of the first and second development phase of the horseshoe housing estate are covered by guidelines that make it easier for the district administration of Neukölln to respond to the pressure for alteration resulting from the privatisation of the houses. A monument preservation plan based upon available documentation of the existing state of the housing estate is currently being established.

Sie geben Auskunft über den Schutzcharakter und denkmalrechtliche Verpflichtungen

Ausstellungen sowie andere Aktivitäten zur Vermittlung der Bedeutung des Welterbes in Zusammenarbeit mit Berliner Institutionen, wie im Zusammenhang mit den Kooperationspartnern dargestellt

Medieninformationen einschließlich einer verstärkten Präsentation im Internet

Die Aufstellung von Informationstafeln in den Siedlungen

Bürgerversammlungen und Vorträge

Tage der Offenen Tür, wie der jährlich stattfindende „Tag des offenen Denkmals" (European Heritage Day)

**Tourismuskonzept**
Mit Fördermitteln für die Tourismusentwicklung sollte ein touristisches Vermarktungs- und Vertriebskonzept entwickelt werden, dass die üblichen Angebote von der Internet- und Messepräsentation bis hin zur Wegweisung, aber auch Übernachtungs-, Rundfahrt oder Führungsangebote umfasst. Mit Unterstützung der Senatsverwaltung für Wirtschaft und ihrer Tourismuspartner ist die Federführung bei der Erarbeitung sowie die Aufgabenverteilung bei der Umsetzung zu klären.

Es ist zu erwarten, dass viele der o. g. Kooperationspartner in die Erarbeitung und Umsetzung des Tourismuskonzepts einbezogen werden können. Besonders hilfreich dürfte auch die Mitarbeit in den schon bestehenden Vermarktungsaktivitäten des Vereins UNESCO-Welterbestätten Deutschland e.V. sein.

Langfristiges Ziel sollte eine touristische Themenroute zu den bedeutenden Stätten der Moderne sein, wie sie mit EU-Fördermitteln bereits als „Straße der Backsteingotik" aufgebaut wurde und gerade für die historischen Festungsanlagen im Ostseeraum aufgebaut wird.

**V. Kontrolle und Überwachung (Monitoring)**
Es ist erforderlich, über ein Instrumentarium zur Überwachung des Erhaltungszustandes und der Erneuerung zu verfügen, das die Einhaltung denkmalpflegerischer Grundsätze und Kriterien sowie die damit verbundenen qualitativen Veränderungen dokumentiert und bewertet. Dazu werden vorrangig laufend verfügbare Informationen zusammengetragen und ggf. ergänzende Erkenntnisse durch Begutachtung oder Begehung gewonnen. Ziel ist es, hohe Aussagekraft der Daten und Bewertungen mit möglichst geringem Erhebungsaufwand für alle Beteiligten zu verbinden.

In diese regelmäßig stattfindenden Datenerhebungen sind naturgemäß die Eigentümer der Siedlungen eingebunden, im Einzelfall auch Architekten, Landschaftsarchitekten und Sonderfachleute. Gegenstand der Kontrollen bilden die unter der Ziffer 6.A genannten Schlüsselindikatoren und die mit ihnen verbundenen Abfrageprotokolle. Zudem werden die auf der Basis von Bestandsuntersuchungen genehmigten Veränderungen dokumentiert, so dass diese Dokumentationen beim Monitoring zur Verfügung stehen.

Abb. 104: Großsiedlung Siemensstadt, Plan: Gartendenkmalpflegerische Zielplanung, Teil des Parkpflegewerks von 2003

Fig. 104: Großsiedlung Siemensstadt, plan: plan for preservation of historic garden, part of the park maintenance plan of 2003

**Public relations activities**
Planned activities to date:

A comprehensive publication presenting the world heritage housing estates together with the application for inscription into the world heritage list

Brochures on the history and significance of the individual housing estates, their state of conservation and measures for their renewal

Leaflets for the individual private owners with information on how to treat the monument; these leaflets will provide information on the character of protection and the obligations for preserving the monuments

Exhibitions and other activities to demonstrate the importance of the world heritage (in cooperation with Berlin institutions as shown in the chapter on cooperation partners)

Media information inclusive of more extensive presentation on the Internet

Setting up of information tables in the housing estates

Citizens' meetings and lectures

Public presentation days like the annual "Tag des offenen Denkmals" (European Heritage Day)

**Tourism concept**
Grants for developing tourism are to be used for creating a tourism marketing and sales concept which covers the usual offers, ranging from presentations on the Internet and at fairs, to setting up sign posts, to offers for overnight stays, round trips through the locations and guided tours. We will cooperate with the ministry of economics and its partners in the tourism industry to decide who will be responsible for coordinating the creation of the concept and its implementation.

We expect that many of the above mentioned cooperation partners can be involved in creating and implementing the tourism concept. Our cooperation in the existing marketing activities of the association UNESCO-Welterbestätten Deutschland e.V. (UNESCO World Heritage Locations Germany) will certainly be very useful in this respect.

The long-term objective of this activity should be to set up a tourism route around the important locations of the Modern Style as it has been already created with EU financial support under the title of "Backstein Gothic route" which is currently being extended to cover also the historic fortresses in the Baltic Sea region.

**V. Control and reporting (monitoring)**
Monitoring the state of conservation and the renewal of the monuments requires a set of instruments which document and assess the adherence to the principles and criteria of monument protection and preservation and the qualitative changes resulting from any renewal activities. To achieve this purpose, the relevant persons collect available information on an ongoing basis and they may acquire additional

5.F **Quellen und Umfang der Finanzierung**

Die Bauunterhaltung und Erneuerung aller sechs Siedlungen ist Aufgabe der Eigentümer (vgl. Ziffer 5.A), die in der Regel hierfür die Finanzmittel zur Verfügung stellen. Durch die Mieteinnahmen ist die Refinanzierung der laufenden Bauunterhaltung gesichert.

Aus dem Denkmalschutzgesetz von Berlin (DSchG Bln) vom 24. April 1995 ergibt sich eine Verpflichtung des Eigentümers, „ein Denkmal im Rahmen des Zumutbaren instand zu halten und instand zu setzen" (§ 8 Abs. 1). Im Einzelfall können Fördermittel des Landes Berlin für denkmalpflegerische Mehraufwendungen in Anspruch genommen werden. Außerdem haben die Eigentümer der nominierten Siedlungen die Möglichkeit, nach der bestehenden Einkommensteuergesetzgebung ihre Aufwendungen für Maßnahmen zur Erhaltung oder sinnvollen Nutzung der Baudenkmale vom zu versteuernden Einkommen über mehrere Jahre hinweg erhöht abzusetzen.

In der Vergangenheit konnten beim Pilotprojekt der Sanierung der Häuser der Wohnstadt Carl Legien 1994 auch Zuwendungen der Deutschen Stiftung Denkmalschutz eingesetzt werden.

Für die Unterhaltung der öffentlichen Straßen, Wege und Freiflächen werden im Rahmen des laufenden Landeshaushaltes Mittel bereitgestellt.

knowledge by means of tours through and inspections of the monuments. The purpose of the system is to acquire high quality data and assessments with as little effort and expense as possible for all parties involved.

The owners of the housing estates are of course involved in the regular activities for acquiring data, and architects, landscape architects and other experts also occasionally participate. The activities focus on acquiring information on the key indicators mentioned in 6.A and on using the questionnaires related to the key indicators. Additionally, the alterations that are approved on the basis of investigations into the existing monuments will also be documented, such that these documentations are available for the monitoring.

5.F **Sources and scope of financing**

The owners are responsible for maintaining and renewing all six housing estates (see Item 5.A) and usually they also provide the necessary financing for these purposes. Refinancing of the expenses for current maintenance is assured by the rental revenues.

The Berlin Law on the Preservation of Historic Places and Monuments (DSchG Bln) of 24th April 1995 stipulates that owners are obliged "to take reasonable measures for preserving and repairing monuments" (Section 8, Paragraph 1). In individual cases, owners may claim grants by the federal state of Berlin for covering additional expenses resulting from the obligation to preserve and restore monuments. Furthermore, the current income tax law provides that expenses for the reasonable preservation or reasonable use of architectural monuments may be used for several years for deductions from taxable income at a rate that is above the usual deductions, thus creating a tax privilege for the owners of the nominated housing estates.

Abb. 105: Orientierungstafeln in der Großsiedlung Siemensstadt, 2005

Fig. 105: Orientation boards in the Großsiedlung Siemensstadt, 2005

Abb. 106: Orientierungstafel in der Großsiedlung Siemensstadt, 2005

Fig. 106: Orientation board in the Großsiedlung Siemensstadt, 2005

## 5.G Fachwissen und Schulung bezüglich Denkmalpflege und Verwaltung

Für die Erhaltung und Unterhaltung der Siedlungen ist gewährleistet, dass die Betreuung des Denkmalbestandes durch das wissenschaftliche Fachpersonal in den Berliner Denkmalbehörden erfolgt. Die Mitarbeiter sind ausgebildete Kunsthistoriker, Architekten, Landschaftsarchitekten oder Restauratoren.

Auch die Mitglieder des Landesdenkmalrates, der als verwaltungsexternes Fachgremium gemäß § 7 des Denkmalschutzgesetzes von Berlin das für den Denkmalschutz zuständige Mitglied des Senats von Berlin berät, unterstützt mit seiner Erfahrung bei Denkmalschutzfragen oder konkreten Planungen die Denkmalpflege und gibt Empfehlungen ab.

Darüber hinaus verfügen die Eigentümergesellschaften über erfahrene Mitarbeiter, in der Regel Architekten und Bauingenieure, für laufende Instandsetzungs- und Unterhaltungsmaßnahmen.

Planungen für Grundinstandsetzungen und zum Teil auch deren Überwachung werden an denkmalerfahrene Architektenbüros vergeben. Denkmalerfahrene Architekten, Landschaftsarchitekten, Restauratoren und Fachingenieure sind in Berlin ausreichend vorhanden. Auf diesem Sektor forschen und lehren in Berlin mehrere universitäre Einrichtungen und Fachhochschulen. Ebenso sind geeignete bauausführende Fach- und Handwerksfirmen in Berlin und im Brandenburger Umland ausreichend verfügbar.

## 5.H Besuchereinrichtungen und -statistik

Die Siedlungen können im öffentlich zugänglichen Bereich jederzeit besichtigt werden. Die Besichtigungen werden überwiegend individuell vorgenommen, Statistiken werden hierüber nicht geführt. Am „Tag des offenen Denkmals" werden jährlich von Fachpersonal stark nachgefragte Führungen durch die Siedlungen veranstaltet. Auf Anfrage bei den Eigentümern und den Denkmalbehörden sind auch Führungen darüber hinaus möglich.

In der Großsiedlung Siemensstadt sind auf den öffentlichen Wegen von der Wohnungsbaugesellschaft 2003 Orientierungstafeln aufgestellt worden, die auf die Baugeschichte und Bedeutung der Ringsiedlung und ihrer einzelnen Bauteile hinweisen. Darüber hinaus ist geplant, zu jeder Siedlung Informationsmaterial herauszugeben, das über Geschichte, Architektur und Städtebau, Gartenkunst sowie über die Denkmalbedeutung und Erneuerungsmaßnahmen Auskunft gibt. Zudem ist vorgesehen, Informationen über die Berliner Welterbestätten im Internet anzubieten.

In den Siedlungen der GSW (Weiße Stadt und Großsiedlung Siemensstadt) gibt es Gästewohnungen, die von auswärtigen Besuchern angemietet werden können. Es wird angestrebt, für alle Siedlungen ein vernetztes System solcher Wohnungen für Fachtouristen und interessierte Laien zu entwickeln. So sind bereits in der Wohnstadt Carl Legien zwei Wohnungen mit der Tautschen Originalfarbigkeit rekonstruiert worden, die besichtigt werden können.

Abb. 107: Informationsbroschüre der GEHAG für die Eigentümer der Reihenhäuser in der Großsiedlung Britz, um 2003

Fig. 107: Information brochure issued by GEHAG for the owners of the row houses in the Großsiedlung Britz, approximately 2003

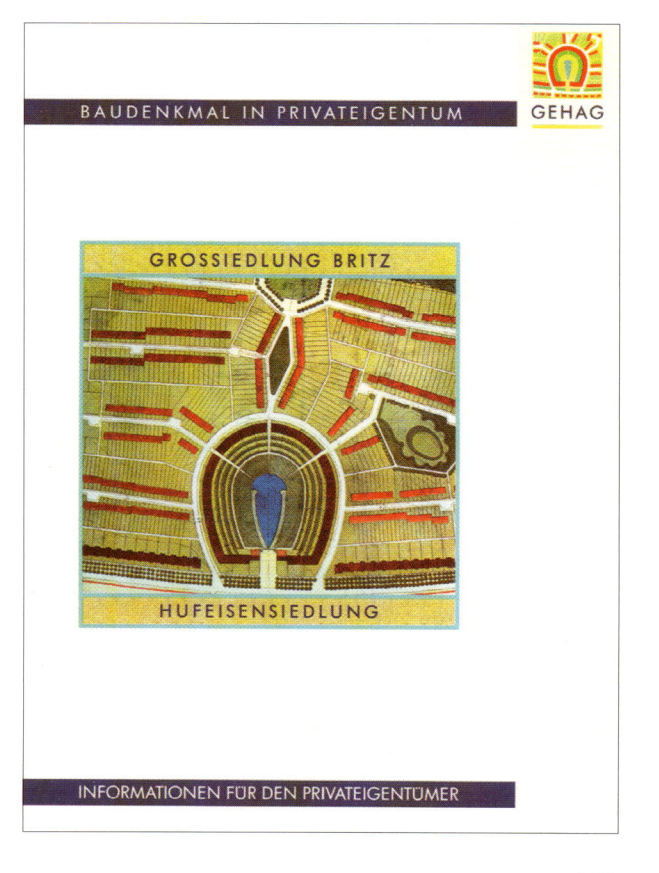

The pilot project of restoring the houses of Wohnstadt Carl Legien in 1994 was further supported by grants provided by Deutsche Stiftung Denkmalschutz (German Foundation for Preservation of Monuments).

Finance for the maintenance of public roads, paths and outdoor facilities is provided by the current state budget.

## 5.G Sources of expertise and training in conservation and management techniques

The preservation and maintenance of the housing estates is supported by the scientific staff of the Berlin monument preservation authorities. The relevant employees are trained art historians, architects, landscape architects or restorers.

With their experience, the members of the State Monument Council give recommendations or support the involved parties in case specific plans are being produced. The State Monument Council (Landesdenkmalrat) is an expert body which is separate from the administration and according to Section 7 of the Berlin Law on the Preservation of Historic Places and Monuments it acts as a consultant for that member of the Berlin government who is responsible for the preservation of monuments.

Moreover, the owners also have experienced employees for current repair and maintenance measures. Most of these are architects and civil engineers.

When thorough refurbishment works have to be planned or supervised, the relevant contracts are often awarded to architectural agencies having experience in the preservation of monuments. Berlin has a sufficient number of archi-

Auch in der Siedlung Schillerpark ist geplant, eine derartig wiederhergestellte Wohnung der Öffentlichkeit zugänglich zu machen.

Weitergehende Einrichtungen zur Besucherbetreuung existieren bisher nicht.

### 5.1 Grundlagen und Programme für die Öffentlichkeitsarbeit

Seit der Wiederentdeckung der architektonischen und städtebaulichen Qualitäten der Berliner Siedlungen aus der Weimarer Zeit gegen Ende der 1970er Jahre sind die nominierten Siedlungen über Ausstellungen und Publikationen einer breiteren Öffentlichkeit bekannt gemacht worden. Bis in die jüngste Zeit haben neben den Fachverwaltungen des Senats von Berlin auch die Eigentümergesellschaften Broschüren zur Bau- und Kulturgeschichte ihrer Wohnanlagen sowie zum Thema Denkmalschutz herausgebracht. Als letztes erschien 2004 eine Broschüre der Berliner Bau- und Wohnungsgenossenschaft von 1892 eG mit dem Titel: „Genossenschaftliche Wohnanlagen von Messel und Taut".

Vonseiten der Denkmalbehörden sind Beratungseinrichtungen vorgesehen, um die Denkmaleigentümer in Fragen der Bauunterhaltung und des Denkmalstatus zu beraten und denkmalunverträgliche Eingriffe zu vermeiden.

Wichtiges Mittel, die sechs Siedlungen der Bevölkerung zu präsentieren, ist der jährlich stattfindende und vom Landesdenkmalamt Berlin organisierte „Tag des offenen Denkmals" unter der Beteiligung der Berliner Denkmalbehörden, an dem fachkundige Betreuer Interessierte durch die Siedlungen führen. Es ist geplant, zu jeder Siedlung Materialien für Bewohner, Eigentümer und Interessierte als Begleitinformation zu diesem Antrag herauszugeben. Außerdem soll der Antrag in einer Publikation vorgestellt werden. Beide Vorhaben werden dazu beitragen, den Bekanntheitsgrad der sechs Siedlungen zu erhöhen und ihre Wertschätzung zu vertiefen.

Es ist beabsichtigt, die Siedlungen auch über die Berliner Tourismuswerbung bundesweit und international bekannt zu machen und hierfür ein Marketingkonzept zu entwickeln. Als eine erste Maßnahme sind in der Großsiedlung Siemensstadt, jeweils bei den verschiedenen Bauteilen der beteiligten Architekten, Hinweistafeln aufgestellt worden, die Auskunft über Bau- und Entwicklungsgeschichte geben. Es ist auch geplant, die Siedlungen in das im Aufbau befindliche touristische Leitsystem Berlins einzubinden und über Medieninformationen, einschließlich einer verstärkten Informationsvermittlung im Internet, einen breiten Kreis von Interessierten anzusprechen.

### 5.J Vorhandenes Personal

Bei den Unteren Denkmalschutzbehörden und dem Landesdenkmalamt stehen diplomierte, zum Teil promovierte Absolventen der Fachrichtungen „Architektur", „Garten- und Landschaftsarchitektur", „Kunstgeschichte und Bauingenieurswesen" zur Verfügung, die im Rahmen der Geschäftsverteilung selbstständig Entscheidungen treffen und tects, landscape architects, restorers and engineers who have such experience. Several university departments and technical colleges are engaged in research and training in this field. Berlin and the surrounding state of Brandenburg have a sufficient number of suitable companies for executing the measures.

### 5.H Visitor facilities and statistics

The publicly accessible parts of the housing estates may be visited any time. Visits are usually made on an individual basis. There are no statistics on the visits. Each year on "European Heritage Day," when monuments are open to the public, experts conduct guided tours through the estates. These tours always meet an enormous demand. Additional tours may be done on the basis of applications which have to be submitted to the owners and the monument preservation authorities.

Within the Großsiedlung Siemensstadt, its owner, the housing company, set up information boards along the public pedestrian paths in 2003. These boards provide information on the history and significance of the Ringsiedlung and its parts. The authorities intend to issue material with information on the history, architecture, urban development and garden architecture for each of the housing estates, as well as on the significance of the monuments and restoration measures. They further intended to offer on the Berlin world heritage locations on the Internet information.

In the housing estates owned by GSW (Weiße Stadt and Siemensstadt), guest apartments exist which may be rented by visitors. The involved parties intend to develop a network of these flats for visiting experts and interested lay people. In Wohnstadt Carl Legien, for instance, two flats have been restored with the original colour scheme by Taut and these flats may be visited. There are plans to make a flat in the housing estate publicly accessible after a corresponding restoration.

No further visitors' facilities exist to date.

### 5.I Policies and programmes related to the presentation and promotion of the property

Since the architectural and urban development qualities of the Berlin housing estates from the period of the Weimar Republic were re-discovered in the late 1970s, the nominated housing estates have been made known to a wider public by means of exhibitions and publications. Until the recent past, both the special purpose authorities of the Berlin government and the owners have published brochures on the building and cultural history of their housing estates as well as on the topic of monument preservation. The most recent publication is a brochure of the Berliner Bau- und Wohnungsgenossenschaft von 1892 eG published in 2004 with the title "Genossenschaftliche Wohnanlagen von Messel und Taut" ("Cooperative Housing Facilities by Messel and Taut").

The monument preservation authorities provide advice for the owners concerning the maintenance and the status of

Abb. 108: Informationsbroschüre der GSW zur Baugeschichte und zu denkmalpflegerischen Maßnahmen in der Weißen Stadt, 1980er Jahre

Fig. 108: Information brochure issued by GSW on building history and monument preservation activities in Weiße Stadt, 1980s

monuments and to prevent actions that might interfere with the monuments.

An important instrument for presenting the six housing estates to the population is the annual "Heritage Day", which is organized by the Berlin State Monument Office in cooperation with the monument authorities. On this day, experts guide interested persons through the housing estates. There are plans to produce material on each of the housing estates for the inhabitants, owners and interested parties as information accompanying this application. There are also plans to present this application in a publication. Both actions will contribute to making the six housing estates better known and win them more appreciation.

The relevant parties also intend to make the housing estates better known everywhere in Germany and abroad by means of Berlin tourism advertisement and to develop a marketing concept for this purpose. The first of these actions was to set up information boards at each of the sections by the various architects in the Großsiedlung Siemensstadt that provide information on their building and development history. Furthermore, there are plans for integrating the housing estates in the tourist guidance system for Berlin that is currently under development and to approach a wide circle of interested parties through various media including more extensive dissemination through the Internet.

### 5.1 Staffing levels

Among the employees of the lower monument preservation authorities and the Landesdenkmalamt are licensed architects, garden and landscape architects, art historians and civil engineers (some with a doctor's degree), who make autonomous decisions and take on responsibilities in accordance with their respective realm of duties. Maintenance must be provided by the relevant owners who are obliged to adhere to the stipulations of the Berlin Law on the Preservation of Historic Places and Monuments.

Verantwortung wahrnehmen. Die Bauunterhaltung obliegt den jeweiligen Eigentümergesellschaften, die dabei die Bestimmungen des Berliner Denkmalschutzgesetzes zu beachten haben.

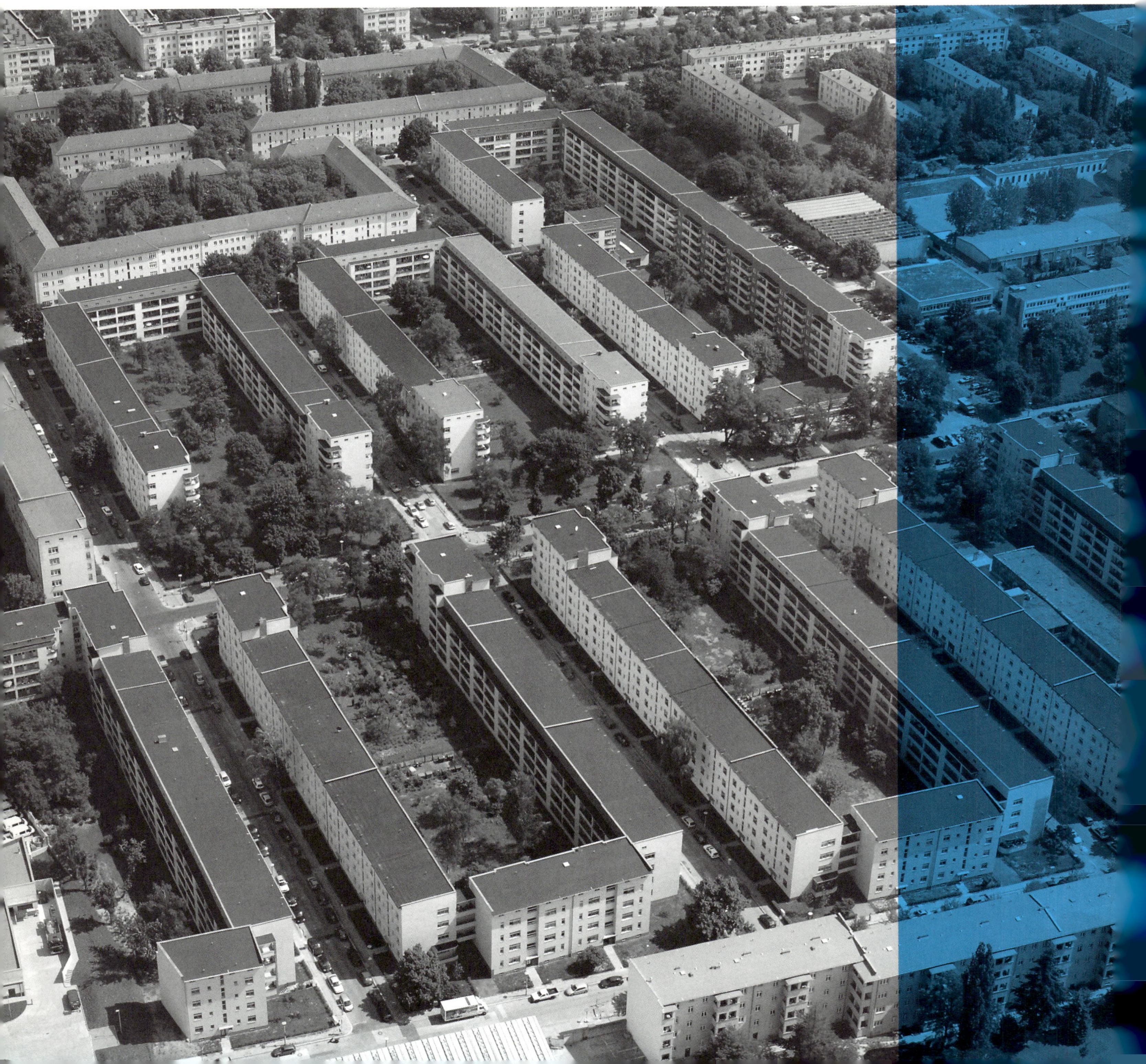

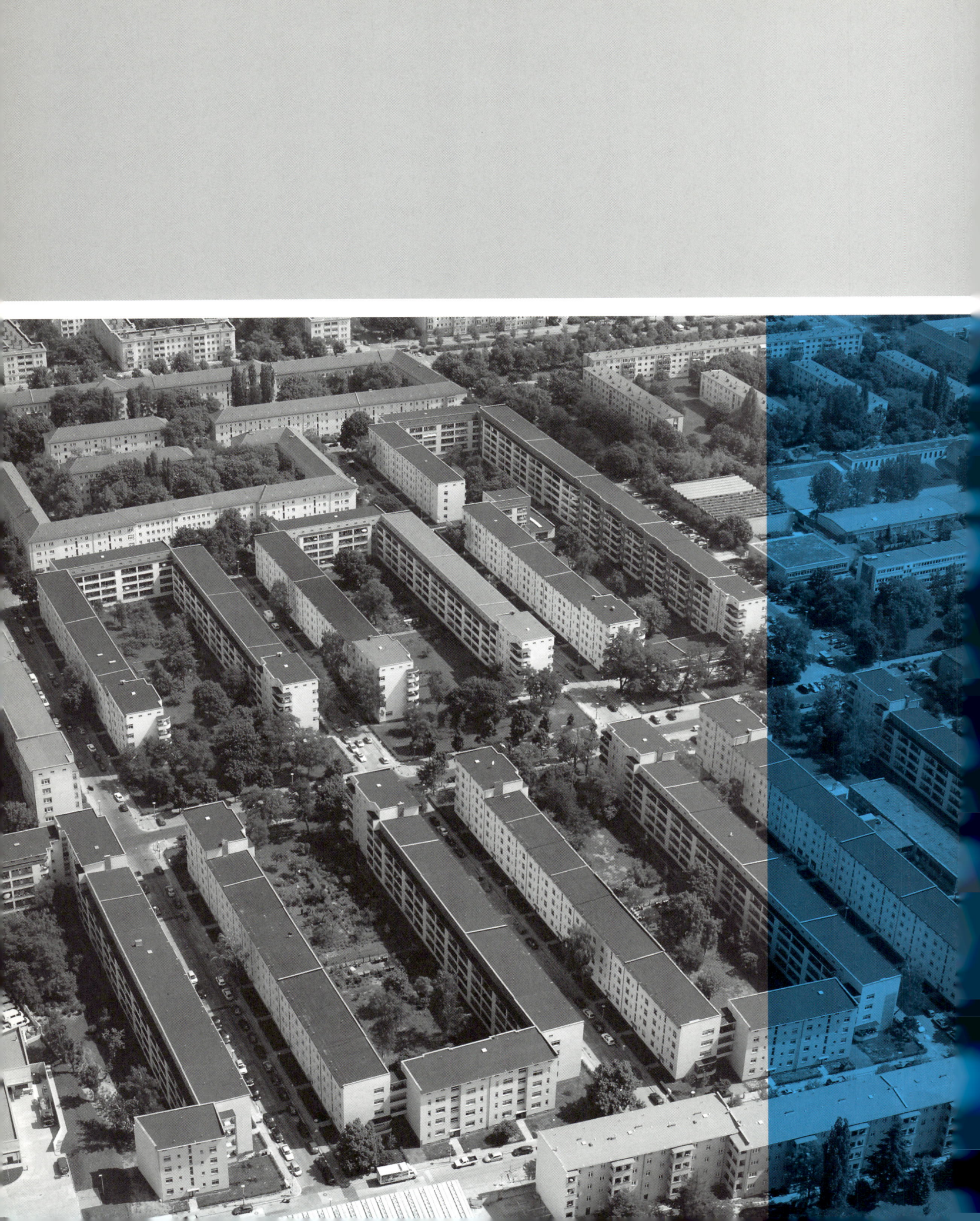

# 6

**ÜBERWACHUNG**
**MONITORING**

## 6. A Schlüsselindikatoren zur Bestimmung des Erhaltungszustandes

Um den Erhalt des Denkmalbestandes sicherzustellen und um zu gewährleisten, dass Bauunterhalt und Erneuerungsmaßnahmen nach denkmalpflegerischen Grundsätzen und Kriterien erfolgen, sind Schlüsselindikatoren zur Überwachung vorgesehen. Bei den turnusmäßig stattfindenden Monitorings wird mit Hilfe von Fragekatalogen, die auf den Schlüsselindikatoren des Managementplanes basieren, der jeweilige Erhaltungszustand dargestellt bzw. werden die dazugehörigen Daten festgehalten.

Die Datenerhebungen für die Schlüsselindikatoren verteilen sich auf verschiedene Behörden und Eigentümergesellschaften, die an den Monitorings beteiligt sind.

Indikatoren, zu denen Erhebungen seitens der Denkmalbehörden erfolgen:

Pflege- und Erhaltungszustand des Denkmalbestandes
Stand der denkmalgerechten Wiederherstellungen
Höhe der Denkmalfördermittel, die zur Erhaltung und zur Wiederherstellung aufgewendet wurden
Denkmalrechtliche Genehmigungen zur Wiederherstellung und Pflege des Denkmalbestandes
Steuerbescheinigungen für denkmalpflegerische Maßnahmen
Verfügbare Personalressourcen für die Betreuung

Indikatoren, zu denen Erhebungen in Zusammenarbeit mit anderen Fachbehörden erfolgen:

Planerische Vorgaben (Änderung der Bauleitpläne)
Infrastruktur (Anzahl und Lage der PKW- Stellplätze, Art der Erschließung, Oberflächenbeschaffenheit der Wege und Straßen)
Belastungen aus dem Verkehr (Straßen- und Luftverkehr)
Sozialstruktur der Bewohner
Mietspiegel und Bodenrichtwerte
Informationsangebote und Besucheraufkommen (Zugriffe auf Websites)

Indikatoren, zu denen Erhebungen in Zusammenarbeit mit den Eigentümergesellschaften erfolgen:

Stand der Umsetzung von Instandsetzungskonzepten
Entwicklung des Pflegezustandes
Finanzielle Aufwendungen zu Instandsetzung, Bauunterhaltung und Pflege
Eigentumsstruktur (Privatisierungen)
Verwaltungsstruktur
Nutzungsstruktur (Leerstand von Wohnungen, Gewerbe- und Versorgungseinrichtungen)

## 6. A Key indicators for measuring state of conservation

Key indicators have been created for assuring that the monuments are preserved and that maintenance and renewal measures apply the principles and criteria for restoration. Regular monitoring actions use questionnaires which have been established on the basis of the key indicators of the management scheme for recording the state of preservation or the relevant data.

The data recordings concerning the key indicators are distributed to the various authorities and owners which are involved in the monitoring activities.

The monument preservation authorities make recordings for the following indicators:

State of preservation and repair of the monuments
State of restoration
Amount of grants paid for preservation and restoration
Approvals for restoring and maintaining the monuments
Tax certificates concerning restoration and monument preservation measures
Personnel available for the preservation of the monuments

Recordings on the following indicators are made in cooperation with other special purpose authorities:

Planning (amendments of the development plans)
Infrastructure (number and location of parking lots, type of servicing, pavings)
Burdens resulting from traffic (road and air traffic)
Social structure of the inhabitants
Average rents and land values
Offered information and number of visitors (access to websites)

Recordings on the following indicators are made in cooperation with the owners:

Status of implementation of restoration concepts
Development of state of preservation
Financial expenses for repair, maintenance and care
Owners (privatisations)
Administrative structure
Utilisation (disused flats, commercial and service facilities)

## 6.B Administrative Regelungen für die Überwachung der Anlagen

Verantwortlich für die turnusmäßige Überwachung der nominierten Siedlungen sind die zuständigen Denkmalbehörden. Sie sollen die regelmäßigen Erhebungen bzw. Berichte über den Denkmalzustand organisieren und durchführen. Neben anderen Fachbehörden werden an den „Monitorings" auch die Eigentümergesellschaften beteiligt.

Grundlage für die „Monitorings" sind die in Abfrageprotokolle aufgenommenen Schlüsselindikatoren (Ziffer 6.A) sowie ggfs. weitere Zustandsermittlungen wie Fotodokumentationen und Planunterlagen. Die Abfrageprotokolle bzw. die ermittelten Daten werden entsprechend den aktuellen Bedingungen fortgeschrieben.

Darüber hinaus wird der Zustand der sechs Siedlungen durch regelmäßige Kontrollgänge von Mitarbeitern der Eigentümergesellschaften (siehe Ziffer 5.A) überwacht, die zum Teil in den Siedlungsgebieten ansässige Verwalterbüros unterhalten.

## 6.C Ergebnisse früherer Berichterstattungen

Die zur Zeit verfügbaren Berichte und Dokumentationen, die Aussagen über den Konservierungszustand der Siedlungen treffen, sind unter den Ziffern 7.B und 7.C (Bestandsgutachten mit fotografischen Aufnahmen, Befunduntersuchungen etc.) aufgeführt und unter der Ziffer 4.A berücksichtigt. Eine Verschlechterung des Erhaltungszustandes in den Siedlungen, die noch nicht vollständig denkmalpflegerisch wiederhergestellt sind – Weiße Stadt und die Großsiedlungen Britz und Siemensstadt –, ist nicht zu erkennen, da auch dieser Zustand von den Eigentümergesellschaften im Rahmen des laufenden Bauunterhalts gepflegt wird.

## 6.B Administrative arrangements for monitoring property

The relevant monument preservation authorities are responsible for the regular monitoring of the nominated housing estates. They have to organize and carry out the regular monitoring and the corresponding reporting. In addition to other special purpose authorities also the owners (housing companies) are invited to participate in the monitoring activities.

The monitoring activities are based on the key indicators which are contained in the questionnaires (Item 6.A) and occasionally on further investigations into the state (for instance photographs and planning documents). The questionnaires and the date are continuously recorded as they are found.

In addition to the above employees of the owners monitor the state of the six housing estates by means of regular inspections (see Item 5.A). Some of the owners (housing companies) have in the very housing estates offices for administering the housing estates.

## 6.C Results of previous reporting

All currently available reports and documentations which contain information on the state of preservation of the housing estates are contained under Items 7.B and 7.C (expert opinions on existing state with photographs, investigations, etc.) and under Item 4.A. We do not perceive a deterioration of the state of preservation in those housing estates whose restoration has not been completed to date (Großsiedlung Britz, Weiße Stadt and Siemensstadt) since the housing companies which own them provide proper current maintenance.

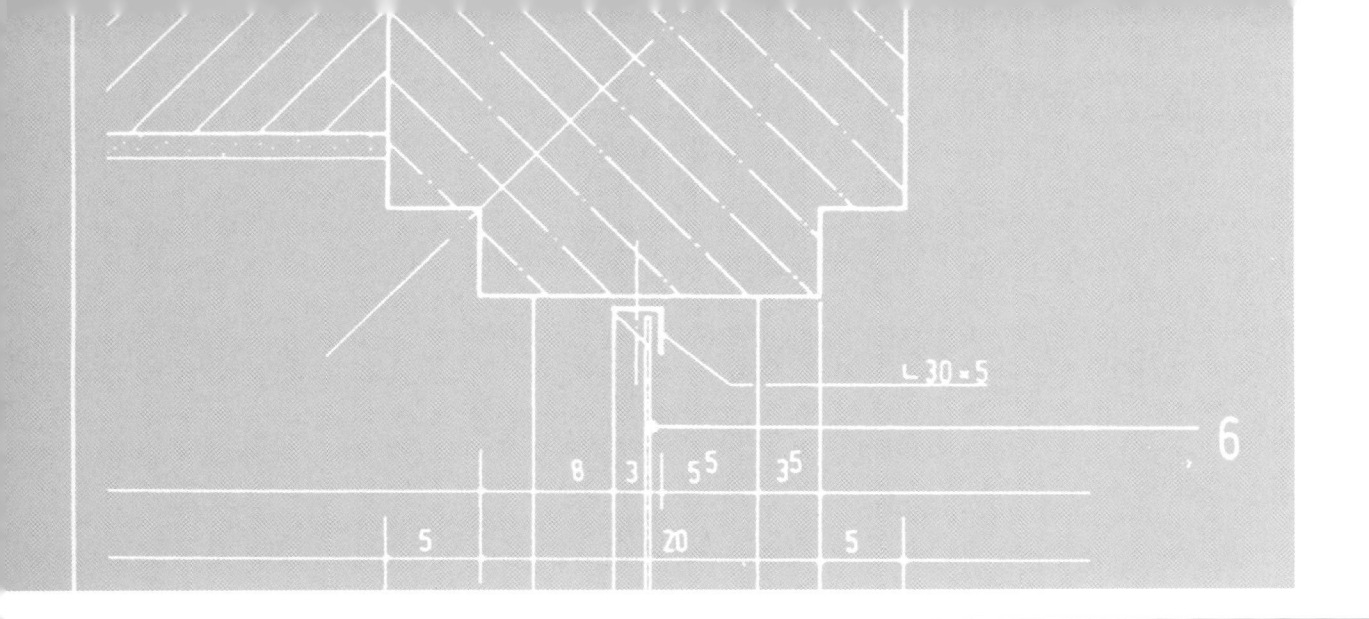

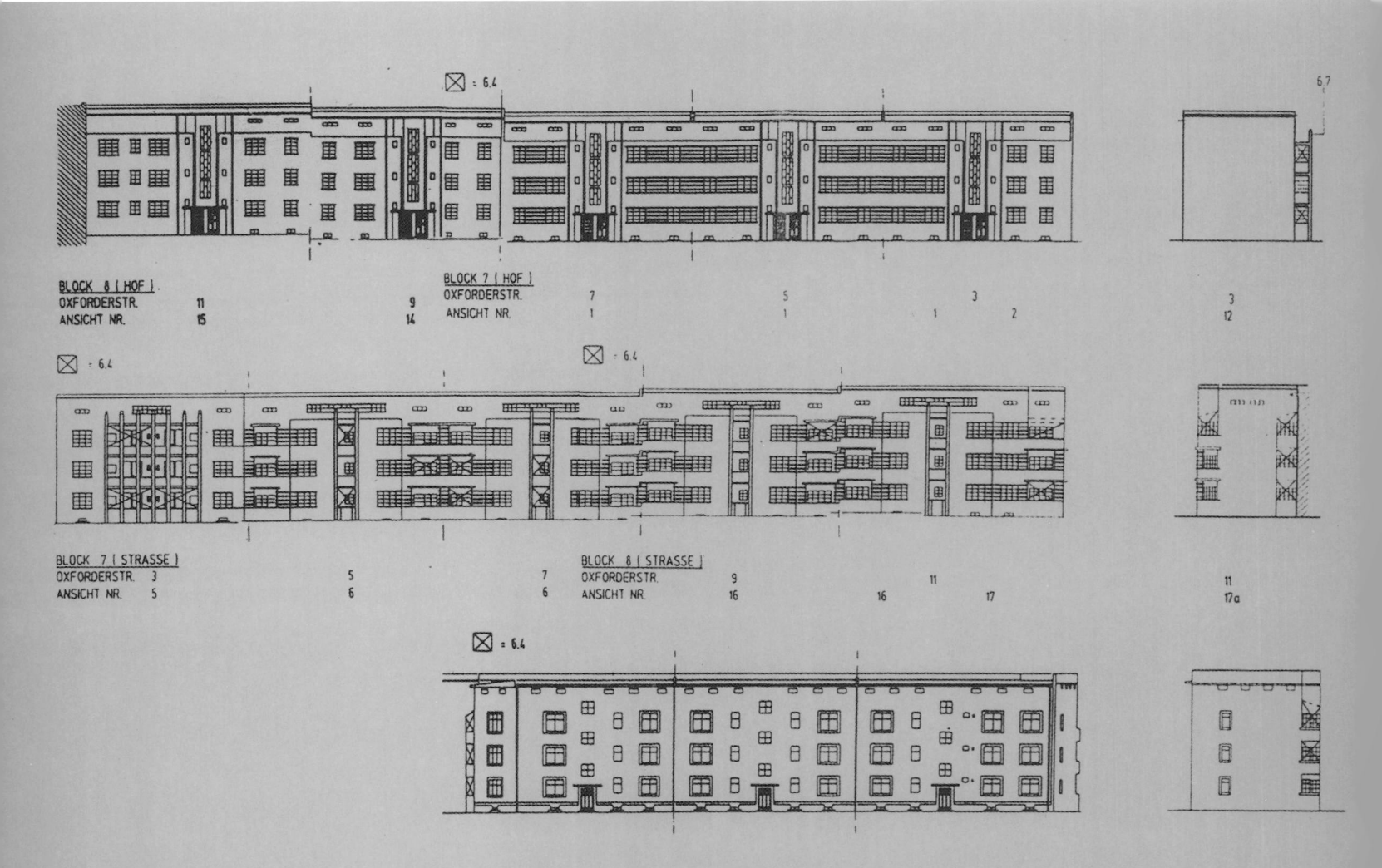

| BLOCK 8 (HOF) | | BLOCK 7 (HOF) | | | | |
|---|---|---|---|---|---|---|
| OXFORDERSTR. | 11 | 9 | OXFORDERSTR. | 7 | 5 | 3 | 3 |
| ANSICHT NR. | 15 | 14 | ANSICHT NR. | 1 | 1 | 1 | 2 | 12 |

| BLOCK 7 (STRASSE) | | | BLOCK 8 (STRASSE) | | | |
|---|---|---|---|---|---|---|
| OXFORDERSTR. | 3 | 5 | 7 | OXFORDERSTR. | 9 | 11 | 11 |
| ANSICHT NR. | 5 | 6 | 6 | ANSICHT NR. | 16 | 16 | 17 | 17a |

# 7

**DOKUMENTATION**
**DOCUMENTATION**

### 7.A Photographien, Dias, Bildnachweis und Bildrechte sowie sonstiges audiovisuelles Material

Sämtliche verwendeten Fotos sind separat zum Antragsformular auf einer gesonderten CD-ROM als Bilddateien im tif-, jpg- oder pdf-Format abgespeichert, einschließlich einer Liste mit Numerierung, Bildunterschrift und Bildnachweis, und als Dias angefertigt worden.
Der UNESCO wird zugestanden das Foto- und Abbildungsmaterial zu nutzen und zu verbreiten. Kosten für Bildrechte und Nutzungsgebühren entstehen nicht, bzw. werden vom Antragsteller übernommen. Die Erlaubnis zur uneingeschränkten Nutzung und Verbreitung der Foto- und Bildvorlagen beinhaltet allerdings keine Übertragung der Bildrechte an die UNESCO zwecks exklusiver Vermarktung.

### 7.A Photographs, slides, image inventory and authorization table and other audiovisual materials

All photographs used in the application are stored as image files in the formats tif or jpg or pdf on a separate CD-ROM inclusive of a list with their numbers, captions and sources and have also been produced as slides.
UNESCO is entitled to use and disseminate the photographs and images. There is no charge for image rights and use of the images and photographs, or any costs shall be borne by the applicant. However, permission to unlimitedly use and disseminate the photographs and images does not constitute a transfer of the rights of the photographs and images to UNESCO for exclusive marketing.

**Abbildungsnachweis/Picture credits**

*Institutionen und Einrichtungen/Institutions and agencies*
Akademie der Künste Berlin:
Abb./fig. VI, 32, 37–40, 42, 44, 49, 116, 117, 121, 123

Architekturwerkstatt Pitz/Brenne, Berlin:
Abb./fig. 103, 109–114; S./p. 216

Bauhaus-Archiv Museum für Gestaltung Berlin:
Abb./fig. 124

Berliner Bau- und Wohnungsgenossenschaft von 1892, Berlin:
Abb./fig. 35, 36, 61

Bezirksamt Neukölln von Berlin:
Abb./fig. 95

Bezirksamt Pankow von Berlin:
Abb./fig. 102

Bildarchiv Preußischer Kulturbesitz Berlin:
Abb./fig. III, IV, VII; S./p. 12

Courtesy of The Art Institute of Chicago:
Abb./fig. VIII

Winfried Brenne Architekten, Berlin:
Abb./fig. 5–17, 19–21, 23–25, 27, 50–57, 59, 71–79, 83, 85, 87, 88, 90, 91, 93, 105, 106; S./p. 38, 39, 42, 43, 46, 52, 53, 56, 57, 60, 61, 66, 80, 164

Richard Büning, Köln:
Abb./fig. 119

Filmmuseum Berlin:
Abb./fig. II, V

GEHAG GmbH, Berlin:
Abb./fig. 41, 46, 107; S./p. 47

Gemeinnützige Siedlungs- und Wohnungsbaugesellschaft Berlin mbH (GSW), Berlin:
Abb./fig. 108

Landesarchiv Berlin:
Abb./fig. 66

Landesdenkmalamt Berlin:
Abb./fig. X, XI, XII, XIII/XIV, XV, XVI, 28 (Reuss)

Katrin Lesser, Landschaftsarchitektin, Berlin:
Abb./fig. 128

Schmidt-Seifert, Landschaftsarchitektur, Berlin:
Abb./fig. 26, 58, 81, 104, 115; S./p. 184

Senatsverwaltung für Stadtentwicklung, Berlin:
Abb./fig. XVII, XVIII, 1–3, 18, 22, 82, 84, 86, 89, 92, 94, 96–101; S./p. 32, 33, 40, 41, 44, 45, 48, 49, 50, 51, 54, 55, 58, 59, 62–65, 212, 213, 242, 243

Siemens-Museum, Bildarchiv, Siemens AG, München:
Abb./fig. IX

Privatbesitz/In private hands:
Abb./fig. 120, 126

*Literatur/Literature*
Adler, Leo, Neuzeitliche Miethäuser und Siedlungen. Berlin 1931, S./p. 53, 164:
Abb./fig. 4, 67

Alvar Aalto, Band/vol. I 1922–1962, Zürich 1970³, S./p. 101
Abb./Fig. 130

Bauwelt (21) 1930, Nr./No. 48, S./p. 6:
Abb./fig. 43

Bredow, Jürgen/Lerch, Helmut, Materialien zum Werk des Architekten Otto Bartning. Darmstadt 1983:
Abb./fig. 125

La Construction Moderne (47) 1932, Nr./No. 16:
Abb./fig. 45

Deutsche Bauausstellung Berlin 1931. Berlin 1931:
Abb./fig. 118

Foltyn, Ladislav, Slowakische Architektur und die tschechische Avantgarde 1918–1939, Dresden 1991, S./p. 172
Abb./fig. 132

Gartenstadt-Mitteilungen der Deutschen Gartenstadtgesellschaft (7) 1913, Nr./No. 5, S./p. 83:
Abb./fig. 60

Gartenstadt-Mitteilungen der Deutschen Gartenstadtgesellschaft (7) 1913, Nr./No. 6, S./p. 112:
Abb./fig. 31

GEHAG: Die Gehag-Wohnung. Berlin 1931:
Abb./fig. 47, 48, S./p. 118

Geist, Johann F./Kürvers, Klaus, Das Berliner Mietshaus
1962–1945. München 1984, S./p. 462:
Abb./fig. 30

Karl Schneider – Leben und Werk (1892–1945), hrsg. von/
ed. by R. Koch und/and E. Pook, Hamburg, 1992, S./p. 114
Abb./Fig. 133

Keimsche Mineralfarben (Firmenschrift/Advertising).
Lohwald bei/near Augsburg, um/approximately 1931:
Abb./fig. 68

Kommunaler Wohnbau in Wien. Aufbruch – 1923–1934
– Ausstrahlung. Stadt Wien (Hg./Ed.). Wien 1977:
Abb./fig. 63

Konservierung der Moderne? ICOMOS Hefte des
Deutschen Nationalkomitees XXIV. Leipzig 1997:
Abb./fig. I

Leberecht Migge 1881–1935. Hg./Ed. von der/by
Gesamthochschule Kassel. Worpswede 1981, S./p. 8:
Abb./fig. 127

Mohr, Christoph/Müller, Michael, Funktionalität und
Moderne. Köln 1984, S./p. 249:
Abb./fig. 64

Oelker, Simone/Otto Haesler. Eine Architektenkarriere in
der Weimarer Republik. Hamburg 2002, S./p. 154:
Abb./fig. 65

Posener, Julius, Berlin auf dem Wege zu einer neuen
Architektur. München 1979, S./p. 343:
Abb./fig. 29

Rassegna (5) 1983, Nr./No. 15, S./p. 26:
Abb./fig. 122

Taut, Bruno, Bauen – Der Neue Wohnbau, Leipzig, Berlin
1927, Titelblatt/cover, S./p. 54
Abb./fig. 69, 70

Taut, Bruno, Die Neue Baukunst in Europa und Amerika,
Stuttgart 1929, S./p. 149, 159
Abb./fig. 129, 131

Wattjes, Jannes Gerjardis, Nieuw-Nederlandsche
Bouwkunst. Amsterdam 1926, S./p. 61:
Abb./fig. 62

Wohnungswirtschaft (3) 1926, Nr./No. 11/12:
Abb./fig. 34

Wohnungswirtschaft (4) 1927, Nr./No. 1/2:
Abb./fig. 33

## 7.B Texte, die sich auf den Schutzstatus beziehen, Kopien bestehender Planungen oder Managementsysteme und Auszüge aus sonstigen für die Anlagen relevanten Plänen

Die folgenden Dokumente stellen Auszüge aus bestehenden Dokumentationen (Bestandsuntersuchungen, Instandsetzungskonzepte, Maßnahmenpläne) zur Siedlung Schillerpark dar, die zum Teil als mehrbändige Gutachten zum Bestand vorhanden sind. Die getroffene Auswahl soll exemplarisch Aufbau und Tiefe der Dokumentationen vor Augen führen, die in ähnlicher Form auch für die anderen zur Nominierung vorgesehenen Siedlungen vorliegen

## 7.B Texts relating to protective designation, copies of property management plans or documented management systems and extracts of other plans relevant to the property

The documents mentioned below constitute excerpts from existing documentation (investigations into the existing monuments, restoration concepts, action plans) concerning the Siedlung Schillerpark, some of which are expert opinions consisting of several volumes. The chosen documents are to stand as examples for the composition and depth of the documentation which similarly also exists for the other nominated housing estates.

Abb./fig. 109–112
Auszüge aus der Bestandsuntersuchung: Siedlung am Schillerpark. Dokumentation und Rekonstruktion des Originalzustandes der Siedlung. Angef. von der Architekturwerkstatt Helge Pitz/Winfried Brenne mit Franz Jaschke. 2 Bde. Berlin 1990

Excerpts from the investigations into the existing monument: Siedlung am Schillerpark. Dokumentation und Rekonstruktion des Originalzustandes der Siedlung. Produced by Architekturwerkstatt Helge Pitz/Winfried Brenne with Franz Jaschke. 2 vol. Berlin 1990

Abb./fig. 113–114
Auszüge aus dem Instandsetzungskonzept: Siedlung am Schillerpark. Instandsetzungskonzept im Rahmen des Denkmalschutzes. Angef. von der Architekturwerkstatt Helge Pitz/Winfried Brenne mit Franz Jaschke.
Berlin 1991

Excerpts from the restoration concept: Siedlung am Schillerpark. Instandsetzungskonzept im Rahmen des Denkmalschutzes. Produced by Architekturwerkstatt Helge Pitz/Winfried Brenne with Franz Jaschke. Berlin 1991

Abb./fig. 115
Gartendenkmalpflegerischer Maßnahmenplan, aus: Siedlung Schillerpark. Gartendenkmalpflegerisches Gutachten. Anlagegeschichte und Dokumentation. Angef. vom Büro Hackenberg/Annett Gries im Auftrag der Berliner Bau- und Wohnungsgenossenschaft von 1892. Berlin 2003

Action plan for the preservation and restoration of the historic garden, from: Siedlung Schillerpark. Gartendenkmalpflegerisches Gutachten. Anlagegeschichte und Dokumentation. Produced by Büro Hackenberg/Annett Gries by order of Berliner Bau- und Wohnungsgenossenschaft von 1892. Berlin 2003

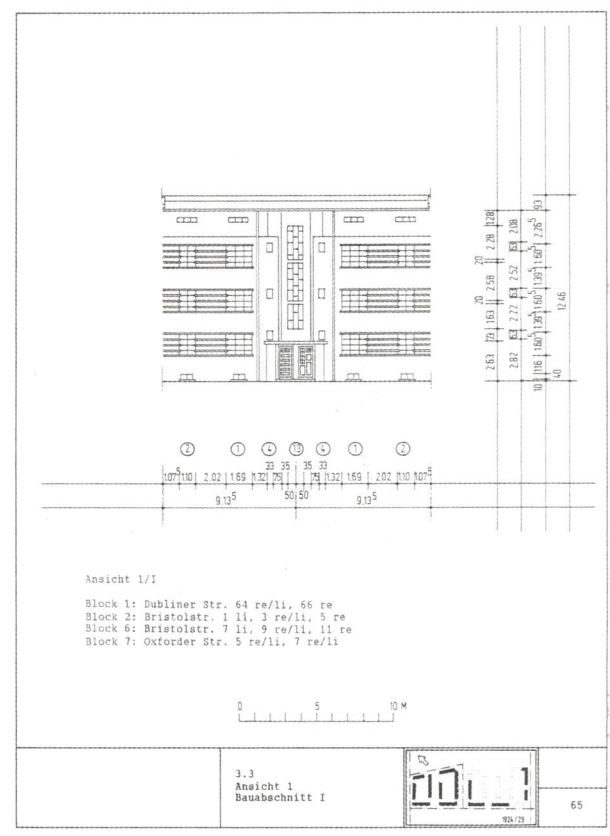

Abb./Fig. 109

Abb./Fig. 110

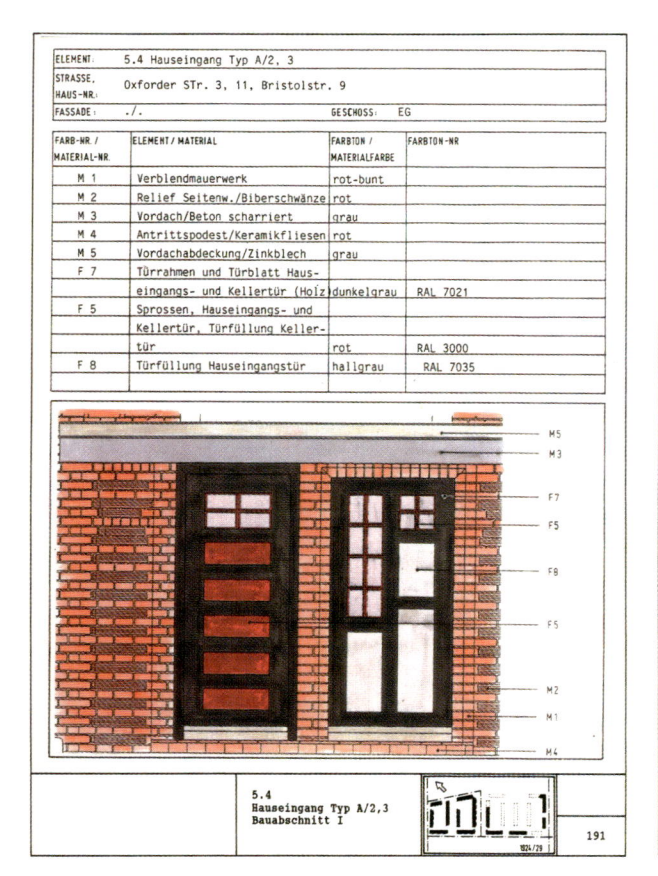

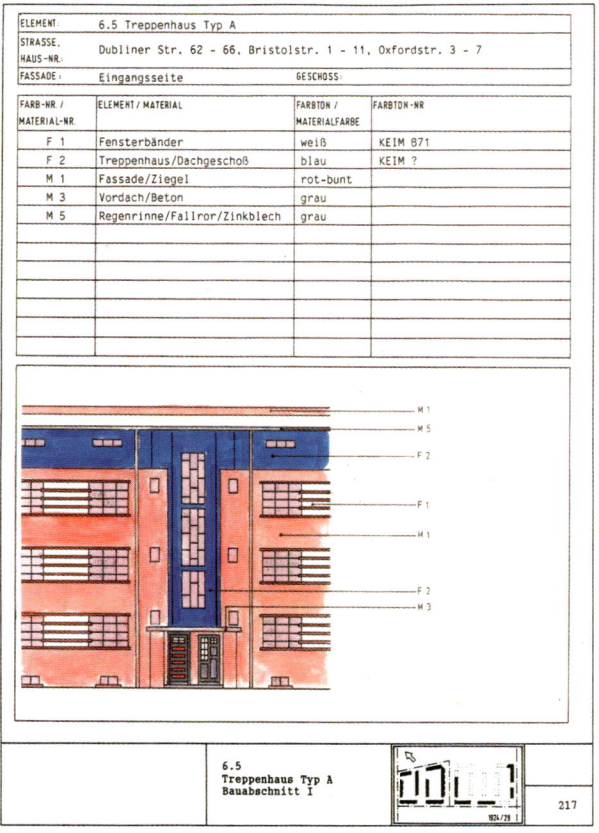

Abb./Fig. 111

Abb./Fig. 112

**SIEDLUNG AM SCHILLERPARK   BERLIN-WEDDING**

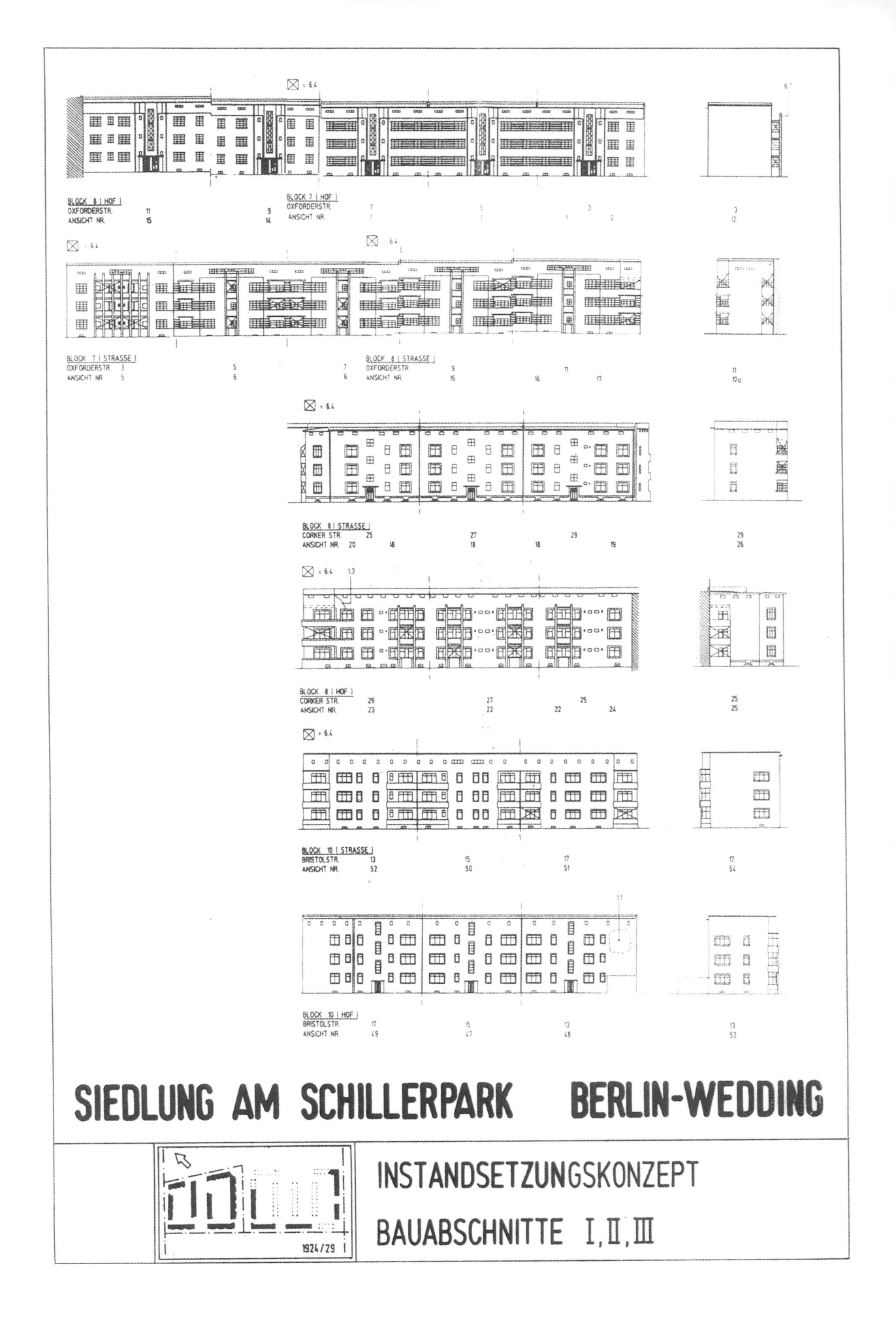

**INSTANDSETZUNGSKONZEPT**

**BAUABSCHNITTE I, II, III**

Abb./Fig. 113

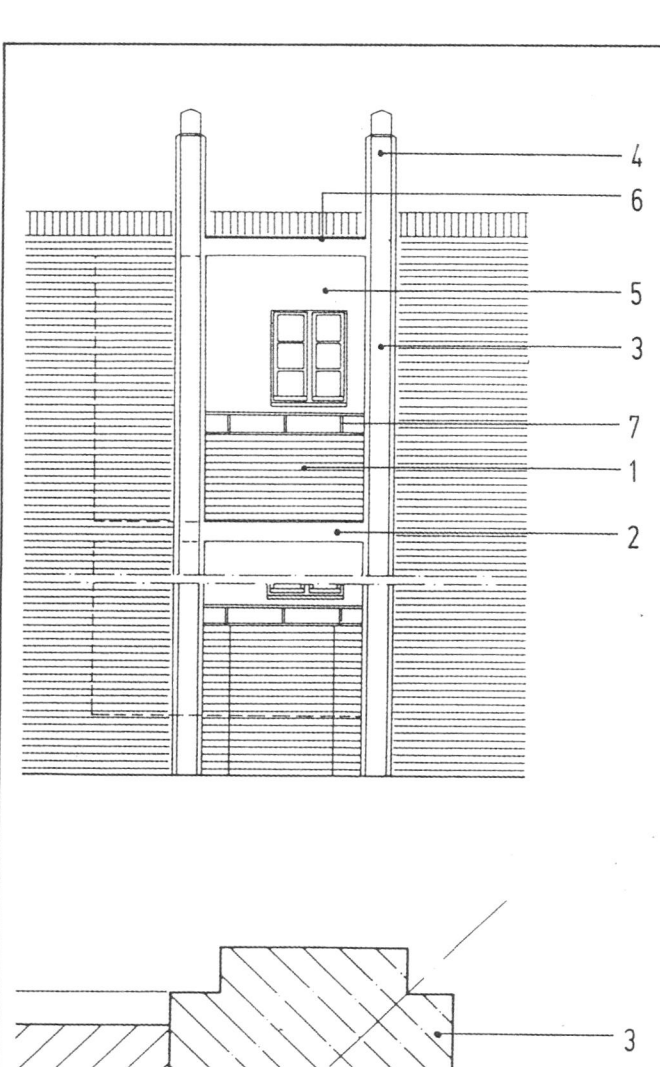

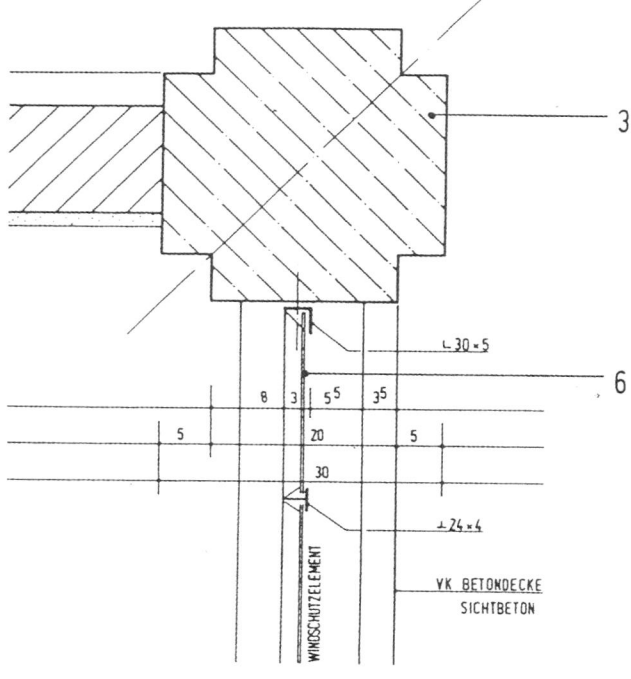

1. Brüstung
   - Außenseite entspr. 1.1 instandsetzen
   - Innenseite entspr. 3.1 Originalputz überarbeiten
   - ggf. entspr. 3.2 neuen Glattputz herstellen
   - Oberkante mit Binderschicht entspr. 1.2 und Blechverwahrung entspr. 7.1 überarbeiten bzw. wieder herstellen

2. Deckenunterseite und -stirnfläche
   - entspr. 2.1 instandsetzen
   - entspr. 4.4 lasierender Anstrich

3. Betonpfeiler entspr. 2.1 instandsetzen
   - entspr. 4.4 lasierenden Anstrich

4. Pfeilerspitzen entspr. 2.3 nach Rekonstruktion neu herstellen (s. Detail)

5. Rückwand und Seitenwände
   - entspr. 3.1 Originalputz überarbeiten
   - ggf. entspr. 3.2 neuen Glattputz herstellen
   - entspr. 4.2 bzw. 4.3 Mineralfarbenanstrich

6. Windschutzelement
   - entspr. 6.2 überarbeitern
   - entspr. 4.5 Anstrich mit Lackfarbe (F3, weiß, RAL 9010)

7. Blumenkastenhalterung
   - entspr. 6.5 überarbeiten
   - entspr. 4.5 Anstrich mit Lackfarbe (F4, schwarz, RAL 9005)

Maßnahmen Balkone BA I

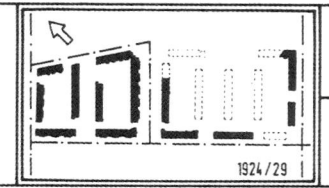

115

Abb./Fig. 114

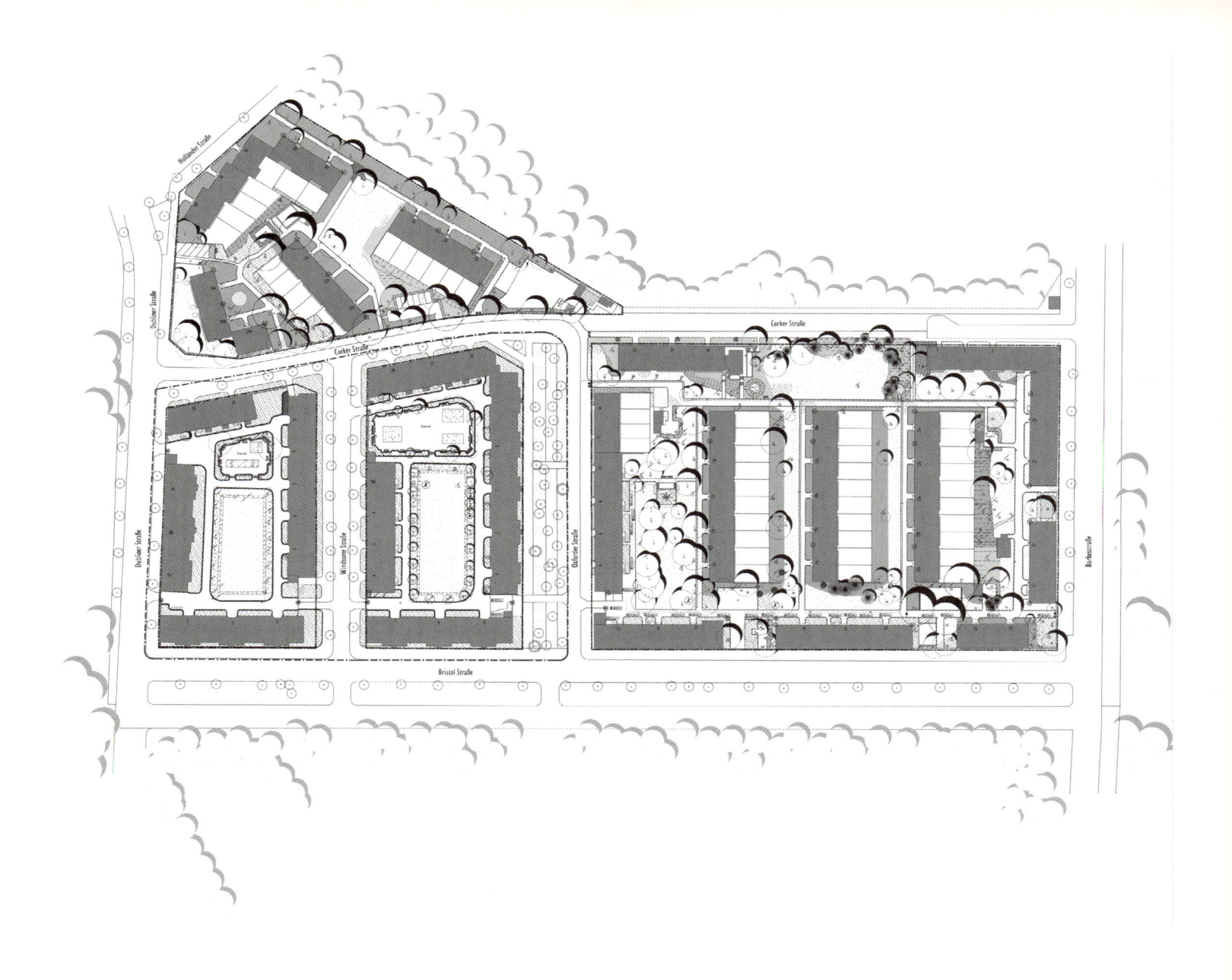

Abb./Fig. 115

## 7.C Form und Datum jüngerer Publikationen und Bestandsaufnahmen/Form and date of most recent records and inventory of property

### Gartenstadt Falkenberg

Die Gartenstadt Falkenberg ist als ein bedeutendes Werk von Bruno Taut und des Reformwohnungsbaues in Deutschland Gegenstand ständiger wissenschaftlicher Auseinandersetzung (vgl. Ziffer 7.E). Als zuletzt erschienene Publikationen, die Aspekte der Gartenstadt Falkenberg behandeln, sind zu nennen:

As an important work by Bruno Taut and an outstanding example of reform housing development in Germany, Gartenstadt Falkenberg is subject to ongoing scientific investigation (see Item 7.E). The most recent publications dealing with aspects of Gartenstadt Falkenberg are:

Manfred Speidel, Bruno Taut Retrospektive 1880–1938. Natur und Fantasie (= Katalog zur Ausstellung vom 11. Mai bis 30. Juli 1995 in Magdeburg). Berlin 1995, S./p. 117–124

Katrin Lesser-Sayrac u. a./et al., Ludwig Lesser (1869–1957). Erster freischaffender Gartenarchitekt in Berlin und seine Werke im Bezirk Reinickendorf. Beiträge zur Denkmalpflege in Berlin. Heft/No. 4. Berlin 1995

Astrid Holz, Die Farbigkeit in der Architektur von Bruno Taut – Konzeption oder Intuition? Ein Beitrag zur Farbigkeit in der Architektur der Moderne. Dissertation Kiel 1996, Dissertationsdruck 1997

Kristina Hartmann, Bruno Taut, der Architekt und Planer von Gartenstädten und Siedlungen. In: Bruno Taut 1880–1938. Architekt zwischen Moderne und Avantgarde. Hg. von/Ed. by W. Nerdinger, K. Hartmann, M. Schirren, M. Speidel. Stuttgart/München 2001, S./p. 142–145

Winfried Brenne, Wohnbauten von Bruno Taut. Erhaltung und Wiederherstellung farbiger Architektur. In: Bruno Taut 1880–1938. Architekt zwischen Moderne und Avantgarde. Hg. von/Edited by W. Nerdinger, K. Hartmann, M. Schirren, M. Speidel. Stuttgart/München 2001, S./p. 275–298

Winfried Brenne, Zum baulichen Umgang mit dem Erbe von Bruno Taut. In: Genossenschaftliche Wohnanlagen von Messel und Taut. Zur Wiederentdeckung baulicher und kultureller Höhepunkte der Berliner Bau- und Wohnungsgenossenschaft von 1892 eG. Berlin 2004, S./p. 36–41

Katrin Lesser, Die historische Grünplanung und ihre denkmalgerechte Wiederherstellung. In: Genossenschaftliche Wohnanlagen von Messel und Taut. Zur Wiederentdeckung baulicher und kultureller Höhepunkte der Berliner Bau- und Wohnungsgenossenschaft von 1892 eG. Berlin 2004, S./p. 42–45

Im Zusammenhang mit Grundinstandsetzungen und denkmalpflegerischen Erneuerungen wurden Untersuchungen über die ursprüngliche Farbfassung sowie Bestandsaufnahmen zur Ermittlung des originalen Zustandes der Gebäude erstellt. Für die Ende der 1960er Jahre vorgenommenen ersten Instandsetzungen und Erneuerungen des Farbanstriches fand eine Analyse der ursprünglichen Farbgebung statt:

Investigations into the original colouring and stock takings for establishing the original state of the buildings were carried out in connection with the thorough refurbishment and restoration works. An analysis of the original colouring was carried out for the first refurbishment works and renewal of the facades' paint coating in the late 1960s:

Berthold Staake, Die Farben der Gartenstadt (restauratorische Untersuchung anlässlich der Restaurierung der Siedlung in den 1960er Jahren). Typoskript/Typoscript. Berlin 1966/67

Eine grundlegende Erforschung des ursprünglichen Zustandes mit detaillierten farbrestauratorischen Untersuchungen erfolgte 1991–95. Sie umfasst die Beschreibung der Baugeschichte mit einer Dokumentation der Archivalien und der Literatur, die zeichnerische Erfassung des Baubestandes mit einem Schadenskatalog, die Ermittlung originaler Bauelemente mit restauratorischen Befunduntersuchungen sowie Vorschläge für denkmalpflegerische Maßnahmen. Außerdem wurde vom Landesdenkmalamt Berlin, Fachreferat Gartendenkmalpflege ein Wiederherstellungskonzept für die zukünftige Rekonstruktion der gärtnerischen Freiflächen und Gärten in Auftrag gegeben. Es handelt sich um folgende Schriften und Dokumentationen:

In 1991–95, thorough investigations were carried out into the original state together with studies of the colouring for restoration purposes. The corresponding documentation includes a description of the building history with a documentation on archive material and literature, drawings of the existing buildings with a register of the damages, the definition of original building elements with studies of the state for restoration purposes as well as proposals for restoration and conservation measures. The department for conservation of historic gardens of Landesdenkmalamt of Berlin ordered the production of a refurbishment concept for the future reconstruction of the outdoor facilities and gardens. The entire set consists of the following papers and documentation:

Gartenstadt Falkenberg. Denkmalpflegerische Maßnahmekataloge. Angef. von/Produced by Winfried Brenne Architekten im Auftrag der/in order of Berliner Bau- und Wohnungsgenossenschaft von 1892 e. G. analog den Bauabschnitten der Instandsetzungen/in accordance with the refurbishment phases. Berlin 1991

Gartenstadt Falkenberg. Bauhistorische Bestandsaufnahme und Ermittlung des originalen Zustandes der Gebäude als Grundlage für zukünftige Erneuerungs- und Instandhaltungsmaßnahmen im Rahmen des Denkmalschutzes. Angef. von/Produced by Winfried Brenne Architekten (Bd./Vol. 1 Baugeschichte von/by Jürgen Tomisch) im Auftrag der/by order of Berliner Bau- und Wohnungsgenossenschaft von 1892 e. G. 8 Bde./Vol. Berlin 1994/95

Katrin Lesser, Gartenstadt Falkenberg. Gartendenkmalpflegerisches Gutachten. Historischer Zustand, Bestand, Konzept. Angef. von/Produced by Katrin Lesser im Auftrag der/by order of Berliner Bau- und Wohnungsgenossenschaft von 1892 e. G. Berlin 2001

**Siedlung Schillerpark**
Im Rahmen der jüngsten wissenschaftlichen Auseinandersetzung mit dem Œuvre von Bruno Taut ist auch die Siedlung Schillerpark wiederholt abgehandelt worden. Auch auf dem Forschungsgebiet „Genossenschaftlicher Wohnungsbau" kam es zu Veröffentlichungen, die ebenfalls die Geschichte der Siedlung und die des „Berliner Spar- und Bauvereins", jetzt „Berliner Bau- und Wohnungsgenossenschaft von 1892", betrafen. Zu nennen sind die Publikationen:

In connection with the recent scientific studies on Bruno Taut and his works, the Siedlung Schillerpark has also been treated in several publications. Other publications have been produced on the topic of "cooperative housing development" which also cover the history of this housing estate and of "Berliner Spar- und Bauverein" (now "Berliner Bau- und Wohnungsgenossenschaft von 1892"). These publications are:

Klaus Novy/Barbara von Neumann-Cosel (Hg./Ed.), Zwischen Tradition und Innovation. 100 Jahre Berliner Bau- und Wohnungsgenossenschaft von 1892. Berlin 1992, S./p. 51, 75–79, 94, 99, 142 f.

Bettina Zöller-Stock, Bruno Taut. Die Innenraumentwürfe des Berliner Architekten. Stuttgart 1993, S./p. 91–93

Gabi Dolff-Bonekämper, Die Schillerpark-Siedlung in Berlin-Wedding – ein Beitrag zum Wohnungsbau der 20er Jahre. In: Denkmalschutz und Denkmalpflege in Berlin. Jahrbuch/Yearbook 1994 (= Beiträge zur Denkmalpflege in Berlin, Heft/No. 7). Berlin 1996, S./p. 57–60

Bruno Taut 1880–1938. Architekt zwischen Moderne und Avantgarde. Hg. von/Ed. by W. Nerdinger, K. Hartmann, M. Schirren, M. Speidel. Stuttgart/München 2001

Denkmaltopographie Bundesrepublik Deutschland. Denkmale in Berlin. Bezirk Mitte. Ortsteile Wedding und Gesundbrunnen. Hg. von/Ed. by Landesdenkmalamt Berlin. Berlin 2004, S./p. 237 f.

Annett Gries/Klaus-Peter Hackenberg, Vom grünen Hof zur Stadtlandschaft. Die Berliner Siedlung – ein Beitrag zur Freiraumgestaltung im urbanen Siedlungsbau der 1920er und 1950er Jahre. In: Stadt + Grün (53) 2004, S./p. 44–52

Eine grundlegende denkmalpflegerische Analyse des Baubestandes und der erhaltenen Bauelemente fand Ende der 1980er Jahre statt, wobei auch statische Ermittlungen über die Festigkeit und Tragfähigkeit der Eisenbetonstützen der Loggien-Balkone vorgenommen wurden. Sie beinhaltete eine Auswertung der Archivalien und der Literatur, die zeichnerische Erfassung des Baubestandes und die Ermittlung originaler Bauelemente mit restauratorischen Befunduntersuchungen. Die Ergebnisse der Untersuchungen dienten als Grundlage für die anschließende, nunmehr größtenteils abgeschlossene Instandsetzung und Restaurierung. Es handelt sich um folgende Gutachten und Dokumentationen:
In the late 1980s, a thorough analysis of the existing monuments and of the preserved building elements was conducted for restoration purposes. These investigations also included static studies on the strength and load-bearing capacity of the reinforced concrete pillars of the loggias and balconies. The activities included studies of archive material and literature, the production of drawings of the existing structures and the definition of original building elements with analyses of the existing state for restoration purposes. The results of these investigations were used as a basis for the subsequent refurbishment and restoration, which is now almost complete. The entire set consists of the following expert opinions and documentations:

Siedlung am Schillerpark. Dokumentation und Rekonstruktion des Originalzustandes der Siedlung. Grundlage für zukünftige Erneuerungs- und Instandhaltungsmaßnahmen im Rahmen des Denkmalschutzes. Architekturwerkstatt Helge Pitz/Winfried Brenne mit Franz Jaschke. 2 Bde./Vol. Berlin 1990

Siedlung am Schillerpark. Instandsetzungskonzept im Rahmen des Denkmalschutzes. Architekturwerkstatt Helge Pitz/Winfried Brenne mit Franz Jaschke. Berlin 1991

Im Auftrag der Baugenossenschaft konnte 2003 ein Denkmalpflegeplan für die Freianlagen der 1920er und 1950er Jahre erarbeitet werden. Seit 2004 liegt darüber hinaus eine gartendenkmalpflegerische Entwicklungskonzeption für alle Siedlungsteile vor:
In 2003, a plan for preserving the monument's outdoor facilities of the 1920s and 1950s was established by order of the building cooperative. Since 2004, a development concept for the restoration and preservation of the garden architecture has also been in existence:

Siedlung Schillerpark. Gartendenkmalpflegerisches Gutachten. Anlagegeschichte und Dokumentation. Angef. vom/Produced by Büro Hackenberg/Annett Gries im Auftrag der/by order of Berliner Bau- und Wohnungsgenossenschaft von 1892. Berlin 2003

## Großsiedlung Britz (Hufeisensiedlung)

Seit ihrer Erbauung steht die Großsiedlung Britz im Brennpunkt journalistischen und wissenschaftliches Interesses (vgl. Ziffer 7.E). Eine ausführliche geschichtliche Beschreibung lieferte 1984 Annemarie Jaeggi in dem von Norbert Huse herausgegebenen Ausstellungskatalog: Siedlungen der zwanziger Jahre – heute. Vier Berliner Großsiedlungen 1924–1984. Im Rahmen der jüngsten Auseinandersetzung mit dem Œuvre von Bruno Taut ist auch die Britzer Siedlung wiederholt abgehandelt worden. Ebenso kam es auf dem Forschungsgebiet „gewerkschaftlich-genossenschaftlicher Wohnungsbau" zu Veröffentlichungen, die die Geschichte der Siedlung und die der GEHAG betrafen. Zu nennen sind die Publikationen:
Since it was erected, the Großsiedlung Britz has been a point of interest for journalists and scientists (see Item 7.E). In 1984, Annemarie Jaeggi provided a detailed description of its history in the exhibition catalogue edited by Norbert Huse: Siedlungen der zwanziger Jahre – heute. Vier Berliner Großsiedlungen 1924–1984. In connection with the recent studies on Bruno Taut and his works, the housing estate at Britz has also been treated in several publications. Publications on the history of the housing estate and of GEHAG have also been issued in connection with research into trade-union and cooperative housing development. These publications are:

Klaus Novy, M. Prinz, Illustrierte Geschichte der Gemeinwirtschaft. Berlin/Bonn 1985, S./p. 105 ff.

Bettina Zöller-Stock, Bruno Taut. Die Innenraumentwürfe des Berliner Architekten. Stuttgart 1993, S./p. 94–96

T. Shigemura, Der nie zu Ende geträumte Traum vom gemeinschaftlichen Wohnen. In: Manfred Speidel, Bruno Taut Retrospektive 1880–1938. Natur und Fantasie (= Katalog zur Ausstellung vom 11. Mai bis 30. Juli 1995 in Magdeburg). Berlin 1995, S./p. 236–240

Annemarie Jaeggi, Die Berliner Hufeisensiedlung von Bruno Taut, Architektur im Spannungsfeld von Politik und Wirtschaft. In: Festschrift für Johannes Langner. Hg. von /Ed. by K. G. Beuckes und/and A. Jaeggi. Münster 1997, S./p. 273–296

Bruno Taut 1880–1938. Architekt zwischen Moderne und Avantgarde. Hg. von/Ed. by W. Nerdinger, K. Hartmann, M. Schirren, M. Speidel. Stuttgart/München 2001, S./p. 12 f., 107, 148, 363–365

Martin Baumann, Freiraumplanung in den Siedlungen der zwanziger Jahre am Beispiel der Planungen des Gartenarchitekten Leberecht Migge. Halle 2002, S./p. 143–145

Eine denkmalpflegerische Analyse des Baubestandes fand in den 1980ern Jahren statt. Sie beinhaltete auch die zeichnerische Erfassung des Baubestandes und restauratorische Befunduntersuchungen. Die Ergebnisse der Untersuchungen dienten als Grundlage für eine gleichzeitig in Angriff genommene denkmalgerechte Instandsetzung und Restaurierung der Siedlungshäuser, die bis heute anhält. Es handelt sich um folgendes Gutachten:

An analysis for restoration purposes was carried out in the 1980s. In connection with this analysis, drawings of the existing structures were produced and investigations made into the structures for restoration purposes. The results of the investigations were used as a basis for refurbishment and restoration of the houses of this housing estate which began simultaneously with the investigations and continues to date. The results are contained in the following expert opinion.

> Großsiedlung Britz (Hufeisensiedlung). Dokumentation und Rekonstruktion des Originalzustandes. Grundlage für zukünftige Erneuerungs- und Instandhaltungsmaßnahmen im Rahmen des Denkmalschutzes. Architekturwerkstatt Helge Pitz/Winfried Brenne (Bd./Vol. 1 Planungs- und Baugeschichte von/by A. Jaeggi und/and J. Tomisch). Gutachten im Auftrag der/Expert opinion by order of Gemeinnützigen Heimstätten AG. 11 Bde./Vol. Berlin 1984–91

Im Rahmen der Begutachtung des Denkmalwertes der Siedlungsgärten und Freiflächen fanden im Auftrag des Landesdenkmalamtes Berlin, Fachreferat Gartendenkmalpflege, folgende Untersuchungen statt:
The following investigations were carried out by order of the State Monument Preservation Office (Landesdenkmalamt), department for preservation of historic gardens, for the purpose of assessing the value of the housing estate's gardens and outdoor facilities as monuments:

> B. Drescher, R. Mohrmann, S. Stern, Untersuchung des Gehölzbestandes der Hufeisen-Siedlung in Berlin-Britz. Berlin 1981

> Katrin Lesser, Untersuchung der denkmalgeschützten Freiflächen und Konzeption für den zukünftigen Umgang. 3. Bde./Vol. Berlin 2003

Im Auftrag des Bezirksamtes Neukölln wurde 2001 für die ersten beiden Bauabschnitte am Hufeisen folgendes Gutachten erstellt:
In 2001 the following expert opinion was produced by order of the district office of Neukölln for the first two development phases of the horseshoe:

> Untersuchung in Berlin-Neukölln, Hufeisensiedlung, zur Herstellung einer planungsrechtlichen Entscheidungsgrundlage unter Berücksichtigung von denkmalpflegerischen Aspekten. Angef. von/Produced by J. Langeheinecke, C. P. Claussen (Planer in der/Planner in Pankemühle). Berlin 2001

Die zuletzt genannte Untersuchung hatte zum Inhalt, den Bauzustand der Siedlungshäuser fotografisch und textlich zu erfassen, Veränderungen zu registrieren und mittels eines Maßnahmekataloges auf den Veränderungsdruck zu reagieren, der sich aus der Privatisierung der Reihenhäuser ergibt.
The purpose of the above mentioned investigations was to record the state of the houses by means of photographs and verbal descriptions, to register alterations and establish an action list for responding to the pressure for change which results from the privatisation of the row houses.

**Wohnstadt Carl Legien**

Die Wohnstadt Carl Legien ist eingehend im Inventarband der Bau- und Kunstdenkmale der DDR, Hauptstadt I, Berlin 1984, auf den Seiten 412–413 beschrieben worden. Im Rahmen der jüngsten wissenschaftlichen Auseinandersetzung mit dem Œuvre von Bruno Taut ist auch die Wohnstadt wiederholt abgehandelt worden. Zu nennen sind die Publikationen und Schriften:
Wohnstadt Carl Legien has been described comprehensively in the inventory volume of the architectural and artistic monuments of the GDR (Inventarband der Bau- und Kunstdenkmale der DDR, Hauptstadt I, Berlin 1984) on pages 412–413. In connection with the recent scientific studies on Bruno Taut and his works, Wohnstadt Carl Legien has also been treated in several publications. These publications and papers are:

> Bettina Zöller-Stock, Bruno Taut. Die Innenraumentwürfe des Berliner Architekten. Stuttgart 1993, S./p. 109–111

> Winfried Brenne, Fazination Farbe. In: Symposium Bruno Taut in Magedeburg, Dokumentation. Hg. vom Stadtplanungsamt Magdeburg/Edited by urban development office Magdeburg (= Schriftenreihe des Stadtplanungsamtes Magdeburg 48 I/II). Magdeburg 1995, S./p. 228–229

> Manfred Speidel, Bruno Taut Retrospektive 1880–1938. Natur und Fantasie (= Katalog zur Ausstellung vom 11. Mai bis 30. Juli 1995 in Magdeburg). Berlin 1995, S./p. 220–226

> Bruno Taut 1880–1938. Architekt zwischen Moderne und Avantgarde. Hg. von/Ed. by W. Nerdinger, K. Hartmann, M. Schirren, M. Speidel. Stuttgart/München 2001, S./p. 376 f.

> Heinz-Josef Klimeczek, Die gesunde Wohnung – Die Genese der Bauordnung vom 3.11.1925 (mit einem Fallballspiel: Die Herstellung gesunder Wohnungen – Die Wohnstadt Carl Legien). Dissertation an der Technischen Universität von Berlin 2005

Eine erste denkmalpflegerische Analyse des Bauzustandes legte 1990 Viola Beil mit ihrer Abschlussarbeit an der Technischen Universität Dresden vor:
In her final thesis at Technische Universität (Technical University) Dresden in 1990, Viola Beil presented a first analysis of the state of the buildings from the point of view of monument preservation.

> Viola Beil, Die Wohnstadt Carl Legien in Berlin-Prenzlauer Berg, von Bruno Taut 1929–1930 erbaut. Erarbeitung einer denkmalpflegerischen Rahmenzielstellung (Abschlussarbeit zum Postgradualstudium Denkmalpflege an der Technischen Universität Dresden 1988/89). Typoskript/Typoscript. Berlin 1990

Anfang der 1990er Jahre begannen erste denkmalpflegerische Bestandsuntersuchungen und restauratorische Befundermittlungen der Fassaden und der Farbigkeit der Treppenhäuser, die sich allerdings auf Blockteile an der Trachtenbrodtstraße 2–18 und Sodtkestraße 20–36 be-

schränkten. Sie dienten als Grundlage für die anschließende denkmalgerechte Wiederherstellung dieses kleinen Teils der Wohnstadt. Es sind folgende detaillierte Untersuchungen:
In the early 1990s, stocktaking activities from the point of view of monument preservation and investigations for restoration purposes of the facades and the colouring of the staircases began, but they were limited to those parts of the block at Trachtenbrodtstraße 2–18 and Sodtkestraße 20–36. The results provided the basis for the subsequent proper restoration of this small part of the Wohnstadt. The following papers resulted from the investigations:

Wohnstadt Carl Legien. Dokumentation und Rekonstruktion des Originalzustandes der Gebäude als Grundlage für zukünftige Erneuerungs- und Instandsetzungsmaßnahmen im Rahmen des Denkmalschutzes. Blockabschnitt Trachtenbrodtstraße 2–18, Winfried Brenne Architekten im Auftrag der/by order of GEHAG. 2 Bde./Vol. Berlin 1993

Wohnstadt Carl Legien. Dokumentation des Originalzustandes und Maßnahmenkatalog für die Wiederherstellung. Blockabschnitt Sodtkestraße 20–36. Winfried Brenne Architekten im Auftrag der/by order of GEHAG. 2 Bde./Vol. Berlin 1995

Im Rahmen der folgenden und 2005 abgeschlossenen denkmalgerechten Sanierung der Wohnstadt wurden weitere vorbereitende restauratorische Gutachten erstellt:
The subsequent proper restoration of the Wohnstadt Carl Legien was completed in 2005 and resulted in the production of another expert opinion preparing further restorations:

Wohnstadt Carl Legien. Dokumentation zur restauratorischen Farb- und Putzuntersuchung der Kopfbauten. Angef. von/Produced by Christine Becker. Berlin 2000

Wohnstadt Carl Legien. Dokumentation zur restauratorischen Farbuntersuchung der Blöcke A–G. Angef. von/Produced by Christine Becker. Berlin 2000

2001 beauftragte das Landesdenkmalamt Berlin, Fachreferat Gartendenkmalpflege, ein Gutachten als Grundlage für die sukzessive Wiederherstellung der Freiflächen:
In 2001, the department for the preservation of historic gardens of the Berlin State Monument Office ordered the production of an expert opinion which was to be used as basis for the gradual restoration of the outdoor facilities:

Wohnstadt Carl Legien. Gartendenkmalpflegerische Recherche und Analyse des „Außenwohnraums" in der Wohnstadt. Atelier Schreckenberg Partner. Juni/June 2001

**Weiße Stadt**
Seit dem es Ende der 1970er Jahre zur Wiederentdeckung der architektonischen und städtebaulichen Qualitäten der Berliner Siedlungen aus der Weimarer Zeit kam, steht auch die Großsiedlung „Weiße Stadt" im Mittelpunkt wissenschaftlichen und denkmalpflegerischen Interesses. Zu nennen sind die Publikationen:
Since the re-discovery of the architectural and urban development qualities of the Berlin housing estates from the period of the Weimar Republic, the large housing estate "Weiße Stadt" has also been moved into the focus of scientists and urban preservationists. The publications to be mentioned in this respect are:

Klaus-Peter Kloß, Siedlungen der 20er Jahre. Berlin 1982, S./p. 56–68

Norbert Huse (Hg./Ed.), Siedlungen der zwanziger Jahre – heute. Vier Berliner Großsiedlungen 1924–1984. Berlin 1984, und darin/and in this:

Annemarie Jaeggi, Weiße Stadt, Planungs- und Baugeschichte. In: Siedlungen der zwanziger Jahre – heute. Vier Berliner Großsiedlungen 1924–1984. Hg. von/Ed. by Nobert Huse. Berlin 1984, S./p. 181–200

Jürgen Tomisch, Rainer Schomann, Denkmaltopographie Bundesrepublik Deutschland, Baudenkmale in Berlin, Bezirk Reinickendorf, Ortsteil Reinickendorf, hg. vom Senator für Stadtentwicklung und Umweltschutz/edited by the Minister for Urban Development and Environmental Protection. Berlin o. J./without year, S./p. 68–70, 94, 168–171

Eine umfangreiche denkmalpflegerische Analyse des Baubestandes fand Ende der 1970er Jahre statt. Sie beinhaltete eine Auswertung der Archivalien und der Literatur, eine bau- und planungsgeschichtliche Beschreibung, die zeichnerische Erfassung des Baubestandes und die Ermittlung originaler Bauelemente mit restauratorischen Befunduntersuchungen. Die Ergebnisse der Untersuchungen dienten als Grundlage für die anschließende und bis heute anhaltende Instandsetzung und Restaurierung der Siedlungshäuser. Es handelt sich um folgende im Auftrag des Landesdenkmalamtes Berlin, Fachreferat Baudenkmalpflege, und der GSW als Eigentümerin der Siedlung erstellte Dokumentation:
An analysis for restoration purposes was carried out in the late 1970s. The activities included studies of archive material and literature, a description of the building and planning history, the production of drawings of the existing structures and the definition of original building elements with analyses of the existing state for restoration purposes. The results of these investigations were used as a basis for the subsequent and still ongoing refurbishment and restoration of the houses of the housing estate. The results have been laid down in the following documentation, which was produced by order of the Berlin Landesdenkmalamt (State Monument Preservation Office) and GSW (owner of the housing estate):

Architekturwerkstatt Pitz/Brenne, Uli Böhme, Jürgen Tomisch, Weiße Stadt Berlin Reinickendorf, Dokumentation der 50jährigen Geschichte, Erarbeitung des Originalzustandes sowie der Grundlagen für zukünftige denkmalpflegerische Maßnahmen. Gutachten in 6 Bänden im Auftrag der GSW/Expert opinion in 6 volumes ordered by GSW. Berlin 1981

Im Auftrag der GSW wurden 2000 zwei denkmalpflegerische Instandsetzungskonzepte erstellt, die zum einen den Zeilenbau von Wilhelm Büning an der Aroser Allee 141–

147 und zum anderen den langen Randbau von Otto Rudolf Salvisberg an der Aroser Allee 155–191 betrafen:
In 2000, two restoration concepts were produced by order of GSW. They covered the ribbon building by Wilhelm Büning at Aroser Allee and the long margin building by Otto Rudolf Salvisberg at Aroser Allee:

> Winfried Brenne Architekten, Wohnbebauung Aroser Allee 141–147, Denkmalpflegerische Bestandsaufnahme und Maßnahmenkatalog. Erstellt im Auftrag der/Produced by order of GSW. Berlin 2000
>
> Winfried Brenne Architekten, Denkmalpflegerisches Konzept zur Erneuerung der Wintergartenfenster und der Rückfassaden Aroser Allee 155–191. Erstellt im Auftrag der/Produced by order of GSW. Berlin 2000

Im Laufe der Wiederherstellung des ursprünglichen Zustandes fanden auch eine Reihe von ausführlichen gartendenkmalpflegerischen Untersuchungen und Konzeptionsüberlegungen statt. Es sind dies:
At the same time as the restoration of the buildings, a number of investigations were carried out into the historic garden areas and concepts for these outdoor facilities were drafted. These are:

> Ralf Klinger/Hans-Jürgen Pröbster, Gartendenkmalpflegerisches Gutachten Weiße Stadt – Berlin Reinickendorf, Gutachten im Auftrag des Senators für Stadtentwicklung und Umweltschutz, Abt. III – Gartendenkmalpflege/Expert opinion by order of the Minister for Urban Development and Environmental Protection, Dept. III – preservation of historic gardens. Berlin 1984
>
> Wilmer Loger/Christa Ringkamp u. a./et al., Hortec Garten- und Landschaftsplanung GBR, Gartendenkmalpflegerische Wiederherstellungsplanung, Weiße Stadt Reinickendorf. Gutachten im Auftrag der/Expert opinion produced by order of GSW. 3 Bde./Vol. Berlin 1985
>
> Schmidt-Seifert, „Weiße Stadt" Berlin Reinickendorf. Umsetzung der gartendenkmalpflegerischen Konzeption, Gutachten von Peter Schmidt-Seifert, Stefan Helmich im Auftrag der GSW, Berlin 2000

**Großsiedlung Siemensstadt**
Die Großsiedlung Siemensstadt ist eingehend in den Inventarbänden „Die Bauwerke und Kunstdenkmäler" der Bezirke Charlottenburg 1961, Seite 458–460, und Spandau 1971, Seite 303–305, beschrieben worden. Gegen Ende der 1970er Jahre wurden die architektonischen und städtebaulichen Qualitäten der Berliner Siedlungen aus der Weimarer Zeit durch die Forschung und die Denkmalpflege wiederentdeckt. Zu nennen sind die Publikationen:
The Großsiedlung Siemensstadt has been described in detail in the inventory volumes "Die Bauwerke und Kunstdenkmäler" for the districts of Charlottenburg, 1961, pages 458–460 and Spandau 1971, pages 303–305. In the late 1970s researchers and urban preservationists re-discovered the architectural and urban development qualities of the Berlin housing estates from the period of the Weimer Republic. The publications to be mentioned in this respect are:

> Klaus-Peter Kloß, Siedlungen der 20er Jahre. Berlin 1982, S./p. 42–55
>
> Norbert Huse (Hg./Ed.), Siedlungen der zwanziger Jahre – heute. Vier Berliner Großsiedlungen 1924–1984. Berlin 1984, und darin/and in this:
>
> Annemarie Jaeggi, Siemensstadt, Planungs- und Baugeschichte. In: Siedlungen der zwanziger Jahre – heute. Vier Berliner Großsiedlungen 1924–1984. Hg. von/Ed. by Norbert Huse. Berlin 1984, S./p. 159–180
>
> Martin Baumann, Freiraumplanung in den Siedlungen der zwanziger Jahre am Beispiel der Planungen des Gartenarchitekten Leberecht Migge. Halle 2002, S./p. 137–139, 155–157

Eine denkmalpflegerische Bestandsanalyse fand Anfang der 1980er Jahre statt. Sie beinhaltete eine Auswertung der Archivalien und der Literatur, eine bau- und planungsgeschichtliche Beschreibung, die zeichnerische Erfassung des Baubestandes, bautechnische und statische Untersuchungen beim Bauteil Häring sowie eine Ermittlung originaler Bauelemente mit restauratorischen Befunduntersuchungen in allen Siedlungsteilen.
In the early 1980s, a stocktaking was carried out from the point of view of restoration. The activities included studies of archive material and literature, a description of the building and planning history, the production of drawings of the existing structures, investigations into the constructional state and structural stability of the buildings designed by Häring and the definition of original building elements with analyses of the existing state for restoration purposes in all parts of the housing estate.

Die Ergebnisse der Untersuchungen dienten als Grundlage für die anschließende Instandsetzung und Restaurierung einzelner Siedlungsteile (Bauabschnitte von Hans Scharoun und Hugo Häring) und werden auch bei zukünftigen denkmalgerechten Erneuerungen herangezogen. Nach dem Ende der Restaurierungen wurden die Ergebnisse in entsprechenden Dokumentationen festgehalten. Es handelt sich um folgende im Auftrag des Landesdenkmalamtes, Fachreferat Baudenkmalpflege und Fachreferat Gartendenkmalpflege, und der GSW als Eigentümerin der Siedlung erstellte Dokumentationen:
The results of these investigations were used as a basis for the subsequent refurbishment and restoration of individual parts of the housing estate (development phases by Hans Scharoun and Hugo Häring) and they will also be used for future restoration works. After the end of the restorations, their results were recorded in corresponding documentations. These are the following documentations that were produced by order of the departments for urban preservation and for historic gardens of the Berlin Landesdenkmalamt and GSW (owner of the housing estate):

> Großsiedlung Siemensstadt. Dokumentation und Rekonstruktion des Originalzustandes der Gebäude. Achitekturwerkstatt Helge Pitz/Winfried Brenne (Bd./Vol. 1 Planungs- und Baugeschichte von Jürgen Tomisch). Gutachten im Auftrag der/Expert opinion produced by order of GSW. 8 Bde./Vol. Berlin 1984

Großsiedlung Siemensstadt. Bauabschnitt Hugo Häring. Dokumentation der historisch-technischen Betreuung der Erneuerungs- und Instandsetzungsmaßnahmen im Rahmen des Denkmalschutzes 1984/85. Achitekturwerkstatt Helge Pitz/Winfried Brenne. Berlin 1986

Großsiedlung Siemensstadt. Bauabschnitt Hans Scharoun. Dokumentation der historisch-technischen Betreuung der Erneuerungs- und Instandsetzungsmaßnahmen im Rahmen des Denkmalschutzes 1985/86. Achitekturwerkstatt Helge Pitz/Winfried Brenne. Berlin 1986

Farbgestaltung der Fassaden bei den Gebäuden Goebelstraße 12–118 von Hugo Häring in Berlin, Siemensstadt. Gutachten angefertigt von/Expert opinion produced by H. Cabanis, A. Höß und/and Menrad. Berlin 1984

Gartendenkmalpflegerisches Gutachten. Angef. von/Produced by Ralf Klinger, Hans-Jürgen Pröbster. Berlin 1984

Gartendenkmalpflegerische Wiederherstellungsplanung. Siemensstadt – Charlottenburg Nord. Angef. von/Produced by Hortec – Garten- und Landschaftsplanung GBR im Auftrag der/by order of GSW. 3 Bde./Vol. Berlin 1985

Büro Schmidt-Seifert, Parkpflegewerk Siemensstadt. Großsiedlung Siemensstadt und Charlottenburg-Nord. Angef. von/Produced by Peter Schmidt-Seifert, Stefan Helmich. Gutachten im Auftrag des Landesdenkmalamtes Berlin, Abteilung Gartendenkmalpflege/Expert opinion by order of the department for historic gardens of Landesdenkmalamt Berlin. Berlin 2003

## 7.D Anschriften der Einrichtungen, bei denen Bestandsunterlagen, Berichte und Archivalien verwahrt werden/Addresses where inventory, records and archives are held

**Denkmalpflegebehörden/Monument preservation authorities**

*Denkmalfachbehörde (Landesdenkmalamt)*
Hier werden für alle nominierten Siedlungen Unterlagen archiviert (Gutachten, Dokumentationen, Befunduntersuchungen, Pflegewerke, Bildarchiv, Akten etc).

*Special purpose authority for monument preservation (Landesdenkmalamt – state monument preservation office)*
This authority keeps documents on all of the nominated housing estates in its archives (expert opinions, documentations, investigations into the existing state of the buildings, preservation schemes, image archives, files, etc.).

Landesdenkmalamt Berlin
Klosterstraße 47
10179 Berlin

*Untere Denkmalschutzbehörden*
Hier werden Unterlagen für diejenige Anlage verwahrt, die sich im entsprechenden Bezirksgebiet befindet.

*Untere Denkmalschutzbehörden*
These authorities keep in their archives the documents for those monuments which are located in their territories.

Großsiedlung Siemensstadt (Ringsiedlung):
Bezirksamt Charlottenburg-Wilmersdorf von Berlin
Fehrbelliner Platz 4
10707 Berlin

Großsiedlung Siemensstadt (Ringsiedlung):
Bezirksamt Spandau von Berlin
Carl-Schurz-Str. 2–6
13597 Berlin

Großsiedlung Britz (Hufeisensiedlung):
Bezirksamt Neukölln von Berlin
Karl-Marx-Straße 83
12040 Berlin

Wohnstadt Carl Legien:
Bezirksamt Pankow (Prenzlauer Berg) von Berlin
Storkower Straße 139 c
10407 Berlin

Siedlung Schillerpark:
Bezirksamt Mitte (Wedding) von Berlin
Iranische Straße 3
13347 Berlin

Gartenstadt Falkenberg:
Bezirksamt Treptow-Köpenick von Berlin
Alt-Köpenick 21
12414 Berlin

Weiße Stadt:
Bezirksamt Reinickendorf von Berlin
Eichborndamm 215–239
13437 Berlin

**Eigentümergesellschaften/Owners**

Hier werden in der Regel Kopien oder Originale der beauftragten Gutachten und Untersuchungen wie auch Vorgänge, die den Bauunterhalt betreffen, verwahrt. Bei der GEHAG, der GSW und der Berliner Bau- und Wohnungsgenossenschaft von 1892 sind auch Bildarchive oder andere Archivalien vorhanden.

They usually keep copies or originals of the ordered expert opinions and investigation results as well as documents referring to the maintenance of the buildings. GEHAG, GSW and Berliner Bau- und Wohnungsgenossenschaft von 1892 also keep images and other material in their archives.

Gartenstadt Falkenberg und/and Siedlung Schillerpark:
Berliner Bau- und Wohnungsgenossenschaft von 1892 e. G.
Knobelsdorffstr. 96
14050 Berlin

Großsiedlungen Siemensstadt und/and Weiße Stadt:
G S W
Gemeinnützige Siedlungs- und
Wohnungsbaugesellschaft Berlin mbH
Kochstraße 22
10969 Berlin

Großsiedlung Britz (Hufeisensiedlung):
GEHAG GmbH
Mecklenburgische Str. 57
14197 Berlin

Wohnstadt Carl Legien:
BauBeCon Immobilien GmbH
Schützenallee 3
30519 Hannover

## 7. E Bibliographie/Bibliography

**Architektur des 20. Jahrhunderts – allgemeine Darstellungen/Architecture of the 20th century – general presentations**

Banham, Reyner, Theory and design in the first machine age. London 1960

Benevolo, Leonardo, Storia dell'architettura moderna. Bari 1960

Casteels, Maurice, Die Sachlichkeit in der modernen Kunst. Leipzig 1930

CIAM – Dokumente 1928–1939. Hg. von/Ed. by Martin Steinmann, Schriftenreihe des Instituts für Geschichte und Theorie der Architektur an der ETH Zürich (Bd./Vol. 11). Basel, Stuttgart 1979

Collins, Peter, Changing ideals in modern architecture 1750–1950. London 1965

Conrads, Ulrich, Programme und Manifeste zur Architektur des 20. Jahrhunderts. Stuttgart 1983[2]

Curtis, William J. R., Modern architecture since 1900. London 1982

De Fusco, Renato, Storia dell'architettura contemporanea. Bari 1974

Frampton, Kenneth, Modern architecture. A critical history. London 1992[3]

Giedion, Sigfried, Space, time and architecture. Cambridge, Mass. 1962[3]

Giedion, Sigfried, Befreites Wohnen. Zürich, Leipzig 1929

Gropius, Walter, Internationale Architektur (Bauhausbücher 1). München 1925

Hatje, Gerd (Hg./Ed.), Knaurs Lexikon der modernen Architektur. München 1963

Hilberseimer, Ludwig, Internationale Neue Baukunst. Stuttgart 1927

Hitchcock, Henry-Russel, Architecture nineteenth and twentieth centuries. Harmondsworth 1958 (deutsch/german: Die Architektur des 19. und 20. Jahrhunderts. München 1994)

Hitchcock, Henry-Russel/Johnson, Philip, The International Style. Architecture since 1922. New York 1932

Hitchcock, Henry-Russel, Modern architecture. Romanticism and reintegration. New York 1929

Joedicke, Jürgen, Geschichte der modernen Architektur. Stuttgart 1958

Joedicke, Jürgen, Moderne Architektur. Stuttgart 1969

Kultermann, Udo, Die Architektur im 20. Jahrhundert. Köln 1977

Magnago Lampugnani, Vittorio, Architektur und Städtebau des 20. Jahrhunderts. Stuttgart 1980

Magnago Lampugnani, Vittorio (Hg./Ed.), Hatje Lexikon der modernen Architektur, Stuttgart 1983

Mendelsohn, Erich, Russland – Europa – Amerika. Berlin 1928

Pevsner, Nikolaus, Pioneers of modern design. Harmondsworth 1960[3]

Pevsner, Nikolaus, The sources of modern architecture and design. London 1968

Sartoris, Alberto, Gli elementi dell'architettura funzionale. Mailand 1932

Sharp, Dennis, Sources of modern architecture. A bibliography. London 1967

Sharp, Dennis, Modern architecture and expressionism. London 1966

Taut, Bruno, Die neue Baukunst in Europa und Amerika. Stuttgart 1929

Whittick, Arnold, European architecture in the twentieth century. Aylesbury 1974.

Zevi, Bruno, Storia dell'architettura moderna. Turin 1955[3]

**Architektur der Moderne in Deutschland und Berlin/
Modern Age Architecture in Germany and Berlin**

Adler, Leo, Neuzeitliche Miethäuser und Siedlungen. Berlin 1931

Architekten- und Ingenieurverein zu Berlin (Hg./Ed.), Berlin und seine Bauten. Berlin, München, Düsseldorf 1964 ff.

Bauen in Berlin 1900–2000, Stadt der Architektur – Architektur der Stadt, Josef Paul Kleihues, Thorsten Scheer, Jan Gerd Becker-Schwering, Paul Kahlfeldt (Hg./Ed.), 2 Bde./Vol. Berlin 2000

Bayer, Herbert/Gropius, Walter/Gropius, Ise, Bauhaus 1919–1928. New York 1938 (deutsch/german: Stuttgart 1955)

Behne, Adolf, Neues Wohnen – Neues Bauen. Leipzig 1927

Behne, Adolf, Der moderne Zweckbau, München 1926

Behne, Adolf, Die Wiederkehr der Kunst. Leipzig 1919

Behrendt, Walter Curt, Der Sieg des neuen Baustils. Stuttgart 1927

Berning, Maria, Berliner Wohnquartiere. Ein Führer durch 60 Siedlungen in Ost und West. Berlin 1994

Block, Fritz, Probleme des Bauens. Potsdam 1928

Buddensieg, Tilmann (Hg./Ed.), Berlin 1900–1933. Architecture and design. Architektur und Design. New York, Berlin 1987

Burckhardt, Lucius (Hg./Ed.), Der Werkbund in Deutschland, Österreich und der Schweiz. Form ohne Ornament. Stuttgart 1978

Busche, Ernst A. 1918–1933. Laboratorium Wohnen und Weltstadt. In: Kleihues, Josef Paul (Hg./Ed.): 750 Jahre Architektur und Städtebau. Stuttgart 1987, S./p. 153 ff.

Campbell, Joan, The German Werkbund. The politics of reform in the applied arts. Princeton 1978

Conrads, Ulrich/Sperlich, Hans G., Phantastische Architektur. Stuttgart 1983[2]

Durth, Werner, Deutsche Architekten. Biografische Verflechtungen 1900–1933. Braunschweig, Wiesbaden 1987[2]

Freiheit, Gleichheit, Brüderlichkeit, Ausstellungskatalog/Exhibition catalogue 43. Ruhrfestspiele Recklinghausen. Recklinghausen 1989

de Fries, Heinrich, Junge Baukunst in Deutschland. Berlin 1926

GAGFAH 1918–1993. Innovation aus Tradition, 75 Jahre GAGFAH, Berlin 1993

Gut, Albert, Der Wohnungsbau in Deutschland nach dem Weltkriege. München 1928

Hajos, Maria Elisabeth/Zahn, Leopold, Berliner Architektur der Nachkriegszeit. Berlin 1928

Hartmann, Kristiana, Deutsche Gartenstadtbewegung. Kulturpolitik und Gesellschaftsreform. München 1976

Hartmann, Kristiana (Hg./Ed.), trotzdem modern. Die wichtigsten Texte zur Architektur in Deutschland 1919–1933. Braunschweig–Wiesbaden 1994

Hegemann, Werner, Das steinerne Berlin. Berlin 1930

Henning-Schefold, M./Schaefer, I., Frühe Moderne in Berlin. Winterthur 1967

Herzberg, Ursula, Geschichte der Berliner Wohnungswirtschaft. Unter besonderer Berücksichtigung der gemeinnützigen (Klein-)Wohnungswirtschaft. Hamburg 1957

Hilberseimer, Ludwig, Berliner Architektur der 20er Jahre. Mainz 1967

Huse, Norbert, „Neues Bauen" 1918 bis 1933 – Moderne Architektur in der Weimarer Republik. München 1975

Hüter, Karl Heinz, Architektur in Berlin. 1900–1933. Dresden, Stuttgart 1988

Johannes, Heinz, Neues Bauen in Berlin. Berlin 1931

Junghanns, Kurt, Der Deutsche Werkbund. Sein erstes Jahrzehnt. Berlin 1982

Kähler, Gert, Wohnung und Stadt. Massenwohnungsbau der zwanziger Jahre – Hamburg, Frankfurt, Wien, Wiesbaden 1985

Kloß, Klaus-Peter, Siedlungen der 20er Jahre, (= Berliner Sehenswürdigkeiten Heft 4). Berlin 1982

Konservierung der Moderne? Icomos. Hefte des deutschen Nationalkomitees XXIV. München 1997

Las cuatro colonias Berlinesas en la republica de Weimar, Ausstellungskatalog. Madrid 1992

Magnago Lampugnani, Vittorio / Schneider, Romana, Moderne Architektur in Deutschland 1900–1950: Reform und Tradition (Bd./Vol. 1). Frankfurt/Main 1992; Expressionismus und Neue Sachlichkeit (Bd./Vol. 2). Frankfurt/Main 1994

Massenwohnungsbau und Denkmalpflege (Arbeitsberichte des Landesamtes für Denkmalpflege Sachsen-Anhalt 2), Berlin 1997

Miller Lane, Barbara, Architecture and politics in Germany 1918–1945. Cambridge (Mass.) 1968

Müller-Wulckow, Walter, Bauten der Gemeinschaft. Königstein, Leipzig 1928

Müller-Wulckow, Walter, Wohnbauten und Siedlungen. Königstein, Leipzig 1928

Müller-Wulckow, Walter, Bauten der Arbeit und des Verkehrs. Königstein, Leipzig 1925

Novy, Klaus/von Neumann-Cosel, Barbara (Hg./Ed.), Wohnreform in Berlin – Ein Arbeitsprogramm wird vorgestellt. Berlin 1991

Novy, Klaus/von Neumann-Cosel, Barbara (Hg./Ed.), Zwischen Tradition und Innovation. 100 Jahre Berliner Bau- und Wohnungsgenossenschaft von 1982. Berlin 1992

Novy, Klaus/Prinz, Michael, Illustrierte Geschichte der Gemeinwirtschaft. Wirtschaftliche Selbsthilfe in der Arbeiterbewegung von den Anfängen bis 1945. Berlin, Bonn 1985

Pehnt, Wolfgang, Deutsche Architektur seit 1900. München 2005

Pehnt, Wolfgang, Die Architektur des Expressionismus. Ostfildern-Ruit 1998³

Planen und Bauen in Europa 1913–1933. Von der futuristischen zur funktionellen Stadt. Berlin 1978

Platz, Gustav Adolf, Die Baukunst der neuesten Zeit. Berlin 1927

Posener, Julius, Anfänge des Funktionalismus. Berlin, Frankfurt 1964

Posener, Julius, Berlin auf dem Wege zu einer neuen Architektur – Das Zeitalter Wilhelms II. München 1979

Posener, Julius, Vorlesungen zur Geschichte der neuen Architektur 1750–1933. In: arch+ 1979 (Nr./No. 48), 1980 (Nr./No. 53), 1981 (Nr./No. 59), 1982 (Nr./No. 63–64), 1983 (Nr./No. 69–70)

Rave, Rolf/Knöfel, Hans-Joachim, Bauen seit 1900. Ein Führer durch Berlin. Berlin 1968

Rasch, Heinz und Bodo, Wie bauen? Stuttgart 1927

Schäche, Wolfgang (Hg./Ed.), 75 Jahre GEHAG 1924–1999. Berlin 1999

Schallenberger, Jakob/Kraffert, Hans, Berliner Wohnungsbauten aus öffentlichen Mitteln. Berlin 1926

Schallenberger, Jakob/Gutkind, Erwin, Berliner Wohnbauten der letzten Jahre. Berlin 1931

Schirren, Matthias, Geist und Tat – Architektur und Städtebau der Avantgarde im Berlin der Zwanziger Jahre. In: Berlin – Moskau 1900–1950, Ausstellungskatalog hg. von/Exhibition catalogue edited by Irina Antonowa, Jörn Merkert. München 1995, S./p. 211–215

Schmidt, Friedrich/Ebel, Martin, Wohnungsbau der Nachkriegszeit in Deutschland. Berlin 1927

Siedlungen der zwanziger Jahre – heute. Ausstellungskatalog/Exhibition catalogue Bauhaus-Archiv Berlin, Berlin 1984 (2. Ausgabe/2nd edition: Vier Berliner Siedlungen der Weimarer Republik. Britz, Onkel Toms Hütte, Siemensstadt, Weiße Stadt. Berlin 1987; spanische Ausgabe/spanish edition: Cuatro Siedlungen Berlinesas en la republica de Weimar. Madrid 1992)

Siedlungen der 20er Jahre. Dokumentation der Tagung des Deutschen Nationalkomitees für Denkmalschutz (= Bd./Vol. 28 der Schriftenreihe des DNK). Bonn 1985

Tendenzen der Zwanziger Jahre, 15. Europäische Kunstausstellung, Ausstellungskatalog/Exhibition catalogue. Berlin 1977

Ungers, Liselotte, Die Suche nach einer neuen Wohnform. Siedlungen der zwanziger Jahre damals und heute. Stuttgart 1983

Ungers, Oswald Matthias/Kultermann, Udo (Hg./Ed.), Die gläserne Kette. Visionäre Architekturen aus dem Kreis um Bruno Taut 1919–1920. Leverkusen, Berlin 1963

Wem gehört die Welt? – Kunst und Gesellschaft in der Weimarer Republik, hg. von der/edited by Neuen Gesellschaft für Bildende Kunst. Berlin 1977

Wingler, Hans M., Das Bauhaus 1919–1933. Weimar Dessau Berlin. Bramsche 1962

Wohnen in Berlin. 100 Jahre Wohnungsbau in Berlin, Ausstellungskatalog/Exhibition catalogue. Berlin 1999

Wohnen und Bauen – Housing and Building – Habitation et Construction. Kongresspublikation/Congress publication. Berlin 1931

Wohnhäuser und Wohnviertel in Berlin. Die GSW im Dienste Berlins und ihrer Mieter 1914–1999. Berlin 1999

Wolf, Paul, Wohnung und Siedlung. Berlin 1926

Zukowsky, John (Hg./Ed.), Architektur in Deutschland 1919 bis 1939. Die Vielfalt der Moderne. München 1994

**Die einzelnen Siedlungen/The individual housing estates**

**Gartenstadt Falkenberg**
Behne, Adolf, Die Bedeutung der Farbe in Falkenberg. In: Gartenstadt-Mitteilungen der deutschen Gartenstadtgesellschaft (7) 1913, Heft/No. 12, S./p. 240–250

Behne, Adolf, Die Wiederkehr der Kunst. Leipzig 1919

Die Berliner Vororte, Ein Handbuch für Haus- und Grundstückskäufer, Baulustige, Wohnungssuchende, Grundstücksbesitzer. Berlin 1908, S./p. 70 f.

Biel, F., Wirtschaftliche und technische Gesichtspunkte zur Gartenstadtbewegung. Leipzig (o. J./without year) um/approx. 1913, S./p. 115, 120

Bollerey, Franziska/Hartmann, Kristiana/Bruno Taut. Vom phantastischen Ästheten zum ästhetischen Sozial(ideal)isten. In: Ausst. Kat./Exhibition catalogue Bruno Taut 1880–1938 (Berlin 1980), S./p. 50 ff.

Brenne, Winfried, Gartenstadt Falkenberg. Denkmalpflegerische Maßnahmekataloge. Winfried Brenne Architekten im Auftrag der/by order of Berliner Bau- und Wohnungsgenossenschaft von 1892 e. G., analog den Bauabschnitten der Instandsetzungen/coordinated with the development phases of the refurbishment works. Berlin 1991 ff.

Brenne, Winfried, Gartenstadt Falkenberg. Bauhistorische Bestandsaufnahme und Ermittlung des originalen Zustandes der Gebäude als Grundlage für zukünftige Erneuerungs- und Instandhaltungsmaßnahmen im Rahmen des Denkmalschutzes. Winfried Brenne Architekten (Bd./Vol. 1 Baugeschichte von Jürgen Tomisch) im Auftrag der/by order of Berliner Bau- und Wohnungsgenossenschaft von 1892 e. G. 11 Bde./Vol. Berlin 1994/95

Brenne, Winfried, Creating a cosmos of colours – Bruno Taut's housing estates in Berlin. In: Modern Colour Technology – Ideals and Conservation, hg. von do.co.mo.mo international working party (= preservation technology, dossier 5) Leuven 2002, S./p. 23, 37

Brenne, Winfried, Réhabiliter l'architecture colorée de Bruno Taut. In: L'architecture d'aujourd'hui (71) 2001, Nr./No. 334, S./p. 46–51

Brenne, Winfried, On the Reconstruction of Bruno Taut's Colored Architecture. In: a+u Architecture and Urbanism, Nr./No. 384, Japan, September 2002, S./p. 124–127

Brenne, Winfried, Die „farbige Stadt" und die farbige Siedlung. In: Mineralfarben – Beiträge zur Geschichte und Restaurierung von Fassadenmalereien und Anstrichen. Zürich 1998, S./p. 70–71

Brenne, Winfried, Wohnbauten von Bruno Taut. Erhaltung und Wiederherstellung farbiger Architektur. In: Bruno Taut 1880–1938. Architekt zwischen Moderne und Avantgarde. Hg. von/Ed. by W. Nerdinger, K. Hartmann, M. Schirren, M. Speidel. Stuttgart/München 2001

Brenne, Winfried, Faszination Farbe. In: Symposium Bruno Taut in Magdeburg, Dokumentation. Hg. vom Stadtplanungsamt Magdeburg/Ed. by urban development office Magdeburg (= Schriftenreihe des Stadtplanungsamtes Magdeburg 48 I/II). Magdeburg 1995, S./p. 218–222

Brenne, Winfried, Zum baulichen Umgang mit dem Erbe von Bruno Taut. In: Genossenschaftliche Wohnanlagen von Messel und Taut. Zur Wiederentdeckung baulicher und kultureller Höhepunkte der Berliner Bau- und Wohnungsgenossenschaft von 1892 eG. Berlin 2004, S./p. 36–41

Brenne, Winfried, Deutscher Werkbund Berlin (Hg./Ed.), Bruno Taut. Meister des farbigen Bauens in Berlin, Berlin 2005, S./p. 56–61

Der Falkenberg. Zwanglose Worte zum Weiterdenken. Mitteilungsblatt der Gartenvorstadt Nr./No. 3, 1916, S./p. 12

Der Falkenberg 1913–1923. Denkschrift zum 10jährigen Bestehen der Gartenstadt-Siedlung Falkenberg-Grünau. Hg. von/Ed. by Robert Tautz. Falkenberg-Altglienicke, 1. Oktober 1923/1st October 1923 (= Der Falkenberg. Zwanglose Worte zum Weiterdenken. Mitteilungsblatt der Gartenvorstadt, Nr./No. 6)

Fuchs, Carl-Johannes, Die Wohnungs- und Siedlungsfrage nach dem Kriege. Stuttgart 1918, S./p. 166 f.

Die Gartenstadtbewegung in Groß-Berlin. Beginn der Bautätigkeit in der Siedlung Falkenberg. In: Die Bauwelt (4) 1913, Heft 21, S./p. 21–24

Die Gartenstadt Falkenberg bei Grünau. In: Zentralblatt für das deutsche Baugewerbe (12) 1913, Nr./No. 43, S./p. 373–374

Gartenvorstadt Falkenberg bei Grünau i. Mark. In: Baugewerks-Zeitung (45) 1913, Heft/No. 86, S./p. 861 f.

Gartenstadt Falkenberg (Werbeschrift/Advertisement). Hg. von der/Ed. by Bauabteilung der Deutschen Gartenstadtgesellschaft, o. J./without year (ca./approx. 1913/14)

Gartenstadtkolonie Falkenberg in Grünau. In: Neuköllnische Zeitung (41) 1913, Nr./No. 243

Gartenstadt-Mitteilungen der deutschen Gartenstadtgesellschaft (5) 1911, S./p. 3, 12, 73, 118, 176

Gartenstadt-Mitteilungen der deutschen Gartenstadtgesellschaft (6) 1912, S./p. 10, 70, 72, 103 f., 144, 220

Gartenstadt-Mitteilungen der deutschen Gartenstadtgesellschaft (7) 1913, S./p. 37 ff, 55, 70 f., 111 ff., 119, 186

Gartenstadt-Mitteilungen der deutschen Gartenstadtgesellschaft (8) 1914 S./p. 41, 64, 132, 206

Gartenstadtsiedlung bei Berlin. In: Zeitschrift für Wohnungswesen (10) 1912, Heft/No. 15, S./p. 220

Haeselmann, J. F., Kriegerheimstätten. In: Der Profanbau, 1915, S./p. 317 ff.

Kästner, Wilhelm, Stadtbaurat Bruno Taut, Magdeburg. In: Moderne Bauformen (21) 1922, S./p. 289 ff.

Hartmann, Kristiana, Deutsche Gartenstadtbewegung, Kulturpolitik und Gesellschaftsreform. München 1976, S./p. 102 ff.

Hartmann, Kristiana, Bernoulli, Salvisberg, Taut: Architektur und Reformpolitik. In: Im Grünen wohnen – im Blauen planen. Ein Lesebuch zur Gartenstadt. Hg. von/Ed. by F. Bollerey/G. Fehl/K. Hartmann. Hamburg 1990, S./p. 397 f.

Hartmann, Kristina, Die Berliner Gartenstadt Falkenberg. Ein Planungsbeispiel der deutschen Gartenstadtbewegung. In: Wald, Garten und Park. Hg. von/Ed. by B. Kirchgässner / J. B. Schultis (= Stadt in der Geschichte. Bd. 18. Veröffentlichungen des Südwestdeutschen Arbeitskreises für Stadtgeschichtsforschung). Sigmaringen 1993, S./p. 83–95

Hartmann, Kristiana, Bruno Taut, der Architekt und Planer von Gartenstädten und Siedlungen. In: Bruno Taut 1880–1938. Architekt zwischen Moderne und Avantgarde. Hg. von/Ed. by W. Nerdinger, K. Hartmann, M. Schirren, M. Speidel. Stuttgart/München 2001

Hüter, Karl-Heinz, Architektur in Berlin 1900–1933. Dresden 1988, S./p. 193 ff.

Junghanns, Kurt, Bruno Taut und seine internationale Bedeutung als Städtebauer. In: Fünfzig Jahre Gartenstadt Falkenberg (1912–1963). Berlin 1963

Junghanns, Kurt, Bruno Taut 1880–1938. Berlin 1983

Kampffmeyer, Bernhard/Otto, Adolf, Die architektonische Einheitlichkeit in der Siedlung Falkenberg bei Grünau. Grundsätze und Bestimmungen für ihre Durchführung. Hg. von/Ed. by Bauabteilung der Deutschen Gartenstadt-Gesellschaft GmbH. Berlin 1913

Kampfmeyer, Hans, Die deutsche Gartenstadtbewegung – zusammenfassende Darstellung über den heutigen Stand der Bewegung. Berlin 1911, S./p. 61

Lesser, Ludwig, Der Kleingarten, seine zweckmässige Anlage und Bewirtschaftung. Berlin 1915

Lesser-Sayrac, Katrin u. a./et al., Ludwig Lesser (1869–1957). Erster freischaffender Gartenarchitekt in Berlin und seine Werke im Bezirk Reinickendorf. Beiträge zur Denkmalpflege in Berlin. Heft/No. 4. Berlin 1995

Lesser, Katrin, Gartenstadt Falkenberg. Gartendenkmalpflegerisches Gutachten. Historischer Zustand, Bestand, Konzept. Katrin Lesser im Auftrag der/by order of Berliner Bau- und Wohnungsgenossenschaft von 1892 eG. Berlin 2001

Lesser, Katrin, Die historische Grünplanung und ihre denkmalgerechte Wiederherstellung. In: Genossenschaftliche Wohnanlagen von Messel und Taut. Zur Wiederentdeckung baulicher und kultureller Höhepunkte der Berliner Bau- und Wohnungsgenossenschaft von 1892 eG. Berlin 2004, S./p. 42–45

Kolonie Tuschkasten. In: Berliner Tageblatt, Jg./Vol. 45, 1915, Nr./No. 349 vom/of 11.7.1915

Mebes, Paul, Das zweigeschossige Haus. In: Volkswohnung (1) 1919, S./p. 167 ff.

Michaelis, Marco de, Heinrich Tessenow 1876–1950. Das architektonische Gesamtwerk. Stuttgart 1991, S./p. 238

Mietskaserne oder Gartenstadthaus? Hg. von/Ed. by Gemeinnützige Baugenossenschaft Gartenvorstadt Groß-Berlin. (Werbebroschüre/Advertising brochure) Berlin o. J./without year (ca./approx. 1914)

Das Mietskasernen-Elend … Hg. von/Ed. by Gemeinnützige Baugenossenschaft Gartenvorstadt Groß-Berlin. (Werbebroschüre/Advertising brochure) Berlin o. J./without year (ca./approx. 1914)

Novy, Klaus/von Neumann-Cosel, Barbara, Zwischen Tradition und Innovation. 100 Jahre Berliner Bau- und Wohnungsgenossenschaft von 1892. Berlin 1992

Otto, Adolf, Wie es war und wurde. In: Der Falkenberg 1913–1923. Denkschrift zum 10jährigen Bestehen der Gartenstadt-Siedlung Falkenberg-Grünau. Hg. von/Ed. by Robert Tautz

Falkenberg-Altglienicke, 1. Oktober 1923/1st October 1923 (= Der Falkenberg. Zwanglose Worte zum Weiterdenken. Mitteilungsblatt der Gartenvorstadt, Nr./No. 6)

Pehnt, Wolfgang, Ferne Ziele, große Hoffnungen. Der Deutsche Werkbund 1918–1924. In: L. Burckhardt (Hg./Ed.), Der Werkbund in Deutschland, Österreich und der Schweiz (Stuttgart 1978), S./p. 72–80

Posener, Julius, Bruno Taut. Eine Rede zu seinem fünfzigsten Todestag (= Anmerkungen zur Zeit, Heft/No. 28, hg. von der/ed. by Akademie der Künste) Berlin 1989, S./p. 26 ff.

Posener, Julius, Berlin auf dem Wege zu einer neuen Architektur – Das Zeitalter Wilhelms II. München 1979, S./p. 555 f.

Rahmenplanung für die Gartenstadtsiedlung Am Falkenberg, Gutachten im Auftrag der Senatsverwaltung für Bau- und Wohnungswesen in Zusammenarbeit mit dem Bezirk Treptow/Expert opinion by order of Senatsverwaltung für Bau- und Wohnungswesen in cooperation with the district of Treptow, Arge Gartenstadt Falkenberg, Berlin 1991

Scharf, Armin, Farbe in der Architektur – Gestaltungskriterien und Beispiele für den Wohnungsbau. München 2002, S./p. 102–105

Seifert, Clemens, Feiern und Feste des Berliner Proletariats. 65 Jahre Gartenstadt Falkenberg. In: Kultur und Lebensweise des Proletariats. Arbeitsmaterial des Zentralen Fachausschusses Kulturgeschichte / Volkskunde beim Kulturbund der DDR. Berlin 1980

Speidel, Manfred, Bruno Taut Retrospektive 1880–1938. Natur und Fantasie (= Katalog zur Ausstellung vom 11. Mai bis 30. Juli 1995 in Magdeburg). Berlin 1995

Staake, Berthold, Die Farben der Gartenstadt, restauratorische Untersuchung anläßlich der Restaurierung der Siedlung in den 1960er Jahren. (Typoskript/Typoscript) Berlin 1966/67

Strey, Waltraut, Die Zeichnungen von Heinrich Tessenow. Der Bestand in der Kunstbibliothek Berlin. Berlin 1981, S./p. 17 f, Tafel/Image S. 58

Taut, Bruno, Die Gartenstadt Falkenberg b. Berlin. Der neue Bebauungsplan. In: Gartenstadt-Mitteilungen der deutschen Gartenstadtgesellschaft (8) 1914 Nr./No. 3, S./p. 49–51

Taut, Bruno, Stellungnahme zum Artikel/Statement concerning the article „Wohnungsbau in Einheitsformen"

(von/by Gustav Wolf, in: Der Baumeister (13) 1915, Nr./No. 4). In: Der Baumeister (13) 1915, Nr./No. 8, S./p. 62 f.

Taut, Bruno, Architektonisches zum Siedlungswerk. In: Der Siedler (1) 1918, Nr./No. 6, S./p. 252

Taut, Bruno, Gartenstadtsiedlung Falkenberg in Grünau bei Berlin. In: Der Siedler (1) 1918/19, Nr./No. 7, S./p. 307 f.

Taut, Bruno, Beobachtungen über Farbenwirkung aus meiner Praxis. In: Bauwelt (10) 1919, Nr./No. 38, S./p. 12

Taut, Bruno, Drei Siedlungen. Gartenstadt-Siedlung bei Berlin. In: Wasmuths Monatshefte für Baukunst (4) 1919, S./p. 183 ff.

Taut, Bruno, Der Regenbogen. Aufruf zum farbigen Bauen. Zitiert nach/Quoted from: B. Taut. Frühlicht 1920–1922. Eine Folge für die Verwirklichung des neuen Baugedankens (Berlin/Frankfurt a. M./Wien 1963), S./p. 97 f.

Taut, Bruno, Die Gartenstadtkrone. In: Der Falkenberg 1913–1923. Denkschrift zum 10jährigen Bestehen der Gartenstadt-Siedlung Falkenberg-Grünau. Hg. von/Ed. by Robert Tautz. Falkenberg-Altglienicke, 1. Oktober 1923/1st October 1923 (= Der Falkenberg. Zwanglose Worte zum Weiterdenken. Mitteilungsblatt der Gartenvorstadt, Nr./No. 6)

Taut, Bruno, Volksfest-Haus und Siedlung Falkenberg bei Grünau. In: Die Bauwelt (15) 1924, Heft/No. 11, S./p. 571

Taut, Bruno, Siedlungsmemoiren. In: Architektur der DDR (24) 1975, Nr./No. 12, S./p. 761

Taut, Bruno, Der neue Wohnbau. Leipzig/Berlin 1927

Tautz, Robert, Piefke! In: Der Falkenberg. Zwanglose Worte zum Weiterdenken. Mitteilungsblatt der Gartenvorstadt, Nr./No. 7

Tessenow, Heinrich, Der Wohnungsbau. München 1909

Tessenow, Heinrich, Hausbau und dergleichen. Berlin 1916, S./p. 25 f., 102–105

„Tuschkastensiedlung" Falkenberg, Alt-Glienicke (Treptow). In: Reparieren, Renovieren, Restaurieren – Vorbildliche Denkmalpflege in Berlin, hg. vom/ed. by Landesdenkmalamt Berlin. Berlin 1998, S./p. 63–64

Unsere Kriegsinvaliden, Heim und Werkstatt in Gartensiedlungen. Denkschrift der Deutschen Gartenstadt-Gesellschaft über den Dienst des Vaterlandes an den Kriegsinvaliden und den Hinterbliebenen der gefallenen Krieger. Leipzig 1915, S./p. 52–62

Wangerin, Gerda/Weiss, Gerhard, Heinrich Tessenow. Ein Baumeister 1876–1950. Leben, Lehre, Werk. Essen 1976, S./p. 122, 211

**Siedlung Schillerpark**
Architekturwerkstatt Helge Pitz/Winfried Brenne mit Franz Jaschke. Siedlung am Schillerpark. Dokumentation und Rekonstruktion des Originalzustandes der Siedlung. Grundlage für zukünftige Erneuerungs- und Instandhaltungsmaßnahmen im Rahmen des Denkmalschutzes. (Typoskript/Typoscript). 2 Bde./Vol. Berlin 1990

Architekturwerkstatt Helge Pitz/Winfried Brenne mit Franz Jaschke. Siedlung am Schillerpark. Instandsetzungskonzept im Rahmen des Denkmalschutzes. (Typoskript/Typoscript). Berlin 1991

Ardizzola, Paola, Am Schillerpark, Berlino 1924. La Siedlung dimenticata di Bruno Taut. In: Opus 7 (2003/2004), S./p. 453–466

Bauwelt (18) 1927, S./p. 38–39 (= Heft/No. 2, Beilage/Supplement „Der neue Bau", S./p. 46–47)

Berlin und seine Bauten. Hg. von/Ed. by Architekten- und Ingenieur-Verein zu Berlin. Teil IV A. Berlin/München/Düsseldorf 1970, S./p. 270 f., Obj. 105 II

Berlin und seine Bauten. Hg. von/Ed. by Architekten- und Ingenieur-Verein zu Berlin. Teil IV B. Berlin/München/Düsseldorf 1974, S./p. 24, Obj. 905, S./p. 372 f.

Berliner Wohnungsbauten aus öffentlichen Mitteln. In: Baugewerkszeitung (58) 1926, S./p. 547–548

75 Jahre Berliner Bau- und Wohnungsgenossenschaft von 1892. Berlin 1967

Bothe, Rolf, Bruno Tauts Siedlung Schillerpark, „eine bewußte Scheußlichkeit"? In: Schlösser, Gärten, Berlin. Festschrift für Martin Sperlich zum 60. Geburtstag 1979 (= Kunstwissenschaftliche Studien, Technische Universität Berlin. Hg. von/Ed. by Detlef Heikamp. Bd./Vol. 1. Tübingen 1980, S./p. 179–200

Bothe, Rolf, Erker, Balkons und Loggien und die Bedeutung des „Außenwohnraums" bei Bruno Taut. Die Siedlung Schillerpark in Berlin-Wedding. In: neue heimat. Monatshefte für neuzeitlichen Wohnungs- und Städtebau, 1980, Nr./No. 5, S./p. 38–47, 100

Brenne, Winfried, Creating a cosmos of colours – Bruno Taut's housing estates in Berlin. In: Modern Colour Technology – Ideals and Conservation, hg. von/ed. by do.co.mo.mo international working party (= preservation technology, dossier 5). Leuven 2002, S./p. 23–24

Brenne, Winfried, On the Reconstruction of Bruno Taut's Colored Architecture. In: a+u Architecture and Urbanism, Nr./No. 384, Japan, September 2002, S./p. 128–131

Brenne, Winfried, Deutscher Werkbund Berlin (Hg./Ed.), Bruno Taut. Meister des farbigen Bauens in Berlin, Berlin 2005, S./p. 68–73

Dolff-Bonekämper, Gabi, Die Schillerpark-Siedlung in Berlin-Wedding – ein Beitrag zum Wohnungsbau der 20er Jahre. In: Denkmalschutz und Denkmalpflege in Berlin.

Jahrbuch/Yearbook 1994 (= Beiträge zur Denkmalpflege in Berlin, Heft/No. 7). Berlin 1996, S./p. 57–60

Brunner, Karl-Heinz, Das großstädtische Mietshaus. In: Zeitschrift für Bauwesen (79) 1929, S. 10

Denkmaltopographie Bundesrepublik Deutschland. Denkmale in Berlin. Bezirk Mitte. Ortsteile Wedding und Gesundbrunnen. Petersberg 2004, S./p. 238 f.

Dehio, Handbuch der deutschen Kunstdenkmäler. Berlin. München 1994, S./p. 526 f.

Die Form (1) 1925/26, Taf. von S./Image p. 25

Gries, Annett/Hackenberg, Klaus-Peter, Siedlung Schillerpark. Gartendenkmalpflegerisches Gutachten. Anlagegeschichte und Dokumentation. Büro Hackenberg/Annett Gries im Auftrag der/by order of Berliner Bau- und Wohnungsgenossenschaft von 1892. Berlin 2003

Gries, Annett, Hackenberg, Klaus-Peter, Vom grünen Hof zur Stadtlandschaft. Die Berliner Siedlung – ein Beitrag zur Freiraumgestaltung im urbanen Siedlungsbau der 1920er und 1950er Jahre. In: Stadt + Grün (53) 2004, S./p. 44–52

Die neue GEHAG Siedlung in Berlin. In: Wohnungswirtschaft (7) 1930, Nr./No. 14/15, S./p. 269 f.

Junghanns, Kurt, Bruno Taut 1880–1933. Berlin 1983 (2. Auflage/2nd Edition), S./p. 69–71, Abb./fig. 139–146

Für die neue Baukunst Berlins! In: Wohnungswirtschaft (2) 1925, Nr./No. 1, S./p. 3–5

Neue Berliner Siedlungen. In: Deutsche Bauhütte (31) 1927, S./p. 163

Novy, Klaus/von Neumann-Cosel, Barbara (Hg./Ed.), Zwischen Tradition und Innovation. 100 Jahre Berliner Bau- und Wohnungsgenossenschaft von 1892. Berlin 1992, S./p. 51, 75–79, 94, 99, 105–107, 142 f., 146 f.

Schallenberger, Jacob/Kraffert, Hans, Berliner Wohnungsbauten aus öffentlichen Mitteln. Berlin 1926, S./p. 108–109

Schallenberger, Jacob/Gutkind, Erwin, Berliner Wohnbauten der letzten Jahre. Berlin 1931, S./p. 102

Schmidt, Friedrich, Ebel/Martin, Wohnungsbau der Nachkriegszeit in Deutschland. Bd./Vol. 1. Berlin-Brandenburg. Berlin 1929, S./p. 196

Soziale Bauwirtschaft (8) 1928, S./p. 27

Taut, Bruno, Die Lücke im Baublock – eine Lücke in der Bauordnung von Berlin. In: Bauwelt (18) 1927, S./p. 791–793

Bruno Taut 1880–1938 (Katalog zur Ausstellung der Akademie der Künste vom 29.6–3.8.1980). Berlin 1980, Kat. Nr./Cat. No. 101.1–101.16, 102–105, Abb. S./fig. p. 221

Bruno Taut 1880–1938. Architekt zwischen Moderne und Avantgarde. Hg. von/Ed. by W. Nerdinger, K. Hartmann, M. Schirren, M. Speidel. Stuttgart/München 2001, S./p. 355–357

Umbreit, Paul, Warum Wohnstadt Carl Legien ? In: Wohnungswirtschaft (7) 1930, Nr./No. 14/15, S./p. 271

Zöller-Stock, Bettina, Bruno Taut. Die Innenraumentwürfe des Berliner Architekten. Stuttgart 1993, S./p. 91–93

## Großsiedlung Britz (Hufeisensiedlung)

Adler, Leo, Siedlungen in Berlin-Britz. In: Wasmuths Monatshefte für Baukunst. (11) 1927. Nr./No. 10, S./p. 385–390

Adler, Leo, Neuzeitliche Miethäuser und Siedlungen. Berlin 1931, S./p. 164 f.

Architekturwerkstatt Helge Pitz/Winfried Brenne, Großsiedlung Britz (Hufeisensiedlung). Dokumentation und Rekonstruktion des Originalzustandes. Grundlage für zukünftige Erneuerungs- und Instandhaltungsmaßnahmen im Rahmen des Denkmalschutzes. Architekturwerkstatt Helge Pitz/Winfried Brenne (Bd./Vol. 1 Planungs- und Baugeschichte von/by A. Jaeggi, J. Tomisch). Gutachten im Auftrag der/Expert opinion by order of Gemeinnützigen Heimstätten AG. 11 Bde./Vol. Berlin 1984–91

Bätzner, Nike, Die Hufeisensiedlung Britz. Symbol einer idealen Gemeinschaft. In: Das XX. Jahrhundert. Ein Jahrhundert der Kunst. Köln 1999, S./p. 32–33

Baumann, Martin, Freiraumplanung in den Siedlungen der zwanziger Jahre am Beispiel der Planungen des Gartenarchitekten Leberecht Migge. Halle 2002, S./p. 143–145

Behrendt, W. C., Die Form unserer Zeit. In: Gartenkunst (42) 1929, Sonderheft/Special issue, S./p. 21–22

Berlin und seine Bauten. Hg. von/Ed. by Architekten- und Ingenieur-Verein zu Berlin. Teil IV A. Berlin/München/Düsseldorf 1970, S./p. 162, 163, 360, 361

Berlin und seine Bauten. Hg. von/Edited by Architekten- und Ingenieur-Verein zu Berlin. Teil IV B. Berlin/München/Düsseldorf 1974, S./p. 509–514

Brenne, Winfried, Wie die Siedlungen gebaut wurden. Damals – Heute. Bautechnik, Konstruktion und Ausstattung. In: N. Huse (Hg./Ed.). Siedlungen der zwanziger Jahre – heute. Berlin 1984. S./p. 47 f.

Brenne, Winfried, Die „farbige Stadt" und die farbige Siedlung. In: Mineralfarben – Beiträge zur Geschichte und Restaurierung von Fassadenmalereien und Anstrichen. Zürich 1998, S./p. 73–74

Brenne, Winfried, Creating a cosmos of colours – Bruno Taut's housing estates in Berlin. In: Modern Colour Technology – Ideals and Conservation, hg. von/ed. by do.co.mo.mo international working party (= preservation technology, dossier 5). Leuven 2002, S./p. 23–24, 38

Brenne, Winfried, Deutscher Werkbund Berlin (Hg./Ed.), Bruno Taut. Meister des farbigen Bauens in Berlin, Berlin 2005, S./p. 90–97

Bruno Taut: Colonia Hufeisen, Berlin-Britz, 1925–1927. In: AV monografias 1995, Nr./No. 56, S./p. 22–23

Dexel, Grete/Dexel, Walter, Das Wohnhaus von heute, Leipzig 1928, S./p. 70–71, Abb./fig. 48–51

Drescher, Barbara/Mohrmann, Rita/Stern, S., Untersuchung des Gehölzbestandes der Hufeisen-Siedlung in Berlin-Britz. Berlin 1981 (Typoskript/Typoscript)

Gut, Albert, Der Wohungsbau in Deutschland nach dem Weltkriege. München 1928, S./p. 539–543 u. Tafel/and Image XI

Hilpert, Thilo, Die andere Moderne. Bruno Tauts Stadtvision und die Hufeisensiedlung Britz. In: Ute Schmidt-Krafft (Hg./Ed.): Symposium Bruno Taut. Magdeburg 1995, S./p. 80–89

Hilpert, Thilo, Hufeisensiedlung in Britz. 1926–1980. Ein alternativer Siedlungsbau der 20er Jahre als Studienobjekt. Berlin 1980 (TU Berlin: Dokumente aus Forschung und Lehre, Nr./No. 1)

Hoh-Slodczyk, Christine, Siedlungsbau als Aufgabe und die Antworten der Architekten. In: N. Huse (Hg./Ed.), Siedlungen der zwanziger Jahre – heute. Berlin 1984. S./p. 34 ff.

Die Hufeisensiedlung in Britz. In: Einfa-Nachrichten (4) 1933. Nr./No. 5/7, S./p. 3–5

Jaeggi, Annemarie, Hufeisensiedlung Britz. Planungs- und Baugeschichte. In: Nobert Huse (Hg./Ed.), Siedlungen der zwanziger Jahre – heute, Berlin 1984. S./p. 111–136

Jaeggi, Annemarie, Die Berliner Hufeisensiedlung von Bruno Taut, Architektur im Spannungsfeld von Politik und Wirtschaft. In: Festschrift für Johannes Langner. Hg. von/Ed. by K. G. Beuckes und/and A. Jaeggi. Münster 1997, S./p. 273–296

Johannes, Heinz, Neues Bauen in Berlin. Berlin 1931. S./p. 69–73

Junghanns, Kurt, Bruno Taut, 1880–1938. Berlin 1983, S./p. 73–76, Abb./fig. 152–168

Kloß, Klaus-Peter, Siedlungen der 20er Jahre. Berlin 1982, S./p. 14–27

Langeheinecke, J., Untersuchung in Berlin-Neukölln, Hufeisensiedlung zur Herstellung einer planungsrechtlichen Entscheidungsgrundlage unter Berücksichtigung von denkmalpflegerischen Aspekten. Angef. von/Produced by J. Langeheinecke, C. P. Claussen (Planer in der/Planner in Pankemühle). Berlin 2001

Lesser, Katrin, Untersuchung der denkmalgeschützten Freiflächen und Konzeption für den zukünftigen Umgang. 3. Bde../Vol. Berlin 2003 (Typoskript/Typoscript)

Linneke, Richard, Zwei Jahre Gehag-Arbeit. In: Wohnungswirtschaft. (3) 1926, Nr./No. 8, S./p. 53–60

Migge, Leberecht, Höfe und Gärten bei Miethausblöcken. In: Wohnungswirtschaft (4) 1927 Nr./No. 20, S./p. 165–170

Migge, Leberecht, Groß-Berliner Siedlungsfreiraum. In: Die Wohnung (5) 1930. Nr./No. 4, S./p. 97–108

Neue Berliner Siedlungen. In: Deutsche Bauhütte (31) 1927, S./p. 163

Novy, Klaus/Prinz, M., Illustrierte Geschichte der Gemeinwirtschaft. Berlin/Bonn 1985, S./p. 105 ff.

Pitz, Helge, Die Farbigkeit der vier Siedlungen – Ein Werkstattbericht. In: Norbert Huse (Hg./Ed.), Siedlungen der zwanziger Jahre – heute. Berlin 1984. S./p. 59

Rotival, Maurice, Les grandes ensembles. In: L'architecture d'aujourd'hui (6) 1935, Heft/No. 6, S./p. 68

Schmidt, Friedrich/Ebel, Martin, Wohnungsbau der Nachkriegszeit in Deutschland. Bd./Vol. 1. Berlin-Brandenburg. Berlin 1929, S./p. 182, 183, 198, 199

Shigemura, T., Der nie zu Ende geträumte Traum vom gemeinschaftlichen Wohnen. In: Manfred Speidel, Bruno Taut Retrospektive 1880–1938. Natur und Fantasie (= Katalog zur Ausstellung vom 11. Mai bis 30. Juli 1995 in Magdeburg). Berlin 1995, S./p. 236–240

Siedlung Britz. In: Neues Berlin, 1929, S./p. 18 f.

Die sozialen Baubetriebe Berlins. In: Soziale Bauwirtschaft (7) 1927, S./p. 18–20, 263 f.

Taut, Bruno, Neue und alte Form im Bebauungsplan. Wohnungswirtschaft (3) 1926, Nr./No. 24, S./p. 198 f.

Taut, Bruno, Der Außenwohnraum. In: Gehag-Nachrichten (2) 1931, Nr./No. 1/2, S./p. 9 ff

Taut, Bruno, Die Jugend muß bauen. In: Wohnungswirtschaft (4) 1927, Nr./No. 20, S./p. 163–165

Taut, Bruno, Siedlungsmemoiren, Erstveröffentlichung des 1936 verfassten Artikels in/First publication of the article of 1936 in: Architektur der DDR (24) 1975, Nr./No. 12, S./p. 761 ff.

Bruno Taut 1880–1938. Architekt zwischen Moderne und Avantgarde. Hg. von/Ed. by W. Nerdinger, K. Hartmann, M. Schirren, M. Speidel. Stuttgart/München 2001, S./p. 12 f., 107, 148, 363–365

Wagner, Martin, Großsiedlung, der Weg zur Rationalisierung des Wohnungsbaues. In: Wohnungswirtschaft (3) 1926, Nr./No. 11/14, S./p. 81–114

1000 Wohnungen – Siedlung in Britz. In: Bauwelt. (18) 1927, Nr./No. 9, Beilage/supplement, S./p. 12–14

Wittkower, Käthe, Les nouvelles cités-jardins du Grand Berlin. In: Art et décoration (55) 1929, S./p. 145–160

Wedemeyer, Alfred, Die Großsiedlung Britz in Berlin Neukölln. In: Deutsche Bauzeitung (61) 1927, Heft/No. 98, S./p. 801–808 und Heft/No. 99, S./p. 809–815

Zöller-Stock, Bettina, Bruno Taut. Die Innenraumentwürfe des Berliner Architekten. Stuttgart 1993, S./p. 94–96

**Wohnstadt Carl Legien**
Adler, Leo, Neuzeitliche Miethäuser und Siedlungen. Berlin 1931, S./p. 159–161

Atelier Schreckenberg, Wohnstadt Carl Legien. Gartendenkmalpflegerische Recherche und Analyse des „Außenwohnraums" in der Wohnstadt. Atelier Schreckenberg Partner. Juni/June 2001

Die Bau- und Kunstdenkmale in der DDR. Hauptstadt Berlin I. Hg. von/Ed. by Institut für Denkmalpflege der DDR. Berlin 1983, S./p. 412 f.

Becker, Christine, Wohnstadt Carl Legien. Dokumentation zur restauratorischen Farb- und Putzuntersuchung der Kopfbauten. Berlin 2000

Becker, Christine, Wohnstadt Carl Legien. Dokumentation zur restauratorischen Farbuntersuchung der Blöcke A–G. Berlin 2000

Beil, Viola, Die Wohnstadt Carl Legien in Berlin-Prenzlauer Berg, von Bruno Taut 1929–1930 erbaut. Erarbeitung einer denkmalpflegerischen Rahmenzielstellung (Abschlußarbeit zum Postgradualstudium Denkmalpflege an der Technischen Universität Dresden 1988/89). Typoskript/Typoscript. Berlin 1990.

Berlin und seine Bauten. Hg. von/Ed. by Architekten- und Ingenieur-Verein zu Berlin. Teil IV A. Berlin/München/Düsseldorf 1970, S./p. 85 f., 176, 273 Obj. 110, I

Berlin und seine Bauten. Hg. von/Ed. by Architekten- und Ingenieur-Verein zu Berlin. Teil IV B. Berlin/München/Düsseldorf 1974, S./p. 24 f., S./p. 381 f., Obj. 916

Berliner Groß-Bauten des Jahres 1930. In: Bauwelt (22) 1931, S./p. 633 (= Nr./No. 19, Beilage/supplement, S./p. 11)

Die Berliner Wohnungsbauten der letzten Jahre. In: Die Bauzeitung (41) 1931, S./p. 272

Blunck, Erich, Berliner Bauten aus neuester Zeit. In: Deutsche Bauzeitung (65) 1931, S./p. 8

Brenne, Winfried, Wohnstadt Carl Legien. Dokumentation und Rekonstruktion des Originalzustandes der Gebäude als Grundlage für zukünftige Erneuerungs- und Instandhaltungsmaßnahmen im Rahmen des Denkmalschutzes. Blockabschnitt Trachtenbrodtstraße 2–18. Winfried Brenne Architekten im Auftrag der/by order of GEHAG. 2 Bde./Vol. Berlin 1993

Brenne, Winfried, Wohnstadt Carl Legien. Dokumentation des Originalzustandes und Maßnahmenkatalog für die Wiederherstellung. Blockabschnitt Sodtkestraße 20–36. Winfried Brenne Architekten im Auftrag der/by order of GEHAG. 2 Bde./Vol. Berlin 1995

Brenne, Winfried, Fazination Farbe. In: Symposium Bruno Taut in Magedeburg, Dokumentation. Hg. vom Stadtplanungsamt Magdeburg/Edited by urban development office Magdeburg (= Schiftenreihe des Stadtplanungsamtes Magdeburg 48 I/II) Magdeburg 1995, S./p. 228–229

Brenne, Winfried, Die „farbige Stadt" und die farbige Siedlung. In: Mineralfarben – Beiträge zur Geschichte und Restaurierung von Fassadenmalereien und Anstrichen. Zürich 1998, S./p. 75

Brenne, Winfried, Creating a cosmos of colours – Bruno Taut's housing estates in Berlin, in: Modern Colour Technology – Ideals and Conservation, hg. von/ed. by do.co.mo.mo international working party (= preservation technology, dossier 5) Leuven 2002, S./p. 23–24

Brenne, Winfried, Deutscher Werkbund Berlin (Hg./Ed.), Bruno Taut. Meister des farbigen Bauens in Berlin, Berlin 2005, S./p. 140–145

Les cités-jardins de Berlin. In: L'architecture d'aujourd'hui 1993, Nr./No. 287, S./p. 49

Deutsche Bauzeitung (65) 1931, S./p. 173 (Bauwirtschaft und Baurecht)

Die schöne Großstadtwohnung. Die Wohnstadt Carl Legien. In: Einfa Nachrichten (3) 1932, Nr./No. 9/10, S./p. 2 f.

Huth, Wohnstadt Carl Legien, Berlin N. In: Deutsche Bauhütte (34) 1930, S./p. 313–314

Johannes, Heinz, Neues Bauen in Berlin. Berlin 1931, S./p. 79

Junghanns, Kurt, Bruno Taut 1880–1933. Berlin 1983 (2. Auflage/2nd Edition), S./p. 76–77, Abb./fig. 169–177

Junghanns, Kurt, Das Grün in den Wohnanlagen von Bruno Taut. In: Landschaftsarchitektur (2) 1973, Nr./No. 2, S./p. 77–79

Klimeczek, Heinz-Josef, Die gesunde Wohnung – Die Genese der Bauordnung vom 3.11.1925 (mit einem Fallbeispiel: Die Herstellung gesunder Wohnungen – Die Wohnstadt Carl Legien). Dissertation an der Technischen Universität von Berlin 2005

Ostdeutsche Bauzeitung (29) 1931, S./p. 218–219

Rohloff, Kurt, Baufinanzierung und Miete der Berliner Wohnungen. In: Die Baugilde (13) 1931, S./p. 846

Schallenberger, Jacob/Gutkind, Erwin, Berliner Wohnbauten der letzten Jahre. Berlin 1931, S./p. 108–109

Speidel, Manfred, Bruno Taut Retrospektive 1880–1938. Natur und Fantasie (= Katalog zur Ausstellung vom 11. Mai bis 30. Juli 1995 in Magdeburg). Berlin 1995, S./p. 220–226

Snodgrass, Karin M., A Visonary in Practice. Bruno Taut and his Wohnstadt Carl Legien. Senior Honours Dissertation, University of St. Andrews, Department or Art History 1995 (Typoskript/Typoscript)

Bruno Taut 1880–1938 (Katalog zur Ausstellung der Akademie der Künste vom 29.6–3.8.1980). Berlin 1980, Kat. Nr./Cat. No. 115.1–115.14, S./p. 81, 223–234

Bruno Taut 1880–1938. Architekt zwischen Moderne und Avantgarde. Hg. von/Ed. by W. Nerdinger, K. Hartmann, M. Schirren, M. Speidel. Stuttgart/München 2001, S./p. 376 f.

Wedemeyer, Alfred, Die Wohnstadt Carl Legien in Berlin. In: Deutsche Bauzeitung (65) 1931, S./p. 29–33

Wohnstadt Carl Legien. In: Einfa Nachrichten (1) 1930, Heft/No. 3

Zöller-Stock, Bettina, Bruno Taut. Die Innenraumentwürfe des Berliner Architekten. Stuttgart 1993, S./p. 109–111

**Weiße Stadt**
Adler, Leo, Neuzeitliche Miethäuser und Siedlungen. Berlin 1931, S./p. 172–177

Architekturwerkstatt Pitz/Brenne/Böhme, U. /Tomisch, J., Weiße Stadt Berlin Reinickendorf, Dokumentation der 50jährigen Geschichte, Erarbeitung des Originalzustandes sowie der Grundlagen für zukünftige denkmalpflegerische Maßnahmen (Typoskript/Typoscript). 6 Bde./Vol. Berlin 1981

Behne, Adolf, Städtebauer auf neuen Wegen. Siedlungen Siemensstadt und Reinickendorf in Berlin. In: Berliner Illustrierte Zeitung vom/of 15.6.1930

Berlin und seine Bauten. Hg. von/Ed. by Architekten- und Ingenieur-Verein zu Berlin. Teil IV A. Berlin/München/Düsseldorf 1970, S./p. 165–167, 195, 376–378, Obj. 254

Berlin und seine Bauten. Hg. von/Ed. by Architekten- und Ingenieur-Verein zu Berlin. Teil IV B. Berlin/München/Düsseldorf 1974, Obj. 1088–1090

Blunck, Erich, Berliner Bauten aus neuester Zeit im Rahmen einer neuen deutschen Baukunst. In: Deutsche Bauzeitung, 1931, S./p. 8

Brenne, Winfried Architekten, Wohnbebauung Aroser Allee 141–147, Denkmalpflegerische Bestandsaufnahme und Maßnahmenkatalog. Erstellt im Auftrag der/Produced by order of GSW. Berlin 2000

Brenne, Winfried Architekten, Denkmalpflegerisches Konzept zur Erneuerung der Wintergartenfenster und der Rückfassaden Aroser Allee 155–191. Erstellt im Auftrag der/Produced by order of GSW. Berlin 2000

Brenne, Winfried, Preservation of steel frame windows – The Weiße Stadt Estate in Berlin-Reinickendorf 1929–30. In: Reframing the Modern – Substitute Windows and Glass, hg. von/ed. by do.co.mo.mo international working party (= preservation technology, dossier 3). Delft 2000, S./p. 83–87

Das Fernheizwerk am Schillerring in Berlin-Reinickendorf. In: Deutsche Bauzeitung (65) 1931, S./p. 236–238

Duvigneau, Hans Jörg, Wohnhäuser und Wohnviertel in Berlin, Die GSW im Dienste Berlins und ihrer Mieter 1924–1999, hg. von der/ed. by GSW, Berlin 1999

Großsiedlung Berlin-Reinickendorf, Schillerpromenade. In: Bauwelt (21) 1930, Nr./No. 48, Sonderbeilage/Special Supplement, S./p. 1–24

Hart, R., Gedanken zur Frage der Großsiedlungsgärten. In: Deutsche Bauhütte (35) 1931, S./p. 80, 82

Hüter, Karl-Heinz, Architektur in Berlin. 1900–1933. Dresden 1987. S./p. 224–227

Huth, Friedrich, Ein Massen-Kleinwohnungsbau in Berlin-Reinickendorf. In: Deutsche Bauhütte (34) 1930, S./p. 253–255

Jaeggi, Annemarie, Weiße Stadt, Planungs- und Baugeschichte. In: Siedlungen der zwanziger Jahre – heute. Vier Berliner Großsiedlungen 1924–1984. Hg. von/Ed. by Nobert Huse. Berlin 1984, S./p. 181–200

Johannes, Heinz, Neues Bauen in Berlin. Berlin 1931, S./p. 79

Klinger, Ralf/Pröbster, Hans-Jürgen, Gartendenkmalpflegerisches Gutachten Weiße Stadt – Berlin Reinickendorf, Gutachten im Auftrag des Senators für Stadtentwicklung und Umweltschutz, Abt. III – Gartendenkmalpflege (Typoskript/Typoscript). Berlin 1984

Kloß, Klaus-Peter, Siedlungen der 20er Jahre. Berlin 1982, S./p. 56–68

Kloß, Klaus-Peter, Vier Siedlungen der 20er Jahre als Projekt der Denkmalpflege. In: Siedlungen der zwanziger Jahre – heute. Vier Berliner Großsiedlungen 1924–1984. Hg. von/Ed. by Nobert Huse. Berlin 1984, S./p. 91–106

Lesser, Ludwig, Billige Gärten bei Großsiedlungen. Die Gärten vor den Bauten an der Berliner Schillerpromenade. In: Deutsche Bauhütte (35) 1931, S./p. 80 ff.

Lesser-Sayrac, Katrin, Ludwig Lesser (1869–1957). Erster freischaffender Gartenarchitekt in Berlin und seine Werke im Bezirk Reinickendorf. In: Beiträge zur Denkmalpflege in Berlin, Nr./No. 4, hg. von der/ed. by Senatsverwaltung für Stadtentwicklung und Umweltschutz. Berlin 1995, S./p. 43–46

Loger, Wilmer/Ringkamp, Christa u. a./et al. (= Hortec Garten- und Landschaftsplanung GBR) Gartendenkmalpflegerische Wiederherstellungsplanung, Weisse Stadt Rei-

nickendorf. Gutachten im Auftrag der/Expert opinion by order of GSW (Typoskript/Typoscript). Berlin 1985

Pitz, Helge, Die Farbigkeit der vier Siedlungen – Ein Werkstattbericht. In: Siedlungen der zwanziger Jahre – heute. Hg. von/Ed. by Norbert Huse. Vier Berliner Großsiedlungen 1924–1984. Berlin 1984, S./p. 59–61

Posener, Julius, Grand Lotissement à Berlin-Reinickendorf. In: L'architecture d'aujourd'hui (2) 1931, Nr./No. 5, S./p. 38–43

Schallenberger, Jacob/Gutkind, Erwin, Berliner Wohnbauten der letzten Jahre. Berlin 1931, S./p. 110–114

Büro Schmidt-Seifert, „Weiße Stadt" Berlin Reinickendorf. Umsetzung der gartendenkmalpflegerischen Konzeption, Gutachten angef. von/Expert opinion produced by Peter Schmidt-Seifert, Stefan Helmich im Auftrag der/by order of GSW, Berlin 2000.

Tomisch, Jürgen/Schomann, Rainer, Denkmaltopographie Bundesrepublik Deutschland, Baudenkmale in Berlin, Bezirk Reinickendorf, Ortsteil Reinickendorf, hg. vom Senator für Stadtentwicklung und Umweltschutz/ed. by the Minister for Urban Development and Environmental Protection. Berlin, o. J./without year (1988), S./p. 68–70, 94, 168–171

Wagner, Martin/Behne, Adolf, Bebauungsplan Reinickendorf. In: Das Neue Berlin, 1929, S./p. 82 f.

## Großsiedlung Siemensstadt
Adler, Leo, Neuzeitliche Miethäuser und Siedlungen. Berlin 1931, S./p. 144–157

Achitekturwerkstatt Helge Pitz/Winfried Benne. Großsiedlung Siemensstadt. Dokumentation und Rekonstruktion des Originalzustandes der Gebäude. (Bd./Vol. 1 Planungs- und Baugeschichte von Jürgen Tomisch). Gutachten im Auftrag der/Expert opinion by order of GSW. (Typoskript/Typoscript). 8 Bde../Vol. Berlin 1984

Achitekturwerkstatt Helge Pitz/Winfried Brenne. Großsiedlung Siemensstadt. Bauabschnitt Hugo Häring. Dokumentation der historisch-technischen Betreuung der Erneuerungs- und Instandsetzungsmaßnahmen im Rahmen des Denkmalschutzes 1984/85. (Typoskript/Typoscript). Berlin 1986

Achitekturwerkstatt Helge Pitz/Winfried Brenne. Großsiedlung Siemensstadt. Bauabschnitt Hans Scharoun. Dokumentation der historisch-technischen Betreuung der Erneuerungs- und Instandsetzungsmaßnahmen im Rahmen des Denkmalschutzes 1985/86. (Typoskript/Typoscript). Berlin 1986

Badovici, J., L'architecture en Allemagne. In: L'architecture vivante. (37) 1931, S./p. 5–9

Bauer, F., Eine moderne Großsiedlung in Berlin-Siemensstadt. In: Architektur und Bautechnik (18) 1931, S./p. 97–99, 118–122, 111–112, 105, 110, 113–117

Baumann, Martin, Freiraumplanung in den Siedlungen der zwanziger Jahre am Beispiel der Planungen des Gartenarchitekten Leberecht Migge. Halle 2002, S./p. 137–139, 155–157

Behne, Adolf, Städtebauer auf neuen Wegen. Siedlungen Siemensstadt und Reinickendorf in Berlin. In: Berliner Illustrierte Zeitung vom/of 15.6.1930

Berlin und seine Bauten. Hg. von/Ed. by Architekten- und Ingenieur-Verein zu Berlin. Teil IV A. Berlin/München/Düsseldorf 1970, S./p. 174–176, 183, 284 f., Obj. 129 A

Berlin und seine Bauten. Hg. von/Ed. by Architekten- und Ingenieur-Verein zu Berlin. Teil IV B. Berlin/München/Düsseldorf 1974, S./p. 25–29, 399–405, Obj. 941–946

Berliner Siedlungsbauten. In: Ostdeutsche Bau-Zeitung (29) 1931, Nr./No. 22, S./p.181–183

Blunck, Erich, Berliner Bauten aus neuester Zeit. In: Deutsche Bauzeitung (65) 1931, S./p. 263–268

Cabanis, H. u. a./et al., Farbgestaltung der Fassaden bei den Gebäuden Goebelstraße 12–118 von Hugo Häring in Berlin, Siemensstadt. Gutachten angefertigt von/Expert opinion produced by H. Cabanis, A. Höß und Menrad. Berlin 1984

Chermayeff, Serge, Film shots in Germany. In: The Architectural Review (70) 1931, S./p. 131–133, Nr./No. 27–32, A. 33

La Cité Siemensstadt à Berlin. (Par Walter Gropius et Otto Bartning, Architectes). In: La Construction Moderne (46) 1931, Nr./No. 23, S./p. 358–363, 365, T./I. 89–92; Nr./No. 32, Titelseite/front page, S./p. 500–504, T./I. 125–128

Czeminski, F., Berlin. In: Wohnen und Bauen (3) 1931, Nr./No. 1/2, S./p. 6–12, 27–30

Forbat, Fred, Großsiedlung Siemensstadt. In: Bauwelt (22) 1931, Heft/No. 47, S./p. 33–38

Gorgas, Carl, Großsiedlung Siemensstadt, Berlin. In: Bauwelt (21) 1930, Sonderbeilage/special supplement, Nr./No. 46, S./p. 1–24

Groß-Siedlung Siemensstadt. Erbaut durch die Gemeinnützige Baugesellschaft Berlin-Heerstraße mbH. In: Wohnen und Bauen, (3) 1931, Nr./No. 1/2

Groupe d'habitations à Berlin-Siemensstadt. In: L'architecture d'aujourd'hui (33) 1962, Nr./No. 104, S./p. 36–39.

Gutkind, Erwin, Wohnungsbauten in Berlin-Siemensstadt. In: Die Baugilde (12) 1930, Nr./No. 23, S./p. 2137–2145

Häring, Hugo, Künstlerische Probleme des Städtebaues. In: Deutsche Bauzeitung (65) 1931, Nr./No. 43/44, S./p. 253–256

Henning, Paul-Rudolf, Berliner Wohnbauten. In: Zentralblatt der Bauverwaltung (52) 1932, Nr./No. 6, S./p. 61–66.

Hortec – Garten- und Landschaftsplanung GBR, Gartendenkmalpflegerische Wiederherstellungsplanung. Siemensstadt – Charlottenburg Nord. Angef. von/Produced by Hortec – Garten- und Landschaftsplanung GBR. im Auftrag der/by order of GSW. 3 Bde./Vol. Berlin 1985

Hüter, Karl-Heinz, Architektur in Berlin. 1900–1933. Dresden 1987. S./p. 136, 224–236

Huse, Norbert (Hg./Ed.), Siedlungen der zwanziger Jahre – heute, vier Berliner Großsiedlungen 1924–1984. Eine Ausstellung vom 24.10.1984–7.1.1985 im Bauhaus-Archiv, Museum für Gestaltung. Berlin 1984

Jaeggi, Annemarie, Die Planungs- und Baugeschichte der vier Siedlungen, Großsiedlung Siemensstadt. In: Siedlungen der zwanziger Jahre – heute, vier Berliner Großsiedlungen 1924–1984, eine Ausstellung vom 24.10.1984–07.01.1985 im Bauhaus-Archiv, Museum für Gestaltung. Berlin 1984, S./p. 159–180

Jahn, Günter, Die Bauwerke und Kunstdenkmäler von Berlin. Stadt und Bezirk Spandau. Berlin 1971, S./p. 303–305, Abb./fig. 381–384

Johannes, Heinz, Neues Bauen in Berlin. Berlin 1931, S./p. 90–91

Klinger, Ralf/Pröbster, Hans-Jürgen, Gartendenkmalpflegerisches Gutachten. Angef. von/Produced by Ralf Klinger, Hans-Jürgen Pröbster. Berlin 1984

Kloß, Klaus-Peter, Siedlungen der 20er Jahre. Berlin 1982, S./p. 42–55

Lepointe, E., La Cité Siemensstadt à Berlin. In: La Construction Moderne (47) 1932, Nr./No. 16, Titelblatt/front page, S./p. 248–254, T./I. 61–64.

Marconi, Federico, Il quartiere Siemensstadt Berlino 1930. In: Casabelle cintinuità 1959, Nr./No. 223, S./p. 35–39

Mengeringhausen, Max, Fernheizung, Warmwasserversorgung und Waschanlage der Siedlung Siemensstadt. In: Bauwelt (21) 1930, Heft/No. 46, S./p. 1494–1496

Migge, Leberecht, Groß-Berliner Siedlungsfreiraum. In: Die Wohnung (5) 1930, Heft/No. 4, S./p. 97–108

Rading, Adolf, Bebauungsplan Siemensstadt. In: Das neue Berlin (1) 1929, Heft/No. 3, S./p. 60, 61

Rotival, M., Les Grandes Ensembles. In: L'architecture d'aujourd'hui (6) 1935, Nr./No. 6, S./p. 64–65.

Schallenberger, Jacob/Gutkind, Erwin, Berliner Wohnbauten der letzten Jahre. Berlin 1931, S./p. 114–123, S./p. 126

Hans Scharoun. Bauten, Entwürfe, Texte. Hg. von/Ed. by Peter Pfankuch. Berlin 1974, S./p. 249, 394, Obj. 195

Scharoun, Hans, Charlottenburg-Nord – Sechzig Jahre Entwicklung der Siemensstadt. In: Neue Heimat, 1962, Nr./No. 2, S./p. 18–32

Schmidt-Seifert, Parkpflegewerk Siemensstadt. Großsiedlung Siemensstadt und Charlottenburg-Nord. Angef. von Peter Schmidt-Seifert, Stefan Helmich. Gutachten im Auftrag des Landesdenkmalamtes Berlin, Abteilung Gartendenkmalpflege/Expert opinion by order of the department for historic gardens of Landesdenkmalamt Berlin. Berlin 2003

Slapeta, Lubomir/Slapeta, Cestmir, Siedlung Siemensstadt. In: STAVBA (10) 1931, Nr./No. 1, S./p. 2–4

STAVBA (11) 1932, Nr./No. 9, S./p. 144–145, 166–167

Thiele, Klaus-Jakob, 60 Jahre Berlin-Siemensstadt. In: Bauwelt (53) 1962, Nr./No. 15/16, S./p. 399–415

40 Jahre Großsiedlung Siemensstadt. In: Bauwelt (62) 1971, S./p. 1907–1911

Wirth, Ingrid, Die Bauwerke und Kunstdenkmäler von Berlin. Stadt und Bezirk Charlottenburg. Berlin 1961, S./p. 298f., 458–460, 463f., 522, Tafelband Abb./Image volume fig. 587–591, 603

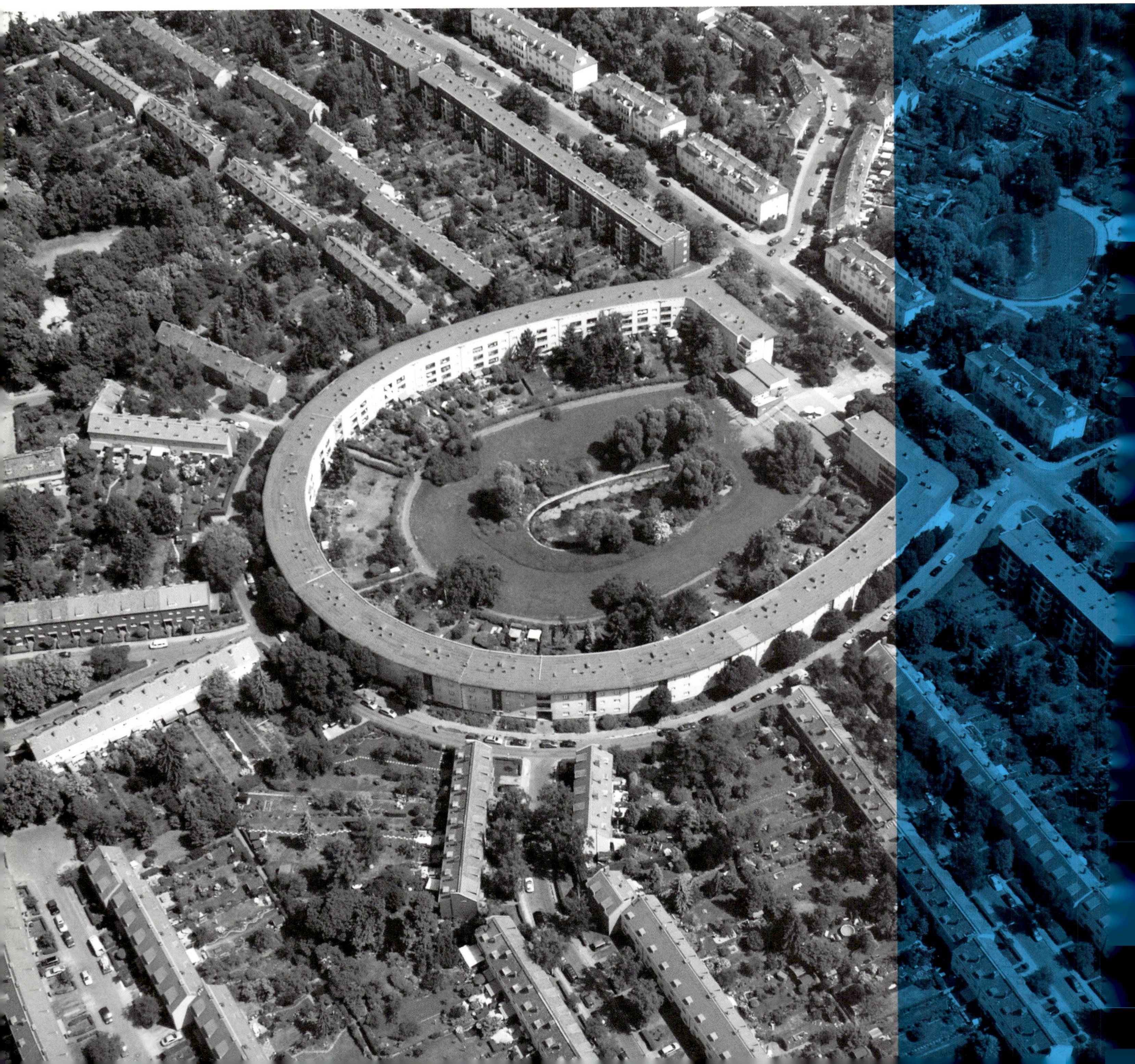

# 8
**ANGABEN ZU DEN ZUSTÄNDIGEN BEHÖRDEN**
CONTACT INFORMATION OF RESPONSIBLE AUTHORITIES

## 8.A Vorbereitung

Senatsverwaltung für Stadtentwicklung –
Landesdenkmalamt Berlin
Klosterstraße 47
10179 Berlin

## 8.B Örtlich zuständige Einrichtung/Behörde

Senatsverwaltung für Stadtentwicklung – OD
Brückenstraße 6
10179 Berlin

Landesdenkmalamt Berlin
Klosterstraße 47
10179 Berlin

## 8.C Sonstige örtliche Einrichtungen

Bezirksamt Charlottenburg-Wilmersdorf von Berlin – UD
Fehrbelliner Platz 4, 10707 Berlin

Bezirksamt Mitte von Berlin – UD
Iranische Straße 3, 13341 Berlin

Bezirksamt Neukölln von Berlin – UD
Karl-Marx-Straße 83, 12040 Berlin

Bezirksamt Pankow von Berlin – UD
Storkower Straße 139 C, 10407 Berlin

Bezirksamt Reinickendorf von Berlin – UD
Eichborndamm 215/239, 13437 Berlin

Bezirksamt Spandau von Berlin – UD
Carl-Schurz-Straße 2/6, 13597 Berlin

Bezirksamt Treptow-Köpenick von Berlin – UD
Alt-Köpenick 21, 12555 Berlin

## 8.D Offizielle Internetadresse

http://www.stadtentwicklung.berlin.de

Unterschrift für den Vertragsstaat

Ingeborg Junge-Reyer
Senatorin für Stadtentwicklung

aktualisiert Oktober 2006

## 8.A Preparer

Senatsverwaltung für Stadtentwicklung – LDA-Berlin
(Senate Department for Urban Development)
Klosterstraße 47
D-10179 Berlin

## 8.B Official local institution/agency

Senatsverwaltung für Stadtentwicklung – OD
(Senate Department for Urban Development)
Brückenstraße 6
D-10179 Berlin

Landesdenkmalamt Berlin
Klosterstraße 47
D-10179 Berlin

## 8.C Other local institutions

Bezirksamt Charlottenburg-Wilmersdorf von Berlin – UD
Fehrbelliner Platz 4, D-10707 Berlin

Bezirksamt Mitte von Berlin – UD
Iranische Straße 3, D-13341 Berlin

Bezirksamt Neukölln von Berlin – UD
Karl-Marx-Straße 83, D-12040 Berlin

Bezirksamt Pankow von Berlin – UD
Storkower Straße 139 C, D-10407 Berlin

Bezirksamt Reinickendorf von Berlin – UD
Eichborndamm 215/239, D-13437 Berlin

Bezirksamt Spandau von Berlin – UD
Carl-Schurz-Straße 2/6, D-13597 Berlin

Bezirksamt Treptow-Köpenick von Berlin – UD
Alt-Köpenick 21, D-12555 Berlin

## 8.D Official Web address

http://www.stadtentwicklung.berlin.de

Signature on Behalf of the State Party

Ingeborg Junge-Reyer
Senatorin für Stadtentwicklung

last updated October 2006

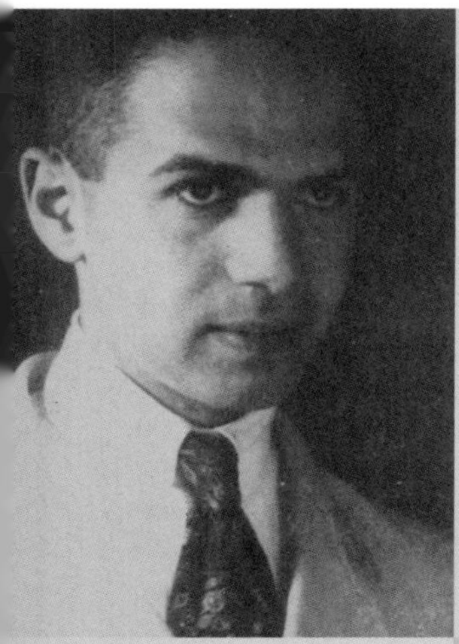

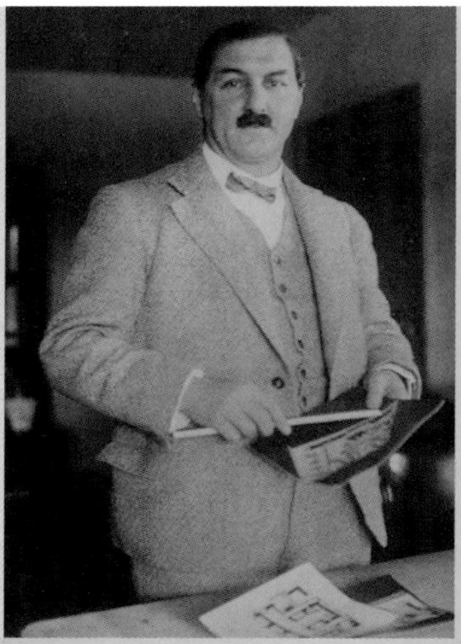

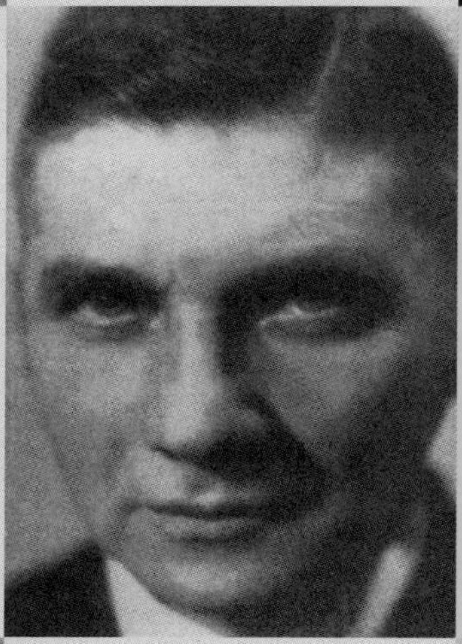

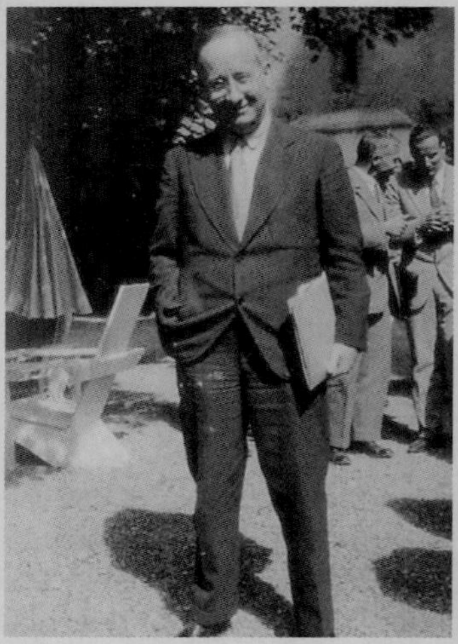

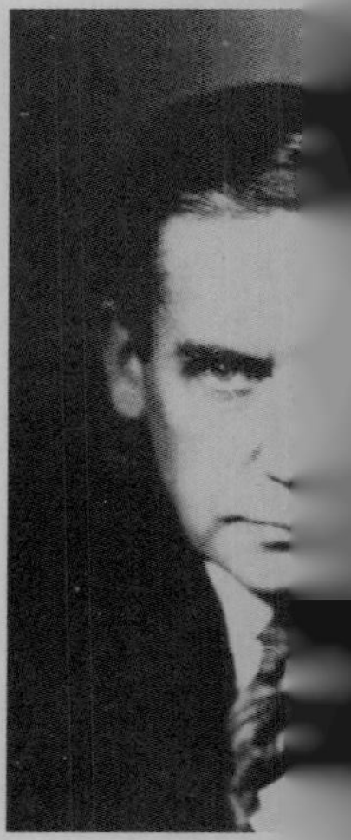

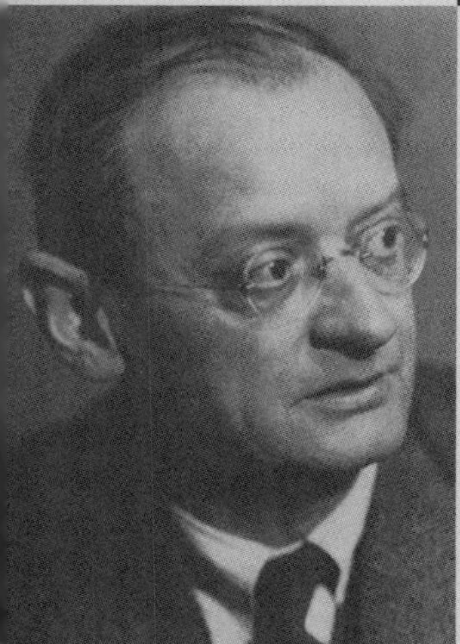

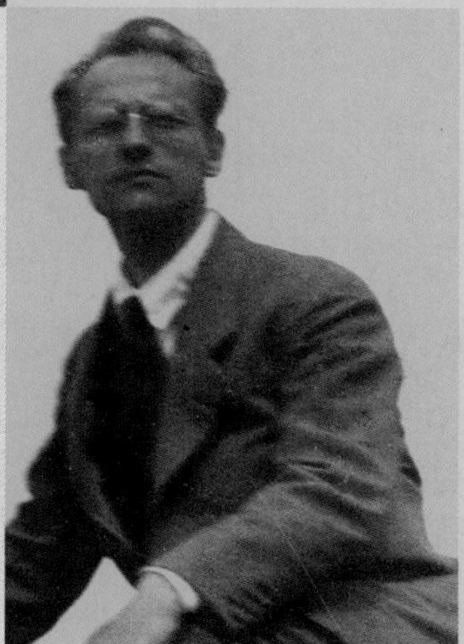

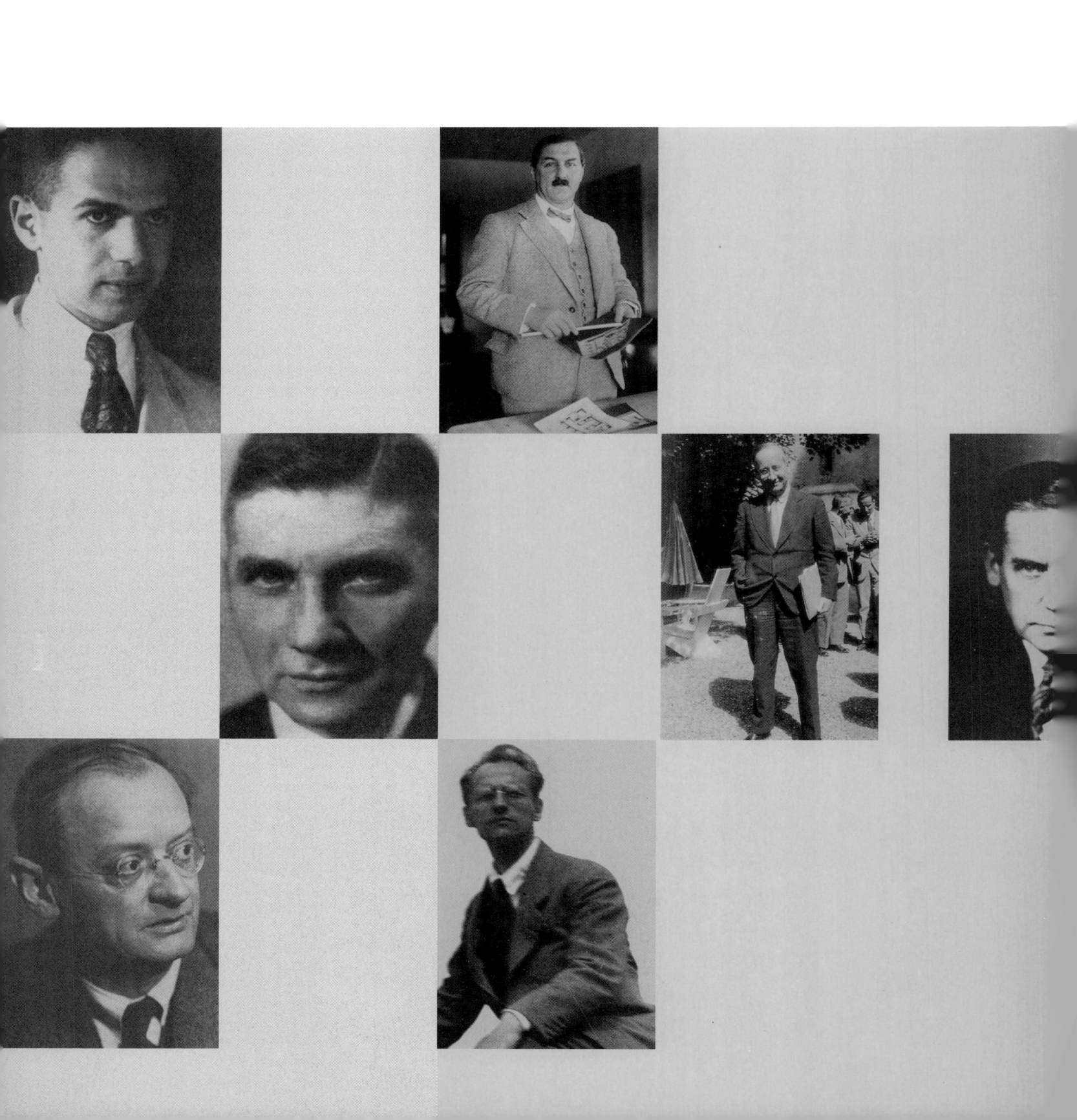

# ANHANG
## ATTACHMENT

Abb. 116:
Bruno Taut, 1933

Fig. 116:
Bruno Taut, 1933

## Bruno Taut

| | |
|---|---|
| 4.5.1880 | geboren in Königsberg/Ostpreußen |
| 1897–1901 | Besuch der Baugewerkschule in Königsberg/Ostpreußen |
| 1910 | Mitglied im Deutschen Werkbund |
| 1918 | Mitglied der Novembergruppe und Mitbegründer des Arbeitsrates für Kunst |
| 1921–1924 | Stadtbaurat in Magdeburg |
| 1924 | Mitglied der Berliner Architektenvereinigung „Zehnerring" (ab 1926 „Der Ring") |
| 1924–1931 | zahlreiche Wohnungsbauprojekte für verschiedene Baugesellschaften und -genossenschaften |
| 1927 | Mitglied der Reichsforschungsgesellschaft für Wirtschaftlichkeit im Bau- und Wohnungswesen (RfG) |
| 1931 | Mitglied der Preußischen Akademie der Künste Berlin |
| 1933 | Emigration nach Japan |
| 1936 | Emigration in die Türkei, Berufung an die Akademie der Künste Istanbul, Professur in der Architekturabteilung |
| 24.12.1938 | gestorben in Istanbul-Ortaköy |

*wichtige Bauten:*

| | |
|---|---|
| 1913–1916 | Gartenstadt Falkenberg, Berlin-Treptow |
| 1913–1930 | Gartenstadt Kolonie Reform, Magdeburg |
| 1924–1930 | Siedlung Schillerpark, Berlin-Wedding |
| 1925–1930 | Großsiedlung Britz, Berlin-Neukölln |
| 1926–1931 | Waldsiedlung Zehlendorf „Onkel Toms Hütte", Berlin-Zehlendorf |
| 1927 | Beteiligung an der Werkbundausstellung „Die Wohnung", Stuttgart-Weißenhof |
| 1928–1930 | Wohnstadt Carl Legien, Berlin-Prenzlauer Berg |

*wichtige Schriften:*

**Taut, Bruno,** Architekturlehre. Grundlagen, Theorie und Kritik, Beziehungen zu den anderen Künsten und zur Gesellschaft, hg. von Tilmann Heinisch und Goerd Peschken. Hamburg 1977 (verfasst 1936/1937. Erstveröffentlichung Tokio 1948)
**Taut, Bruno,** Bauen. Der neue Wohnbau. Leipzig 1927
**Taut, Bruno,** Die neue Wohnung – Die Frau als Schöpferin. Leipzig 1924
**Taut, Bruno,** Die Auflösung der Städte. Hagen 1920
**Taut, Bruno,** Die Stadtkrone. Jena 1919

*Literatur:*

**Brenne, Winfried** (Hg.), Bruno Taut. Meister des farbigen Bauens in Berlin. Berlin 2005
**Junghanns, Kurt,** Bruno Taut 1880–1938. Architektur und sozialer Gedanke. Leipzig 1983
**Nerdinger, Winfried/Hartmann, Kristiana** (Hg.), Bruno Taut 1880–1938. Architekt zwischen Tradition und Avantgarde. Stuttgart 2001
**Speidel, Manfred,** Bruno Taut 1880–1938. Natur und Fantasie. Berlin 1995
(Erstveröffentlichung: Bruno Taut Retrospective – Nature and Fantasy. Tokio 1994)

## Bruno Taut

| | |
|---|---|
| 4.5.1880 | born at Königsberg (Kaliningrad)/East Prussia |
| 1897–1901 | training at "Baugewerkschule" (building crafts school) at Königsberg/East Prussia |
| 1910 | member of Deutscher Werkbund |
| 1913 | consultant architect: Deutsche Gartenstadtgesellschaft (German garden city society) |
| 1918 | member of Novembergruppe and co-founder of Arbeitsrat für Kunst (Working Council for Art) |
| 1921–1924 | urban development councillor at Magdeburg |
| 1924 | member of the Berlin association of architects "Zehnerring" (as from 1926 "Der Ring") |
| 1924–1931 | many residential projects for various building societies and cooperatives |
| 1927 | member of "Reichsforschungsgesellschaft" für Wirtschaftlichkeit im Bau- und Wohnungswesen (RfG) |
| 1931 | member of the Prussian Academy of Arts, Berlin |
| 1933 | emigration to Japan |
| 1936 | emigration to Turkey, appointment at Academy of Arts Istanbul, professor at department of architecture |
| 24.12.1938 | died at Istanbul-Ortaköy |

*important works:*

| | |
|---|---|
| 1913–1916 | Gartenstadt Falkenberg, Berlin-Treptow |
| 1913–1930 | garden town "Reform" at Magdeburg |
| 1924–1930 | Siedlung Schillerpark at Berlin-Wedding |
| 1925–1930 | Großsiedlung Britz at Berlin-Neukölln |
| 1926–1931 | Waldsiedlung Zehlendorf "Onkel-Toms-Hütte" at Berlin-Zehlendorf |
| 1927 | participation in Werkbund exhibition "Die Wohnung" at Stuttgart-Weißenhof |
| 1928–1930 | Wohnstadt Carl Legien at Berlin-Prenzlauer Berg |

*important publications:*

**Taut, Bruno,** Architekturlehre. Grundlagen, Theorie und Kritik, Beziehungen zu den anderen Künsten und zur Gesellschaft, edited by Tilmann Heinisch and Goerd Peschken. Hamburg 1977 (written 1936/1937/first publication Tokyo 1948)
**Taut, Bruno,** Bauen. Der neue Wohnbau. Leipzig 1927
**Taut, Bruno,** Die neue Wohnung – Die Frau als Schöpferin. Leipzig 1924
**Taut, Bruno,** Die Auflösung der Städte. Hagen 1920
**Taut, Bruno,** Die Stadtkrone. Jena 1919

*literature:*

**Brenne, Winfried** (Ed.), Bruno Taut. Meister des farbigen Bauens in Berlin. Berlin 2005
**Junghanns, Kurt,** Bruno Taut 1880–1938. Architektur und sozialer Gedanke. Leipzig 1983
**Nerdinger, Winfried/Hartmann, Kristiana** (Ed.), Bruno Taut 1880–1938. Architekt zwischen Tradition und Avantgarde. Stuttgart 2001
**Speidel, Manfred,** Bruno Taut 1880–1938. Natur und Fantasie. Berlin 1995 (first publication: Bruno Taut Retrospective – Nature and Fantasy. Tokyo 1994)

## Martin Wagner

| | |
|---|---|
| 5.11.1885 | geboren in Königsberg/Ostpreußen |
| ab 1905 | Architekturstudium an der Technischen Hochschule in Berlin-Charlottenburg |
| 1909–1910 | Städtebau- und Volkswirtschaftsstudium in Dresden |
| 1911–1914 | Stadtbaumeister in Rüstringen bei Wilhelmshaven |
| 1914–1918 | im „Zweckverband Groß-Berlin" tätig |
| 1918–1920 | Stadtbaurat von Berlin-Schöneberg |
| 1919 | Mitbegründer der „Deutschen Bauhütte" soziale Baugesellschaft mbH |
| 1920–1924 | Geschäftsführer des „Verbandes sozialer Baubetriebe" |
| 1924–1926 | Geschäftsführer der „Deutschen Wohnungsfürsorge AG" für Beamte, Angestellte und Arbeiter |
| 1926–1933 | Stadtbaurat von Groß-Berlin |
| 1927 | Mitglied der Reichsforschungsgesellschaft für Wirtschaftlichkeit im Bau- und Wohnungswesen (RfG) |
| 1933 | Entlassung aus dem öffentlichen Dienst |
| 1935 | Emigration in die Türkei, Städtebauberater in Ankara und Istanbul |
| 1938 | Übersiedlung in die USA |
| 1938–1950 | Lehrtätigkeit an der Harvard University in Cambridge, Mass. (USA) |
| 28.5.1957 | gestorben in Cambridge, Mass. (USA) |

**wichtige Bauten:**

| | |
|---|---|
| 1918–1919 | Siedlung Lindenhof, Berlin-Schöneberg |
| 1925–1927 | Großsiedlung Britz (Hufeisensiedlung), Berlin-Neukölln |
| 1929–30 | Strandbad Wannsee (zusammen mit Richard Ermisch), Berlin-Zehlendorf, Strandbad Müggelsee (zusammen mit Hennings), Berlin-Köpenick, Messegelände, Berlin-Charlottenburg |

**wichtige Schriften:**

**Wagner, Martin** (Hg.), Das Neue Berlin – Monatshefte für Probleme der Großstadt. Berlin 1929
**Wagner, Martin**, Gross-Siedlung – Der Weg zur Rationalisierung des Wohnungsbaues. In: Wohnungswirtschaft (3) 1926, Nr.11/14, S. 75–114
**Wagner, Martin**, Neue Wege zum Kleinwohnungsbau. Berlin 1924
**Wagner, Martin**, Das sanitäre Grün der Städte. Ein Beitrag zur Freiflächentheorie. Diss. Berlin 1915

*Literatur:*
**Scarpa, Ludovica**, Martin Wagner und Berlin. Architektur und Städtebau in der Weimarer Republik. Braunschweig 1986
**Martin Wagner** 1885–1957. Wohnungsbau und Weltstadtplanung. Die Rationalisierung des Glücks, Ausstellungskatalog. Berlin 1985

## Martin Wagner

| | |
|---|---|
| 5.11.1885 | born at Königsberg (Kaliningrad)/East Prussia |
| as from 1905 | studies of architecture at the technical colleges at Berlin-Charlottenburg |
| 1909–1910 | studies of urban development and economics at Dresden |
| 1911–1914 | chief architect at Rüstringen near Wilhelmshaven |
| 1914–1918 | working in the „Zweckverband Groß-Berlin" (special purpose association of Greater Berlin) |
| 1918–1920 | chief architect of Berlin-Schöneberg |
| 1919 | co-founder of „Deutsche Bauhütte" soziale Baugesellschaft mbH (social housing construction company) |
| 1920–1924 | manager of „Verband sozialer Baubetriebe" (association of social construction companies) |
| 1924–1926 | manager of „Deutsche Wohnungsfürsorge AG" für Beamte, Angestellte und Arbeiter (social housing company for civil servants, white and blue collar employees) |
| 1926–1933 | urban development councillor of Greater Berlin |
| 1927 | member of Reichsforschungsgesellschaft für Wirtschaftlichkeit im Bau- und Wohnungswesen (RfG) |
| 1933 | dismissed from public service |
| 1935 | emigration to Turkey, consultant for urban development at Ankara and Istanbul |
| 1938 | moves to the USA |
| 1938–1950 | teacher at Harvard University (Cambridge, Mass.) (USA) |
| 28.5.1957 | died at Cambridge, Mass. (USA) |

*important works:*

| | |
|---|---|
| 1918–1919 | Siedlung Lindenhof at Berlin-Schöneberg |
| 1925–1927 | Großsiedlung Britz at Berlin-Neukölln |
| 1929–30 | Strandbad Wannsee (with Richard Ermisch) at Berlin-Zehlendorf, Strandbad Müggelsee (with Hennings) at Berlin-Köpenick, Messegelände at Berlin-Charlottenburg |

*important publications:*

**Wagner, Martin** (Ed.), Das Neue Berlin – Monatshefte für Probleme der Großstadt. Berlin 1929
**Wagner, Martin**, Gross-Siedlung – Der Weg zur Rationalisierung des Wohnungsbaues. In: Wohnungswirtschaft (3) 1926, No.11/14, p. 75–114
**Wagner, Martin**, Neue Wege zum Kleinwohnungsbau. Berlin 1924
**Wagner, Martin**, Das sanitäre Grün der Städte. Ein Beitrag zur Freiflächentheorie. Doctoral thesis. Berlin 1915

*literature:*
**Scarpa, Ludovica**, Martin Wagner und Berlin. Architektur und Städtebau in der Weimarer Republik. Braunschweig 1986
**Martin Wagner** 1885–1957. Wohnungsbau und Weltstadtplanung. Die Rationalisierung des Glücks, exhibition catalogue. Berlin 1985

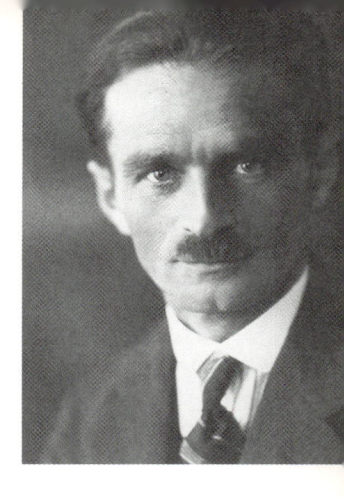

Abb. 117:
Martin Wagner, 1930

Fig. 117:
Martin Wagner, 1930

Abb. 118:
Bruno Ahrends, 1931

Fig. 118:
Bruno Ahrends, 1931

**Bruno Ahrends**

| | |
|---|---|
| 9.4.1887 | geboren in Berlin |
| 1898–1903 | Architekturstudium an der Technischen Universität Berlin |
| ab 1905 | Mitglied im Architekten- und Ingenieurverein Berlin |
| 1910–1914 | Architekturbüro mit Heinrich Schweitzer in Berlin |
| 1914–1933 | eigenes Büro in Berlin, zahlreiche Villen- und Landhausprojekte |
| 1927 | Mitglied der Reichsforschungsgesellschaft für Wirtschaftlichkeit im Bau- und Wohnungswesen (RfG) |
| 1931 | Mitarbeit bei der Deutschen Bauausstellung, Bereich ländlicher Siedlungsbau |
| 1936 | Emigration nach Italien |
| 1939 | Emigration nach England |
| 1948 | Übersiedlung nach Südafrika |
| 24.7.1948 | in Kapstadt (Südafrika) gestorben |

*wichtige Bauten:*

| | |
|---|---|
| 1919–1920 | Kleinhaussiedlung Johannisthal, Berlin-Treptow |
| 1921–1925 | Doppelhäuser in der Kriegerheimstättensiedlung Lübars, Berlin-Reinickendorf |
| 1925–1930 | Wohnanlage am Archibaldweg, Berlin-Lichtenberg |
| 1929–1931 | Wohnbauten und Kinderheim in der Siedlung Weiße Stadt, Berlin-Reinickendorf |

*wichtige Schriften:*

**Ahrends, Bruno,** Die ländliche Siedlung. In: Wasmuths Lexikon der Baukunst. Band 4. Berlin 1932, S. 375–389
**Ahrends, Bruno,** Die Küche im Rahmen des Kleinwohnungsproblems. In: Die Küche der Klein- und Mittelwohnung, Sonderheft 2 der RFG (1)1928, S. 22–26

*Literatur:*

**Benton, Charlotte,** A different World – Emigre Architects in Britain 1928–1958. London 1995, S. 80–81, 137–138
**Schlüter, Sabine,** Studien zum Werk des Berliner Architekten Bruno Ahrends. Magisterarbeit Technische Universität Berlin 1991
**Stahl, Fritz,** Bruno Ahrends (Reihe Kunst und Architektur der Gegenwart). Berlin 1927
**Warhaftig, Myra,** Deutsche jüdische Architekten vor und nach 1933 – Das Lexikon. Berlin 2005, S.41–43

**Bruno Ahrends**

| | |
|---|---|
| 9.4.1887 | born at Berlin |
| 1898–1903 | studies of architecture at Technische Universität Berlin |
| as from 1905 | member of Architekten- und Ingenieurverein (association of architects and engineers) Berlin |
| 1910–1914 | architects' practice together with Heinrich Schweitzer at Berlin |
| 1914–1933 | own office at Berlin, many villa and country-house projects |
| 1927 | member of Reichsforschungsgesellschaft für Wirtschaftlichkeit im Bau- und Wohnungswesen (RfG) (Research society of the Reich for economics in civil engineering and housing) |
| 1931 | collaboration in Deutsche Bauausstellung (German exhibition of architecture), department of rural housing estate development |
| 1936 | emigration to Italy |
| 1939 | emigration to England |
| 1948 | moves to South Africa |
| 24.7.1948 | died at Cape Town (South Africa) |

*important works:*

| | |
|---|---|
| 1919–1920 | housing estate of small houses at Johannisthal, Berlin-Treptow |
| 1921–1925 | double-houses at Kriegerheimstättensiedlung (housing estate homesteads for military personnel) at Lübars (Berlin-Reinickendorf) |
| 1925–1930 | residential estate at Archibaldweg, Berlin-Lichtenberg |
| 1929–1931 | residential buildings and children's home at housing estate Weiße Stadt at Berlin-Reinickendorf |

*important publications:*

**Ahrends, Bruno,** Die ländliche Siedlung. In: Wasmuths Lexikon der Baukunst. vol. 4. Berlin 1932, p. 375–389
**Ahrends, Bruno,** Die Küche im Rahmen des Kleinwohnungsproblems. In: Die Küche der Klein- und Mittelwohnung, special issue 2, RFG (1)1928, p. 22–26

*literature:*

**Benton, Charlotte,** A different World – Emigre Architects in Britain 1928–1958. London 1995, p. 80–81, 137–138
**Schlüter, Sabine,** Studien zum Werk des Berliner Architekten Bruno Ahrends, Magisterarbeit Technische Universität Berlin 1991
**Stahl, Fritz,** Bruno Ahrends (series Kunst und Architektur der Gegenwart). Berlin 1927
**Warhaftig, Myra,** Deutsche jüdische Architekten vor und nach 1933 – Das Lexikon. Berlin 2005, p. 41–43

## Wilhelm Büning

| | |
|---|---|
| 4.4.1881 | geboren in Borken/Westfalen |
| | Architekturstudium an den Technischen Hochschulen in München, Berlin-Charlottenburg und Dresden |
| 1913 | Mitglied im Deutschen Werkbund |
| 1921 | Professor an den Vereinigten Staatsschulen für freie und angewandte Kunst Berlin, der Technischen Hochschule Berlin und der Hochschule für Bildende Künste Berlin |
| ab 1930 | Sonderforschungsgebiet „Tageslicht im Hochbau" |
| 1950er Jahre | Professor für architektonisches Entwerfen, Baukonstruktion und Hygiene im Bauwesen an der Hochschule für Bildende Künste Berlin |
| 2.8.1958 | in Berlin gestorben |

*wichtige Bauten:*

| | |
|---|---|
| 1926–1927 | Wohnanlage am Tile-Brügge-Weg, Berlin-Reinickendorf |
| 1929–1931 | Zeilenbauten und Heizkraftwerk in der Siedlung Weiße Stadt, Berlin-Reinickendorf |

*wichtige Schriften:*
**Büning, Wilhelm,** Angemessenes Tageslicht im Wohnungsbau. Stuttgart 1953
**Büning, Wilhelm,** Bauanatomie – Handwerklich technische Grundlagen des Wohnbaues als Einführung in die Baukunst. Berlin 1928 (1947 als überarbeitete Neuauflage unter dem Titel „Die neue Bauanatomie")

*Literatur:*
**Büning, Wilhelm.** In: Allgemeines Künstlerlexikon, Band 15, München/Leipzig 1997, S. 44

## Wilhelm Büning

| | |
|---|---|
| 4.4.1881 | born at Borken/Westphalia |
| | studies of architecture at the Technische Hochschulen (technical colleges) at Munich, Berlin-Charlottenburg and Dresden |
| 1913 | member of Deutscher Werkbund |
| 1921 | professor at Vereinigte Staatsschulen für freie und angewandte Kunst (united state schools for free and applied arts) Berlin, Technische Hochschule Berlin and Hochschule für Bildende Künste (college for fine arts) Berlin |
| as from 1930 | special research on "daylight in civil engineering" |
| 1950s | professor for architectural design, constructive design and hygiene in civil engineering at Hochschule für Bildende Künste Berlin |
| 2.8.1958 | died at Berlin |

*important works:*

| | |
|---|---|
| 1926–1927 | residential estate at Tile-Brügge-Weg at Berlin-Reinickendorf |
| 1929–1931 | ribbon buildings and heating plant at housing estate Weiße Stadt at Berlin-Reinickendorf |

*important publications:*
**Büning, Wilhelm,** Angemessenes Tageslicht im Wohnungsbau. Stuttgart 1953
**Büning, Wilhelm,** Bauanatomie – Handwerklich technische Grundlagen des Wohnbaues als Einführung in die Baukunst. Berlin 1928 (1947 as revised new edition with the title "Die neue Bauanatomie")

*literature:*
**Büning, Wilhelm.** In: Allgemeines Künstlerlexikon, vol. 15, München/Leipzig 1997, p. 44

Abb. 119:
Wilhelm Büning, 1931

Fig. 119:
Wilhelm Büning, 1931

Abb. 120:
Otto Rudolf Salvisberg, 1928

Fig. 120:
Otto Rudolf Salvisberg, 1928

## Otto Rudolf Salvisberg

| | |
|---|---|
| 19.10.1882 | geboren in Könitz bei Bern (Schweiz) |
| 1901–1904 | Studium an der Bauschule im Technikum Biel (Schweiz) |
| 1908–1913 | Tätigkeit in den Architekturbüros von Johann Emil Schaudt und Paul Zimmerreimer in Berlin |
| 1914–1929 | selbständiger Architekt in Berlin, intensive Siedlungsbautätigkeit |
| 1922 | Eröffnung eines zweiten Büros in Bern (zusammen mit Otto Brechbühl) |
| 1927 | Mitglied der Reichsforschungsgesellschaft für Wirtschaftlichkeit im Bau- und Wohnungswesen (RfG) |
| 1928 | Mitglied im Deutschen Werkbund |
| 1929 | Professor für Architektur an der Eidgenössischen Technischen Hochschule Zürich (ETH) |
| 1930 | Hausarchitekt des Pharmakonzerns Hoffmann-La Roche |
| 23.12.1940 | gestorben in Arosa (Schweiz) |

*wichtige Bauten:*

| | |
|---|---|
| 1916–1919 | Werkssiedlung der Mitteldeutschen Reichswerke, Piesteritz bei Wittenberg |
| 1919–1929 | Siedlung Elsengrund, Berlin-Köpenick |
| 1924–1926 | Wohnanlage am Botanischen Garten, Berlin-Steglitz |
| 1926–1928 | Reihenhäuser in der Waldsiedlung Zehlendorf „Onkel Toms Hütte", Berlin-Zehlendorf |
| 1927–1928 | Wohnanlage an der Knobelsdorffstraße, Berlin-Charlottenburg |
| 1928–1929 | Stadtrandsiedlung Mittelheide, Berlin-Köpenick |
| 1929–1931 | Wohnbebauung mit Brückenhaus Aroser Allee in der Siedlung Weiße Stadt, Berlin-Reinickendorf |
| 1930 | Wohnanlage Attilahöhe, Berlin-Tempelhof |

*Literatur:*

**Lichtenstein, Claude,** O. R. Salvisberg – Die andere Moderne. Zürich 1985

**Neuere Arbeiten von O. R. Salvisberg.** Mit einer Einleitung von Paul Westheim (Reihe „Neue Werkkunst"). Berlin/Leipzig/Wien 1927 (Reprint mit einem Nachwort von Matthias Noell, Berlin 2000)

**Schaefer, Paul,** Otto Rudolf Salvisberg. In: Neue Baukunst (4) 1928, Nr. 5

## Otto Rudolf Salvisberg

| | |
|---|---|
| 19.10.1882 | born at Könitz near Bern (Switzerland) |
| 1901–1904 | studies at the civil engineering department of Technikum Biel (Switzerland) |
| 1908–1913 | work at the architects' practices of Johann Emil Schaudt and Paul Zimmerreimer at Berlin |
| 1914–1929 | free-lance architect at Berlin, many housing estate projects |
| 1922 | opening a second office at Bern (together with Otto Brechbühl) |
| 1927 | member of Reichsforschungsgesellschaft für Wirtschaftlichkeit im Bau- und Wohnungswesen (RfG) (Research society of the Reich for economics in civil engineering and housing) |
| 1928 | member of Deutscher Werkbund |
| 1929 | professor for architecture at Eidgenössische Technische Hochschule Zurich (ETH) |
| 1930 | in-house architect of pharmaceuticals concern Hoffmann-La Roche |
| 23.12.1940 | died at Arosa (Switzerland) |

*important works:*

| | |
|---|---|
| 1916–1919 | company housing estate of Mitteldeutsche Reichswerke at Piesteritz near Wittenberg |
| 1919–1929 | housing estate Elsengrund at Berlin-Köpenick |
| 1924–1926 | residential estate at Botanischer Garten (Berlin-Steglitz) |
| 1926–1928 | row houses for Waldsiedlung Zehlendorf "Onkel-Toms-Hütte" at Berlin-Zehlendorf |
| 1927–1928 | residential estate at Knobelsdorffstrasse (Berlin-Charlottenburg) |
| 1928–1929 | housing estate Mittelheide at margin of the city (Berlin-Köpenick) |
| 1929–1931 | residential buildings with bridge house at Aroser Allee in housing estate Weiße Stadt at Berlin-Reinickendorf |
| 1930 | residential estate Attilahöhe at Berlin-Tempelhof |

*literature:*

**Lichtenstein, Claude,** O. R. Salvisberg – Die andere Moderne. Zurich 1985

**Neuere Arbeiten von O. R. Salvisberg.** With an introduction by Paul Westheim (series "Neue Werkkunst"). Berlin/Leipzig/Wien 1927 (Reprint with an epilogue by Matthias Noell, Berlin 2000)

**Schaefer, Paul,** Otto Rudolf Salvisberg. In: Neue Baukunst (4) 1928, No. 5

## Hans Scharoun

| | |
|---|---|
| 20.9.1895 | geboren in Bremen |
| 1912–1914 | Studium an der Fakultät für Architektur der Technischen Hochschule Berlin-Charlottenburg |
| 1919 | Mitarbeiter im „Arbeitsrat für Kunst" (nicht Mitglied), Mitglied der von Bruno Taut geleiteten Architektengemeinschaft „Gläserne Kette", Mitglied im Deutschen Werkbund |
| 1925–1932 | Professor an der Staatlichen Akademie für Kunst und Kunstgewerbe Breslau |
| 1926 | Mitglied der Architektenvereinigung „Der Ring" |
| 1945–1946 | Leiter der Abteilung Bau- und Wohnungswesen des Magistrats von Groß-Berlin |
| 1946–1958 | Professor an der Fakultät für Architektur der Technischen Universität Berlin, Lehrstuhl am Institut für Städtebau |
| 1955–1968 | Präsident der Akademie der Künste, Berlin |
| 25.11.1972 | in Berlin gestorben |

*wichtige Bauten:*

| | |
|---|---|
| 1927 | Einfamilienhaus Werkbundausstellung „Die Wohnung", Stuttgart-Weißenhof |
| 1928–1929 | Appartmenthäuser Kaiserdamm / Königin-Elisabeth-Straße, Berlin-Charlottenburg |
| 1929 | Wohnheim Werkbundausstellung „Wohnung und Werkraum", Breslau |
| 1929/30 | Appartmenthäuser Hohenzollerndamm / Mansfelder Straße, Berlin-Wilmersdorf |
| 1930 | Großsiedlung Siemensstadt (Block 1, 2), Berlin-Spandau |
| 1954–1959 | Wohnhochhausgruppe „Romeo und Julia", Stuttgart-Zuffenhausen |
| 1955 | Bebauungsplan im Hansaviertel (mit Hubert Hoffmann, Sergius Ruegenberg, Alfred Schinz), Berlin-Tiergarten |
| 1955 | Laubenganghaus Goebelstr. 1–9 (Großsiedlung Siemensstadt), Berlin-Charlottenburg |
| 1960–1963 | Philharmonie, Berlin-Tiergarten |
| 1967–1976 | Staatsbibliothek, Berlin-Tiergarten |

*Literatur:*

**Hans Scharoun.** Architekt in Deutschland 1893–1972, hrsg. von Christine Hoh-Slodzyck, Norbert Huse, Günter Kühne und Andreas Tönnesmann. München 1992
**Jones, Peter Blundell,** Hans Scharoun. London 1995
**Pfankuch, Peter** (Hg.), Hans Scharoun. Bauten. Entwürfe. Texte. Berlin 1993

## Hans Scharoun

| | |
|---|---|
| 20.9.1895 | born at Bremen |
| 1912–1914 | studies at the department for architecture at Technische Hochschule Berlin-Charlottenburg |
| 1919 | cooperates in "Arbeitsrat für Kunst" (not member), member of "Gläserne Kette" – an association of architects headed by Bruno Taut, member of Deutscher Werkbund |
| 1925–1932 | professor at Staatliche Akademie für Kunst und Kunstgewerbe (State academy for arts and crafts) at Breslau (Wrocław) |
| 1926 | member of architects' association "Der Ring" |
| 1945–1946 | head of the department for civil engineering and housing of the government of Greater Berlin |
| 1946–1958 | professor at department for architecture at Technische Universität Berlin, chair, institute for urban development |
| 1955–1968 | president of the Akademie der Künste (Academy of Arts), Berlin |
| 25.11.1972 | died at Berlin |

*important works:*

| | |
|---|---|
| 1927 | single family house for Werkbund exhibition "Die Wohnung" at Stuttgart-Weißenhof |
| 1928–1929 | apartment houses at Kaiserdamm / Königin-Elisabeth-Straße (Berlin-Charlottenburg) |
| 1929 | hostel at Werkbund exhibition "Wohnung und Werkraum", Breslau |
| 1929/30 | apartment houses at Hohenzollerndamm / Mansfelder Straße (Berlin-Wilmersdorf) |
| 1930 | Großsiedlung Siemensstadt (blocks 1 and 2) at Berlin-Spandau |
| 1954–1959 | group high-rise residential buildings "Romeo und Julia" at Stuttgart-Zuffenhausen |
| 1955 | development plan for Hansaviertel (together with Hugo Hoffmann, Segius Ruegenberg, Alfred Schinz) at Berlin-Tiergarten |
| 1955 | gallery block of Goebelstraße 1–9 (Großsiedlung Siemensstaadt) at Berlin-Charlottenburg |
| 1960–1963 | Philharmonie (building for philharmonic orchestra) at Berlin-Tiergarten |
| 1967–1976 | State Library at Berlin-Tiergarten |

*literature:*

**Hans Scharoun.** Architekt in Deutschland 1893–1972, ed. by Christine Hoh-Slodzyck, Norbert Huse, Günter Kühne and Andreas Tönnesmann. Munich 1992
**Jones, Peter Blundell,** Hans Scharoun. London 1995
**Pfankuch, Peter** (Ed.), Hans Scharoun. Bauten. Entwürfe. Texte. Berlin 1993

Abb. 121:
Hans Scharoun, 1933

Fig. 121:
Hans Scharoun, 1933

Abb. 122:
Walter Gropius, 1930

Fig. 122:
Walter Gropius, 1930

## Walter Gropius

| | |
|---|---|
| 18.5.1883 | geboren in Berlin |
| vor 1908 | Architekturstudium an den Technischen Hochschulen in München und Berlin-Charlottenburg |
| 1908–1910 | Mitarbeiter bei Peter Behrens in Berlin |
| 1910–1918 | selbstständiger Architekt in Berlin, Arbeitsgemeinschaft mit dem Architekten Adolf Meyer |
| 1912 | Mitglied im Deutschen Werkbund |
| 1918 | Mitbegründer des Arbeitsrates für Kunst |
| 1919–1925 | Leiter des „Staatlichen Bauhauses" in Weimar |
| 1925–1928 | Direktor der „Bauhaus Dessau-Hochschule für Gestaltung" |
| 1924 | Mitglied der Berliner Architektenvereinigung „Zehnerring" (ab 1926 „Der Ring") |
| 1927 | Mitglied der Reichsforschungsgesellschaft für Wirtschaftlichkeit im Bau- und Wohnungswesen (RfG) |
| 1930 | Vizepräsident der CIAM |
| 1934 | Emigration nach England |
| 1937 | Übersiedlung in die USA, Professor für Architektur an der Harvard University in Boston (Mass.) |
| 1938–1952 | Leiter der Harvard-Architekturabteilung, bis 1941 Büropartnerschaft mit dem ehemaligen Bauhausmeister Marcel Breuer |
| 1942–1952 | Zusammenarbeit mit Konrad Wachsmann bei der Herstellung von Sperrholzhäusern (General Panel Corporation) |
| 1945 | Gründung von „The Architects Collaborative" (TAC) |
| 1948–1950 | Präsident der CIAM |
| 05.07.1969 | gestorben in Boston (USA) |

*wichtige Bauten:*

| | |
|---|---|
| 1911–1914 | Faguswerke (Schuhleistenfabrik Benscheidt), Alfeld a.d. Leine |
| 1925–1926 | Bauhausgebäude und Meisterhäuser, Dessau |
| 1926–1928 | Siedlung Dessau-Törten |
| 1928 | Wohnhäuser der Siedlung Dammerstock, Karlsruhe |
| 1929–1930 | Großsiedlung Siemensstadt (Block 4 und 9), Berlin-Charlottenburg |
| 1955–1957 | Wohnhochhaus für die INTERBAU im Hansaviertel, Berlin-Tiergarten |
| ab 1959 | Generalplanung für die Großsiedlung Britz-Buckow-Rudow (Gropiusstadt), Berlin-Neukölln |

*wichtige Schriften:*
**Gropius, Walter,** Dammerstock-Siedlung. Die Gebrauchswohnung. Ausstellungskatalog. Karlsruhe 1929
**Gropius, Walter,** Internationale Architektur. München 1925

*Literatur:*
**Isaacs, Reginald R.,** Walter Gropius. Der Mensch und sein Werk. Berlin 1983–1984
**Nerdinger, Winfried,** Der Architekt Walter Gropius. Berlin 1985
**Probst, Hartmut/Schädlich, Christian,** Walter Gropius, Berlin 1985–1987 (3 Bde.)

## Walter Gropius

| | |
|---|---|
| 18.5.1883 | born at Berlin |
| before 1908 | studies of architecture at the technical colleges at Munich and Berlin-Charlottenburg |
| 1908–1910 | working with Peter Behrens at Berlin |
| 1910–1918 | free-lance architect in Berlin, cooperation with the architect Adolf Meyer |
| 1912 | member of Deutscher Werkbund |
| 1918 | co-founder of the "Arbeitsrat für Kunst" |
| 1919–1925 | director of "Staatliches Bauhaus" (State Bauhaus) at Weimar |
| 1925–1928 | director of "Bauhaus Dessau Hochschule für Gestaltung" |
| 1924 | member of the Berlin association of architects "Zehnerring" (as from 1926 „Der Ring") |
| 1927 | member of "Reichsforschungsgesellschaft" (RfG) (Research society of the Reich for economics in civil engineering and housing) |
| 1930 | vice-president of CIAM |
| 1934 | emigration to England |
| 1937 | moves to USA; professor for architecture at Harvard university, Boston (Mass.) |
| 1938–1952 | head of the department of architecture at Harvard, until 1941 office partnership with Marcel Breuer, former Bauhaus-Master |
| 1942–1952 | cooperation with Konrad Wachsmann in producing plywood houses (General Panel Corporation) |
| 1945 | founding The Architects Collaborative (TAC) |
| 1948–1950 | president of CIAM |
| 05.07.1969 | died at Boston (USA) |

*important works:*

| | |
|---|---|
| 1911–1914 | Faguswerke (shoe last factory Benscheidt), Alfeld a.d. Leine |
| 1925–1926 | Bauhaus building and Meisterhäuser (master houses) at Dessau |
| 1926–1928 | housing estate at Dessau-Törten |
| 1928 | residential buildings of housing estate Dammerstock at Karlsruhe |
| 1929–1930 | Großsiedlung Siemensstadt (blocks 4 and 9) at Berlin-Charlottenburg |
| 1955–1957 | high-rise residential building for INTERBAU at Hansaviertel (Hansa quarter) at Berlin-Tiergarten |
| as from 1959 | master plan for large housing estate Britz-Buckow-Rudow (Gropiusstadt) at Berlin-Neukölln |

*important publications:*
**Gropius, Walter,** Dammerstock-Siedlung. Die Gebrauchswohnung. Ausstellungskatalog. Karlsruhe 1929
**Gropius, Walter,** Internationale Architektur. Munich 1925

*literature:*
**Isaacs, Reginald R.,** Walter Gropius. Der Mensch und sein Werk. Berlin 1983–1984
**Nerdinger, Winfried,** Der Architekt Walter Gropius. Berlin 1985
**Probst, Hartmut/Schädlich, Christian,** Walter Gropius, Berlin 1985–1987 (3 vols.)

## Hugo Häring

| | |
|---|---|
| 22.5.1882 | geboren in Biberach/Riß |
| 1899–1903 | Studium an der Technischen Hochschule Stuttgart bei Theodor Fischer |
| 1901–1903 | Studium an der Technischen Hochschule Dresden, u.a. bei Fritz Schumacher und Paul Wallot |
| 1921 | Übersiedlung nach Berlin, freier Architekt (bis 1943), Mitglied der Novembergruppe |
| 1924 | Mitglied der Berliner Architektenvereinigung „Zehnerring" (ab 1926 „Der Ring") |
| 1926 | Vorstandsmitglied des Deutschen Werkbundes |
| 1928 | Teilnahme an der Gründungsveranstaltung des CIAM |
| 1932 | Teilnahme an der Werkbundausstellung in Wien |
| 1935–43 | „Kunst- und Werkprivatschule für Gestaltung" in Berlin, Lehrtätigkeit und Leitung |
| 1947 | Berufung in die Forschungsgemeinschaft „Bauen und Wohnen" |
| 1950 | Ehrendoktor der Technischen Hochschule in Stuttgart |
| 1956 | Kunstpreis der Stadt Berlin |
| 17.5.1958 | in Göppingen gestorben |

*wichtige Bauten:*
| | |
|---|---|
| 1922–1928 | Gut Garkau bei Lübeck |
| 1926–1927 | Reihenhausbauten Waldsiedlung Zehlendorf „Onkel-Toms-Hütte", Berlin-Zehlendorf |
| 1928–1030 | Wohnbauten Stockholmer Straße, Berlin-Wedding |
| 1929–1930 | Zeilenbauten in der Großsiedlung Siemensstadt, Berlin-Charlottenburg |
| 1932–1933 | Reichsforschungssiedlung Haselhorst, Berlin-Spandau, Bauabschnitt mit 300 Wohnungen |

*wichtige Schriften:*
**Häring, Hugo,** Die Ausbildung des Geistes zur Arbeit an der Gestalt. Fragmente. Berlin 1968
**Häring, Hugo,** Vom neuen Bauen. Über das Geheimnis der Gestalt. Berlin 1957

*Literatur:*
**Joedicke, Jürgen/Lauterbach, Heinrich,** Hugo Häring. Schriften. Entwürfe. Bauten. Stuttgart 1965
**Jones, Peter Blundell,** Hugo Häring. The Organic versus the Geometric. Stuttgart 1999
**Kremer, Sabine,** Hugo Häring (1882–1958). Wohnungsbau in Theorie und Praxis. Stuttgart 1984
**Schirren, Matthias,** Hugo Häring. Architekt des Neuen Bauens 1882–1958. Mit einem kritischen Werkkatalog von Sylvia Claus. Ostfildern-Ruit 2001

## Hugo Häring

| | |
|---|---|
| 22.5.1882 | born at Biberach/Riss |
| 1899–1903 | student of professor Theodor Fischer at Technische Hochschule Stuttgart |
| 1901–1903 | studies at Technische Hochschule Dresden, e.g. with professors Fritz Schumacher and Paul Wallot |
| 1921 | moving to Berlin, free-lance architect (until 1943), member of Novembergruppe (November group) |
| 1924 | member of the Berlin association of architects "Zehnerring" (as from 1926 "Der Ring") |
| 1926 | member of executive of Deutscher Werkbund |
| 1928 | participation in founding event for CIAM |
| 1932 | participation in exhibition of Werkbund at Vienna |
| 1935–43 | teacher and director of "Kunst- und Werkprivatschule für Gestaltung" (private arts and crafts school) at Berlin |
| 1947 | appointed member of Forschungsgemeinschaft "Bauen und Wohnen" (research association construction and housing) |
| 1950 | honorary doctor of Technische Hochschule at Stuttgart |
| 1956 | arts award of the city of Berlin |
| 17.5.1958 | died at Göppingen |

*important works:*
| | |
|---|---|
| 1922–1928 | Gut (estate) Garkau near Lübeck |
| 1926–1927 | row houses for Waldsiedlung Zehlendorf "Onkel-Toms-Hütte" at Berlin-Zehlendorf |
| 1928–1030 | residential buildings at Stockholmer Straße, Berlin-Wedding |
| 1929–1930 | ribbon buildings at Großsiedlung Siemensstadt, Berlin-Charlottenburg |
| 1932–1933 | research housing estate of the Reich at Haselhorst, Berlin-Spandau, phase of construction with 300 flats |

*important publications:*
**Häring, Hugo,** Die Ausbildung des Geistes zur Arbeit an der Gestalt. Fragmente. Berlin 1968
**Häring, Hugo,** Vom neuen Bauen. Über das Geheimnis der Gestalt. Berlin 1957

*literature:*
**Joedicke, Jürgen/Lauterbach, Heinrich,** Hugo Häring. Schriften. Entwürfe. Bauten. Stuttgart 1965
**Jones, Peter Blundell,** Hugo Häring. The Organic versus the Geometric. Stuttgart 1999
**Kremer, Sabine,** Hugo Häring (1882–1958). Wohnungsbau in Theorie und Praxis. Stuttgart 1984
**Schirren, Matthias,** Hugo Häring. Architekt des Neuen Bauens 1882–1958. With a critical catalogue of the works by Sylvia Claus. Ostfildern-Ruit 2001

Abb. 123:
Hugo Häring, 1930

Fig. 123:
Hugo Häring, 1930

Abb. 124:
Fred Forbat, 1930

## Fred Forbat

| | |
|---|---|
| 31.3.1897 | geboren in Pécs (Ungarn) |
| vor 1918 | Architektur- und Kunstgeschichtsstudium in Budapest (Ungarn) |
| 1918 | Student an der Technischen Hochschule in München bei Theodor Fischer |
| 1920–1922 | Mitarbeit im Atelier Gropius in Weimar |
| 1922 | Mitarbeit beim Projekt zur Bauhaussiedlung Am Horn in Weimar |
| 1925–1928 | Chefarchitekt beim Sommerfeld-Konzern, Berlin |
| seit 1928 | eigenes Atelier in Berlin, Mitglied der CIAM |
| 1932 | Mitarbeiter bei Ernst May in Moskau |
| 1933 | Mitarbeiter von Prof. Dörpfeld bei seinen archäologischen Forschungen in Olympia (Griechenland) |
| 1933–1938 | freier Architekt in Pécs (Ungarn) |
| seit 1938 | als Architekt und Stadtplaner in Schweden tätig |
| 22.5.1972 | in Vällingby (Schweden) gestorben |

*wichtige Bauten:*
| | |
|---|---|
| 1929–1930 | Großsiedlung Siemensstadt, Berlin-Charlottenburg, Block 6 und 7 |
| 1931 | Reichsforschungssiedlung Haselhorst, Berlin-Spandau, westlicher Bauabschnitt |

*Literatur:*
**Architekt Fred Forbat.** In: Bauwelt (22) 1931, S. 1475–1486
**International Biographical Dictionary of Central European Emigrés.** 1933–1945. München/New York/London/Paris 1983
**Folkesdotter, Gärd,** Fred Forbat och den funktionalistiska stadsbyggnadskonsten. In: Bebyggelsehistorisk tidskrift 1990, no. 20, S. 157–172

## Fred Forbat

| | |
|---|---|
| 31.3.1897 | born at Pécs (Hungary) |
| before 1918 | studies of architecture and history of arts at Budapest (Hungary) |
| 1918 | student of professor Theodor Fischer at Technische Hochschule Munich |
| 1920–1922 | member of Atelier (studio) Gropius at Weimar |
| 1922 | participation in the project of Bauhaussiedlung (Bauhaus housing estate) Am Horn at Weimar |
| 1925–1928 | chief architect of Sommerfeld concern, Berlin |
| since 1928 | own studio at Berlin, member of CIAM |
| 1932 | member of group of Ernst May at Moscow |
| 1933 | member of group of professor Dörpfeld during his archaeological research at Olympia (Greece) |
| 1933–1938 | free architect at Pécs (Hungary) |
| since 1938 | work as architect and urban planner in Sweden |
| 22.5.1972 | died at Vällingby (Sweden) |

*important works:*
| | |
|---|---|
| 1929–1930 | Großsiedlung Siemensstadt, Berlin-Charlottenburg, blocks 6 and 7 |
| 1931 | research housing estate of the Reich at Haselhorst, Berlin-Spandau, western phase of construction |

*literature:*
**Architekt Fred Forbat.** In: Bauwelt (22) 1931, p. 1475–1486
**International Biographical Dictionary of Central European Emigrés.** 1933–1945. München/New York/London/Paris 1983
**Folkesdotter, Gärd,** Fred Forbat och den funktionalistiska stadsbyggnadskonsten. In: Bebyggelsehistorisk tidskrift 1990, no. 20, p. 157–172

## Otto Bartning

| | |
|---|---|
| 12.4.1883 | geboren in Karlsruhe |
| 1904–1908 | Architekturstudium in Berlin und Karlsruhe |
| 1908 | Mitglied im Deutschen Werkbund, von 1919–1923 Vorstandsmitglied |
| 1918 | Mitglied im „Arbeitsrat für Kunst" |
| 1924 | Mitglied der Berliner Architektenvereinigung „Zehnerring" (ab 1926 „Der Ring") |
| 1926–1930 | Professor und Direktor der Bauhochschule in Weimar |
| 1926 | Mitbegründer der Reichsforschungsgesellschaft für Wirtschaftlichkeit im Bau- und Wohnungswesen (RfG) |
| 1948–1950 | Programm für Notkirchen aus vorgefertigten Teilen |
| 1950–1959 | Präsident des Bundes Deutscher Architekten (BDA) |
| 1955 | Städtebaulicher Berater der Stadt Berlin und Vorsitzender des Leitenden Ausschusses der „INTERBAU" |
| 20.2.1959 | in Darmstadt gestorben |

*wichtige Bauten:*

| | |
|---|---|
| 1921–1924 | Wohnhaus Schuster, Wylerberg/Kleve |
| 1926–1928 | Großsiedlungsprojekt, Berlin-Schöneberg für 48.000 Wohnungen |
| 1928 | Stahlkirche auf der „Pressa" in Köln |
| 1929–1930 | Randbebauung mit Heizwerk und Wäscherei der Großsiedlung Siemensstadt, Berlin-Charlottenburg |
| 1931–1934 | Gustav-Adolf-Kirche, Berlin-Charlottenburg |
| 1932–1933 | Reichsforschungssiedlung Haselhorst, Berlin-Spandau, Bauabschnitt mit 300 Wohnungen |

*wichtige Schriften:*
**Bartning, Otto,** Vom Raum der Kirche. Bramsche 1958
**Bartning, Otto,** Vom neuen Kirchbau. Berlin 1919

*Literatur:*
**Bredow, Jürgen/Lerch, Helmut,** Materialien zum Werk des Architekten Otto Bartning. Darmstadt 1983
**Nicolaisen, Dörte** (Hg.), Das andere Bauhaus. Otto Bartning und die Staatliche Bauhochschule in Weimar 1926–1930. Berlin 1996
**Mayer, K. F. Hans,** Der Baumeister Otto Bartning und die Wiederentdeckung des Raumes. Heidelberg 1951
**Pollack, Ernst,** Der Baumeister Otto Bartning. Bonn 1926
**Posener, Julius,** Otto Bartning. Berlin 1983

Abb. 125:
Otto Bartning, um 1950

Abb. 126:
Hugo Häring, 1930

Fig. 126:
Hugo Häring, 1930

**Paul Rudolf Henning**

| | |
|---|---|
| 16.8.1886 | geboren in Berlin |
| 1903–1907 | Studium der Architektur und Bildhauerei an der Technischen Hochschule in Berlin |
| 1905 | Studien an der Kunstakademie in Dresden bei Wilhelm Kreis und bei Fritz Schumacher an der dortigen Technischen Hochschule |
| 1907 | Eröffnung eines eigenes Ateliers in Berlin, Beginn der künstlerischen Tätigkeit als Bildhauer und Keramiker |
| 1913 | Mitglied im Deutschen Werkbund |
| 1919 | Berufung in den „Arbeitsrat für Kunst" |
| 1928 | Mitglied beim Internationalen Verband für Städtebau und Wohnungswesen |
| nach 1945 | städtebauliche Planungen für Siedlungsprojekte in Berlin |
| 11.10.1986 | in Berlin gestorben |

*wichtige Bauten:*

| | |
|---|---|
| 1921–1923 | Zusammenarbeit mit Erich Mendelsohn beim Verlagshaus Mosse, Berlin-Mitte |
| 1930 | Wohnblock Baumschulenweg, Berlin-Treptow |
| 1930/31 | Wohnhauszeilen in der Großsiedlung Siemensstadt, Berlin-Charlottenburg |
| 1930–1931 | eigenes Wohnhaus mit Atelier, Berlin-Lankwitz |
| nach 1933 | Einfamilienhausprojekte, verschiedene Planungen für Wohnblöcke in Berlin-Lichtenberg |

**Literatur:**
**Paul Rudolf Henning.** Der Verlust der Utopie in der modernen Architektur. Ausstellungskatalog Berlin 1991

**Paul Rudolf Henning**

| | |
|---|---|
| 16.8.1886 | born at Berlin |
| 1903–1907 | studies of architecture and sculpture at Technische Hochschule Berlin |
| 1905 | studies at the Academy of Arts at Dresden (professors Wilhelm Kreis) and at Technische Hochschule Dresden (professor Fritz Schumacher) |
| 1907 | opening an own studio at Berlin, beginning work at sculptor and ceramist |
| 1913 | member of Deutscher Werkbund |
| 1919 | appointed member of „Working Council for Art" |
| 1928 | member of Internationaler Verband für Städtebau und Wohnungswesen (International Association for Urban Development and Housing) |
| after 1945 | urban development plans for housing estates in Berlin |
| 11.10.1986 | died at Berlin |

*important works:*

| | |
|---|---|
| 1921–1923 | cooperation with Erich Mendelsohn in designing the building of Verlagshaus (publishing house) Mosse at Berlin-Mitte |
| 1930 | residential block at Baumschulenweg, Berlin-Treptow |
| 1930/31 | ribbon buildings (residential) at Großsiedlung Siemensstadt, Berlin-Charlottenburg |
| 1930–1931 | own residential building with studio at Berlin-Lankwitz |
| after 1933 | single family houses, several designs for residential blocks at Berlin-Lichtenberg |

**literature:**
**Paul Rudolf Henning.** Der Verlust der Utopie in der modernen Architektur. Exhibition catalogue, Berlin 1991

## Leberecht Migge

| | |
|---|---|
| 20.3.1881 | geboren in Danzig |
| 1904–1913 | Mitarbeiter, später künstlerischer Leiter in der Gartenbaufirma Ochs in Hamburg |
| 1910 | Englandreise mit Auswirkungen auf Migges Konzept einer Gartenkultur des 20. Jahrhunderts |
| 1912 | Mitglied im Deutschen Werkbund |
| 1920 | Ansiedlung auf dem Sonnenhof in Worpswede und Gründung der „Siedlerschule Worpswede" |
| 1923–1929 | Herausgeber der Zeitschrift „Siedlungswirtschaft" |
| 1926–1935 | eigenes Büro in Berlin mit Kontakten zu den Architekten der Wohnungsreformbewegung |
| 30.5.1935 | in Flensburg gestorben |

*wichtige Projekte:*

| | |
|---|---|
| 1918–1920 | Gartengestaltung der Siedlung Lindenhof (Architekt: M. Wagner), Berlin-Schöneberg |
| 1924 | Kleinhaussiedlung „Neu-Jerusalem" (Architekt: Erwin Gutkind), Berlin-Spandau |
| 1925 | Großsiedlung Britz (Hufeisensiedlung), I/II. Bauabschnitt, Berlin-Neukölln |
| 1926 | Siedlung Georgsgarten (Architekt: Otto Haesler), Celle |
| 1926–1930 | Siedlung Römerstadt (Architekt: Ernst May), Frankfurt/Main |
| 1926–1929 | Waldsiedlung Onkel-Toms-Hütte, Berlin-Zehlendorf |
| 1927–1928 | Siedlung Praunheim (Architekt: Ernst May), Frankfurt/Main |
| 1929–1931 | Großsiedlung Siemensstadt, Berlin-Spandau |

*wichtige Schriften:*

**Migge, Leberecht,** Deutsche Binnenkolonisation. Sachgrundlagen des Siedlungswesens. Berlin 1926 (Reprint 1999 unter dem Titel: „Der soziale Garten. Das grüne Manifest")
**Migge, Leberecht,** Jedermann Selbstversorger. Eine Lösung der Siedlungsfrage durch neuen Gartenbau. Jena 1918
**Migge, Leberecht,** Die Gartenkultur des 20. Jahrhunderts. Jena 1913

*Literatur:*

**Baumann, Martin,** Freiraumplanung in den Siedlungen der Zwanziger Jahre am Beispiel der Planungen des Gartenarchitekten Leberecht Migge. Halle 2002
**Leberecht Migge**. 1881–1935. Gartenkultur des 20. Jahrhunderts, hg. vom Fachbereich Stadt- und Landschaftsplanung der Gesamthochschule Kassel. Worpswede 1981
**Haney, David Henderson,** Leberecht Migge (1881–1935) and the modern garden in Germany. Dissertation an der Universität von Pennsylvania (USA) 2005
**Hulbusch, I. M.,** „Jedermann Selbstversorger". Das koloniale Grün Leberecht Migges. Von der Flucht ins harmonische Landleben zur Konzeption einer sozial engagierten Gartenarchitektur. In: Lucius Burckhardt (Hg.): Der Werkbund in Deutschland, Österreich und der Schweiz. Form ohne Ornament. Stuttgart 1978, S. 66–71

Abb. 127:
Leberecht Migge, um 1930

Abb. 128:
Ludwig Lesser, 1930

Fig. 128:
Ludwig Lesser, 1930

## Ludwig Lesser

| | |
|---|---|
| 3.2.1869 | geboren in Berlin |
| 1884–1885 | gärtnerische Ausbildung im Frankfurter Palmengarten unter Leitung des Direktors August Siebert |
| ab 1902 | freier Gartenarchitekt in Berlin, zahlreiche Privatgärten in Berlin und Umgebung |
| 1908 | Gartendirektor der „Berliner Terrain-Centrale" und der „Zehlendorf-West Terrain AG" |
| 1913 | Mitbegründer des „Deutschen Volksparkbundes" |
| 1914 | Mitglied im Deutschen Werkbund |
| 1919 | Berufung in das Präsidium der Deutschen-Gartenbau-Gesellschaft, von 1923 bis 1933 deren Präsident |
| 1913–1933 | Lehrtätigkeit an der Berliner Universität |
| 1939 | Emigration nach Schweden |
| 25.12.1957 | in Vallentuna bei Stockholm (Schweden) gestorben |

*wichtige Projekte:*

| | |
|---|---|
| ab 1909 | Gartenstadt Frohnau, Berlin-Reinickendorf, Villenkolonien Grunewald und Zehlendorf-West, Berlin-Zehlendorf |
| 1913–1916 | Gartenstadt Falkenberg (Architekt: Bruno Taut), Berlin-Treptow |
| 1914–1917 | Gartenstadt Staaken (Architekt: Paul Schmitthenner), Berlin-Spandau |
| 1929–1931 | Siedlung Weiße Stadt (Architekten: Salvisberg, Büning, Ahrends), Berlin-Reinickendorf |
| 1932 | Ausstellung „Sonne, Luft und Haus für alle" auf dem Messegelände am Funkturm |

*wichtige Schriften:*
**Lesser, Ludwig,** Volksparke Heute und Morgen. Berlin 1927
**Lesser, Ludwig,** Der Kleingarten. Berlin 1915

*Literatur:*
**Lesser-Sayrac, Katrin,** Ludwig Lesser (1869–1957) – Erster freischaffender Gartenarchitekt in Berlin (Beiträge zur Denkmalpflege in Berlin, Heft 4). Berlin 1995

## Ludwig Lesser

| | |
|---|---|
| 3.2.1869 | born at Berlin |
| 1884–1885 | training as gardener at Palmengarten Frankfurt under August Siebert, director |
| as from 1902 | free-lance garden architect at Berlin, many private gardens in and around Berlin |
| 1908 | gardening director of "Berliner Terrain-Centrale" and "Zehlendorf-West Terrain AG" |
| 1913 | co-founder of "Deutscher Volksparkbund" (German public park federation) |
| 1914 | member of Deutscher Werkbund |
| 1919 | appointment to the presidium of Deutsche-Gartenbau-Gesellschaft (German horticultural society), president of the society from 1923 until 1933 |
| 1913–1933 | teacher at the Berlin university |
| 1939 | emigration to Sweden |
| 25.12.1957 | died at Vallentuna near Stockholm (Sweden) |

*important projects:*

| | |
|---|---|
| as from 1909 | garden city Frohnau at Berlin-Reinickendorf, colonies of villas at Grunewald and Zehlendorf-West (Berlin-Zehlendorf) |
| 1913–1916 | Gartenstadt Falkenberg (Garden town Falkenberg); (architect: Bruno Taut) at Berlin-Treptow |
| 1914–1917 | Gartenstadt Staaken (Garden town Staaken); (architect: Paul Schmitthenner) at Berlin-Spandau |
| 1929–1931 | residential estate Weiße Stadt (architects: Salvisberg, Büning, Ahrends) at Berlin-Reinickendorf |
| 1932 | exhibition "Sonne, Luft und Haus für alle" (sun, air and house for all) on Messegelände (fairgrounds) at Funkturm |

*important publications:*
**Lesser, Ludwig,** Volksparke Heute und Morgen. Berlin 1927
**Lesser, Ludwig,** Der Kleingarten. Berlin 1915

*literature:*
**Lesser-Sayrac, Katrin,** Ludwig Lesser (1869–1957) – Erster freischaffender Gartenarchitekt in Berlin (Beiträge zur Denkmalpflege in Berlin, No. 4). Berlin 1995

# GUTACHTEN
# EXPERT`S REVIEW

**Berliner Siedlungen der Moderne (1913 – 1932)**
*Antrag auf Eintragung in die UNESCO-Welterbeliste*

1871 wurde Berlin die Hauptstadt des von Bismarck neugegründeten Deutschen Reiches. In den darauf folgenden Jahren führte die industrielle Revolution zu tiefgreifenden Veränderungen der Stadt, deren Aussehen und Struktur durch den schnellen Fortschritt stark beeinflusst wurden. Ein Netz von Straßen, Eisenbahnlinien und Wasserstraßen wurde für die schnell wachsende Industrie geschaffen und verband die verschiedenen Teile des städtischen Ballungsraumes miteinander. Um die Verteilung der Waren zu erleichtern, wurden Bahnhöfe, Häfen, Markthallen und Warenhäuser errichtet. Durch diese Bautätigkeit wurde die städtische Struktur bis zur Unkenntlichkeit verändert und Berlin in eine moderne Stadt verwandelt. Mit dem Anwachsen des Volumens der Industrieproduktion kamen viele Immigranten in die Stadt, die auf der Suche nach Arbeit und Wohnung waren. Mietshäuser mit vielen Hinterhöfen waren bald bis an die äußersten Grenzen ihrer Kapazität belegt. Es entwickelte sich ein enormer Wohnraummangel und wahrscheinlich war die Lage in keiner anderen Stadt Europas so kritisch wie in der deutschen Metropole. Von 900.000 im Jahre 1871 wuchs die Bevölkerungszahl auf mehr als 2.700.000 im Jahre 1900 und auf mehr als 4 Millionen zu Anfang der 1920er Jahre. In seinem bekannten Buch „Das steinerne Berlin" beschreibt Werner Hegemann die Stadt als die „größte Mietskasernenstadt der Welt". Diese Entwicklung führte zu einer schweren Wohnungsnot

**Berlin housing estates in the modern style (1913 – 1932)**
*Application for the UNESCO-World Heritage List*

In 1871, Berlin became the capital of Bismarck's newly founded German Empire. In the ensuing years, an industrial revolution changed the city dramatically as rapid progress profoundly influenced its face and structure. A network of roads, railways and waterways was created for the rapidly growing industry, interconnecting parts of the city agglomeration, and railway stations, ports, market halls and department stores were built to make the distribution of products easier. These building interventions changed the urban structure beyond recognition and transformed Berlin into a modern large city. As industrial production grew in volume, vast numbers of immigrants came into the city, seeking work and cheap housing. Residential blocks with numerous backyards were soon filled to their utmost capacity. A grave housing shortage arose, and probably in no other big city in Europe was the situation as critical as in the German metropolis. The population of the city and the industrial agglomeration grew from 900,000 in 1871 to more than 2,700,000 in 1900 and to over 4 million at the beginning of the 1920s. In his well-known book "Das steinerne Berlin", Werner Hegemann characterised the city as the "largest barracks-to-rent city in the world" ("die größte Mietskasernenstadt der Welt"). The situation resulted in a housing shortage, and this became even worse during the First World War, which put an end to all construction, and during the great inflation in the

Abb. 129: Siedlung an der Bruchfeldstraße in Frankfurt/Main, 1925–1929 von Ernst May, 1929

Fig. 129: Housing estate at Bruchfeldstraße in Frankfurt/Main, 1925–1929 by Ernst May, 1929

und die Situation verschlechterte sich während des Ersten Weltkrieges, der zur Einstellung sämtlicher Bautätigkeit führte, und während der großen Inflation zu Anfang der 1920er Jahre noch weiter. Die Wohnungsnot war besonders groß in den während der sogenannten Gründerzeit errichteten Stadtteilen, wo Häuser mit vielen Hinterhöfen errichtet worden waren. Dort wohnten mehr als vier Menschen jeweils in einem Raum und mehr als 600.000 Einwohner der Stadt lebten unter solchen Bedingungen. Sogar 1925 lebten noch 70.000 Einwohner der Stadt in Kellerwohnungen.

Das Gartenstadtkonzept, wie es von Ebenezer Howard und Raymond Unwin in England entwickelt wurde, oder dessen deutsche Formen (wie zum Beispiel Hellerau, eine Gartenstadt in Dresden, entworfen von Richard Riemerschmid und Heinrich Tessenow) oder die utopischen, visionären Konzepte konzentrisch angelegter städtischer Bereiche, wie sie von Bruno Taut kurz vor Beginn des Ersten Weltkrieges entwickelt wurden, reichten nicht mehr aus, um dieses schwerwiegende Problem zu lösen. Auch die Ausstellungen des Werkbundes, errichtet zwischen 1927 und 1932 in Stuttgart-Weißenhof, Brünn-Wilson Forest, Breslau-Grüneiche, Zürich-Neubühl, Prag-Baba und Wien-Lainz, konnten nur Musterhäuser darstellen. Es handelte sich dabei um Einfamilienhäuser, Doppel- oder Dreifachhäuser für die obere Mittelklasse oder um Reihenhäuser (mit Ausnahme der Mietshäuser von Ludwig Mies van der Rohe und Peter Behrens in Stuttgart sowie der Kollektivhäuser von Scharoun und Rading in Breslau) und nicht um Beispiele für die weite Verbreitung und Nutzung durch alle Gesellschaftsklassen. Die Lösung konnte nur in der Errichtung großer Siedlungen im Grünen mit modernen Bebauungsplänen und rationell gestalteten Grundrissen, gebaut nach den Prinzipien neuer, rational geführter Wohnungsorganisationen liegen. Dies wurde durch die Konsolidierung

early 1920s. The housing shortage was especially serious in the city districts built in the so-called "Gründerzeit" period, where the houses had been designed with many backyards. There, each room had more than 4 occupants, and this was the situation for more than 600,000 residents. More than 70,000 residents lived in basements even as late as 1925.

The experience of the garden city concept of Ebenezer Howard and Raymond Unwin from England, and their German modifications (such as Hellerau, a garden city in Dresden designed by Richard Riemerschmid and Heinrich Tessenow) or the utopian visionary concepts of concentric urban units, as proposed by Bruno Taut shortly before World War I, could no longer suffice to solve this critical situation. Similarly, the Werkbund exhibition estates, built between 1927 and 1932 in Stuttgart-Weissenhof, Brno-Wilson Forest, Breslau-Grüneiche, Zurich-Neubühl, Prague-Baba and Vienna-Lainz, could only present "Musterhäuser" (Model Houses), single-family houses and semi-detached or triple houses for upper middle class customers or terraced houses (with the exception of tenement houses by Ludwig Mies van der Rohe and Peter Behrens in Stuttgart and collective houses by Scharoun and Rading in Breslau), and not everyday examples for all social classes. The solution could only be found in large housing developments in green surroundings with modern master plans and rationally formulated floor plans, built according to the principles of new, rational housing organization. This was made possible by the consolidation of the economy after the inflation, beginning in 1924, and by the emergence of a new generation of architects, led by city building counsellor (Stadtbaurat) Martin Wagner and architect Bruno Taut. These men had not only been influenced by the idea of garden cities but also by "Taylorism" – American organization of rationalised building production – and

der Wirtschaft ab 1924 nach der Inflation und das Erscheinen einer neuen Generation von Architekten, angeführt von Stadtbaurat Martin Wagner und dem Architekten Bruno Taut ermöglicht. Diese Männer waren nicht nur von den Ideen der Gartenstadtbewegung beeinflusst, sondern auch durch die des Taylorismus und durch innovative Möglichkeiten der Finanzierung von Wohnungsbautätigkeit unter der Führung der deutschen Wohnungsbaugesellschaft.

Die während der Weimarer Republik zwischen 1924 und 1932 (bis zur Einführung der Brüning'schen Notverordnungen) errichteten Siedlungen mit 135.000 Wohneinheiten sind zweifellos zu den größten Errungenschaften der Berliner Architektur zu zählen, und zwar nicht nur wegen ihrer architektonischen Qualität, sondern auch aufgrund ihres Wertes als soziale und wirtschaftliche Leistung.

Hier wurde eine neue Strategie fortschrittlicher Lebensweise geboten, die sich grundlegend von den Wohnkomplexen der Gründerzeit des ausgehenden 19. und beginnenden 20. Jahrhunderts unterschied. Diese älteren Wohnkomplexe wurden unter Stadtbaurat Ludwig Hoffmann, dem Vorgänger von Martin Wagner errichtet und waren Häuser im Stil des Historismus, die auf langen, schmalen Grundstücken errichtet worden waren und wo die hygienischen Bedingungen aufgrund der geschlossenen Blöcke und der engen Hinterhöfe alles andere als gut waren. „Licht, Luft und Sonne" war das Motto, unter dem die neuen Siedlungen in den Außenbezirken der Stadt errichtet wurden. Sie waren umgeben von Grün und boten gute öffentliche Verkehrsverbindungen zum Stadtzentrum und den Arbeitsplätzen. Diese Strategie beruhte auf der fortschrittlichen sozialdemokratischen Vision einer neuen Gesellschaft, die während der Weimarer Republik von vielen geteilt wurde.

Auch in anderen deutschen und ehemals deutschen Städten findet man Siedlungen aus den 1920er Jahren, insbe-

by innovative ways of financing housing construction under the auspices of the German housing society.

The housing developments built in the time of the Weimar Republic between 1924 and 1932 (until the introduction of Brüning's emergency measures) – when 135,000 apartments were built – can doubtlessly be declared one of the supreme achievements of Berlin architecture, and not only because of their architectural qualities but also because of their value as a great social and economic act.

Here, a new strategy of avant-garde living was offered, quite unlike the "Gründerzeit" housing complexes from the end of the 19th and beginning of the 20th century, the time of Martin Wagner's predecessor, city building counsellor Ludwig Hoffmann, where historical style houses were built on long, narrow plots and where the hygienic conditions of block housing with cramped backyards were far from satisfactory: "Light, air, and sun" was the motto for the new housing projects on the outskirts of the city, surrounded by greenery and provided with convenient public transport connections to the city centre and to job opportunities. This strategy was based on the progressive social democratic vision of a new society, shared by many in the Weimar Republic.

Housing developments from the 1920s can also be found in many other German and former German Cities, especially in Frankfurt am Main, Karlsruhe, Magdeburg, Gera, Leipzig, Dresden, Celle, Breslau (present-day Wrocław), and elsewhere. Some of them, however, bear traditionalist features (Breslau), others – in Karlsruhe (Dammerstock – Gropius), Leipzig (Neu Gohlis – Mebes and Emmerich) and Magdeburg (Bruno Taut) are the works of Berlin architects or local architects copying Berlin models (Haesler – Celle, Hans Richter – Dresden-Trachau, Schoder – Gera). The housing estates in Hamburg have a strong regional

Abb. 130: Reihenhäuser für Angestellte der Zellulosefabrik Sunila (Finnland), 1936–1939 von Alvar Aalto

Fig. 130: Semi-detached houses for the employees of the cellulose factory at Sunila (Finland), 1936–1939 by Alvar Aalto

Abb. 131: Siedlung in Hoek van Holland (Niederlande), 1924–1927 von J. J. P. Oud, um 1928

Fig. 131: Housing estate in Hoek van Holland (Netherlands), 1924–1927 by J. J. P. Oud, approximately 1928

sondere in Frankfurt am Main, Karlsruhe, Madgeburg, Gera, Leipzig, Dresden, Celle, Breslau (heute Wrocław) sowie in anderen Städten. Einige davon tragen aber noch traditionalistische Züge (Breslau), andere – z.B. Karlsruhe-Dammerstock von Gropius, Leipzig Neu-Gohlis von Mebes und Emmerich sowie Projekte in Magdeburg von Bruno Taut – sind Arbeiten von Berliner Architekten oder die von lokalen Architekten, die Berliner Modelle kopiert haben (Haesler in Celle, Hans Richter in Dresden-Trachau, Schoder in Gera). Die Siedlungen in Hamburg haben einen sehr regionalen Charakter mit ihren Ziegelfassaden und einigen originellen urbanen Zügen, insbesondere in den Arbeiten von Karl Schneider.

Die Siedlungen in Frankfurt am Main, die während der Zeit von Ernst May als Stadtarchitekt zwischen 1925 und 1930 errichtet wurden, sind die einzige Ausnahme. May hatte in London mit Raymond Unwin zusammengearbeitet und als Direktor der Schlesischen Heimstätte in Breslau (von 1920 bis 1925) hatte er nach der Volksabstimmung zur Grenze zwischen Polen und Deutschland den Bau von mehr als 15.000 Wohnungen für Immigranten in Ober- und Niederschlesien organisiert. In Frankfurt am Main wandte er seine früher in England und Schlesien, von woher er einige Mitarbeiter mitgebracht hatte (H. C. Rudloff, Hans Leistikow), gemachten Erfahrungen an und er lud auch Kollegen aus Wien (Margarethe Schütte-Lihotzky, Anton Brenner, Franz Schuster), aus den Niederlanden (Mart Stam) und der Schweiz (Karl Steiger) ein, bei der Errichtung des Neuen Frankfurt mitzuarbeiten.

Betrachtet man ihren rationalen Ansatz beim städtebaulichen Entwurf, ihre lichten, klaren Grundrisse, ihre Verwendung von Farbe, den Standard von Ausstattung und Sanitäreinrichtungen sowie die rationalisierte Produktion,

character with the use of brick surfaces and some original urban gestures, especially in the work of Karl Schneider.

The housing developments in Frankfurt am Main built in the time of Ernst May, city architect between 1925 and 1930, are the only exception. May had worked together with Raymond Unwin in London, and as the director of Schlesische Heimstätte in Breslau (from 1920 to 1925) he had organised the building of more than 15,000 dwellings for immigrants to Upper and Lower Silesia after the plebiscite on the border between Poland and Germany. In Frankfurt am Main he used his own earlier experience from England and Silesia, from where he had brought several collaborators (H. C. Rudloff, Hans Leistikow) and also invited colleagues from Vienna (Margarethe Schütte-Lihotzky, Anton Brenner, Franz Schuster) and from the Netherlands (Mart Stam) and Switzerland (Karl Steiger) to create "Das Neue Frankfurt" (The new Frankfurt).

Judged by the rational approach in their urban design, their lucid, clear floor plans, their use of colours, their standard of interior and sanitary facilities and their rationalised production, May's housing developments – "Das Neue Frankfurt" - bear comparison with those in Berlin. Sadly, the case is different with their present condition which, from the point of view of monument care, would not stand comparison with the Berlin housing complexes.

Last but not least to mention is the size of the housing developments in the other cities, which never reached the big city scale of the Berlin projects as far as size and impact on the society's way of life is concerned.

A comparison between the Berlin housing developments and their counterparts in other countries would lead to

Abb. 132: Genossenschaftswohnbauten in Kosice (Slowakei), 1930–1931 von Josef Polasek, um 1931

Fig. 132: Cooperative housing estates in Kosice (Slovakia), 1930–1931 by Josef Polasek, approximately 1931

so scheinen die Siedlungen des Neuen Frankfurt von May durchaus einem Vergleich mit denen in Berlin standzuhalten. Leider trifft dies jedoch nicht auf ihren gegenwärtigen Erhaltungszustand zu, der aus der Sicht der Denkmalpflege nicht mit dem der Berliner Siedlungen vergleichbar ist.

Außerdem muss auch die Größe der Siedlungen in den anderen Städten berücksichtigt werden, die niemals dasselbe Niveau wie in Berlin erreicht hat, weder was den Umfang noch was die Auswirkungen auf die Lebensweise der Gesellschaft angeht.

Ein Vergleich zwischen den Berliner Siedlungen und deren Entsprechungen in anderen Ländern würde zu ähnlichen Ergebnissen führen. Die in Wien in den 1920er Jahren unter Bürgermeister Karl Seitz errichteten „Super-Blöcke" waren in ihrer Massigkeit und Einfachheit immer noch dem modernen Traditionalismus aus der Zeit vor dem Krieg und der „Großstadtarchitektur" des Großmeisters Otto Wagner verhaftet. Mit ihren halboffenen oder geschlossenen Innenhöfen waren die Häuser als Volkswohnungspaläste mit Geschäften, Clubs und Gemeinschaftsräumen auf Straßenebene geplant und hatten damit noch einen sehr urbanen Charakter. Manchmal erinnern sie sogar etwas an Festungen (Karl-Marx-Hof, Lasalle-Hof). Im Detail waren sie jedoch noch mit der industriellen Kunst und dekorativen Tradition verbunden, deren Feinheit in scharfem Widerspruch zu dem bescheidenen Ausstattungsgrad der Wohnungen ohne Bäder stand. Mehrgeschossige Wohnhäuser in Amsterdam, die während des Ersten Weltkrieges errichtet wurden, z.B. die Siedlung Eigen Haard von Michel de Klerk, und zu denen ganz Europa aufsah, wiesen den expressionistischen Stil der Amsterdamer Schule mit ihren detailreichen Reliefs und Backsteinfassaden auf. Obwohl dieser Stil in den Arbeiten anderer Architekten derselben Gruppe (P. Krämer, J. Ruetgers, H. T. Wijdeveld, M. Krop-

similar conclusions. The "superblocks" built in Vienna in the 1920s under Mayor Karl Seitz were, by their massiveness and simplicity, still connected to the pre-war modern traditionalism and the "Großstadtarchitektur" idea of the grand seigneur Otto Wagner. With their inner courtyards, semi-open or enclosed, the houses were designed as "people's housing palaces" (Volkswohnungspaläste) with stores, clubs and social meeting rooms on street level, thus retaining a strongly urban character, at times even reminiscent of fortifications (Karl-Marx-Hof, Lasalle-Hof). In detail, however, they were still connected to industrial arts and the decorative tradition, the intricacy of which contrasted sharply with the modest facilities of apartments designed without bathrooms. Residential blocks in Amsterdam built during World War I – such as Michel de Klerk's Eigen Haard – which all post-war Europe looked up to, were designed in the expressionist style of the Amsterdam School, with a relief craft detail of brick-faced walls. Although the style became more moderate in the buildings of other architects of the group (P. Kramer, J. Ruetgers, H. T. Wijdeveld, M. Kropholler, and others) who participated in the development of Amsterdam-South, designed according to the urban plan of H. P. Berlage, it did not follow the tendency toward rationalised mass production which had been followed in Berlin from the very beginning. Nor did the size of the living area and the hygienic standard (no bathrooms) reach the level that had been aimed at in Berlin. Parallel to Amsterdam, other experimental brick-faced apartment blocks were built in Rotterdam: Spangen (M. Brinkman) and – after Jacobus J. P. Oud was appointed city architect – Tusschendijken which, unlike their Amsterdam counterparts, suggested a shift toward a more rational architectural form. In the housing developments of Hoek van Holland (1924–1927) and De Kiefhoek in Rotterdam (1925–1929), J. J. P. Oud harmonised ingenious minimalist concepts of the plan with rational construction and pure

holler und anderen), die an der Errichtung von Amsterdam-Süd nach einem Bebauungsplan von H. P. Berlage beteiligt waren, etwas moderater wurde, gab es hier nicht den Trend hin zur rationalisierten Massenproduktion, die in Berlin von Anfang an eine wichtige Rolle spielte. Auch die Größe des Wohnraumes und die hygienischen Standards (keine Bäder) erreichten nicht das in Berlin angestrebte Niveau. Parallel zu Amsterdam wurden in Rotterdam andere mehrgeschossige Wohnhäuser mit Backsteinfassaden errichtet: die Siedlungen Spangen (M. Brinkman) und – nach der Ernennung von J. J. P. Oud zum Stadtarchitekten – Tusschendijken, die im Gegensatz zu den Amsterdamer Siedlungen eine Bewegung hin zu rationelleren Bauformen widerspiegeln. In den Siedlungen Hoek van Holland (1924–1927) und De Kiefhoek in Rotterdam (1925–1929) brachte Oud geniale minimalistische Gestaltungskonzepte in Einklang mit rationellem Bauen und den reinen Architekturformen der Traditionen von „De Stijl". Durch diese Projekte wurde er einer der international führenden Architekten des Neuen Bauen, eine Stilrichtung, die später in Amerika in „International Style" umbenannt wurde. Was die Wohnbedingungen, den urbanen Maßstab und die sanitären Einrichtungen (noch ohne Bäder) angeht, können diese Siedlungen allerdings nicht mit denen in Berlin und deren großstädtischem Charakter verglichen werden.

Die Siedlungen in Berlin spielen also in der Entwicklung des Wohnungsbaus des 20. Jahrhunderts auch aus internationaler Sicht eine einzigartige Rolle. Ihre Einzigartigkeit wird in einer Reihe von Aspekten deutlich.

### Bebauungspläne

Jedes der sechs ausgewählten Beispiele beruht auf einem höchst originellen Bebauungsplan, allerdings wurden von der Gartenstadt Falkenberg zwischen 1913 und 1915 nur zwei Teilbereiche errichtet. Der Akazienhof wurde als privater Bereich mit einem kleinen Platz gestaltet, während die Bebauung entlang des Gartenstadtweges einfühlsam auf den Geländeverlauf eingeht. Beim Entwurf des Schillerparks hatte Bruno Taut zum ersten Mal nach der Inflation 1924 Gelegenheit, halboffene mehrgeschossige Wohnbauten zu planen. Bei dem Projekt ließ er sich von der holländischen Backsteinarchitektur inspirieren und die Finanzierung beruhte auf einem neuen System – der Hauszinssteuer. Die Hufeisensiedlung von Bruno Taut (Baubeginn 1925) stellt eine bemerkenswerte Übergangsstufe von der städtebaulichen Form der Gartenstadt zur Großsiedlung dar. Damit verbinden sich in ihr die Verwendung von Reihenhäusern und mehrgeschossigen Wohnhäusern sowie private und öffentliche Grünflächen. Die Gebäude sind im zentralen Bereich der Siedlung axial angeordnet (die Reihenhäuser als „Hüsung" und die mehrgeschossigen Häuser als „Hufeisen"), und schaffen so symbolhafte städtebauliche Formen, um die herum sich die anderen Teile der Siedlung (zum überwiegenden Teil aus Reihenhäusern und mehrgeschossigen Miethäusern bestehend) gruppieren. Die übrigen drei Siedlungen – die Weiße Stadt, Siemensstadt und die Wohnsiedlung Carl Legien – stellen drei unterschiedliche Ansätze an großstädtisches Bauen dar. In der Siedlung Carl Legien (1928–1930) gestaltete Bruno Taut eine rippenartige Komposition U-förmiger mehrgeschossiger Wohnbauten entlang der Erich-Weinert-Straße als Hauptachse. Die zu den halboffenen Höfen und der Hauptachse weisenden Fassaden sind durch ein System von Loggien und

architectural forms in the tradition of "De Stijl." It was these projects that made him one of the leading international architects of the "Neues Bauen" style, later renamed the "International Style" in America. In terms of living area standards, urban scale and sanitary facilities (bathrooms were still lacking), however, these housing complexes cannot be compared to the metropolitan character of the developments in Berlin.

The housing complexes of Berlin, therefore, play a unique role in the development of 20th century housing, even from the international perspective. Their uniqueness is seen in a number of aspects:

### Master Plan

The master plan is very original in all of the six examples chosen, although only two fragments of the Falkenberg garden city were built between 1913 and 1915. Akazienhof is designed as a private area with a small square; in Gartenstadtweg the development responds sensitively to the sloping terrain. Schillerpark was Bruno Taut's first opportunity to build semi-open apartment blocks after the great inflation in 1924. The project was inspired by Dutch brick architecture and relied on the new system of housing financing based on the house tax (Hauszinssteuer). Bruno Taut's Hufeisensiedlung, begun in 1925, represents a remarkable transition phase between the urban forms of the garden city and housing development. As such, it combines the use of row houses and apartment buildings with private and public green areas. The buildings are arranged axially in the central part of the development, the row houses as "Hüsung" and the apartment blocks as "Hufeisen" ("horseshoe"), creating symbolic urban figures around which the other part of the housing development (consisting mostly of row houses and tenement houses) is arranged. The other three housing complexes – Die Weiße Stadt (the White City), Siemensstadt and Carl-Legien-Stadt – represent three various metropolitan urban approaches. In Carl-Legien-Stadt (1928–1930), Bruno Taut designed a rib-like composition of U-shaped apartment blocks along the main axis of Erich Weinert-Straße. In the direction toward the semi-open courts and toward the main axis, the facade is decorated by a system of loggias and balconies which gives the entire space a unified urban character.

The entry to the "Weiße Stadt" (White City) housing development (1929–1931) is accentuated by Bruno Ahrends' symmetrically situated tower apartment buildings and further complemented by a fan-shaped composition of tenement houses by Wilhelm Büning. Otto Rudolf Salvisberg's gallery-access house arches as a bridge over the main boulevard, Schillerpromenade. The location of the main streets was kept unchanged by the architects, in accordance with the 1913 regulation. Finally, Hans Scharoun as the architect of the master plan of the Siemensstadt housing development (1929–1931) did not content himself with a schematic linear development in greenery but designed a funnel-like symbolic urban figure at the entry to the development, consisting of three apartment houses of his own design with an original relief "navy" detail on the balconies, which earned one of the houses the nickname "Panzerkreuzer" (the Cruiser).

In all these cases, the significant metropolitan urban form, the expression created by outstanding architects (Ahrends,

Balkonen gestaltet, die dem gesamten Raum einen einheitlichen städtebaulichen Ausdruck verleihen.

Der Eingang zur Weißen Stadt (1929–1931) wird durch die symmetrisch angeordneten, turmartigen Wohnhäuser von Bruno Ahrends betont und durch die fächerförmig angeordneten Mietshäuser von Wilhelm Büning ergänzt. Das Laubenganghaus von Rudolf Salvisberg liegt als Brücke über der Hauptpromenade, der Schillerpromenade. Der Verlauf der Hauptstraßen entspricht dem 1913 festgelegten Plan und wurde von den Architekten nicht verändert. Hans Scharoun, der den Bebauungsplan für die Großsiedlung Siemensstadt (1929–1931) entwarf, gab sich nicht mit der schematischen Anordnung von Zeilen in Grünflächen zufrieden, sondern gestaltete eine trichterartige, symbolhafte städtebauliche Figur am Eingang zu dieser Siedlung, die aus drei von ihm selbst entworfenen Wohnhäusern mit originellen „maritimen" Reliefs an den Balkonen besteht. Wegen dieser Details erhielt eines der Häuser den Beinamen „Panzerkreuzer".

In all diesen Fällen hebt sich die bedeutende großstädtische Gestaltung, der von hervorragenden Architekten (Ahrends, Salvisberg, Scharoun, Bruno Taut, Gropius und Häring) geschaffene Ausdruck über den Schematismus und die Banalität einfacher Zeilenbauten heraus.

*Funktionalität*
Im Gegensatz zu den früheren Blöcken mit ihren vielen tiefen und dunklen Hinterhöfen stellte das System der schlanken, von Grün umgebenen Wohnblöcke am Rande der Stadt ein neues Wohnungsbauprogramm dar, das von dem Motto „Licht, Luft und Sonne" beschrieben wird. Die Funktionalität wird nicht nur im Bebauungsplan deutlich, sondern auch in einem neuen Grundrisskonzept, bei dem eine zentrale tragende Wand es ermöglicht, die wesentlichen Funktionen nach den Himmelsrichtungen auszurichten. Die Anordnung der Balkone sorgt für die Verbindung von Innen- und Außenraum und schafft eine dreidimensionale rhythmische Gliederung der Fassade und weist so auf die Bestimmung des Gebäudes für Wohnzwecke hin. Die Größe der Wohnungen und die Ausstattung mit sanitären Einrichtungen (jede Wohnung verfügt über ein eigenes Bad) übersteigt bei weitem den früheren im sozialen Wohnungsbau üblichen Standard und setzte Maßstäbe, die später auch in anderen europäischen Ländern übernommen wurden.

*Detailreichtum*
Die Berliner Siedlungen haben viele originelle architektonische Details: Gesimse, Hauseingänge, Balkone, Fenster, Türen, Veranden, Ecken mit Keilsteinen, Schornsteine usw., die mit relativ geringem Aufwand herzustellen sind, aber eine lange Lebensdauer aufweisen. Sie spiegeln den individuellen Stil des jeweiligen Architekten wider und reichen über alle Formen des Neuen Bauens hinweg, beginnend mit dem rationalistischen Ansatz von Walter Gropius bis zum Marinestil von Hans Scharoun und den organischen Formen von Hugo Häring.

Abb. 133: Wohnblock Habichtsplatz/Habichtstraße in Hamburg, 1927–1928 von Karl Schneider, Foto 1928

Fig. 133: Block at Habichtsplatz/Habichtstraße in Hamburg, 1927–1928 by Karl Schneider, 1928

Salvisberg, Scharoun, Bruno Taut, Gropius and Häring), surpassed the schematism and banality of a simple linear development.

*Functionality*
In contrast to previous block development with many deep and dark yards, the system of slender apartment houses surrounded by greenery at the outskirts of the city represented a new housing programme, characterised by the motto "light, air, and sun." The functional composition shows not only in the master plan but also in a new concept of the floor plan, where a central supporting wall makes it possible to distribute the basic functions rationally with respect to the cardinal points. The system of balconies provides a connection of interior and exterior spaces and creates a rhythmic three-dimensional articulation of the front facade, thus signalling the house's residential function. The size of the apartments and the level of the sanitary facilities (each apartment had its own bathroom) definitely surpassed what had up to that point been common in social housing, and created standards which were later also accepted in other European countries.

*Sensibility of detail*
The Berlin housing developments offer a wide range of original architectural details: cornices, entrances, balconies, windows, doors, porches, quoins, chimneys, etc., made at a relatively small cost but of great durability. They reveal the architects' individual styles and cover all the nuances of "Neues Bauen" architecture – from the rationalist approach of Walter Gropius to the navy style of Hans Scharoun and the organic approach of Hugo Häring.

## Farbe

Alle Berliner Siedlungen zeichnen sich durch ihre Farbigkeit aus. In der Gartenstadt Falkenberg experimentierte Bruno Taut mit einer ganzen Palette expressionistischer Farbkombinationen von schwarz über blau, grün, rot, terrakotta, gelb und ocker bis zu weiß. In der Siedlung Schillerpark erschienen bündige Ziegelflächen in Kombination mit weißer Farbe. Die Hufeisensiedlung zeigt mehr von Tauts expressionistischen Farbkombinationen, während in der Siedlung Carl Legien die Farbe etwas zurückhaltender verwendet wird. Hier sind die Fassaden großflächig grün, blau, gelb oder rot mit weißen oder beigefarbenen Gruppen von Loggien und vorgesetzten Balkonen. Blaue, braune und beigefarbene Fensterrahmen bringen Leben in die Weiße Stadt. Die Farben der Siemensstadt werden bestimmt von der Kombination von weißem Putz und Naturmaterialien, d.h. den gelben Backsteinen aus der Niederlausitz. Das Farbkonzept war ein wesentlicher Teil der Gesamtplanung all dieser Siedlungen, und es ist höchst anerkennenswert, dass dieser Aspekt bei den Wiederherstellungsarbeiten in den 1980er Jahren und danach mit großer Sorgfalt und Aufmerksamkeit behandelt wurde.

## Landschaftsplanung

Die Landschaftsgestaltung bildete bei den sechs Siedlungen einen festen Bestandteil des Entwicklungskonzeptes und mit wenigen Ausnahmen wurde sie von hervorragenden Landschaftsarchitekten dieser Zeit (Ludwig Lesser für Falkenberg und die Weiße Stadt, Leberecht Migge für die Hufeisensiedlung und Siemensstadt) geschaffen. Die Gartenstadt Falkenberg weist die Atmosphäre und die Größenordnungen einer ländlichen Idylle auf. Die Landschaftsgestaltung der Hufeisensiedlung weist zum Teil Elemente des Gartenstadtgedankens auf (Mietergärten), zum Teil aber auch Elemente in großem Maßstab, wie im Falle der zentralen Freifläche, d.h. des Hufeisens selbst. In der Weißen Stadt und Siemensstadt verbessern großzügige öffentliche Grünanlagen zwischen den Bauten die Qualität der Umwelt.

Abgesehen davon sind die sechs ausgewählten Siedlungen – Falkenberg, Schillerpark, Hufeisensiedlung, Weiße Stadt, Siemensstadt und Carl Legien – charakteristische Vertreter aller Entwicklungsstufen des Wohnungsbaus zwischen 1913 und 1932 von der Gartenstadt (Falkenberg) bis zu den mehrgeschossigen Wohnbauten, beeinflusst von den holländischen Siedlungen (Schillerpark) über die Übergangsform zwischen Gartenstadt und Großsiedlungen (Hufeisensiedlung) und zuletzt bis hin zu städtischen Großsiedlungen mit Grünflächen in drei unterschiedlichen Formen (Weiße Stadt, Siemensstadt, Wohnsiedlung Carl Legien). Sie sind über das gesamte Berliner Stadtgebiet von Nord nach Süd und von Ost nach West verteilt und liegen sowohl auf früherem Ost- als auch West-Berliner Gebiet. Die Architekten, die am Bau dieser Siedlungen beteiligt waren, zählten zu den führenden Architekten ihrer Zeit: Bruno Taut, Martin Wagner, Otto Rudolf Salvisberg, Walter Gropius, Hans Scharoun, Otto Bartning, Hugo Häring, Fred Forbat und andere.

Schon während ihrer Errichtung zogen die Berliner Großsiedlungen große internationale Aufmerksamkeit auf sich. In führenden Fachzeitschriften in aller Welt erschienen Veröffentlichungen über sie. Sie erschienen in Büchern

## Colours

All of the Berlin housing developments are characterised by colourfulness: In the Falkenberg garden city, Bruno Taut experimented with a whole range of expressionist colour combinations from black to blue, green, red, terracotta, yellow and ochre to white; Schillerpark combines fair-faced brickwork and white colour. The Hufeisensiedlung shows more of Bruno Taut's very colourful expressionist combinations, and finally the use of colours becomes somewhat more moderate in Carl-Legien-Stadt, where the front facades are designed as large areas of green, blue, yellow or red colour with white or beige groups of loggias and attached balconies. Blue, brown and beige window frames bring life to the Weiße Stadt; the colours of Siemensstadt are determined by the combination of white plaster and natural material, i.e., the yellow brick of Lower Lusatia (Niederlausitz). The colour concept was an important part of the complex design of all these housing developments, and it is praiseworthy indeed that the reconstructions in the 1980s and later handled the problem with great care and attention.

## Landscape planning

The landscaping design of the six housing developments formed an integral part of their concept and was, with just minor exceptions, prepared by outstanding landscape architects of the period – Ludwig Lesser (Falkenberg and Weiße Stadt), Leberecht Migge (Hufeisensiedlung, Siemensstadt). Falkenberg garden city retains the atmosphere and scale of a rural idyll; the landscape design of Hufeisensiedlung borrows partly from the garden city idea (the tenants' gardens) and also from large-scale landscape design in the case of the Hufeisen (horseshoe) central park. In Weiße Stadt and Siemensstadt, public green areas were designed generously between the blocks, thus improving the environment quality. Apart from that, the six housing projects chosen – Falkenberg, Schillerpark, Hufeisensiedlung, Weiße Stadt, Siemensstadt and Carl-Legien-Stadt – are characteristic representatives of all the phases of housing development between 1913 and 1932 – from the garden city (Falkenberg) to residential blocks influenced by the Dutch complexes (Schillerpark) to the transitional stage between the garden city and the housing development form (Hufeisensiedlung) and to big city housing complexes with green areas, in three different variations (Weiße Stadt, Siemensstadt, Carl-Legien-Stadt). They cover the entire Berlin agglomeration from north to south and from east to west, as well as the area of both former East and West Berlin. The architects who participated in these projects were the leading architects of the period: Bruno Taut, Martin Wagner, Otto Rudolf Salvisberg, Walter Gropius, Hans Scharoun, Otto Bartning, Hugo Häring, Fred Forbat, and others.

The Berlin housing developments drew broad international attention already at the time they were built. They were published in major professional journals worldwide, in books on modern architecture and town planning, and they were the focus of attention at the Berlin Building Exhibition in 1931. With the high level of urban design, living area standards, sanitary and technical facilities (e.g., they were originally equipped mostly with communal laundries) and integration into the landscape, they immediately became models for further social housing construction in

über moderne Architektur und Städtebau und sie standen im Mittelpunkt der Aufmerksamkeit während der Berliner Bauausstellung 1931. Mit ihrem hohen Standard der städtebaulichen Gestaltung, des Wohnraumes, der sanitären und technischen Ausstattung (die meisten von ihnen hatten ursprünglich zum Beispiel Gemeinschaftswäschereien) und durch ihre Einbettung in die Landschaft wurden sie sofort zu Vorbildern für den künftigen sozialen Wohnungsbau in anderen europäischen Ländern. Anfang der 1930er Jahre schloss sich die Tschechoslowakei dieser Entwicklung an mit dem Grünen Fuchs (Zelená liška) in Prag-Pankrác (von F. A. Libra, J. Kan, B. Kozák) und Siedlungen in Brünn und Košice von Josef Polášek. Die skandinavischen Länder kamen später hinzu mit den dänischen Siedlungen in Klampenborg (Bellavista von Arne Jacobsen) und in Kopenhagen (Klokkergarden von Povl Baumann und Knud Hansen), mit mehreren Gebäuden von Kay Fisker, Projekten in der finnischen Industriestadt Sunila in Kotka (Alvar Aalto) und zuletzt den Vororten von Helsinki (Hilding Ekelund, Yrjö Lindegren) sowie von Stockholm (Sven Backström und Leif Reinius). Der Trend hin zu einer noch größeren Harmonie von Landschaft und Gebäuden erreichte mit dem Bau von Tapiola, einer Satellitenstadt, die von einer Reihe führender finnischer Architekten (Blomstedt, Revell, Siren und anderen) geplant wurde, in den frühen 1950er Jahren seinen Höhepunkt.

Bisher sind die Errungenschaften der ersten Hälfte des 20. Jahrhunderts auf der Welterbeliste der UNESCO noch kaum vertreten. Das Haus von Rietveld Schröder in Utrecht, die Tugendhat-Villa in Brünn von Ludwig Mies van der Rohe und die Bauhaus-Anlagen in Weimar und Dessau sind mehr oder weniger einzigartige und hervorragende Beispiele exklusiver Einzelgebäude. Nur die Weiße Stadt in Tel Aviv – nach einem Bebauungsplan von Patrick Geddes – ist ein Ausdruck einer neuen Urbanität und sozialen Bewegung, verbunden mit der Gründung des Staates Israel. Ohne das Wissen von den Berliner Siedlungen wäre die Weiße Stadt von Tel Aviv allerdings undenkbar: Viele der Architekten, Planer und Erbauer, die sich an ihrer Planung und Errichtung beteiligten, sind mit ihren Erfahrungen aus Berlin nach Palästina gekommen.

Die Stadt Le Havre von Auguste Perret wurde erst jüngst in die Welterbeliste aufgenommen als Beispiel für den Wiederaufbau eines durch den Krieg zerstörten strategischen Hafens auf der Grundlage eines klaren kartesischen Planes mit anspruchsvoller französischer Standardisierung und Vorfertigung, wodurch die Grundlagen für neue Strategien für den Wohnungsbau in der zweiten Hälfte des 20. Jahrhunderts geschaffen wurden.

Die Gruppe der Berliner Siedlungen stellt auch eine der größten Errungenschaften des International Style (Neues Bauen) der 1920er Jahre dar und ist eng mit der gesellschaftlichen Vision einer gerechteren Gesellschaft und eines besseren Lebensstandards für alle Klassen der Bevölkerung verbunden. Die Gruppe der ausgewählten Berliner Siedlungen, die seit beinahe 25 Jahren das Ziel umfassender denkmalpflegerischer Tätigkeit sind, verdient also, in die Welterbeliste der UNESCO aufgenommen zu werden – nicht nur als hervorragendes Beispiel für den Städtebau und die Architektur des 20. Jahrhunderts, sondern auch wegen ihrer beispielhaften sozialen Intentionen.

other European countries. Czechoslovakia followed at the very beginning of the 1930s with the Green Fox (Zelená liska) in Prague-Pankrác (by F. A. Libra, J. Kan, B. Kozák) and housing estates in Brno and Kosice, designed by Josef Polásek. The Scandinavian countries joined later with the Danish housing developments in Klampenborg (Bellavista by Arne Jacobsen) and in Copenhagen (Klokkergarden by Povl Baumann and Knud Hansen), and several blocks by Kay Fisker, and in the Finnish industrial city Sunila at Kotka (Alvar Aalto), and finally in the 1940s with the suburbs of Helsinki (Hilding Ekelund, Yrjö Lindegren) and of Stockholm (Sven Backström and Leif Reinius). The tendency toward a yet closer harmony of landscape and housing then reached its peak in the early 1950s in the building of Tapiola, a satellite town designed by a number of leading Finnish architects (Blomstedt, Revell, Siren and others).

The first half of the 20th century is until now only barely represented in the UNESCO World Heritage List. Rietveld Schröder's house in Utrecht, the Tugendhat villa in Brno designed by Ludwig Mies van der Rohe and the Bauhaus sites in Weimar and Dessau are more or less unique, brilliant examples of exclusively solitary buildings. Only the White City of Tel Aviv, based on an urban plan by Patrick Geddes, is an expression of new urbanism and social movement, connected with the foundation of the state of Israel. However, without knowledge of the Berlin housing estates, the White City of Tel Aviv would not be thinkable: Many of the architects, planners and builders who participated in the planning and execution had arrived in Palestine with experience from Berlin.

The city of Le Havre by Auguste Perret has very recently been added to the World Heritage List as an example of reconstruction of a war-destroyed strategic seaport, based on a clear Cartesian plan and sophisticated French standardisation and prefabrication, which opens the era of housing strategies in the second half of the 20th century.

The set of Berlin housing estates is also one of the most important achievements of the International Style ("Neues Bauen") in the 1920s, and is closely connected to a social vision of a more just society, offering a higher standard of living for all social classes. Therefore, the selected set of Berlin housing developments, which have been an important target of monument care efforts for the last 25 years, deserves to be inscribed in the UNESCO World Heritage List not only as an excellent example of 20th century town planning and architecture but also as an exceptional social act.

Prof. Ing.-Arch. Vladimír Šlapeta, Dr. Sc.
Hon FRIBA, Hon FAIA, BDA Eh.
Dekan an der Fakultät für Architektur, Tschechische Technische Universität in Prag, August 2005
Dean at the Faculty of Architecture, Czech Technical University in Prague, August 2005

## Impressum | Imprint

Die Deutsche Bibliothek verzeichnet diese Publikation in der Deutschen Nationalbibliographie; detaillierte bibliographische Daten sind im Internet abrufbar über: http://dnb.ddb.de

ISBN 978-3-938780-20-6

© 2007 by Verlagshaus Braun
www.verlagshaus-braun.de

Dieses Werk ist urheberrechtlich geschützt. Jede Verwertung außerhalb der engen Grenzen des Urheberrechtsgesetzes ist ohne Zustimmung des Verlags unzulässig und strafbar. Dies gilt insbesondere für Vervielfältigungen, Übersetzungen, Mikroverfilmungen sowie die Einspeicherung und Verarbeitung in elektronischen Systemen.

1. Auflage 2007

The Deutsche Bibliothek is registering this publication in the Deutsche Nationalbibliographie; detailed bibliographical information can be found on the internet at http://dnb.ddb.de

ISBN 978-3-938780-20-6

© 2007 by Verlagshaus Braun
www.verlagshaus-braun.de

The work is copyright protected. Any use outside of the close boundaries of the copyright law, which has not been granted permission by the publisher, is unauthorized and liable for prosecution. This especially applies to duplications, translations, microfilming, and any saving or processing in electronic systems.

1st edition 2007

Herausgeber | Edited by:
Landesdenkmalamt Berlin im Auftrag der Senatsverwaltung für Stadtentwicklung Berlin

Projektleitung | Project management:
Winfried Brenne (Winfried Brenne Architekten Berlin), Jörg Haspel (Landesdenkmalamt Berlin), Manfred Kühne (Senatsverwaltung für Stadtentwicklung Berlin)

Koordination und Redaktion | Coordination and editorial staff:
Markus Jager (Landesdenkmalamt Berlin), Joachim Günther, Sigrid Kayser, Manfred Kühne (Senatsverwaltung für Stadtentwicklung), Ulrich Borgert, Winfried Brenne (Winfried Brenne Architekten), Peter Schmidt-Seifert (Schmidt-Seifert Landschaftsarchitektur Berlin), Frank Hesse, Klaus Lingenauber, Hubert Staroste (Landesdenkmalamt Berlin)

Manuskripterstellung | Compilation of the script:
Gabi Dolff-Bonekämper (Landesdenkmalamt Berlin), Ulrich Borgert (Winfried Brenne Architekten), Peter Schmidt-Seifert (Schmidt-Seifert Landschaftsarchitektur Berlin), Jürgen Tomisch (Büro für Stadt- und Baugeschichte), Matthias Dunger, Wilhelm Fuchs, Frank Hesse, Anna Maria Odenthal, Gabriele Schulz, Sibylle Schulz, Hubert Staroste (Landesdenkmalamt Berlin)

Schriftleitung, Lektorat deutsche Fassung und Schlussredaktion | Editorship, correction German text and final editing:
Ulrich Borgert (Winfried Brenne Architekten), Hubert Staroste (Landesdenkmalamt Berlin), Franziska Nauck (Verlagshaus Braun)

Übersetzung | Translation:
lost in translation – Sprachservice Gunhild Blankenstein

Lektorat englische Fassung | Correction English text:
Claudia Ade Team

Grafikkonzept und Layout | Graphic design and layout:
Kraft plus Wiechmann, Glenn Vincent Kraft

Repro | Litho:
LVD Gesellschaft für Datenverarbeitung mbH, Berlin